CLASSICAL AND MEDIEVAL LITERARY CRITICISM

CLASSICAL AND MEDIEVAL LITERARY CRITICISM

Translations and Interpretations

EDITED BY

ALEX PREMINGER

LEON GOLDEN

O. B. HARDISON, JR.

KEVIN KERRANE

FREDERICK UNGAR PUBLISHING CO.

NEW YORK

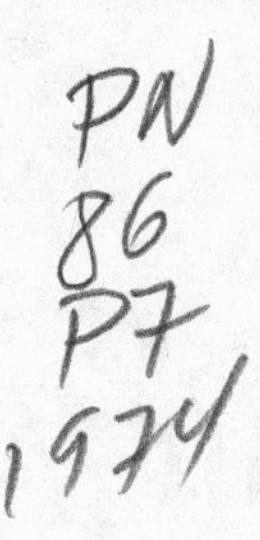

Printed in the United States of America
Designed by Irving Perkins
Library of Congress Catalog Card Number: 73-84722
ISBN: 0-8044-3257-0

Second Printing, 1983

ACKNOWLEDGMENTS

Acknowledgment is gratefully made to the following who have granted permission to use copyrighted material.

Clarendon Press, for "Ion" and selections from "Gorgias," "Laws," "Phaedrus," "Republic," and "Symposium" from *The Dialogues of Plato*, tr. by B. Jowett, 4th ed. (Oxford 1953); and for *"Longinus" on Sublimity*, tr. by D. A. Russell, copyright 1965 by Oxford University Press.

Mrs. Norman J. DeWitt, for translation of Horace's *Ars Poetica* by Norman J. DeWitt.

Drama Survey, for translation of Horace's *Ars Poetica* by Norman J. DeWitt in the October 1961 issue, by permission of John D. Hurrell on behalf of *Drama Survey*.

Duke University Press, for O.B. Hardison's "The Place of Averroes' Commentary on the *Poetics* in the History of Medieval Criticism" in *Medieval and Renaissance Studies*, no. 4., ed. by John Lievsay, copyright 1970 Duke University Press and reprinted here in abridged and modified form.

Faber and Faber Ltd., for passages from Plotinus: *The Enneads*, 4th ed., copyright 1969 Faber and Faber Ltd. and copyright 1969 Random House, reprinted by permission of Faber and Faber Ltd.

Harvard University Press, for selections from Book X of Quintilian, *Institutio Oratoria*, tr. H. E. Butler and reprinted by permission of the publisher and The Loeb Classical Library.

Richmond Lattimore, for translation from Aristophanes, *The Frogs*.

Macmillan & Co., Ltd., for chapters X-XIII of Dionysius of Halicarnassus, *On Literary Composition*, tr. by W. Rhys Roberts and reprinted by permission of the publisher.

Pontifical Institute of Mediaeval Studies, for selections from *The Poetria Nova* of Geoffrey of Vinsauf, tr. by Margaret F. Nims and reprinted by permission of the translator and of the President of the Pontifical Institute.

Prentice-Hall, Inc., for the translation of the *Poetics* from Leon Golden and O. B. Hardison, Jr., *Aristotle's Poetics: A Translation and Commentary for Students of Literature*, copyright 1968. By permission of Prentice-Hall, Inc., Englewood Cliffs, New Jersey.

Random House, Inc., for passages from *The Enneads*, 4th ed., by Plotinus, copyright 1969 Faber and Faber Ltd. and copyright 1969 Random House (Pantheon Books, a Division of Random House, Inc.). All rights reserved.

University of Michigan Press, for an extract from Aristophanes, *The Frogs*, tr. by Richmond Lattimore, copyright 1962 by William Arrowsmith.

University of Toronto Press, for selection from *A Greek Critic: Demetrius on Style*, by G.M.A. Grube, by permission of University of Toronto Press. Copyright, Canada, 1961 by University of Toronto Press.

CONTENTS

MEDIEVAL LITERARY CRITICISM
O. B. Hardison, Jr.

PREFACE

One of the controlling premises of this anthology is that the truest history of literary theory is a history of major documents. The opening sentence of our first general introduction—"Classical criticism was born of classical philosophy"—reflects our belief that the most significant critical works embody sustained analysis and argumentative rigor, and that the methods a critic uses to arrive at his conclusions can be as important as the conclusions themselves. Consequently, we have tried to avoid relying on short or truncated selections. We have focused on influential texts, reprinting whole chapters and even complete works whenever possible. In addition to works which are significant in themselves and seminal in the history of poetics, we have included texts which, though generally neglected, are historically important and are genuine contributions to critical thought.

It was our aim to provide accurate and readable translations. For Plato, we have used Jowett's translation, still unsurpassed for its fluid and easy style. On the other hand, Leon Golden's translation of Aristotle's *Poetics* is a new one, based on a review of all the important Greek texts from Bywater to Kassel. Latin medieval texts are difficult to translate into an easy modern style. Where possible, established translations have been used, but in three cases new ones have been made.

Our major aim has been to provide interpretation in depth. Thus about forty percent of this volume has been given over to general and individual introductions, notes, annotated bibliographies, to a glossary of proper names, and to indexes.

The selection from each critic is prefaced by an introductory essay, prepared by Leon Golden for the classical section, and O. B. Hardison for the medieval section, which places the critic's work in the context of its time, summarizes its substance and method, assesses its influences on later poetics, and points out significant problems. We have also provided a "General Introduction" for each of our two major sections, emphasizing larger historical movements in criticism, and commenting on critics and texts not represented in this collection.

The result is, we hope, something substantially more than a conventional anthology. While one of its functions is to make available important texts, another is to provide the framework of an interpretation of the history of classical and medieval criticism. In addition this volume offers, by means of a sufficiently extensive bibliography, guidance to those seeking further information.

The general introduction and the introductions to the individual selections for the medieval section are longer and more detailed, generally, than the corresponding material in the classical section. The reason for this is that the medieval selections are much less familiar and need more explanation. Secondary studies, though readily available for classical critics, are often inadequate, difficult to obtain, or nonexistent for medieval critics.

Taken together, the two general introductions reveal certain strong lines of continuity in pre-Renaissance criticism. One of these may be called "Platonic." This strain of thought is concerned with the moral utility of literature and its philosophical "content." Such topics, first explored systematically in Plato's *Republic* and *Laws*, recur in medieval criticism—not only in such consciously Neoplatonic writings as the essays of Proclus, but also in the work of Christian critics, especially those concerned with the issue of assimilating classical culture to the New Dispensation. But this same Platonic strain of thought provided a counteremphasis. Beginning with Plato's *Ion*, and continuing through the writings of Neoplatonists and medieval Christian critics, the theory of inspiration asserts that the soul of the true artist is attuned to the "One," and that his work is imbued with the quality of revelation. A similar positive and mystical emphasis recurs in the tradition of allegorical interpretation; the major classical proponents of this critical approach were the Sophists and the Stoics, but the theory that authors who were inspired concealed their truths under the veil of myth or fiction became standard with later Neoplatonists (Proclus) and Christians (Fulgentius), and still enjoyed wide popularity in the Age of Dante.

A second line of continuity might be termed "rhetorical." Through its basic perception of literature as a means to an end, this critical approach also raised moral issues—as in the classical writings of Plutarch and "Longinus." Its major emphasis, however, was practical and stylistic. Such classical treatises as the anonymous *Rhetorica ad Herennium*, Cicero's *De Inventione*, Horace's *Ars Poetica* and Demetrius' *On Style* bequeathed to later critics a host of concepts and terms: a system of genres correlated with various compositional formulae and levels of style; the quantitative division of a literary work along the lines of an oration; decorum of character and language (often in terms of Horatian formulae); and—perhaps most important—techniques for the exhaustive analysis of stylistic figures. Medieval critics frequently merged the study of grammar with rhetorical criticism. This approach is best exemplified in medieval commentaries and glosses (Servius' discussion of Vergil), treatments of prosody (Bede's *De Arte Metrica*), and the type of schematic critical treatment known as the *accessus* (a direct influence on Dante's *Letter to Can Grande della Scala*).

Both general introductions make clear the fact that Aristotle's *Poetics*, the most sophisticated and modern of all the works of pre-Renaissance criticism, exerted little direct influence on subsequent classical or medieval writers. It appears likely that Aristotle's text was simply unavailable to most of these writers; but even if it had been known, its essentially aesthetic insights would have run counter to the didactic and rhetorical nature of later criticism. Only in the late medieval period, in an incredibly garbled series of paraphrases and translations from Greek to Syriac to Arabic to Latin, did the *Poetics* become a factor in critical theory. The medieval *Poetics* has only a tenuous relation to Aristotle's thought. It remained for Renaissance scholars, with access to Aristotle's texts in Greek, to show just how seminal a document the *Poetics* is.

A special note of appreciation is due Professor Leon Golden, whose help went far beyond the boundary of his own important contribution. We are grateful for advice, concrete suggestions, and criticism received from Professors Merton Christensen, Procope S. Costas, Gerald F. Else, Aldo Scaglione, and Roy Arthur Swanson. We also wish to thank Professor Antoinette Ciolli for her contribution, Frances McConney for typing the manuscript, and Calliope Scumas of Frederick Ungar Publishing Co. for her invaluable assistance. Finally, we would like to acknowledge with appreciation a grant from The City University of New York Faculty Research Award Program, which helped to expedite this work.

THE EDITORS

CLASSICAL LITERARY CRITICISM

Leon Golden

GENERAL INTRODUCTION

Classical literary criticism was born of classical philosophy. In the fourth century B.C., through systematic investigations by Plato and Aristotle into the nature of artistic imitation and specific poetic techniques, Western literary criticism first emerged as a distinct and rigorous inquiry. Much of the enduring influence of classical criticism derives from this philosophical orientation—a comprehensiveness and complexity in practical analysis, and a vocabulary and perspective for discussing the value of literature itself among the manifold activities of man.

But the liveliness and force of classical criticism are also embodied in the writings of numerous poets, scholars, and rhetoricians who—without benefit of a clear critical terminology or an explicit theory of literature—offered opinions on matters of style, pronounced judgment on particular poems, and struggled to articulate some larger questions about literary art. This vitality is clearly evident in the stage of "proto-criticism" that preceded the work of Plato and Aristotle. The poets themselves, from Homer to Aristophanes, in exploring issues relating to their own art, dealt with topics that were to preoccupy the later theorists. Although this early criticism was generally intuitive and unsystematic, and can only be pieced together from scattered references in literary works, it is a key to understanding many of the premises and themes of the whole classical tradition in criticism.

GREEK PROTO-CRITICISM

The earliest classical criticism focuses on the social role of the poet. He is viewed as a moral teacher, and as thus in need of occasional censorship. But most often he is simply venerated—usually through the claim that he is protected and inspired by a divine muse, who enables him to please his audience through stories and words that convey a unique kind of knowledge. This claim, suggesting man's early identification of the poet's role with that of priest and prophet, is close in spirit to the modern romantic image of the artist—and it may reflect the basic aesthetic insight that the workings of imagination are mysterious, irreducible to sheer logical explanation. At any rate, when this theme found its fullest classical expression in Plato's dialogue *Ion,* it must already have been a commonplace of critical thinking, for it appears explicitly in the writings of Homer, Hesiod, and Pindar.

Homer (ca. 8th century B.C.) addresses the muse in his own poetic invocations, but his most striking references to inspiration appear in his characterizations of two poets in the *Odyssey*. In Book VIII Homer describes the banquet which King Alcinous holds in honor of Odysseus. Here the bard Demodocus is presented as a man cherished by the muse: although she took away his sight, she granted him the sweet gift of song. Homer later says that all men owe honor to the poets, for they are dear to the muse, who puts upon their lips the ways of life. In Book XXII (344–49) Phemios the minstrel, pleading for his life amid the slaughter of the suitors, tells Odysseus that a god shaped the songs which it is his gift to sing.

Similarly, Hesiod (8th or 7th century B.C.) claims in the invocation to his *Theogony* that the muses, daughters of Zeus, taught him his lovely songs. He credits them with having given him a divine voice to sing of the future and the past, and he asserts that inspired poetry can give a pleasure so great as to charm away the melancholy of any man. Hesiod's own poetry is far more didactic than Homer's, dealing less with heroic legends than with theology (stories of the gods) and practical instruction. Thus he seems led to express an ethical concern that the poet can relate falsehoods in the form of truths. This concern, which later assumed great importance in the Platonic approach to art, is also reflected in the writings of such early classical moralists as Solon and Xenophanes (6th century B.C.). Xenophanes, for example, scorns the anthropomorphic gods of the epics, objecting to the presentation of theft, lying, and adultery as divine attributes (Fragment II).

Pindar (518–438 B.C.) also expresses moral criticism of certain episodes in the epics, claiming that Homer's vast artistic skill makes some of his poetry all the more capable of leading men astray (*Nemean* VII.22). "Inspiration," he says, must be tempered by "accuracy" (*Pythian* IV.279). Usually, however, Pindar discusses the poet's role in much more positive terms. In *Pythian* (I.41–42) he asserts that the gods provide the means for achieving every excellence, and he includes here wisdom, might of hand, and skill of speech. Elsewhere he indicates his agreement with Hesiod's view of poetry as a healing agent (*Olympian* II.14–15; *Pythian* I.6–14; *Nemean* IV.1–5). He suggests that the poet serves as a mediator between men and the gods who are so often indifferent to them, and as the agent who makes eternal the glory won by men in athletic contests.

Aristophanes (ca. 450–385 B.C.) was much more concerned with the social and political aspects of poetry than with the question of its divine origin. Eleven of his plays have survived, and nearly all of them investigate with brilliant and often sardonic humor the disintegration of the quality of Athenian life in the latter decades of the fifth century B.C. Aristophanes' stance is that of a social and political conservative who looks back to a "golden age": the austere, salubrious morality of a predominantly rural Greek culture. This conservatism guides Aristophanes' caricatures of sophistic and militaristic mentalities, and also leads him to use his satire for the purpose of literary criticism. Aristophanes often focuses on contemporary poetry, attacking literary trends which, in his opinion, were operating together with the sophistic movement and political demogoguery to subvert the integrity of society.

One of Aristophanes' consistent targets was Euripides. In the *Acharnians* (393–489) Euripides is presented as a destructive realist, lowering tragedy from an ideal to an ordinary level. In *Peace* Aristophanes begins by ridiculing Euripides for excessive experimentation in stage spectacle. But the *Frogs,* written shortly after Euripides' death, offers a more balanced assessment: Euripides, although ultimately judged as inferior to Aeschylus, is clearly perceived as a great poet. The plot of the *Frogs* involves nothing less than a venture in practical literary criticism, for it turns upon a contest for the Chair of Tragedy in the Underworld: Dionysus, god of tragedy, attempts to judge between the idealism and grand style of Aeschylus and the realism and novelty of Euripides. This play is the high point of Greek proto-criticism. It abounds in critical insights and sharply focuses on one of the most important and persistent problems in the evaluation of literature as it portrays the conflicting views of Aeschylus and Euripides. For Aeschylus represents the position, favored by Aristophanes himself, that poets are ethical teachers and that art has a moral purpose to fulfil. By contrast, Euripides represents the view that the essential goal of art is the illumination of reality without regard to moral or ethical consideration.

PLATO AND ARISTOTLE

Aristophanes' concern with art as a social influence anticipates much of the work of Plato (ca. 429–347 B.C.). But Plato's writings on poetry constitute the emergence of proto-criticism into true literary criticism. His position is far more sophisticated than Aristophanes': his preoccupation with the moral force of literature cannot be isolated from a larger, more "philosophical," view of the nature of art. In Plato's work, literary criticism became a discipline, an intellectual enterprise requiring analytical rigor and sustained argumentation.

Much of Plato's literary criticism is marked by a strong hostility to art. First, as a metaphysician Plato argues that an artistic fiction is an "imitation," one degree removed from real experience, and thus two degrees removed from the ultimate reality which is ideal. Since for Plato the pursuit of this ultimate truth is the most significant of all human activities, he is extremely cautious about the "knowledge" that art conveys. Second, as a moralist Plato argues that poetry feeds and waters the passions, elements of personality that need to be controlled and disciplined by reason. Viewing the epics as repositories of dangerous moral examples, Plato is finally led to declare a "feud" between poetry and philosophy.

Once the distance between art and reality is recognized, however, Plato can find a positive role for proper kinds of literary imitation. Abundant evidence can be found in Plato's dialogues (themselves works of art) to demonstrate that certain metaphors, myths, and fictions represent necessary stages in the gradual progress men must make as they travel from spiritual darkness to spiritual light. Moreover, Plato's apparent acceptance of the ancient notion of divine inspiration would elevate the status of poetry. Although Plato's most sustained discussion of inspiration, the dialogue *Ion,* may have ironic overtones, the speaker Socrates decides that the real power possessed by the rhapsode Ion must derive from a sacred "madness" imparted by the muse.

Aristotle (384–322 B.C.) began his philosophical career as one of Plato's students, but in almost every area of intellectual inquiry he eventually diverged radically from Plato, even while addressing himself to the very questions that Plato raised. Aristotle's literary criticism follows this pattern. Although Plato is never mentioned by name in Aristotle's *Poetics,* Plato's critical position seems to be used as a point of departure. Like Plato, Aristotle defines poetic art as a kind of "imitation," but he effectively rids this term of any pejorative connotations. Aristotle's orientation is aesthetic: he considers an artistic imitation as the creation of an object with its own ontology and its own unique internal logic. Moreover, he emphasizes the capacity of art to illuminate human existence. In Chapter 4 of the *Poetics* he declares that the pleasure man obtains from all forms of artistic imitation is predicated on a process of learning. In Chapter 9 Aristotle argues that poetry is more significant and more philosophical than history: poetry aims at universals, whereas history is concerned with particulars. For Aristotle poetry has an essentially intellectual goal, the unified presentation of insights into human action.

Aristotle's controversial term *katharsis* (Chapter 6) seems directly related to his theory of imitation. Scholars have traditionally interpreted it as an emotional process—for example, the "purging" of the audience's emotions of pity and fear through their witnessing of an imitation in tragic form, the essential pleasure being a sense of relief from oppressive feelings. But Aristotle's statement in Chapter 4 that a kind of "learning" is the essential pleasure produced by artistic imitations suggests an alternate, and more positive, interpretation. It is possible to render *katharsis* as "intellectual clarification," thus confirming a notion of art as illuminatory. Aristotle may have meant that a tragedy gives clarity to incidents involving pity and fear, that the dramatist's particular insight into the human condition becomes the "theme" around which the work is organized.

The relationship of art and morality is not discussed explicitly in the

Poetics. In the treatment of the ideal tragic hero in Chapter 13 certain moral factors are relevant, but on the whole the *Poetics* deals strictly with questions of artistic effectiveness—emphasizing "probability" (internal coherence) rather than fidelity to some external norm. Aristotle does speak about the relation of art to morality in the *Politics,* where certain types of artistic imitation are accepted or excluded from the educational process in the state, on the basis of whether or not they contribute to social goals. This is an issue which Aristotle places outside the province of literary criticism itself, and he maintains a far stricter distinction between the aesthetic and ethical realms than any other critic of the classical era—or, for that matter, any Western theorist up to the time of Immanuel Kant.

Aristotle views poetry as a craft which the artist must master to achieve success. Thus the *Poetics* deals extensively with all aspects of the art of poetry, from larger philosophical and psychological questions to specific discussions of plot, characterization, and diction. This emphasis on the technical aspect of art was to reappear in the rhetorical orientation of later classical critics, but it is given its fullest and most aesthetic expression in the *Poetics.*

Unlike Plato, Aristotle has little to say about inspiration. His one reference to it in the *Poetics* appears in a disputed passage in Chapter 17, where he says either that the poet must be talented *or* mad, or that the poet must be talented *rather than* mad. The first interpretation might be related to the theme of divine "furor" described in Plato's *Ion,* but the idea of "talent" could also stand as a rationalized version of inspiration. Clearly Aristotle recognized, as did the early proto-critics, the existence of some innate power, beyond the diligent study of the rules of art, by which an individual artist performs effectively. Nevertheless, Aristotle's major emphasis remains on poetry as a *technê,* a body of knowledge governed by observable principles.

HELLENISTIC AND HORATIAN CRITICISM

Unfortunately, Aristotle's *Poetics* exerted no observable influence in the classical period. It appears likely that the treatise was unavailable to subsequent critics; but even if it had been known, the practical and didactic temper of later classical criticism would probably have insured the rejection of its aesthetic thesis. From the third to the first century B.C., as Greek culture itself became more diffuse, literary criticism—as distinguished (which it rarely was) from the study of rhetoric—belonged primarily to two groups: philosophical moralists and professional scholars.

The followers of the Epicurean school, like the members of the Platonic Academy, were hostile to poetry, considering it an emotional danger to the potentially wise man. One late Epicurean, however, offered a surprising alternative to this view: Philodemus of Gadara (ca. 110–40/35 B.C.) was himself a poet, and his fragmentary *Poetics* provides the closest Hellenistic analogue to Aristotelian criticism. Philodemus dismissed orthodox moral criticism, arguing that a true judgment of a poem cannot separate content from form. He insisted on the poet's freedom to treat any subject, even an imaginary one, and he rejected all rigid critical "rules" which would subvert the wholeness and integrity of the work of art.

More typical of Hellenistic philosophical criticism is the Stoic school, which usually drew a firm distinction between content and form. The Stoics tended to judge literature by ethical and utilitarian standards, although they were far less negative than most Platonists and Epicureans. Their main distinction was a penchant for allegorical interpretation.

The use of allegorizing as a critical method had begun early in classical criticism, perhaps with Theagenes of Rhegium (6th century B.C.), and it was occasionally used by the Sophists. It could serve as a defense for morally questionable poetry—for example, in taking the quarrels among Homer's gods as a cosmological allegory of the contention of the physical elements in nature. Plato, in Book II of the *Republic,* refers explicitly to this technique, but declares it useless: unsophisticated readers, especially impressionable youths, would still be vulnerable to bad moral examples as presented in poetry. The Stoics, however, carried out critical allegorizing on a large scale, using it not only to "rescue" allegedly dangerous poetry, but also to confirm specific Stoic beliefs. This trend is best illustrated by a work probably written in the first century A.D., the *Quaestiones Homericae* by Heraclitus (otherwise unknown). Treating the *Iliad* and the *Odyssey* in detail, Heraclitus extracts from the poems "hidden" meanings which adumbrate Stoic doctrines. Like other Stoic interpreters, Heraclitus not only focuses on major episodes, but also delves into stylistics: he examines figures of speech as means of conveying "secondary" meanings, and emphasizes etymologies as guides to allegorical intentions.

A more standard stylistic criticism was practiced by the Hellenistic scholars—many of them grammarians, editors of texts, and antiquarians associated with libraries and royal courts. Although little of their own criticism is extant, it is clear that they used stylistics as a means of discussing broader poetic issues. What set them apart from contemporaneous rhetorical critics was a thoroughgoing "classicism," with strong prescriptive and conservative attitudes. The scholars at Alexandria, for example, devised an elaborate schema of genres, with each poetic type governed by "rules" regarding subject matter, verse form, and diction. Their work seemed to suggest that all true examples of literary excellence lay in the Greek past; they venerated the ancients by drawing up official lists of the great models in each poetic form.

Horace (65–8 B.C.) transformed this kind of classicism into vital criticism. His eloquent and urbane *Ars Poetica* embodies a complex sensibility, balancing a classicist conservatism and penchant for rule-making with a lively wit, a tone of common sense, and an unremitting commitment to poetry as a demanding but noble craft. This sensibility is evident when Horace considers a critical commonplace of the Hellenistic period: whether natural aptitude or acquired technical skill is the more essential attribute for a poet. Horace takes a middle ground and asserts the need for both powers, but he concludes his verse-essay with a highly amusing caricature of the "mad" poet, vulgar and pompous, a disgrace both to his family name and to the discipline of literature.

Horace also takes a middle ground in regard to the ultimate value of poetry, asserting that the poet must both profit and please his audience. Both of these goals require an understanding of the truths of human nature. "Profit" for Horace means the moral advantages gained from precepts expressed in the poet's work, insights perhaps similar to those which dominate so many of Horace's own odes and humane satires. The "pleasure" Horace mentions is explicitly related to poetic realism ("verisimilitude") and decorum. Most of Horace's essay deals with techniques and procedures for achieving such literary propriety; despite his recognition of the moral aspects of art, it is this sense of poetry as a precise craft that controls the *Ars Poetica.*

RHETORICAL CRITICISM

The Alexandrian classicism on which Horace drew was deeply influenced by the study of rhetoric, but the *Ars Poetica* also owes a great debt to Roman rhetoric. The modern scholars George C. Fiske and Mary A. Grant have even approached Horace's treatise in terms of Cicero's *De Oratore* and *Orator* rather than earlier poetic treatises, pointing out such parallel topics as decorum of character, the dual goals of instruction and delight, and the emulation of great models as a means of training. This kind of overlap between poetry and rhetoric is typical of the classical tradition: both arts were usually subsumed under a larger concept—"effective expression"—and Aristotle's *Poetics* was the only major critical document of the period which did not rely heavily on rhetorical theory. The significance of classical rhetoric for the study of literature is most obvious in three areas: stylistics, moral issues, and motivation.

The discipline of rhetoric first attracted significant attention in Athens in 427 B.C., through the visit of Gorgias of Leontini. For Gorgias rhetoric was concerned only with style: as a Sophist he maintained that the effectiveness of a speech depended not on its truth value, but on the skill with which the orator used stylistic devices to appeal to his audience. Consequently, Gorgias' work emphasizes the importance of various sound effects and rhetorical figures.

The contribution to literary criticism of Gorgias' rhetorical approach was the development of a methodology and working vocabulary which could be used to study the verbal complexities of poetry. Such stylistic analysis was carried further by Aristotle's student Theophrastus (ca. 370–288/85 B.C.), Cicero (106–43 B.C.), and Demetrius (1st century B.C.?)—all of whom recommended to students of rhetoric well-chosen *poetic* illustrations of the subtle and telling ways that language can be manipulated. In fact, one justification for the study of poetry within the classical grammar curriculum was to illustrate rhetorical figures that the student might use in prose orations.

Cicero's early thinking on rhetoric is emphatically in the Gorgian tradition, and is typified by *De Inventione,* a treatise focusing on technical terms and formulae. Together with the anonymous *Rhetorica ad Herennium* (once thought erroneously to have been written by Cicero), *De Inventione* provided a terminology for the qualitative and quantitative parts of rhetoric—a terminology used extensively in the literary criticism of the Middle Ages and early Renaissance, when Aristotle's *Poetics* was unknown and the structural vocabulary of criticism was relatively impoverished.

Qualitatively, Cicero divides rhetoric into invention, arrangement, style, memory, and delivery. Quantitatively, he divides a speech into exordium, statement of the case (*narratio*), partition, proof, refutation, and peroration. He also treats rhetorical figures in detail, and discusses the three kinds of style—high, middle, and low (which the *Rhetorica ad Herennium* correlates with the various poetic genres). Demetrius, in the selection reprinted in this anthology, provides a good example of the late classical approach to high style. "Longinus," on the other hand, departs from purely stylistic rhetoric: his discussion of high style is really a discussion of a certain kind of moral excellence, and is related to a second major movement in rhetorical criticism.

The movement was begun by Gorgias' pupil Isocrates (436–338 B.C.) who, departing from the sophistic orientation of his teacher, viewed rhetoric as a subject as well as a method, a discipline involving genuine philosophical and moral principles. Isocrates insisted that the truly effective orator must possess moral goodness. Plato, in the dialogues *Gorgias* and *Phaedrus,* made clear his admiration for this idealized theory, and much of Plato's literary criticism is, for all intents and purposes, the application to literature of Isocrates' rhetorical approach—that is, literature as a means of moral education.

Cicero's mature writings on rhetoric follow this lead. In *De Oratore, Orator,* and *Brutus* he rejects the notion that rhetoric is merely a technical discipline, arguing that it has significant relationships to philosophy, law, and history, and that it requires a proper moral disposition. Other critics in the same tradition are Dionysius of Halicarnassus (1st century B.C.), Quintilian (ca. 30/35–100 A.D.), and Plutarch (before 50–after 120 A.D.). Although these writers are sensitive to stylistic issues, their real status as "rhetorical" critics derives from their view of literature as a form of ethical persuasion.

The third major force in classical rhetoric was Aristotle's systematic formulation of the principles of argumentation. Unlike the followers of Isocrates, Aristotle denied that rhetoric has a specific subject matter and a moral basis; he viewed rhetoric as an amoral "faculty" which enables its possessor to express himself most effectively. But unlike the followers of Gorgias, Aristotle thought of style as much less important than other means of influencing an audience. In Book II of his *Rhetoric* he focuses on three major forms of rhetorical appeal: *ethos* (the character of the speaker), *pathos* (the audience's emotions), and *dianoia* (lines of logical argument). The last two of these modes of appeal are especially relevant to literature.

Although Aristotle always maintained the distinction between rhetoric (which aims at persuasion) and literature (which aims at imitation, and hence aesthetic experience), his rhetorical approach allows for a complex examination of two kinds of motivation in literature: the artist's control of audience-response, and his development of characterization within his work. In his analysis of *pathos* Aristotle treats specific emotions (such as pity, fear, and indignation), emphasizing the stimuli most likely to arouse them. Many of Aristotle's examples constitute what Kenneth Burke has called "epitomized situations," and they seem closely related to the dynamics of drama. Aristotle's exploration of *pathos* continues with a discussion of various character-types in relation to age, fortune, and moral quality. These thumbnail sketches are offered ostensibly as abstracts of hypothetical audiences the orator may encounter, but they also provide handy formulae for literary figures, and they might be compared to Aristotle's requirements for dramatic characters in Chapter 15 of the *Poetics.*

Aristotle's subsequent discussion focuses on intellectual modes of appeal, and he explains twenty-eight "topics," lines of argument, that the expert orator should know how to use. Some of these topics, such as *a fortiori* argumentation, are analogous to the kinds of logic that may control a thematic work of literature, and Aristotle again seems to be offering many "epitomized situations." In addition, it is noteworthy that the term *dianoia,* used to refer to the intellectual modes of appeal, is used in the *Poetics* as one of the six qualitative parts of drama: "thought," the substance and rhetorical form of the dramatic speeches. In Chapter 19 of the *Poetics* Aristotle develops this concept by referring explicitly to his *Rhetoric.* His general meaning seems to be that the dramatist—in order to create "probable" speeches that reveal character, elucidate the action, and guide the audience's responses—must have a mastery of the faculty of rhetoric.

Because of its unusual approach, neither moral nor emphatically stylistic, Aristotle's *Rhetoric* exerted relatively little influence on the work of subsequent classical rhetoricians. And in the area of literary criticism its only direct effect stemmed from Aristotle's treatment (in Book I) of "epideictic" as one of the three main kinds of oratory. As contrasted with political and legal oratory, epideictic is primarily ceremonial: the listener is addressed not as a *kritēs,* a judge who must render a decision, but as a *theōros,* similar to a spectator at a play. Epideictic oratory is concerned with "praise and blame," and its characteristic form, according to Aristotle, is the encomium or panegyric. The *Rhetoric* analyzes this form in detail, recommending special techniques of amplification to the prospective orator.

Late classical rhetoricians—especially Aphthonius and Menander (4th century A.D.)—supplemented Aristotle by providing formulae for other epideictic types: the praise of seasons, cities, rulers, and so forth, with emphasis on special "occasions" (birthday, marriage, funeral). Many of the techniques of these epideictic types are similar to those of "occasional poetry," and it is significant that from the late classical period through the Middle Ages epideictic formulae were used in the teaching of poetry. They provided, in effect, standard "topics," offering rhetorical approaches to a rhetorically-oriented literature.

LONGINIAN AND NEOPLATONIC CRITICISM

"Longinus" is the name given to the unknown author of *On the Sublime,* a rhetorical treatise probably written in the first century A.D. This work typifies the classical overlap of literature and rhetoric, for "Longinus" treats sublime expression in general, instructing the prospective orator by pointing out passages of poetry worthy of emulation. His approach seems close to those of Isocrates and the mature Cicero: although most of the treatise examines such practical skills as rhetorical figures and the arrangement of words, the concept of "the sublime" goes far beyond the traditional notion of high style. "Longinus" frames his discussion by considering sublimity in philosophical terms. He insists that the true artist (poet or orator) must possess a sublime nature, a moral elevation, and greatness of soul. The pleasure which "Longinus" attributes to the experience of the sublime is that of "transport" (*ecstasis*), by which he seems to mean an exciting intensification of the audience's capacity for moral and intellectual judgment, a sense of elevation that unites reason and emotion.

"Longinus" was once believed to have been a third-century disciple of Plotinus, and much of *On the Sublime* is easily compatible with the Neoplatonic approach to art. The philosophical emphasis of the treatise is on a goal at once moral and aesthetic, a stage of consciousness in which truth and beauty are perceived as one. As a rhetorical theorist "Longinus" seems to be making a transition from morality to mysticism.

The first stirrings of Neoplatonic criticism appeared in Alexandria in the first century A.D., in the commentaries on Genesis written by the Jewish philosopher Philo Judaeus. These commentaries emphasize the compatibility of Moses' vision with Plato's philosophy, and they explore the possibilities of allegorical exegesis. A similar kind of exegesis was used by some early Christian writers—

Clement of Alexandria in the late second century, Origen in the early third century—who began to develop a method for interpreting the pagan classics (especially Homer) in Christian terms. Their theories were based largely on the Platonic notions of inspiration and the essential oneness behind all truth.

Neoplatonism first became a fully developed approach to art in the work of Plotinus (205–269/270 A.D.). According to Plotinus, the soul of the true artist is attuned to the "One," and his work is thus inspired, possessing an essentially moral quality of revelation. The work of art is beautiful because it participates in the transcendent "Idea" of beauty; it achieves and expresses a vision of ultimate reality. Plotinus thus uses Plato's remarks on inspiration (as found in the *Ion*) to surmount Plato's objections to art as a secondary imitation (as found in the *Republic*). This positive emphasis was carried from aesthetics into literary criticism by two of Plotinus' students, Proclus and Porphyry. And Plotinus' general method reappears in the work of most idealistic critics—Christians, humanists, or romantics—from the Middle Ages onward.

This introduction was prepared jointly by Leon Golden and Kevin Kerrane.

ARISTOPHANES

(ca. 450–385 B.C.)

INTRODUCTION

In his play *The Frogs* Aristophanes expands the boundaries of classical poetics by providing an early and very perceptive example of practical criticism, a comparison of the world views and dramatic styles of Aeschylus and Euripides. The first part of the play centers on Dionysus' adventures as he attempts to bring Euripides back from the dead. In the second half of the play, Dionysus adjudicates a contest between Aeschylus and Euripides as to who is really the best poet and deserves to return to the world, and it is here that we find many important statements of Aristophanes' view of literature.

The struggle between Aeschylus and Euripides is based both on philosophical and stylistic issues. Euripides berates Aeschylus for his use of strange, new, and very long words which are difficult to understand. Aeschylus counters that the nobility of his themes requires such language. Euripides proudly claims that he has made tragedy more realistic by using everyday speech and characters out of ordinary life. Aeschylus, in turn, denounces Euripides for degrading the stage by introducing to it language and incidents from the more sordid aspects of life.

Aeschylus proudly points to the fact that he wrote plays such as the *Seven Against Thebes,* which inspired men to want to fight for their country, and the *Persians,* which filled them with patriotic fervor, while Euripides presented the morally and ethically degraded on the stage. Aeschylus sees himself as a part of the noble tradition of poet-teachers which includes Orpheus, who taught mystic religious rites and the horror of murder; Musaeus, who explained the healing of illnesses and the meaning of oracles; Homer, who described the art of war; and Hesiod, who taught the tilling of the soil. The Aeschylean position strongly affirms the role of the poet as priest and moral instructor to his people.

Euripides is placed by Aristophanes in the position of defending the view that art has a right to depict the sordid aspects of reality and to use appropriate diction and costuming in the process. When Aeschylus denounces him for introducing psychologically abnormal and morally degraded figures into his dramas, Euripides demands to know if his description of Phaedra's love for her stepson was untrue. Aeschylus accepts the truth of Euripides' description but asserts that the task of the poet is to be the teacher of mankind and that he should not portray events which subvert the morality of the audience.

There is a deep philosophical difference in the attitudes toward art expressed by Aeschylus and Euripides. For Aeschylus the artist is, as we have indicated, both a priest and teacher of his fellow men and his essential task is to present in his artistic work themes and actions which will uplift his audience morally and instruct them in a proper social and personal ethic. Both subject matter and style must be chosen so as to conform to this essential goal. Euripides argues for a very different concept of art, one in which the poet's essential task is to express reality no matter how vile or immoral it may be. The Euripidean position sees art as an investigation into the nature of reality and not as a means for achieving moral and social goals. The serious problem raised by the clashing arguments of Aeschylus and Euripides will play a prominent role in the history of classical literary criticism.

Aeschylus' elevated diction and Euripides' more pedestrian style are attributed in this passage to the character of the themes the two poets present. Aristophanes uses this occasion for some very perceptive, but frequently quite technical, stylistic criticism of both poets. He parodies both the rugged, sometimes unclear, diction of Aeschylus and the plain, sometimes pedestrian and mechanical, style of Euripides. In having his characters cite and analyze specific passages, Aristophanes functions as the first practical critic in the classical poetic tradition.

The translation which follows (and most of the notes) are by Richmond Lattimore and taken from Aristophanes, *The Frogs* (Ann Arbor: University of Michigan Press, 1962) by permission of the publisher.

The numbers inserted in the translation give the approximate location of every tenth line in the Greek text.

from THE FROGS

AESCHYLUS

The whole business gives me a pain in the middle, my rage and resentment are heated
at the idea of having to argue with *him*. But so he can't say I'm defeated,
here, answer me, you. What's the poet's duty, and why is the poet respected?

EURIPIDES

Because he can write, and because he can think, but mostly because he's injected some virtue into the body politic.

AESCHYLUS

What if you've broken your trust,
and corrupted good sound right-thinking people and filled them with treacherous lust?
If poets do that, what reward should they get?

DIONYSOS

The axe. That's what we should do with 'em.

AESCHYLUS

Then think of the people *I* gave him, and think of the people when he got through with 'em.
I left him a lot of heroic six-footers, a grand generation of heroes,
unlike our new crop of street-corner loafers and gangsters and decadent queer-os.
Mine snorted the spirit of spears and splendor, of white-plumed helmets and stricken fields,
of warrior heroes in shining armor and greaves[1] and sevenfold-oxhide shields.

DIONYSOS

And that's a disease that never dies out. The munition-makers will kill me.

EURIPIDES

Just what did you do to make them so noble? Is that what you're trying to tell me?

DIONYSOS

Well, answer him, Aeschylus, don't withdraw into injured dignity. That won't go.

AESCHYLUS

I made them a martial drama.

DIONYSOS

Which?

AESCHYLUS

Seven Against Thebes, if you want to know.
Any man in an audience sitting through that would aspire to heroic endeavor.

DIONYSOS
That was a mistake, man. Why did you make the Thebans more warlike than ever
and harder to fight with? By every right it should mean a good beating for you.

AESCHYLUS
To the audience
Well, *you* could have practiced austerity too. It's exactly what *you* wouldn't *do.*
Then I put on my *Persians,*[2] and anyone witnessing that would promptly be smitten
with longing for victory over the enemy. Best play I ever have written.

DIONYSOS
Oh, yes, I loved that, and I thrilled where I sat when I heard old Dareios was dead
and the chorus cried "wahoo" and clapped with their hands. I tell you, it went to my head.

AESCHYLUS
There, there is work for poets who also are MEN. From the earliest times
incitement to virtue and useful knowledge have come from the makers of rhymes.
There was Orpheus first. He preached against murder, and showed us the heavenly way.
Musaeus taught divination and medicine; Hesiod, the day-after-day cultivation
of fields, the seasons, and plowings. Then Homer, divinely inspired,
is a source of indoctrination to virtue. Why else is he justly admired
than for teaching how heroes armed them for battle?

DIONYSOS
He didn't teach Pantakles, though.
He can't get it right. I watched him last night. He was called to parade, don't you know,
and he put on his helmet and tried to tie on the plume when the helm was on top of his head.

AESCHYLUS
Ah, many have been my heroic disciples; the last of them, Lamachos (recently dead).
The man in the street simply has to catch something from all my heroics and braveries.
My Teucers and lion-hearted Patrokloses lift him right out of his knaveries
and make him thrill to the glory of war and spring to the sound of the trumpet.
But I never regaled you with Phaidra the floozie—or Sthenoboia[3] the strumpet.
I think I can say that a lovesick woman has never been pictured by me.

EURIPIDES
Aphrodite never did notice you much.

AESCHYLUS
Aphrodite can go climb a tree.
But you'll never have to complain that she didn't bestow her attentions on you.
She got you in person, didn't she?

DIONYSOS
Yes, she did, and your stories came true.
The fictitious chickens came home to roost.

EURIPIDES
But tell me, o man without pity:
suppose I did write about Sthenoboia. What harm has she done to our city?

AESCHYLUS
Bellerophon-intrigues, as given by you, have caused the respectable wives
of respectable men, in shame and confusion, to do away with their lives.

EURIPIDES
But isn't my story of Phaidra a story that really has happened?

AESCHYLUS
So be it.
It's true. But the poet should cover up scandal, and not let anyone see it.
He shouldn't exhibit it out on the stage. For the little boys have their teachers
to show them example, but when they grow up we poets must act as their preachers,
and what we preach should be useful and good.

EURIPIDES
But you, with your massive construction,
huge words and mountainous phrases, is that what you call useful instruction?
You ought to make people talk like people.

AESCHYLUS
Your folksy style's for the birds.
For magnificent thoughts and magnificent fancies, we must have magnificent words.
It's appropriate too for the demigods of heroic times to talk bigger

than we. It goes with their representation as grander in costume and figure.
I set them a standard of purity. You've corrupted it.

EURIPIDES

How did I do it?

AESCHYLUS

By showing a royal man in a costume of rags, with his skin showing through it.
You played on emotions.

EURIPIDES

But why should it be so wrong to awaken their pity?

AESCHYLUS

The rich men won't contribute for warships.[4] You can't find one in the city
who's willing to give. He appears in his rags, and howls, and complains that he's broke.

DIONYSOS

But he always has soft and expensive underwear under the beggarman's cloak.
The liar's so rich and he eats so much that he has to feed some to the fishes.

AESCHYLUS

You've taught the young man to be disputatious. Each argues as long as he wishes.
You've emptied the wrestling yards of wrestlers. They all sit around on their fannies
and listen to adolescent debates. The sailormen gossip like grannies
and question their officers' orders. In my time, all that they knew how to do
was to holler for rations, and sing "yeo-ho," and row, with the rest of the crew.

DIONYSOS

And blast in the face of the man behind, that's another thing too that they knew how to do.
And how to steal from the mess at sea, and how to be robbers ashore.
But now they argue their orders. We just can't send them to sea any more.

AESCHYLUS

That's what he's begun. What hasn't he done?
His nurses go propositioning others.
His heroines have their babies in church
or sleep with their brothers

or go around murmuring: "*Is* life life?"[5]
So our city is rife
with the clerk and the jerk,
the altar-baboon, the political ape,
and our physical fitness is now a disgrace
with nobody in shape
to carry a torch in a race.

PLATO

(ca. 429–347 B.C.)

INTRODUCTION

Alfred North Whitehead once observed that the history of Western philosophy is basically a series of "footnotes" to Plato. To a lesser extent, the same observation might be made about the history of Western poetics. Plato, the formulator of man's first general theory of art, has had an immense influence on nearly every generation of Western literary critics.

It is significant, however, that this influence has been so diverse. On the one hand, Plato's position is reflected in the antagonism of religious, radically humanistic, and politically totalitarian forces to aesthetic freedom and to art as an end in itself. On the other hand, Plato has served as the patron saint of scores of critics who wish to glorify the artist and the role of art in human life. These strikingly different emphases are possible because of the rich complexity of Plato's theory of art.

Plato's most famous statements about art occur in Book X of the *Republic*, where the decision is made to banish nearly all poetry from the ideal state. The surprisingly intense opposition to art exhibited in Book X derives from two kinds of Platonic premises: metaphysical and ethical. First, as a philosophical idealist principally concerned with the apprehension of ultimate reality, Plato is antagonistic to artistic *fictions*, which necessarily distort what limited vision of truth man possesses. In Book X of the *Republic* Plato argues that works of art are at best trivial, being merely imperfect reflections of the literal world, which is in turn a pale reflection of the ideal. Using the example of a bed, Plato cites the necessary existence of the idea of the bed, an eternally existing model for all actual beds—which can themselves be called "imitations" of this idea. Thus, a painting or a literary description of a bed would be an "imitation of an imitation," standing three degrees removed from reality itself.

Plato's second basis of opposition to art also appears in Book X of the *Republic*: he suggests that art is not only inherently trivial but also potentially dangerous, that it poses ethical as well as metaphysical problems. Imitative art has a powerful emotional effect on its audience. Plato, unlike Aristotle, identifies this effect as unhealthy, a reversal of the control that reason should always have over the passions. According to Plato, the imitative poet establishes a "badly governed state" within the soul of each member of the audience. Moreover, the power of art to mold men's attitudes and values means that the philosopher has the right to object to (and to censor) any artistic imitation which deviates from approved themes and representations.

Many discussions of Plato's theory of art begin and end with Book X of the *Republic*, but distinguished work by Richard McKeon and W. J. Verdenius, among others, has shown that Plato's view of art is deeper and much more complex than the preceding summary might suggest.[1] Plato's remarks in Book X cannot be isolated from the logic that controls the *Republic* as a whole, or from the general attitudes expressed in other dialogues.

In contrast to the *Laws*, where an attempt is made to depict a fairly realistic state, the *Republic* is an inquiry into the principles of an ideal state, one existing in accordance with *absolute* truth and justice. Thus, whereas the *Laws* significantly modifies most of the "Platonic" restrictions against art, the *Republic* denies toleration to any activities which might subvert the absolute social, moral, and philosophical goals of the state. In Book III of the *Republic* Plato not only justifies stringent censorship (e. g., of poems which portray wickedness triumphant), but also demands that poets tell "profitable" stories which can help to inculcate such virtues as courage and temperance.

Plato also sees the form or style of a literary work as having a moral potency. He argues that the completely imitative mode (i. e., drama) is the worst; in tragedies and comedies evil is represented directly, and thus becomes more potentially attractive to the audience. On the other hand, a totally narrative style, while avoiding the direct representation of evil, also prevents the direct representation of the morally good. Plato finally affirms a mixed style, in which there is a small amount of direct representation of the morally good and a large amount of narration. (Plato's remarks in Book III provide an interesting counterpoint to those of Aristotle in the *Poetics*. Aristotle, who sees as "imitative" *all* the styles that Plato mentions, argues on aesthetic grounds for the superiority of the dramatic mode. Moreover, Plato's insistence in Book III on "poetic justice"—goodness rewarded and vice punished—would seem to make Aristotle's ideal literary form, tragedy, almost impossible.)

Many of Plato's negative comments about art are repeated in other dialogues. Poetry is attacked for one of two reasons—its moral dangers or its distance from absolute truth. In the *Gorgias*, for example, poetry and music are described as forms of flattery, in that their goal is "pleasure" rather than the moral improvement of the audience. In the *Phaedrus* Plato uses the myth of Theuth to contrast the stasis of art with the dynamism of philosophical dialectic; artistic imitations, and the "written word" in general, are compared unfavorably to the "living word" of the never-ending dialectical process.

Nevertheless, it is precisely this concern with a dialectic of spiritual growth that leads Plato to allow for a more positive view of art. In Book V of the *Republic* (516 A-B) Plato compares the intellectual process of moving from opinion to knowledge with the sense experience of moving from the depths of a cave to open sunlight. He notes that a person could not endure the blinding light of the sun after long exposure to darkness: such a person would have to accommodate himself *gradually* to increasing levels of light before he could view the bright sun. Similarly, the person who is proceeding from spiritual darkness to spiritual light must adjust himself to the new experience gradually. He will need, therefore, to traverse a series of imitations of reality that come ever closer to absolute truth. Artistic imitations which perform this role thus have a significant place in the Platonic system.

As long as a man maintains a clear and absolute distinction between the imitation and reality, a work of art may provide him with a means of spiritual growth. In the *Laws* (668 A-B) such worthwhile imitations are identified as having truth (similarity to the model) rather than pleasure as their goal. Obviously, the poet should have sound knowledge of his subject matter. In the *Sophist* (267 B) we are told that some imitators have knowledge of what they imitate, while others do not; imitations accomplished by those who have knowledge will, by virtue of similarity to models, be able to illuminate reality itself. In the *Symposium* Diotima eloquently praises the "children of the spirit"—by which she means all of the intellectual achievements of man, including the works of Hesiod and Homer. Diotima's remarks make it clear that literary works can be a useful (though lower) stage in the quest for an understanding of absolute beauty.

The *Laws*, which—as has been noted—delineates the concept of a political state more realistic than that of the *Republic*, presents a liberalization of many strictures against art—again because of Plato's concern with a dialectic of spiritual growth. Plato deals with literature and music as elements of the educational process, stressing the moral possibilities of various kinds of art. In the state envisioned by the *Laws* both comedy and tragedy have a place, and the reasoning that Plato uses to "defend" them indicates that he is concerned with the moral dimension of literature in a newer, more subtle way. Comedy is to be admitted because man, in learning the nature of the ignoble and the ridiculous, may be better able to understand and pursue the noble and the virtuous. Tragedy is to be allowed because, when it conforms to the morality approved by the state, it illuminates the noble aspects of human existence. The standard for judging tragedy is to be found in the wisdom of the philosopher-statesman, for the *Laws* tells us that the whole state "is an imitation of the best and noblest life, which we affirm to be indeed the very truth of tragedy."

Plato's positive view of artistic imitation is supported by the formal qualities of his own dialogues. His frequent use of key images, such as the cave, is an example of imitation used to express a truth that could not be expressed in any other way. Moreover, the larger and more extended metaphors that we call "myths" occur at many crucial places in the dialogues, providing imaginative clarification of Plato's themes. Finally, it is significant that Aristotle (in Chapter I of the *Poetics*) classified the Platonic dialogues themselves as forms of "imitation." Plato is, in fact, one of the most poetic of all philosophers.

Admitting all of this, however, Plato's theory remains troublesome: its didactic emphasis seems too crude to be aesthetically satsifying. Generations of Neoplatonic critics, from Plotinus to Shelley, have attempted to remedy this problem by locating another, more powerful positive emphasis in Plato's poetic: a doctrine of inspiration, in which the poet is seen as the direct imitator of ultimate reality, not a mere copier of the images of physical nature. This doctrine, which makes of the poet a mystic visionary, accords art a supreme role in human life, far beyond that of a "beginning stage" for spiritual growth.

The putative basis for this doctrine is Plato's *Ion*, an investigation into the nature of the skill and knowledge of the poet and rhapsode. Ion, an elocutionist extremely talented in interpreting Homer, is nevertheless puzzled by his inability to interpret other poets equally well. Socrates proceeds to show that Ion lacks a truly scientific command of his subject matter—i.e., medicine, military strategy, and other areas of knowledge within the Homeric poems. (When Ion momentarily anticipates Aristotle by asking whether the province of poetic knowledge is really "the entire poems" rather than any separable discipline discussed in the poems, Socrates disregards the question.) According to Socrates, the kind of knowledge possessed by a poet or rhapsode must be based on divine inspiration, since it obviously cannot be based on scientific expertise. Socrates uses the image of a magnetic field to explain the nature of inspiration. The muse of poetry is the source of a power which pulls the poet's soul toward the ideal; the poet in turn influences the rhapsode (Ion) who finally communicates this influence to the audience.

Despite the strong possibility that Plato is being ironic, that he is using the disjunction which concludes *Ion* to satirize the pretentiousness of poets and rhapsodes,[2] the concept of *furor poeticus*, inspiration in which the poet is "possessed" and unconscious of what he is doing, has become a commonplace of literary theory. In the two great periods of Plato's critical influence—the Italian Renaissance and the romantic movements of the nineteenth century—*furor poeticus* has been used as a supplement for Plato's didacticism—rendering more aesthetically palatable a theory of poetry as metaphysical or ethical "truth." Renaissance Neoplatonists (e.g., Ficino and Politian) sometimes spoke of art almost as a humanistic religion, an inspired presentation of ultimate reality. For romantic critics (especially Shelley and Emerson) Plato's didactic and inspirational emphases were almost perfectly consonant with the concept of the transcendental imagination.

Generally speaking, the poetic world-view of twentieth-century criticism is far more Aristotelian than Platonic. Nevertheless, whenever a critic tries to deal fully with the truth-value, the ethical implications, or the social significance of literature, he is almost certain to provide one more "footnote" to Plato.

The translations of the selections used here (and most of the notes) are Benjamin Jowett's. They are reprinted from *The Dialogues of Plato*, 4th ed. (Oxford: Clarendon Press, 1953) by permission of the publisher. The numbers inserted in the translations are those of Stephanus (the sixteenth century scholar-printer Henri Estienne) and are generally given in editions of Plato. In the following English selections, these numbers appear in the approximate location in which they occur in the original. Stephanus' subdivisions (A, B, etc.) have been omitted.

from THE SYMPOSIUM

[*Socrates*] "Assuming Love to be such as you say, what is the use of him to men?" [*Diotima*] "That, Socrates," she replied, "I will attempt to unfold: of his nature and birth I have already spoken; and you acknowledge that love is of the beautiful. But someone will say: What does it consist in, Socrates and Diotima? Or rather let me put the question more clearly, and ask: When a man loves the beautiful, what does his love desire?" I answered her "That the beautiful may be his." "Still," she said, "the answer suggests a further question: What is given by the possession of beauty?" "To what you have asked," I replied, "I have no answer ready." "Then," she said, "let me put the word 'good' in the place of the beautiful, and repeat the question once more: If he who loves loves the good, what is it then that he loves?" "The possession of the good." "And what does he gain who possesses the good?" "Happiness," I replied; "there is less difficulty in answering that question." (205) "Yes," she said, "the happy are made happy by the acquisition of good things. Nor is there any need to ask why a man desires happiness; the answer is already final." "You are right," I said. "And is this wish and this desire common to all? And do all men always desire their own good, or only some men?—What say you?" "All men," I replied; "the desire is common to all." "Why, then," she rejoined, "are not all men, Socrates, said to love, but only some of them? whereas you say that all men are always loving the same things." "I myself wonder," I said, "why this is." "There is nothing to wonder at," she replied; "the reason is that one part of love is separated off and receives the name of the whole, but the other parts have other names." "Give an illustration," I said. She answered me as follows: "There is creative activity which, as you know, is complex and manifold. All that causes the passage of non-being into being is a 'poesy' or creation, and the processes of all art are creative; and the masters of arts are all poets or creators." "Very true." "Still," she said, "you know that they are not called poets, but have other names; only that one portion of creative activity which is separated off from the rest, and is concerned with music and meter is called by the name of the whole and is termed poetry, and they who possess poetry in this sense of the word are called poets." "Very true," I said. "And the same holds of love. For you may say generally that all desire of good and happiness is only the great and subtle power of love; but they who are drawn towards him by any other path, whether the path of money-making or gymnastics or philosophy, are not called lovers—the name of the whole is appropriated to those whose desire takes one form only—they alone are said to love, or to be lovers." "I dare say," I replied, "that you are right." "Yes," she added, "and you hear people say that lovers are seeking for their other half; but I say that they are seeking neither for the half of themselves, nor for the whole, unless the half or the whole be also a good; men will cut off their own hands and feet and cast them away, if they think them evil. They do not, I imagine, each cling to what is his own, unless perchance there be someone who calls what belongs to him the good, and what belongs to another the evil; (206) for there is nothing which men love but the good. Is there anything?" "Certainly, I should say, that there is nothing." "Then," she said, "the simple truth is, that men love the good." "Yes," I said. "To which must be added that they love the possession of the good?" "Yes, that must be added." "And not only the possession, but the everlasting possession of the good?" "That must be added too." "Then love," she said, "may be described generally as the love of the everlasting possession of the good?" "That is most true."

"Then if this be always the nature of love, can you tell me further," she went on, "what is the manner of the pursuit? what are they doing who show all this eagerness and heat which is called love? And what is the object which they have in view? Answer me." "Nay, Diotima," I replied, "if I knew, I should not be wondering at your wisdom, neither should I come to learn from you about this very matter." "Well," she said, "I will teach you: The object which they have in view is birth in beauty, whether of body or soul." "I do not understand you," I said; "the oracle requires an explanation." "I will make my meaning clearer," she replied. "I mean to say, that all men are bringing to the birth in their bodies and in their souls. There is a certain age at which human nature is desirous of procreation—procreation which must be in beauty and not in deformity. The union of man and woman is a procreation; it is a divine thing, for conception and generation are an immortal principle in the mortal creature, and in the inharmonious they can never be. But the deformed is inharmonious with all divinity, and the beautiful harmonious. Beauty, then, is the destiny or goddess of parturition who presides at birth, and therefore, when approaching beauty, the procreating power is propitious, and expansive, and benign, and bears and produces fruit: at the sight of ugliness she frowns and contracts and has a sense of pain, and turns away, and shrivels up, and not without a pang refrains from procreation. And this is the reason why, when the hour of procreation comes, and the teeming nature is full, there is such a flutter and ecstasy about beauty whose approach is the alleviation of the bitter pain of travail. For love, Socrates, is not, as you imagine, the love of the beautiful only." "What then?" "The love of generation and of birth in beauty." "Yes," I said. "Yes, indeed," she replied. "But why of generation? Because to the mortal creature, generation is a sort of eternity and immortality, and if, as has been already admitted, love is of the everlasting possession of the good, all men will necessarily desire immortality together with good: (207) whence it must follow that love is of immortality."

All this she taught me at various times when she spoke of love. And I remember her once saying to me, "What is the cause, Socrates, of love, and the attendant desire? See you not how all animals, birds as well as beasts, in their desire of procreation, are in agony when they take the infection of love, which begins with the desire of union and then passes to the care of offspring, on whose behalf the weakest are ready to battle against the strongest even to the uttermost, and to die for them, and will let themselves be tormented with hunger, or make any other sacrifice, in order to maintain their young. Man may be supposed to act thus from reason; but why should animals have these passionate feelings? Can you tell my why?" Again I replied that I did not know. She said to me: "And do you expect ever to become a master in the art of love, if you do not know this?" "But I have told you already, Diotima, that my ignorance is the reason why I come to you, for I am conscious that I want a teacher; tell me then the cause of this and of the other mysteries of love." "Marvel not," she said, "if you believe that love is of the immortal, as we have several times acknowledged; for here again, and on the same principle too, the mortal nature is seeking as far as is possible to be everlasting and immortal: and this is only to be attained by generation, because generation always leaves behind a new and different existence in the place of the old. Nay, even in the life of the same individual there is succession and not absolute uniformity: a man is called the same, and yet in the interval between youth and age, during which every animal is said to have life and identity, he is undergoing a perpetual process of loss and reparation—hair, flesh, bones, blood, and the whole body are always changing. Which is true not only of the body, but also of the soul, whose habits, tempers, opinions, desires, pleasures, pains, fears, never remain the same way in any one of us, but are always coming and going. What is still more surprising, it is equally true of science; (208) not only do some of the sciences come to life in our minds, and others die away, so that we are never the same in regard to them either, but the same fate happens to each of them individually. For what is implied in the word 'recollection,' but the departure of knowledge, which is ever being forgotten, and is renewed and preserved by recollection, and appears to be the same although in reality new, according to that law by which all mortal things are preserved, not absolutely the same, but by substitution, the old worn-out mortality leaving another new and similar existence behind—unlike the divine, which is wholly and eternally the same? And in this way, Socrates, the mortal body, or mortal anything, partakes of immortality; but the immortal in another way. Marvel not then at the love which all men have of their offspring; for that universal love and interest is for the sake of immortality."

I was astonished at her words, and said: "Is this really true, O most wise Diotima?" And she answered with all the authority of an accomplished sophist: "Of that, Socrates, you may be assured; think only of the ambition of men, and you will wonder at the senselessness of their ways, unless you consider how they are stirred by the passionate love of fame. They are ready to run all risks, even greater than they would have run for their children, and to pour out money and undergo any sort of toil, and even to die, 'if so they leave an everlasting name.' Do you imagine that Alcestis would have died to save Admetus, or Achilles to avenge Patroclus, or your own Codrus in order to preserve the kingdom for his sons, if they had not imagined that the memory of their virtues, which still survives among us, would be immortal? Nay," she said, "I am persuaded that all men do all things, and the better they are the more they do them, in hope of the glorious fame of immortal virtue; for they desire the immortal.

"Those who are pregnant in the body only, betake themselves to women and beget children—this is the the character of their love; their offspring, as they hope, will preserve their memory and give them the blessedness and immortality which they desire for all future time. (209) But souls which are pregnant—for there certainly are men who are more creative in their souls than in their bodies, creative of that which is proper for the soul to conceive and bring forth: and if you ask me what are these conceptions, I answer, wisdom, and virtue in general—among such souls are all creative poets and all artists who are deserving of the name inventor. But the greatest and fairest sort of wisdom by far is that which is concerned with the ordering of states and families, and which is called temperance and justice. And he who in youth has the seed of these implanted in his soul, when he grows up and comes to maturity desires to beget and generate. He wanders about seeking beauty that he may get offspring—for from deformity he will beget nothing—and naturally embraces the beautiful rather than the deformed body; above all, when he finds a fair and noble and well-nurtured soul, he embraces the two in one person, and to such a one he is full of speech about virtue and the nature and pursuits of a good man, and he tries to educate him. At the touch and in the society of the beautiful which is ever present to his memory, even when absent, he brings forth that which he had conceived long before, and in company with him tends that which he brings forth; and they are married by a far nearer tie and have a closer friendship than those who beget mortal children, for the children who are their common offspring are fairer and more immortal. Who, when he thinks of Homer and Hesiod and other great poets, would not rather have their children than ordinary human ones? Who would not emulate them in the creation of children such as theirs, which have preserved their memory and given them everlasting glory? Or who would not have such children as Lycurgus left behind him to be the saviors, not only of Lacedaemon, but of Hellas, as one may say? There is Solon, too, who is the revered father of Athenian laws; and many others there are in many other places, both among Hellenes and barbarians, who have given to the world many noble works, and have been the parents of virtue of every kind; and many temples have been raised in their honor for the sake of children such as theirs; which were never raised in honor of anyone, for the sake of his mortal children.

"These are the lesser mysteries of love, into which even you, Socrates, may enter; (210) to the greater and more hidden ones which are the crown of these, and to which, if you pursue them in a right spirit, they will lead, I know not whether you will be able to attain. But I will do my utmost to inform you, and do you follow if you can. For he who would proceed aright in this matter should begin in youth to seek the company of corporeal beauty; and first, if he be guided by his instructor aright, to love one beautiful body only—out of that he should create fair thoughts; and soon he will of himself perceive that the beauty of one body is akin to the beauty of another; and then if beauty of form in general is his pursuit, how foolish would he be not to recognize that the beauty in every body is one and the same! And when he perceives this he will abate his violent love of the one, which he will despise and deem a small thing, and will become a steadfast lover of all beautiful bodies. In the next stage he will consider that the beauty of the soul is more precious than the beauty of the outward form; so that if a virtuous soul have but a little comeliness, he will be content to love and tend him, and will search out and bring to the birth thoughts which may improve the young, until he is compelled next to contemplate and see the beauty in institutions and laws, and to understand that the beauty of them all is of one family, and that personal beauty is a trifle; and after institutions his guide will lead him on to the sciences, in order that, beholding the wide region already occupied by beauty, he may cease to be like a servant in love with one beauty only, that of a particular youth or man or institution, himself a slave mean and narrow-minded; but drawing towards and contemplating the vast sea of beauty, he will create many fair and noble thoughts and discourses in boundless love of wisdom, until on that shore he grows and waxes strong, and at last the vision is revealed to him of a single science, which is the science of beauty everywhere. To this I will proceed; please give me your very best attention:

"He who has been instructed thus far in the things of love, and who has learned to see the beautiful in due order and succession, when he comes toward the end will suddenly perceive a nature of wondrous beauty (and this, Socrates, is the final cause of all our former toils)—a nature which in the first place is everlasting, (211) knowing not birth or death, growth or decay; secondly, not fair in one point of view and foul in another, or at one time or in one relation or at one place fair, at another time or in another relation or at another place foul, as if fair to some and foul to others, or in the likeness of a face or hands or any other part of the bodily frame, or in any form of speech or knowledge, or existing in any individual being, as for example, in a living creature, whether in heaven, or in earth, or anywhere else; but beauty absolute, separate, simple, and everlasting, which is imparted to the ever growing and perishing beauties of all other beautiful things, without itself suffering diminution, or increase, or any change. He who, ascending from these earthly things under the influence of true love, begins to perceive that beauty, is not far from the end. And the true order of going, or being led by another, to the things of love, is to begin from the beauties of earth and mount upwards for the sake of that other beauty, using these as steps only, and from one going on to two, and from two to all fair bodily forms, and from fair bodily forms to fair practices, and from fair practices to fair sciences, until from fair sciences he arrives at the science of which I have spoken, the science which has no other object than absolute beauty, and at last knows that which is beautiful by itself alone. This, my dear Socrates," said the stranger of Mantinea [Diotima], "is that life above all others which man should live, in the contemplation of beauty absolute; a beauty which if you once beheld, you would see not to be after the measure of gold, and garments, and fair boys and youths, whose presence now entrances you; and you and many a one would be content to live seeing them only and conversing with them without meat or drink, if that were possible—you only want to look at them and to be with them. But what if a man had eyes to see the true beauty—the divine beauty, I mean, pure and clear and unalloyed, not infected with the pollutions of the flesh and all the colors and vanities of mortal life—thither looking, and holding converse with the true beauty simple and divine? (212) Remember how in that communion only, beholding beauty with that by which it can be beheld, he will be enabled to bring forth, not images of beauty, but realities (for he has hold not of an image but of a reality), and bringing forth and nourishing true virtue will properly become the friend of God and be immortal, if mortal man may. Would that be an ignoble life?"

from PHAEDRUS

SOCRATES. I dare say that you are thoroughly at home in the views of Tisias. Now we have one more thing to ask him. Does he not define probability to be that which the many think?

PHAEDRUS. Certainly, he does.

SOC. I believe that he has a clever and ingenious case of this sort: He supposes a feeble and valiant man to have assaulted a strong and cowardly one, and to have robbed him of his coat or of something or other; he is brought into court, and then Tisias says that both parties should tell lies: the coward should say that he was assaulted by more men than one; the other should prove that they were alone, and should argue thus: "How could a weak man like me have assaulted a strong man like him?" The complainant will not like to confess his own cowardice, and will therefore invent some other lie which his adversary will thus gain an opportunity of refuting. And there are other devices of the same kind which have a place in the system. Am I not right, Phaedrus?

PHAEDR. Certainly.

SOC. Bless me, what a wonderfully mysterious art is this which Tisias or some other gentleman, in whatever name or country he rejoices, has discovered. Shall we say a word to him or not?

PHAEDR. What shall we say to him?

SOC. Let us tell him that, before he appeared, you and I were saying that the probability of which he speaks was engendered in the minds of the many by the likeness of the truth, and we had just been affirming that he who knew the truth would always know best how to discover the resemblances of the truth. If he has anything else to say about the art of speaking we should like to hear him; but if not, we are satisfied with the view recently expressed, that unless a man estimates the various characters of his hearers and is able to divide all things into classes and to comprehend every one under single ideas, he will never be a skillful rhetorician even within the limits of human power. And this skill he will not attain without a great deal of trouble, which a good man ought to undergo, not for the sake of speaking and acting before men, but in order that he may be able to say what is acceptable to God and always to act acceptably to Him as far as in him lies; for there is a saying of wiser men than ourselves, that a man of sense should not try to please his fellow servants (at least this should not be his first object) but his good and noble masters; (274) and therefore, Tisias, if the way is long and circuitous, marvel not at this, for, where the end is great, there we may take the longer road, but not for lesser ends such as yours. However, our argument says that even these are best secured as the consequence of higher aims.

PHAEDR. I think, Socrates, that this is admirable, if only practicable.

SOC. But provided one's aim is honorable, so is any ill success which may ensue.

PHAEDR. True.

SOC. Enough appears to have been said by us of a true and false art of speaking.

PHAEDR. Certainly.

SOC. But there is something yet to be said of propriety and impropriety of writing.

PHAEDR. Yes.

SOC. Do you know how you can speak or act about rhetoric in a manner which will be acceptable to God?

PHAEDR. No, indeed. Do you?

SOC. I have heard a tradition of the ancients, whether true or not they only know; although if we had found the truth ourselves, do you think that we should care much about the opinions of men?

PHAEDR. Your question needs no answer; but simply tell me what you say that you have heard.

SOC. At the Egyptian city of Naucratis there was a famous old god whose name was Theuth; the bird which is called the Ibis is sacred to him, and he was the inventor of many arts, such as arithmetic and calculation and geometry and astronomy as well as draughts and dice, but his great discovery was the use of letters. Now in those days [the god] Thamus was the king of the whole country of Egypt; and he dwelt in that great city of Upper Egypt which the Hellenes call Egyptian Thebes, and the god himself is called by them Ammon. To him came Theuth and showed his inventions, desiring that the other Egyptians might be allowed to have the benefit of them; he enumerated them, and Thamus inquired about their several uses, and praised some of them and censured others, as he approved or disapproved of them. It would take a long time to repeat all that Thamus said to Theuth in praise or blame of the various arts. But when they came to letters, Theuth said: O king, here is a study which will make the Egyptians wiser and give them better memories; it is a specific both for the memory and for the wit. Thamus replied: O most ingenious Theuth, the parent or inventor of an art is not always the best judge of the utility or inutility of his own inventions to the users of them. (275) And in this instance, you who are the father of letters, from a paternal love of your own children have been led to attribute to them a quality which they cannot have; for this discovery of yours will create forgetfulness in the learners' souls, because they will not use their memories; they will trust to the external written characters and not remember of themselves. And so the specific which you have discovered is an aid not to memory, but to reminiscence. As for wisdom, it is the reputation, not the reality, that you have to offer to those who learn from you; they will have heard many things and yet received no teaching; they will appear to be omniscient and will generally know nothing; they will be tiresome company, having acquired not wisdom, but the show of wisdom.

PHAEDR. Yes, Socrates, you can easily invent tales of Egypt, or of any other country.

SOC. There was a tradition in the temple of Dodona[1] that oaks first gave prophetic utterances. The men of old, far simpler than you sophisticated young men, deemed that if they heard the truth even from "oak or rock," it was enough; whereas you seem to consider not whether a thing is or is not true, but who the speaker is and from what country the tale comes.

PHAEDR. I acknowledge the justice of your rebuke; and I think that the Theban is right in his view about letters.

SOC. He would be a very simple person, and quite a stranger to the oracles of Thamus or Ammon, who should suppose that he had left his "Art" in writings or who should accept such an inheritance in the hope that the written word would give anything intelligible or certain; or who deemed that writing could be any more than a reminder to one who already knows the subject.

PHAEDR. That is most true.

SOC. I cannot help feeling, Phaedrus, that writing has one grave fault in common with painting; for the creations of the painter have the attitude of life, and yet if you ask them a question they preserve a solemn silence. And the same may be said of books. You would imagine that they had intelligence, but if you require any explanation of something that has been said, they preserve one unvarying meaning. And when they have been once written down they are tumbled about anywhere, all alike, among those who understand them and among strangers, and do not know to whom they should or should not reply: and, if they are maltreated or abused, they have no parent to protect them; for the book cannot protect or defend itself.

PHAEDR. That again is most true.

(276) SOC. Is there not another kind of word or speech far better than this, and having far greater power—a son of the same family, but lawfully begotten?

PHAEDR. Whom do you mean, and what is his origin?

SOC. I mean an intelligent word graven in the soul of the learner, which can defend itself, and knows with whom to speak and with whom to be silent.

PHAEDR. You mean the living word of knowledge which has a soul, and of which the written word is properly no more than an image?

SOC. Yes, of course that is what I mean. And now may I be allowed to ask you a question?: Would a husbandman, who is a man of sense, take seeds which he values and which he wishes to bear fruit, and in sober seriousness plant them during the heat of summer, in some garden of Adonis, that he may rejoice when he sees them in eight days appearing in beauty? At least he would do so, if at all, only for the sake of amusement and for show. But when he is in earnest he employs his art of husbandry and sows in fitting soil, and is satisfied if in eight months the seeds which he has sown arrive at perfection?

PHAEDR. Yes, Socrates, that will be his way when he is in earnest; he might act otherwise for the reasons which you give.

SOC. And can we suppose that he who knows the just and good and honorable has less understanding than the husbandman about his own seeds?

PHAEDR. Certainly not.

SOC. Then he will not seriously incline to "write" his thoughts "in water" with pen and ink, sowing words which can neither speak for themselves nor teach the truth adequately to others?

PHAEDR. No, that is not likely.

SOC. No, that is not likely—in the garden of letters he will sow and plant, but only for the sake of recreation and amusement; he will write them down as memorials to be treasured against the forgetfulness of old age, by himself, or by any other man who is treading the same path. He will rejoice in beholding their tender growth; and while others are refreshing their souls with banqueting and the like, this will be the pastime in which his days are spent.

PHAEDR. A pastime, Socrates, as noble as the other is ignoble, the pastime of a man who can be amused by serious talk, and can discourse merrily about justice and the like.

SOC. True, Phaedrus. But nobler far is the serious pursuit of the dialectician, who, finding a congenial soul, by the help of science sows and plants therein words which are able to defend themselves and him who planted them, (277) and are not unfruitful, but have in them a seed which others brought up in different soils render immortal, making the possessors of it happy to the utmost extent of human happiness.

PHAEDR. Far nobler, certainly.

SOC. And now at last, Phaedrus, having agreed upon this, we may decide the original question.

PHAEDR. What question was that?

SOC. I mean those problems, in trying to solve which we have made our way hither; we wished to examine the censure passed on Lysias for his professional speech-writing, and to distinguish the speech composed with art from that which is composed without art. And I think that we have now pretty well distinguished the artistic from its opposite.

PHAEDR. Yes, I thought so, but I wish that you would repeat what was said.

SOC. Until a man knows the truth of the several particulars of which he is writing or speaking, and is able to define them as they are, and having defined them again to divide them until they can be no longer divided; and until in like manner he is able to discern the nature of the soul, and discover the different modes of discourse which are adapted to different natures, and to arrange and dispose them in such a way that the simple form of speech may be addressed to the simpler nature, and the complex form, with many variations of key, to the more complex nature—until he has accomplished all this, he will be unable to handle arguments according to rules of art, as far as their nature allows them to be subjected to art, either for the purpose of teaching or persuading;—such is the view which is implied in the whole preceding argument.

PHAEDR. Yes, that was our view, certainly.

SOC. Secondly, as to the censure which was passed on the speaking or writing of discourses, and when they might be rightly or wrongly censured—did not our previous argument show—?

PHAEDR. Show what?

SOC. That whether Lysias or any other writer that ever was or will be, whether private man or statesman, proposes laws and so becomes the author of a political treatise, fancying that there is any great certainty and clearness in his performance, the fact of his so writing is only a disgrace to him, whatever men may say. For not to know the nature of justice and injustice, and good and evil, and not to be able to distinguish the dream from the reality, cannot in truth be otherwise than disgraceful to him, even though he have the applause of the whole world.

PHAEDR. Certainly.

SOC. But he who thinks that in the written word, whatever its subject, there is neccessarily much which is not serious, and that no discourse worthy of study has ever yet been written in poetry or prose, and that spoken ones are no better if, like the recitations of rhapsodes, they are delivered for the sake of persuasion, and not with any view to criticism or instruction; (278) and who thinks that even the best of writings are but a memorandum for those who know, and that only in principles of justice and goodness and nobility taught and communicated orally for the sake of instruction and graven in the soul, which is the true way of writing, is there clearness and perfection and seriousness, and that such principles should be deemed a man's own and his legitimate offspring;—being, in the first place, the word which he finds in his own bosom; secondly, the brethren and descendants and relations of his idea which have been duly implanted by him in the souls of others;—and who cares for them and no others—this is the right sort of man; and you and I, Phaedrus, would pray that we may become like him.

PHAEDR. That is most assuredly my desire and prayer.

SOC. And now the play is played out; and of rhetoric enough. Go and tell Lysias that to the fountain and school of the Nymphs we went down, and were bidden by them to convey a message to him and to other composers of speeches—to Homer and other writers of poems, whether set to music or not; and to Solon and others who have composed writings in the form of political discourses which they would term laws—to all of them we are to say that if their compositions are based on knowledge of the truth, and they can defend or prove them, when they are put to the test, by spoken arguments, which leave their writings poor in comparison of them, then they are to be called, not only poets, orators, legislators, but are worthy of a higher name, befitting the serious pursuit of their life.

PHAEDR. What name would you assign to them?

SOC. Wise, I may not call them; for that is a great name which belongs to God alone,—lovers of wisdom or philosophers is their modest and befitting title.

PHAEDR. Very suitable.

SOC. And he who cannot rise above his own compilations and compositions, which he has been long patching and piecing, adding some and taking away some, may be justly called poet or speech-maker or law-maker.

from GORGIAS

SOCRATES. Can you tell me the pursuits which delight mankind—or rather, if you would prefer, let me ask, and do you answer, which of them belong to the pleasurable class, and which of them not? In the first place, what do you say of flute-playing? Does not that appear to be an art which seeks only pleasure, Callicles, and thinks of nothing else?

CALLICLES. I assent.

SOC. And is not the same true of all similar arts, as, for example, the art of playing the lyre at festivals?

CAL. Yes.

SOC. And what do you say of the choral art and of dithyrambic poetry? Are not they of the same nature? Do you imagine that Cinesias the son of Meles cares about what will tend to the moral improvement of his hearers, or about what will give pleasure to the multitude? (502)

CAL. There can be no mistake about Cinesias, Socrates.

SOC. And what do you say of his father, Meles the harp-player? When he sang to the harp, did you suppose that he had his eye on the highest good? Perhaps he indeed could scarcely be said to regard even the greatest pleasure, since his singing was an infliction to his audience? In fact, would you not say that all music of the harp and dithyrambic poetry in general have been invented for the sake of pleasure?

CAL. I should.

SOC. And as for the Muse of Tragedy, that solemn and august personage —what are her aspirations? Is all her aim and desire only to give pleasure to the spectators, or does she strive to refrain her tongue from all that pleases and charms them but is vicious? To proclaim, in speech and song, truth that is salutary but unpleasant, whether they welcome it or not? Which in your judgment is of the nature of tragic poetry?

CAL. There can be no doubt, Socrates, that Tragedy has her face turned towards pleasure and the gratification of the audience.

SOC. And is not that the sort of thing, Callicles, which we were just now describing as flattery?

CAL. Quite true.

SOC. Well now, suppose that we strip all poetry of melody and rhythm and meter, there will remain speech?

CAL. To be sure.

SOC. And this speech is addressed to a crowd of people?

CAL. Yes.

SOC. Then poetry is a sort of public speaking?

CAL. True.

SOC. And it is a rhetorical sort of public speaking; do not the poets in the theatres seem to you to be rhetoricians?

CAL. Yes.

SOC. Then now we have discovered a sort of rhetoric which is addressed to a crowd of men, women, and children, freemen and slaves. And it is not much to our taste, for we have described it as having the nature of flattery.

CAL. Quite true.

SOC. Very good. And what do you say of that other rhetoric which addresses the Athenian Assembly and the assemblies of freemen in other states? Do the rhetoricians appear to you always to aim at what is best, and do they seek to improve the citizens by their speeches, or are they too, like the rest of mankind, bent upon giving them pleasure, forgetting the public good in the thought of their own interest, playing with the people as with children, and trying only to gratify them, but never considering whether they will be better or worse for this? (503)

CAL. The question does not admit of a simple answer. There are some who have a real care of the public in what they say, while others are such as you describe.

SOC. That is enough for me. If rhetoric also is twofold, one part of it will be mere flattery and disgraceful declamation; the other noble, aiming at the improvement of the souls of the citizens, and striving to say what is best, whether welcome or unwelcome to the audience. But you have never known such a rhetoric; or if you have, and can point out any rhetorician who is of this stamp, who is he?

CAL. But, indeed, I am afraid that I cannot tell you of any such among the orators who are at present living.

ION

(530) SOCRATES. Welcome, Ion. Are you from your native city of Ephesus?

ION. No, Socrates; but from Epidaurus, where I attended the festival of Aesculapius.

SOC. Indeed! Do the Epidaurians have a contest of rhapsodes[1] in his honor?

ION. O yes; and of other kinds of music.

SOC. And were you one of the competitors—and did you succeed?

ION. I—we—obtained the first prize of all, Socrates.

SOC. Well done; now we must win another victory, at the Panathenaea.[2]

ION. It shall be so, please heaven.

SOC. I have often envied the profession of a rhapsode, Ion; for it is a part of your art to wear fine clothes and to look as beautiful as you can, while at the same time you are obliged to be continually in the company of many good poets, and especially of Homer, who is the best and most divine of them, and to understand his mind, and not merely learn his words by rote; all this is a thing greatly to be envied. I am sure that no man can become a good rhapsode who does not understand the meaning of the poet. For the rhapsode ought to interpret the mind of the poet to his hearers, but how can he interpret him well unless he knows what he means? All this is much to be envied, I repeat.

ION. Very true, Socrates; interpretation has certainly been the most laborious part of my art; and I believe myself able to speak about Homer better than any man; and that neither Metrodorus of Lampsacus, nor Stesimbrotus of Thasos, nor Glaucon, nor anyone else who ever was, had as good ideas about Homer as I have, or as many.

SOC. I am glad to hear you say so, Ion; I see that you will not refuse to acquaint me with them.

ION. Certainly, Socrates; and you really ought to hear how exquisitely I display the beauties of Homer. I think that the Homeridae should give me a golden crown.[3]

SOC. I shall take an opportunity of hearing your embellishments of him at some other time. (531) But just now I should like to ask you a question: Does your art extend to Hesiod and Archilochus, or to Homer only?

ION. To Homer only; he is in himself quite enough.

SOC. Are there any things about which Homer and Hesiod agree?

ION. Yes; in my opinion there are a good many.

SOC. And can you interpret what Homer says about these matters better than what Hesiod says?

ION. I can interpret them equally well, Socrates, where they agree.

SOC. But what about matters in which they do not agree? For example, about divination of which both Homer and Hesiod have something to say—

ION. Very true.

SOC. Would you or a good prophet be a better interpreter of what these two poets say about divination, not only when they agree, but when they disagree?

ION. A prophet.

SOC. And if you were a prophet, and could interpret them where they agree, would you not know how to interpret them also where they disagree?

ION. Clearly.

SOC. But how did you come to have this skill about Homer only, and not about Hesiod or the other poets? Does not Homer speak of the same themes which all other poets handle? Is not war his great argument? And does he not speak of human society and of intercourse of men, good and bad, skilled and unskilled, and of the gods conversing with one another and with mankind, and about what happens in heaven and in the world below, and the generations of gods and heroes? Are not these the themes of which Homer sings?

ION. Very true, Socrates.

SOC. And do not the other poets sing of the same?

ION. Yes, Socrates; but not in the same way as Homer.

SOC. What, in a worse way?

ION. Yes, in a far worse.

SOC. And Homer in a better way?

ION. He is incomparably better.

SOC. And yet surely, my dear friend Ion, where many people are discussing numbers, and one speaks better than the rest, there is somebody who can judge which of them is the good speaker?

ION. Yes.

SOC. And he who judges of the good will be the same as he who judges of the bad speakers?

ION. The same.

SOC. One who knows the science of arithmetic?

ION. Yes.

SOC. Or again, if many persons are discussing the wholesomeness of food, and one speaks better than the rest, will he who recognizes the better speaker be a different person from him who recognizes the worse, or the same?

ION. Clearly the same.

SOC. And who is he, and what is his name?

ION. The physician.

SOC. And speaking generally, in all discussions in which the subject is the same and many men are speaking, will not he who knows the good know the bad speaker also? (532) For obviously if he does not know the bad, neither will he know the good, when the same topic is being discussed.

ION. True.

SOC. We find, in fact, that the same person is skillful in both?

ION. Yes.

SOC. And you say that Homer and the other poets, such as Hesiod and Archilochus, speak of the same things, although not in the same way; but the one speaks well and the other not so well?

ION. Yes; and I am right in saying so.

SOC. And if you know the good speaker, you ought also to know the inferior speakers to be inferior?

ION. It would seem so.

SOC. Then, my dear friend, can I be mistaken in saying that Ion is equally skilled in Homer and in other poets, since he himself acknowledges that the same person will be a good judge of all those who speak of the same things; and that almost all poets do speak of the same things?

ION. Why then, Socrates, do I lose attention and have absolutely no ideas of the least value and practically fall asleep when anyone speaks of any other poet; but when Homer is mentioned, I wake up at once and am all attention and have plenty to say?

SOC. The reason, my friend, is not hard to guess. No one can fail to see that you speak of Homer without any art or knowledge. If you were able to speak of him by rules of art, you would have been able to speak of all other poets; for poetry is a whole.

ION. Yes.

SOC. And when anyone acquires any other art as a whole, the same may be said of them. Would you like me to explain my meaning, Ion?

ION. Yes, indeed, Socrates; I very much wish that you would: for I love to hear you wise men talk.

SOC. O that we were wise, Ion, and that you could truly call us so; but you rhapsodes and actors, and the poets whose verses you sing, are wise; whereas I am a common man, who only speak the truth. For consider what a very commonplace and trivial thing is this which I have said—a thing which any man might say: that when a man has acquired a knowledge of a whole art, the inquiry into good and bad is one and the same. Let us consider this matter; is not the art of painting a whole?

ION. Yes.

SOC. And there are and have been many painters good and bad?

ION. Yes.

SOC. And did you ever know anyone who was skillful in pointing out the excellences and defects of Polygnotus the son of Aglaophon, but incapable of criticizing other painters; (533) and when the work of any other painter was produced, went to sleep and was at a loss, and had no ideas; but when he had to give his opinion about Polygnotus, or whoever the painter might be, and about him only, woke up and was attentive and had plenty to say?

ION. No indeed, I have never known such a person.

SOC. Or take sculpture—did you ever know of anyone who was skillful in expounding the merits of Daedalus the son of Metion, or of Epeius the son of Panopeus, or of Theodorus the Samian, or of any individual sculptor; but when the works of sculptors in general were produced, was at a loss and went to sleep and had nothing to say?

ION. No indeed; no more than the other.

SOC. And if I am not mistaken, you never met with anyone among flute-players or harp-players or singers to the harp or rhapsodes who was able to discourse of Olympus or Thamyras or Orpheus, or Phemius the rhapsode of Ithaca, but was at a loss when he came to speak of Ion of Ephesus, and had no notion of his merits or defects?

ION. I cannot deny what you say, Socrates. Nevertheless I am conscious in my own self, and the world agrees with me, that I do speak better and have more to say about Homer than any other man; but I do not speak equally well about others. After all, there must be some reason for this; what is it?

SOC. I see the reason, Ion; and I will proceed to explain to you what I imagine it to be. The gift which you possess of speaking excellently about Homer is not an art, but, as I was just saying, an inspiration; there is a divinity moving you, like that contained in the stone which Euripides calls a magnet, but which is commonly known as the stone of Heraclea. This stone not only attracts iron rings, but also imparts to them a similar power of attracting other rings; and sometimes you may see a number of pieces of iron and rings suspended from one another so as to form quite a long chain: and all of them derive their power of suspension from the original stone. In like manner the Muse first of all inspires men herself; and from these inspired persons a chain of other persons is suspended, who take the inspiration. For all good poets, epic as well as lyric, compose their beautiful poems not by art, but because they are inspired and possessed. (534) And as the Corybantian revelers[4] when they dance are not in their right mind, so the lyric poets are not in their right mind when they are composing their beautiful strains: but when falling under the power of music and meter they are inspired and possessed; like Bacchic maidens who draw milk and honey from the rivers when they are under the influence of Dionysus but not when they are in their right mind. And the soul of the lyric poet does the same, as they themselves say; for they tell us that they bring songs from honeyed fountains, culling them out of the gardens and dells of the Muses; they, like the bees, wing-ing their way from flower to flower. And this is true. For the poet is a light and winged and holy thing, and there is no invention in him until he has been inspired and is out of his senses, and reason is no longer in him: no man, while he retains that faculty, has the oracular gift of poetry.

Many are the noble words in which poets speak concerning the actions of men; but like yourself when speaking about Homer, they do not speak of them by any rules of art: they are simply inspired to utter that to which the Muse impels them, and that only; and when inspired, one of them will make dithyrambs,[5] another hymns of praise, another choral strains, another epic or iambic verses, but not one of them is of any account in the other kinds. For not by art does the poet sing, but by power divine; had he learned by rules of art, he would have known how to speak not of one theme only, but of all; and therefore God takes away reason from poets, and uses them as his ministers, as he also uses the pronouncers of oracles and holy prophets, in order that we who hear them may know them to be speaking not of themselves, who utter these priceless words while bereft of reason, but that God himself is the speaker, and that through them he is addressing us. And Tynnichus the Chalcidian affords a striking instance of what I am saying: he wrote no poem that anyone would care to remember but the famous paean[6] which is in everyone's mouth, one of the finest lyric poems ever written, simply an invention of the Muses, as he himself says. For in this way God would seem to demonstrate to us and not to allow us to doubt that these beautiful poems are not human, nor the work of man, but divine and the work of God; and that the poets are only the interpreters of the gods by whom they are severally possessed. (535) Was not this the lesson which God intended to teach when by the mouth of the worst of poets he sang the best of songs? Am I not right, Ion?

ION. Yes, indeed, Socrates, I feel that you are; for your words touch my soul, and I am persuaded that in these works the good poets, under divine inspiration, interpret to us the voice of the gods.

SOC. And you rhapsodists are the interpreters of the poets?

ION. There again you are right.

SOC. Then you are the interpreters of interpreters?

ION. Precisely.

SOC. I wish you would frankly tell me, Ion, what I am going to ask of you: When you produce the greatest effect upon the audience in the recitation of some striking passage, such as the apparition of Odysseus leaping forth on the floor, recognized by the suitors and shaking out his arrows at his feet, or the description of Achilles springing upon Hector, or the sorrows of Andromache, Hecuba, or Priam—are you in your right mind? Are you not carried out of yourself, and does not your soul in an ecstasy seem to be among the persons or places of which you are speaking, whether they are in Ithaca or in Troy or whatever may be the scene of the poem?

ION. That proof strikes home to me, Socrates. For I must frankly confess that at the tale of pity my eyes are filled with tears, and when I speak of horrors, my hair stands on end and my heart throbs.

SOC. Well, Ion, and what are we to say of a man who at a sacrifice or festival, when he is dressed in an embroidered robe, and has golden crowns upon his head, of which nobody has robbed him, appears weeping or panic-stricken in the presence of more than twenty thousand friendly faces, when there is no one despoiling or wronging him—is he in his right mind or is he not?

ION. No indeed, Socrates, I must say that, strictly speaking, he is not in his right mind.

SOC. And are you aware that you produce similar effects on most of the spectators?

ION. Only too well; for I look down upon them from the stage, and behold the various emotions of pity, wonder, sternness, stamped upon their countenances when I am speaking: and I am obliged to give my very best attention to them; for if I make them cry I myself shall laugh, and if I make them laugh I myself shall cry, when the time of payment arrives.

SOC. Do you know that the spectator is the last of the rings which, as I am saying, receive the power of the original magnet from one another? The rhapsode like yourself and the actor are intermediate links, and the poet himself is the first of them. (536) Through all these God sways the souls of men in any direction which He pleases, causing each link to communicate the power to the next. Thus there is a vast chain of dancers and masters and undermasters of choruses, who are suspended, as if from the stone, at the side of the rings which hang down from the Muse. And every poet has some Muse from whom he is suspended, and by whom he is said to be possessed, which is nearly the same thing; for he is taken hold of. And from these first rings, which are the poets, depend others, some deriving their inspiration from Orpheus, others from Musaeus; but the greater number are possessed and held by Homer. Of whom, Ion, you are one, and are possessed by Homer; and when anyone repeats the words of another poet you go to sleep, and know not what to say; but when anyone recites a strain of Homer you wake up in a moment, and your soul leaps within you, and you have plenty to say; for not by art or knowledge about Homer do you say what you say, but by divine inspiration and by possession; just as the Corybantian revelers too have a quick perception of that strain only which is appropriated to the god by whom they are possessed, and have plenty of dances and words for that, but take no heed of any other. And you, Ion, when the name of Homer is mentioned have plenty to say, and have nothing to say of others. You ask, "Why is this?" The answer is that your skill in the praise of Homer comes not from art but from divine inspiration.

ION. That is good, Socrates; and yet I doubt whether you will ever have eloquence enough to persuade me that I praise Homer only when I am mad and possessed; and if you could hear me speak of him I am sure you would never think this to be the case.

SOC. I should like very much to hear you, but not until you have answered a question which I have to ask. On what part of Homer do you speak well?—not surely about every part?

ION. There is no part, Socrates, about which I do not speak well: of that I can assure you.

SOC. Surely not about things in Homer of which you have no knowledge?

ION. And what is there in Homer of which I have no knowledge?

(537) SOC. Why, does not Homer speak in many passages about arts? For example, about driving; if I can only remember the lines I will repeat them.

ION. I remember, and will repeat them.

SOC. Tell me then, what Nestor says to Antilochus, his son, where he bids him be careful of the turn at the horse-race in honor of Patroclus.

ION. "Bend gently," he says, "in the polished chariot to the left of them, and urge the horse on the right hand with whip and voice; and slacken the rein. And when you are at the goal, let the left horse draw near, so that the nave of the well-wrought wheel may appear to graze the extremity; but have a care not to touch the stone."[7]

SOC. Enough. Now, Ion, will the charioteer or the physician be the better judge of the propriety of these lines?

ION. The charioteer, clearly.

SOC. And will the reason be that this is his art, or will there be any other reason?

ION. No, that will be the reason.

SOC. And every art is appointed by God to have knowledge of a certain work; for that which we know by the art of the pilot we shall not succeed in knowing also by the art of medicine?

ION. Certainly not.

SOC. Nor shall we know by the art of the carpenter that which we know by the art of medicine?

ION. Certainly not.

SOC. And this is true of all the arts—that which we know with one art we shall not know with the other? But let me ask a prior question: You admit that there are differences of arts?

ION. Yes.

SOC. You would argue, as I should, that if there are two kinds of knowledge, dealing with different things, these can be called different arts?

ION. Yes.

SOC. Yes, surely; for if the object of knowledge were the same, there would be no meaning in saying that the arts were different—since they both gave the same knowledge. For example, I know that here are five fingers, and you know the same. And if I were to ask whether I and you became acquainted with this fact by the help of the same art of arithmetic, you would acknowledge that we did?

ION. Yes.

(538) SOC. Tell me, then, what I was intending to ask you—whether in your opinion this holds universally? If two arts are the same, must not they necessarily have the same objects? And if one differs from another, must it not be because the object is different?

ION. That is my opinion, Socrates.

SOC. Then he who has no knowledge of a particular art will have no right judgment of the precepts and practice of that art?

ION. Very true.

SOC. Then which will be the better judge of the lines which you were reciting from Homer, you or the charioteer?

ION. The charioteer.

SOC. Why, yes, because you are a rhapsode and not a charioteer.

ION. Yes.

SOC. And the art of the rhapsode is different from that of the charioteer?

ION. Yes.

SOC. And if a different knowledge, then a knowledge of different matters?

ION. True.

SOC. You know the passage in which Hecamede, the concubine of Nestor, is described as giving to the wounded Machaon a posset, as he says, "made with Pramnian wine; and she grated cheese of goat's milk with a grater of bronze, and at his side placed an onion which gives a relish to drink."[8] Now would you say that the art of the rhapsode or the art of medicine was better able to judge of the propriety of these lines?

ION. The art of medicine.

SOC. And when Homer says, "And she descended into the deep like a leaden plummet, which, set in the horn of ox that ranges the fields, rushes along carrying death among the ravenous fishes,"[9] will the art of the fisherman or of the rhapsode be better able to judge what these lines mean, and whether they are accurate or not?

ION. Clearly, Socrates, the art of the fisherman.

SOC. Come now, suppose that you were to say to me: "Since you, Socrates, are able to assign different passages in Homer to their corresponding arts, I wish that you would tell me what are the passages of which the excellence ought to be judged by the prophet and prophetic art"; and you will see how readily and truly I shall answer you. For there are many such passages, particularly in the Odyssey; as, for example, the passage in which Theoclymenus the prophet of the house of Melampus says to the suitors:

> (539) Wretched men! what is happening to you? Your heads
> and your faces and your limbs underneath are shrouded in night;

> and the voice of lamentation bursts forth, and your cheeks are wet with tears. And the vestibule is full, and the court is full, of ghosts descending into the darkness of Erebus, and the sun has perished out of heaven, and an evil mist is spread abroad.[10]

And there are many such passages in the Iliad also; as for example in the description of the battle near the rampart, where he says:

> As they were eager to pass the ditch, there came to them an omen: a soaring eagle, skirting the people on his left, bore a huge blood-red dragon in his talons, still living and panting; nor had he yet resigned the strife, for he bent back and smote the bird which carried him on the breast by the neck, and he in pain let him fall from him to the ground into the midst of the multitude. And the eagle, with a cry, was borne afar on the wings of the wind.[11]

These are the sort of things which I should say that the prophet ought to consider and determine.

ION. And you are quite right, Socrates, in saying so.

SOC. Yes, Ion, and you are right also. And as I have selected from the Iliad and Odyssey for you passages which describe the office of the prophet and the physician and the fisherman, do you, who know Homer so much better than I do, Ion, select for me passages which relate to the rhapsode and the rhapsode's art, and which the rhapsode ought to examine and judge of better than other men.

ION. All passages, I should say, Socrates.

SOC. Not all, Ion, surely. Have you already forgotten what you were saying? A rhapsode ought to have a better memory.

(540) ION. Why, what am I forgetting?

SOC. Do you not remember that you declared the art of the rhapsode to be different from the art of the charioteer?

ION. Yes, I remember.

SOC. And you admitted that being different they would know different objects?

ION. Yes.

SOC. Then upon your own showing the rhapsode, and the art of the rhapsode, will not know everything?

ION. I should exclude such things as you mention, Socrates.

SOC. You mean to say that you would exclude pretty much the subjects of the other arts. As he does not know all of them, which of them will he know?

ION. He will know what a man and what a woman ought to say, and what a freeman and what a slave ought to say, and what a ruler and what a subject.

SOC. Do you mean that a rhapsode will know better than the pilot what the ruler of a sea-tossed vessel ought to say?

ION. No; the pilot will know best.

SOC. Or will the rhapsode know better than the physician what the ruler of a sick man ought to say?

ION. Again, no.

SOC. But he will know what a slave ought to say?

ION. Yes.

SOC. Suppose the slave to be a cowherd; the rhapsode will know better than the cowherd what he ought to say in order to soothe infuriated cows?

ION. No, he will not.

SOC. But he will know what a spinning-woman ought to say about the working of wool?

ION. No.

SOC. At any rate he will know what a general ought to say when exhorting his soldiers?

ION. Yes, that is the sort of thing which the rhapsode will be sure to know.

SOC. What! Is the art of the rhapsode the art of the general?

ION. I am sure that I should know what a general ought to say.

SOC. Why, yes, Ion, because you may possibly have the knowledge of a general as well as that of a rhapsode; and you might also have a knowledge of horsemanship as well as of the lyre, and then you would know when horses were well or ill managed. But suppose I were to ask you: By the help of which art, Ion, do you know whether horses are well managed, by your skill as a horseman or as a performer on the lyre—what would you answer?

ION. I should reply, by my skill as a horseman.

SOC. And if you judged of performers on the lyre, you would admit that you judged of them as a performer on the lyre, and not as a horseman?

ION. Yes.

SOC. And in judging of the general's art, do you judge as a general, or as a good rhapsode?

ION. To me there appears to be no difference between them.

(541) SOC. What do you mean? Do you mean to say that the art of the rhapsode and of the general is the same?

ION. Yes, one and the same.

SOC. Then he who is a good rhapsode is also a good general?

ION. Certainly Socrates.

SOC. And he who is a good general is also a good rhapsode?

ION. No; I do not agree to that.

SOC. But you do agree that he who is a good rhapsode is also a good general.

ION. Certainly.

SOC. And you are the best of Hellenic rhapsodes?

ION. Far the best, Socrates.

SOC. And are you also the best general, Ion?

ION. To be sure, Socrates; and Homer was my master.

SOC. But then, Ion, why in the name of goodness do you, who are the best of generals as well as the best of rhapsodes in all Hellas, go about reciting rhapsodies when you might be a general? Do you think that the Hellenes are in grave need of a rhapsode with his golden crown, and have no need at all of a general?

ION. Why, Socrates, the reason is that my countrymen, the Ephesians, are the servants and soldiers of Athens, and do not need a general; and that you and Sparta are not likely to appoint me, for you think that you have enough generals of your own.

SOC. My good Ion, did you never hear of Apollodorus of Cyzicus?

ION. Who may he be?

SOC. One who, though a foreigner, has often been chosen their general by the Athenians: and there is Phanosthenes of Andros, and Heraclides of Clazomenae, whom they have also appointed to the command of their armies and to other offices, although aliens, after they had shown their merit. And will they not choose Ion the Ephesian to be their general, and honor him, if they deem him qualified? Were not the Ephesians originally Athenians, and Ephesus is no mean city? But, indeed, Ion, if you are correct in saying that by art and knowledge you are able to praise Homer, you do not deal fairly with me, and after all your professions of knowing many glorious things about Homer, and promises that you would exhibit them, you only deceive me, and so far from exhibiting the art of which you are a master, will not, even after my repeated entreaties, explain to me the nature of it. You literally assume as many forms as Proteus, twisting and turning up and down, until at last you slip away from me in the disguise of a general, in order that you may escape exhibiting your Homeric lore. (542) And if you have art, then, as I was saying, in falsifying your promise that you would exhibit Homer, you are not dealing fairly with me. But if, as I believe, you have no art, but speak all these beautiful words about Homer unconsciously under his inspiring influence, then I acquit you of dishonesty, and shall only say that you are inspired. Which do you prefer to be thought, dishonest or inspired?

ION. There is a great difference, Socrates, between the two alternatives; and inspiration is by far the nobler.

SOC. Then, Ion, I shall assume the nobler alternative; and attribute to you in your praises of Homer inspiration, and not art.

THE REPUBLIC

from BOOK III

Persons of the Dialogue

Socrates Adeimantus Glaucon

(386) Then as far as the gods are concerned, I said, such tales are to be told, and such others are not to be told to our disciples from their youth upwards, if we mean them to honor the gods and their parents, and to value friendship with one another.

Yes; and I think that our principles are right, he said.

But if they are to be courageous, must they not learn other lessons besides these, and lessons of such a kind as will take away the fear of death? Can any man be courageous who has the fear of death in him?

Certainly not, he said.

And can he be fearless of death, or will he choose death in battle rather than defeat and slavery, who believes the world below to be real and terrible?

Impossible.

Then we must assume a control over the narrators of this class of tales as well as over the others, and beg them not simply to revile, but rather to commend the world below, intimating to them that their descriptions are untrue, and will do harm to our future warriors.

That will be our duty, he said.

Then, I said, we shall have to obliterate many obnoxious passages, beginning with the verses, "I would rather be a serf on the land of a poor and portionless man than rule over all the dead who have come to nought."[1] We must also expunge the verse, which tells us how Pluto feared: "Lest the mansions grim and squalid which the gods abhor should be seen both of mortals and immortals."[2] And again: "O heavens! verily in the house of Hades there is soul and ghostly form, but no mind at all in them!"[3] Again of Tiresias: "[To him even after death did Persephone grant mind] that he alone should be wise; but the other souls are flitting shades."[4] Again: "The soul flying from the limbs had gone to Hades, lamenting her fate, leaving manhood and youth."[5] Again: "And the soul, with shrilling cry, passed like smoke beneath the earth."[6] (387) And, "As bats in hollow of mystic cavern, whenever any of them has dropped out of the string and falls from the rock, fly shrilling and cling to one another, so did they with shrilling cry hold together as they moved."[7] And we must beg Homer and the other poets not to be angry if we strike out these and similar passages, not because they are unpoetical, or unattractive to the popular ear, but because the greater the poetical charm of them, the less are they meet[8] for the ears of boys and men who are meant to be free, and who should fear slavery more than death.

Undoubtedly.

Also we shall have to reject all the terrible and appalling names which describe the world below—Cocytus and Styx, ghosts under the earth, and sapless shades, and any similar words of which the very mention causes a shudder to pass through the inmost soul[4] of him who hears them. I do not say that these horrible stories may not have a use of some kind; but there is a danger that our guardians may be rendered too excitable and effeminate by them.

There is a real danger, he said.

Then we must have no more of them.

True.

Our poets must sing in another and a nobler strain.

Clearly.

And shall we proceed to get rid of the weepings and wailings of famous men?

They will go with the rest.

But shall we be right in getting rid of them? Reflect: our principle is that the good man will not consider death terrible to any other good man who is his comrade.

Yes; that is our principle.

And therefore he will not sorrow for his departed friend as though he had suffered anything terrible?

He will not.

Another thing which we should say of him is that he is the most sufficient for himself and his own happiness, and therefore is least in need of other men.

True, he said.

And for this reason the loss of a son or brother, or any deprivation of fortune, is to him of all men least terrible.

Assuredly.

And therefore he will be least likely to lament, and will bear with the greatest equanimity any misfortune of this sort which may befall him.

Yes, he will feel such a misfortune far less than another.

Then we shall be right in getting rid of the lamentations of famous men, and making them over to women (and not even to women who are good for anything), (388) or to men of a baser sort, that those who are being educated by us to be the defenders of their country may scorn to do the like.

That will be very right.

Then we will once more entreat Homer and the other poets not to depict Achilles,[9] who is the son of a goddess, first lying on his side, then on his back, and then on his face; then starting up and sailing[10] in a frenzy along the shores of the barren sea; now taking the sooty ashes in both his hands and pouring them

over his head, or weeping and wailing[11] in the various modes which Homer has delineated. Nor should he describe Priam the kinsman of the gods as praying and beseeching, "rolling in the dirt, calling each man loudly by his name."[12] Still more earnestly will we beg of him at all events not to introduce the gods lamenting and saying, "Alas! my misery! Alas! that I bore the bravest to my sorrow."[13] But if he must introduce the gods, at any rate let him not dare so completely to misrepresent the greatest of the gods, as to make him say: "O heavens! with my eyes verily I behold a dear friend of mine chased round and round the city, and my heart is sorrowful."[14] Or again: "Woe is me that I am fated to have Sarpedon, dearest of men to me, subdued at the hands of Patroclus the son of Menoetius."[15] For if, my dear Adeimantus, our young men seriously listen to such unworthy representations of the gods, instead of laughing at them as they ought, hardly will any of them deem that he himself, being but a man, can be dishonored by similar actions; neither will he rebuke any inclination which may arise in his mind to say and do the like. And instead of having any shame or endurance, he will be always whining and lamenting on slight occasions.

Yes, he said, that is most true.

Yes, I replied; but that surely is what ought not to be, as the argument has just proved to us; and by that proof we must abide until it is disproved by a better.

It ought not to be.

Neither ought our guardians to be given to laughter. For a fit of laughter which has been indulged to excess almost always demands a violent reaction.

So I believe.

Then persons of worth, even if only mortal men, must not be represented as overcome by laughter, and still less must such a representation of the gods be allowed.

(389) Still less of the gods, as you say, he replied.

Then we shall not suffer such an expression to be used about the gods as that of Homer when he describes how "inextinguishable laughter arose among the blessed gods, when they saw Hephaestus bustling about the mansion."[16] On your views, we must not admit them.

On my views, if you like to father them on me; that we must not admit them is certain.

Again, truth should be highly valued; if we were right in saying that falsehood is useless to the gods, and useful only as a medicine to men, then the use of such medicines should be restricted to physicians; private individuals have no business with them.

Clearly not, he said.

Then if anyone at all is to have the privilege of lying, the rulers of the state should be the persons; and they, in their dealings either with enemies or with their own citizens, may be allowed to lie for the public good. But nobody else

should meddle with anything of the kind; and although the rulers have this privilege, for a private man to lie to them in return is to be deemed a more heinous fault than for the patient or the pupil of a gymnasium not to speak the truth about his own bodily illnesses to the physician or to the trainer, or for a sailor not to tell the captain what is happening about the ship and the rest of the crew, and how things are going with himself or his fellow sailors.

Most true, he said.

If, then, the ruler catches in a lie anybody beside himself in the state, "any of the craftsmen, whether he be priest or physician or carpenter,"[17] he will punish him for introducing a practice which is equally subversive and destructive of ship or state.

Most certainly, he said, if our talk about the state is ever translated into action.[18]

In the next place our youth must be temperate?

Certainly.

Are not the chief elements of temperance, speaking generally, obedience to commanders and command of oneself in the pleasures of eating and drinking, and of sexual relations?

True.

Then we shall approve such language as that of Diomede in Homer, "Friend, sit still and obey my word,"[19] and the verses which follow, "The Greeks marched breathing prowess,[20] . . . in silent awe of their leaders,"[21] and other sentiments of the same kind.

We shall.

What of this line, "O heavy with wine, who hast the eyes of a dog and the heart of a stag,"[22] and of the words which follow? (390) Would you say that these, or any similar impertinences which private individuals are supposed to address to their rulers, whether in verse or prose, are well or ill spoken?

They are ill spoken.

They may very possibly afford some amusement, but they do not conduce to temperance. And therefore they are likely to do harm to our young men—you would agree with me there?

Yes.

And then, again, to make the wisest of men say that nothing in his opinion is more glorious than "When the tables are full of bread and meat, and the cup-bearer carries round wine which he draws from the bowl and pours into the cups";[23] is it fit or conducive to self-control for a young man to hear such words? Or the verse "The saddest of fates is to die and meet destiny from hunger"?[24] What would you say again to the tale of Zeus, who, while other gods and men were asleep and he the only person awake, lay devising plans, but forgot them all in a moment through his lust, and was so completely overcome at the sight of Hera that he would not even go into the hut, but wanted to lie with her on the ground,

declaring that he had never been in such a state of rapture before, even when they first used to meet one another "without the knowledge of their parents";[25] or that other tale of how Hephaestus, because of similar goings-on, cast a chain around Ares and Aphrodite?[26]

Indeed, he said, I am strongly of opinion that they ought not to hear that sort of thing.

But any instances of endurance of various ills by famous men which are recounted or represented in drama, these they ought to see and hear; as, for example, what is said in the verses, "He smote his breast and thus reproached his heart,/ Endure, my heart; far worse hast thou endured!"[27]

Certainly, he said.

In the next place, we must not let them be receivers of bribes or lovers of money.

Certainly not.

Neither must we sing to them of "gifts persuading gods, and persuading reverend kings."[28] Neither is Phoenix, the tutor of Achilles, to be approved or deemed to have given his pupil good counsel when he told him that if the Greeks offered him gifts he should assist them;[29] but that without a gift he should not lay aside his anger. Neither will we believe or acknowledge Achilles himself to have been such a lover of money that he took Agamemnon's gifts, or that when he had received payment he restored the dead body of Hector, but that without payment he was unwilling to do so.[30]

(391) Undoubtedly, he said, these are not sentiments which can be approved.

Loving Homer as I do,[31] I hardly like to say that to attribute these feelings to Achilles, or to accept such a narrative from others, is downright impiety. As little can I believe the narrative of his insolence to Apollo, where he says, "Thou hast wronged me, O far-darter, most abominable of deities. Verily I would be even with thee, if I had only the power";[32] or his insubordination to the river-god,[33] on whose divinity he is ready to lay hands; or his offering to the dead Patroclus of his own hair,[34] which had been previously dedicated to the other river-god Spercheius, and that he actually performed this vow; or that he dragged Hector round the tomb of Patroclus,[35] and slaughtered the captives at the pyre;[36] all this we shall declare to be untrue, and shall not allow our citizens to be persuaded that he, the wise Cheiron's pupil, the son of a goddess and of Peleus who was the most modest of men and third in descent from Zeus, was so confused within as to be affected with two seemingly inconsistent diseases, meanness, not untainted by avarice, and overweening contempt of gods and men.

You are quite right, he replied.

And let us equally refuse to believe, or allow to be repeated, the tale of Theseus son of Poseidon, and Peirithous son of Zeus, going forth as they did to perpetrate a horrid rape; or of any other hero or son of a god daring to do such impious and dreadful things as they falsely ascribe to them in our day: and let us further compel the poets to declare either that these acts were not done by them, or that they were not the sons of gods—both in the same breath they shall not be permitted to affirm. We will not have them trying to persuade our youth that the gods are the authors of evil, and that heroes are no better than men—sentiments which, as we were saying, are neither pious nor true, for we have already proved that evil cannot come from the gods.

Assuredly not.

And further they are likely to have a bad effect on those who hear them; for everybody will begin to excuse his own vices when he is convinced that similar wickednesses are always being perpetrated by "the kindred of the gods, near descendants of Zeus, who worship him their ancestor at his altar, aloft in air on the peak of Ida," and who have "the blood of deities yet flowing in their veins."[37] And therefore let us put an end to such tales, lest they engender laxity of morals among the young. (392)

By all means, he replied.

But now that we are determining what classes of tales are or are not to be told, let us see whether any have been omitted by us. The manner in which gods and demigods and heroes and the world below should be treated has been already laid down.

Very true.

And it remains for us to decide what to say about men?

Clearly so.

But we are not in a condition to answer this question at present, my friend.

Why not?

Because, if I am not mistaken, we shall have to say that, about men, poets and story-tellers are guilty of making the gravest misstatements when they tell us that wicked men are often happy and the good miserable; and that injustice is profitable when undetected, but that justice is a man's own loss and another's gain—these things we shall forbid them to utter, and command them to sing and describe the opposite.

To be sure we shall, he replied.

But if you admit that I am right in this, then I shall maintain that you have implied the principle for which we have been all along contending.

I grant the truth of your inference.

That such things are or are not to be said about men is a question which we cannot determine until we have discovered what justice is, and how naturally advantageous to the possessor, whether he seem to be just or not.

Most true, he said.

Enough of the subjects of poetry: let us now speak of the style; and when this has been considered, both matter and manner will have been completely treated.

I do not understand what you mean, said Adeimantus.

Then I must make you understand; and perhaps I may be more intelligible if I put the matter in this way. You are aware, I suppose, that all mythology and poetry is a narration of events, either past, present, or to come?

Certainly, he replied.

And narration may be either simple narration, or imitation, or a union of the two?

That again, he said, I do not quite understand.

I fear that I must be an absurdly vague teacher. Like a bad speaker, therefore, I will not take the whole of the subject, but will break a piece off in illustration of my meaning. You know the first lines of the Iliad, in which the poet says that Chryses prayed Agamemnon to release his daughter, and that Agamemnon flew into a passion with him; whereupon Chryses, failing of his object, invoked the anger of the god against the Achaeans. (393) Now as far as these lines, "And he prayed all the Greeks, but especially the two sons of Atreus, the chiefs of the people,"[38] the poet is speaking in his own person; he never even tries to distract us by assuming another character. But in what follows he takes the person of Chryses, and then he does all that he can to make us believe that the speaker is not Homer, but the aged priest himself. And in this double form he has cast the entire narrative of the events which occurred at Troy and in Ithaca and throughout the Odyssey.

Yes.

And a narrative it remains both in the speeches which the poet recites from time to time and in the intermediate passages?

Quite true.

But when the poet speaks in the person of another, may we not say that he assimilates his style to that of the person who, as he informs you, is going to speak?

Certainly we may.

And this assimilation of himself to another, either by the use of voice or gesture, is the imitation of the person whose character he assumes?

Of course.

Then in this case the narrative of the poet, whether Homer or another, may be said to proceed by way of imitation?

Very true.

Or, if the poet were at no time to disguise himself, then again the imitation would be dropped, and his poetry become simple narration. However, in order that you may not have to repeat that you do not understand, I will show how the change might be effected. If Homer had said, "The priest came, having his daughter's ransom in his hands, supplicating the Achaeans, and above all the kings"; and then if, instead of speaking in the person of Chryses, he had continued in his own person, the words would have been, not imitation, but simple narration. The passage would have run as follows (I am no poet, and therefore I drop the meter), "The priest came and prayed the gods on behalf of the Greeks that they might capture Troy and return safely home, but begged that they would give him back his daughter, and take the ransom which he brought, and respect the god. Thus he spoke, and the other Greeks revered the priest and assented. But Agamemnon was wroth, and bade him depart and not come again, lest the staff and chaplets[39] of the god should be of no avail to him, and told him that before his daughter should be released, she should grow old with him in Argos. And then he told him to go away and not to provoke him, if he intended to get home unscathed. (394) And the old man went away in fear and silence, and, when he had left the camp, he called upon Apollo by his many names, reminding him of everything which he had done pleasing to him, whether in building his temples or in offering sacrifice, and praying that his good deeds might be returned to him and that the Achaeans might expiate his tears by the arrows of the god,"—and so on. In this way the whole becomes simple narrative.

I understand, he said.

And you must realize that an opposite case occurs, when the poet's comments are omitted and the passages of dialogue only are left.

That also, he said, I understand; you mean, for example, as in tragedy.

You have conceived my meaning perfectly; and I think I can now make clear what you failed to apprehend before, that some poetry and mythology are wholly imitative (and, as you say, I mean tragedy and comedy); there is likewise the opposite style, in which the poet is the only speaker—of this the dithyramb affords the best example; and the combination of both is found in epic, and in several other styles of poetry. Do I take you with me?

Yes, he said; I see now what you meant.

I will ask you to remember also what I began by saying, that we had done with the subject and might proceed to the style.

Yes, I remember.

In saying this, I intended to imply that we must come to an understanding about the mimetic art—whether the poets, in narrating their stories, are to be allowed by us to imitate, and if so, whether in whole or in part, and if the latter, in what parts; or should all imitation be prohibited?

You mean, I suspect, to ask whether tragedy and comedy shall be admitted into our state?

Perhaps, I said; but there may be more than this in question: I really do not know as yet, but whither the argument may blow, thither we go.

And go we will, he said.

Then, Adeimantus, let me ask you to consider whether our guardians should or should not be fond of imitation; or rather, has not this question been decided by the rule already laid down that one man can only do one thing well, and not many; and that one who grasps at many will altogether fail of gaining much reputation in any?

Certainly.

And this is equally true of imitation; no one man can imitate many things as well as he would imitate a single one?

He cannot.

(395) Then the same person will hardly be able to play a serious part in life, and at the same time to be an imitator and imitate many other parts as well; for even when two species of imitation are nearly allied, the same persons cannot succeed in both, as for example, the writers of tragedy and comedy—did you not just now call them imitations?

Yes, I did; and you are right in thinking that the same persons cannot succeed in both.

Any more than they can be rhapsodists and actors at once?

True.

Neither do comic and tragic writers employ the same actors; yet all these things are imitations.

They are so.

And human nature, Adeimantus, appears to have been coined into yet smaller pieces, and to be as incapable of imitating many things well, as of performing well the actions of which the imitations are copies.

Quite true, he replied.

If then we adhere to our original notion and bear in mind that our guardians, released from every other business, are to dedicate themselves wholly to the maintenance of the freedom of the state, making this their craft and engaging in no work which does not bear on this end, then they ought not to practice or even imitate anything else; if they imitate at all, they should imitate from youth upward only those characters which are suitable to their profession—the courageous, temperate, holy, free, and the like; but they should not depict or be skillful at imitating any kind of illiberality or baseness, lest the fruit of imitation should be reality. Did you never observe how imitations, beginning in early youth and continuing far into life, at length grow into habits and become a second nature, affecting body, voice, and mind?

Yes, certainly, he said.

Then, I said, we will not allow those for whom we profess a care and of whom we say that they ought to be good men, to imitate a woman, whether young or old, quarrelling with her husband, or striving and vaunting against the gods in conceit of her happiness, or when she is in affliction, or sorrow, or weeping; and certainly not one who is in sickness, love, or labor.

Very right, he said.

Neither must they represent slaves, male or female, performing the offices of slaves?

They must not.

And surely not bad men, whether cowards or any others, who do the reverse of what we have just been prescribing, who scold or mock or revile one another in drink or out of drink, (396) or who in any other manner sin against themselves and their neighbors in word or deed, as the manner of such is. Neither should they be trained to imitate the action or speech of madmen; they must be able to recognize madness and vice in man or woman, but none of these things is to be practiced or imitated.

Very true, he replied.

Neither may they imitate smiths or other artificers, or oarsmen, or boatswains, or the like?

How can they, he said, when they are not allowed to apply their minds to the callings of any of these?

Nor may they imitate the neighing of horses, the bellowing of bulls, the murmur of rivers and roll of the ocean, thunder, and all that sort of thing?

Nay, he said, if madness be forbidden, neither may they copy the behavior of madmen.

You mean, I said, if I understand you aright, that there is one sort of narrative style which is likely to be employed by an upright and good man when he has anything to say, and another sort, very unlike it, which will be preferred by a man of an opposite character and education.

And which are these two sorts? he asked.

As for the man of orderly life, I answered, when the time comes to describe some saying or action of another good man,—I think he will be willing to personate him, and will not be ashamed of this sort of imitation: he will be most ready to play the part of the good man when he is acting firmly and wisely; less often and in a less degree when he is overtaken by illness or love or drink, or has met with any other disaster. But when he comes to a character which is unworthy of him, he will not seriously assume the likeness of his inferior, and will do so, if at all, for a moment only when he is performing some good action; at other times he will be ashamed, both because he is not trained in imitation of such characters, and because he disdains to fashion and frame himself after the baser models; he feels the employment of such an art, unless in jest, to be beneath him.

So I should expect, he replied.

Then he will adopt a mode of narration such as we have illustrated out of Homer, that is to say, his style will be both imitative and narrative; but there will be, in a long story, only a small proportion of the former. Do you agree?

Certainly, he said; that is the model which such a speaker must necessarily take. (397)

But there is another sort of character who will narrate anything, and, the worse he is, the more unscrupulous he will be; nothing will be too bad for him: and he will be ready to imitate anything, in right good earnest, and before a large company. As I was just now saying, he will attempt to represent the roll of thunder, the noise of wind and hail, or the creaking of wheels, and pulleys, and the various sounds of flutes, pipes, trumpets, and all sorts of instruments: he will bark like a dog, bleat like a sheep, or crow like a cock; his entire art will consist in imitation of voice and gesture, or will be but slightly blended with narration.

That, he said, will be his mode of speaking.

These, then, are the two kinds of style I had in mind.

Yes.

And you would agree with me in saying that one of them is simple and has but slight changes; and that if an author expresses this style in fitting harmony and rhythm, he will find himself, if he does his work well, keeping pretty much within the limits of a single harmony (for the changes are not great), and in like manner he will make a similar choice of rhythm?

That is quite true, he said.

Whereas the other requires all sorts of harmonies and all sorts of rhythms if the music and the style are to correspond, because the style has all sorts of changes.

That is also perfectly true, he replied.

And do not the two styles, or the mixture of the two, comprehend all poetry and every form of expression in words? No one can say anything except in one or other of them or in both together.

They include all, he said.

And shall we receive into our state all the three styles, or one only of the two unmixed styles? Or would you include the mixed?

I should prefer only to admit the pure imitator of virtue.

Yes, I said, Adeimantus; and yet the mixed style is also charming: and indeed the opposite style to that chosen by you is by far the most popular with children and their attendants, and with the masses.

I do not deny it.

But I suppose you would argue that such a style is unsuitable to our state, in which human nature is not twofold or manifold, for one man plays one part only?

Yes; quite unsuitable.

And this is the reason why in our state, and in our state only, we shall find a shoemaker to be a shoemaker and not a pilot also, and a husbandman to be a husbandman and not a dicast[40] also, and a soldier a soldier and not a trader also, and the same throughout?

True, he said.

(398) And therefore when any one of these pantomimic gentlemen, who are so clever that they can imitate anything, comes to us and makes a proposal to exhibit himself and his poetry, we will fall down and worship him as a sacred, marvellous and delightful being; but we must also inform him that in our state such as he are not permitted to exist; the law will not allow them. And so when we have anointed him with myrrh, and set a garland of wool upon his head, we

shall send him away to another city. For we mean to employ for our souls' health the rougher and severer poet or storyteller, who will imitate the style of the virtuous only, and will follow those models which we prescribed at first when we began the education of our soldiers.

We certainly will, he said, if we have the power.

Then now, my friend, I said, that part of music or literary education which relates to the story or myth may be considered to be finished; for the matter and manner have both been discussed.

I think so too, he said.

Next in order will follow melody and song.

That is obvious.

Everyone now would be able to discover what we ought to say about them, if we are to be consistent with ourselves.

I fear, said Glaucon, laughing, that the word "everyone" hardly includes me, for I cannot at the moment say what they should be, though I have a suspicion.

At any rate you are aware that a song or ode has three parts—the words, the melody, and the rhythm.

Yes, he said; so much as that I know.

And as for the words, there will surely be no difference between words which are and which are not set to music; both will conform to the same laws, and these have been already determined by us?

Yes.

And the melody and rhythm will be in conformity with the words?

Certainly.

We were saying, when we spoke of the subject-matter, that we had no need of lamentation and strains of sorrow?

True.

And which are the harmonies expressive of sorrow? You are musical, and can tell me.

The harmonies which you mean are the mixed or tenor Lydian, and the full-toned or bass Lydian, and such-like.

These then, I said, must be banished; even to women who have a character to maintain they are of no use, and much less to men.

Certainly.

In the next place, drunkenness and softness and indolence are utterely unbecoming the character of our guardians.

Utterly unbecoming.

And which are the soft and convivial harmonies?

The Ionian, he replied, and some of the Lydian which are termed "relaxed."

(399) Well, and are these of any use for warlike men?

Quite the reverse, he replied; and if so the Dorian and the Phrygian are the only ones which you have left.

I answered: Of the harmonies I know nothing, but would have you leave me one which can render the note or accent which a brave man utters in warlike action and in stern resolve; and when his cause is failing, and he is going to wounds or death or is overtaken by disaster in some other form, at every such crisis he meets the blows of fortune with firm step and a determination to endure; and an opposite kind for times of peace and freedom of action, when there is no pressure of necessity, and he is seeking to persuade God by prayer, or man by instruction and admonition, or when on the other hand he is expressing his willingness to yield to the persuasion of entreaty or admonition of others. And when in this manner he has attained his end, I would have the music show him not carried away by his success, but acting moderately and wisely in all circumstances, and acquiescing in the event. These two harmonies I ask you to leave; the strain of necessity and the strain of freedom, the strain of the unfortunate and the strain of the fortunate, the strain of courage, and the strain of temperance; these, I say, leave.

And these, he replied, are the Dorian and Phrygian harmonies of which I was just now speaking.

Then, I said, if these and these only are to be used in our songs and melodies, we shall not want multiplicity of strings or a panharmonic scale?

I suppose not.

Then we shall not maintain the artificers of lyres with three corners and complex scales, or the makers of any other many-stringed, curiously harmonized instruments?

Certainly not.

But what do you say to flute-makers and flute-players? Would you admit them into our state when you reflect that in this composite use of harmony the flute is worse than any stringed instrument; even the panharmonic music is only an imitation of the flute?

Clearly not.

There remain then only the lyre and the harp for use in the city, and the shepherds in the country may have some kind of pipe.

That is surely the conclusion to be drawn from the argument.

The preferring of Apollo and his instruments to Marsyas and his instruments is not at all strange, I said.

Not at all, he replied.

And so, by the dog of Egypt, we have been unconsciously purging the state, which not long ago we termed luxurious.

And we have done wisely, he replied.

Then let us now finish the purgation, I said. Next in order to harmonies, rhythms will naturally follow, and they should be subject to the same rules, for we ought not to seek out complex systems of meter, and a variety of feet, but rather to discover what rhythms are the expressions of a courageous and harmonious life; (400) and when we have found them, we shall adapt the foot and the melody to words having a like spirit, not the words to the foot and melody. To say what these rhythms are will be your duty—you must teach me them, as you have already taught me the harmonies.

But, indeed, he replied, I cannot tell you. I know from observation that there are some three principles of rhythm out of which metrical systems are framed, just as in sounds there are four notes[41] out of which all the harmonies are composed. But of what sort of lives they are severally the imitations I am unable to say.

Then, I said, we must take Damon into our counsels; and he will tell us what rhythms are expressive of meanness, or insolence, or fury, or other unworthiness, and what are to be reserved for the expression of opposite feelings. And I think that I have an indistinct recollection of his mentioning a complex Cretic rhythm; also a dactylic or heroic, and he arranged them in some manner which I do not quite understand, making the rhythms equal in the rise and fall of the foot, long and short alternating; and, unless I am mistaken, he spoke of an iambic as well as of a trochaic rhythm, and assigned to them short and long quantities.[42] Also in some cases he appeared to praise or censure the movement of the foot quite as much as the rhythm; or perhaps a combination of the two; for I am not certain what he meant. These matters, however, as I was saying, had better be referred to Damon himself, for the analysis of the subject would be difficult, you know?

Rather so, I should say.

But it does not require much analysis to see that grace or the absence of grace accompanies good or bad rhythm.

None at all.

And also that good and bad rhythm naturally assimilate to a good and bad style; and that harmony and discord in like manner follow style; for our principle is that rhythm and harmony are regulated by the words, and not the words by them.

Just so, he said, they should follow the words.

And will not the words and the character of the style depend on the temper of the soul?

Yes.

And everything else on the style?

Yes.

Then beauty of style and harmony and grace and good rhythm depend on simplicity—I mean the true simplicity of a rightly and nobly ordered mind and character, not that other simplicity which is only a euphemism for folly?

Very true, he replied.

And if our youth are to do their work in life, must they not make these graces and harmonies their perpetual aim?

They must.

(401) And surely the art of the painter and every other creative and constructive art are full of them—weaving, embroidery, architecture, and every kind of manufacture; also nature, animal and vegetable—in all of them there is grace or the absence of grace. And ugliness and discord and inharmonious motion are nearly allied to ill words and ill nature, as grace and harmony are the twin sisters of goodness and self-restraint and bear their likeness.

That is quite true, he said.

But shall our superintendence go no further, and are the poets only to be required by us to express the image of the good in their works, on pain, if they do anything else, of expulsion from our state? Or is the same control to be extended to other artists, and are they also to be prohibited from exhibiting the opposite forms of vice and intemperance and meanness and deformity in sculpture and building and the other creative arts; and is he who cannot conform to this rule of ours to be prevented from practicing his art in our state, lest the taste of our citizens be corrupted by him? We would not have our guardians grow up amid images of moral deformity, as in some noxious pasture, and there browse and feed upon many a baneful herb and flower day by day, little by little, until they silently gather a festering mass of corruption in their own soul. Let us rather search for artists who are gifted to discern the true nature of the beautiful and graceful; then will our youth dwell in a land of health, amid fair sights and sounds, and receive the good in everything; and beauty, the effluence of fair works, shall flow into the eye and ear, like a health-giving breeze from a purer region, and insensibly draw the soul from earliest years into likeness and sympathy with the beauty of reason.

There can be no nobler training than that, he replied.

And therefore, I said, Glaucon, musical training is a more potent instrument than any other, because rhythm and harmony find their way into the inward places of the soul, on which they mightily fasten, imparting grace, and making the soul of him who is rightly educated graceful, or of him who is ill-educated ungraceful; and also because he who has received this true education of the inner being will most shrewdly perceive omissions or faults in art and nature, (402) and with a true taste, while he praises and rejoices over and receives into his soul the good, and becomes noble and good, he will justly blame and hate the bad, now in the days of his youth, even before he is able to know the reason why; and when reason comes he will recognize and salute the friend with whom his education has made him long familiar.

Yes, he said, I quite agree with you in thinking that it is for such reasons that they should be trained in music.

Just as in learning to read, I said, we were satisfied when we knew the letters of the alphabet, few as they are, in all their recurring combinations; not slighting them as unimportant whether they occupy a space large or small, but everywhere eager to make them out, because we knew we should not be perfect in the art of reading until we could do so:

True—

And as we recognize the reflection of letters in water, or in a mirror, only when we know the letters themselves, the same art and study giving us the knowledge of both:

Exactly—

Even so, as I maintain, neither we nor the guardians, whom we say that we have to educate, can ever become musical until we and they know the essential forms of temperance, courage, liberality, magnanimity, and their kindred, as well as the contrary forms, in all their combinations, and can recognize them and their images wherever they are found, not slighting them either in small things or great, but believing them all to be within the sphere of one art and study.

Most assuredly.

And when nobility of soul is observed in harmonious union with beauty of form, and both are cast from the same mold, that will be the fairest of sights to him who has an eye to see it?

The fairest indeed.

And the fairest is also the loveliest?

That may be assumed.

And it is with human beings who most display such harmony that a musical man will be most in love; but he will not love any who do not possess it.

That is true, he replied, if the deficiency be in the soul; but if there be any bodily defect he will be patient of it, and may even approve it.

BOOK X

Persons of the Dialogue

Socrates Glaucon

(595) Of the many excellences which I perceive in the order of our state, there is none which upon reflection pleases me better than the rule about poetry.

To what do you refer?

To our refusal to admit the imitative kind of poetry, for it certainly ought not to be received; as I see far more clearly now that the parts of the soul have been distinguished.

What do you mean?

Speaking in confidence, for you will not denounce me to the tragedians and the rest of the imitative tribe, all poetical imitations are ruinous to the understanding of the hearers, unless as an antidote they possess the knowledge of the true nature of the originals.

Explain the purport of your remark.

Well, I will tell you, although I have always from my earliest youth had an awe and love of Homer which even now makes the words falter on my lips, for he seems to be the great captain and teacher of the whole of that noble tragic company[1]; but a man is not to be reverenced more than the truth, and therefore I will speak out

Very good, he said.

Listen to me then, or rather, answer me.

Put your question.

Can you give me a general definition of imitation? for I really do not myself understand what it professes to be.

A likely thing, then, that I should know.

(596) There would be nothing strange in that, for the duller eye may often see a thing sooner than the keener.

Very true, he said; but in your presence, even if I had any faint notion, I could not muster courage to utter it. Will you inquire yourself?

Well then, shall we begin the inquiry at this point, following our usual method: Whenever a number of individuals have a common name, we assume that there is one corresponding idea or form[2]—do you understand me?

I do.

Let us take, for our present purpose, any instance of such a group; there are beds and tables in the world—many of each, are there not?

Yes.

But there are only two ideas or forms of such furniture—one the idea of a bed, the other of a table.

True.

And the maker of either of them makes a bed or he makes a table for our use, in accordance with the idea—that is our way of speaking in this and similar instances—but no artificer makes the idea itself: how could he?

Impossible.

And there is another artificer—I should like to know what you would say of him.

Who is he?

One who is the maker of all the works of all other workmen.

What an extraordinary man!

Wait a little, and there will be more reason for your saying so. For this is the craftsman who is able to make not only furniture of every kind, but all that grows out of the earth, and all living creatures, himself included; and besides these he can make earth and sky and the gods, and all the things which are in heaven or in the realm of Hades under the earth.

He must be a wizard and no mistake.

Oh! you are incredulous, are you? Do you mean that there is no such maker or creator, or that in one sense there might be a maker of all these things but in another not? Do you see that there is a way in which you could make them all yourself?

And what way is this? he asked.

An easy way enough; or rather, there are many ways in which the feat might be quickly and easily accomplished, none quicker than that of turning a mirror round and round—you would soon enough make the sun and the heavens, and the earth and yourself, and other animals and plants, and furniture and all the other things of which we were just now speaking, in the mirror.

Yes, he said, but they would be appearances only.

Very good, I said, you are coming to the point now. And the painter too is, as I conceive, just such another—a creator of appearances, is he not?

Of course.

But then I suppose you will say that what he creates is untrue. And yet there is a sense in which the painter also creates a bed? Is there not?

Yes, he said, but here again, an appearance only.

(597) And what of the maker of the bed? Were you not saying that he too makes, not the idea which according to our view is the real object denoted by the word bed, but only a particular bed?

Yes, I did.

Then if he does not make a real object he cannot make what *is*, but only some semblance of existence; and if any one were to say that the work of the maker of the bed, or of any other workman, has real existence, he could hardly be supposed to be speaking the truth.

Not, at least, he replied, in the view of those who make a business of these discussions.

No wonder, then, that his work too is an indistinct expression of truth.

No wonder.

Suppose now that by the light of the examples just offered we inquire who this imitator is?

If you please.

Well then, here we find three beds: one existing in nature, which is made by God, as I think that we may say—for no one else can be the maker?

No one, I think.

There is another which is the work of the carpenter?

Yes.

And the work of the painter is a third?

Yes.

Beds, then, are of three kinds, and there are three artists who superintend them: God, the maker of the bed, and the painter?

Yes, there are three of them.

God, whether from choice or from necessity, made one bed in nature and one only; two or more such beds neither ever have been nor ever will be made by God.

Why is that?

Because even if He had made but two, a third would still appear behind them of which they again both possessed the form, and that would be the real bed and not the two others.

Very true, he said.

God knew this, I suppose, and He desired to be the real maker of a real bed, not a kind of maker of a kind of bed, and therefore He created a bed which is essentially and by nature one only.

So it seems.

Shall we, then, speak of Him as the natural author or maker of the bed?

Yes, he replied; inasmuch as by the natural process of creation He is the author of this and of all other things.

And what shall we say of the carpenter—is not he also the maker of a bed?

Yes.

But would you call the painter an artificer and maker?

Certainly not.

Yet if he is not the maker, what is he in relation to the bed?

I think, he said, that we may fairly designate him as the imitator of that which the others make.

Good, I said; then you call him whose product is third in the descent from nature, an imitator?

Certainly, he said.

And so if the tragic poet is an imitator, he too is thrice removed from the king and from the truth; and so are all other imitators.

That appears to be so.

Then about the imitator we are agreed. And what about the painter? (598) Do you think he tries to imitate in each case that which originally exists in nature, or only the creations of artificers?

The latter.

As they are or as they appear? You have still to determine this.

What do you mean?

I mean to ask whether a bed really becomes different when it is seen from different points of view, obliquely or directly or from any other point of view? Or does it simply appear different, without being really so? And the same of all things.

Yes, he said, the difference is only apparent.

Now let me ask you another question: Which is the art of painting designed to be—an imitation of things as they are, or as they appear—of appearance or of reality?

Of appearance, he said.

Then the imitator is a long way off the truth, and can reproduce all things because he lightly touches on a small part of them, and that part an image. For example: A painter will paint a cobbler, carpenter, or any other artisan, though he knows nothing of their arts; and, if he is a good painter, he may deceive children or simple persons when he shows them his picture of a carpenter from a distance, and they will fancy that they are looking at a real carpenter.

Certainly.

And surely, my friend, this is how we should regard all such claims: whenever anyone informs us that he has found a man who knows all the arts, and all things else that anybody knows, and every single thing with a higher degree of accuracy than any other man—whoever tells us this, I think that we can only retort that he is a simple creature who seems to have been deceived by some wizard or imitator whom he met, and whom he thought all-knowing, because he himself was unable to analyse the nature of knowledge and ignorance and imitation.

Most true.

And next, I said, we have to consider tragedy and its leader, Homer; for we hear some persons saying that these poets know all the arts; and all things human; where virtue and vice are concerned, and indeed all divine things too; because the good poet cannot compose well unless he knows his subject, and he who has not this knowledge can never be a poet. We ought to consider whether here also there may not be a similar illusion. Perhaps they may have come across imitators and been deceived by them; they may not have remembered when they saw their works that these were thrice removed from the truth, (599) and could easily be made without any knowledge of the truth, because they are appearances only and not realities? Or, after all, they may be in the right, and good poets do really know the things about which they seem to the many to speak so well?

The question, he said, should by all means be considered.

Now do you suppose that if a person were able to make the original as well as the image, he would seriously devote himself to the image-making branch? Would he allow imitation to be the ruling principle of his life, as if he had nothing higher in him?

I should say not.

But the real artist, who had real knowledge of those things which he chose also to imitate, would be interested in realities and not in imitations; and would desire to leave as memorials of himself works many and fair; and, instead of being the author of encomiums, he would prefer to be the theme of them.

Yes, he said, that would be to him a source of much greater honor and profit.

Now let us refrain, I said, from calling Homer or any other poet to account regarding those arts to which his poems incidentally refer: we will not ask them, in case any poet has been a doctor and not a mere imitator of medical parlance, to show what patients have been restored to health by a poet, ancient or modern, as they were by Asclepius; or what disciples in medicine a poet has left behind him, like the Asclepiads. Nor shall we press the same question upon them about the other arts. But we have a right to know respecting warfare, strategy, the administration of states and the education of man, which are the chiefest and noblest subjects of his poems, and we may fairly ask him about them. "Friend Homer," then we say to him, "if you are only in the second remove from truth in what you say of virtue, and not in the third—not an image maker, that is, by our definition, an imitator—and if you are able to discern what pursuits make men better or worse in private or public life, tell us what state was ever better governed by your help? The good order of Lacedaemon is due to Lycurgus, and many other cities great and small have been similarly benefited by others; but who says that you have been a good legislator to them and have done them any good? Italy and Sicily boast of Charondas, and there is Solon who is renowned among us; but what city has anything to say about you?" Is there any city which he might name?

I think not, said Glaucon; not even the Homerids themselves pretend that he was a legislator.

(600) Well, but is there any war on record which was carried on successfully owing to his leadership or counsel?

There is not.

Or is there anything comparable to those clever improvements in the arts, or in other operations, which are said to have been due to men of practical genius such as Thales the Milesian or Anacharsis the Scythian?

There is absolutely nothing of the kind.

But, if Homer never did any public service, was he privately a guide or teacher of any? Had he in his lifetime friends who loved to associate with him, and who handed down to posterity an Homeric way of life, such as was established by Pythagoras who was especially beloved for this reason and whose followers are to this day conspicuous among others by what they term the Pythagorean way of life?

Nothing of the kind is recorded of him. For surely, Socrates, Creophylus, the companion of Homer, that child of flesh, whose name always makes us laugh, might be more justly ridiculed for his want of breeding, if what is said is true, that Homer was greatly neglected by him in his own day when he was alive?

Yes, I replied, that is the tradition. But can you imagine, Glaucon, that if Homer had really been able to educate and improve mankind—if he had been capable of knowledge and not been a mere imitator—can you imagine, I say, that he would not have attracted many followers, and been honored and loved by them? Protagoras of Abdera, and Prodicus of Ceos, and a host of others, have only to whisper to their contemporaries: "You will never be able to manage either your own house or your own state until you appoint us to be your ministers of education"—and this ingenious device of theirs has such an effect in making men love them that their companions all but carry them about on their shoulders. And is it conceivable that the contemporaries of Homer, or again of Hesiod, would have allowed either of them to go about as rhapsodists, if they had really been able to help mankind forward in virtue? Would they not have been as unwilling to part with them as with gold, and have compelled them to stay at home with them? Or, if the master would not stay, then the disciples would have followed him about everywhere, until they had got education enough?

Yes, Socrates, that, I think, is quite true.

Then must we not infer that all these poetical individuals, beginning with Homer, are only imitators, who copy images of virtue and the other themes of their poetry, but have no contact with the truth? (601) The poet is like a painter who, as we have already observed, will make a likeness of a cobbler though he understands nothing of cobbling; and his picture is good enough for those who know no more than he does, and judge only by colors and figures.

Quite so.

In like manner the poet with his words and phrases[3] may be said to lay on the colors of the several arts, himself understanding their nature only enough to imitate them; and other people, who are as ignorant as he is, and judge only from his words, imagine that if he speaks of cobbling, or of military tactics, or of anything else, in meter and harmony and rhythm, he speaks very well—such is the sweet influence which melody and rhythm by nature have. For I am sure that you know what a poor appearance the works of poets make when stripped of the colors which art puts upon them, and recited in simple prose. You have seen some examples?

Yes, he said.

They are like faces which were never really beautiful, but only blooming, seen when the bloom of youth has passed away from them?

Exactly.

Come now, and observe this point: The imitator or maker of the image knows nothing, we have said, of true existence; he knows appearances only. Am I not right?

Yes.

Then let us have a clear understanding, and not be satisfied with half an explanation.

Proceed.

Of the painter we say that he will paint reins, and he will paint a bit?

Yes.

And the worker in leather and brass will make them?

Certainly.

But does the painter know the right form of the bit and reins? Nay, hardly even the workers in brass and leather who make them; only the horseman who knows how to use them—he knows their right form.

Most true.

And may we not say the same of all things?

What?

That there are three arts which are concerned with all things: one which uses, another which makes, a third which imitates them?

Yes.

And the excellence and beauty and rightness of every structure, animate or inanimate, and of every action of man, is relative solely to the use for which nature or the artist has intended them.

True.

Then beyond doubt it is the user who has the greatest experience of them, and he must report to the maker the good or bad qualities which develop themselves in use; for example, the flute-player will tell the flute-maker which of his flutes is satisfactory to the performer; he will tell him how he ought to make them, and the other will attend to his instructions?

Of course.

So the one pronounces with knowledge about the goodness and badness of flutes, while the other, confiding in him, will make them accordingly?

True.

The instrument is the same, but about the excellence or badness of it the maker will possess a correct belief, since he associates with one who knows, and is compelled to hear what he has to say; (602) whereas the user will have knowledge?

True.

But will the imitator have either? Will he know from use whether or no that which he paints is correct or beautiful? Or will he have right opinion from being compelled to associate with another who knows and gives him instructions about what he should paint?

Neither.

Then an imitator will no more have true opinion than he will have knowledge about the goodness or badness of his models?

I suppose not.

The imitative poet will be in a brilliant state of intelligence about the theme of his poetry?

Nay, very much the reverse.

And still he will go on imitating without knowing what makes a thing good or bad, and may be expected therefore to imitate only that which appears to be good to the ignorant multitude?

Just so.

Thus far then we are pretty well agreed that the imitator has no knowledge worth mentioning of what he imitates. Imitation is only a kind of play or sport, and the tragic poets, whether they write in iambic or in heroic verse,[4] are imitators in the highest degree?

Very true.

And now tell me, I conjure you—this imitation is concerned with an object which is thrice removed from the truth?

Certainly.

And what kind of faculty in man is that to which imitation makes its special appeal?

What do you mean?

I will explain: The same body does not appear equal to our sight when seen near and when seen at a distance?

True.

And the same objects appear straight when looked at out of the water, and crooked when in the water; and the concave becomes convex, owing to the illusion about colors to which the sight is liable. Thus every sort of confusion is revealed within us; and this is that weakness of the human mind on which the art of painting in light and shadow, the art of conjuring, and many other ingenious devices impose, having an effect upon us like magic.

True.

And the arts of measuring and numbering and weighing come to the rescue of the human understanding—there is the beauty of them—with the result that the apparent greater or less, or more or heavier, no longer have the mastery over us, but give way before the power of calculation and measuring and weighing?

Most true.

And this, surely, must be the work of the calculating and rational principle in the soul?

To be sure.

And often when this principle measures and certifies that some things are equal, or that some are greater or less than others, it is, at the same time, contradicted by the appearance which the objects present?

True.

But did we not say that such a contradiction is impossible—the same faculty cannot have contrary opinions at the same time about the same thing?

We did; and rightly.

(603) Then that part of the soul which has an opinion contrary to measure

can hardly be the same with that which has an opinion in accordance with measure?

True.

And the part of the soul which trusts to measure and calculation is likely to be the better one?

Certainly.

And therefore that which is opposed to this is probably an inferior principle in our nature?

No doubt.

This was the conclusion at which I was seeking to arrive when I said that painting or drawing, and imitation in general, are engaged upon productions which are far removed from truth, and are also the companions and friends and associates of a principle within us which is equally removed from reason, and that they have no true or healthy aim.

Exactly.

The imitative art is an inferior who from intercourse with an inferior has inferior offspring.

Very true.

And is this confined to the sight only, or does it extend to the hearing also, relating in fact to what we term poetry?

Probably the same would be true of poetry.

Do not rely, I said, on a probability derived from the analogy of painting; but let us once more go directly to that faculty of the mind with which imitative poetry has converse, and see whether it is good or bad.

By all means.

We may state the question thus: Imitation imitates the actions of men, whether voluntary or involuntary, on which, as they imagine, a good or bad result has ensued, and they rejoice or sorrow accordingly. Is there anything more?

No, there is nothing else.

But in all this variety of circumstances is the man at unity with himself —or rather, as in the instance of sight there was confusion and opposition in his opinions about the same things, so here also is there not strife and inconsistency in his life? Though I need hardly raise the question again, for I remember that all this has been already admitted; and the soul has been acknowledged by us to be full of these and ten thousand similar oppositions occurring at the same moment?

And we were right, he said.

Yes, I said, thus far we were right; but there was an omission which must now be supplied.

What was the omission?

Were we not saying that a good man, who has the misfortune to lose his son or anything else which is most dear to him, will bear the loss with more equanimity than another?

Yes, indeed.

But will he have no sorrow, or shall we say that although he cannot help sorrowing, he will moderate his sorrow?

The latter, he said, is the truer statement.

(604) Tell me: will he be more likely to struggle and hold out against his sorrow when he is seen by his equals, or when he is alone in a deserted place?

The fact of being seen will make a great difference, he said.

When he is by himself he will not mind saying many things which he would be ashamed of any one hearing, and also doing many things which he would not care to be seen doing?

True.

And doubtless it is the law and reason in him which bids him resist; while it is the affliction itself which is urging him to indulge his sorrow?

True.

But when a man is drawn in two opposite directions, to and from the same object, this, as we affirm, necessarily implies two distinct principles in him?

Certainly.

One of them is ready to follow the guidance of the law?

How do you mean?

The law would say that to be patient under calamity is best, and that we should not give way to impatience, as the good and evil in such things are not clear, and nothing is gained by impatience; also, because no human thing is of serious importance, and grief stands in the way of that which at the moment is most required.

What is most required? he asked.

That we should take counsel about what has happened, and when the dice have been thrown, according to their fall, order our affairs in the way which reason deems best; not, like children who have had a fall, keeping hold of the part struck and wasting time in setting up a howl, but always accustoming the soul forthwith to apply a remedy, raising up that which is sickly and fallen, banishing the cry of sorrow by the healing art.

Yes, he said, that is the true way of meeting the attacks of fortune.

Well then, I said, the higher principle is ready to follow this suggestion of reason?

Clearly.

But the other principle, which inclines us to recollection of our troubles and to lamentation, and can never have enough of them, we may call irrational, useless, and cowardly?

Indeed, we may.

Now does not the principle which is thus inclined to complaint, furnish a great variety of materials for imitation? Whereas the wise and calm temperament, being always nearly equable, is not easy to imitate or to appreciate when imitated, especially at a public festival when a promiscuous crowd is assembled in a theatre. For the feeling represented is one to which they are strangers.

Certainly.

(605) Then the imitative poet who aims at being popular is not by nature made, nor is his art intended, to please or to affect the rational principle in the soul; but he will appeal rather to the lachrymose and fitful temper, which is easily imitated?

Clearly.

And now we may fairly take him and place him by the side of the painter, for he is like him in two ways: first, inasmuch as his creations have an inferior degree of truth—in this, I say, he is like him; and he is also like him in being the associate of an inferior part of the soul; and this is enough to show that we shall be right in refusing to admit him into a state which is to be well ordered, because he awakens and nourishes this part of the soul, and by strengthening it impairs the reason. As in a city when the evil are permitted to wield power and the finer men are put out of the way, so in the soul of each man, as we shall maintain, the imitative poet implants an evil constitution, for he indulges the irrational nature which has no discernment of greater and less, but thinks the same thing at one time great and at another small—he is an imitator of images and is very far removed from the truth.

Exactly.

But we have not yet brought forward the heaviest count in our accusation—the power which poetry has of harming even the good (and there are very few who are not harmed), is surely an awful thing?

Yes, certainly, if the effect is what you say.

Hear and judge: The best of us, as I conceive, when we listen to a passage of Homer or one of the tragedians, in which he represents some hero who is drawling out his sorrows in a long oration, or singing, and smiting his breast—the best of us, you know, delight in giving way to sympathy, and are in raptures at the excellence of the poet who stirs our feelings most.

Yes, of course I know.

But when any sorrow of our own happens to us, then you may observe that we pride ourselves on the opposite quality—we would fain be quiet and patient; this is considered the manly part, and the other which delighted us in the recitation is now deemed to be the part of a woman.

Very true, he said.

Now can we be right in praising and admiring another who is doing that which any one of us would abominate and be ashamed of in his own person?

No, he said, that is certainly not reasonable.

(606) Nay, I said, quite reasonable from one point of view.

What point of view?

If you consider, I said, that when in misfortune we feel a natural hunger and desire to relieve our sorrow by weeping and lamentation, and that this very feeling which is starved and suppressed in our own calamities is satisfied and delighted by the poets—the better nature in each of us, not having been sufficiently trained by reason or habit, allows the sympathetic element to break loose because the sorrow is another's; and the spectator fancies that there can be no disgrace to himself in praising and pitying any one who while professing to be a brave man, gives way to untimely lamentation; he thinks that the pleasure is a gain, and is far from wishing to lose it by rejection of the whole poem. Few persons ever reflect, as I should imagine, that the contagion must pass from others to themselves. For the pity which has been nourished and strengthened in the misfortunes of others is with difficulty repressed in our own.

How very true!

And does not the same hold also of the ridiculous? There are jests which you would be ashamed to make yourself, and yet on the comic stage, or indeed in private, when you hear them, you are greatly amused by them, and are not at all disgusted at their unseemliness—the case of pity is repeated—there is a principle in human nature which is disposed to raise a laugh, and this, which you once restrained by reason because you were afraid of being thought a buffoon, is now let out again; and having stimulated the risible faculty at the theater, you are betrayed unconsciously to yourself into playing the comic poet at home.

Quite true, he said.

And the same may be said of lust and anger and all the other affections, of desire and pain and pleasure, which are held to be inseparable from every action—in all of them poetry has a like effect; it feeds and waters the passions instead of drying them up; she lets them rule, although they ought to be controlled if mankind are ever to increase in happiness and virtue.

I cannot deny it.

Therefore, Glaucon, I said, whenever you meet with any of the eulogists of Homer declaring that he has been the educator of Hellas, and that he is profitable for education and for the ordering of human things, and that you should take him up again and again and get to know him and regulate your whole life according to him, we may love and honor those who say these things—they are excellent people, as far as their lights extend; (607) and we are ready to acknowledge that Homer is the greatest of poets and first of tragedy writers; but we must remain firm in our conviction that hymns to the gods and praises of famous men are the only poetry which ought to be admitted into our state. For if you go beyond this and allow the honeyed Muse to enter, either in epic or lyric verse, not law and the reason of mankind, which by common consent have ever been deemed best,[5] but pleasure and pain will be the rulers in our state.

That is most true, he said.

And now since we have reverted to the subject of poetry, let this our defense serve to show the reasonableness of our former judgment in sending away out of our state an art having the tendencies which we have described; for reason constrained us. But that she may not impute to us any harshness or want of politeness, let us tell her that there is an ancient quarrel between philosophy and poetry; of which there are many proofs, such as the saying of "the yelping hound howling at her lord," or of one "mighty in the vain talk of fools," and "the mob of sages circumventing Zeus," and the "subtle thinkers who are beggars after all";[6] and there are innumerable other signs of ancient enmity between them. Notwithstanding this, let us assure the poetry which aims at pleasure, and the art of imitation, that if she will only prove her title to exist in a well-ordered state we shall be delighted to receive her—we are very conscious of her charms; but it would not be right on that account to betray the truth. I dare say, Glaucon, that you are as much charmed by her as I am, especially when she appears in Homer?

Yes, indeed, I am greatly charmed.

Shall I propose, then, that she be allowed to return from exile, but upon this condition only—that she make a defense of herself in some lyrical or other meter?

Certainly.

And we may further grant to those of her defenders who are lovers of poetry and yet not poets the permission to speak in prose on her behalf: let them show not only that she is pleasant but also useful to states and to human life, and we will listen in a kindly spirit; for we shall surely be the gainers if this can be proved, that there is a use in poetry as well as a delight?

Certainly, he said, we shall be the gainers.

If her defense fails, then, my dear friend, like other persons who are enamored of something, but put a restraint upon themselves when they think their desires are opposed to their interests, so too must we after the manner of lovers give her up, though not without a struggle. We too are inspired by that love of such poetry which the education of noble states has implanted in us, (608) and therefore we shall be glad if she appears at her best and truest; but so long as she is unable to make good her defense, this argument of ours shall be a charm to us, which we will repeat to ourselves while we listen to her strains; that we may not fall away into the childish love of her which captivates the many. At all events we are well aware that poetry,[7] such as we have described, is not to be regarded seriously as attaining to the truth; and he who listens to her, fearing for the safety of the city which is within him, should be on his guard against her seductions and make our words his law.

Yes, he said, I quite agree with you.

Yes, I said, my dear Glaucon, for great is the issue at stake, greater than appears, whether a man is to be good or bad. And what will any one be profited if under the influence of honor or money or power, aye, or under the excitement of poetry, he neglect justice and virtue?

Yes, he said; I have been convinced by the argument, as I believe that anyone else would have been.

And yet we have not described the greatest prizes and rewards which await virtue.

What, are there any greater still? If there are, they must be of an inconceivable greatness.

Why, I said, what was ever great in a short time? The whole period from childhood to age is surely but a little thing in comparison with eternity?

Say rather "nothing," he replied.

And should an immortal being be anxious for this little time rather than for the whole?

For the whole, certainly. But why do you ask?

Are you not aware, I said, that the soul of man is immortal and imperishable?

He looked at me in astonishment, and said: No, by heaven: And are you really prepared to maintain this?

Yes, I said, I ought to be, and you too—there is no difficulty in proving it.

I see a great difficulty; but I should like to hear you state this argument of which you make so light.

Listen then.

I am attending.

There is a thing which you call good and another which you call evil?

Yes, he replied.

Would you agree with me in thinking that the corrupting and destroying element is the evil, and the saving and improving element the good?

True.

And you admit that everything has a good and also an evil; (609) as ophthalmia is the evil of the eyes and disease of the whole body; as blight is of corn, and rot of timber, or rust of copper and iron: in everything, or in almost everything, there is an inherent evil and disease?

Yes, he said.

And any of these evils, when it attacks a thing, first makes it rotten and at last wholly dissolves and destroys it?

True.

The vice and evil which is inherent in each is the destruction of each; or if this does not destroy them there is nothing else that will; for good certainly will never destroy anything, nor, again, will that which is neither good nor evil.

Certainly not.

If, then, we find any nature which has indeed some inherent corruption, but of a kind whereby it cannot be dissolved or destroyed, we many be certain that of such a nature there is no destruction?

That may be assumed.

Well, I said, and is there no evil which corrupts the soul?

Yes, he said, there are all the evils which we were just now passing in review: unrighteousness, intemperance, cowardice, ignorance.

But does any of these dissolve and destroy her? And here do not let us fall into the error of supposing that the unjust and foolish man, when he is detected, perishes through his own injustice, which is an evil of the soul. You should represent it rather in this way: The evil of the body is a disease which dissolves and wastes it, till it is no longer a body at all; and all the things of which we were just now speaking come to annihilation through their own corruption attaching to them and inhering in them and so destroying them. Is not this true?

Yes.

Consider the soul in like manner. Does injustice, or vice in some other form, waste and consume her? Do they by attaching to the soul and inhering in her at last bring her to death, and so separate her from the body?

Certainly not.

And yet, I said, it is unreasonable to suppose that anything can perish under a disease proper to another thing, which could not be destroyed by a corruption of its own?

It is, he replied.

Consider, I said, Glaucon, that even the badness of food, whether staleness, decomposition, or any other bad quality, when confined to the actual food, is not supposed to destroy the body; although, if the badness of food causes the body to become corrupt in its own fashion, then we should say that the body has been destroyed by a corruption of itself, which is disease, brought on by this; (610) but that the body, being one thing, can be destroyed by the badness of food, which is another, unless it has implanted the corruption peculiar to the body—this we shall absolutely deny?

Very true.

On the same principle, then, unless some bodily evil can produce in the soul an evil of the soul, we must not suppose that the soul, which is one thing, can be dissolved, in the absence of its own disease, by an evil which belongs to another?

Yes, he said, there is reason in that.

Either, then, let us refute this conclusion, or, while it remains unrefuted, let us never say that fever, or any other disease, or the knife put to the throat, or even the cutting up of the whole body into the minutest pieces, can destroy the soul, until she herself is proved to become more unholy or unrighteous in consequence of these things being done to the body; but that the soul or anything else can be free from its special evil and yet be destroyed because a foreign evil is found in something else, is not to be affirmed by any man.

And surely, he replied, no one will ever prove that the souls of dying men become more unjust in consequence of death.

But if someone, lest he be obliged to admit the immortality of the soul, boldly goes out to meet our argument, and says that the dying do really become more evil and unrighteous, then, if the speaker is right, I suppose that injustice, like disease, must be assumed to be fatal to the unjust, and that those who take this disorder die by the natural inherent power of destruction which evil has, and which kills them sooner or later, but in quite another way from that in which, at present, the wicked receive death at the hands of others as the penalty of their deeds?

Nay, he said, in that case injustice, if fatal to the unjust, will not be so very terrible to him, for he will thus be delivered from evil. But I rather suspect the opposite will prove to be the truth, and that injustice which, if it have the power, will murder others, gives the murderer greater vitality—aye, and keeps him well awake too; so far removed is her dwelling-place from being a house of death.

True, I said; if the inherent natural vice or evil of the soul has not the force to kill or destroy her, hardly will that which is appointed to be the destruction of some other body destroy a soul, or anything else except that of which it was appointed to be the destruction.

Yes, that can hardly be.

(611) But the soul which cannot be destroyed by any evil, whether its own or that of something else, must exist for ever, and if existing for ever, must be immortal?

Certainly.

Let that be our conclusion, I said; and, if it is a true conclusion, you will observe that the souls must always be the same, for if none be destroyed they will not diminish in number. Neither will they increase, for the increase of the immortal natures must, as you know, come from something mortal, and all things would thus end in immortality.

Very true.

But this we cannot believe—reason will not allow us—any more than we can believe the soul, in her truest nature, to be a thing full of variety and internal difference and dissimilarity.

What do you mean? he said.

It is not easy, I said, for that thing to be immortal which is a compound of many elements not perfectly adapted to each other, as the soul has appeared to us to be.

Certainly not.

Her immortality is demonstrated by the previous argument, and there are many other proofs; but to see her as she really is, not, as we now behold her, marred by association with the body and other miseries, you must contemplate her with the eye of reason, in her original purity; and then her greater beauty will be revealed, and the forms of justice and injustice and all the things which we have described will be more vividly discerned. Thus far, we have spoken the truth concerning her as she appears at present, but we have seen her only in a condition which may be compared to that of the sea-god Glaucus, whose original nature could hardly be discerned by those who saw him because his natural members were either broken off or crushed and damaged by the waves in all sorts of ways, and incrustations had grown over them of seaweed and shells and stones, so that he was more like some monster than to his own natural form. And the soul which we behold is in a similar condition, disfigured by ten thousand ills. But not there, Glaucon, not there must we look.

Where then?

At her love of wisdom. Let us see whom she affects, and what society and converse she seeks in virtue of her near kindred with the immortal and eternal and divine; also how different she would become if wholly following this superior principle, and borne by a divine impulse out of the ocean in which she now is, and disengaged from the stones and shells and things of earth and rock which in wild variety spring up around her because she feeds upon earth, (612) and is overgrown by the good things of this life as they are termed: then you would see her as she is, and know whether she have one shape only or many, or what her nature and state may be. Of her affections and of the forms which she takes in this present life I think that we have now given a very fair description.

True, he replied.

And thus, I said, we have disproved the charges brought against justice without introducing the rewards and glories, which, as you were saying, are to be found ascribed to her in Homer and Hesiod; but justice in her own nature has been shown to be best for the soul in her own nature. Let a man do what is just, whether he have the ring of Gyges or not, and even if in addition to the ring of Gyges he put on the helmet of Hades.

Very true.

And now, Glaucon, there will be no harm in further enumerating how many and how great are the rewards which justice and the other virtues procure to the soul from gods and men, both in life and after death.

Certainly not, he said.

Will you repay me, then, what you borrowed in the argument?

What did I borrow?

The assumption that the just man should appear unjust and the unjust just: for you were of opinion[8] that even if the true state of the case could not possibly escape the eyes of gods and men, still this admission ought to be made for the sake of the argument, in order that pure justice might be weighed against pure injustice. Do you remember?

The injustice would be mine if I had forgotten.

Then, as the cause is decided, I demand on behalf of justice that we should admit the estimation in which she is held by gods and men to be what it really is; since she has been shown to confer the blessings which come from reality, and not to deceive those who truly possess her, let what has been taken from her be given back, that so she may win that palm of appearance which is hers also, and which she gives to her own.

The demand, he said, is just.

In the first place, I said—and this is the first thing which you will have to give back—the nature both of the just and unjust is truly known to the gods.

Granted.

And if they are both known to them, one must be the friend and the other the enemy of the gods, as we admitted from the beginning?

True.

(613) And the friend of the gods may be supposed to receive in its best form whatever the gods bestow, excepting only such evil as may have been the necessary consequence of former sins?

Certainly.

Then this must be our notion of the just man, that even when he is in poverty or sickness, or any other seeming misfortune, these things will bring him finally to some good end, either in life, or perhaps in death; for the gods surely will not neglect anyone whose earnest desire is to become just and by the pursuit of virtue to be like God, as far as man can attain the divine likeness?

Yes, he said; if he is like God he will surely not be neglected by Him.

And of the unjust must not the opposite be supposed?

Certainly.

Such, then, are the palms of victory which the gods give the just?

That, at least, is my conviction.

And what do they receive of men? Look at things as they really are, and you will see that the clever unjust are in the case of runners, who run well from the starting-place to the goal but not back again from the goal: they go off at a great pace, but in the end only look foolish, slinking away with their ears draggling on their shoulders, and without a crown; but the true runner comes to the finish and receives the prize and is crowned. And this is the way with the just; they endure to the end of every action and association, and of life itself, and so win a good report and carry off the prizes which men have to bestow.

True.

Will you then allow me to repeat of the just the blessings which you were attributing to the fortunate unjust? I shall say of them that as they grow older they become rulers in their own city if they care to be; they marry whom they like and give in marriage to whom they will; all that you said of the others I now say of these. And, on the other hand, of the unjust I say that the greater number, even though they escape in their youth, are found out at last and look foolish at the end of their course, and when they come to be old and miserable are flouted alike by stranger and citizen; they are beaten, and then come those things unfit for ears polite, as you truly term them; they will be racked and have their eyes burned out, as you were saying. And you may suppose that I have repeated the remainder of your tale of horrors. I ask once more, will you allow all this?

Certainly, he said, for what you say is true.

(614) These, then, are the prizes and rewards and gifts which are bestowed upon the just by gods and men in this present life, in addition to the other good things which justice of herself provides.

Yes, he said; and they are fair and lasting.

And yet, I said, all these are as nothing either in number or greatness in comparison with those other recompenses which await both just and unjust after death. And you ought to hear them, and then both just and unjust will have received from us a full payment of the debt which the argument owes to them.

Speak, he said; there are few things which I would more gladly hear.

Well, I said, I will tell you a tale; not one of the tales which Odysseus tells[9] to the hero Alcinous, yet this too is a tale of a hero, Er the son of Armenius, a Pamphylian by birth. He was slain in battle, and ten days afterwards, when the bodies of the dead were taken up already in a state of corruption, his body was found unaffected by decay, and carried away home to be buried. And on the twelfth day, as he was lying on the funeral pile, he returned to life and told them what he had seen in the other world. He said that when his soul left the body it went on a journey with a great company, and that they came to a mysterious place at which there were two openings in the earth; they were near together, and over against them were two other openings in the heaven above. In the intermediate space there were judges seated, who commanded the just, after they had given judgment on them and had bound their sentences in front of them, to ascend by the way up through the heaven on the right hand; and in like manner the unjust were bidden by them to descend by the lower way on the left hand; these also bore tokens of all their deeds, but fastened on their backs. He drew near, and they told him that he was to be the messenger who would carry the report of the other world to men, and they bade him hear and see all that was to be heard and seen in that place. Then he beheld and saw on one side the souls departing at either opening of heaven and earth when sentence had been given on them; and at the two other openings other souls, some ascending out of the earth dusty and worn with travel, some descending out of heaven clean and bright. And arriving ever and anon they seemed to have come from a long journey, and they went forth with gladness into the meadow, where they encamped as at a festival; and those who knew one another embraced and conversed, the souls which came from earth curiously inquiring about the things above, and the souls which came from heaven about the things beneath. And they told one another of what had happened by the way, (615) those from below weeping and sorrowing at the remembrance of the things which they had endured and seen in their journey beneath the earth (now the journey lasted a thousand years), while those from above were describing heavenly delights and visions of inconceivable beauty. The full story, Glaucon, would take too long to tell; but the sum was this: He said that for every wrong which they had done and every person whom they had injured they had suffered tenfold; or once in a hundred years—such being reckoned to be the length of man's life, and the penalty being thus paid ten times in a thousand years. If, for example, there were any who had been the cause of many deaths by the betrayal of cities or armies, or had cast many into slavery, or been accessory to any other ill treatment, for all their offences, and on behalf of each man wronged, they were afflicted with tenfold pain, and the rewards of beneficence and justice and holiness were in the same proportion. I need hardly repeat what he said concerning young children dying almost as soon as they were born. Of piety and impiety to gods and parents, and of murder, there were retributions other and greater far which he described. He mentioned that he was present when one of the spirits asked another, "Where is Ardiaeus the Great?" (Now this Ardiaeus lived a thousand years before the time of Er: he had been the tyrant of some city of Pamphylia and had murdered his aged father and his elder brother, and was said to have committed many other abominable crimes.) The answer of the other spirit was: "He comes not hither and will never come. And this," said he, "was one of the dreadful sights which we ourselves witnessed. We were at the mouth of the cavern, and, having completed all our experiences, were about to reascend, when of a sudden, we saw Ardiaeus and several others, most of whom were tyrants; but there were also some private individuals who had been great criminals: they were just, as they fancied, about to return into the upper world, but the mouth, instead of admitting them, gave a roar, whenever any of these whose wickedness was incurable or who had not been sufficiently punished tried to ascend; and then wild men of fiery aspect, who were standing by and heard the sound, seized and carried them[10] off; (616) but Ardiaeus and others they bound head and foot and hand, and threw them down, and flayed them with scourges, and dragged them along the road outside the entrance, carding them on thorns like wool, and declaring to the passers-by what were their crimes, and that they were being taken away to be cast into Tartarus." And of all the many terrors of every kind which they had endured, he said that there was none like the terror which each of them felt at that moment, lest they should hear the voice; and when there was silence, one by one they ascended with exceeding joy. These, said Er, were the penalties and retributions, and there were blessings as great.

Now when each band which was in the meadow had tarried seven days, on the eighth they were obliged to proceed on their journey, and, on the fourth day after, he said that they came to a place where they could see from above a line of light, straight as a column, extending right through the whole heaven and through the earth, in color resembling the rainbow, only brighter and purer; another day's journey brought them to the place, and there, in the midst of the light, they saw the ends of the chains of heaven let down from above: for this light is the belt of heaven, and holds together the circumference of the universe, like the under-girders of a trireme.[11] From these ends is extended the spindle of Necessity, on which all the revolutions turn. The shaft and hook of this spindle are made of adamant, and the whorl is made partly of steel and also partly of other materials. The nature of the whorl is as follows; it is, in outward shape, like the whorl used on earth; and his description of it implied that there is one large hollow whorl which is quite scooped out, and into this is fitted another lesser one, and another, and another, and four others, making eight in all, like vessels which fit into one another; the whorls show their circular edges on the upper side, and on their lower side all together form one continuous whorl. This is pierced by the shaft which is driven home through the centre of the eighth. The first and outermost whorl has the rim broadest, and the seven inner whorls are narrower, in the following proportions—the sixth is next to the first in size, the fourth next to the sixth; then comes the eighth; the seventh is fifth, the fifth is sixth, the third is seventh, last and eighth comes the second. The largest [or fixed stars] is spangled, and the seventh [or sun] is brightest; (617) the eighth [or moon] colored by the reflected light of the seventh; the second and fifth [Saturn and Mercury] are in color like one another, and yellower than the preceding; the third [Venus] has the whitest light; the fourth [Mars] is reddish; the sixth [Jupiter] is in whiteness second. Now the whole spindle has the same motion; but, as the whole revolves in one direction, the seven inner circles move slowly in the other, and of these the swiftest is the eighth; next in swiftness are the seventh, sixth, and fifth, which move together; third in swiftness appeared to move, because of this contrary motion, the fourth; the third appeared fourth and the second fifth. The spindle turns on the knees of Necessity; and on the upper surface of each circle stands a siren, who goes round with them, chanting a single tone or note. The eight together form one harmony; and round about, at equal intervals, there is another band, three in number, each sitting upon her throne: these are the Fates, daughters of Necessity, who are clothed in white robes and have chaplets upon their heads, Lachesis and Clotho and Atropos, who accompany with their voices the harmony of the sirens—Lachesis singing of the past, Clotho of the present,

Atropos of the future; Clotho from time to time assisting with a touch of her right hand the revolution of the outer circle of the whorl or spindle, and Atropos with her left hand touching and guiding the inner ones, and Lachesis laying hold of either in turn, first with one hand and then with the other.

When Er and the spirits arrived, their duty was to go at once to Lachesis; but first of all there came a prophet who arranged them in order; then he took from the knees of Lachesis lots and samples of lives, and having mounted a high pulpit, spoke as follows: "Hear the word of Lachesis, the daughter of Necessity. Mortal souls, behold a new cycle of life and mortality. Your genius will not be allotted to you, but you will choose your genius; and let him who draws the first lot have the first choice, and the life which he chooses shall be his destiny. Virtue is free, and as a man honors or dishonors her he will have more or less of her; the responsibility is with the chooser—God is not responsible." When the Interpreter had thus spoken he scattered lots indifferently among them all, and each of them took up the lot which fell near him, (618) all but Er himself (he was not allowed), and each as he took his lot perceived the number which he had obtained. Then the Interpreter placed on the ground before them the patterns of lives; and there were many more lives than the souls present, and they were of all sorts. There were lives of every animal and of man in every condition. And there were tyrannies among them, some lasting out the tyrant's life, others which broke off in the middle and came to an end in poverty and exile and beggary; and there were lives of famous men, some who were famous for their form and beauty as well as for their strength and success in games, or, again, for their birth and the qualities of their ancestors; and some who were the reverse of famous for the opposite qualities. And of women likewise. The disposition of the soul was not, however, included in them, because the soul, when choosing a new life, must of necessity become different. But there was every other quality, and they all mingled with one another, and also with elements of wealth and poverty, and disease and health; and there were also states intermediate in these respects.

And here, my dear Glaucon, is the supreme peril of our human state; and therefore each one of us must take the utmost care to forsake every other kind of knowledge and seek and study one thing only, if peradventure he may be able to discover someone who will make him able to discern between a good and an evil life, and so to choose always and everywhere the better life as he has opportunity. He should consider the bearing of all these things which have been mentioned severally and collectively upon the excellence of a life; he should know what the effect of beauty is, for good or evil, when combined with poverty or wealth in this or that kind of soul, and what are the good and evil consequences of noble and humble birth, of private and public station, of strength and weakness, of cleverness and dullness, and of all the natural and acquired gifts of the soul, and the operation of them when blended with one another;

he will then look at the nature of the soul, and from the consideration of all these qualities he will be able to determine which is the better and which is the worse; and so he will choose, giving the name of evil to the life which will tend to make his soul more unjust, and good to the life which will make his soul more just; all else he will disregard. For we have seen and know that this is the best choice both in life and after death. (619) A man must take with him into the world below an adamantine faith in truth and right, that there too he may be undazzled by the desire of wealth or the other allurements of evil, lest he be drawn into tyrannies and similar activities, and do irremediable wrongs to others and suffer yet worse himself; but may know how to choose a life moderate in these respects and avoid the extremes on either side, as far as possible, not only in this life but in all that which is to come. For this way brings men to their greatest happiness.

And according to the report of the messenger from the other world this was what the prophet said at the time: "Even for the last comer, if he chooses wisely and will live diligently, there is appointed a happy and not undesirable existence. Let not him who chooses first be careless, and let not the last despair." And when he had spoken, he who had the first choice came forward and in a moment chose the greatest tyranny; his mind having been darkened by folly and sensuality, he had not made any thorough inspection before he chose, and did not perceive that he was fated, among other evils, to devour his own children. But when he had time to examine the lot and saw what was in it, he began to beat his breast and lament over his choice, forgetting the proclamation of the prophet; for, instead of throwing the blame of his misfortune on himself, he accused chance and the gods, and everything rather than himself. Now he was one of those who came from heaven, and in a former life had dwelt in a well-ordered state, virtuous from habit only, and without philosophy. And for the most part it was true of others who were caught in this way, that the greater number of them came from heaven and therefore they had never been schooled by trial, whereas the pilgrims who came from earth having themselves suffered and seen others suffer were not in a hurry to choose. And owing to this inexperience of theirs, and also to the accident of the lot, the majority of the souls exchanged a good destiny for an evil or an evil for a good. For if a man had always on his arrival in this world dedicated himself from the first to sound philosophy, and had been moderately fortunate in the number of the lot, he might, as the messenger reported, be happy here, and also his journey to another life and return to this, instead of being rough and underground, would be smooth and heavenly. Most curious, he said, was the spectacle—sad and laughable and strange; for the choice of the souls was in most cases based on their experience of a previous life. (620) There he saw the soul which had once been Orpheus choosing the life of a swan out of enmity to the race of women, hating to be born of a woman because they had been his murderers; he beheld also the soul of Thamyras choosing the life of a nightingale; birds, on the other hand, like the swan and other musicians, wanting to be men. The soul which obtained the twentieth lot chose the life of a lion, and this was the soul of Ajax the son of Telamon, who would not be a man, remembering the injustice which was done him in the judgment about the arms. The next was Agamemnon, who took the life of an eagle, because, like Ajax, he hated human nature by reason of his sufferings. About the middle came the lot of Atalanta; she, seeing the great fame of an athlete, was unable to resist the temptation: and after her there followed the soul of Epeus the son of Panopeus passing into the nature of a woman skilled in some craft; and far away among the last who chose, the soul of the jester Thersites was putting on the form of a monkey. There came also the soul of Odysseus having yet to make a choice, and his lot happened to be the last of them all. Now the recollection of former toils had disenchanted him of ambition, and he went about for a considerable time in search of the life of a private man who had no cares; he had some difficulty in finding this, which was lying about and had been neglected by everybody else; and when he saw it, he said that he would have done the same had his lot been first instead of last, and gladly chose it. And not only did men pass into animals, but I must also mention that there were animals tame and wild who changed into one another and into corresponding human natures—the righteous into the gentle and the unrighteous into the savage, in all sorts of combinations.

All the souls had now chosen their lives, and they went in the order of their choice to Lachesis, who sent with them the genius whom they had severally chosen, to be the guardian of their lives and the fulfiller of the choice: this genius led the souls first to Clotho, and drew them within the revolution of the spindle impelled by her hand, thus ratifying the destiny of each; and then, when they were fastened to this, carried them to Atropos, who spun the threads and made them irreversible, (621) whence without turning round they passed beneath the throne of Necessity; and when they had all passed, they marched on to the plain of Forgetfulness, in intolerable scorching heat, for the plain was a barren waste destitute of trees and verdure; and then towards evening they encamped by the river of Unmindfulness, whose water no vessel can hold; of this they were all obliged to drink a certain quantity, and those who were not saved by wisdom drank more than was necessary; and each one as he drank forgot all things. Now after they had gone to rest, about the middle of the night there was a thunderstorm and earthquake, and then in an instant they were driven upwards in all manner of ways to their birth, like stars shooting. He himself was hindered from drinking the water. But in what manner or by what means he returned to the body he could not say; only in the morning, awaking suddenly, he found himself lying on the pyre.

And thus, Glaucon, the tale has been saved and has not perished, and will save us if we are obedient to the word spoken; and we shall pass safely over the river of Forgetfulness and our soul will not be defiled. Wherefore my counsel is that we hold fast ever to the heavenly way and follow after justice and virtue always, considering that the soul is immortal and able to endure every sort of good and every sort of evil. Thus shall we live dear to one another and to the gods, both while remaining here and when, like conquerors in the games who go round to gather gifts, we receive our reward. And it shall be well with us both in this life and in the pilgrimage of a thousand years which we have been describing.

LAWS

from BOOK VII

ATHENIAN STRANGER. Let us then affirm the paradox that strains of music are our laws (*nomoi*), and this latter being the name which the ancients gave to lyric songs, they probably would not have very much objected to our proposed application of the word. (800) Some one, either asleep or awake, must have had a dreamy suspicion of their nature. And let our decree be as follows: No one in singing or dancing shall offend against public and consecrated models, and the general fashion among the youth, any more then he would offend against any other law. And he who observes this law shall be blameless; but he who is disobedient, as I was saying, shall be punished by the guardians of the laws, and by the priests and priestesses. Suppose that we imagine this to be our law.

CLEINIAS. Very good.

ATH. Can anyone who makes such laws escape ridicule? Let us see. I think that our only safety will be in first framing certain models for composers. One of these models shall be as follows: If a sacrifice has been offered, and the victims burnt according to law—if, I say, anyone who may be a son or brother, standing by another at the altar and over the victims, horribly blasphemes, will not his words inspire despondency and evil omens and forebodings in the mind of his father and of his other kinsmen?

CLE. Of course.

ATH. And this is just what takes place in almost all our cities. A magistrate offers a public sacrifice, and there come in not one but many choruses, who take up a position a little way from the altar, and from time to time pour forth all sorts of horrible blasphemies on the sacred rites, exciting the souls of the audience with words and rhythms and melodies most sorrowful to hear; and he who at the moment when the city has offered sacrifice makes the citizens weep most, carries away the palm of victory. Now, ought we not to forbid such strains as these? And if ever our citizens must hear such lamentations, then on some unblest and inauspicious day let there be choruses of foreign and hired minstrels, like those hirelings who accompany the departed at funerals with barbarous Carian chants. That is the sort of thing which will be appropriate if we have such strains at all; and let the apparel of the singers of the funeral dirge be, not circlets and ornaments of gold, but the reverse. Enough of all this. I will simply ask once more whether we shall lay down as one of our principles of song——

CLE. What?

(801) ATH. That we should avoid every word of evil omen; let that kind of song which is of good omen be heard everywhere and always in our state. I need hardly ask again, but shall assume that you agree with me.

CLE. By all means; that law is approved by the suffrages of us all.

ATH. But what shall be our next musical law or type? Ought not prayers to be offered up to the gods when we sacrifice?

CLE. Certainly.

ATH. And our third law, if I am not mistaken, will be to the effect that our poets, understanding prayers to be requests which we make to the gods, will take especial heed that they do not by mistake ask for evil instead of good. To make such a prayer would surely be too ridiculous.

CLE. Very true.

ATH. Were we not a little while ago quite convinced that no silver or golden Plutus should dwell in our state?[1]

CLE. To be sure.

ATH. And what has it been the object of our argument to show? Did we not imply that the poets are not always quite capable of knowing what is good or evil? And if one of them utters a mistaken prayer in song or words, he will make our citizens pray for the opposite of what we ordain in matters of the highest import; than which, as I was saying, there can be few greater mistakes. Shall we then propose as one of our laws and models relating to the Muses——

CLE. What? Will you explain the law more precisely?

ATH. Shall we make a law that the poet shall compose nothing contrary to the ideas of the lawful, or just, or beautiful, or good, which are allowed in the state? Nor shall he be permitted to communicate his compositions to any private individuals, until he shall have shown them to the appointed judges and the guardians of the law, and they are satisfied with them. As to the persons whom we appoint to be our legislators about music[2] and as to the director of education,[3] these have been already indicated. Once more then, as I have asked more than once, shall this be our third law, and type, and model—what do you say?

CLE. Let it be so, by all means.

ATH. Then it will be proper to have hymns and praises of the gods,[4] intermingled with prayers; and after the gods prayers and praises should be offered in like manner to demigods and heroes, suitable to their several characters.

CLE. Certainly.

ATH. In the next place there will be no objection to a law, that citizens who are departed and have done good and energetic deeds, either with their souls or with their bodies, and have been obedient to the laws, should receive eulogies; this will be very fitting.

CLE. Quite true. (802)

ATH. But to honor with hymns and panegyrics those who are still alive is not safe; a man should run his course, and make a fair ending, and then we will praise him; and let praise be given equally to women as well as men who have been distinguished in virtue. The order of songs and dances shall be as follows: There are many ancient musical compositions and dances which are excellent, and from these it is fair to select what is proper and suitable to the newly-founded city; and they shall choose judges of not less than fifty years of age, who shall make the selection, and any of the old poems which they deem sufficient they shall include; any that are deficient or altogether unsuitable, they shall either utterly throw aside, or examine and amend, taking into their counsel poets and musicians, and making use of their potential genius; but explaining to them the wishes of the legislator in order that they may regulate dancing, music, and all choral strains, according to the mind of the judges; and not allowing them to indulge, except in some few matters, their individual pleasures and fancies. Now the irregular strain of music is always made ten thousand times better by attaining to law and order, and rejecting the honeyed Muse[5]—not however that we mean wholly to exclude pleasure, which is the characteristic of all music. And if a man be brought up from childhood to the age of discretion and maturity in the use of the orderly and severe music, when he hears the opposite he detests it, and calls it illiberal; but if trained in the sweet and vulgar music, he deems the severer kind cold and displeasing. So that, as I was saying before, while he who hears them gains no more pleasure from the one than from the other, the one has the advantage of making those who are trained in it better men, whereas the other makes them worse.

CLE. Very true.

ATH. Again, we must distinguish and determine on some general principle what songs are suitable to women, and what to men, and must assign to them their proper melodies and rhythms. It is shocking for a whole harmony to be inharmonical, or for a rhythm to be unrhythmical, and this will happen when the melody is inappropriate to them. And therefore the legislator must assign to these also their forms. Now both sexes have melodies and rhythms which of necessity belong to them; and those of women are clearly enough indicated by their natural difference. The grand, and that which tends to courage, may be fairly called manly; (803) but that which inclines to moderation and temperance, may be declared both in law and in ordinary speech to be the more womanly quality. This, then, will be the general order of them.

Let us now speak of the manner of teaching and imparting them, and the persons to whom, and the time when, they are severally to be imparted. As the shipwright first lays down the lines of the keel, and thus, as it were, draws the ship in outline, so do I seek to distinguish the patterns of life, and lay down their keels according to the nature of different men's souls; seeking truly to consider by what means, and in what ways, we may go through the voyage of life best. Now human affairs are hardly worth considering in earnest, and yet we must be in earnest about them—a sad necessity constrains us. And having got thus far, there will be a fitness in our completing the matter, if we can only find some suitable method of doing so. But what do I mean? Someone may ask this very question, and quite rightly, too.

CLE. Certainly.

ATH. I say that about serious matters a man should be serious, and about a matter which is not serious he should not be serious; and that God is the natural and worthy object of our most serious and blessed endeavors, for man, as I said before,[6] is made to be the plaything of God, and this, truly considered, is the best of him; wherefore also every man and woman should walk seriously, and pass life in the noblest of pastimes, and be of another mind from what they are at present.

CLE. In what respect?

ATH. At present they think that their serious pursuits should be for the sake of their sports, for they deem war a serious pursuit, which must be managed well for the sake of peace; but the truth is, that there neither is, nor has been, nor ever will be, either amusement or instruction in any degree worth speaking of in war, which is nevertheless deemed by us to be the most serious of our pursuits. And therefore, as we say, every one of us should live the life of peace as long and as well as he can.[7] And what is the right way of living? Are we to live in sports always? If so, in what kind of sports? We ought to live sacrificing, and singing, and dancing, and then a man will be able to propitiate the gods, and to defend himself against his enemies and conquer them in battle. The type of song or dance by which he will propitiate them has been described, and the paths along which he is to proceed have been cut for him. (804) He will go forward in the spirit of the poet: "Telemachus, some things thou wilt thyself find in thy heart, but other things God will suggest; for I deem that thou wast not born or brought up without the will of the gods."[8] And this ought to be the view of our alumni; they ought to think that what has been said is enough for them, and that any other things their genius and god will suggest to them—he will tell them to whom, and when, and to what gods severally they are to sacrifice and perform dances, and how they may propitiate the deities, and live according to the appointment of nature; being for the most part puppets, but having some little share of reality.

. . . . .

(810) ATH. That is quite true; and you mean to imply that the road which we are taking may be disagreeable to some but is agreeable to as many others, or if not to as many, at any rate to persons not inferior to the others, and in company with them you bid me, at whatever risk, to proceed along the path of legislation which has opened out of our present discourse, and to be of good cheer, and not to faint.

CLE. Certainly.

ATH. And I do not faint; I say, indeed, that we have a great many poets writing in hexameter, trimeter, and all sorts of measures—some who are serious, others who aim only at raising a laugh—and all mankind declare that the youth who are rightly educated should be brought up in them and saturated with them; some insist that they should be constantly hearing them read aloud, and always learning them, so as to get by heart entire poets; (811) while others select choice passages and long speeches, and make compendiums of them, saying that these ought to be committed to memory, if a man is to be made good and wise by experience and learning of many things. And you want me now to tell them plainly in what they are right and in what they are wrong.

CLE. Yes, I do.

ATH. But how can I in one word rightly comprehend all of them? I am of opinion, and, if I am not mistaken, there is a general agreement, that every one of these poets has said many things well and many things the reverse of well; and if this be true, than I do affirm that much learning is dangerous to youth.

CLE. How would you advise the guardian of the law to act?

ATH. In what respect?

CLE. I mean to what pattern should he look as his guide in permitting the young to learn some things and forbidding them to learn others. Do not shrink from answering.

ATH. My good Cleinias, I rather think that I am fortunate.

CLE. How so?

ATH. I think that I am not wholly in want of a pattern, for when I consider the words which we have spoken from early dawn until now, and which, as I believe, have been inspired by heaven, they appear to me to be quite like a poem. When I reflected upon all these words of ours, I naturally felt pleasure, for of all the discourses which I have ever learnt or heard, either in poetry or prose, this seemed to me to be the justest, and most suitable for young men to hear; I cannot imagine any better pattern than this which the guardian of the law who is also the director of education can have. He cannot do better than advise the teachers to teach the young these words and any which are of a like nature, if he should happen to find them, either in poetry or prose, or if he come across unwritten discourses akin to ours, he should certainly preserve them, and commit them to writing. And, first of all, he shall constrain the teachers themselves to learn and approve them, and any of them who will not, shall not be employed by him, but those whom he finds agreeing in his judgment, he shall make use of and shall commit to them the instruction and education of youth. (812) And here and on this wise let my fanciful tale about letters and teachers of letters come to an end.

. . . . . .

(814) ATH. Enough of wrestling; we will now proceed to speak of other movements of the body. Such motion may be in general called dancing, and is of two kinds: one of nobler figures, imitating the honorable, the other of the more ignoble figures, imitating the mean; and of both these there are two further subdivisions. Of the serious, one kind is of those engaged in war and vehement action, and is the exercise of a noble person and a manly heart; the other exhibits a temperate soul in the enjoyment of prosperity and modest pleasures, and may be truly called and is the dance of peace. (815) The warrior dance is different from the peaceful one, and may be rightly termed pyrrhic[9]; this imitates the modes of avoiding blows and missiles by dropping or giving way, or springing aside, or rising up or falling down; also the opposite postures which are those of action, as, for example, the imitation of archery and the hurling of javelins, and of all sorts of blows. And when the imitation is of brave bodies and souls, and the action is direct and muscular, giving for the most part a straight movement to the limbs of the body—that, I say, is the true sort; but the opposite is not right. In the dance of peace what we have to consider is whether a man bears himself naturally and gracefully, and after the manner of men who duly conform to the law. But before proceeding I must distinguish the dancing about which there is any doubt, from that about which there is no doubt. Which is the doubtful kind, and how are the two to be distinguished? There are dances of the Bacchic sort, both those in which, as they say, they imitate drunken men, and which are named after the nymphs, and Pan, and Silenuses, and satyrs; and also those in which purifications are made or mysteries celebrated—all this sort of dancing cannot be rightly defined as having either a peaceful or a warlike character, or indeed as having any meaning whatever, and may, I think, be most truly described as distinct from the warlike dance, and distinct from the peaceful, and not suited for a city at all. There let it lie; and so leaving it to lie, we will proceed to the dances of war and peace, for with these we are undoubtedly concerned. Now the unwarlike muse, which honors in dance the gods and the sons of the

gods, is entirely associated with the consciousness of prosperity; this class may be subdivided into two lesser classes, of which one is expressive of an escape from some labor or danger into good, and has greater pleasures, the other expressive of preservation and increase of former good, in which the pleasure is less exciting—in all these cases, every man when the pleasure is greater, moves his body more, and less when the pleasure is less; and, again, if he be more orderly and has learned courage from discipline he moves less, (816) but if he be a coward, and has no training or self-control, he makes greater and more violent movements, and in general when he is speaking or singing he is not altogether able to keep his body still; and so out of the imitation of words in gestures the whole art of dancing has arisen. And in these various kinds of imitation one man moves in an orderly, another in a disorderly manner; and as the ancients may be observed to have given many names which are according to nature and deserving of praise, so there is an excellent one which they have given to the dances of men who in their times of prosperity are moderate in their pleasures—the giver of names, whoever he was, assigned to them a very true, and poetical, and rational name, when he called them Emmeleiai, or dances of order, thus establishing two kinds of dances of the nobler sort, the dance of war which he called the pyrrhic, and the dance of peace which he called Emmeleia,[10] or the dance of order; giving to each their appropriate and becoming name. These things the legislator should indicate in general outline, and the guardian of the law should inquire into them and search them out, combining dancing with music, and assigning to the several sacrificial feasts that which is suitable to them; and when he has consecrated all of them in due order, he shall for the future change nothing, whether of dance or song. Thenceforward the city and the citizens shall continue to have the same pleasures, themselves being as far as possible alike, and shall live well and happily.

I have described the dances which are appropriate to noble bodies and generous souls. But it is necessary also to consider and know uncomely persons and thoughts, and those which are intended to produce laughter in comedy, and have a comic character in respect of style, song, and dance, and of the imitations which these afford. For serious things cannot be understood without laughable things, nor opposites at all without opposites, if a man is really to have intelligence of either; but he cannot carry out both in action, if he is to have any degree of virtue. And for this very reason he should learn them both, in order that he may not in ignorance do or say anything which is ridiculous and out of place—he should command slaves and hired strangers to imitate such things, but he should never take any serious interest in them himself, nor should any freeman or freewoman be discovered taking pains to learn them; and there should always be some element of novelty in the imitation. Let these then be laid down, both in law and in our discourse, as the regulations of laughable amusements which are generally called comedy. (817) And, if any of the serious poets, as they are termed, who write tragedy, come to us and say: "O strangers, may we go to your city and country or may we not, and shall we bring with us our poetry—what is your will about these matters?" How shall we answer the divine men? I think that our answer should be as follows:[11] Best of strangers, we will say to them, we also according to our ability are tragic poets, and our tragedy is the best and noblest; for our whole state is an imitation of the best and noblest life, which we affirm to be indeed the very truth of tragedy. You are poets and we are poets, both makers of the same strains, rivals and antagonists in the noblest of dramas, which true law can alone perfect, as our hope is. Do not then suppose that we shall all in a moment allow you to erect your stage in the agora,[12] or introduce the fair voices of your actors, speaking above our own, and permit you to harangue our women and children, and the common people, about our institutions, in language other than our own, and very often the opposite of our own. For a state would be mad which gave you this license, until the magistrates had determined whether your poetry might be recited, and was fit for publication or not. Wherefore, O ye sons and scions of the softer Muses, first of all show your songs to the magistrates, and let them compare them with our own, and if they are the same or better we will give you a chorus; but if not, then, my friends, we cannot. Let these, then, be the customs ordained by law about all dances and the teaching of them, and let matters relating to slaves be separated from those relating to masters, if you do not object.

ARISTOTLE

(384–322 B.C.)

INTRODUCTION

The *Poetics* of Aristotle is widely recognized as the most influential document in the history of literary criticism. Its major concepts have become standard points of departure for subsequent discussions of the general nature of literature and the particular structure and function of tragedy. The reasons for the long-standing and widespread popularity of this work are not hard to discern. The *Poetics* not only embodies brilliant, verifiable insights into the nature of the artistic experience; it also links these insights together in a tightly-knit, deductively rigorous argument that further illuminates important aesthetic problems.

A survey of the structure of the *Poetics* clearly reveals its tightly-knit argument. Aristotle begins his discussion with a reference to "first principles," pointing out the essential character of poetry as *mimesis* (imitation). In Chapters 1–3 he introduces the "co-ordinates" of imitation—means, object, and manner—by which all of the various arts can be compared and contrasted. Even at this early point in the *Poetics,* it is obvious that Aristotle wishes to elevate tragedy as the literary form which "imitates" in the fullest, most complex way.

After pointing out the natural origin of poetry in Chapter 4, Aristotle provides a brief sketch of the history of the major literary forms. In Chapters 4 and 5 he is once again focusing on tragedy as the fullest realization of the possibilities of imitation, the highest "evolutionary" development of mimetic form. This emphasis is so pronounced, in fact, that it makes Aristotle's brief history less an empirical survey than a deductive schema.

Chapter 6 opens with a lengthy definition of tragedy which sums up the preceding material: tragedy is categorized in terms of its means, manner, and purpose of imitation. Aristotle then begins a lengthy inquiry (Chapters 6–22) into the six qualitative parts of tragedy: plot, character, thought, diction, melody, and spectacle. As its placement in this sequence suggests, "plot" (*mythos*) is to Aristotle the most important element (the "soul") of a tragedy.

Understood in its fullest sense, plot is what best objectifies the thematic logic of a play, what most fully engages the audience's emotions, and what most directly determines the author's other choices in the act of poetic composition.

In Chapters 7–11 Aristotle discusses specific criteria for plots. A plot must have the proper magnitude, encompassing neither too many nor too few incidents. It must manifest unity of action (the only "unity" Aristotle insists upon), creating a "meaning" of its own by selecting, condensing, shaping, and arranging the materials of real life, rather than trying to present the whole life span of its protagonist. It must, in other words, represent a "universal" action (what a certain type of individual might do) rather than a particular chronicle of events (what a specific, historical individual actually did). In Chapters 10 and 11 Aristotle divides plots into the "simple" and the "complex," the latter involving the elements of Reversal (a change of fortune to the exact opposite state of affairs) and Recognition (a change from ignorance to knowledge). Aristotle's emphasis once again elevates *complexity* as an aesthetic norm.

After a listing of the quantitative parts of drama in Chapter 12, Aristotle begins to shift his attention to "character" (*ethos*), the second qualitative element. The problem he confronts in Chapter 13 is the question of *hamartia*: how can the dramatist portray his tragic protagonist so as to guide the audience's emotional response, generating pity and fear while avoiding a reaction of disgust or pure shock? The logic of Aristotle's answer (discussed below) depends in part on his definitions of pity (aroused by the perception of *undeserved* misfortune) and fear (evoked by the realization that the sufferer is a man *like ourselves*)—but it depends even more on his understanding of "character" as manifesting moral choice (*proairesis*). This premise, in fact, accounts for most of Aristotle's general remarks in Chapter 15 on how the dramatist can develop character effectively.

Chapters 16–18 are difficult to fit into the logical sequence of Aristotle's argument; Chapter 18, for example, offers a somewhat puzzling classification of kinds of tragedies which seems unconnected to Aristotle's earlier comments.[1] In Chapter 19, however, Aristotle returns to a consideration of qualitative parts. "Thought" (*dianoia*) refers to the intellectual content of the speeches, and is related to the art of rhetoric. "Diction" (*lexis*) is treated in Chapters 19–22; Aristotle's discussion moves from the simplest elements of language (letters and syllables) to complexities of poetic metaphor.

Aristotle seems to have felt that the last two qualitative parts of drama, "melody" (*melos*) and "spectacle" (*opsis*) were accidental rather than essential elements of dramatic art, belonging more to the exigencies of stage production than to the craft of composition. In Chapter 23, then, he turns to the genre of epic, the literary form most closely related to tragedy, a form understandable in terms of the four primary qualitative parts. Chapters 23–24 stress that epic aspires to a "dramatic" ideal: unity of action.

The *Poetics* concludes with a consideration of certain technical and critical problems, and a final comparison and contrast of epic and tragedy. These last two chapters not only complete the logic of Aristotle's argument; they also reaffirm his aesthetic orientation. Poetry, in his view, has its own ontology. In the "world" or "whole" (*holos*) of a literary work, internal coherence or "probability" (*to eikos*) takes precedence over verisimilitude. One of the most significant comments in the *Poetics* (in Chapter 25) asserts that "the criticism that a work of art is not a truthful representation can be met by the argument that it represents the situation as it should be."

The original Greek text of the *Poetics* is not extant, but there are three fundamentally important witnesses for it. The most important of these is an eleventh-century manuscript (Paris 1741) which is the primary source for nearly all contemporary texts of the *Poetics.* This is supplemented by an inferior but still quite useful manuscript (Riccardianus 46) of the thirteenth or fourteenth centuries, and, less significantly, by an Arabic translation of the *Poetics* dating from the tenth century and based on a Syriac translation of a seventh-century Greek manuscript. Because difficulties exist in interpreting a number of passages in all three manuscripts, editors have been forced, in varying degrees, to amend the text of the *Poetics.* There has also been considerable speculation in recent years that some sections of the *Poetics* were not written by Aristotle, but were added by later interpolators. For the most part, textual problems do not affect our understanding of the major concepts and themes of the *Poetics.* Still, readers of Aristotle's treatise should be aware of the unsettled and disputed nature of parts of the text they are reading, and that there are differences of judgment, occasionally severe, among editors and translators of the Greek text.

Stylistically, the *Poetics* also offers problems for its readers, translators, and interpreters. The original Greek is extremely terse, sometimes to the point of obscurity, and many passages require "expansion" before they can be made meaningful. Scholars have offered two hypotheses for the special stylistic character of the *Poetics* and some of Aristotle's other works. It has been suggested that these works are really lecture notes, made either by Aristotle or his students, rather than fully developed treatises. An alternative suggestion is based on the distinction between "esoteric" and "exoteric" works. Under this view the *Poetics* would be an esoteric work—i.e., a work meant to be circulated among those already familiar with Aristotle's doctrines, and thus not in need of the complete and detailed account that would be circulated as an exoteric work among those without a specialized knowledge of the subject.

Both for textual and stylistic reasons, therefore, all interpreters of the *Poetics* must provide some expansion of the literal text in order to make the work comprehensible. The most important problem facing the student of the *Poetics,* however, does not result from difficulties in text or style. The wide influence of the *Poetics* is based on the major critical concepts it offers; but while nearly all critics agree on the importance of these major concepts, there exists wide disagreement on the full meaning and scope of a number of them. It is difficult to disentangle any of Aristotle's concepts from the rigorous argument that controls the *Poetics* as a whole, but four key terms seem to stand out from the others and demand special consideration. These terms, all of the highest significance for Aristotle's critical position, are (I) *mimesis* ("imitation"), (II) *katharsis*, (III) *hamartia* ("tragic error"), and (IV) *spoudaios* ("noble" character).

(I) *Mimesis.* The concept of art as imitation is as central to the Aristotelian view as it is to the Platonic, but Aristotle's application of the term *mimesis* is far different from that customarily attributed to Plato.[2] In Book X of the *Republic* Plato regarded poetic imitation as "copying," and on this basis asserted that it is essentially trivial—even less significant than the "copying" of ideas which is embodied in the work of craftsmen. The *Poetics* constitutes an emphatic rejection of the view. Aristotle emphasizes the dynamic, conscious "craft" (*technê*) of art, recognizing the artist's *creativity.* The artist is not a copier, but a "maker" whose products can best be understood as imitations of human action, character, and emotion.

Aristotle's concept of imitation is very much in keeping with the main thrust of modern aesthetic criticism.[3] In his seminal work on the *Poetics*, S. H. Butcher recognized the essential modernity of Aristotle's argument. Butcher pointed out that Aristotle's statement that the artists "may imitate things as they ought to be" is evidence of a very sophisticated concept, far beyond the notion of "copying." Aristotle's phrase "ought to be" implies the existence of an *aesthetic* judgment, and suggests that art is a free activity of the human mind, independent of utilitarian consideration.[4] In effect, the concept of imitation distinguishes between "fine art" and the useful crafts (e.g., carpentry, ship-building); the product of a useful craft is not, strictly speaking, an "imitation" of anything. As John Crowe Ransom has observed, the very term "imitation" implies a variation of the art-for-art's sake position: "not being actual," an imitation "cannot be used; it can only be known."[5]

Aristotle relates imitation to learning. In Chapter 4 he notes that we enjoy seeing artistic representations of even the most disgusting and unpleasant objects, objects we would be repelled by if we saw them in reality. Tragedy, for example, deals with horrible and depressing events, but its representation of these events is itself aesthetically enjoyable. Aristotle's explanation is that in such cases the imitation results in a kind of learning, culminating in an insight that is a source of pleasure for the audience. Here and elsewhere in the *Poetics* Aristotle seems to be arguing that the process of imitation leads from the particular represented in the work of art to a universal which subsumes it, and that this movement from particular to universal is a learning experience which clarifies the particular representation by expressing its essential nature. The act of learning or clarification is specifically identified with the essential human pleasure offered by all forms of imitation. Understood in this way, Aristotle's *mimesis* is generically related to the aesthetic concept of art as a source of insight.

The aesthetic implications of imitation have been analyzed further by O. B. Hardison, who emphasizes that Aristotle's term carries an *active* meaning. *Mimesis* can refer to the actual process of composition. In the writing of a tragedy, "imitation" would involve the construction and articulation of the six component elements enumerated in Chapter 6: plot, character, thought, diction, melody, and spectacle. When this process is carried out according to the laws of probability and necessity (i.e., internal coherence), a universal form is achieved which imparts intelligibility to the particular actions represented by the poet.[6]

(II) *Katharsis.* *Katharsis* is a rare word in the Aristotelian critical vocabulary. It appears twice in the *Poetics*, once in a routine technical sense to describe Orestes' purification from madness and once at the climax of Aristotle's definition of tragedy in Chapter 6, where its appearance has made it the most famous term in Aristotle's impressive critical system. The essential meaning of the concept is still much disputed, despite the interpretative labors of innumerable scholars. Four major theories have been offered to explain catharsis. These may be generally designated as (1) medical or therapeutic, (2) moral, (3) structural, and (4) intellectual.

The medical or therapeutic interpretation relates the term to the ancient theory of homeopathic medicine, which asserted that an illness should be treated by the administration of agents similar to the illness itself (e.g., the application of heat to expel fever). This interpretation is suggested in Milton's preface to *Samson Agonistes*, and was developed into a full-scale theory by H. Weil and J. Bernays in the nineteenth century. Critics who hold this view usually translate *katharsis* as "purgation," and interpret it as a process of purging pity and fear from an audience by exposing that audience to a representation of pitiable and fearful events in tragedy. This theory assumes that all men are subject in varying degrees to excesses of pity and fear, and that the essential pleasure of tragedy is the therapeutic pleasure of removing these excesses.

Those who subscribe to the medical theory of catharsis usually support it by citing a passage from the *Politics* (1341 B 37–42 A 17): Aristotle's reference to the therapeutic use of certain musical melodies to purge the emotional frenzy of some participants in religious observances. Aristotle uses the term *katharsis* to describe this purging, indicating that he will discuss the concept in more detail in his *Poetics*. Many scholars believe that this more explicit treatment of catharsis was presented in a lost second book of the *Poetics*.

From Bernays' time to our own, the medical theory of catharsis has been dominant. Its principal advantage has been that it relates an enigmatic passage in the *Poetics* to a passage in the *Politics* where the relatively rare term *katharsis* appears in the explicit sense of "purgation." But the medical theory has failed to win universal acceptance: many critics and scholars dispute the thesis that Aristotle conceived of art as essentially and regularly a form of therapy directed at relieving audiences of psychic excesses. Such scholars question the validity of applying a discussion in the *Politics* about music as an instrument of education to a sustained argument in a different treatise about the fundamental nature of poetry.[7]

The moral interpretation of catharsis renders the term as "purification." It asserts that the principal goal of a tragedy is to purify the audience's pity and fear of any excess or deficiency, or to correct any misdirection of these emotions with respect to the persons, places, or circumstances toward which they are displayed. The moral interpretation of catharsis is didactic: it sees catharsis as a means of *disciplining* the audience's attitudes toward life in general. The principle evidence for such an interpretation is a passage from the *Nicomachean Ethics* (1106 B 8–23). Here Aristotle explicitly mentions pity among the emotions that must be felt neither in an excessive nor a deficient way, but according to a proper mean. Most interpreters have felt that this evidence is very tenuous, and they have been generally unable to accept the argument that Aristotle saw the primary purpose of art as the moral conditioning of the audience. Lessing is the most significant critic to advocate the moral view of catharsis.[8]

A form of the structural interpretation of catharsis was developed early in the twentieth century by H. Otte, but its most famous and influential formulation is in the work of Gerald Else.[9] Else argues that catharsis is not a major critical concept at all. Instead, he claims, it is a limited, although quite necessary, element in the structure of a tragedy. Else interprets catharsis as a process carried on by the plot, through which the protagonist's tragic deed is shown to be *katharmos*, free from pollution. The protagonist demonstrates to the audience that he did not intend the evils he has caused, or that he wishes to provide expiation for his crime; the audience is then able to respond with the emotions of pity and fear appropriate to a tragedy.

Else's interpretation has the advantage of linking catharsis with other concepts in the *Poetics*, especially *hamartia* and "recognition," and of avoiding vague speculation about the psychological and moral conditioning of the audience. But an important problem in Else's theory is that it removes *katharsis* from its central position of importance as a critical term without adequately explaining the appearance of this term at the climax of Aristotle's definition of tragedy.

This very problem is dealt with directly in the intellectual interpretation of catharsis, an interpretation that renders the term as "intellectual clarification." S. O. Haupt presented a version of this position early in the twentieth century.[10] Haupt's arguments, however, were only partially demonstrable on philological grounds, and his work was soon rejected and forgotten. In 1962 Leon Golden published an article in which the intellectual interpretation was given an independent defense, and he placed special emphasis on the functional role that catharsis (as "intellectual clarification") plays in the total argument of the *Poetics*.[11] In 1966 H. D. F. Kitto published another independent paper confirming a number of the positions taken by Haupt and Golden.[12]

The intellectual interpretation of catharsis rests on three main lines of argument. First, it is in accord with Aristotle's procedure, throughout his total philosophy, of attaching greatest significance to the intellectual value of any activity; his *Nicomachean Ethics*, for example, defines the contemplative mode as the highest form of human life, and his *Metaphysics* defines God as *Nous* ("Mind"). Second, the term *katharsis* was occasionally used in Greek by such authors as Plato, Epicurus, and Philodemus to mean intellectual clarification. Third, and most important, this interpretation stresses the logical coherence of the *Poetics*. The word *katharsis* appears in Chapter 6 of the *Poetics*, in a definition of tragedy prefaced by Aristotle's claim that he is "summing up" what has been said so far. *Katharsis* appears at the climax of the definition, in a position which indicates that it is the goal or final cause of tragedy. But in Chapter 4 Aristotle has already identified the ultimate goal of all artistic imitation (and specifically the representation of "horrible" events) as a learning experience. Learning, Aristotle says, is a source of pleasure for all men. This point also gains support from Aristotle's statement in Chapter 9 that poetry is more philosophical and significant than history: poetry aims at the universal while history deals with the particular.

Whatever theory of catharsis one adopts, it is clear that Aristotle's concept answers Plato's charge, in Book III of the *Republic*, that art is morally harmful. The *Poetics* was probably not written as a direct refutation of Plato, but Aristotle and Plato are at opposite poles on the question of the moral effect of art. For Aristotle the effect is catharsis, and catharsis is beneficial—a form of therapy, a morally refining experience, a release from guilt, or a kind of learning.

(III) *Hamartia.* This important term has most commonly been rendered into English as "tragic flaw," although this translation fails to convey the real nature and full scope of the concept. It was once general practice for interpreters to emphasize the moral overtones of *hamartia*, sometimes by relating the term to its usage in traditional Christian writings; in the Gospel of St. John, for example, *hamartia* means "sin." Under this theory the tragic hero commits a serious moral error and receives condign punishment for it. This line of interpretation has been challenged, however, by a number of scholars who have intensively examined the use of the term *hamartia* by Aristotle and the Greek tragedians. Their investigations, conducted independently over several decades, indicate that *hamartia* should be interpreted primarily as an intellectual error rather than a moral flaw.[13]

Aristotle's analysis of tragedy is based on *Oedipus Rex.* Both in this play and its sequel, *Oedipus at Colonus,* there is strong evidence that Sophocles thought of Oedipus' error as more intellectual than moral; indeed, in *Oedipus at Colonus* Sophocles has Oedipus make the explicit defense that he was ignorant of what he was doing in committing parricide and incest, and that he would never have performed these crimes knowingly. At the very least, Sophocles seems to show that Oedipus' punishment is *in excess* of his crime.

This point may be clarified if *hamartia* is interpreted primarily as an intellectual error. Such an interpretation deemphasizes the notion of "poetic justice," suggesting that Aristotle holds a sophisticated concept of tragedy. Aristotle's argument in Chapter 13 indicates that if a play shows that the protagonist's destruction is exactly what he deserves, there is no true pity and fear; the play is essentially *melodramatic.* In these terms tragedy can be more easily understood as a literary form which avoids demonstrating a perfect justice in this world, a literary form capable of posing such philosophical questions as the meaning of life itself.

In whatever way *hamartia* is interpreted, it must be related to the general line of inquiry in Chapter 13. Aristotle is concerned with the dynamics of audience-response. Given the essential dialectic of tragedy—the passage of a basically good man from happiness to misery—it is necessary for the dramatist to guide the reaction of the audience, preventing a response of revulsion or pure shock at the sight of totally innocent suffering. Thus, the general notion of *hamartia* means that the dramatist must assign *some* responsibility, but not a total responsibility, to the protagonist.

(IV) *Spoudaios* ("Noble" Character). Aristotle defines "character" (*ethos*) as that element in speech or action which manifests a moral choice. He uses this principle as one of the co-ordinates by which genres may be defined: in Chapter 2 he declares that the essential difference between tragedy and comedy is that the former imitates "noble" (*spoudaios*) character while the latter imitates "base" (*phaulos*) character, and in Chapter 5 he finds an essential similarity between tragedy and epic in that both imitate "noble" character.

Aristotle's description of tragic character has often been popularly construed (especially by neoclassical critics) as a social proscription: the tragic hero must be a member of "the nobility," or at least a political or military leader. Arthur Miller has attributed this view to Aristotle himself, attacking it as a social blind spot, an implicit snobbery, in the *Poetics.* According to Miller, a "common man" (such as Willy Loman in *Death of a Salesman*) is as potentially tragic as any protagonist in the works of Sophocles or Shakespeare.[14]

It would appear that Aristotle's position is not antithetical to Miller's, because the "nobility" referred to in the *Poetics* is more moral than social. The adjective *spoudaios* can also be rendered as "serious," "good," or "weighty." Aristotle's tragic protagonist might be defined as a man "weighty" enough to demand the audience's *moral attention.* To put it another way: if the action of a tragedy is viewed as a kind of ritualistic sacrifice, Aristotle's requirement would mean that the protagonist must somehow be made to seem *worth* sacrificing. It may be easier to grant such moral attention to a king or a general (especially because their actions are fraught with consequences for other people), but this is not essential; in our own age, at least, the intensity and cultural relevance of a Willy Loman can make him truly *spoudaios.*

The important point here is that Aristotle is not, as is so often thought, a *soi-disant* maker of prohibitive "rules" (e.g., the non-existent "three unities"). Such a spirit is really more typical of the conservative sensibility of Horace's *Ars Poetica.* By contrast, Aristotle's remarks on tragic character, like his other observations on poetry, are in the nature of a philosophical investigation into the entelechial "perfection" of literary form—and the spirit of this investigation is affirmative rather than negative, comprehensive rather than judicial.

In addition to the four concepts discussed above, there are many other terms and ideas in the *Poetics* which are of great significance to the critic and historian of literature. Fortunately, many of these are not controversial and are clearly defined and explained in the *Poetics.* In this category are such widely used critical concepts as "recognition" (*anagnorisis*), "reversal" (*peripeteia*), "complication" (*desis*), and "resolution" (*lysis*)—as well as such important theoretical discussions as the analysis of the six qualitative parts of tragedy. A few other concepts, however, deserve brief explanation here because of their relevance to the major ideas discussed above. The most noteworthy of these are the role of pity and fear in tragedy, the comparison of a work of art to an organism, and the primacy of plot over the other elements in drama.

One of Aristotle's major contributions to the theory of tragedy is his insistence that the genre is concerned with the representation of the pitiable and fearful rather than with other emotions or experiences. Aristotle defines pity and fear in his *Rhetoric* (Book II, Chapter 5) as well as in the *Poetics* (Chapter 13): fear is an emotion caused by the presence of whatever threatens our own selves with harm or destruction; pity is a variant of the same emotion, directed at the fate of *others* who suffer undeserved misfortune. In Chapter 6 of the *Poetics* Aristotle introduces the concepts of pity and fear in his famous definition of tragedy, and in Chapter 14 he enters into a detailed discussion of the best ways for the tragic dramatist to achieve pity and fear in his work. Aristotle's argument for the essential relation of pity and fear to tragedy is important because it unites with the other aspects of his analysis to form a persuasive and coherent theory of tragedy. For example, the emphasis on pity and fear in tragedy illuminates the need for the tragic hero to be *spoudaios*; only when a "noble" hero falls from happiness to misery, enduring a punishment in excess of his moral offense, can the properly "tragic" emotions be called forth. Thus, this line of thought in the *Poetics* unites the concepts of *katharsis*, *hamartia*, and "noble" character.

In Chapter 7 Aristotle introduces the notion that a work of art should resemble a living organism (*zoön*). His emphasis here differs from the doctrine of "organicism" in many romantic aesthetic theories. Coleridge, for example, posits an "indwelling power" which shapes the work into a living unit, a Platonic whole so perfect that no *word* in a true poem can be changed without damage. By contrast, Aristotle is more functional: he is thinking primarily of *structural* cohesiveness, emphasizing the dramatist's conscious construction of episodes. Most important, Aristotle's concept is related to audience response, and it may support the interpretation of *katharsis* as intellectual clarification: the audience must be able to perceive the coherence of the work of art. Thus, the dramatist's work must be a true "whole"—i.e., with articulated principles of beginning, middle, and end. In order to be aesthetically perceivable, the work must also possess the proper "magnitude"—being neither too large nor too small, neither too simple nor too complex. The relationship between this organic concept and the principle of audience effect is perhaps clearest in Chapter 23: discussing the epic genre, Aristotle argues that the action of the work must be unified "so that, like a single integrated organism, it achieves the pleasure natural to it." Aristotle's meaning might be clarified by a passage from his treatise on the *Parts of Animals* (Book I, Chapter 5): all living creatures, "by disclosing to intellectual perception the artistic spirit that designed them, give immense pleasure to all who can trace links of causation and are inclined to philosophy."

Aristotle's organic analogy is also operative in his attempt to elevate the concept of "plot" (*mythos*). In Chapter 6 Aristotle calls plot the "first principle" or "soul" (*psyche*) of tragedy. Plot is what makes a tragedy dynamic, and it is functionally related to audience response. Moreover, it is on the basis of plot-considerations that the dramatist must manage his characterization, writing of speeches, choice of diction, and so on. In the chapters which follow Aristotle again insists on the crucial importance of structural coherence or logical "universality" (the essential difference between poetry and history) and he demonstrates his aesthetic preference for complex plots (those involving reversal and recognition) and unhappy (i.e., pitiable and fearful) tragic endings.

Aristotle's emphasis on plot leads him to reject the idea that the difference between poetry and non-poetry is the use of verse. For him poetry is the art of fiction rather than the art of writing in verse. According to the standards of the *Poetics*, a novel would be as truly a poem as would *Paradise Lost*. L. J. Potts has stressed this in his translation of the *Poetics* by giving it the title *Aristotle on the Art of Fiction.*

In spite of the seminal quality of Aristotle's ideas, the *Poetics* exerted little influence for approximately 1800 years after its first transcription; it was largely unknown to Horace, Longinus, Plutarch, Augustine, Aquinas, Dante, and Boccaccio. Following the recovery of the *Poetics* by Renaissance scholars, the treatise entered its first period of major popularity: as a core document in the syntheses of neoclassical criticism. For Scaliger, Castelvetro, Sidney, Ben Jonson, Boileau, Pope, and Samuel Johnson, the *Poetics* was valuable as an "authoritative" work which complemented Horace's *Ars Poetica,* thus confirming a generally rhetorical view of literature.

Neoclassical critics tended to ignore Aristotle's argumentative rigor and to narrow the meanings of his major terms—e.g., by construing "probability" in terms of "verisimilitude." The nineteenth century was a period of eclipse for the *Poetics*: romantic critics, operating under new premises—a theory of the poetic imagination rather than a theory based on the materials of poetry—reacted sharply against Aristotle, or at least against the Aristotle of neoclassicism. Their doctrines are often antithetical to the *Poetics*: the exaltation of lyric over drama, of character over plot, of "genius" over "rules," and most importantly, of expression over imitation.

It has remained for twentieth-century scholars and critics to bring the *Poetics* into its second phase of major influence. S. H. Butcher's *Aristotle's Theory of Poetry and Fine Art* (1895) demonstrated the essential kinship between Aristotle and the major romantic theorists—emphasizing that the methodology of the *Poetics* is neither positivistic nor moralistic, but aesthetic. Subsequent adaptations of the *Poetics* support this view, especially in the work of Thomists (Jacques Maritain), phenomenological critics (Roman Ingarden), eclectic critics (Francis Fergusson), "new critics" (John Crowe Ransom), and the "Chicago Neo-Aristotelians" (R. S. Crane). On the other hand, Aristotle's treatise has also remained a source of evidence and insight for psychological and sociological critics (Kenneth Burke), anthropological critics (Gilbert Murray), Marxists (George Thomson), and humanists (Irving Babbitt).

That so many modern theorists, of such differing critical persuasions, have found inspiration and guidance in the *Poetics* suggests that Aristotle's insights have lost none of their vitality after two millennia. There can be little doubt that the *Poetics* will continue to exert a significant influence on the future theory and practice of literature.

The translation is my own and is reprinted from Leon Golden and O. B. Hardison, Jr., *Aristotle's Poetics: A Translation and Commentary for Students of Literature* (Englewood Cliffs: Prentice-Hall, 1968) by permission of the publisher. The numbers inserted in the translation are the page numbers of the Berlin edition of Aristotle by Immanuel Bekker. In the following English version, these numbers, which are used by scholars in the citation of passages from Aristotle's text, appear in the approximate location they occupy in the original. However, Bekker's subdivisions (a and b) have been omitted.

POETICS

I

(1447) Let us discuss the art of poetry, itself, and its species, describing the character of each of them, and how it is necessary to construct plots if the poetic composition is to be successful and, furthermore, the number and kind of parts to be found in the poetic work, and as many other matters as are relevant. Let us follow the order of nature, beginning with first principles.

Now epic poetry, tragedy, comedy, dithyrambic poetry,[1] and most forms of flute and lyre playing all happen to be, in general, imitations, but they differ from each other in three ways: either because the imitation is carried on by different means or because it is concerned with different kinds of objects or because it is presented, not in the same, but in a different manner.

For just as some artists imitate many different objects by using color and form to represent them (some through art, others only through habit), other artists imitate through sound, as indeed, in the arts mentioned above; for all these accomplish imitation through rhythm and speech and harmony, making use of these elements separately or in combination. Flute playing and lyre playing, for example, use harmony and rhythm alone; and this would also be true of any other arts (for example, the art of playing the shepherd's pipe) that are similar in character to these. Dancers imitate by using rhythm without harmony, since they imitate characters, emotions, and actions by rhythms that are arranged into dance-figures.

The art that imitates by words alone, in prose and in verse, and in the latter case, either combines various meters or makes use of only one, has been nameless up to the present time. (1447) For we cannot assign a common name to the mimes[2] of Sophron and Xenarchus and the Socratic dialogues; nor would we have a name for such an imitation if someone should accomplish it through trimeters or elegiacs or some other such meter, except that the public at large by joining the term "poet" to a meter gives writers such names as "elegiac poets" and "epic poets." Here the public classifies all those who write in meter as poets and completely misses the point that the capacity to produce an imitation is the essential characteristic of the poet. The public is even accustomed to apply the name "poet" to those who publish a medical or scientific treatise in verse, although Homer has nothing at all in common with Empedocles except the meter. It is just to call Homer a poet, but we must consider Empedocles a physicist rather than a poet.

And in the same way, if anyone should create an imitation by combining all the meters as Chairemon did when he wrote *The Centaur*, a rhapsody composed by the use of all the meters, he must also be designated a poet. Concerning these matters let us accept the distinctions we have just made.

There are some arts that use all the means that have been discussed, namely, rhythm and song and meter, as in the writing of dithyrambs and nomic poetry[3] and in tragedy and comedy. A difference is apparent here in that some arts use all the various elements at the same time, whereas others use them separately. These, then, are what I call the differences in the artistic means through which the imitation is accomplished.

II

(1448) Artists imitate men involved in action and these must either be noble or base since human character regularly conforms to these distinctions, all of us being different in character because of some quality of goodness or evil. From this it follows that the objects imitated are either better than or worse than or like the norm. We find confirmation of this observation in the practice of our painters. For Polygnotus represents men as better, Pauson as worse, and Dionysius as like the norm. It is clear that each of the above-mentioned forms of imitation will manifest differences of this type and will be different through its choosing, in this way, a different kind of object to imitate. Even in dancing, flute-playing, and lyre-playing it is possible for these differences to exist, and they are seen also in prose, and in verse that does not make use of musical accompaniment, as is shown by the fact that Cleophon represents men like the norm, Homer as better, and both Hegemon the Thasian (who was the first writer of parodies) and Nicochares, the author of the *Deiliad*, as worse. The same situation is found in dithyrambic and nomic poetry,[4] as we see in the way Timotheus and Philoxenus handled the Cyclops theme. It is through the same distinction in objects that we differentiate comedy from tragedy, for the former takes as its goal the representation of men as worse, the latter as better, than the norm.

III

There is, finally, a third factor by which we distinguish imitations, and that is the manner in which the artist represents the various types of object. For, using the same means and imitating the same kinds of object, it is possible for the poet on different occasions to narrate the story (either speaking in the person of one of his characters as Homer does or in his own person without changing roles) or to have the imitators performing and acting out the entire story.

As we said at the beginning, imitations are to be distinguished under these three headings: means, object, and manner. Thus, in one way, Sophocles is the same kind of imitative artist as Homer, since they both imitate noble men; but in another sense, he resembles Aristophanes, since they both imitate characters as acting and dramatizing the incidents of the story. It is from this, some tell us, that these latter kinds of imitations are called "dramas" because they present characters who "dramatize" the incidents of the plot.

By the way, it is also for this reason that the Dorians claim to be the originators of both tragedy and comedy. The Megarians—both those in Megara itself, who assert that comedy arose when democracy was established among them, and those Megarians in Sicily, who point out that their poet Epicharmus far antedates Chionides and Magnes—claim to have originated comedy; in addition, some of the Dorians in the Peloponnesus claim to be the originators of tragedy. As proof of their contentions, they cite the technical terms they use for these art forms; for they say that they call the towns around their city *komai*, but that the Athenians call their towns *demoi*. By this they argue that the root of the name "comedian" is not derived from *komazein* [the word for "reveling"] but from *komai* [their word for the towns] that the comic artists visited in their wanderings after they had been driven in disgrace from the city. (1448) In support of their claim to be the originators of "drama," they point out that the word for "doing" is *dran* in their dialect, whereas Athenians use the word *prattein* for this concept.

Concerning the number and kind of distinctions that characterize "imitations," let us accept what has been said above.

IV

Speaking generally, the origin of the art of poetry is to be found in two natural causes. For the process of imitation is natural to mankind from childhood on: Man is differentiated from other animals because he is the most imitative of them, and he learns his first lessons through imitation, and we observe that all men find pleasure in imitations. The proof of this point is what actually happens in life. For there are some things that distress us when we see them in reality, but the most accurate representations of these same things we view with pleasure—as, for example, the forms of the most despised animals and of corpses. The cause of this is that the act of learning is not only most pleasant to philosophers but, in a similar way, to other men as well, only they have an abbreviated share in this pleasure. Thus men find pleasure in viewing representations because it turns out that they learn and infer what each thing is—for example, that this particular object is that kind of object; since if one has not happened to see the object previously, he will not find any pleasure in the imitation *qua* imitation but rather in the workmanship or coloring or something similar.

Since imitation is given to us by nature, as are harmony and rhythm (for it is apparent that meters are parts of the rhythms), men, having been naturally endowed with these gifts from the beginning and then developing them gradually, for the most part, finally created the art of poetry from their early improvisations.

Poetry then diverged in the directions of the natural dispositions of the poets. Writers of greater dignity imitated the noble actions of noble heroes; the less dignified sort of writers imitated the actions of inferior men, at first writing invectives as the former writers wrote hymns and encomia. We know of no "invective" by poets before Homer, although it is probable that there were many who wrote such poems; but it is possible to attribute them to authors who came after Homer—for example, the *Margites*[5] of Homer himself, and other such poems. In these poems, the fitting meter came to light, the one that now bears the name "iambic" [i.e., invective] because it was originally used by men to satirize each other. Thus, of our earliest writers, some were heroic and some iambic poets. And just as Homer was especially the poet of noble actions (for he not only handled these well but he also made his imitations dramatic), so also he first traced out the form of comedy by dramatically presenting not invective but the ridiculous. For his *Margites* has the same relation to comedy as the *Iliad* and *Odyssey* have to tragedy. (1449) But when tragedy and comedy began to appear, poets were attracted to each type of poetry according to their individual natures, one group becoming writers of comedies in place of iambics, and the other, writers of tragedies instead of epics because these genres were of greater importance and more admired than the others.

Now then, the consideration of whether or not tragedy is by now sufficiently developed in its formal elements, judged both in regard to its essential nature and in regard to its public performances, belongs to another discussion. What is relevant is that it arose, at first, as an improvisation (both tragedy and comedy are similar in this respect) on the part of those who led the dithyrambs, just as comedy arose from those who led the phallic songs that even now are still customary in many of our cities. Tragedy, undergoing many changes (since our poets were developing aspects of it as they emerged), gradually progressed until it attained the fulfillment of its own nature. Aeschylus was the first to increase the number of actors from one to two; he also reduced the role of the chorus and made the dialogue the major element in the play. Sophocles increased the number of actors to three and introduced scene painting. Then tragedy acquired its magnitude. Thus by developing away from a satyr-play[6] of short plots and absurd diction, tragedy achieved, late in its history, a dignified level. Then the iambic meter took the place of the tetrameter. For the poets first used the trochaic tetrameter because their poetry was satyric and very closely associated with dance; but when dialogue was introduced, nature itself discovered the appropriate meter. For the iambic is the most conversational of the meters—as we see from the fact that we speak many iambs when talking to each other, but few [dactylic] hexameters, and only when departing from conversational tone. Moreover, the number of episodes was increased. As to the other elements by which, we are told, tragedy was embellished, we must consider them as having been mentioned by us. For it would probably be an enormous task to go through each of these elements one by one.

V

As we have said, comedy is an imitation of baser men. These are characterized not by every kind of vice but specifically by "the ridiculous," which is a subdivision of the category of "deformity." What we mean by "the ridiculous" is some error or ugliness that is painless and has no harmful effects. The example that comes immediately to mind is the comic mask, which is ugly and distorted but causes no pain.

Now then, the successive changes in the history of tragedy and the men who brought them about have been recorded; but the analogous information about the history of comedy is lacking because the genre was not treated, at the beginning, as a serious art form. (1449) It was only recently that the archons[7] began to grant choruses to the comic poets; until then, the performers were all volunteers. And it was only after comedy had attained some recognizable form that we began to have a record of those designated as "comic poets." Who introduced masks or prologues, who established the number of actors, and many other matters of this type, are unknown. The creation of plots came first from Sicily, where it is attributed to Epicharmus and Phormis; and it was the first Crates among the Athenian poets who departed from iambic [or invective] poetry and began to write speeches and plots of a more universal nature.

Now epic poetry follows the same pattern as tragedy insofar as it is the imitation of noble subjects presented in an elevated meter. But epic differs from tragedy in that it uses a single meter, and its manner of presentation is narrative. And further, there is a difference in length. For tragedy attempts, as far as possible, to remain within one circuit of the sun or, at least, not depart from this by much. Epic poetry, however, has no limit in regard to time, and differs from tragedy in this respect; although at first the poets proceeded in tragedy in the same way as they did in epic. Some of the parts of a poem are common to both tragedy and epic, and some belong to tragedy alone. Therefore, whoever can judge what is good and bad in tragedy can also do this in regard to epic. For whatever parts epic poetry has, these are also found in tragedy; but, as we have said, not all of the parts of tragedy are found in epic poetry.

VI

We shall speak about the form of imitation that is associated with hexameter verse and about comedy later. Let us now discuss tragedy, bringing together the definition of its essence that has emerged from what we have already said. Tragedy is, then, an imitation of a noble and complete action, having the proper magnitude;[8] it employs language that has been artistically enhanced by each of the kinds of linguistic adornment, applied separately in the various parts of the play; it is presented in dramatic, not narrative form, and achieves, through the representation of pitiable and fearful incidents, the catharsis of such pitiable and fearful incidents. I mean by "language that has been artistically enhanced," that which is accompanied by rhythm and harmony and song; and by the phrase "each of the kinds of linguistic adornment applied separately in the various parts of the play," I mean that some parts are accomplished by meter alone and others, in turn, through song.

And since [in drama] agents accomplish the imitation by acting the story out, it follows, first of all, that the arrangement of the spectacle should be, of necessity, some part of the tragedy as would be melody and diction, also; for these are the means through which the agents accomplish the imitation. I mean by diction the act, itself, of making metrical compositions, and by melody, what is completely obvious. Since the imitation is of an action and is accomplished by certain agents, the sort of men these agents are is necessarily dependent upon their "character" and "thought." It is, indeed, on the basis of these two considerations that we designate the quality of actions, (1450) because the two natural causes of human action are thought and character. It is also in regard to these that the lives of all turn out well or poorly. For this reason we say that tragic plot is an imitation of action.

Now I mean by the plot the arrangement of the incidents, and by character that element in accordance with which we say that agents are of a certain type; and by thought I mean that which is found in whatever things men say when they prove a point or, it may be, express a general truth. It is necessary, therefore, that tragedy as a whole have six parts in accordance with which, as a genre, it achieves its particular quality. These parts are plot, character, diction, thought, spectacle, and melody. Two of these parts come from the means by which the imitation is carried out; one from the manner of its presentation, and three from the objects of the imitation. Beyond these parts there is nothing left to mention. Not a few poets, so to speak, employ these parts; for indeed, every drama [theoretically] has spectacle, character, plot, diction, song, and thought.

The most important of these parts is the arrangement of the incidents; for tragedy is not an imitation of men, *per se,* but of human action and life and happiness and misery. Both happiness and misery consist in a kind of action; and the end of life is some action, not some quality.[9] Now according to their characters men have certain qualities; but according to their actions they are happy or the opposite. Poets do not, therefore, create action in order to imitate character; but character is included on account of the action. Thus the end of tragedy is the presentation of the individual incidents and of the plot; and the end is, of course, the most significant thing of all. Furthermore, without action tragedy would be impossible, but without character it would still be possible. This point is illustrated both by the fact that the tragedies of many of our modern poets are characterless, and by the fact that many poets, in general, experience this difficulty. Also, to take an example from our painters, Zeuxis illustrates the point when compared to Polygnotus; for Polygnotus is good at incorporating character into his painting, but the work of Zeuxis shows no real characterization at all. Furthermore, if someone arranges a series of speeches that show character and are well-constructed in diction and thought, he will not, by this alone, achieve the end of tragedy; but far more will this be accomplished by the tragedy that employs these elements rather inadequately but, nevertheless, has a satisfactory plot and arrangement of incidents. In addition to the arguments already given, the most important factors by means of which tragedy exerts an influence on the soul are parts of the plot, the reversal, and the recognition. We have further proof of our view of the importance of plot in the fact that those who attempt to write tragedies are able to perfect diction and character before the construction of the incidents, as we see, for example, in nearly all our early poets.

The first principle, then, and to speak figuratively, the soul of tragedy, is the plot; and second in importance is character. A closely corresponding situation exists in painting. (1450) For if someone should paint by applying the most beautiful colors, but without reference to an over-all plan, he would not please us as much as if he had outlined the figure in black and white. Tragedy, then, is an imitation of an action; and it is, on account of this, an imitation of men acting.

Thought is the third part of tragedy and is the ability to say whatever is pertinent and fitting to the occasion, which, in reference to the composition of speeches, is the essential function of the arts of politics and rhetoric. As proof of this we point out that our earlier poets made their characters speak like statesmen, and our contemporary poets make them speak like rhetoricians. Now character is that part of tragedy which shows an individual's purpose by indicating, in circumstances where it is not clear, what sort of things he chooses or rejects. Therefore those speeches do not manifest character in which there is absolutely nothing that the speaker chooses or rejects. Thought we find in those speeches in which men show that something is or is not, or utter some universal proposition.

The fourth literary part is diction, and I mean by diction, as has already been said, the expression of thoughts through language which, indeed, is the same whether in verse or prose.

Of the remaining parts, melody is the greatest of the linguistic adornments; and spectacle, to be sure, attracts our attention but is the least artistic and least essential part of the art of poetry. For the power of tragedy is felt even without a dramatic performance and actors. Furthermore, for the realization of spectacle, the art of the costume designer is more effective than that of the poet.

VII

Now that we have defined these terms, let us discuss what kind of process the arrangement of incidents must be, since this is the first and most important element of tragedy. We have posited that tragedy is the imitation of a complete and whole action having a proper magnitude. For it is possible for something to be a whole and yet not have any considerable magnitude. To be a whole is to have a beginning and a middle and an end. By a "beginning" I mean that which is itself not, by necessity, after anything else but after which something naturally is or develops. By an "end" I mean exactly the opposite: that which is naturally after something else, either necessarily or customarily, but after which there is nothing else. By a "middle" I mean that which is itself after something else and which has something else after it. It is necessary, therefore, that well-constructed plots not begin by chance, anywhere, nor end anywhere, but that they conform to the distinctions that have been made above.

Furthermore, for beauty to exist, both in regard to a living being and in regard to any object that is composed of separate parts, not only must there be a proper arrangement of the component elements, but the object must also be of a magnitude that is not fortuitous. For beauty is determined by magnitude and order; therefore, neither would a very small animal be beautiful (for one's view of the animal is not clear, taking place, as it does, in an almost unperceived length of time), nor is a very large animal beautiful (1451) (for then one's view does not occur all at once, but, rather, the unity and wholeness of the animal are lost to the viewer's sight as would happen, for example, if we should come across an animal a thousand miles in length). So that just as it is necessary in regard to bodies and animals for there to be a proper magnitude—and this is the length that can easily be perceived at a glance—thus, also, there must be a proper length in regard to plots, and this is one that can be easily taken in by the memory. The limit of length in regard to the dramatic contests and in terms of the physical viewing of the performance is not a matter related to the art of poetry. For if it were necessary for a hundred tragedies to be played, they would be presented by timing them with water clocks as we are told happened on some occasions in the past. The limit, however, that is set in regard to magnitude by the very nature of the subject itself is that whatever is longer (provided it remains quite clear) is always more beautiful. To give a general rule, we say that whatever length is required for a change to occur from bad fortune to good or from good fortune to bad through a series of incidents that are in accordance with probability or necessity, is a sufficient limit of magnitude.

VIII

A plot is a unity not, as some think, merely if it is concerned with one individual, for in some of the many and infinitely varied things that happen to any one person, there is no unity. Thus, we must assert, there are many actions in the life of a single person from which no over-all unity of action emerges. For this reason all those poets seem to have erred who have written a *Heracleid* and a *Theseid* and other poems of this type; for they think that since Heracles was one person it is appropriate for his story to be one story. But Homer, just as he was superior in other respects, also seems to have seen this point well, whether through his technical skill or his native talent, since in making the *Odyssey* he did not include all the things that ever happened to Odysseus. (For example, it happened that Odysseus was wounded on Parnassus and that he feigned madness at the time of the call to arms; but between these two events there is no necessary or probable relation.) Homer, rather, organized the *Odyssey* around one action of the type we have been speaking about and did the same with the *Iliad*. Necessarily, then, just as in other forms of imitation, one imitation is of one thing, so also, a plot, since it is an imitation of an action, must be an imitation of an action that is one and whole. Moreover, it is necessary that the parts of the action be put together in such a way that if any one part is transposed or removed, the whole will be disordered and disunified. For that whose presence or absence has no evident effect is no part of the whole.

IX

It is apparent from what we have said that it is not the function of the poet to narrate events that have actually happened, but rather, events such as might occur and have the capability of occurring in accordance with the laws of probability or necessity. (1451) For the historian and the poet do not differ by their writing in prose or verse (the works of Herodotus might be put into verse but they would, nonetheless, remain a form of history both in their metrical and prose versions). The difference, rather, lies in the fact that the historian narrates events that have actually happened, whereas the poet writes about things as they might possibly occur. Poetry, therefore, is more philosophical and more significant than history, for poetry is more concerned with the universal, and history more with the individual. By the universal I mean what sort of man turns out to say or do what sort of thing according to probability or necessity—this being the goal poetry aims at, although it gives individual names to the characters whose actions are imitated. By the individual I mean a statement telling, for example, "what Alcibiades did or experienced."

Now then, this point has already been made clear in regard to comedy; for the comic poets, once they have constructed the plot through probable incidents, assign any names that happen to occur to them, and they do not follow the procedure of the iambic poets who write about specific individuals. In regard to tragedy, however, our poets cling to the names of the heroes of the past on the principle that whatever is clearly capable of happening is readily believable. We cannot be sure that whatever has not yet happened is possible; but it is apparent that whatever has happened is also capable of happening for, if it were not, it could not have occurred. Nevertheless in some tragedies one or two of the names are well known and the rest have been invented for the occasion; in others not even one is well-known, for example, Agathon's *Antheus,* since in this play both the incidents and the names have been invented, and nonetheless they please us. Thus we must not seek to cling exclusively to the stories that have been handed down and about which our tragedies are usually written. It would be absurd, indeed, to do this since the well-known plots are known only to a few, but nevertheless please everyone. It is clear then from these considerations that it is necessary for the poet to be more the poet of his plots than of his meters, insofar as he is a poet because he is an imitator and imitates human actions. If the poet happens to write about things that have actually occurred, he is no less the poet for that. For nothing prevents some of the things that have actually occurred from belonging to the class of the probable or possible, and it is in regard to this aspect that he is the poet of them.

Of the simple plots and actions the episodic are the worst; and I mean by episodic a plot in which the episodes follow each other without regard for the laws of probability or necessity. Such plots are constructed by the inferior poets because of their own inadequacies, and by the good poets because of the actors. For since they are writing plays that are to be entered in contests (and so stretch the plot beyond its capacity) they are frequently forced to distort the sequence of action. (1452)

Since the imitation is not only a complete action but is also of fearful and pitiable incidents, we must note that these are intensified when they occur unexpectedly, yet because of one another. For there is more of the marvelous in them if they occur this way than if they occurred spontaneously and by chance. Even in regard to coincidences, those seem to be most astonishing that appear to have some design associated with them. We have an example of this in the story of the statue of Mitys in Argos killing the man who caused Mitys' death by falling upon him as he was a spectator at a festival. The occurrence of such an event, we feel, is not without meaning and thus we must consider plots that incorporate incidents of this type to be superior ones.

X

Plots are divided into the simple and the complex, for the actions of which the plots are imitations are naturally of this character. An action that is, as has been defined, continuous and unified I call simple when its change of fortune arises without reversal and recognition, and complex when its change of fortune arises through recognition or reversal or both. Now these aspects of the plot must develop directly from the construction of the plot, itself, so that they occur from prior events either out of necessity or according to the laws of probability. For it makes quite a difference whether they occur *because* of those events or merely *after* them.

XI

Reversal is the change of fortune in the action of the play to the opposite state of affairs, just as has been said; and this change, we argue, should be in accordance with probability and necessity. Thus, in the *Oedipus* the messenger comes to cheer Oedipus and to remove his fears in regard to his mother; but by showing him who he actually is he accomplishes the very opposite effect. And in *Lynceus,*[10] Lynceus is being led away to die and Danaus is following to kill him; but it turns out, because of the action that has taken place, that Danaus dies and Lynceus is saved. Recognition, as the name indicates, is a change from ignorance to knowledge, bringing about either a state of friendship or one of hostility on the part of those who have been marked out for good fortune or bad. The most effective recognition is one that occurs together with reversal, for example, as in the *Oedipus.* There are also other kinds of recognition for, indeed, what we have said happens, in a way, in regard to inanimate things, even things of a very casual kind; and it is possible, further, to "recognize" whether someone has or has not done something. But the type of recognition that is especially a part of the plot and the action is the one that has been mentioned. For such a recognition and reversal will evoke pity or fear, and we have defined tragedy as an imitation of actions of this type; (1452) and furthermore, happiness and misery will appear in circumstances of this type. Since this kind of recognition is of persons, some recognitions that belong to this class will merely involve the identification of one person by another when the identity of the second person is clear; on other occasions it will be necessary for there to be a recognition on the part of both parties: for example, Iphigenia is recognized by Orestes from her sending of the letter; but it is necessary that there be another recognition of him on her part.

Now then, these are two parts of the plot, reversal and recognition, and there is also a third part, suffering. Of these, reversal and recognition have been discussed; the incident of suffering results from destructive or painful action such as death on the stage, scenes of very great pain, the infliction of wounds, and the like.

XII

The parts of tragedy that we must view as formal elements we have discussed previously; looking at the quantitative aspect of tragedy and the parts into which it is divided in this regard, the following are the distinctions to be made: prologue, episode, exode, and the choral part, which is divided into parode and stasimon. These are commonly found in all plays, but only in a few are found songs from the stage and *kommoi.* The prologue is the complete section of a tragedy before the parode of the chorus; an episode is the complete section of a tragedy between complete choric songs; the exode is the complete section of a tragedy after which there is no song of the chorus. Of the choral part, the parode is the entire first speech of the chorus, the stasimon is a song of the chorus without anapests and trochees, and a *kommos* is a lament sung in common by the chorus and the actors. The parts of tragedy that we must view as formal elements we have discussed previously; the above distinctions have been made concerning the quantitative aspect of tragedy, and the parts into which it is divided in this regard.

XIII

What goals poets must aim at, what difficulties they must be wary of when constructing their plots, and how the proper function of tragedy is accomplished are matters we should discuss after the remarks that have just been made.

Since the plots of the best tragedies must be complex, not simple, and the plot of a tragedy must be an imitation of pitiable and fearful incidents (for this is the specific nature of the imitation under discussion), it is clear, first of all, that unqualifiedly good human beings must not appear to fall from good fortune to bad; for that is neither pitiable nor fearful; it is, rather, repellent. Nor must an extremely evil man appear to move from bad fortune to good fortune for that is the most untragic situation of all because it has none of the necessary requirements of tragedy; it both violates our human sympathy and contains nothing of the pitiable or fearful in it. (1453) Furthermore, a villainous man should not appear to fall from good fortune to bad. For, although such a plot would be in accordance with our human sympathy, it would not contain the necessary elements of pity and fear; for pity is aroused by someone who undeservedly falls into misfortune, and fear is evoked by our recognizing that it is someone like ourselves who encounters this misfortune (pity, as I say, arising for the former reason, fear for the latter). Therefore the emotional effect of the situation just mentioned will be neither pitiable nor fearful. What is left, after our considerations, is someone in between these extremes. This would be a person who is neither perfect in virtue and justice, nor one who falls into misfortune through vice and depravity; but rather, one who succumbs through some miscalculation. He must also be a person who enjoys great reputation and good fortune, such as Oedipus, Thyestes, and other illustrious men from similar families. It is necessary, furthermore, for the well-constructed plot to have a single rather than a double construction, as some urge, and to illustrate a change of fortune not from bad fortune to good but, rather, the very opposite, from good fortune to bad, and for this to take place not because of depravity but through some great miscalculation on the part of the type of person we have described (or a better rather than a worse one).

A sign of our point is found in what actually happens in the theater. For initially, our poets accepted any chance plots; but now the best tragedies are constructed about a few families, for example, about Alcmaeon, Oedipus, Orestes, Meleager, Thyestes, Telephon, and any others who were destined to experience, or to commit, terrifying acts. For as we have indicated, artistically considered, the best tragedy arises from this kind of plot. Therefore, those critics make the very mistake that we have been discussing who blame Euripides because he handles the material in his tragedies in this way, and because many of his plots end in misfortune. For this is, indeed, the correct procedure, as we have said. The very great proof of this is that on the stage and in the dramatic contests such plays appear to be the most tragic, if they are properly worked out; and Euripides, even if, in other matters he does not manage things well, nevertheless appears to be the most tragic of the poets. The second ranking plot, one that is called first by some, has a double structure of events, as in the *Odyssey,* ending in opposite ways for the better and worse characters. It seems to be first on account of the inadequacy of the audience. For our poets trail along writing to please the tastes of the audience. But this double structure of events involves a pleasure that is not an appropriate pleasure of tragedy but rather of comedy. For in comedy, whoever are the greatest enemies in the story —for example, Orestes and Aegisthus—becoming friends at the end, go off together, and no one is killed by anyone.

XIV

(1453) Pity and fear can arise from the spectacle and also from the very structure of the plot, which is the superior way and shows the better poet. The poet should construct the plot so that even if the action is not performed before spectators, one who merely hears the incidents that have occurred both shudders and feels pity from the way they turn out. That is what anyone who hears the plot of the *Oedipus* would experience. The achievement of this effect through the spectacle does not have much to do with poetic art and really belongs to the business of producing the play. Those who use the spectacle to create not the fearful but only the monstrous have no share in the creation of tragedy; for we should not seek every pleasure from tragedy but only the one proper to it.

Since the poet should provide pleasure from pity and fear through imitation, it is apparent that this function must be worked into the incidents. Let us try to understand what type of occurrences appear to be terrifying and pitiable. It is, indeed, necessary that any such action occur either between those who are friends or enemies to each other, or between those who have no relationship, whatsoever, to each other. If an enemy takes such an action against an enemy, there is nothing pitiable in the performance of the act or in the intention to perform it, except the suffering itself. Nor would there be anything pitiable if neither party had any relationship with the other. But whenever the tragic incidents occur in situations involving strong ties of affection—for example, if a brother kills or intends to kill a brother or a son a father or a mother a son or a son a mother or commits some equally terrible act—there will be something pitiable. These situations, then, are the ones to be sought. Now, it is not possible for a poet to alter completely the traditional stories. I mean, for example, the given fact that Clytemnestra dies at the hands of Orestes, and Eriphyle at the hands of Alcmaeon; but it is necessary for the poet to be inventive and skillful in adapting the stories that have been handed down. Let us define more clearly what we mean by the skillful adaptation of a story. It is possible for the action to occur, as our early poets handled it, with the characters knowing and understanding what they are doing, as indeed Euripides makes Medea kill her children. It is also possible to have the deed done with those who accomplish the terrible deed in ignorance of the identity of their victim, only later recognizing the relationship as in Sophocles' *Oedipus*. The incident, here, is outside the plot, but we find an example of such an incident in the play itself, in the action of Astydamas' *Alcmaeon* or of Telegonus in the *Wounded Odys-*

seus;[11] and there is further a third type in addition to these that involves someone who intends to commit some fatal act through ignorance of his relationship to another person but recognizes this relationship before doing it. Beyond these possibilities, there is no other way to have an action take place. For it is necessary either to do the deed or not and either knowingly or in ignorance.

Of these possibilities, the case in which one knowingly is about to do the deed and does not is the worst; for it is repellent and not tragic because it lacks the element of suffering. (1454) Therefore, no one handles a situation this way, except rarely; for example, in the *Antigone,* Haemon is made to act in this way toward Creon. To do the deed knowingly is the next best way. Better than this is the case where one does the deed in ignorance and after he has done it recognizes his relationship to the other person. For the repellent aspect is not present, and the recognition is startling. But the most effective is the final type, for example, in the *Cresphontes,* where Merope is going to kill her son and does not, but, on the contrary, recognizes him, and in the *Iphigenia,* where a sister is involved in a similar situation with a brother, and in the *Helle,* where a son who is about to surrender his mother recognizes her.[12]

It is for this reason that, as we have said previously, tragedies are concerned with a few families. For proceeding not by art, but by trial and error, poets learned how to produce the appropriate effect in their plots. They are compelled, therefore, to return time and again to that number of families in which these terrifying events have occurred. We have now spoken sufficiently about the construction of the incidents and of what type the plot must be.

XV

In regard to character, there are four points to be aimed at. First and foremost, character should be good. If a speech or action has some choice connected with it, it will manifest character, as has been said, and the character will be good if the choice is good. Goodness is possible for each class of individuals. For, both a woman and a slave have their particular virtues even though the former of these is inferior to a man, and the latter is completely ignoble. Second, character must be appropriate. For it is possible for a person to be manly in terms of character, but it is not appropriate for a woman to exhibit either this quality or the intellectual cleverness that is associated with men. The third point about character is that it should be like reality, for this is different from making character virtuous and making it appropriate, as we have defined these terms. The fourth aspect of character is consistency. For even if it is an inconsistent character who is the subject of the imitation (I refer to the model that suggested the kind of character being imitated), it is nevertheless necessary for him to be consistently inconsistent. We have an example of unnecessarily debased character in the figure of Menelaus in the *Orestes,* of unsuitable and inappropriate character in the lament of Odysseus in the *Scylla*[13] and the speech of Melanippe,[14] and of inconsistency of character in *Iphigenia at Aulis* where the heroine's role as a suppliant does not fit in with her character as it develops later in the play.

In character, as in the construction of the incidents, we must always seek for either the necessary or the probable, so that a given type of person says or does certain kinds of things, and one event follows another according to necessity or probability. (1454) Thus, it is apparent that the resolutions of the plots should also occur through the plot itself and not by means of the *deus ex machina,*[15] as in the *Medea,* and also in regard to the events surrounding the departure of the fleet in the *Iliad*. The *deus ex machina* must be reserved for the events that lie outside the plot, either those that happened before it that are not capable of being known by men, or those that occur after that need to be announced and spoken of beforehand. For we grant to the gods the power of seeing all things. There should, then, be nothing improbable in the action; but if this is impossible, it should be outside the plot as, for example, in Sophocles' *Oedipus*.

Because tragedy is an imitation of the nobler sort of men it is necessary for poets to imitate the good portrait painters. For even though they reproduce the specific characteristics of their subjects and represent them faithfully, they also paint them better than they are. Thus, also, the poet imitating men who are prone to anger or who are indifferent or who are disposed in other such ways in regard to character makes them good as well, even though they have such characteristics, just as Agathon and Homer portray Achilles.

It is necessary to pay close attention to these matters and, in addition, to those that pertain to the effects upon an audience that follow necessarily from the nature of the art of poetry. For, indeed, it is possible frequently to make mistakes in regard to these. We have spoken sufficiently about these matters in our published works.

XVI

What we mean by "recognition" we have indicated previously. Of the kinds of recognition that occur, there is one, first of all, that is least artistic, which poets mainly use through the poverty of their inspiration. This is the form of recognition that is achieved through external signs; some of these are birthmarks, for example, "the spearhead which the Earth-born are accustomed to bear,"[16] or the "stars" such as Carcinus wrote about in his *Thyestes*. Then there are characteristics that we acquire after birth. Of these some are found on the body, for example, scars; and others are external to the body, such as necklaces, and as another example, the ark through which the recognition is accomplished in the *Tyro*.[17] It is also possible to employ these recognitions in better and worse ways; for example, Odysseus was recognized through his scar in one way by the nurse and in another way by the swineherds. Now those recognitions are less artistic that depend on signs as proof, as well as all that are similar to these; but those that derive from the reversal of action, as in the Bath Scene of the *Odyssey,* are better.

In second place come those recognitions that have been contrived for the occasion by the poet and are therefore inartistic. For example, the way Orestes in the *Iphigenia* makes known that he is Orestes; for Iphigenia made herself known through the letter, but he himself says what the poet wishes him to say but not what the plot requires. Therefore this type of recognition is rather close to the error that has already been mentioned; for it would have been just as possible for him to carry tokens with him. Another example of this type of recognition is the use of the "voice of the shuttle"[18] in the *Tereus* of Sophocles.

The third type arises from our being stimulated by something that we see to remember an event that has an emotional significance for us. (1455) This type of recognition occurs in the *Cyprioe* of Dicaeogenes where the sight of the painting brings forth tears, and also in the story of Alcinous where Odysseus hears the lyre player and, reminded of his past fortunes, weeps; in both instances, it was by their emotional reactions that the characters were recognized.

The fourth type of recognition occurs through reasoning, for example, in the *Choëphoroe*[19] it is achieved by the deduction: Someone like me has come; there is no one resembling me except Orestes; he, therefore, has come. Another recognition of this type was suggested by Polyidus the Sophist in regard to Iphigenia; for it was reasonable for Orestes to infer that, since his sister was sacrificed, he was also going to be sacrificed. Again, in the *Tydeus* of Theodectes, the deduction is made that he who had come to find a son was, himself, to perish. Another example is in the *Phinidae*[20] where the women, when they had seen the place, inferred their destiny: that since they had been exposed there, they were fated to die there.

There is also a type of composite recognition from false reasoning on the part of another character, for example, in the story of Odysseus, the False Messenger; for he said that he would know the bow that he had not seen, but it is false reasoning to suppose through this that he *would* recognize it again (as if he had seen it before).

The best recognition is the one that arises from the incidents themselves, striking us, as they do, with astonishment through the very probability of their occurrence as, for example, in the action of the *Oedipus* of Sophocles and in the *Iphigenia*, where it is reasonable for the heroine to wish to dispatch a letter. Such recognitions, alone, are accomplished without contrived signs and necklaces. The second best type of recognition is the one that is achieved by reasoning.

XVII

In constructing plots and working them out with diction, the poet must keep the action as much as possible before his eyes. For by visualizing the events as distinctly as he can, just as if he were present at their actual occurrence, he will discover what is fitting for his purpose, and there will be the least chance of incongruities escaping his notice. A sign of this is found in the criticism that is made of Carcinus. For Amphiarus is coming back from the temple, a point that would have escaped the audience's notice if it had not actually seen it; and on the stage, the play failed because the audience was annoyed at this incongruity.

As much as is possible the poet should also work out the action with gestures. For, given poets of the same natural abilities, those are most persuasive who are involved in the emotions they imitate; for example, one who is distressed conveys distress, and one who is enraged conveys anger most truly. Therefore, the art of poetry is more a matter for the well-endowed poet than for the frenzied one. For poets marked by the former characteristic can easily change character, whereas those of the latter type are possessed.

In regard to arguments, both those that already are in existence and those he himself invents, the poet should first put them down in universal form and then extend them by adding episodes. (1455) I mean that the poet should take a general view of the action of the play, like, for example, the following general view of the *Iphigenia*: A young girl had been sacrificed and had disappeared in a way that was obscure to the sacrificers. She settled in another country in which it was the custom to sacrifice strangers to the goddess, and she came to hold the priesthood for this sacrifice. Later, it turned out that the brother of the priestess came to this country (the fact that the god, for some reason, commanded him to come is outside the argument; the purpose of his coming is outside of the plot). When he came he was seized, and on the point of being sacrificed he made himself known, either as Euripides handled the situation or as Polyidus arranged it, by his saying, in a very reasonable way, that not only had it been necessary for his sister to be sacrificed but also for him; and from this came his deliverance. After this, when the names have already been assigned, it is necessary to complete the episodes. The episodes must be appropriate, as, for example, the madness of Orestes through which he was captured and his deliverance through purification.

In drama, the episodes are short, but epic achieves its length by means of them. For the argument of the *Odyssey* is not long: A certain man is away from home for many years, closely watched by Poseidon but otherwise completely alone. His family at home continually faces a situation where his possessions are being squandered by the suitors who plot against his son. Storm-driven, he arrives home and, having made certain people acquainted with him, he attacks the suitors and, while destroying his enemies, is himself saved. This is the essence of the story; everything else is episode.

XVIII

In every tragedy, we find both the complication and the resolution of the action. Frequently some matters outside the action together with some within it comprise the complication, and the rest of the play consists of the resolution. By complication I mean that part of the play from the beginning up to the first point at which the change occurs to good or to bad fortune. By resolution I mean the part of the play from the beginning of the change in fortune to the end of the play. For example, in the *Lynceus* of Theodectes, the complication comprises everything done before the action of the play begins and the seizing of the child, and, in turn, of the parents; the resolution comprises all that happens from the accusation of murder to the end of the play.[21]

There are four kinds of tragedy (for that number of parts has been mentioned): the complex, which consists wholly in reversal and recognition; the tragedies of suffering, for example, the *Ajaxes* and *Ixions* that have been written; (1456) the tragedies of character, for example, the *Phthiotian Women* and the *Peleus*.[22] And a fourth type [the tragedy of spectacle], for example, is *The Daughters of Phorcis* and *Prometheus*[23] and those plays that take place in Hades. Now it is necessary to attempt, as much as possible, to include all elements in the play, but if that is not possible, then as many as possible and certainly the most important ones. This is especially so now, indeed, when the public unjustly criticizes our poets. For although there have been poets who were outstanding in regard to each kind of tragedy, the public now demands that one man be superior to the particular virtue of each of his predecessors.

It is correct to speak of a tragedy as different from or similar to another one on the basis of its plot more than anything else: that is, in regard to an action having the same complication and resolution. Many poets are skillful in constructing their complications, but their resolutions are poor. It is, however, necessary for both elements to be mastered.

The poet, as has frequently been said, must remember not to make a tragedy out of an epic body of incidents (by which I mean a multiple plot), [as would be the case], for example, if someone should construct a plot out of the entire *Iliad*. For, there, because of the length, the parts take on the appropriate magnitude, but the same plot used in the drama turns out quite contrary to one's expectations. A sign of this is that so many as have written about the entire destruction of Troy (and not of sections of it, as Euripides) or about the entire story of Niobe (and not just a part, as Aeschylus) either completely fail on stage or do badly, since even Agathon failed for this reason alone. But in their reversals and in their simple plots, these poets aim with marvelous accuracy at the effects that they wish for: that is, whatever is tragic and touches our human sympathy. This occurs whenever a clever but evil person is deceived, as Sisyphus, or a brave but unjust man is defeated. Such an event is probable, as Agathon says, because it is probable for many things to occur contrary to probability.

It is necessary to consider the chorus as one of the actors and as an integral part of the drama; its involvement in the action should not be in Euripides' manner but in Sophocles'. In the hands of our later poets, the songs included in the play are no more a part of that particular plot than they are of any other tragedy. They have been sung, therefore, as inserted pieces from the time Agathon first introduced this practice. And yet what difference does it make whether one sings an inserted song or adopts a speech or a whole episode from one play into another?

XIX

We have already spoken about other matters; it remains for us to discuss diction and thought. Concerning thought, let it be taken as given what we have written in the *Rhetoric,* for this is more appropriately a subject of that discipline. All those matters pertain to thought that must be presented through speech; and they may be subdivided into proof and refutation and the production of emotional effects, for example, pity or fear or anger or other similar emotions. (1456) Indications of the importance or insignificance of anything also fall under this heading. It is clear that we must employ thought also in actions in the same ways [as in speech] whenever we aim at the representation of the pitiable, the terrible, the significant, or the probable, with the exception of this one difference —that the effects arise in the case of the incidents without verbal explanation, whereas in the speech they are produced by the speaker and arise because of the speech. For what would be the function of the speaker if something should appear in the way that is required without being dependent on the speech?

Concerning diction one kind of study involves the forms of diction that are investigated by the art of elocution and are the concern of the individual who considers this his guiding art, for example, what a command is and what a prayer is, what a statement is, and threat and question and answer and any other such matters. For in regard to the knowledge or ignorance of these matters, no censure worth taking seriously can be made against the art of poetry. Why should any one accept as an error Protagoras' censure of Homer on the grounds that when he said, "Sing, O goddess, of the wrath . . ."[24] he gave a command, although he really wished to utter a prayer. For Protagoras says to order someone to do something or not is a command. Let us, therefore, disregard such a consideration as being a principle of some other art, not the art of poetry.

XX

The following parts comprise the entire scope of diction: letter, syllable, connective, noun, verb, inflection and sentence. A letter is an indivisible sound; not every such sound is a letter, however, but only one from which a compound sound can be constructed. For I would call none of the individual sounds uttered by wild animals letters. The subdivisions of this category of "letter" are vowel, semivowel, and mute. A vowel is a sound that is audible without the contact of any of the physical structures of the mouth, a semivowel is a sound that is audible with the contact of some of the physical structures of the mouth, for example, the *S* and *R* sounds; and a mute is a letter produced by the contact of the physical structures of the mouth, but inaudible in itself, although it becomes audible when it is accompanied by letters that are sounded, for example, the *G* and *D* sounds. These letters differ in the positions taken by the mouth to produce them, in the places in the mouth where they are produced, in aspiration and smoothness, in being long or short and, furthermore, in having an acute, grave, or middle [circumflex] pitch accent. The detailed investigation concerning these matters belongs to the study of metrics.

A syllable is a nonsignificant sound constructed from a mute and a vowel. For, indeed, *GR* without an *A* is a syllable and also with it, for example, *GRA*. However, it is the business of the art of metrics also to investigate distinctions in this area.[25]

(1457) A connective is a nonsignificant sound that neither hinders nor promotes the creation of one significant sound from many sounds and that it is not appropriate to place at the beginning of a speech that stands independently, for example, *men, dē, toi, de*. Or it is a nonsignificant sound that is naturally able to make one significant sound from a number of sounds, for example, *amphi, peri,* and others like them. There is also a kind of connective that is a nonsignificant sound that shows the beginning, end, or division of a sentence and that may naturally be placed at either end or in the middle of a sentence.

A noun is a compound significant sound, not indicating time, no part of which is significant by itself. For in compound nouns we do not consider each part of the compound as being significant in itself; for example, in the name "Theodore" the root *dor* [gift] has no significance.

A verb is a compound significant sound indicating time, no part of which is significant by itself in the same way as has been indicated in regard to nouns. For "man" or "white" do not tell us anything about "when"; but "He goes" or "He has gone" indicate the present and the past.

Inflection is a characteristic of a noun or verb signifying the genitive or dative relation, or other similar ones, or indicating the singular or plural, that is, man or men, or is concerned with matters that fall under the art of elocution, for example, questions and commands; for the phrases, "Did he go?" or "Go!" involve inflections of the verb in regard to these categories.

A speech is a compound, significant sound some of whose parts are significant by themselves. For not every speech is composed of verbs and nouns but it is possible to have a speech without verbs (for example, the definition of man). However, part of the speech will always have some significance, for example, "Cleon" in the phrase "Cleon walks." A speech is a unity in two ways. Either it signifies one thing or it is a unity through the joining together of many speeches. For example, the *Iliad* is a unity by the process of joining together many speeches, and the definition of man by signifying one thing.

XXI

Nouns are either simple, by which I mean constructed solely from nonsignificant elements, for example *gē* [earth], or compound. This latter category is divided into nouns that are constructed from both significant and nonsignificant elements (except that neither element is significant within the compound word itself) and nouns that are composed solely out of significant elements. Nouns may also be made up of three, four, or more parts, for example, many of the words in the Massilian vocabulary, such as Hermocaicoxanthus. . . .[26]

(1457) Every word is either standard, or is a strange word, or is a metaphor, or is ornamental, or is a coined word, or is lengthened, or contracted, or is altered in some way. I mean by standard, words that everyone uses, and by a strange word, one that foreigners use. Thus, it is apparent, the same word can be both strange and ordinary but not, of course, to the same persons. The word *sigunon* [spear] is ordinary for the Cyprians and strange to us.

Metaphor is the transference of a name from the object to which it has a natural application; this transference can take place from genus to species or species to genus or from species to species or by analogy. I mean by from genus to species, for example, "This ship of mine stands there." For to lie at anchor is a species of standing. An example of the transference from species to genus, "Odysseus has truly accomplished a myriad of noble deeds." For a myriad is the equivalent of "many," for which the poet now substitutes this term. An example of the transference from species to species is "having drawn off life with a sword" and also "having cut with unyielding bronze." For here to draw off is to cut and to cut is called to draw off, for both are subdivisions of "taking away."

I mean by transference by analogy the situation that occurs whenever a second element is related to a first as a fourth is to a third. For the poet will then use the fourth in place of the second or the second in place of the fourth, and sometimes poets add the reference to which the transferred term applies. I mean, for example, that a cup is related to Dionysus as a shield is to Ares. The poet will, therefore, speak of the cup as the shield of Dionysus and the shield as the cup of Ares. The same situation occurs in regard to the relation of old age to life and evening to day. A poet will say that evening is the old age of day, or however Empedocles expressed it, and that old age is the evening of life or the sunset of life. In some situations, there is no regular name in use to cover the analogous relation, but nevertheless the related elements will be spoken of by analogy; for example, to scatter seed is to sow, but the scattering of the sun's rays has no name. But the act of sowing in regard to grain bears an analogous relation to the sun's dispersing of its rays, and so we have the phrase "sowing the god-created fire."

It is also possible to use metaphor in a different way by applying the transferred epithet and then denying some aspect that is proper to it—for example, if one should call the shield not the cup of Ares but the wineless cup. A coined word is one that is not in use among foreigners but is the invention of the poet. There seem to be some words of this type, for example, horns [*kerata*] called "sprouters" [*ernuges*], and a priest [*iereus*] called "supplicator" [*arētēr*].

A word may be lengthened or contracted. (1458) It is lengthened if it makes use of a longer vowel than is usual for it, or a syllable is inserted in it; and it is contracted if any element is removed from it. An example of lengthening is *poleōs* to *polēos* and *Pēleidou* to *Pēlēiadeō:* an example of contraction is *krī* and *dō* and *ops* in *"mia ginetai amphoterōn ops."*

A word is altered whenever a poet utilizes part of the regular name for the object he is describing and invents part anew, for example, in the phrase "*deksiteron kata mazon*" the use of *deksiteron* in place of *deksion*.[27]

Nouns are subdivided into masculine, feminine, and neuter. Those are masculine that end in nu, rho, and sigma and in the two letters psi and ksi that are constructed in combination with sigma. Those nouns are feminine that end in the vowels that are always long, the eta and omega, and that end (in regard to the vowels subject to lengthening) in the lengthened alpha. Thus it turns out that there are an equal number of terminations for masculine and feminine nouns since psi and ksi are subdivisions of sigma. No noun ends in a mute nor in a short vowel. Only three end in iota, *meli, kommi, peperi,* and five end in upsilon. Neuter nouns end in these vowels and in nu and sigma.

XXII

Diction achieves its characteristic virtue in being clear but not mean. The clearest style results from the use of standard words; but it is also mean, as can be seen in the poetry of Cleophon and Sthenelus. A really distinguished style varies ordinary diction through the employment of unusual words. By unusual I mean strange words and metaphor and lengthened words and everything that goes beyond ordinary diction. But if someone should write exclusively in such forms the result would either be a riddle or a barbarism. A riddle will result if someone writes exclusively in metaphor; and a barbarism will result if there is an exclusive use of strange words. For it is in the nature of a riddle for one to speak of a situation that actually exists in an impossible way. Now it is not possible to do this by the combination of strange words; but it can be done by metaphor, for example, "I saw a man who welded bronze on another man by fire," and other metaphors like this. A statement constructed exclusively from strange words is a barbarism.

It is therefore necessary to use a combination of all these forms. The employment of strange words and metaphor and ornamental words and the other forms of speech that have been mentioned will prevent the diction from being ordinary and mean; and the use of normal speech will keep the diction clear. (1458) The lengthening and contraction of words and alterations in them contribute in no small measure to the diction's clarity and its elevation above ordinary diction. For because such words are different they will prevent the diction from being ordinary through their contrast with the ordinary expression; and because they have a share in the customary word, they will keep the diction clear.

Thus, the criticism is not well-taken on the part of those who censure this way of using language and who mock the poet, as the elder Euclid did, on the grounds that it is easy to write poetry if you are allowed to lengthen forms as much as you want; Euclid composed a satiric verse in the very words he used, *Epicharēn eidon Marathōnade badizonta* and *ouk an g'eramenos ton ekeinou elleboron.*[28]

Now then, the employment of the technique of lengthening in excess is ridiculous, and moderation is a quality that is commonly needed in all aspects of diction. For, indeed, if one employs metaphors and strange words and other forms in an inappropriate way and with intended absurdity, he can also accomplish the same effect. When the ordinary words are inserted in the verse, it can be seen how great a difference the appropriate use of lengthening makes in epic poetry. If someone should also change the strange words and metaphors and other forms to ordinary words, he would see the truth of what we have said. For example, Aeschylus and Euripides wrote the same iambic line, but Euripides changed one word and instead of using a standard one employed a strange one; his line thus has an elegance to it, whereas the other is mean. For Aeschylus wrote in his *Philoctetes:*[29] "*phagedaina hē mou sarkas esthiei podos*" [this cancerous sore eats the flesh of my leg]. Euripides in place of "eats" substitutes *thoinatai* [feasts upon]. A similar situation would occur in the line "*nun de m'eōn oligos te kai outidanos kai aeikēs*"[30] if someone should substitute the ordinary words "*nun de m'eōn mikros te kai asthenikos kai aeidēs*" or if we changed the line "*diphron aeikelion katatheis oligēn te trapezan"*[31] to "*diphron moxthēron katatheis mikran te trapezan*" or for *ēiones boōosin,* we substituted *ēiones krazousin.*[32] Furthermore, Ariphrades mocked the tragedians because no one would use their style in conversation; for example, the word order *dōmatōn apo* in place of *apo dōmatōn,* and the word *sethen,* and the phrase *egō de nin,* and the word order *Achilleōs peri* in place of *peri Achilleōs,* and many other similar expressions. (1459) For he missed the point that the virtue of all these expressions is that they create an unusual element in the diction by their not being in ordinary speech.

It is a matter of great importance to use each of the forms mentioned in a fitting way, as well as compound words and strange ones, but by far the most important matter is to have skill in the use of metaphor. The skill alone it is not possible to obtain from another; and it is, in itself, a sign of genius. For the ability to construct good metaphors implies the ability to see essential similarities.

In regard to words, compounds are especially suitable for dithyrambs, strange words for heroic verse, and metaphors for iambic verse; in heroic verse all the forms mentioned are serviceable; but in iambic verse, because as much as possible it imitates conversation, only those words are appropriate that might be used in prose. Of this nature are standard words, metaphors, and ornamental words.

Now, then, concerning tragedy and the imitation that is carried out in action, let what has been said suffice.

XXIII

Concerning that form of verse imitation that is narrative, it is necessary to construct the plot as in tragedy in a dramatic fashion, and concerning a single action that is whole and complete (having a beginning, middle, and end) so that, like a single integrated organism, it achieves the pleasure natural to it.

The composition of incidents should not be similar to that found in our histories, in which it is necessary to show not one action but one period of time and as many things as happened in this time, whether they concern one man or many, and whether or not each of these things is related to the others. For just as there occurred in the same period of time a sea battle at Salamis and a battle with the Carthaginians in Sicily, but these did not at all lead to a common goal, thus also in the sequence of time, occasionally one event happens after another without there being a common goal to join them.

However, almost all the poets commit this error. Also in this, then, Homer would appear to be of exceptional skill in relation to other poets, as we have already said, since he did not attempt to write about the complete war, although it had a beginning and end; for that would have been a very large subject and could not have been taken in easily in a single view; or even if its magnitude were moderate, the story still would be tangled because of the diversity of incidents. But note how although treating only one part of the war, he also introduces many of the other episodes in the war, for example, the catalogue of ships and others, by which he gives variety to his poem. (1459) Others write about one man and about one period and one action with diverse parts, for example, the poet who wrote the *Cypria*[33] and the *Little Iliad*.[34] Therefore from the *Iliad* and *Odyssey* one or two tragedies apiece are constructed; but from the *Cypria* many tragedies are constructed and from the *Little Iliad* eight, for example, *The Award of the Arms, Philoctetes, Neoptolemus,*[35] *Eurypylus, The Beggar, The Laconian Woman, The Sack of Troy, The Return Voyage,* and a *Sinon,* and a *Women of Troy*.[36]

XXIV

Moreover, it is necessary for epic poetry to exhibit the same characteristic forms as tragedy; for it is either simple or complex, displays character or suffering, and is composed of the same parts, with the exception of song and spectacle. In epic, there is also a necessity for reversals, recognitions, and the depiction of suffering. Here too, thought and diction must be handled with skill. Homer used all these elements first and in a proper way. For each of his poems is well-constructed; the *Iliad* is simple and exhibits suffering, whereas the *Odyssey* is complex (for there is recognition throughout) and shows character. In addition to these matters, Homer outstrips all others in diction and thought.

Epic differs from tragedy in regard to the length of the plot, and the meter. The sufficient limit of length has been mentioned, for we have noted that it must be possible to take in the plot's beginning and end in one view. This would occur if the plots were shorter than those of the old epics but would extend to the length of the number of tragedies that are designated for one performance. For the purpose of extending its length, epic poetry has a very great capacity that is specifically its own, since it is not possible in tragedy to imitate many simultaneous lines of action but only that performed by the actors on the stage. But because of the narrative quality of epic it is possible to depict many simultaneous lines of action that, if appropriate, become the means of increasing the poem's scope. This has an advantage in regard to the elegance of the poem and in regard to varying the interest of the audience and for constructing a diverse sequence of episodes. For the rapid overloading of tragedies with the same kind of incident is what makes tragedies fail.

The heroic meter[37] has been found appropriate to epic through practical experience. If someone should write a narrative imitation in another meter, or in a combination of meters, we would feel it to be inappropriate. For the heroic is the stateliest and most dignified meter, and therefore it is especially receptive to strange words and metaphors, for narrative poetry in this regard is exceptional among the forms of imitation; the iambic and the trochaic tetrameter are expressive of motion, the latter being a dance meter and the former displaying the quality of action. (1460) Furthermore, it makes a very strange impression if someone combines these meters as Chairemon did. Therefore no one has written a long poem in a meter other than the heroic; but, as we said, nature herself teaches us to choose the appropriate meter.

Homer deserves praise for many qualities and, especially, because alone of the poets he is not ignorant of the requirements of his craft. For it is necessary for the poet himself to speak in his own person in the poem as little as possible, because he is not fulfilling his function as an imitator when he appears in this way. Now the other poets are themselves active performers throughout the poem, and they perform their imitative function infrequently and in regard to only a few objects. Homer, on the other hand, when he has made a brief prelude immediately brings in a man or woman or some other character; and all his figures are expressive of character, and none lacks it.

Now then, it is necessary in tragedy to create the marvelous, but the epic admits, even more, of the irrational, on which the marvelous especially depends, because the audience does not see the person acting. The whole business of the pursuit of Hector would appear ridiculous on the stage with some men standing about and not pursuing and Achilles nodding at them to keep them back; but in the narrative description of epic, this absurdity escapes notice.

The marvelous is pleasant, and the proof of this is that everyone embellishes the stories he tells as if he were adding something pleasant to his narration. Homer has especially taught others how it is necessary to lie, and this is through the employment of false reasoning. For whenever one event occurs or comes into existence and is naturally accompanied by a second event, men think that whenever this second event is present the first one must also have occurred or have come into existence. This, however, is a fallacy. Therefore, if the first event mentioned is false but there is another event that must occur or come into existence when the first event occurs, we feel compelled to join the two events in our thought. For our mind, through knowing that the second event is true, falsely reasons that the first event must have occurred or have come into existence also. There is an example of this type of fallacy in the Bath Scene in the *Odyssey*.

The use of impossible probabilities is preferable to that of unpersuasive possibilities. We must not construct plots from irrational elements, and we should especially attempt not to have anything irrational at all in them; but if this is not possible, the irrational should be outside the plot (as in Oedipus' ignorance of how Laius died); it should not be in the drama itself, as occurs in the *Electra* concerning those who bring news of the Pythian games,[38] or in the *Mysians,*[39] concerning the man who has come from Tegea to Mysia without speaking. To say that without the use of such incidents the plot would have been ruined is ridiculous. For it is necessary, right from the beginning, not to construct such plots.

If the poet takes such a plot and if it appears to admit of a more probable treatment, the situation is also absurd, since it is clear that even the improbable elements in the *Odyssey* concerning the casting ashore of Odysseus would not be bearable if a poor poet had written them. (1460) Here the poet conceals the absurdity by making it pleasing through his other skillful techniques. It is necessary to intensify the diction only in those parts of the poem that lack action and are unexpressive of character and thought. For too brilliant a diction conceals character and thought.

XXV

Concerning the number and character of the problems that lead to censure in poetry and the ways in which this censure must be met, the following considerations would be apparent to those who study the question. Since the poet is an imitator, like a painter or any maker of likenesses, he must carry out his imitations on all occasions in one of three possible ways. Thus, he must imitate the things that were in the past, or are now, or that people say and think to be or those things that ought to be. The poet presents his imitation in standard diction, as well as in strange words and metaphors and in many variations of diction, for we grant this license to poets. In addition to this, there is not the same standard of correctness for politics and poetry, nor for any other art and poetry. In regard to poetry itself, two categories of error are possible, one essential, and one accidental. For if the poet chose to imitate but imitated incorrectly, through lack of ability[40] the error is an essential one; but if he erred by choosing an incorrect representation of the object (for example, representing a horse putting forward both right hooves) or made a technical error, for example, in regard to medicine or any other art, or introduced impossibilities of any sort, the mistake is an accidental, not an essential, one.

As a result, we must meet the criticisms of the problems encountered in poetry by taking these points into consideration. First, in regard to the problems that are related to the essential nature of art: if impossibilities have been represented, an error has been made; but it may be permissible to do this if the representation supports the goal of the imitation (for the goal of an imitation has been discussed) and if it makes the section in which it occurs, or another part of the poem, more striking. An example of such a situation is the pursuit of Hector in the *Iliad*. If, indeed, the goal of the imitation admits of attainment as well, or better, when sought in accordance with technical requirements, then it is incorrect to introduce the impossible. For, if it is at all feasible, no error should be committed at all. Further, we must ascertain whether an error originates from an essential or an accidental aspect of the art. For it is a less important matter if the artist does not know that a hind does not have horns than if he is unskillful in imitating one. In addition, the criticism that a work of art is not a truthful representation can be met by the argument that it represents the situation as it should be. For example, Sophocles said that he himself created characters such as should exist, whereas Euripides created ones such as actually do exist. If neither of the above is the case, the criticism must be met by reference to men's opinions, for example, in the myths that are told about the gods. For, perhaps, they do not describe a situation that is better than actuality, nor a true one, but they are what Xenophanes said of them—in accordance, at any rate, with men's opinions. (1461) Perhaps the situation described by the artist is not better than actuality but was one that actually existed in the past, for example, the description of the arms that goes, "The spears were standing upright on their butt spikes"; for once this was customary, as it is now among the Illyrians. Now to judge the nobility or ignobility of any statement made or act performed by anyone, we must not only make an investigation into the thing itself that has been said or done, considering whether it is noble or ignoble, but we must also consider the one who does the act or says the words in regard to whom, when, by what means, and for what purpose he speaks or acts—for example, whether the object is to achieve a greater good or to avoid a greater evil.

We must meet some kinds of criticism by considering the diction, for example, by reference to the use of a strange word, as in the phrase, *ourēas men prōton.*[41] The word oureas here could cause some difficulty because perhaps the poet does not mean mules but guards. Dolon's statement, "I who was badly formed,"[42] has a similar difficulty involved in it; for he does not mean that he was misshapen in body but that he was ugly, because the Cretans use *eueidēs* [of fair form] to denote "handsome." A difficulty might arise in the phrase "mix the drink purer,"[43] which does not mean stronger, as if for drunkards, but faster. Difficulties arise in thoughts that are expressed in metaphors, for example, "All the gods and men slept the entire night through," which is said at the same time as "When truly he turned his gaze upon the Trojan plain, and heard the sound of flutes and pipes." "All" is used here metaphorically in place of "many," since "all" is some division of "many." The phrase "alone, she has no share"[44] shows a similar use of metaphor, since the best known one is "alone." A problem may arise from the use of accent; Hippias the Thasian solved such a problem in the phrase, *didomen de oi* and similarly, in the phrase, *to men hoi katapythetai ombrō.*[45] Some difficulties are solved through punctuation, for example, in Empedocles' statement that "Suddenly things became mortal that had previously learned to be immortal and things unmixed before mixed."[46] Some problems are solved by reference to ambiguities, for example, "more than two thirds of night has departed" because "more" is ambiguous here.[47] Some difficulties are met by reference to customary usages in our language. Thus, we call "wine" the mixture of water and wine; and it is with the same justification that the poet writes of "a greave of newly wrought tin"; and iron workers are called *chalkeas,* literally, copper smiths; and it is for this reason that Ganymede is called the wine pourer of Zeus, although the gods do not drink wine. This would also be justified through metaphor.

Whenever a word seems to signify something contradictory, we must consider how many different meanings it might have in the passage quoted; for example, in the phrase "the bronze spear was held there," we must consider how many different senses of "to be held" are possible, whether by taking it in this way or that one might best understand it. The procedure is opposite to the one that Glaucon mentions in which people make an unreasonable prior assumption and, (1461) having themselves made their decree, they draw their conclusions, and then criticize the poet as if he had said whatever they think he has said if it is opposed to their thoughts. We have had this experience in regard to discussions of the character Icarius.[48] People assume that he was a Spartan; but then it appears ridiculous that Telemachus did not meet him in Sparta when he visited there. Perhaps the situation is as the Cephallenians would have it, for they say that Odysseus married amongst them and that there was an Icadius involved, but no Icarius. Thus, it is probable that the difficulty has arisen through a mistake.

Speaking generally, the impossible must be justified in regard to the requirements of poetry, or in regard to what is better than actuality, or what, in the opinion of men, is held to be true. In regard to the art of poetry, we must prefer a persuasive impossibility to an unpersuasive possibility. Perhaps it is impossible[49] for the kind of men Zeuxis painted to exist; but they illustrate what is better than the actual. For whatever is a model must express superior qualities. The irrational must be justified in regard to what men say and also on the grounds that it is, sometimes, not at all irrational. For it is reasonable that some things occur contrary to reason.

We must consider contradictions in the same way as the refutation of arguments is carried on: that is, with reference to whether the same object is involved, and in the same relationship, and in the same sense, so that the poet, indeed, has contradicted himself in regard to what he himself says or what a sensible person might assume. There is justifiable censure for the presence of irrationality and depravity where, there being no necessity for them, the poet makes no use of them, as Euripides' handling of Aegeus in the *Medea* (in regard to the irrational) or in the same poet's treatment of the character of Menelaus in the *Orestes* (in regard to depravity). Criticisms of poetry, then, derive from five sources: either that the action is impossible or that it is irrational or that it is morally harmful or that it is contradictory or that it contains technical errors. The answers to these criticisms must be sought from the solutions, twelve in number, that we have discussed.

XXVI

The problem of whether epic or tragedy is the better type of imitation might be raised. For if whatever is less common is better, that art would be superior that is directed at the more discriminating audience; and it is very clear that the art that imitates every detail is common. For on the grounds that the audience does not see the point unless they themselves add something, the actors make quite a commotion; for example, the poorer sort of flute players roll about the stage if they must imitate a discus throw and drag their leader about if they are playing the *Scylla.* Now tragedy is considered to be of the same character that our older actors attribute to their successors; for, indeed, Mynescus called Callippides an ape on the grounds of overacting, and such an opinion was also held about Pindarus. (1462) As these two types of actor are related to each other, so the whole art of tragedy is thought to be related to epic by some people, who then conclude that epic is oriented toward a reasonable audience that does not at all require gestures, but that tragedy is disposed toward a less sophisticated audience. If, then, tragedy is directed toward a more common audience, it would be clear that it is the inferior art form.

Now then, first, this accusation is made against the art of acting, not poetry, since it is possible to overdo gestures both in epic recitations as Sosistratus did, and in song competitions as Mnasitheus the Opuntian did. Then, too, not every movement is to be rejected, if dancing indeed is not to be condemned, but only the movements of the ignoble, a point that was criticized in Callippides and now in others, since, it was charged, they were not representing free-born women. Further, tragedy even without action achieves its function just as epic does; for its character is apparent simply through reading. If, then, tragedy is better in other respects, this defect is not essential to it. We argue, next, that it is better since it contains all of the elements that epic has (for it is even possible to use epic meter in tragedy) and, further, it has no small share in music and in spectacle, through which pleasure is very distinctly evoked. Tragedy also provides a vivid experience in reading as well as in actual performance. Further, in tragedy the goal of the imitation is achieved in a shorter length of time (for a more compact action is more pleasant than one that is much diluted). (1462) I mean, for example, the situation that would occur if someone should put Sophocles' *Oedipus* into an epic as long as the *Iliad*. Further, the imitation of an epic story is less unified than that of tragedy (a proof of this is that a number of tragedies can be derived from any one epic). So that if epic poets write a story with a single plot, that plot is either presented briefly and appears to lack full development, or, if it follows the accustomed length of epic, it has a watered-down quality (I mean, for example, if the epic should be composed of very many actions in the same way as the *Iliad* and *Odyssey* have many such elements that also have magnitude in themselves). And yet these poems are constructed in the best possible way and are, as much as possible, the imitations of a single action.

If, then, tragedy is superior in all these areas and, further, in accomplishing its artistic effect (for it is necessary that these genres create not any chance pleasure, but the one that has been discussed as proper to them), it is apparent that tragedy, since it is better at attaining its end, is superior to epic.

Now then, we have expressed our view of tragedy and epic, both in general, and in their various species, and of the number and differences in their parts, as well as of some of the causes of their effectiveness or ineffectiveness, and the criticisms that can be directed against them, and the ways in which these criticisms must be answered. . . .

DEMETRIUS

(1st century B.C.?)

INTRODUCTION

The actual date and authorship of *On Style* are in doubt. The work was originally attributed, on significant manuscript authority, to Demetrius of Phalerum, a student of Theophrastus, who died in 283 B.C. This attribution has been questioned for a variety of reasons. First, Demetrius of Phalerum is himself mentioned in the text in a way that would appear strange if he is the author of it. Second, Demetrius of Phalerum is known to have favored a florid style of rhetoric, and many scholars feel that a critic with such a tendency would not have been capable of writing the eminently fair and balanced treatment of the various rhetorical styles which we have in this treatise. Third, the treatment of rhetoric according to classes or types of style which characterizes this work is a practice which began much later than the third century B.C. Finally, the language of the treatise offers many examples of post-classical forms and there are a number of details of grammar and syntax that indicate composition at a later date than the third century B.C.

Although there are still important scholarly views to the contrary, the current consensus is that this work was probably written in the first century B.C. by a critic named Demetrius. The work itself shows that this Demetrius was greatly influenced by Aristotle and Theophrastus, but we are unable to identify him further, although a number of possible candidates have been suggested.

The treatise *On Style* begins with an introductory section on clauses and periods and then systematically treats the four principal rhetorical styles: the elevated, the elegant, the plain, and the forceful. In each case the qualities of diction, composition, and subject matter that produce the various styles are discussed, as are the faults to which each style is liable.

As a representative example of Demetrius' method, the section of his treatise dealing with the elevated style is included in this collection. Demetrius' procedure is to survey all of the means by which elevation can be achieved in style. He points out that certain types of rhythmic clauses can add dignity to expression, and he cites the initial and final paeon (—UUU and UUU—) as accomplishing this purpose. Lengthened clauses and periodic sentence structure are seen as further ways of enhancing the grandeur of the elevated style. Demetrius recommends that the arrangement of words in this style be from least vivid to most vivid and that connectives and expletives be mixed to intensify the elevation of the style.

The elevated style requires that a dignified and impressive subject matter be chosen and that it be framed in impressive diction. Among figures of speech, metaphors contribute most of all to the elevation of style. Demetrius also recommends the use of allegory, statements added at the end of the work, and poetic language as means of achieving the goals of the elevated style.

The stylistic fault which corresponds to the stylistic excellence of the elevated style is that of frigidity, which arises whenever the legitimately elevated style is distorted by the expression of what is exaggerated or impossible. This may occur when an excessively unrealistic thought is expressed or when the literary style is characterized by a very inappropriate use of elevated diction, rhythm, and meter.

Demetrius' treatment of the "high style" might be compared with "Longinus'" *Peri Hypsous,* especially since both critics consider stylistic questions as pertaining equally to literary and rhetorical works. Unlike "Longinus," Demetrius does not probe into the philosophical basis of art; his concern does not transcend the stylistic phenomena of artistic expression. Nevertheless, in this area he provides some of the best classical analyses of how diction, rhythm, and figures of speech can be used.

The translation here used (and most of the notes) are taken from G. M. A. Grube, *A Greek Critic: Demetrius on Style* (Toronto, University of Toronto Press, 1961) and reprinted by permission of the publisher.

from ON STYLE

36. There are four simple types of style: the plain, the grand, the elegant, and the forceful. The rest are combinations of these, but not all combinations are possible: the elegant can be combined with both the plain and the grand, and so can the forceful; the grand alone does not mix with the plain; these two face one another as opposite extremes. That is why some critics recognize only these last two as styles, and the other two as intermediate. They class the elegant rather with the plain, because the elegant is somewhat slight and subtle; while the forceful, which has weight and dignity, is classed with the grand.

37. Such a theory is absurd. With the exception of the two opposite extremes mentioned (the plain and the grand), we find combinations of all these types in the Homeric epic, in the works of Plato, Xenophon, Herodotus, and many other writers who display a frequent mixture of grandeur, forcefulness, and charm, so that the number of types is such as we have indicated, and the manner of expression appropriate to each will be seen in what follows.

IMPRESSIVE WORD-ARRANGEMENT

38. I shall begin with the grand or impressive manner which is today called eloquence. Grandeur resides in three things: the content, the diction, and the appropriate arrangement of words. This last is impressive, as Aristotle says, if it is paeonic in rhythm.[1] There are two kinds of paeon: the initial paeon which consists of one long followed by three shorts, for example

ērxătŏ dĕ

and the final paeon, its opposite, in which three shorts are followed by one long, for example

Ărăbĭā

39. In impressive speech, the clauses should begin with the initial paeon and the final paeon comes later. We may take an example from Thucydides:

ērxătŏ dĕ to kakon ex Aithĭŏpĭās (the evil began in Ethiopia).[2]

Why did Aristotle advise this? Because the start and opening of a clause should impress at once, and so should the end. We will achieve this by using a long syllable in both places. A long syllable has a natural dignity; it impresses at the start and leaves a strong impression at the end. All of us particularly remember the initial and final words and are affected by them but what comes in between has less effect on us, as if it were hidden and obscured.

40. This is obvious in Thucydides. In almost every instance, his impressiveness is wholly due to long-syllable rhythms. The grandeur of the man is many-sided, but it is this kind of word-arrangement which is the sole, or at any rate the main, factor in his greatest effects.

41. We should realize, however, that if we cannot have a paeon exactly at the beginning and at the end of each clause, we can still make our arrangement generally paeonic by at least beginning and ending with long syllables. This would seem to be what Aristotle advises us to do but he goes into details about the two kinds of paeon for no purpose except greater accuracy. Hence Theophrastus gives as an example of the grand manner a clause[3] of which the rhythm does not consist of exact paeons, yet it is paeonic in its general effect. We should therefore incorporate paeons into our prose; it is a measure mixing

long and short, and less risky than others. The long syllables give dignity, while the shorts preserve the character of prose.

42. As for the other meters, the heroic is stately but unsuited to prose; it resounds too much. It is not a good rhythm, indeed it is not a rhythm at all when it becomes a mere succession of long syllables,[4] for the number of longs is far too great for prose rhythm.

43. The iambus (∪—) is commonplace and like the rhythm of ordinary speech. Many people converse in iambics without knowing it. The paeon is a mean between the heroic and the iambic and is a mixture of the two. One should use the paeonic rhythm in impressive passages in some such way as we have indicated.

44. Lengthy clauses also make for grandeur, as in "Thucydides of Athens wrote this account of the war between the Peloponnesians and the Athenians,"[5] and "The history of Herodotus the Halicarnassian is here set forth." To end quickly with a short clause lowers the dignity of the sentence even if there is grandeur in the thought or in the words.

45. A rounded sentence-structure also contributes to grandeur, as in Thucydides': "After flowing from Mount Pindus through Dolopia and the land of the Agrianians and Amphilochians, and passing inland by Stratus, the river Achelous, as it makes its way to the sea near Oeniadae, surrounds that city with a marsh, thus making a winter attack on it impossible because of the water."[6] All the grandeur of this sentence is due to its periodic structure, and to the fact that Thucydides never allows himself or his reader to pause.

46. Now break up the sentence and say: "The river Achelous flows from Mount Pindus; it runs into the sea near Oeniadae; it turns the nearby plain of Oeniadae into a marsh; the water forms a natural protection against winter attacks." Written like this, there are many pauses, but the grandeur has vanished.

47. Long journeys seem shorter if one stops frequently at an inn; on the other hand, a deserted road makes even a short journey seem long. The same is true of clauses.

48. A harsh joining of sounds often makes for impressiveness, as in: "Aias the massive aimed always at Hector's bronze casque."[7] The clash of sounds is not in other ways euphonious but its very exaggeration suggests the greatness of the hero. Smoothness and euphony have no place in the grand style, except occasionally. Thucydides almost always avoids what is smooth and even; his word-order stumbles like men walking along a rough path. For example: "from other outbreaks of disease the year, it was agreed, was free."[8] This could have been put more easily and pleasingly, as "all agreed that the year was free from other diseases," but it is no longer impressive.

49. Harsh-sounding words make for grandeur, as does the juxtaposition of harsh sounds in the arrangement of words. "Shrieking" (*kekragōs*) has a harsher sound than "calling" (*boōn*), and "bursting" (*rhēgnumenon*) than

"going" (*pheromenon*). Thucydides uses all these harsh words; he chooses his words to fit his arrangement of them, and *vice versa.*

50. We should also arrange our words in the following manner: those that are not very vivid should come first, and the more vivid second and last. The sense of vividness then increases from one word to the next. The opposite order gives a feeling of weakness, of lapsing, as it were, from the stronger word to the weaker.

51. Plato has the following example: "When a man allows music to play upon him, and to flood through his ears into his soul," where the second verb is much more vivid than the first. He then goes on: "when the flood does not cease but puts a spell upon him, it weakens and melts his spirit."[9] Here "melts" is a stronger word than "weakens" and closer to poetry. If the second word had been first, the addition of "weakens" would have seemed rather feeble.

52. Homer too, in his description of the Cyclops, continually increases the hyperbole and seems to rise higher and higher with it: "He was not like a mortal man but like a wooded hilltop,"[10] and he goes on to speak of a high mountain towering over its fellows. The things mentioned first are big, but they seem small as bigger things follow.

53. Connectives should not correspond exactly, a *de* after a *men*, for instance, for there is something petty in precise writing. Impressiveness requires a certain disorder, as in a passage of Antiphon[11] where we have *men* used three times before one answering *de* occurs.

54. However, it often happens that a succession of connectives magnifies even trifling things. Homer joins together the names of the Boeotian cities, in themselves ordinary and unimportant, by a string of connectives and this gives them a certain weight and impressiveness: "And Schoinos and Scolos and many-topped Eteonos. . . ."[12]

55. Expletive connectives should not be used as mere empty fillers, like superfluities or excrescences, as some writers use *dē* (then, indeed) without reason, and *nu* (now), and *pote* (ever), but only when they contribute to the impressiveness of what is said.

56. So in Plato's "And in the heavens then (*dē*) the great Zeus,"[13] and Homer's "when they came then (*dē*) to the ford of the wide-flowing river."[14] Thus placed near the beginning of the clause the connective separates it from what precedes and adds a certain impressiveness. To amplify the beginnings of sentences lends dignity. If Homer had merely said: "When they came to the ford of the river" this would have seemed but a trivial description of one particular event.

57. The particle *dē* is also frequently used to express strong emotion, as in Calypso's words to Odysseus, "God-born son of Laertes, wily Odysseus, do you then (*dē*) long so much for your beloved land?"[15] If you remove the expletive, you will destroy the emotional tone. Altogether, as Praxiphanes says,

such particles were employed instead of groans and lamentations, like *ai ai* (Ah! Ah!) or *pheu* (Alas) or *poion ti esti* (what is it?). And he points out too that the connective *kai nu ke* in Homer's line[16] is appropriate to lamentation and has the same effect as a word expressing sorrow.

58. Praxiphanes says that those who use expletive as mere fillers are like actors who add a word here and there without reason, as if one said:

> This country, Calydon, of Pelops' land
> Alas!
> The opposite shore, fertile and happy plains
> Ah me! Ah me!

Just as here "Alas" and "Ah me" only distract the audience's attention, so connectives scattered everywhere without reason have the same effect.

FIGURES OF SPEECH

59. Connectives then can make the word-arrangement impressive, as we said. Figures of speech are themselves a kind of word-arrangement. For to say the same thing twice by repetition, by *epanaphora* or by *anthypallagē*, is to order and arrange the words in a different way. We must assign to each style the figures that are appropriate to it. The following are appropriate to the grand style which is our present concern.

60. First there is anthypallagē (the substitution of one case for another). When Homer says: "The two rocks, one reaching to the sky . . ."[17] he uses a much more impressive construction than if he had used the usual genitive: "Of the two rocks, one reaching to the sky . . . ," for what is customary is trivial and fails to arouse wonder.

61. Nireus is not himself important in the *Iliad*, and his contribution is even less so, three ships and a few men, but Homer makes him appear important and his contribution great instead of small by using and combining two figures, epanaphora and *dialysis*. "Nireus brought three ships," he says, "Nireus, son of Aglaïa," "Nireus, who was the most beautiful man."[18] The epanaphora as a figure of speech in connection with the same name, and the dialysis give an impression of abundant possessions, even though it is only two or three ships.

62. Although Nireus is mentioned only once in the action, we remember him as well as Achilles and Odysseus who are talked about in almost every line. This is due to the effectiveness of the figure of speech. If Homer had said: "Nireus, the son of Aglaïa brought three ships from Syme," he might as well not have mentioned him. At banquets a few well-arranged dishes give an impression of plenty; the same is true in discourse.

63. Frequently, however, impressiveness can be achieved by the opposite

of lack of connectives, namely by *synapheia*, as in: "On this campaign went the Greeks and the Carians and the Lycians and the Pamphilians and the Phrygians."[19] Here it is the repetition of the same connective which gives the impression of large numbers.

64. In such a phrase as "high-arched, white-crested"[20] on the other hand, it is the absence of the connective "and" which makes for greater impressiveness than if he had said "high-arched and white-crested."

65. Impressiveness by means of figures is also attained by varying the case, as in Thucydides: "First to step on the gangway to land he fainted, and as he fell among the oars . . ."[21] This is much more impressive than if he had retained the same case and said: "he fell among the oars and lost his shield."

66. *Anadiplōsis* also heightens the effect, as when Herodotus says: "The serpents in the Caucasus are large, large and numerous."[22] The repetition of "large" gives weight to the style.

67. One should avoid crowding the figures, for this argues a lack of taste and indicates an uneven style. It is true that the old writers use many figures; but because they use them skillfully, their style is more natural than that of those who do not use figures at all.

68. Opinions vary about the clashing of vowels (in hiatus). Isocrates[23] and his school took care to avoid it; others have paid no heed to it at all. We should neither arrange our words so that they ring in our ears through haphazard collisions, for these interrupt our flow with stops and jerks, nor altogether avoid such collisions. Total avoidance of hiatus would, it is true, make our words flow more smoothly, but the result would be flat and unmusical, without the euphony which often results from a clash of vowels.

69. We should in the first place note that customary speech, which certainly favors euphony, itself does bring vowels together within such words as *Aiakos* and *chiōn* (snow); indeed there are words which consist entirely of vowel sounds, for example, *Aiaiē* and *Euios*.[24] These words are no harsher than others; indeed they are perhaps more musical.

70. Poetic forms such as *ēelios* (sun) and *oreōn* (of mountains) with their deliberate lengthening of the words and the resulting clash of vowels, are more euphonious than the shorter forms *hēlios* and *orōn*. The resolving of one syllable into two clashing vowels introduces an added effect not unlike singing.[25] There are many other words which, when run together by elision or contraction, are less harmonious and, when resolved with resulting hiatus, they are more euphonious. Running the sounds together is both harsher in sound and more commonplace.

71. The priests of Egypt, when singing hymns to their gods, utter the seven vowels[26] in succession and men listen to the singing sound of these vowels instead of to the flute or the lyre, because it is so euphonious. It follows that to remove the hiatus is to deprive language of its song and its music. But this is perhaps not the time to pursue the subject further.

72. The grand style favors the clash of long vowels. This is obvious in Homer's *lāan anō ōtheske* (he pushed the stone uphill).[27] The line acquires length through the juxtaposition of long vowels; it imitates the violent straining of the stone uphill. The same is true in the phrase of Thucydides *to mē ēpeiros einai* (not being the mainland),[28] and you will find clashing diphthongs in that sentence of his which describes the founding of Epidamnus by the Corcyraeans.[29]

73. As the clash of the same long vowels or diphthongs makes for impressiveness, the clash of different sounds may have the same result, and it provides variety as well—as in *ēōs* (dawn) or *hoiēn* (such). Not only are the sounds different, but the breathings also, one being rough and the other smooth, so that there is much variety.

74. In songs too there can be musical variations on the same long vowel, like song upon song, so that the clash of similar vowels can be regarded as part of a song or a musical variation. This is enough about the clash of vowels and about the impressive kind of word-arrangement.

IMPRESSIVE SUBJECT MATTER

75. The grandeur may lie also in the subject matter—a great and notable battle on land or sea, or when there is talk of the heavens, or of the earth. When one hears a person discoursing on an impressive subject one is at once apt to think his style impressive even when it is not. One should consider the manner of his discourse, rather than the matter, for an important subject may be dealt with in a trifling and quite unsuitable manner. Some authors, like Theopompus, are considered forceful when in fact it is their subject, not their style, that is forceful.

76. Nicias, the painter, used to say that to choose a great subject is in itself no small part of the painter's art and that he should not fritter away his talent on trifling themes like birds or flowers. Rather he should choose cavalry charges or naval battles as his subjects, where he could introduce many horses galloping, rearing or crouching, many bowmen shooting, many riders falling from their chargers. Nicias considered the choice of theme to be itself a part of the art of painting just as it is of the poet's art. We should therefore not be surprised if, even in prose, great subjects have their own impressiveness.

IMPRESSIVE DICTION

77. The grand style requires the diction to be distinguished, out of the ordinary, unusual. It will then have weight, whereas current and customary language makes for clarity, but it is also commonplace.

METAPHORS

78. In the first place, we should use metaphors. They contribute more than anything else to delight and impressiveness of style. They should not be too numerous, however, or our prose will turn into dithyramb, nor too far-fetched, but arise spontaneously from a true likeness in things. For example, a general, a pilot, and a charioteer all rule over something; one can therefore safely call the general the pilot of his city, or again the pilot the ruler of his ship.

79. Not all metaphors, however, are interchangeable like those just mentioned. The poet (Homer) could call the lower slopes of Ida its foot, but he could not call a man's foot his slope.[30]

80. Whenever a metaphor seems too bold, we can change it into a simile, which is safer. A simile is an extended metaphor, as when instead of: "then the orator Python, rushing upon us, a torrent of words"[31] you add to it and say: "then *like a* torrent of words, the orator Python. . . ." Now you have a simile which is a safer method of expression, while the first is a metaphor which is more chancy. Plato is thought to take more chances because he uses metaphors more freely than similes, while Xenophon makes greater use of similes.

81. Aristotle thought that the best type of metaphor is the so-called active metaphor,[32] by which inanimate things are represented as acting like living things, as in Homer's reference to the arrow as "sharp-pointed, eager to fly into the throng," and to the waves as "high-arched, foam-crested," for these epithets imply the actions of living creatures.

82. Some things are expressed more clearly and properly by a metaphor than by the proper terms themselves, as, for example: "the battle shivered." The meaning could not be more truly or lucidly expressed by changing the phrase and using the proper terms. The confused motion of spears and their continuous subdued sound are rendered by "the shivering battle."[33] At the same time the poet is using the active type of metaphor just described, for he says that the battle shivers like a living creature.

83. We should not forget, however, that the effect of certain metaphors is paltry rather than impressive, even though the metaphor is intended to achieve grandeur, as when Homer says that "the wide sky trumpeted about them."[34] A noise ringing through the high heavens should not be compared to the sound of a trumpet, unless indeed one were to defend Homer by saying that the high heavens resounded as if the whole sky were trumpeting.

84. Let us then consider this other kind of metaphor which makes for triviality instead of grandeur. Metaphors should be transferred from the greater

to the smaller and not *vice versa.* Xenophon says, for example: "On the march a part of the line surged out"[35] and compares the disorder in the line to the surge of the sea. But if one were to reverse this and say that the sea swerved, the metaphor would be inappropriate and certainly trivial.

85. When they consider metaphors too bold, some writers try to make them more acceptable by adding an epithet, as Theognis speaks of the bow of an archer in the act of shooting as "a tuneless lyre."[36] To call a bow a lyre is a bold metaphor, and it is softened by the adjective "tuneless."

86. Common usage is a good teacher in all things, but especially in the use of metaphor. We do not notice that it expresses almost everything by metaphors because they are inoffensive, like "a clear voice," "a sharp man," "a rough character," "a lengthy speaker," and so on. These metaphors are so appropriate that they seem like proper terms.

87. I make the art—or is it the naturalness?—of common usage the criterion of a good metaphor in prose. For usage has produced some metaphors so successfully that we no longer need the proper term and the metaphor has usurped its place, as in "the eye of the vine"[37] and other such expressions.

88. Certain parts of the body[38] derive their names not from a metaphorical usage but from their physical resemblance to other objects.

89. When we turn a metaphor into a simile, as mentioned above, we should aim at brevity, and add only the word "like" (*hōsper*) before it. Otherwise it will not be a simile but a poetic comparison. When Xenophon says: "As a noble hound leaps at a boar without caution," or again: "Like a horse let loose, kicking and prancing in a meadow"[39] he is no longer using similes but poetic comparisons.

90. Such poetic comparisons should not be freely used in prose, but with the greatest caution. And this is a sufficient outline on the subject of metaphors.

COMPOUND WORDS

91. We should also use compound words but we should avoid dithyrambic formations such as "the heaven-portented wanderings" and "the fiery-lanced host of stars." Our compounds should be like those which are formed by usage, for in usage I see the universal criterion of good diction. It forms without challenge such words as lawgiver,[40] and the like.

92. A compound word, because of its composite nature, will also provide a certain ornamental variety and dignity, as well as brevity. One word will take the place of a whole phrase, "corn-supply,"[41] for example, instead of "the supplying of corn," and this is much more impressive. Sometimes, however, this greater effect is better obtained by resolving one word into a phrase, for example, by saying "the supply of corn" instead of "the corn-supply."

93. A word replaces a whole phrase, for example, when Xenophon says: "it was impossible to catch a wild ass unless the hunters took up positions at intervals and hunted in relays."[42] By the word "relays" he means that some riders pursued the animal from behind, while others met it head on so that the wild ass was caught between them.

We should be careful not to combine words already compound. Such double combinations are not suitable in prose.

NEW WORDS

94. Newly-coined words are usually defined as words used to imitate some emotion or action like "sizzled" and "lapping."[43]

95. These words are impressive because they imitate noises, and mostly because they are strange. The poet is not using existing words, for this is their first occurrence. Making a new word is thought to be a clever thing, as if one were creating a usage of one's own. For by creating new words one seems to act in the same way as the originators of language.

96. When coining a new word we should aim at clarity and remain within the bounds of usage. The new coinage should be analogous to existing words, for one should not appear to use Scythian or Phrygian expressions when writing Greek.

97. We should make new words where no existing names are available, as when someone called the kettledrums and other instruments used in effeminate ritual "lewderies" or when Aristotle spoke of an elephant-driver as an "elephanteer."[44] Or we may make new derivatives from existing forms, as someone called a man who rows a boat a "rowman," and Aristotle spoke of a man who dwelt alone as "selfsome."

98. We read in Xenophon: "The army battle-shouted." He makes a kindred verb from the battle-shout the army was raising continually. As I said, this is a risky business, even for a poet. Any compound word, however, is a sort of coined word, for what is composite must have been built from its parts.

99. *Allēgoria* (hidden meaning) is also impressive, especially in threats such as that of Dionysius: "Their grasshoppers will sing to them from the ground."[45]

100. If he had simply said that he would ravage the country of Locris, he would have sounded angrier but more commonplace. As it is, he uses allēgoria to camouflage his meaning. What is implied is always more frightening, for different interpretations are possible. What is clear and obvious is likely to be considered commonplace, like men without their clothes.

101. That is why mystic formulae are expressed by means of allēgoria, to frighten people and make them shudder as they do in the dark and at night. Allēgoria is not unlike darkness and night.

102. A succession of such veiled expressions should, however, be avoided, for then we would be writing riddles like that of the doctor's cupping-glass, "I saw a man who had welded bronze upon another man."[46] The Spartans too used many veiled threats, as when they said to Philip: "Dionysius [is] in Corinth,"[47] and on many other occasions.

103. Sometimes it is impressive to express a thought briefly, and most impressive not to express it at all, for there are things which increase in importance by not being spoken but implied.[48]

At other times, however, to be brief is to be trivial, and grandeur is found in repetition, as when Xenophon says: "The chariots drove on; some drove through the lines of their friends, others through the lines of their foes,"[49] which is much more impressive than if he had said: "The chariots drove on through the lines of friend and foe."

104. An oblique construction is frequently more impressive than a straightforward one: "The decision was of charging the Greek lines and breaking through them,"[50] instead of "They decided to charge and break through."

105. Words similar in sound and an apparent lack of euphony may also contribute to impressiveness. For what is not euphonious often gives an impression of weight. In the line which describes the attack of Ajax upon Hector[51], the combination of these two factors makes us realize the greatness of Ajax better than his shield of seven layers of ox-hide.

106. The so-called *epiphōnēma* might be described as an added ornamentation. It is most impressive in prose. One part of a passage serves to express the thought, the other part is added to embellish it. In the following lines of Sappho the thought is expressed in these words: "The mountain-hyacinths are trodden down/By shepherds' boots" and then comes the epiphōnēma: "and on the ground/The purple blooms lie bleeding." This has obviously been added to what precedes, as a beautiful ornament.

107. Homer's poetry is full of these ornamental additions. For example:

> I've put the arms away, out of the smoke.
> They are already quite unlike the armor
> Odysseus left when he set out for Troy.
> And I bethought me of a graver matter:
> I feared that, flushed with wine and prone to quarrel,
> You wound each other.

Then comes the added phrase: "Steel makes men reckless."[52]

108. Altogether, the epiphōnēma may be compared to those external displays of riches: cornices, triglyphs, and broad purples.[53] The epiphōnēma too is a sign of riches, verbal riches.

109. The enthymeme might be thought to be a kind of epiphōnēma, but it is not. It is added in order to prove something, not to embellish. However it may be added at the end, like the epiphōnēma.

110. The maxim too is an addition like the epiphōnēma, but it is not an

epiphōnēma. It often stands at the beginning, although at times it fills the place of an epiphōnēma.

111. A line like: "Fool! He was not to escape his evil doom"[54] is not an epiphōnēma either. It does not come at the end and it does not beautify. Indeed, it is quite unlike an epiphōnēma and more like a form of address or a rebuke.

112. Even a blind man can see, as the saying is, that poetic language gives a certain grandeur to prose, except that some writers imitate the poets quite openly, or rather they do not so much imitate them as transpose their words into their own work, as Herodotus does.

113. When Thucydides, on the other hand, takes over some expression from a poet, he uses it in his own way and makes it his own. The poet said of Crete, for example, "Crete lies in the midst of the wine-dark sea,/A land comely and fertile, ocean-bound."[55] Homer uses the word "ocean-bound" with impressive effect. Thucydides considers it a fine thing for the Sicilians to have a common policy, since they are the denizens of one land, and that ocean-bound. He uses all the same words as the poet; he says land instead of island but calls it ocean-bound in the same way. Yet one feels that he is not saying what Homer said. The reason is that he uses the word not in order to impress but to underline the need for a common policy.

So much for the grand manner.

FRIGIDITY

114. Every attractive quality has as its neighbor a specific weakness: rashness is close to bravery, and shame is close to respect; similarly, successful styles have certain faulty styles lurking nearby.

We shall deal first with the fault which borders on the grand style. We call it frigidity, and Theophrastus defined the frigid as that which overshoots its appropriate expression. For example, to say "Unbaséd goblets cannot tabled be" instead of "goblets without a base cannot be put on a table" is frigid because the trivial subject cannot carry such weighty words.

115. Frigidity, like grandeur, arises in three ways: it may be in the thought, as when a certain writer said in describing the Cyclops hurling a rock at the ship of Odysseus: "As the rock hurtled through the air, goats were grazing upon it." This is frigid because the thought is exaggerated and impossible.

116. There are, according to Aristotle, four sources of frigidity of diction. [It is due to the use of unnecessary epithets][56] as in Alcidamas' "damp sweat," or to a compound where the nature of the double word is dithyrambic, like "lone-journeyed" or some such overelaborate word; or it may be due to a metaphor such as "pallid and tremulous troubles." These then are the four kinds of frigidity of diction.

117. The arrangement of words is frigid when the rhythm is poor, as when, in a phrase, all the syllables are long.[57] This deserves censure, for it is not like prose.

118. On the other hand, a succession of metrical phrases is equally frigid. Some writers write like that, but the meters are obvious because they follow one another. Verse is out of place in prose, and therefore frigid, as is everything which is too metrical.

119. Generally speaking, pretence and frigidity are alike. The writer who deals with a trivial subject in weighty language is like a man who pretends to qualities he does not possess, undeterred by his lack of them, or like a man who boasts about trifles. To discuss trivialities in an exalted style is, as the saying is, like beautifying a pestle.

120. Yet some people say we should discourse in the grand manner on trivialities and they think that this is a proof of outstanding oratorical talent. Now I admit that Polycrates, the rhetorician, eulogized [Thersites][58] as if he were Agamemnon and in so doing used antitheses, metaphors, and every device used in encomia. But he was doing this in jest, not writing a serious eulogy, and the dignified tone of the whole work was itself a game. Let us be playful by all means, but we must also observe what is fitting in each case: that is, we must write in the appropriate manner, lightly when our subject is slight, impressively when it is impressive.

121. Xenophon says of the small, pretty river Teleboas: "This river was not large, it was pretty though."[59] The short sentence, and its ending with "though" makes us almost see the little river. But when another writer says of a similar stream "from its source in the mountains of Laurium it flows into the sea,"[60] one would think he was describing the cataracts of the Nile or the Danube pouring into the sea. All such writing is called frigid.

122. Small matters can be magnified in another way without inappropriateness, and sometimes this has to be done. We may, for example, want to exalt a general after a slight military success, or the punishment inflicted by the Spartan ephor[61] who had a man whipped for playing ball earnestly and in an un-Spartan way. One is at once struck by the trifling nature of the offence, but we can dramatize its importance by saying that to ignore the formation of bad habits in small things is to open the door to more serious crimes, and that, therefore, it is the lesser, not the graver, infractions of the law that must be punished more severely. We shall then bring in the proverb about "work begun is work half-done"[62] as applying to these trivial offences, or indeed as showing that no offence is trivial.

123. A trivial success may thus be greatly magnified without doing anything inappropriate. Just as it is often useful to minimize what is important, so the unimportant may be magnified.

124. The most frigid of all devices is the hyperbole. It is of three kinds; one thing is said to be like another, as in "they run like the wind"; or one thing

may be made superior to another, for example, "whiter than snow"[63]; or, thirdly, what is said is impossible: "her head reached unto heaven."

125. Every hyperbole is really impossible.[64] Nothing is whiter than snow, no horse can run like the wind, but the type mentioned just now is especially called so. It is precisely because every hyperbole states an impossibility that every hyperbole is thought to be frigid.

126. Hence comic poets use hyperbole very freely, and they make the impossibility a source of laughter, as when someone said hyperbolically, in connection with the insatiability of the Persians: "their excrements covered the plains," and again "they carry oxen between their jaws."[65]

127. Of the same type are the well-known "balder than a cloudless sky" and "healthier than a pumpkin." As for Sappho's phrase "more golden than gold," although it is expressed as a hyperbole and is indeed an impossibility, it is the more charming because impossible. Indeed it is a most admirable feature of the divine Sappho's art, that she extracts great charm from devices which are in themselves questionable and difficult.

So much for frigidity and hyperbole, and we now turn to the elegant style.

HORACE

(65–8 B.C.)

INTRODUCTION

In form the *Ars Poetica* of Horace is a letter of advice to young acquaintances who are contemplating a career as poets. It thus has a more informal tone than most other works of literary criticism, but it also represents an extremely serious statement of a major poet's aesthetic theory. Scholars have observed underneath the relaxed surface of the poem a firm structure that is modeled on the traditional Hellenistic form for a treatise on literary criticism. This structure requires a discussion of *poiesis* or poetic subject matter, *poema* or poetic form, and *poeta* or the nature of the poet himself. As we shall see, each one of these themes is treated by Horace.

Scholars have identified Neoptolemus of Parium as the Hellenistic critic who, in a work now lost to us, exerted the major positive influence on Horace. Another important Hellenistic critic, Philodemus, is known to have been Horace's teacher for a time, but there are major differences between Horace's critical principles and those of his teacher.

Horace is not a critic in the mold of a Plato or an Aristotle intent on searching out the essential nature of art and its relationship to all other human activities. He is, rather, a practical poet-critic concerned with finding ways of improving the artistic efforts of his contemporaries. His most basic norm is one of "sensibility"—a disciplined and civilized, yet flexible, "taste." Although Horace's methodology is far removed from Aristotle's kind of rigorous theoretical analysis, the *Ars Poetica* does contain judgments of universal value which have been highly influential in the subsequent history of literary criticism. Especially noteworthy are Horace's many admiring references to the great achievements of Greek civilization. Throughout the *Ars Poetica* examples from Greek literature are cited as models worthy of Roman imitation although Horace is, of course, aware that even great Homer nods (*bonus dormitat Homerus*).

Horace begins his study with a discussion of poetic subject matter (*poiesis*). The large concept of "appropriateness"—the idea of decorum which was to become an important principle in literary criticism—is used as the standard against which all aspects of the treatment of subject matter are judged. Horace demands that a poet choose a subject appropriate to his abilities and experience and that he include in his work only elements that make an appropriate contribution to the subject. Once the subject has been chosen the poet must then use the specific meter that is appropriate for heroic, tragic, comic, or lyric content.

One important way to achieve appropriateness in the handling of subject matter is to aim at realism, and Horace strongly recommends that if a poet or actor wants his audience to feel a strong emotion he must first experience that emotion himself. The poet must also be careful to see that the emotions expressed by a character are appropriate to his traditional status, age, and station in life. If a poet is to present traditional stories successfully, therefore, he must portray Achilles as implacable in his anger, Medea as fierce in her pursuit of vengeance, and Orestes as strongly grieved by his father's murder and the matricide it necessitates. It is in judgments such as these that Horace's norm of verisimilitude seems to replace Aristotle's concern with "probability" (*internal* coherence). The *Ars Poetica* has a strong rhetorical orientation, generally based on a sense of what the audience will accept.

This same orientation is evident in Horace's discussion of appropriate narrative technique. Here, as in so much of the *Ars Poetica,* Homer serves as the model. According to Horace, the proper way to begin a poem is exemplified in the technique of the *Odyssey*: Homer starts in a minor key and then rushes *in medias res* (into the midst of things) to the presentation of the great events of the story. This method permits the appropriate development of poetic intensity, and avoids the diminution of interest that would result from a movement from more significant to less significant action.

After a discussion of poetic subject matter (*poiesis*), Hellenistic literary criticism regularly required a treatment of poetic form (*poema*). Horace discusses several poetic forms, but gives his most detailed treatment to drama. Here, too, appropriateness is the standard against which dramatic techniques and procedures are judged. Horace's first prescription is that nothing excessively violent or monstrous can be presented on stage. In regard to the formal structure of tragedy Horace argues that appropriate practice requires that a play consist of five acts, that a *deus ex machina* not be employed unless absolutely necessary, and that the chorus should be directly involved in the action of the drama and should be a spokesman for what is morally right. These strictures are more extreme than Aristotle's, precisely because they derive from a concept of "sensibility" rather than from an aesthetic argument. Exemplifying the quality of "classical restraint," the *Ars Poetica* encourages a notion of poetry as a discipline and of the poem as a finished product. In this regard, Horace enunciates the doctrine of *ut pictura poesis*: a poem should be a kind of static beauty analogous to that of a painting.

These premises also control the third part of Horace's treatise, the consideration of the character of the poet (*poeta*). Horace discusses the sources of poetic achievement, concluding that it is necessary for the successful poet to possess both natural genius and a capacity for diligent practice. Throughout the *Ars Poetica* as a whole, however, Horace is primarily concerned with giving advice to prospective poets, and thus he tends to place more emphasis on the second quality: mastery of artistic techniques. Discussing pitfalls the poet faces, he mentions, among others, the incongruous use of purple patches (*purpureus pannus*), the tendency to become obscure when trying to be brief (*brevis esse laboro, obscurus fio*), and to forfeit punch and vitality while straining for smoothness and polish (*sectantem levia nervi deficiunt animique*). Horace also admonishes the aspiring author not to rush into print (*nonumque prematur in annum*) and encourages "imitation"—which is not the *mimesis* propounded by either Plato or Aristotle, but rather the young poet's attempt to emulate the spirit of great models.[1]

One of the most important passages in the *Ars Poetica* is Horace's discussion of the ultimate goal of poetry: *aut prodesse volunt aut delectare poetae.* Almost all modern commentators interpret this as an either/or judgment; the successful poet aims *either* at being useful (communicating philosophical or moral teachings beneficial to the audience) *or* at producing pleasure. Such a view directly conflicts with Horace's statement: *omne tulit punctum qui miscuit utile dulci, lectorem delectando pariterque monendo* (that poet carries every vote who mixes the useful with the pleasant, equally delighting and teaching the reader). For Horace the ideal poet is one who can combine both aims, and the major tradition of Western criticism has taken Horace's dictum as an inclusive judgment. An excellent example of this is Sir Philip Sidney's quasi-Aristotelian argument in his *Defence of Poesie*: "Poetry, therefore, is an art of imitation, for so Aristotle termeth it in the word *Mimesis,* that is to say, a representing, counterfeiting, or figuring forth: to speak metaphorically, a speaking picture, with this end, to teach and delight."[2]

As Sidney's comment indicates, Renaissance critics tended to use the *Ars Poetica* as a "key" to the recently-rediscovered *Poetics*.[3] Horace's sensibility matched their own, and the civilized restraint preached in the *Ars Poetica* also helped to make it the core document of neo-classical syntheses from Ben Jonson to the late Augustans. To Pope in *An Essay on Criticism* (653–60),

> Horace still charms with graceful negligence,
> And without method talks us into sense;
> Will, like a friend, familiarly convey
> The truest notions in the easiest way.
> He who supreme in judgment, as in wit,
> Might boldly censure, as he boldly writ,
> Yet judged with coolness, though he sung with fire;
> His precepts teach but what his works inspire.

Horace's sensibility was naturally at odds with that of most romantic critics, especially in their emphasis on expression, spontaneity, and genius. And the temper of most modern criticism exalts "delight," but not "utility," as the ultimate goal of poetry. To modern humanists, however, the *Ars Poetica* has retained much of its original viability. In the writings of Matthew Arnold, Irving Babbitt, and T. S. Eliot, Horace is frequently echoed; and his sensibility is re-embodied.

The translation which follows is by Norman DeWitt. It appeared first in *Drama Survey,* October, 1961 and is reprinted here with the permission of Mrs. Lois DeWitt and Professor John D. Hurrell, the former editor of *Drama Survey.*

The numbers inserted in the translation give the approximate location of every tenth line in the Latin text.

ARS POETICA

Suppose a painter meant to attach a horse's neck to the head of a man, and to put fancy-work of many-colored feathers on limbs of creatures picked at random; the kind of thing where the torso of a shapely maiden merges into the dark rear half of a fish; would you smother your amusement, my friends, if you were let in to see the result?

Believe me, Pisones,[1] a book will be very much like that painting if the meaningless images are put together like the dreams of a man in a fever, to the end that the head and the foot do not match the one body.

"Poets and painters have always enjoyed this fair privilege, of experimenting however they will."

I know it; and I claim that privilege as a poet and, as a poet, I grant it to the painter; but not to the extent that vicious creatures mate with gentle ones, that snakes are paired with birds, lambs with tigers.

When a poem has a pretentious introduction, promising great themes, a bright red patch or two is usually stitched on, to achieve an expansive, colorful effect, as when a sacred grove and an altar of Diana are described, or a hurrying rivulet of water wandering through the lovely meadows, or the river Rhine, or a rainbow. All very well; but there was no place for these scenes at this point in the poem.

And perhaps you know how to represent a cypress tree: what good is this when the client who has paid your fee in advance is swimming for his life in the picture from the wreckage of his ship?[2] I have started to mould a two-handled jar to hold wine: why does a pitcher come off the potter's turning wheel? What I am getting at is this: let the work of art be whatever you want, as long as it is simple and has unity.

To you, Piso senior, and to you sons worthy of your father, I admit that the majority of us poets are tricked by our own standards. I work hard to be brief; I turn out to be obscure. When I try to achieve smoothness and polish, I lose punch, the work lacks life; the poet who proposes grandeur is merely pompous; the poet who tries to be too conservative creeps on the ground, afraid of gusts of wind; if he is anxious to lend marvellous variety to a single subject, he paints a dolphin in the forest, a boar in the breakers. The avoidance of mistakes leads to serious defects if one is lacking in artistic sense. The sculptor in the last studio around the [gladiatorial] school of Aemilius will mould fingernails and imitate wavy hair in bronze, but the net effect of the work will be unfortunate because he will not know how to represent the whole. If I wanted to make a comparison, I would not care to be like him any more than to go through life with an ugly nose but good-looking otherwise, with dark eyes and dark hair.

If you plan to write, adopt material to match your talents, and think over carefully what burdens your shoulders will not carry and how strong they really are. When a writer's chosen material matches his powers, the flow of words will not fail nor will clarity and orderly arrangement. This is the virtue and charm of such arrangement, unless I am mistaken: that one says now what ought to be said and puts off for later and leaves out a great deal for the present. The author of a poem that has been [asked for and] promised likes one thing and rejects another, is sensitive and careful in putting words together.

Again, you will have expressed yourself with distinction if a clever association gives an old word new meaning. If it turns out to be necessary to explain recent discoveries with new terms, you will be allowed to invent words never heard by the Cethegi[3] in their loin-cloths; and license will be given if you exercise it with due restraint; and new words, recently invented, will win acceptance if they spring from a Greek source with a minor twist in meaning. For that matter, what will a Roman grant to Caecilius and Plautus that he takes away from Vergil and Varius? As for me, why should I be criticized if I add a few words to my vocabulary, when the language of Cato and Ennius enriched the speech of our fathers and produced new names for things? It has always been permissible, and always will be, to mint words stamped with the mark of contemporary coinage.

As the forests change their foliage in the headlong flight of years, as the first leaves fall, so does the old crop of words pass away, and the newly born, like men in the bloom of their youth, come then to the prime of their vigor. We and our works are mortgaged to die. It may be that the land embraces Neptune and diverts the north wind from our navy, the engineering of a king;[4] or a swamp, long unproductive, and good only for boating, now feeds nearby towns and feels the heavy burden of the plow;[5] or it may be that a river, a ravager of fruitful fields, has changed its course, has been taught to follow a better channel:[6] no matter, human accomplishments will pass away, much less does the status of speech endure and popular favor persist. Many things are resurrected which once had passed away, and expressions which are now respected in turn will pass, if usage so decrees—the usage over which the authority and norm of daily speech have final jurisdiction.

The careers of kings and leaders, and sorrow-bringing battles: the meter[7] in which to compose these, Homer has shown us. Laments were first expressed in couplets of unequal lines;[8] later, sentiments of vows fulfilled were included [in this verse] as well. However, what author first published dainty elegiacs, the philologists are arguing, and up to now the dispute rests unresolved. A nasty temper armed Archilochus with his specialty, iambic lines;[9] the sock [10] of comedy and the elevated boot[11] of tragedy took on this meter, just the thing for on-stage conversation, to rise above the noisy audience and quite natural for relations of events. The Muse gave men of wealth and sons of gods, and the victor in the boxing ring and the horse first in the contest, and the heartaches of youth and relaxing wine, to lyric poetry to sing about.

The standard distinctions and overtones of poetic forms: why should I be addressed as a poet if I cannot observe and know nothing about them? Why should I, with a feeble sense of shame, prefer to be ignorant rather than learn them? A comic situation does not want to be treated in tragic verse forms; in the same way, the banquet of Thyestes repudiates a telling in the lines of every-day affairs, close to the level of comedy.

Let each form of poetry occupy the proper place allotted to it.

There are times, however, when comedy raises its voice and an angry Chremes scolds in fury with his swollen cheeks; and, in tragedy, Telephus and Peleus[12] very often express their pain in prose, when the penniless hero and the exile both project inflated lines and complicated compound words, if they are anxious to touch the hearts of the audience with their complaints of deep distress.

It is not enough for poems to be pretty; they must have charm and they must take the heart of the hearer wheresoever they will. Just as the faces of men smile back at those who smile at them, so they join with those who weep. If you want me to weep, you must first feel sorrows yourself; then your misfortunes, Telephus or Peleus, hurt me, too. If you speak your lines badly, I'll go to sleep—or laugh out loud. Sad words fit a mournful face, words full of threats an angry face, playful words a face in fun, words seriously expressed, a sober face. I mean that Nature has already shaped us inwardly for every phase of fortune: fortune makes us happy, or drives us into anger or brings us down to earth with a burden of grief and then torments us. Afterwards it brings out our emotions and our tongue acts as interpreter. If the lines do not correspond to the emotional state of the speaker, the members of the Roman audience will burst out laughing, regardless of their income bracket.

It will make a great deal of difference whether a comedy slave or a tragic hero is speaking, or a man of ripe old age, or a hothead in the flower of youth, or a great lady, or a worrying nursemaid, or a traveling merchant or the farmer of a few flourishing acres, a character from Colchis or an Assyrian, a native of Thebes or of Argos.

You have two choices: either follow the conventions of the stage or invent materials that are self-consistent.

If, as a writer, you happen to bring back on the stage an Achilles whose honor has been satisfied, energetic, hotheaded, ruthless, eager, let him claim that laws were not made for him, that there is nothing not subject to possession by force. Let Medea be wild and untamed, Ino an object of pity and tears, Ixion treacherous, Io a wanderer, Orestes depressed.

If you risk anything new and original on the stage and have the courage to invent a new character, let it maintain to the very end the qualities with which it first appeared—and let it be self-consistent.

It is difficult to develop everyday themes in an original way, and you would do better to present the *Iliad* in dramatic form than if you were the first to produce unknown materials never used before on stage. Material in the public domain will become your private property if you do not waste your time going around in worn-out circles, and do not be a literal translator, faithfully rendering word for word from Greek, and do not be merely an imitator, thereby getting yourself into a hole from which either good conscience, or the laws of the work itself, will forbid you to climb out.

And do not start off like this, the way a cyclic[13] poet once did: "I shall sing of the fate of Priam and a war of renown." What did this promise produce to match such a wide open mouth? The mountains will go into labor and deliver a silly mouse! How much more properly this poet began who undertook nothing in poor taste: "Sing to me, Muse, of the man who, after the time of the capture of Troy, saw the ways of numbers of men and their cities."[14] He gives thought to producing a light from the smoke, not smoke from the gleam of the firelight, so that he may bring forth beauty thereafter, and wonder, Antiphates and Scylla and with the Cyclops, Charybdis; nor does he in detail relate the return of Diomedes after the passing of Meleager, or the story of the Trojan War, starting with the twin eggs.[15] He speeds always on to the outcome, and rushes his hearer into the midst of the action just as if the setting were known, and the events that he cannot hope to treat with brilliance, he omits. And then, too, his inventions are such that fiction is mingled with fact to the end that the middle may match with the start and the end with the middle.

Listen to me: here is what I look for in a play, and with me, the public.

If you want a fan in the audience who waits for the final curtain and stays in his seat to the very end, when the singer says, "Give us a hand," you must observe the habits and manners of each period in men's lives, and the proper treatment must be given to their quickly changing characters and their years. The little boy who already knows how to talk plants his feet firmly on the ground, and is eager to play with boys of his own age, and loses his temper and for no good reason gets it back, and changes his disposition every hour.

The adolescent boy with no beard as yet, when [to his relief] he at last is on his own, has fun with hounds and horses and the turf of the sunny Campus,[16] soft as wax to be moulded to folly, resentful of advice, slow to anticipate what is good for him, throwing his money around, high-spirited and eager, quick to change his interests.

The age of maturity brings a change of interests, and the manly character seeks influence and friends, becomes a slave to ambition and is wary of commitments that he will soon have to break off with great difficulty.

Many disagreeable circumstances surround the old man; for example, he still seeks for wealth and, poor fellow, shrinks from spending it. or, again, his management of everything is over-cautious and without any fire, he is indecisive, hopeful without reason, slow to act, grasping for time, hard to get along with, always complaining, always praising the way things were when he was a boy, scolding and correcting the young generation. The years as they come bring with them many advantages, and as they go, take many things away.

Do not by any chance let the character of the elderly be assigned to a younger man, or a man to a boy; we shall always insist upon the qualities of character joined and fitted to the proper age of man.

An event is either acted on the stage or is reported as happening elsewhere. Events arouse our thoughts more slowly when transmitted through the ears than when presented to the accuracy of the eye and reported to the spectator by himself. On the other hand, do not bring out on stage actions that should properly take place inside, and remove from view the many events which the descriptive powers of an actor present on the stage will soon relate. Do not have Medea butcher her sons before the audience, or have the ghoulish Atreus cook up human organs out in public, or Procne turn into a bird, Cadmus into a snake. If you show me anything of this kind, I will not be fooled and I shall resent it.

Do not let a play consist of less than five acts or be dragged out to more than this length, if you want it to enjoy popular demand and have a repeat performance.

Do not have a god intervene unless the complication of the plot turns out to be appropriate to divine solution; and do not have a fourth leading character working hard to get in with his lines.

Have the chorus carry the part of an actor and take a manly role in the play, and do not let them sing anything between the acts which does not contribute to the plot and fit properly into it. The chorus should side with the good and give friendly advice, curb those who are angry and befriend those who fear to do wrong; the chorus should praise a dinner which has but few courses, healthy legal processes and law, and the conditions of peace when the gates of the city stand open; the chorus will keep secrets, entreat the gods and pray that good fortune will come back to the afflicted and desert the over-confident.

The pipes (not, as now, displaced by the brass and their rival the trumpet, but slender in tone and simple, with only a few stops) used to be helpful in accompanying and supporting the chorus and in filling the auditorium (which was not, in those days, overcrowded) with its music—the audience in which the entire community gathered was then such as one could count, what with its small size; it was thrifty, moral and proper.

After the community began to win wars and extend its domain, and the walls of the city enclosed a wider area, and one's guardian spirit was appeased on holidays without reproach with wine in the daytime, greater license in meters and modes came to the theater. This is to say: what critical sense could an ignorant community have when freed from work, the farmer mingling with the townsman, the commoner with the gentleman? And so the flute player added movement and display to the old-fashioned art and trailed his costume about on the platform. And so, again, they invented special notes for the once sober lyre, and the unrestrained speech of the chorus gave rise to a new kind of eloquence, wise in advice on matters of state, and its divine utterances of things to come were quite in the oracular manner of Delphic ambiguities.

The writer who entered the contest for a common goat[17] in tragic verse soon added rustic satyrs with scanty clothing, and crudely tried his hand at humor without loss of tragic dignity, for the reason that the member of the audience had to be kept in his seat by the enticements of novelties, because after taking part in the Bacchic rituals, he was drunk and rowdy. But it is expedient, nonetheless, to sanction the merry, impudent satyrs, to turn solemnity into jest, so that whatever god, whatever hero, may have been but now presented on the stage in gold and royal purple, shall not move into the slums, use vulgar speech, or, while avoiding the ground, grasp at verbal clouds and empty words.

Tragedy is above spouting frivolous lines, like a modest matron told to dance on festive days; she [tragedy] will have little to do, as a respectable woman, with the boisterous satyrs.

As a writer of satyr-plays,[18] my Pisones, I for one will not favor the commonplace and current nouns and verbs, and I shall not try to differ in vocabulary, from the speech that gives tragedy its color; it will make a difference whether Davus is speaking and the saucy Pythias who has swindled a talent out of Simo,[19] or Silenus, the guardian and attendant of a divine foster child.

I shall follow a poetic style from well-known material, just the same as anyone may expect to do himself; and just the same, if he tries it, he will perspire freely and make little progress: that's how difficult the order and connections of words are: that's how much distinction is attached to our everyday vocabulary.

Fauns imported from the woodlands, in my opinion, should be careful not to carouse around in polished lines, like boys reared at the four corners and practically brought up in the Forum, nor shout out dirty words, make scandalous remarks. I mean, they will offend members of the audience who have a house, a distinguished father, and wealth, who will not accept calmly and give the prize to entertainment that pleases the purchaser of dried peas and nuts.

A long syllable following a short is called "iambic," a rapid foot; for this reason, it had the name "three-measure iambic" [trimeter] applied to itself although the beat, the same from first to last, adds up to six per line. Not so very long ago, so that the line might come to the ear more slowly and with a little more weight, the iambic shared its traditional privileges with the steady spondee, accommodating and tolerant, with the reservation that the iambic foot would not, as a partner, move out of its first and fourth position. The spondee, I may add, rarely appears in Accius' "noble"[20] trimeters; and it burdens Ennius' verses, sent ponderously out on the stage, with the charge of overhasty work and the lack of care and attention, or shameful neglect of the principles of art.

No critic whom you may name in Rome can see that a poem is unmusical; and Roman poets have been given unwarranted freedom. Because of that, am I to wander around and write free verse? Or am I to assume that everyone will see my mistakes and play it safe and stay cautiously within the limits of the license I may be granted? No; what I have been saying simply amounts to this: I have merely managed to escape criticism; I have not earned praise.

You—turn our Greek models in your hands at night, turn them in the daytime. But, you say, your forefathers praised the lives and jokes of Plautus; they were much too tolerant of both; they admired him, if I may say so, stupidly, assuming that you and I know how to tell the difference between expressions in poor and good taste, and have had enough experience to tell, on our fingers and by ear, when a sound has been produced according to the rules of meter.

Thespis is said to have discovered the form of tragic poetry and to have hauled his plays around on carts: plays sung and acted by those who had smeared their faces with sediment from wine jars.

After Thespis: the discoverer of the mask and colorful costume, Aeschylus, also constructed the stage on a limited scale, and taught how to speak in lofty style and to walk in the high boots of tragedy.

After these came old comedy, not without considerable popular approval; but its freedom of speech fell off into license and a violence that deserved restraint by law: law was acknowledged and the chorus was disgraced into silence when its right to libel was removed.

Our Roman poets have not failed to try all forms of drama; they deserve no honor whatsoever for venturing to desert the trail blazed by the Greeks and attempting to give fame to Roman events—those who presented serious history or comedies of daily life. Nor would the land of the Latins be more mighty in valor and glory in war than in words, if the toil of time and polish did not discourage our poets, every one of them. As for you, who represent the bloodline of Pompilius, see that you are severe in your censure of a poem that many a day and many an erasure has not trimmed down, and not corrected ten times by the test of a newly-cut fingernail.

Because Democritus believed natural talent to contribute more to success than pitiful technical competence, he barred from Helicon all poets who were mentally well-balanced; most poets do not bother to trim their nails, their beards, they look for out-of-the-way places, steer clear of the baths. I mean, one will acquire the title of poet and the reputation, if he never entrusts his head—too crazy to be cured by medicine even from three Anticyras[21]—to Licinus the barber.

Oh, how inept I am! I have myself purged of bile as the spring season comes on! Otherwise no man could write a better poem. But it isn't worth the trouble. I'll play the role of whetstone, which is good enough to put an edge on iron but is out of luck when it comes to cutting. While I write nothing myself, I'll teach the gift, the business of the poet, where he gets his material, what nourishes and forms the poet, what is appropriate, the way of right and wrong.

The origin and source of poetry is the wisdom to write according to moral principles: the Socratic dialogues will be able to clarify your philosophy, and the words themselves will freely follow the philosophy, once it has been seen before you write. The man who has learned what he owes to his country, what he owes to his friends, what love is due a father, how a brother and a family friend are loved, what the duties of a senator are, what the duties of a judge, what roles a leader sent to war should play: he knows, as a matter of course, how to assign to each character what is appropriate for it.

I shall tell you to respect the examples of life and of good character—you who have learned the art of imitation—and from this source bring forth lines that live. Quite often a play which is impressive in spots and portrays good character, but with no particular charm, without real content and really good writing, will give the public more pleasure and hold them better than lines without ideas and with resounding platitudes.

To the Greeks, genius, the gift of speaking in well-rounded phrases—these the Muse presented. The Greeks are greedy for nothing save acclaim. The Roman boys learn to calculate percentages of money by long division. "Let the son of Albinus tell me: if one-twelfth is taken from five-twelfths, what's the remainder? You should have been able to tell us by this time." "*One-third.*" "*Très bien*! You'll make a good businessman. Add a twelfth, what happens?" "One-half." When this smut, this worrying about business arithmetic, has permeated our minds, do you think we can expect to put together poems to be treated with oil of cedar and kept in cypress-wood cases?

Poets aim either to help or to amuse the reader, or to say what is pleasant and at the same time what is suitable. Whatever you have in the way of a lesson, make it short, so that impressionable minds can quickly grasp your words and hold them faithfully: every unnecessary word spills over and is lost to a heart that is already filled up to the brim.

Whatever you invent to please, see that it is close to truth, so your play does not require belief in anything it wants; do not have it pull a living child from Lamia's[22] insides just after she has eaten lunch.

The centuries[23] of elders in the audience cannot stand a play that has no moral; the noble young gentlemen ignore an austere composition; but the writer who has combined the pleasant with the useful [*miscuit utile dulci*] wins on all points, by delighting the reader while he gives advice. This kind of book makes money for the Sosii;[24] this kind of book is sold across the sea and prolongs the famous writer's age.

There are, however, faults which I should like to overlook: I mean that the string, when plucked, does not give forth the sound that heart and hand desire; it very often gives back a high note when one calls for a low; and the arrow does not always hit precisely the mark at which it aimed and threatened. So, when most of the passages are brilliant, I am personally not bothered by blots, which are spattered here and there by oversight or those which human nature failed to guard against enough.

Well, what's the point?

If a library copyist keeps on making the same mistake, even though he has been warned about it, there is no excuse for him, and a lyre player who always strikes the same sour note is laughed at; so a writer who is consistently sloppy is in a class with Choerilus—you know who I mean—whom I regard with amused admiration if he happens to write two or three good passages. Similarly, I think it's too bad whenever good old Homer dozes off, as he does from time to time, but when all is said and done, it is natural enough for drowsiness to creep up on a long job of writing. A poem is like a painting: you will find a picture which will attract you more if you stand up close, another if you stand farther back. This picture favors shadow, another likes to be viewed in the light—neither has apprehensions about the keen perceptions of the good critic. Here's one that pleases you only once; here's another that you'll like if you come back to it ten times.

And now to address the older of the two of you: ah, even though your tastes have been formed to appreciate the right things by your father (as well as by others), and you have much good sense of your own, acknowledge what I am going to say and remember it: perfectly proper concessions are made to second-raters in certain fields. A second-rate legal authority and member of the bar can be far from having the qualities of Messala, a very able speaker, and not be as learned as Casellius Aulus, but still he has a certain value—*a second-rate poet gets no advertising posters from either men, gods, or booksellers.*

You know how music off-key grates on your nerves at an otherwise pleasant banquet, and greasy ointment for your hair, and bitter honey from Sardinia mixed with poppy seeds, because the banquet could be carried on without them. That is how it is with poetry: created and developed to give joy to human hearts; but if it takes one step down from the very highest point of merit, it slides all the way back to the bottom.

The lad who does not know how to take part in sports keeps out of the cavalry exercises in the Campus; and if he has not learned how to work with the ball, the disc or the hoop—he sits where he is because he is afraid that the spectators, jammed together, will laugh at his expense—there will be nothing he can do about it. For all of that, the man who has no notion of how to compose poetry has the nerve to go ahead anyhow. Why shouldn't he? After all, he's a free man and born free and what's more to the point, his income is in the top brackets—which puts him beyond criticism.

As for you, my boy, don't do or say anything that Minerva would not approve: that's your standard of judgment, that's your philosophy. However, if you ever do write something, see that it comes into court—to the ears of Maecius as critic, or your father's, or mine, and also see that it is weighted down in storage, put away between the leaves of parchment; you can always edit what you haven't published: the word that is uttered knows no return.

Orpheus, a holy man and spokesman for the gods, forced the wild men of the woods to give up human killing and gruesome feasting; he is said, because of these powers, to soothe tigers and the raging of the lion; yes, and Amphion, the builder of the city of Thebes, is said to move rocks with his lyre and with the softness of song to lead them where he will.

I will tell you what was once the poet's wisdom: to decide what were public and what were private suits at law, to say what was sacred and what was not, to enjoin from sexual license, provide a code of conduct for marriage, to build up towns, and carve the laws on wooden tablets. This was the way honor and renown came to god-like poet-preachers and their songs.

After these, Homer gained renown, and Tyrtaeus with his verses whetted the spirits of males for Mars and war; oracles were given in the form of poems and the way of life was shown; the favor of kings was sought in Pierian[25] strains; and dramatic festivals were invented and thus the end of a long task [of development]—in case the Muse in her lyric artistry and Apollo with his song embarrass you.

The question has been asked: is good poetry created by nature or by training?

Personally, I cannot see what good enthusiasm is or uncultivated talent without a rich vein of genius; each requires the help of the other and forms a friendly compact. The would-be poet whose passion is to reach the hoped-for goal in this race for fame, has worked hard in boyhood and endured a great deal, has sweated and shivered, abstained from women and wine; the artist who plays the pipe at the Pythian games[26] has first learned his art and lived in terror of a teacher. Nowadays it's enough to have said, "I beat out wonderful poems; the hell with the rest of the mob; it's a dirty deal for me to be left at the starting line and admit that I obviously don't know what I never learned."

Like a huckster who collects a crowd to buy his wares, the poet with his wealth in land, with wealth resting on coin put out at interest, tells yes-men to come to his readings for gain. Yes, indeed; if there is a man who can set out a really fat banquet, and co-sign notes for irresponsible paupers, and save the neck of the client tangled in a murder trial, I'll be surprised if, for all his wealth, he can tell the difference between a liar and an honest friend! Whether you have already given someone a present or only expect to do so, don't let him near your verses when he's full of joy: I mean, he'll gush "Lovely! Great! Swell!" On top of this, he'll turn pale, he'll even squeeze drops of dew from sympathetic eyes, leap to his feet and stamp on the ground.

The way hired mourners wail at a funeral and—so they say—carry on more painfully than those who sorrow quite sincerely, thus the critic with his tongue in cheek is more deeply moved than the ordinary flatterer. Rich men are said to keep pushing glasses of wine at, and to torment with wine poured straight, the man whom they are trying hard to see through—to see if he is worthy of friendship. If you will put together poems, motives disguised with a foxy expression will never deceive you.

If you were to read anything to Quintilius, "Change this, please, he kept saying, "and this." If you said you couldn't do better, you'd tried twice, three times, with no success, Quintilius used to say to rub it out and put back on the anvil the lines that were spoiled on the lathe. If you preferred to defend your mistake, not revise it, he would not waste another word or go to more useless trouble to keep you from being your only friend, with no competitors.

A true critic and wise one will scold you for weak lines, blame you for rough ones, he'll indicate unpolished lines with a black crossmark made with his pen, he'll cut out pretentious embellishments, make you clarify obscure phrases, remove ambiguities, mark things to be changed, he'll turn into an Aristarchus, and he will not say, "Why should I hurt the feelings of a friend over these trifles?" Well, these trifles will get you into serious trouble once you have been laughed down and given a poor reception.

As in the case of a man with a bad attack of the itch or inflammation of the liver or one who's offended Diana—he's moon-struck—everyone with any sense is afraid to touch the madman and keeps out of the way of the poet; small boys pester him and don't know any better than to follow him around. If, while burping out his lines and thinking they're sublime, he goes off the roadway, falls into an excavation or a well, like a hunter intent on his blackbirds—he can yell so you can hear him a mile away, "Help! Hey, neighbors!"—no one would be worried about fishing him out. (460) If someone should get excited about rescuing him and let down a rope, I'll say, "How do you know that he didn't do it on purpose when he threw himself down there, and doesn't want to be rescued?" And I'll tell the story about the death of the Sicilian poet.

While he had a yearning to be regarded as an immortal god, Empedocles was cool enough to jump down into the red-hot crater of Aetna. Let poets have the right to perish; issue them a license! When you rescue a man against his will, you do the same as kill him. This isn't the first time he's done it, either; and if he's hauled out, he still won't behave like a human and give up his love of dying for publicity. And it isn't very clear, either, why he keeps on grinding out his verses, (470) whether he's used his father's funeral urn as a pisspot or whether he's tampered with the boundary markers of a holy plot of ground—an act of sacrilege. He's crazy, that's sure; and like a bear that's powerful enough to break the bars at the front of his cage, this dedicated elocutionist puts to flight the scholar and the layman without discrimination. Yes, and when he catches one, he'll hold on to him and recite him to death. You can be sure he won't let go of the hide of his victim until he's as full of blood as a leech.

DIONYSIUS OF HALICARNASSUS

(1st century B.C.)

INTRODUCTION

Other than his work, most of which has fortunately survived, we have no significant biographical data about Dionysius of Halicarnassus. His most important treatise, *On Literary Composition*, is represented in this collection by the selections that follow. The complete work consists of an introduction on the nature of literary composition, a discussion of the techniques of intensifying the effect of words, an analysis of the arrangement of clauses, an important discussion of the basis of charm and beauty of expression in words, and a conclusion devoted to the relationship between poetry and prose.

The wide range of Dionysius' interests as a critic is seen in the subject matter of his other works. In his *On Ancient Orators* an account is given of earlier rhetoricians who could serve as models for the contemporary period. *On Thucydides* is a study of the subject matter and style of the historian, while *On Dinarchus* attempts to distinguish between the orator's genuine and spurious speeches. The *First Letter to Ammaeus* shows that Demosthenes' speeches preceded Aristotle's *Rhetoric* and could not have been dependent for their technical inspiration on that work; and the *Second Letter to Ammaeus* is a study of the grammatical and linguistic characteristics of Thucydides' style. The *Letter to Gnaeus Pompeius* defends Dionysius' critical attitude toward aspects of Plato's literary style; and *On Imitation*, which exists only as a fragment, originally was a study of (1) the nature of imitation in general, (2) the choice of authors for imitation, and (3) the proper method of imitation.

As in the case of other critics of this period, Dionysius' major purpose was the establishment of high standards for rhetorical and other literature. He went back to the literature of classical Greece as a model for contemporary writers and he set down as requirements for literary achievement the possession of natural talent, the capacity for careful study, and the willingness to endure the rigors of the intensive practice of one's art.

In the selections included in this collection Dionysius indicates that the two essential qualities of good composition are charm and beauty. These two concepts are closely related but they are not identical. Thus Dionysius is able to cite works in which both qualities are present as well as those in which only one is found. He indicates that the four most important sources of charm and beauty in literary composition are (1) melody, (2) rhythm, (3) variety, and (4) appropriateness. In terms of charm these sources result in freshness, grace, euphony, sweetness, persuasivness, and similar qualities; in terms of beauty they result in grandeur, impressiveness, solemnity, dignity, mellowness, and related qualities.

According to Dionysius, the ear of the audience is delighted first by melody, second by rhythm, third by variety, and fourth by appropriateness. These effects are found in all arts where language is used, and the difference between music and oratory, according to Dionysius, is one of degree. Dionysius then shows how the very accents of Greek words produce a verbal music insofar as the Greek accent was a pitch accent involving a change of tone for the syllable being accented.

Dionysius recognizes that some sounds are naturally beautiful and others are not, and thus there is a necessity to combine these sounds in order to obtain a pleasant effect. He also indicates the need to avoid monotony in sounds, words, and metaphors and the need to use words that are melodious, rhythmical, and euphonious. Wherever possible, words that possess these qualities should be interwoven with others which lack them. According to Dionysius, the proper use of these techniques of literary composition will create both beauty and charm, the objectives of good style.

The selections included here show Dionysius' major quality as a critic: his sensitivity to the stylistic elements that contribute significantly to the emotional effect of a work of art. Any analysis of the impact of a work of art must include a study of the qualities which Dionysius discusses so well in *On Literary Composition.*

The translation used here is by W. Rhys Roberts and reprinted from Dionysius of Halicarnassus, *On Literary Composition* (London: Macmillan, 1910).

from ON LITERARY COMPOSITION

X
Aims and Methods of Good Composition

Now that I have laid down these broad outlines, the next step will be to state what should be the aims kept in view by the man who wishes to compose well, and by what methods his object can be attained. It seems to me that the two essentials to be aimed at by those who compose in verse and prose are charm and beauty. The ear craves for both of these. It is affected in somewhat the same way as the sense of sight which, when it looks upon molded figures, pictures, carvings, or any other works of human hands, and finds both charm and beauty residing in them, is satisfied and longs for nothing more. And let not anyone be surprised at my assuming that there are two distinct objects in style, and at my separating beauty from charm; nor let him think it strange if I hold that a piece of composition may possess charm but not beauty, or beauty without charm. Such is the verdict of actual experience; I am introducing no novel axiom. The styles of Thucydides and of Antiphon of Rhamnus are surely examples of beautiful composition, if ever there were any, and are beyond all possible cavil from this point of view, but they are not remarkable for their charm. On the other hand, the style of the historian Ctesias of Cnidus, and that of Xenophon the disciple of Socrates, are charming in the highest possible degree, but not as beautiful as they should have been. I am speaking generally, not absolutely; I admit that in the former authors there are instances of charming, in the latter of beautiful arrangement. But the composition of Herodotus has both these qualities; it is at once charming and beautiful.

XI
General Discussion of the Sources of Charm and Beauty in Composition

Among the sources of charm and beauty in style there are, I conceive, four which are paramount and essential—melody, rhythm, variety, and the appropriateness demanded by these three. Under "charm" I class freshness, grace, euphony, sweetness, persuasiveness, and all similar qualities; and under "beauty" grandeur, impressiveness, solemnity, dignity, mellowness, and the like. For these seem to me the most important—the main heads, so to speak, in either case. The aims set before themselves by all serious writers in epic, dramatic, or lyric poetry, or in the so-called "language of prose," are those specified, and I think these are all. There are many excellent authors who have been distinguished in one or both of these qualities. It is not possible at present to adduce examples from the writings of each one of them; I must not waste time over such details; and besides, if it seems incumbent on me to say something about some of them individually, and to quote from them anywhere in support of my views, I shall have a more suitable opportunity for doing so, when I sketch the various types of literary arrangement. For the present, what I have said of them is quite sufficient. So I will now return to the division I made of composition into charming and beautiful, in order that my discourse may "keep to the track," as the saying is.

Well, I said that the ear delighted first of all in melody, then in rhythm, thirdly in variety, and finally in appropriateness as applied to these other qualities. As a witness to the truth of my words I will bring foward experience itself, for it cannot be challenged, confirmed as it is by the general sentiment of mankind. Who is there that is not enthralled by the spell of one melody while he remains unaffected in any such way by another,—that is not captivated by this rhythm while that does but jar upon him? Before now I myself, even in the most popular theatres, thronged by a mixed and uncultured multitude, have seemed to observe that all of us have a sort of natural appreciation for correct melody and good rhythm. I have seen an accomplished harpist, of high repute, hissed by the public because he struck a single false note and so spoilt the melody. I have seen, too, a fluteplayer, who handled his instrument with the practiced skill of a master, suffer the same fate because he blew thickly or, through not compressing his lips, produced a harsh sound or so-called "broken note" as he played. Nevertheless, if the amateur critic were summoned to take up the instrument and himself to render any of the pieces with whose performance by professionals he was just now finding fault, he would be unable to do it. Why so? Because this is an affair of technical skill, in which we are not all partakers; the other of feeling, which is nature's universal gift to man. I have noticed the same thing occur in the case of rhythms. Everybody is vexed and annoyed when a performer strikes an instrument, takes a step, or sings a note, out of time, and so destroys the rhythm.

Again, it must not be supposed that, while melody and rhythm excite pleasure, and we are all enchanted by them, variety and appropriateness have less freshness and grace, or less effect on any of their hearers. No, these too fairly enchant us all when they are really attained, just as their absence jars upon us intensely. This is surely beyond dispute. I may refer, in confirmation, to the case of instrumental music, whether it accompanies singing or dancing; if it attains grace perfectly and throughout, but fails to introduce variety in due season or deviates from what is appropriate, the effect is dull satiety and that disagreeable impression which is made by anything out of harmony with the subject. Nor is my illustration foreign to the matter in hand. The science of public oratory is, after all, a sort of musical science, differing from vocal and instrumental music in degree, not in kind. In oratory, too, the words involve melody, rhythm, variety, and appropriateness; so that, in this case also, the ear delights in the melodies, is fascinated by the rhythms, welcomes the variations, and craves always what is in keeping with the occasion. The distinction between oratory and music is simply one of degree.

Now, the melody of spoken language is measured by a single interval, which is approximately that termed a *fifth.* When the voice rises towards the acute, it does not rise more than three tones and a semitone; and, when it falls towards the grave, it does not fall more than this interval. Further, the entire utterance during one word is not delivered at the same pitch of the voice throughout, but one part of it at the acute pitch, another at the grave, another at both. Of the words that have both pitches, some have the grave fused with the acute on one and the same syllable—those which we call circumflexed; others have both pitches falling on separate syllables, each retaining its own quality. Now in disyllables there is no space intermediate between low pitch and high pitch; while in polysyllabic words, whatever their number of syllables, there is but one syllable that has the acute accent (high pitch) among the many remaining graves ones. On the other hand, instrumental and vocal music uses a great number of intervals, not the fifth only; beginning with the octave, it uses also the fifth, the fourth, the third, the tone, the semitone, and, as some think, even the quarter-tone in a distinctly perceptible way. Music, further, insists that the words should be subordinate to the tune, and not the tune to the words. Among many examples in proof of this, let me especially instance those lyrical lines which Euripides has represented Electra as addressing to the Chorus in the *Orestes* (140–42): "Hush, hush! Light be the tread / Of the sandal; not a sound! / This way, far, far from his bed." In these lines the words *sîga sîga leukón* are sung to one note; and yet each of the three words has both low pitch and high pitch. And the word *arbúles* has its third syllable sung at the same pitch as its middle syllable, although it is impossible for a single word to take two acute accents. The first syllable of *títhete* is sung to a lower note, while the two that follow it are sung to the same high note. The circumflex accent of *ktupeîte* has disappeared, for the two syllables are uttered at one and the same pitch. And the word *apopróbate* does not receive the acute accent on the middle syllable; but the pitch of the third syllable has been transferred to the fourth.

The same thing happens in rhythm. Ordinary prose speech does not violate or interchange the quantities in any noun or verb. It keeps the syllables long or short as it has received them by nature. But the arts of rhythm and music alter them by shortening or lengthening, so that often they pass into their opposites: the time of production is not regulated by the quantity of the syllables, but the quantity of the syllables is regulated by the time.

The difference between music and speech having thus been shown, some other points remain to be mentioned. If the melody of the voice—not the singing voice, I mean, but the ordinary voice—has a pleasant effect upon the ear, it will be called melodious rather than in melody. So also symmetry in the quantities of words, when it preserves a lyrical effect, is rhythmical rather than in rhythm. On the precise bearing of these distinctions I will speak at the proper time. For the present I will pass on to the next question, and try to show how a style of civil oratory can be attained which, simply by means of the composition, charms the ear with its melody of sound, its symmetry of rhythm, its elaborate variety, and its appropriateness to the subject. These are the headings which I have set before myself.

XII
How to Render Composition Charming

It is not in the nature of all the words in a sentence to affect the ear in the same way, any more than all visible objects produce the same impression on the sense of sight, things tasted on that of taste, or any other set of stimuli upon the sense to which they correspond. No, different sounds affect the ear with many different sensations of sweetness, harshness, roughness, smoothness, and so on. The reason is to be found partly in the many different qualities of the letters which make up speech, and partly in the extremely various forms in which syllables are put together. Now since words have these properties, and since it is impossible to change the fundamental nature of any single one of them, we can only mask the uncouthness which is inseparable from some of them, by means of mingling and fusion and juxtaposition—by mingling smooth with rough, soft with hard, cacophonous with melodious, easy to pronounce with hard to pronounce, long with short; and generally by happy combinations of the same kind. Many words of few syllables must not be used in succession (for this jars upon the ear), nor an excessive number of polysyllabic words; and we must avoid the monotony of setting side by side words similarly accented or agreeing in their quantities. We must quickly vary the cases of substantives (since, if continued unduly, they greatly offend the ear); and in order to guard against satiety, we must constantly break up the effect of sameness entailed by placing many nouns, or verbs, or other parts of speech, in close succession. We must not always adhere to the same figures, but change them frequently; we must not reintroduce the same metaphors, but vary them; we must not exceed due measure by beginning or ending with the same words too often.

Still, let no one think that I am proclaiming these as universal rules—that I suppose keeping them will always produce pleasure, or breaking them always produce annoyance. I am not so foolish. I know that pleasure often arises from both sources—from similarity at one time, from dissimilarity at another. In every case we must, I think, keep in view good taste, for this is the best criterion of charm and its opposite. But about good taste no rhetorician or philosopher has, so far, produced a definite treatise. The man who first undertook to write on the subject, Gorgias of Leontini, achieved nothing worth mentioning. The nature of the subject, indeed, is not such that it can fall under any comprehensive and systematic treatment, nor can good taste in general be apprehended by science, but only by personal judgment. Those who have continually trained this latter faculty in many connections are more successful than others in attaining good taste, while those who leave it untrained are rarely successful, and only by a sort of lucky stroke.

To proceed. I think the following rules should be observed in composition by a writer who looks to please the ear. Either he should link to one another melodious, rhythmical, euphonious words, by which the sense of hearing is touched with a feeling of sweetness and softness—those which, to put it broadly, come home to it most; or he should intertwine and interweave those which have no such natural effect with those that can so bewitch the ear that the unattractiveness of the one set is overshadowed by the grace of the other. We may compare the practice of good tacticians when marshalling their armies: they mask the weak portions by means of the strong, and so no part of their force proves useless. In the same way I maintain we ought to relieve monotony by the tasteful introduction of variety, since variety is an element of pleasure in everything we do. And last, and certainly most important of all, the setting which is assigned to the subject matter must be appropriate and becoming to it. And, in my opinion, we ought not to feel shy of using any noun or verb, however hackneyed, unless it carries with it some shameful association; for I venture to assert that no part of speech which signifies a person or a thing will prove so mean, squalid, or otherwise offensive as to have no fitting place in discourse. My advice is that, trusting to the effect of the composition, we should bring out such expressions with a bold and manly confidence, following the example of Homer, in whom the most commonplace words are found, and of Demosthenes and Herodotus and others, whom I will mention a little later so far as is suitable in each case. I think I have now spoken at sufficient length on charm of style. My treatment has been but a brief survey of a wide field, but will furnish the main heads of the study.

XIII
How to Render Composition Beautiful

So far, so good. But, if some one were to ask me in what way, and by attention to what principles, literary structure can be made beautiful, I should reply: In no other way, believe me, and by no other means, than those by which it is made charming, since the same elements contribute to both, namely noble melody, stately rhythm, imposing variety, and the appropriateness which all these need. For as there is a charming diction, so there is another that is noble; as there is a polished rhythm, so also is there another that is dignified; as variety in one passage adds grace, so in another it adds mellowness; and as for appropriateness, it will prove the chief source of beauty, or else the source of nothing at all. I repeat, the study of beauty in composition should follow the same lines throughout as the study of charm. The prime cause, here as before, is to be found in the nature of the letters and the phonetic effect of the syllables, which are the raw material out of which the fabric of words is woven. The time may perhaps now have come for redeeming my promise to discuss these.

QUINTILIAN

(ca. 30/35–ca. 100 A.D.)

INTRODUCTION

From 68 to about 88 A.D. Quintilian was the leading teacher of rhetoric at Rome. On his retirement from teaching he wrote a treatise *On the Decay of Oratory,* which is no longer extant, and in 93 A.D. he wrote the *Institutio Oratoria,* a broad-ranging investigation of all phases of the training of an orator. This treatise stands as one of the most important statements of Roman rhetorical theory and practice. The work was undertaken at the behest of friends who wanted authoritative guidance in rhetoric. In addition to its vast amount of factual material, it offers an occasional insight into the personality and emotions of its author. The most moving of these occasions is found in the introduction to Book VI where Quintilian speaks somberly of the death of his son, for whom this volume was to have been a legacy, and expresses his deep despair over the previous deaths of his wife and another son. Now he faces the prospect of a lonely old age.

Central to Quintilian's theory of rhetoric is the belief he shares with Plato, Horace, "Longinus," and others that a good orator must be a good human being. The *Institutio Oratoria* indicates in its twelve books the appropriate course of technical training that would permit a good human being to achieve success as a rhetorician. Book I opens with a survey of the preliminary education a student should undergo prior to the actual study of rhetoric. Book II is devoted to an investigation of the aims and nature of rhetoric. Books III–VII are concerned with many technical features of oratory, such as the invention and arrangement of arguments, with major emphasis on forensic speeches. Books VIII–X deal with oratorical style, and Book XI is concerned with the memorization and oral delivery of speeches. The final book discusses the nature of the perfect orator.

The selections from the *Institutio Oratoria* included in this collection are taken from Book X. The first selection—from Quintilian's famous and very concise history of literature—deals with Homer. Quintilian's judgments of literary works are based principally on their value for oratorical training, and this orientation must be kept in mind when assessing them. Quintilian covers the entire field of classical literature, beginning with Homer, by providing brief critical assessments of each author discussed.

The analysis of Homer, whom Quintilian admires as a poet of supreme genius, is a good place to observe his approach to the evaluation of literature, because the discussion here is more extensive than that given to other writers. Quintilian praises Homer's ability to deal with both large and small subjects successfully, and he commends Homer's appropriateness in using a variety of styles, expansive and brief, gentle and forceful. He applauds Homer's ability to achieve both poetic and rhetorical excellence as exhibited in the laudatory, exhortatory, and consolatory speeches in his poems. Quintilian points out that Homer established the rules for proper rhetorical presentation by, first, favorably disposing his audience toward him through his invocation of the muse of poetry; second, seizing the attention of the audience by the very grandeur of his subject; and, finally, making his audience eager for further information by setting forth a concise but comprehensive view of his entire subject. Quintilian also praises Homer for his knowledge of all emotions, subtle and intense, for his great skill in all forms of establishment and refutation of proof, and for his expert use of similes, amplifications, and illustrations. As a rhetorical standard of excellence Quintilian cites Priam's speech to Achilles in which the bereaved father begs for the return of his son's body. In similar fashion, principally emphasizing the rhetorical qualities of the author under discussion, Quintilian proceeds through the history of Greek and Latin literature.

The second selection from Quintilian included here is the entire second chapter of Book X, which deals with the subject of mimesis or imitation. In this context the term is subjected to an interpretation that is quite different from those of Plato and Aristotle and comes to mean essentially "copying." Quintilian recommends that students of rhetoric imitate the virtues they find in the works of others. He rates invention as more significant than imitation, but he declares that it is important to take advantage of qualities that have already been proved successful by incorporating them into one's own style. Complete reliance on imitation is, however, rejected by Quintilian on the grounds that it would prevent (or, at least, obstruct) future progress in the field of rhetoric.

Quintilian urges that the student must imitate only what is best in the authors chosen for imitation, and that he must do this in a skillful and effective way. The student must also choose for imitation models that are naturally suited to his own natural abilities. Quintilan further recommends that the student imitate the virtues of many authors, instead of choosing to rely on only one, and that, in doing so, the student combine his own good qualities with those observed in each model. In this way Quintilian expresses the hope that every generation may be able to provide models of excellence for emulation by rhetoricians of the future.

As we have seen, Quintilian's primary interests are rhetorical, and this gives a special orientation to his use and evaluation of literature. But Quintilian's rhetorical emphasis, like that of Cicero and "Longinus," is united with a strong moral impulse. The balance between these two elements made the *Institutio Oratoria* a work of enduring popularity. Although it was known only in fragmentary versions in the Middle Ages, it still became for scholars a standard reference work in rhetoric. The *Institutio Oratoria* attained its highest critical status from the late Renaissance through the neoclassical period. (The complete text, discovered in 1417, was edited by Cardinal Campano in 1470.) Thus, for about three hundred years, Quintilian, like Aristotle, was used to supplement and enlarge an essentially Horatian poetic. And, as Pope's tribute to Quintilian indicates, the adaptation of "rules" of rhetoric became relevant to the evaluation of literary works:

In grave Quintilian's copious work, we find
The justest rules, and clearest method joined.
Thus useful arms in magazines we place,
All ranged in order, and disposed with grace;
But less to please the eye, than arm the hand,
Still fit for use, and ready at command.
(*An Essay on Criticism* 669–74)

The translation which follows is by H. E. Butler and has been taken from Quintilian, *Institutio Oratoria.* 4 vols. (Cambridge: Harvard University Press, 1958–60) with the permission of the publisher.

INSTITUTIO ORATORIA

from BOOK X

(I.46.) I shall, I think, be right in following the principle laid down by Aratus in the line, "With Jove let us begin,"[1] and in beginning with Homer. He is like his own conception of Ocean,[2] which he describes as the source of every stream and river; for he has given us a model and an inspiration for every department of eloquence. It will be generally admitted that no one has ever surpassed him in the sublimity with which he invests great themes or the propriety with which he handles small. He is at once luxuriant and concise, sprightly and serious, remarkable at once for his fullness and his brevity, and supreme not merely for poetic, but for oratorical power as well. (47.) For, to say nothing of his eloquence, which he shows in praise, exhortation, and consolation, do not the ninth book containing the embassy to Achilles, the first describing the quarrel between the chiefs, or the speeches delivered by the counsellors in the second, display all the rules of art to be followed in forensic or deliberative oratory? (48.) As regards the emotions, there can be no one so ill-educated as to deny that the poet was the master of all, tender and vehement alike. Again, in the few lines with which he introduces both of his epics, has he not, I will not say observed, but actually established the law which should govern the composition of the exordium?[3] For, by his invocation of the goodnesses believed to preside over poetry he wins the goodwill of his audience, by his statement of the greatness of his themes he excites their attention and renders them receptive by the briefness of his summary. (49.) Who can narrate more briefly than the hero[4] who brings the news of Patroclus' death, or more vividly than he[5] who describes the battle between the Curetes and the Aetolians? Then consider his similes, his amplifications, his illustrations, digressions, indications of fact, inferences, and all the other methods of proof and refutation which he employs. They are so numerous that the majority of writers on the principles of rhetoric have gone to his works for examples of all these things. (50.) And as for perorations, what can ever be equal to the prayers which Priam addresses to Achilles[6] when he comes to beg for the body of his son? Again, does he not transcend the limits of human genius in his choice of words, his reflections, figures, and the arrangement of his whole work, with the result that it requires a powerful mind, I will not say to imitate, for that is impossible, but even to appreciate his excellences? (51.) But he has in truth outdistanced all that have come after him in every department of eloquence, above all, he has outstripped all other writers of epic, the contrast in their case being especially striking owing to the similarity of the material with which they deal.

(II.1) It is from these and other authors worthy of our study that we must draw our stock of words, the variety of our figures and our methods of composition, while we must form our minds on the model of every excellence. For there can be no doubt that in art no small portion of our task lies in imitation, since, although invention came first and is all-important, it is expedient to imitate whatever has been invented with success. (2.) And it is a universal rule of life that we should wish to copy what we approve in others. It is for this reason that boys copy the shapes of letters that they may learn to write, and that musicians take the voices of their teachers, painters the works of their predecessors, and peasants the principles of agriculture which have been proved in practice, as models for their imitation. In fact, we may note that the elementary study of every branch of learning is directed by reference to some definite standard that is placed before the learner. (3.) We must, in fact, either be like or unlike those who have proved their excellence. It is rare for nature to produce such resemblance, which is more often the result of imitation. But the very fact that in every subject the procedure to be followed is so much more easy for us than it was for those who had no model to guide them, is a positive drawback, unless we use this dubious advantage with caution and judgment.

(4.) The first point, then, that we must realise is that imitation alone is not sufficient, if only for the reason that a sluggish nature is only too ready to rest content with the inventions of others. For what would have happened in the days when models were not, if men had decided to do and think of nothing that they did not know already? The answer is obvious: nothing would ever have been discovered. (5.) Why, then, is it a crime for us to discover something new? Were primitive men led to make so many discoveries simply by the natural force of their imagination, and shall we not then be spurred on to search for novelty by the very knowledge that those who sought of old were rewarded by success? (6.) And seeing that they, who had none to teach them anything, have handed down such store of knowledge to posterity, shall we refuse to employ the experience which we possess of some things, to discover yet other things, and possess nought that is not owed to the beneficent activity of others? Shall we follow the example of those painters whose sole aim is to be able to copy pictures by using the ruler and the measuring rod?[7] (7.) It is a positive disgrace to be content to owe all our achievement to imitation. For what, I ask again, would have been the result if no one had done more than his predecessors? Livius Andronicus would mark our supreme achievement in poetry and the annals of the *Pontifices*[8] would be our *ne plus ultra* in history. We should still be sailing on rafts, and the art of painting would be restricted to tracing a line round a shadow thrown in the sunlight. (8.) Cast your eyes over the whole of history; you will find that no art has remained just as it was when it was discovered, nor come to a standstill at its very birth, unless indeed we are ready to pass special condemnation on our own generation on the ground that it is so barren of invention that no further development is possible; and it is undoubtedly true that no development is possible for those who restrict themselves to imitation. (9.) But if we are forbidden to add anything to the existing stock of knowledge, how can we ever hope for the birth of our ideal orator? For of all the greatest orators with whom we are as yet acquainted, there is not one who has not some deficiency or blemish. And even those who do not aim at supreme excellence, ought to press toward the mark rather than be content to follow in the tracks of others. (10.) For the man whose aim is to prove himself better than another, even if he does not surpass him, may hope to equal him. But he can never hope to equal him, if he thinks it his duty merely to tread in his footsteps: for the mere follower must always lag behind. Further, it is generally easier to make some advance than to repeat what has been done by others, since there is nothing harder than to produce an exact likeness, and nature herself has so far failed in this endeavor that there is always some difference which enables us to distinguish even the things which seem most like and most equal to one another. (11.) Again, whatever is like another object, must necessarily be inferior to the object of its imitation, just as the shadow is inferior to the substance, the portrait to the features which it portrays, and the acting of the player to the feelings which he endeavors to reproduce. The same is true of oratory. For the models which we select for imitation have a genuine and natural force, whereas all imitation is artificial and molded to a purpose which was not that of the original orator. (12.) This is the reason why declamations have less life and vigor than actual speeches, since the subject is fictitious in the one and real in the other. Again, the greatest qualities of the orator are beyond all imitation, by which I mean, talent, invention, force, facility and all the qualities which are independent of art. (13.) Consequently, there are many who, after excerpting certain words from published speeches or borrowing certain particular rhythms, think that they have produced a perfect copy of the works which they have read, despite the fact that words become obsolete or current with the lapse of years, the one sure standard being contemporary usage; and they are not good or bad in virtue of their inherent nature (for in themselves they are no more than mere sounds), but solely in virtue of the aptitude and propriety (or the reverse) with which they are arranged, while rhythmical composition must be adapted to the theme in hand and will derive its main charm from its variety.

(14.) Consequently the nicest judgment is required in the examination of everything connected with this department of study. First we must consider whom to imitate. For there are many who have shown a passionate desire to imitate the worst and most decadent authors. Secondly, we must consider what it is that we should set ourselves to imitate in the authors thus chosen. (15.) For even great authors have their blemishes, for which they have been censured by competent critics and have even reproached each other. I only wish that imitators were more likely to improve on the good things than to exaggerate the blemishes of the authors whom they seek to copy. And even those who have sufficient critical acumen to avoid the faults of their models will not find it sufficient to produce a copy of their merits, amounting to no more than a superficial resemblance, or rather recalling those sloughs which, according to Epicurus, are continually given off by material things. (16.) But this is just what happens to those who mold themselves on the first impressions derived from the style of their model, without devoting themselves to a thorough investigation of its good qualities, and, despite the brilliance of their imitation and the close resemblance of their language and rhythm, not only fail absolutely to attain the force of style and invention possessed by the original, but as a rule degenerate into something worse, and achieve merely those faults which are hardest to distinguish from virtues: they are turgid instead of grand, bald instead of concise, and rash instead of courageous, while extravagance takes the place of wealth, over-emphasis the place of harmony and negligence of simplicity. (17.) As a result, those who flaunt tasteless and insipid thoughts, couched in an uncouth and inharmonious form, think that they are the equals of the ancients; those who lack ornament and epigram, pose as Attic; those who darken their meaning by the abruptness with which they close their periods, count themselves the superiors of Sallust and Thucydides; those who are dreary and jejune, think that they are serious rivals to Pollio, while those who are tame and listless, if only they can produce long enough periods, swear that this is just the manner in which Cicero would have spoken. (18.) I have known some who thought that they had produced a brilliant imitation of the style of that divine orator, by ending their periods with the phrase *esse videatur*.[9] Consequently it is of the first importance that every student should realize what it is that he is to imitate, and should know why it is good.

(19.) The next step is for each student to consult his own powers when he shoulders his burden. For there are some things which, though capable of imitation, may be beyond the capacity of any given individual, either because his natural gifts are insufficient or of a different character. The man whose talent is for the plain style should not seek only what is bold and rugged, nor yet should he who has vigor without control suffer himself through love of subtlety at once to waste his natural energy and fail to attain the elegance at which he aims: for there is nothing so unbecoming as delicacy wedded to ruggedness. (20.) True, I did express the opinion that the instructor whose portrait I painted in my second book, should not confine himself to teaching those things for which he perceived his individual pupils to have most aptitude. For it is his further duty to foster whatever good qualities he may perceive in his pupils, to make good their deficiencies as far as may be, to correct their faults and turn them to better things. For he is the guide and director of the minds of others. It is a harder task to mold one's own nature. (21.) But not even our ideal teacher, however much he may desire that everything that is correct should prevail in his school to the fullest extent, will waste his labor in attempting to develop qualities to the attainment of which he perceives nature's gifts to be opposed.

It is also necessary to avoid the fault to which the majority of students are so prone, namely, the idea that in composing speeches we should imitate the poets and historians, and in writing history or poetry should copy orators and declaimers. (22.) Each branch of literature has its own laws and its own appropriate character. Comedy does not seek to increase its height by the buskin and tragedy does not wear the slipper of comedy. But all forms of eloquence have something in common, and it is to the imitation of this common element that our efforts should be confined.

(23.) There is a further fault to which those persons are liable who devote themselves entirely to the imitation of one particular style: if the rude vigor of some particular author takes their fancy, they cling to it even when the case on which they are engaged calls for an easy and flowing style; if, on the other hand, it is a simple or agreeable style that claims their devotion, they fail to meet the heavy demands of severe and weighty cases. For not only do cases differ in their general aspect, but one part of a case may differ from another, and some things require a gentle and others a violent style, some require an impetuous and others a calm diction, while in some cases it is necessary to instruct and in others to move the audience, in all these instances dissimilar and different methods being necessary. (24.) Consequently I should be reluctant even to advise a student to select one particular author to follow through thick and thin. Demosthenes is by far the most perfect of Greek orators, yet there are some things which others have said better in some contexts as against the many things which he has said better than others. But it does not follow that because we should select one author for special imitation, he should be our only model. (25.) What then? Is it not sufficient to model our every utterance on Cicero? For my own part, I should consider it sufficient, if I could always imitate him successfully. But what harm is there in occasionally borrowing the vigor of Caesar, the vehemence of Caelius, the precision of Pollio or the sound judgment of Calvus? (26.) For quite apart from the fact that a wise man should always, if possible, make whatever is best in each individual author his own, we shall find that, in view of the extreme difficulty of our subject, those who fix their eyes on one model only will always find some one quality which it is almost impossible to acquire therefrom. Consequently, since it is practically impossible for mortal powers to produce a perfect and complete copy of any one chosen author, we shall do well to keep a number of different excellences before our eyes, so that different qualities from different authors may impress themselves on our minds, to be adopted for use in the place that becomes them best.

(27.) But imitation (for I must repeat this point again and again) should not be confined merely to words. We must consider the appropriateness with which those orators handle the circumstances and persons involved in the various cases in which they were engaged, and observe the judgment and powers of arrangement which they reveal, and the manner in which everything they say, not excepting those portions of their speeches which seem designed merely to delight their audience, is concentrated on securing the victory over their opponents. We must note their procedure in the exordium, the method and variety of their statement of facts, the power displayed in proof and refutation, the skill revealed in their appeal to every kind of emotion, and the manner in which they make use of popular applause to serve their case, applause which is most honorable when it is spontaneous and not deliberately courted. If we have thoroughly appreciated all these points, we shall be able to imitate our models with accuracy. (28.) But the man who to these good qualities adds his own, that is to say, who makes good deficiencies and cuts down whatever is redundant, will be the perfect orator of our search; and it is now above all times that such perfection should be attained when there are before us so many more models of oratorical excellence than were available for those who have thus far achieved the highest success. For this glory also shall be theirs, that men shall say of them that while they surpassed their predecessors, they also taught those who came after.

"LONGINUS"

(1st century A.D.?)

INTRODUCTION

The actual authorship and date of *On Sublimity* are in doubt. Because the name "Longinus" appears in the manuscript attributions of authorship, scholars originally accorded the work to Cassius Longinus, a writer of the third century A.D. More careful scrutiny of the manuscripts later showed, however, that the name is actually given at one point as "Dionysius Longinus" and at another point as "Dionysius" *or* "Longinus." No such critic as Dionysius Longinus is known to us, and it seems probable that the original attribution to "Dionysius" or "Longinus" was a guess by Byzantine scholars, who, uncertain of the author's identity, thought it likely that he was either Dionysius of Halicarnassus, the famous critic of the first century A.D., or the third-century Cassius Longinus.

Modern scholars have adduced two major arguments against third-century authorship. First, there are no references in the treatise to literature written after the first century A.D.—and the absence of such references in a well informed third-century critical work would be quite surprising. Second, *On Sublimity* explores themes commonly discussed in the first century, and it involves an explicit refutation of the work of a first-century critic, Caecilius. Contemporary scholars thus ascribe the work to a perceptive first-century critic whom they continue to call "Longinus," although for all practical purposes he is anonymous. Some scholars conclude from the reference to Genesis (Chapter 9) that "Longinus" was a Greek with both Roman and Jewish contacts, but no certain biographical knowledge is possible.

The work as we have it is fragmentary, with perhaps one-third missing from various parts of the treatise. One principal manuscript exists, the tenth-century Paris 2036; a number of other manuscripts, deriving from this source, come from the fifteenth and sixteenth centuries. In addition to its lacunae, the Greek text offers certain difficulties of interpretation for editors and translators, but the general line of argument is quite clear.

On Sublimity is a kind of textbook for prospective orators; its title, *Peri Hypsous,* can also be rendered as "On the High Style," referring primarily to the art of rhetoric. Nevertheless, the treatise has a valid claim to honor as a document in literary criticism: "Longinus" is concerned with a profundity of thought and an excellence of high technique which overlap the area of literary art. Moreover, he does not hesitate to recommend passages of poetry as examples of the sublimity that the orator should strive for.

To assist in introducing his topic and to conclude his general argument, "Longinus" relies on a method of negative development. Chapters 3–5 treat stylistic vices (e. g., bombast) which constitute a *false* sublime. Chapters 41–43 return to this issue in more detail, and the treatise then closes with an analysis of what "Longinus" perceives as a decline of sublimity in his own day. The sublimity that "Longinus" discusses in this final chapter is emphatically moral, not merely a rhetorical quality. The force of his concluding remarks serves in fact to characterize his general critical approach: a consideration of *style* as a bridge between the aesthetic and the ethical modes of criticism.

This general intent seems to be confirmed in "Longinus' " positive development of his topic: his description of the effects of the sublime, and his investigation of the sources of the sublime. The main effect of the sublime, according to "Longinus," is neither persuasion nor pleasure, but an intense experience of "transport" (*ecstasis*). The audience is carried out of itself, entranced by a stylistic power which reveals itself like a flash of lightning (Chapter 1). But "Longinus" insists that the sublime is no mere wave of sentimentality. It produces a controlled kind of ecstasy, depending largely on diction and imagery that are precise, not vague. "Transport" is no momentary emotional thrill, but a significant psychological experience that is capable of being sustained. And perhaps most importantly, it has serious ethical implications—e.g., the disposing of the mind to "lofty ideas" (Chapter 7).

"Longinus" now passes to the central section of his treatise (Chapters 8–40), an exploration of five major sources of the sublime. Two of these (*noesis* and *pathos*) are qualities which the orator or poet must possess "by nature," and three are technical skills (competence in rhetorical figures, diction, and arrangement of words) which can be studied and developed.

Noesis, the first innate quality, is a power of "great intellectual conception," by which the artist is able to frame thoughts that are awe-inspiring in themselves (as exemplified in many passages from Homer, or in the opening of Genesis). But "Longinus" also elucidates *noesis* in a much broader sense. First, he stresses its ethical implications: sublime thoughts are possible only to an artist whose nature is itself sublime, who possesses true "nobility of soul." Thus *noesis* connotes not only a powerful intellect, but an essential high-mindedness. Second, "Longinus" seems to subsume under *noesis* various elements of rhetorical and poetic craft that unify the finished work and imbue it with telling detail and appropriateness of tone (Chapters 10–15): the artist's inherent skill at selection and organization, amplification, emulation of great works, and vivid representation.

To illustrate how selection and organization of material contribute to the achievement of the sublime, "Longinus" comments perceptively on the famous ode of Sappho which deals with the tormenting emotions of love. He shows how Sappho skillfully selected the essential details and unified them to create an intense effect. He concludes that in this poem, and in all other works of similar excellence, nothing irrelevant or inappropriate weakens or clashes with the poet's intention.

This discussion of selection and arrangement leads "Longinus" to a consideration of the proper amplification of material. The term "amplification" (*auxesis*) pertains to the theory of rhetoric, and it was used by earlier writers to refer to quantitative elaboration, the "piling up" of details to support an argumentative point. "Longinus" explicitly rejects this definition. Although his discussion is interrupted by a lacuna in the text, he seems to be aiming at a definition predicated on quality rather than quantity, a concept of amplification as relevant to poetry as to rhetoric. The sublime can be achieved through the artist's inherent skill at using small details, but the avoidance of redundancy is essential. In an eloquent passage "Longinus" compares the widely divergent but equally effective skills of Demosthenes and Cicero, both successful at "elevated" amplification.

Still another aspect of *noesis* is the artist's talent for "imitation" (*mimesis*) of other great writers. The sublime can often be attained if the artist judiciously attempts to emulate the way that Homer, Plato, or Demosthenes would have expressed a thought. Using such spiritual models, the artist tends to rise to their level—and perhaps even to participate in their visions, much as the priestess at Delphi became the inspired and possessed instrument of the will of Apollo himself. Clearly no mere "copying" is involved; instead, the process encourages the raising of oneself to the level of the sublime thought and expression that characterizes great human beings.

The artist's inherent talent for vivid representation (*phantasia*) is one of the most important aspects of *noesis*. Indeed, a major difference between sublimity and mere bombast is the presence in a poem or speech of precise, evocative images. To startle, move, and uplift his audience, the artist must be able to utilize imagery as a medium. (In one sense, "Longinus' " argument anticipates modern notions of an "objective correlative.")

The text of *On Sublimity* includes only a brief treatment (in Chapter 8) of *pathos,* the second innate quality of the successful artist. Yet several of "Longinus' " other discussions—e.g., his analysis of Sappho's ode—have significant implications for this topic. By *pathos* "Longinus" means the artist's capacity for strong and inspired emotion. He asserts that an emotional "gust" in a speech or poem can be an invaluable aid in the quest for sublimity, but he also implies that this power is to be tempered by *noesis,* that the ideal artist maintains the two faculties in delicate conjunction. In fact, one classical scholar has recently suggested that this aspect of "Longinus' " theory approximates T. S. Eliot's concept of the ideal artist's "unified sensibility."[1]

The concepts of *noesis* and *pathos* continue to underlie "Longinus' " thinking even after he turns (in Chapter 16) to a lengthy discussion of stylistic skills that the prospective artist can consciously study and practice. In analyzing the contribution to sublimity made by various devices of style, "Longinus" usually speaks in terms of their emotional appeal, but he often warns against excess and asserts the need for intellectual control. He proceeds to elucidate the use of such devices as oaths, rhetorical questions, asyndeton (lack of connectives between words and phrases), anaphora (repetition), hyperbaton (abnormal sequence of words and thoughts), the imaginary second person, and periphrasis. In these chapters "Longinus' " technical explanations are fairly traditional, but his true quality as a critic shows forth in his brilliant analyses of the excellence of the passages he chooses for illustration. His discussion of the intellectual and emotional connotations of the oath in Demosthenes' *On the Crown* (Chapter 16) is representative of his best critical technique.

"Longinus' " technical analysis is interrupted in Chapters 33–37. Here he poses a question of great importance in criticism, and his answer extends and clarifies his own philosophy of the sublime. "Longinus" asks whether a poet who has no great virtues but makes no technical errors is superior to one who displays genius but commits errors as well. Would one rather be Homer who occasionally nods amidst much overwhelming greatness, or Apollonius of Rhodes who makes no technical mistakes but never sounds the note of genius? For "Longinus" sublimity is manifestly a product of genius: it cannot be subverted by any quantity of minor errors, and it cannot be achieved by any quantity of mere technical skills. In a passage of surpassing eloquence "Longinus" envisions mankind as having been created by nature to be spectators of the awesome magnificence of the universe. Whenever the grandeur and transcendent beauty of this universe is expressed successfully in art, the sublime is achieved. Such an artistic symbolization of cosmic magnificence is grandly unaffected by the existence of minor technical errors.

"Longinus' " treatise has enjoyed a wide influence in post-Renaissance literary criticism. Popularized by Boileau's translation in 1674, *On the Sublime* became a key document in the critical syntheses of the neoclassical age. It served partly as a necessary supplement to Horace's *Ars Poetica,* "Longinus' " stirring affirmation of "sublimity" balancing Horace's more conservative insistence on "decorum." Alexander Pope in his *Essay on Criticism* (1709) asserted that the great poets were able to "snatch a grace beyond the reach of art," and he praised "Longinus" as a critic "Whose own example strengthens all his laws,/ And is himself the great Sublime he draws." Joseph Addison's *Spectator* essays on *Paradise Lost* (1711–12) relied explicitly on "Longinus" for a critical rationale: according to Addison, the grandeur and sweep of Milton's epic, its essential "sublimity," rendered irrelevant any violation of traditional rules.

The increased influence of *On Sublimity* in eighteenth-century criticism was in part a prefiguration of romantic poetics.[2] In the philosophical treatises on sublimity presented by Edmund Burke and Immanuel Kant, "Longinus' " remarks became the starting point for new idealist philosophies. More significantly, "Longinus' " emphasis on the personality of the artist, especially in regard to inspiration and "genius," helped to prepare for the critical orientation of the major German and British romantics. Ironically, however, most nineteenth-century romantics tended to neglect "Longinus," apparently with the feeling that his outlook was too elementary.[3]

In the modern era, however, the influence of *On Sublimity* has been diverse. Matthew Arnold used "Longinus' " method in "The Study of Poetry" (1880), attempting to define a quality of greatness in literature by isolating eleven short passages as "touchstones," their beauty to be recognized by a flash of insight rather than by rigorous analysis. Carl Jung used the notion of *ecstasis* in 1925 to describe man's aesthetic encounter with the world of archetypal images: "No wonder, then, that at the moment when a typical situation occurs, we feel suddenly aware of an extraordinary release, as though transported, or caught up by an overwhelming power. At such moments we are no longer individuals, but the race: the voice of all mankind resounds in us."[4] Northrop Frye has used *ecstasis* as a companion concept to Aristole's *katharsis*: works of literature may be tentatively categorized according to which of the two responses they encourage.[5]

"Longinus' " greatest influence in modern criticism has been in the area of stylistics. The American "new critics," in particular, have returned to Longinian co-ordinates of criticism; according to Allen Tate, "Longinus' " great relevance derives from the fact that he "implicitly claims for Thought and Diction, two of the nonstructural elements in Aristotle's analysis of tragedy, a degree of objectivity that Aristotle's rhetorical view of poetic language could not include."[6] Significantly, the neo-Aristotelian "Chicago critics" have found "Longinus" to be one of the very few thinkers other than Aristotle himself whose outlook is compatible with theirs, and they have occasionally attempted to balance a sense of Aristotelian "structure" with a sense of Longinian "style," especially in trying to come to terms with lyric poetry.[7]

In both the range and depth of his influence, then, the anonymous rhetorician who wrote *Peri Hypsous* continues as a major force in Western criticism.

The text which follows (and most of the notes) are from D. A. Russell, tr. "Longinus," *On Sublimity* (Oxford: Clarendon Press, 1965) and reprinted by permission of the publisher.

ON SUBLIMITY

PREFACE

(I.1.) You will recall, my dear Postumius Terentianus, that when we were reading together Caecilius' monograph *On Sublimity*, we felt that it was inadequate to its high subject, and failed to touch the essential points. Nor indeed did it appear to offer the reader much practical help, and this ought to be a writer's principal object. Two things are required of any text-book: first, that it should explain what its subject is; second, and more important, that it should explain how and by what methods we can achieve it. Caecilius tries at immense length to explain to us what sort of thing "the sublime" is, as though we did not know; but he has somehow passed over as unnecessary the question how we can develop our nature to some degree of greatness. (2.) However, we ought perhaps not so much to blame our author for what he has left out as to commend him for his originality and enthusiasm. You have urged me to set down a few notes on sublimity for your own use. Let us then consider whether there is anything in my observations which may be thought useful to public men. You must help me, my friend, by giving your honest opinion in detail, as both your natural candor and your friendship with me require. It was well said that what man has in common with the gods is "doing good and telling the truth." (3.) Your own wide culture dispenses me from any long preliminary definition. Sublimity is a kind of eminence or excellence of discourse. It is the source of the distinction of the very greatest poets and prose writers and the means by which they have given eternal life to their own fame. (4.) For grandeur produces ecstacy rather than persuasion in the hearer; and the combination of wonder and astonishment always proves superior to the merely persuasive and pleasant. This is because persuasion is on the whole something we can control, whereas amazement and wonder exert invincible power and force and get the better of every hearer. Experience in invention and ability to order and arrange material cannot be detected in single passages; we begin to appreciate them only when we see the whole context. Sublimity, on the other hand, produced at the right moment, tears everything up like a whirlwind, and exhibits the orator's whole power at a single blow.

(II.1.) Your own experience will lead you to these and similar considerations. The question from which I must begin is whether there is in fact an art of sublimity or profundity.[1] Some people think it is a complete mistake to reduce things like this to technical rules. Greatness, the argument runs, is a natural product, and does not come by teaching. The only art is to be born like that. They believe moreover that natural products are very much weakened by being reduced to the bare bones of a textbook. (2.) In my view, these arguments can be refuted by considering three points: (i) Though nature is on the whole a law unto herself in matters of emotion and elevation, she is not a random force and does not work altogether without method. (ii) She is herself in every instance a first and primary element of creation, but it is method that is competent to provide and contribute quantities and appropriate occasions for everything, as well as perfect correctness in training and application. (iii) Grandeur is particularly dangerous when left on its own, unaccompanied by knowledge, unsteadied, unballasted, abandoned to mere impulse and ignorant temerity. It often needs the curb as well as the spur.

(3.) What Demosthenes[2] said of life in general is true also of literature: good fortune is the greatest of blessings, but good counsel comes next, and the lack of it destroys the other also. In literature, nature occupies the place of good fortune, art that of good counsel. Most important of all, the very fact that some things in literature depend on nature alone can itself be learned only from art. If the critic of students of this subject will bear these points in mind, he will, I believe, come to realize that the examination of the question before us is by no means useless or superfluous. [Lacuna equivalent to about three printed pages]

FAULTS INCIDENT TO THE EFFORT TO ACHIEVE SUBLIMITY: TURGIDITY, PUERILITY, FALSE EMOTION, FRIGIDITY

(III.1.) . . . restrain the oven's mighty glow.
For if I see but one beside his hearth,
I'll thrust in just one tentacle of storm,
And fire his roof and turn it all to cinders.
I've not yet sung my proper song.[3]

This is not tragedy; it is a parody of the tragic manner—tentacles, vomiting to heaven, making Boreas a flute-player, and so on. The result is not impressiveness but turbid diction and confused imagery. If you examine the details closely, they gradually sink from the terrifying to the contemptible.

Now if untimely turgidity is unpardonable in tragedy, a genre which is naturally magniloquent and tolerant of bombast, it will scarcely be appropriate in writing which has to do with real life. (2.) Hence the ridicule attaching to Gorgias of Leontini's "Xerxes, the Persians' Zeus" and "their living tombs, the vultures," or to various things in Callisthenes, where he has not so much risen to heights as been carried off his feet. Clitarchus is an even more striking example; he is an inflated writer, and, as Sophocles has it, "Blows at his tiny flute, the mouth-band off."[4] Amphicrates, Hegesias, Matris—they are all the same. They often fancy themselves possessed when they are merely playing the fool. (3.) Turgidity is a particularly hard fault to avoid, for it is one to which all who aim at greatness naturally incline, because they seek to escape the charge of weakness and aridity. They act on the principle that "to slip from a great prize is yet a noble fault." (4.) In literature as in the body, puffy and false tumors are bad, and may well bring us to the opposite result from that which we expected. As the saying goes, there is nothing so dry as a man with dropsy. While turgidity is an endeavor to go above the sublime, puerility is the sheer opposite of greatness; it is a thoroughly low, mean and ignoble vice. What do I mean by "puerility"? A pedantic thought, so over-worked that it ends in frigidity. Writers slip into it through aiming at originality, artifice, and (above all) charm, and then coming to grief on the rocks of tawdriness and affection.

(5.) A third kind of fault—what Theodorus called "the pseudo-bacchanalian" —corresponds to these in the field of emotion. It consists of untimely or meaningless emotion where none is in place, or immoderate emotion where moderate is in place. Some people often get carried away, like drunkards, into emotions unconnected with the subject, which are simply their own pedantic invention. The audience feels nothing, so that they inevitably make an exhibition of themselves, parading their ecstasies before an audience which does not share them.

(IV.1.) But I reserve the subject of emotion for another place,[5] returning meanwhile to the second fault of those I mentioned: frigidity. This is a constant feature in Timaeus, who is in many ways a competent writer, not without the capacity for greatness on occasion, learned and original, but as unconscious of his own faults as he is censorious of others', and often falling into the grossest childishness through his passion for always starting exotic ideas. (2.) I will give one or two examples; Caecilius has already cited most of those available. (i) In praise of Alexander the Great, Timaeus writes: "He conquered all Asia in fewer years than it took Isocrates to write the *Panegyricus* to advocate the Persian war." What a splendid comparison this is—the Macedonian king and the sophist! On the same principle, the Lacedaemonians were very much less brave than Isocrates: it took them thirty years to capture Messene,[6] whereas he took only ten to write the *Panegyricus*! (3.) (ii) Listen also to Timaeus' comment on the Athenians captured in Sicily. "They were punished for their impiety to Hermes and mutilation of his statues, and the main agent of their punishment was one who had a family connection with their victim, Hermocrates the son of Hermon." I cannot help wondering, my dear Terentianus, why he does not also write about the tyrant Dionysius, "Because he was impious towards Zeus and Heracles, Dion and Heraclides robbed him of his throne."[7] (4.) But why speak of Timaeus, when those heroes of letters, Xenophon and Plato, for all that they were trained in Socrates' school, forget themselves sometimes for the sake of similar petty pleasures? Thus Xenophon writes in *The Constitution of the Lacedaemonians:* "You could hear their voice less than the voice of stone statues, you could distract their eyes less than the eyes of bronze images; you would think them more bashful than the very maidens in the eyes."[8] It would have been more in keeping with Amphicrates' manner than Xenophon's to speak of the pupils of our eyes as bashful maidens. And what an absurd misconception to think of everybody's pupils as bashful! The shamelessness of a person, we are told, appears nowhere so plainly as in the eyes. Remember the words Achilles used to revile Agamemnon's violent temper: "Drunken sot, with a dog's *eyes!*"[9] (5.) Timaeus, unable to keep his hands off stolen property, as it were, has not left the monopoly of this frigid conceit to Xenophon. He uses it in connection with Agathocles, who eloped with his cousin from the unveiling ceremony of her marriage to another: "Who would have done this, if he had not had harlots in his eyes for pupils (*koras*)?"[10]

(6.) Now here is Plato, the otherwise divine Plato. He wants to express the idea of writing-tablets. "They shall write," he says, "and deposit in the temples memorials of cypress."[11] Again: "As for walls, Megillus, I should concur with Sparta in letting walls sleep in the earth and not get up."[12] (7.) Herodotus' description[13] of beautiful women as "pains on the eyes" is the same sort of thing, though it is to some extent excused by the fact that the speakers are barbarians and drunk—not that it is a good thing to make an exhibition of the triviality of one's mind to posterity, even through the mouths of characters like these.

(V.) All such lapses from dignity arise in literature through a single cause: that desire for novelty of thought which is all the rage today. Evils often come from the same source as blessings; and so, since beauty of style, sublimity, and charm all conduce to successful writing, they are also causes and principles not only of success but of failure. Variation, hyperbole, and the use of plural for singular are like this too; I shall explain below the dangers which they involve.[14]

SOME MARKS OF TRUE SUBLIMITY

At this stage, the question we must put to ourselves for discussion is how to avoid the faults which are so much tied up with sublimity. (VI.) The answer, my friend, is: by first of all achieving a genuine understanding and appreciation of true sublimity. This is difficult; literary judgment comes only as the final product of long experience. However, for the purposes of instruction, I think we can say that an understanding of all this can be acquired. I approach the problem in this way:

(VII.1.) In ordinary life, nothing is truly great which it is great to despise; wealth, honor, reputation, absolute power—anything in short which has a lot of external trappings—can never seem supremely good to the wise man; because it is no small good to despise them. People who could have these advantages if they chose but disdain them out of magnanimity are admired much more than those who actually possess them. It is much the same with elevation in poetry and literature generally. We have to ask ourselves whether any particular example does not give a show of grandeur which, for all its accidental trappings, will, when dissected, prove vain and hollow, the kind of thing which it does a man more honor to despise than to admire. (2.) It is our nature to be elevated and exalted by true sublimity. Filled with joy and pride, we come to believe we have created what we have only heard. (3.) When a man of sense and literary experience hears something many times over, and it fails to dispose his mind to greatness or to leave him with more to reflect upon than was contained in the mere words, but comes instead to seem valueless on repeated inspection, this is not true sublimity: it endures only for the moment of hearing. Real sublimity contains much food for reflection, is difficult or rather impossible to resist, and makes a strong and ineffaceable impression on the memory. (4.) In a word, reckon those things which please everybody all the time as genuinely and finely sublime. When people of different training, way of life, tastes, age, and manners all agree about something, the judgment and assent, as it were, of so many distinct voices lends strength and irrefutability to the conviction that their admiration is rightly directed.

THE FIVE SOURCES OF SUBLIMITY; THE PLAN OF THE BOOK

(VIII.1.) There are, one may say, five most productive sources of sublimity. (Competence in speaking is assumed as a common foundation for all five; nothing is possible without it.) (i) The first and most important is the power to conceive great thoughts; I defined this in my work on Xenophon. (ii) The second is strong and inspired emotion. (These two sources are for the most part natural; the remaining three involve art.) (iii) Certain kinds of figures. (These may be divided into figures of thought and figures of speech.) (iv) Noble diction. This has as subdivisions choice of words and the use of metaphorical and artificial language.[15] (v) Finally, to round off the whole list, dignified and elevated word-arrangement.[16] Let us now examine the points which come under each of these heads. I must first observe, however, that Caecilius has omitted some of the five—emotion, for example. (2.) Now if he thought that sublimity and emotion were one and the same thing and always existed and developed together, he was wrong. Some emotions, such as pity, grief, and fear, are found divorced from sublimity and with a low effect. Conversely, sublimity often occurs apart from emotion. Of the innumerable examples of this I select Homer's bold account of the Aloadae: "Ossa upon Olympus they sought to heap; and on Ossa/Pelion with its shaking forest, to make a path to heaven—" and the even more impressive sequel—"And they would have finished their work. . . ."[17] (3.) In orators, encomia and ceremonial or exhibition pieces always involve grandeur and sublimity, though they are generally devoid of emotion. Hence those orators who are best at conveying emotion are least good at encomia, and conversely the experts at encomia are not conveyors of emotion. (4.) On the other hand, if Caecilius thought that emotion had no contribution to make to sublimity and therefore thought it not worth mentioning, he was again completely wrong. I should myself have no hesitation in saying that there is nothing so productive of grandeur as noble emotion in the right place. It inspires and possesses our words with a kind of madness and divine spirit.

GREATNESS OF THOUGHT

(IX.1.) The first source, natural greatness, is the most important. Even if it is a matter of endowment rather than acquisition, we must, so far as possible, develop our minds in the direction of greatness and make them always pregnant with noble thoughts. (2.) You ask how this can be done. I wrote elsewhere something like this: "sublimity is the echo of a noble mind." This is why a mere idea, without verbal expression, is sometimes admired for its nobility—just as Ajax's silence in the Vision of the Dead is grand and indeed more sublime than any words could have been.[18] (3.) First then we must state what sublimity comes from: the orator must not have low or ignoble thoughts. Those whose thoughts and habits all their lives are trivial and servile cannot possibly produce anything admirable or worthy of eternity. Words will be great if thoughts are weighty. (4.) This is why splendid remarks come naturally to the proud; the man who, when Parmenio said, "I should have been content". . . .[19] [Lacuna equivalent to about nine pages]

SUCCESSFUL AND UNSUCCESSFUL WAYS OF REPRESENTING SUPERNATURAL BEINGS AND OF EXCITING AWE

. . . the interval between earth and heaven. (5.) One might say that this is the measure not so much of strife as of Homer.[20] Contrast the line about Darkness in Hesiod—if the *Shield* is by Hesiod: "Mucus dripped from her nostrils."[21] This gives a repulsive picture, not one to excite awe. But how does Homer magnify the divine power? "As far as a man can peer through the mist,/Sitting on watch, looking over the wine-dark sea,/So long is the stride of the gods' thundering horses."[22] He uses a cosmic distance to measure this speed. This enormously impressive image would make anybody say, and with reason that, if the horses of the gods took two strides like that, they would find there was not enough room in the world. (6.) The imaginative pictures in the Battle of the Gods are also very remarkable:

> And the great heavens and Olympus trumpeted
> around them.
> Aïdoneus, lord of the dead, was frightened in his
> depths;
> And in fright he jumped from his throne, and shouted,
> For fear the earth-shaker Poseidon might break
> through the ground,
> And gods and men might see
> The foul and terrible halls, which even the gods
> detest.[32]

Do you see how the earth is torn from its foundations, Tartarus laid bare, and the whole universe overthrown and broken up, so that all things—Heaven and Hell, things mortal and things immortal—war together and are at risk together in that ancient battle? (7.) But, terrifying as all this is, it is blasphemous and indecent unless it is interpreted allegorically; in relating the gods' wounds, quarrels, revenges, tears, imprisonments, and manifold misfortunes, Homer, as it seems to me, has done his best to make the men of the Trojan war gods, and the gods men. If men are unhappy, there is always death as a harbor in trouble; what he has done for his gods is to make them immortal indeed, but immortally miserable.

(8.) Much better than the Battle of the Gods are the passages which represent divinity as genuinely unsoiled and great and pure. The lines about Poseidon, much discussed by my predecessors, exemplify this:

> The high hills and the forest trembled,
> And the peaks and the city of Troy and the Achaean
> ships
> Under the immortal feet of Poseidon as he went his
> way.
> He drove over the waves, and the sea-monsters gam-
> bolled around him,
> Coming up everywhere out of the deep; they recog-
> nized their king.
> The sea parted in joy; and the horses flew onward.[24]

(9.) Similarly, the lawgiver of the Jews, no ordinary man—for he understood and expressed God's power in accordance with its worth—writes at the beginning of his *Laws*: "God said"—now what?—" 'Let there be light,' and there was light; 'Let there be earth,' and there was earth."[25]

(10.) Perhaps it will not be out of place, my friend, if I add a further Homeric example—from the human sphere this time—so that we can see how the poet is accustomed to enter into the greatness of his heroes. Darkness falls suddenly. Thickest night blinds the Greek army. Ajax is bewildered. "O Father Zeus," he cries, "Deliver the sons of the Achaeans out of the mist,/Make the sky clear, and let us see;/In the light—kill us."[26] The feeling here is genuinely Ajax's. He does not pray for life—that would be a request unworthy of a hero—but having no good use for his courage in the paralyzing darkness, and so angered at his inactivity in the battle, he asks for light, and quickly: he will at all costs find a shroud worthy of his valor, though Zeus be arrayed against him.

COMPARISON BETWEEN THE ILIAD AND THE ODYSSEY

(11.) In this passage, it is the real Homer, the gale of whose genius fans the excitement of battle; the poet "Rages like Ares, spear-brandishing, or the deadly fire/Raging in the mountains, in the thickets of the deep wood./Foam shows at his mouth."[27] In the *Odyssey*, on the other hand—and there are many reasons for adding this to our inquiry—he demonstrates that when a great mind begins to decline, a love of story-telling characterizes its old age. (12.) We can tell that the *Odyssey* was his second work from various considerations, in particular from his insertion of the residue of the Trojan troubles in the poem in the form of episodes, and the way in which he pays tribute of lamentation and pity to the heroes, treating them as persons long known. The *Odyssey* is simply an epilogue to the *Iliad*: "There lies warlike Ajax, there Achilles,/There Patroclus, the gods' peer as a counsellor,/And there my own dear son."[28] (13.) For the same reason, I maintain, he made the whole body of the *Iliad*, which was written at the height of his powers, dramatic and exciting, whereas most of the *Odyssey* consists of narrative, which is a characteristic of old age. Homer in the *Odyssey* may be compared to the setting sun: the size remains without the force. He no longer sustains the tension as it was in the tale of Troy, nor the consistent level of elevation which never admitted any falling off. The outpouring of passions crowding one or another has gone; so has the versatility, the realism, the abundance of imagery taken from the life. We see greatness on the ebb. It is as though the Ocean were withdrawing into itself and flowing quietly in its own bed. Homer is lost in the realm of the fabulous and incredible. (14.) In saying this, I have not forgotten the storms in the *Odyssey*, the story of Cyclops, and a few other episodes; I am speaking of old age—but it is the old age of a Homer. The point about all these stories is that the mythical element in them predominates over the realistic.

I digressed into this topic, as I said, to illustrate how easy it is for great genius to be perverted in decline into nonsense. I mean things like the story of the wineskin, the tale of the men kept as pigs in Circe's palace ("howling piglets," Zoilus called them), the feeding of Zeus by the doves (as though he were a chick in the nest), the ten days on the raft without food, and the improbabilities of the murder of the suitors.[29] What can we say of all this but that it really is "the dreaming of a Zeus"? (15.) There is also a second reason for discussing the *Odyssey*. I want you to understand that the decline of emotional power in great writers and poets turns to a capacity for depicting manners. The realistic description of Odysseus' household forms a kind of comedy of manners.

SELECTION AND ORGANIZATION OF MATERIAL

(X.1.) Now have we any other means of making our writing sublime? Every topic naturally includes certain elements which are inherent in its raw material. It follows that sublimity will be achieved if we consistently select the most important of these inherent features and learn to organize them as a unity by combining one with another. The first of these procedures attracts the reader by the selection of details, the second by the compression of those selected.

Consider Sappho's treatment of the feelings involved in the madness of being in love. She uses the attendant circumstances and draws on real life at every point. And in what does she show her quality? In her skill in selecting the outstanding details and making a unity of them:

(2.) To me he seems a peer of the gods, the man who sits facing
you and hears your sweet voice
And lovely laughter; it flutters my heart in my breast.
When I see you only for a moment, I cannot speak;
My tongue is broken, a subtle fire runs under my skin; my
eyes cannot see, my ears hum;
Cold sweat pours off me; shivering grips me all over; I am
paler than grass; I seem near to dying;
But all must be endured. . . .[30]

(3.) Do you not admire the way in which she brings everything together—mind and body, hearing and tongue, eyes and skin? She seems to have lost them all, and to be looking for them as though they were external to her. She is cold and hot, mad and sane, frightened and near death, all by turns. The result is that we see in her not a single emotion, but a complex of emotions. Lovers experience all this; Sappho's excellence, as I have said, lies in her adoption and combination of the most striking details.

A similar point can be made about the descriptions of storms in Homer who always picks out the most terrifying aspects. (4.) The author of the *Arimaspea* on the other hand expects these lines to excite terror:

This too is a great wonder to us in our hearts:
There are men living on water, far from land, on the deep sea:
Miserable they are, for hard is their lot;

They give their eyes to the stars, their lives to the sea;
Often they raise their hands in prayer to the gods,
As their bowels heave in pain.[31]

Anyone can see that this is more polished than awe-inspiring. (5.) Now compare it with Homer (I select one example out of many):

He fell upon them as upon a swift ship falls a wave,
Huge, wind-reared by the clouds. The ship
Is curtained in foam, a hideous blast of wind
Roars in the sail. The sailors shudder in terror:
They being carried away from under death, but only just.[32]

(6.) Aratus rtied to transfer the same thought: "A little plank wards off Hades."[33] But this is smooth and unimpressive, not frightening. Moreover, by saying "a plank wards off Hades," he has got rid of the danger. The plank *does* keep death away. Homer, on the other hand, does not banish the cause of fear at a stroke; he gives a vivid picture of men, one might almost say, facing death many times for every wave that comes. Notice also the forced combination of naturally uncompoundable prepositions: *hupek*, "away from under." Homer has tortured the words to correspond with the emotion of the moment, and expressed the emotion magnificently by thus crushing words together. He has in effect stamped the special character of the danger on the diction: "they are being carried away from under death."

(7.) Compare Archilochus on the shipwreck, and Demosthenes on the arrival of the news ("It was evening . . .").[34] In short, one might say that these writers have taken only the very best pieces, polished them up and fitted them together. They have inserted nothing inflated, undignified, or pedantic. Such things ruin the whole effect, because they produce, as it were, gaps or crevices, and so spoil the impressive thoughts which have been built into a structure whose cohesion depends upon their mutual relations.

AMPLIFICATION

(XI.1.) The quality called "amplification" is connected with those we have been considering. It is found when the facts or the issues at stake allow many starts and pauses in each section. You wheel up one impressive unit after another to give a series of increasing importance. (2.) There are innumerable varieties of amplification: it may be produced by commonplaces, by exaggeration or intensification of facts or arguments, or by a build-up of action or emotion. The orator should realize, however, that none of these will have its full effect without sublimity. Passages expressing pity or disparagement are no doubt an exception; but in any other instance of amplification, if you take away the sublime element, you take the soul away from the body. Without the strengthening influence of the sublimity, the effective element in the whole loses all its vigor and solidity. (3.) What is the difference between this precept and the point made above about the inclusion of vital details and their combination in a unity? What in general is the difference between amplification and sublimity? I must define my position briefly on these points, in order to make myself clear.

(XII.1.) I do not feel satisfied with the definition given by the rhetoricians: "amplification is expression which adds grandeur to its subject." This might just as well be a definition of sublimity or emotion or tropes. All these add grandeur of some kind. The difference lies, in my opinion, in the fact that sublimity depends on elevation, whereas amplification involves extension; sublimity exists often in a single thought, amplification cannot exist without a certain quantity and superfluity. (2.) To give a general definition, amplification is an aggregation of all the details and topics which constitute a situation, strengthening the argument by dwelling on it; it differs from proof in that the latter demonstrates the point made. . . . [Lacuna equivalent to about three pages]

SAME GENERAL SUBJECT CONTINUED: A COMPARISON BETWEEN PLATO AND DEMOSTHENES, WITH A WORD ON CICERO

(3.) . . . spreads out richly in many directions into an open sea of grandeur. Accordingly, Demosthenes, the more emotional of the two, displays in abundance the fire and heat of passion, while Plato, consistently magnificent, solemn and grand, is much less intense—without of course being in the least frigid. (4.) These seem to me, my dear Terentianus—if a Greek is allowed an opinion—to be also the differences between the grandeur of Cicero and the grandeur of Demosthenes. Demosthenes has an abrupt sublimity; Cicero spreads himself. Demosthenes burns and ravages; he has violence, rapidity, strength and force, and shows them in everything; he can be compared to a thunderbolt or a flash of lightning. Cicero, on the other hand, is like a spreading conflagration. He ranges everywhere and rolls majestically on. His huge fires endure; they are renewed in various forms from time to time and repeatedly fed with fresh fuel.—(5.) But this is a comparison which your countrymen can make better than I. Anyway, the place for the intense, Demosthenic kind of sublimity is in indignant exaggeration, the violent emotion, and in general wherever the hearer has to be struck with amazement. The place for expansiveness is where he has to be deluged with words. This treatment is appropriate in *loci communes,* epilogues, digressions, all descriptive and exhibition pieces, historical or scientific topics, and many other departments.

(XIII.1.) To return to Plato, and the way in which he combines the "soundless flow"[35] of his smooth style with grandeur. A passage you have read in the

Republic[36] makes the point: "Men without experience of wisdom and virtue and always occupied with feasting and that kind of thing naturally go downhill and wander through life on a low plane of existence. They never look upwards to the truth and never rise, they never taste certain or pure pleasure. Like cattle, they always look down, bowed earthwards and tablewards; they feed and they breed, and their greediness in these directions makes them kick and butt till they kill one another with iron horns and hooves, because they can never be satisfied."

IMITATION OF EARLIER WRITERS AS A MEANS TO SUBLIMITY

(2.) Plato, if we will read him with attention, illustrates yet another road to sublimity, besides those we have discussed. This is the way of imitation and emulation of great writers of the past. Here too, my friend, is an aim to which we must hold fast. Many are possessed by a spirit not their own. It is like what we are told of the Pythia at Delphi: she is in contact with the tripod near the cleft in the ground which (so they say) exhales a divine vapor, and she is thereupon made pregnant by the supernatural power and prophesies as one inspired. Similarly, the genius of the ancients acts as a kind of oracular cavern, and effluences flow from it into the minds of their imitators. Even those previously not much inclined to prophesy become inspired and share the enthusiasm which comes from the greatness of others. (3.) Was Herodotus the only "most Homeric" writer? Surely Stesichorus and Archilochus earned the name before him. So, more than any, did Plato, who diverted to himself countless rills from the Homeric spring. (If Ammonius had not selected and written up detailed examples of this, I might have had to prove the point myself.) (4.) In all this process there is no plagiarism. It resembles rather the reproduction of good character in statues and works of art.[37] Plato could not have put such a brilliant finish on his philosophical doctrines or so often risen to poetical subjects and poetical language, if he had not tried, and tried wholeheartedly, to compete for the prize against Homer, like a young aspirant challenging an admired master. To break a lance in this way may well have been a brash and contentious thing to do, but the competition proved anything but valueless. As Hesiod says, "this strife is good for men."[38] Truly it is a noble contest and prize of honor, and one well worth winning, in which to be defeated by one's elders is itself no disgrace.

(XIV.1.) We can apply this to ourselves. When we are working on something which needs loftiness of expression and greatness of thought, it is good to imagine how Homer would have said the same thing, or how Plato or Demosthenes or (in history) Thucydides would have invested it with sublimity. These great figures, presented to us as objects of emulation and, as it were, shining before our gaze, will somehow elevate our minds to the greatness of which we form a mental image. (2.) They will be even more effective if we ask ourselves "How would Homer or Demosthenes have reacted to what I am saying, if he had been here? What would his feelings have been?" It makes it a great occasion, if you imagine such a jury or audience for your own speech, and pretend that you are answering for what you write before judges and witnesses of such heroic stature. (3.) Even more stimulating is the further thought: "How will posterity take what I am writing?" If a man is afraid of saying anything which will outlast his own life and age, the conceptions of his mind are bound to be incomplete and abortive; they will miscarry and never be brought to birth whole and perfect for the day of posthumous fame.

VISUALIZATION (PHANTASIA)

(XV.1.) Another thing which is very productive of grandeur, magnificence, and urgency, my young friend, is visualization (*phantasia*). I use this word for what some people call image-production. The term *phantasia* is used generally for anything which in any way suggests a thought productive of speech;[39] but the word has also come into fashion for the situation in which enthusiasm and emotion make the speaker *see* what he is saying and bring it *visually* before his audience. (2.) It will not escape you that rhetorical visualization has a different intention from that of the poets: in poetry the aim is astonishment, in oratory it is clarity. Both, however, seek emotion and excitement: "Mother, I beg you, do not drive them at me, / The women with the blood in their eyes and the snakes—They are here, they are here, jumping right up to me."[40] Or again: "O, O! She'll kill me. Where shall I escape?"[41] The poet himself saw the Erinyes, and has as good as made his audience see what he imagined. (3.) Now Euripides devotes most pains to producing a tragic effect with two emotions, madness and love. In these he is supremely successful. At the same time, he does not lack the courage to attempt other types of visualization. Though not formed by nature for grandeur, he often forces himself to be tragic. When the moment for greatness comes, he (in Homer's words) "Whips flank and buttocks with his tail / And drives himself to fight."[42] (4.) For example, here is Helios handing the reins to Phaethon:

"Drive on, but do not enter Libyan air—
It has no moisture in it, and will let
Your wheel fall through—"

and again:

"Steer towards the seven Pleiads."
The boy listened so far, then seized the reins,
Whipped up the winged team, and let them go.
To heaven's expanse they flew.
His father rode behind on Sirius,
Giving the boy advice: "That's your way, there:
Turn here, turn there."[43]

May one not say that the writer's soul has mounted the chariot, has taken wing with the horses and shares the danger? Had it not been up among those heavenly bodies and moved in their courses, he could never have visualized such things. Compare, too, his Cassandra: "Ye Trojans, lovers of horses . . ."[44] (5.) Aeschylus, of course, ventures on the most heroic visualizations; he is like his own Seven against Thebes—

Seven men of war, commanders of companies,
Killing a bull into a black-bound shield,
Dipping their hands in the bull's blood,
Took oath by Ares, by Enyo, by bloodthirsty Terror—

in a joint pledge of death in which they showed themselves no mercy. At the same time, he does sometimes leave his thoughts unworked, tangled, and hard. The ambitious Euripides does not shirk even these risks. (6.) For example, there is in Aeschylus a remarkable description of the palace of Lycurgus in its divine seizure at the moment of Dionysus' epiphany: "The palace was possessed, the house went bacchanal." Euripides expresses the same thought less harshly: "The whole mountain went bacchanal with them."[45] (7.) There is another magnificent visualization in Sophocles' account of Oedipus dying and giving himself burial to the accompaniment of a sign from heaven,[46] and in the appearance of Achilles to the departing fleet over his tomb.[47] Simonides has perhaps described this scene more vividly than anyone else; but it is impossible to quote everything. (8.) The poetical examples, as I said, have a quality of exaggeration which belongs to fable and goes far beyond credibility. In an orator's visualizations, on the other hand, it is the element of fact and truth which makes for success; when the content of the passage is poetical and fabulous and does not shrink from any impossibility, the result is a shocking and outrageous abnormality. This is what happens with the shock orators of our own day; like tragic actors, these fine fellows *see* the Erinyes, and are incapable of understanding that when Orestes says "Let me go; you are one of my Erinyes, / You are hugging me tight, to throw me into Hell."[48] he visualizes all this because he is mad.

(9.) What then is the effect of rhetorical visualization? There is much it can do to bring urgency and passion into our words; but it is when it is closely involved with factual arguments that it enslaves the hearer as well as persuading him. "Suppose you heard a shout this very moment outside the court, and someone said that the prison had been broken open and the prisoners had escaped—no one, young or old, would be so casual as not to give what help he could. And if someone then came forward and said 'This is the man who let them out,' our friend would never get a hearing; it would be the end of him."[49] (10.) There is a similar instance in Hyperides' defense of himself when he was on trial for the proposal to liberate the slaves which he put forward after the defeat.[50] "It was not the proposer," he said, "who drew up this decree: it was the battle of Chaeronea." Here the orator uses a visualization actually in the moment of making his factual argument, with the result that his thought has taken him beyond the limits of mere persuasiveness. (11.) Now our natural instinct is, in all such cases, to attend to the stronger influence, so that we are diverted from the demonstration to the astonishment caused by the visualization, which by its very brilliance conceals the factual aspect. This is a natural reaction: when two things are joined together, the stronger attracts to itself the force of the weaker. (12.) This will suffice for an account of sublimity of thought produced by greatness of mind, imitation, or visualization.

FIGURES

An Example to Illustrate the Right Use of Figures: The "Oath" in "On the Crown"

(XVI.1.) The next topic is that of figures. Properly handled, figures constitute, as I said, no small part of sublimity. It would be a vast, or rather infinite, labor to enumerate them all; what I shall do is to expound a few of those which generate sublimity, simply in order to confirm my point.

(2.) Here is Demosthenes putting forward a demonstrative argument on behalf of his policy.[51] What would have been the natural way to put it? "You have not done wrong, you who fought for the liberty of Greece; you have examples to prove this close at home: the men of Marathon, of Salamis, of Plataea did not do wrong." But instead of this he was suddenly inspired to give voice to the oath by the heroes of Greece: "By those who risked their lives at Marathon, you have not done wrong!" Observe what he effects by this single figure of conjuration, or "apostrophe" as I call it here. He deifies his audience's ancestors, suggesting that it is right to take an oath by men who fell so bravely, as though they were gods. He inspires the judges with the temper of those who risked their lives. He transforms his demonstration into an extraordinary piece of sublimity and passion, and into the convincingness of this unusual and amazing oath. At the same time he injects into his hearers' minds a healing specific, so as to lighten their hearts by these paeans of praise and make them as proud of the battle with Philip as of the triumphs of Marathon and Salamis. In short, the figure enables him to run away with his audience. (3.) Now the origin of this oath is said to be in the lines of Eupolis: "By Marathon, by *my* battle, / No one shall grieve me and escape rejoicing."[52] The greatness therefore depends not on the mere form of the oath, but on place, manner, occasion, and purpose. In Eupolis, there is nothing but the oath; he is speaking to the Athenians while their fortunes are still high and they need no comfort; and instead of immortalizing the men in order to engender in the audience a proper estimation of their valor, he wanders away from the actual people who risked their lives to an inanimate object, namely the battle. In Demosthenes, on the other hand, the oath is addressed to a defeated nation, to make them no longer think of Chaeronea as a disaster. It embraces, as I said, a demonstration that they "did no wrong," an illustrative example, a confirmation, an encomium, and an exhortation. (4.) Moreover, because he was faced with the possible objection "your policies brought us to defeat—and yet you swear by victories!" he brings his thought back under control and makes it safe and unanswerable, showing that sobriety is needed even under the influence of inspiration: "By those who *risked their lives* at Marathon, and *fought in the ships* at Salamis and Artemisium, and *formed the line* at Plataea!" He never says *conquered;* throughout he withholds the word for the final issue, because it was a happy issue, and the opposite to that of Chaeronea. From the same motives he forestalls his audience by adding immediately: "all of whom were buried at the city's expense, Aeschines—all, not only the successful."

THE RELATION BETWEEN FIGURES AND SUBLIMITY

(XVII.1.) At this point, my friend, I feel I ought not to pass over an observation of my own. It shall be very brief: figures are natural allies of sublimity and themselves profit wonderfully from the alliance. I will explain how this happens. Playing tricks by means of figures is a peculiarly suspect procedure. It raises the suspicion of a trap, a deep design, a fallacy. It is to be avoided in addressing a judge who has power to decide, and especially in addressing tyrants, kings, governors, or anybody in a high place. Such a person immediately becomes angry if he is led astray like a foolish child by some skillful orator's figures. He takes the fallacy as indicating contempt for himself. He becomes like a wild animal. Even if he controls his temper, he is now completely conditioned against being convinced by what is said. A figure is therefore generally thought to be best when the fact that it is a figure is concealed. (2.) This sublimity and emotion are a defense and a wonderful aid against the suspicion which the use of figures engenders. The artifice of the trick is lost to sight in the surrounding brillance of beauty and grandeur, and it escapes all suspicion. "By the men of Marathon . . ." is proof enough. For how did Demosthenes conceal the figure in that passage? By sheer brilliance of course. As fainter lights disappear when the sunshine surrounds them, so the sophisms of rhetoric are dimmed when they are enveloped in encircling grandeur. Something like this happens in painting: when light and shadow are juxtaposed in colors on the same plane, the light seems more prominent to the eye, and both stands out and actually appears much nearer. Similarly, in literature, emotional and sublime features seem closer to the mind's eye, both because of a certain natural kinship[53] and because of their brilliance. Consequently, they always show up above the figures, and overshadow and eclipse their artifice.

RHETORICAL QUESTIONS

(XVIII.1.) What are we to say of inquiries and questions? Should we not say that they increase the realism and vigor of the writing by the actual form of the figure?[54] "Or—tell me—do you want to go round asking one another 'Is there any news?' ? What could be hotter news than that a Macedonian is conquering Greece? 'Is Philip dead?' 'No, but he's ill.' What difference does it make to you? If anything happens to him, you will soon create another Philip."[55] Again: "Let us sail to Macedonia. 'Where shall we anchor?' says someone. The war itself will find out Philip's weak spots."[56] Put in the straightforward form, this would have been quite insignificant; as it is, the impassioned rapidity of question and answer and the device of making an objection to oneself have made the remark, in virtue of its figurative form, not only more sublime but more credible. (2.) For emotion carries us away more easily when it seems to be generated by the occasion rather than deliberately assumed by the speaker, and the self-directed question and its answer represent precisely this momentary quality of emotion. Just as people who are unexpectedly plied with questions become annoyed and reply to the point with vigor and exact truth, so the figure of question and answer arrests the hearer and cheats him into believing that all the points made were raised and are being put into words on the spur of the moment. Again—this sentence in Herodotus is believed to be a particularly fine example of sublimity— . . . [Lacuna equivalent to about three pages]

ASYNDETON

(XX.1.) The conjunction of several figures in one phrase also has a very stirring almost getting ahead of the speaker: "Engaging their shields, they pushed, fought, slew, died" (Xenophon.)[57] (2.) "We went as you told us, noble Odysseus, up the woods,/ We saw a beautiful palace built in the glades," says Homer's Eurylochus.[58] Disconnected and yet hurried phrases convey the impression of an agitation which both obstructs the reader and drives him on. Such is the effect of Homer's asyndeta.

ASYNDETON COMBINED WITH ANAPHORA

(XX.1.) The conjunction of several figures in one phrase also has a very stirring effect. Two or three may be joined together in a kind of team, jointly contributing strength, persuasiveness, charm. An example is the passage in *Against Midias,*[59] where asyndeton is combined with anaphora and vivid description. "The aggressor would do many things—some of which his victim would not even be able to tell anyone else—with gesture, with look, with voice." (2.) Then, to save the sentence from monotony and a stationary effect—for this goes with inertia, whereas disorder goes with emotion, which is a disturbance and movement of the mind—he leaps immediately to fresh instances of asyndeton and epanaphora: "With gesture, with look, with voice, when he insults, when he acts as an enemy, when he slaps the fellow, when he slaps him on the ears. . . ." The orator is doing here exactly what the bully does—hitting the jury in the mind with blow after blow. (3.) Then he comes down with a fresh onslaught, like a sudden squall: ". . . when he slaps the fellow, when he slaps him on the ears. That rouses people, that makes them lose control, when they are not used to being insulted. No one could bring out the horror of such a moment by a mere report." Here Demosthenes keeps up the natural effect of epanaphora and asyndeton by frequent variation. His order becomes disorderly, and his disorder in turn acquires a certain order.

POLYSYNDETON

(XXI.1.) Now add the conjunctions, as Isocrates' pupils do. "Again, one must not omit this point that the aggressor would do many things, first with gesture, then with look, and finally with voice." As you proceed with these insertions, it will become clear that the urgent and harsh character of the emotion loses its sting and becomes a spent fire as soon as you level it down to smoothness by the conjunctions. (2.) If you tie a runner's arms to his side, you take away his speed; likewise, emotion frets at being impeded by conjunctions and other additions, because it loses the free abandon of its movement, and the sense of being, as it were, catapulted out.

HYPERBATON

(XXII.1.) Hyperbaton belongs to the same general class. It is an arrangement of words or thoughts which differs from the normal sequence. . . .[60] It is a very real mark of urgent emotion. People who in real life feel anger, fear, or indignation, or are distracted by jealousy or some other emotion (it is impossible to say how many emotions there are; they are without number), often put one thing forward and then rush off to another, irrationally inserting some remark, and then hark back again to their first point. They seem to be blown this way and that by their excitement, as if by a veering wind. They inflict innumerable variations on the expression, the thought, and the natural sequence. Thus hyperbaton is a means by which, in the best authors, imitation approaches the effect of nature. Art is perfect when it looks like nature, nature is felicitous when it embraces concealed art. Consider the words of Dionysius of Phocaea in Herodotus: "Now, for our affairs are on the razor's edge, men of Ionia, whether we are to be free or slaves—and worse than slaves, runaways—so if you will bear hardships now, you will suffer temporarily but be able to overcome your enemies."[61] (2.) The natural order of thought would have been: "Men of Ionia, now is the time for you to bear hardships, for our affairs are on the razor's edge." The speaker has displaced "men of Ionia"; he begins with the cause of fear, as though the alarm was so pressing that he did not even have time to address the audience by name. He has also diverted the order of thought. Before saying that they must suffer hardship themselves (that is the gist of his exhortation), he first gives the reason why it is necessary, by saying "our affairs are on the razor's edge." The result is that he seems to be giving not a premeditated speech but one forced on him by the circumstances. (3.) It is even more characteristic of Thucydides to show ingenuity in separating by transpositions even things which are by nature completely unified and indivisible. Demosthenes is less wilful in this than Thucydides, but no one uses this kind of effect more lavishly. His transpositions produce not only a great sense of urgency but the appearance of extemporization, as he drags his hearers with him into the hazards of his long hyperbata. (4.) He often holds in suspense the meaning which he set out to convey and, introducing one extraneous item after another in an alien and unusual place before getting to the main point, throws the hearer into a panic lest the sentence collapse altogether, and forces him in his excitement to share the speaker's peril, before, at long last and beyond all expectation, appositely paying off at the end the long due conclusion; the very audacity and hazardousness of the hyperbata add to the astounding effect. There are so many examples that I forbear to give any.

CHANGES OF CASE, TENSE, PERSON, NUMBER, GENDER; PLURAL FOR SINGULAR AND SINGULAR FOR PLURAL

(XXIII.1.) What is called polyptoton, like accumulation, variation, and climax, is, as you know, extremely effective and contributes both to ornament and to sublimity and emotion of every kind.[62] How do variations in case, tense, person, number, and gender diversify and stimulate the style? (2.) My answer to this is that, as regards variations of number, the lesser effect (though a real one) is produced by instances in which singular forms are seen on reflection to be plural in sense: "The innumerable host/Were scattered over the sandy beach, and shouted." More worthy of note are the examples in which plurals give a more grandiose effect, and court success by the sense of multitude expressed by the grammatical number. (3.) An example comes in Sophocles, where Oedipus says:

Weddings, weddings,
You bred me and again released my seed,

Made fathers, brothers, children, blood of the kin,
Brides, wives, mothers—all
The deeds most horrid ever seen in men.[63]

All this is about Oedipus on the one hand and Jocasta on the other, but the expansion of the number to the plural forms pluralizes the misfortunes also. Another example is: "Hectors and Sarpedons came forth."[64] Another is the Platonic passage about the Athenians, which I have quoted elsewhere:[65] (4.) "No Pelopses or Cadmuses or Aegyptuses or Danauses or other barbarians by birth have settled among us; we are pure Greeks, with no barbarian blood," and so on. Such an agglomeration of names in crowds naturally makes the facts sound more impressive. But the practice is only to be followed when the subject admits amplification, abundance, hyperbole, or emotion—one or more of these. Only a sophist has bells on his harness wherever he goes.

(XXIV.1.) The contrary device—the contraction of plurals into singulars—also sometimes produces a sublime effect. "The whole Peloponnese was divided."[66] "When Phrynichus produced *The Capture of Miletus* the theater burst into tears" ("theater" for "spectators.").[67] To compress the separate individuals into the corresponding unity produces a more solid effect. (2.) The cause of the effect is the same in both cases. Where the nouns are singular, it is a mark of unexpected emotion to pluralize them.[68] Where they are plural, to unite the plurality under one well-sounding word is again surprising because of the opposite transformation of the facts.

VIVID PRESENT TENSE

(XXV.) To represent past events as present is to turn a narrative into a thing of immediate urgency. "A man who has fallen under Cyrus' horse and is being trampled strikes the horse in the belly with his sword. The horse, convulsed, shakes Cyrus off. He falls." (Xenophon[69]). This is common in Thucydides.

IMAGINARY SECOND PERSON

(XXVI.1.) Urgency may also be conveyed by the replacement of one grammatical person by another. It often gives the hearer the sense of being in the midst of the danger himself. "You would say they were tireless, never wearied in war,/So eagerly they fought" (Homer[70]). "May you never be drenched in the sea in that month!" (Aratus[71]). (2.) "You will sail upstream from Elephantine, and then you will come to a smooth plain. After crossing this, you will embark on another boat and sail for two days. Then you will come to a great city called Meroe" (Herodotus[72]). Do you see, my friend, how he grips your mind and takes it on tour through all these places, making hearing as good as seeing? All such forms of expression, being directed to an actual person, bring the hearer into the presence of real events. (3.) Moreover, if you speak as though to an individual and not to a large company, you will affect him more and make him more attentive and excited, because the personal address stimulates: "You could not tell with whom Tydides stood."[73]

LAPSES INTO DIRECT SPEECH

(XXVII.1.) Sometimes a writer, in the course of a narrative in the third person, makes a sudden change and speaks in the person of his character. This kind of thing is an outburst of emotion.

> Hector shouted aloud to the Trojans
> To rush for the ships, and leave the spoils of the dead.
> "If I see anyone away from the ships of his own accord,
> I will have him killed on the spot." [74]

Here the poet has given the narrative to himself, as appropriate to him, and then suddenly and without warning has put the abrupt threat in the mouth of the angry prince. It would have been flat if he had added "Hector said." As it is, the change of construction is so sudden that it has outstripped its creator. (2.) Hence the use of this figure is appropriate when the urgency of the moment gives the writer no chance to delay, but forces on him an immediate change from one person to another. "Ceyx was distressed at this, and ordered the children to depart. 'For I am unable to help you. Go therefore to some other country, so as to save yourselves without harming me' " (Hecataeus[75]). (3.) Somewhat different is the method by which Demosthenes in *Against Aristogiton*[76] makes variation of person produce the effect of strong emotion and rapid change of tone: "Will none of you be found to feel bile or anger at the violence of this shameless monster, who—you vile wretch, your right of free speech is barred not by gates and doors which can be opened, but . . . !" He makes the change before the sense is complete, and in effect divides a single thought between two persons in his passion ("who—you vile wretch . . . !"), as well as turning to Aristogiton and giving the impression of abandoning the course of his argument—with the sole result, so strong is the emotion, of giving it added intensity. (4.) So also Penelope:

> Herald, why have the proud suitors sent you here?
> Is it to tell Odysseus' maidservants
> To stop their work and get dinner for them?
> After their wooing, may they never meet again!

May this be their last dinner here—
You who gather together so often and waste wealth,
Who never listened to your fathers when you were children
And they told you what kind of man Odysseus was![77]

PERIPHRASIS

(XXVIII.1.) No one, I fancy, would question the fact that periphrasis is a means to sublimity. As in music the melody is made sweeter by what is called the accompaniment, so periphrasis is often heard in concert with the plain words and enhances them with a new resonance. This is especially true if it contains nothing bombastic or tasteless but only what is pleasantly blended. (2.) There is a sufficient example in Plato, at the beginning of the Funeral Speech: "These men have received their due, and having received it they go on their fated journey, escorted publicly by their country and privately each by his own kindred."[78] Plato here calls death a "fated journey" and the bestowal of regular funeral rites a public escort by the country. This surely adds no inconsiderable impressiveness to the thought. He has lyricized the bare prose, enveloping it in the harmony of the beautiful periphrasis. (3.) "You believe labor to be the guide to a pleasant life; you have gathered into your souls the noblest and most heroic of possessions: you enjoy being praised more than anything else in the world" (Xenophon[79]). In this passage "you make labor the guide to a pleasant life" is put for "you are willing to labor." This and the other expansions invest the praise with a certain grandeur of conception. (4.) Another example is the inimitable sentence of Herodotus: "The goddess struck the Scythians who plundered the temple with a feminine disease."[80]

(XXIX.1.) Periphrasis, however, is a particularly dangerous device if it is not used with moderation. It soon comes to be heavy and dull, smelling of empty phrases and coarseness of fiber. This is why Plato—who is fond of the figure and sometimes uses it unseasonably—is ridiculed for the sentence in the *Laws*[81] which runs: "Neither silvern wealth nor golden should be permitted to establish itself in the city." If he had wanted to prohibit cattle, says the critic, he would have talked of "ovine and bovine" wealth.

CONCLUSION OF THE SECTION ON FIGURES

(2.) So much, my dear Terentianus, by way of digression on the theory of the use of those figures which conduce to sublimity. They all make style more emotional and excited, and emotion is as essential a part of sublimity as characterization is of charm.[82] [Lacuna of about three pages]

DICTION

General Remarks

(XXX.1.) Thought and expression are of course very much involved with each other. We have therefore next to consider whether any topics still remain in the field of diction. The choice of correct and magnificent words is a source of immense power to entice and charm the hearer. This is something which all orators and other writers cultivate intensely. It makes grandeur, beauty, old-world charm, weight, force, strength, and a kind of luster bloom upon our words as upon beautiful statues; it gives things life and makes them speak. But I suspect there is no need for me to make this point; you know it well. (2.) It is indeed true that beautiful words are the light that illuminates thought. Magniloquence, however, is not always serviceable: to dress up trivial material in grand and solemn language is like putting a huge tragic mask on a little child. In poetry and history, however. . . . [Lacuna equivalent to about three pages]

USE OF EVERYDAY WORDS

(XXXI.1.) . . . and productive, as is Anacreon's "I no longer turn my mind to the Thracian filly."[83] Similarly, Theopompus' much admired phrase seems to me to be particularly expressive because of the aptness of the analogy, though Caecilius manages to find fault with it: "Philip was excellent at stomaching facts." An idiomatic phrase is sometimes much more vivid than an ornament of speech, for it is immediately recognized from everyday experience, and the familiar is inevitably easier to credit. "To stomach facts" is thus used vividly of a man who endures unpleasantness and squalor patiently, and indeed with pleasure, for the sake of gain. (2.) There are similar things in Herodotus: "Cleomenes in his madness cut his own flesh into little pieces with a knife till he had sliced himself to death," "Pythes continued fighting on the ship until he was cut into joints."[84] These phrases come within an inch of being vulgar, but they are so expressive that they avoid vulgarity.

METAPHORS

(XXXII.1) As regards number of metaphors, Caecilius seems to agree with the propounders of the rule that not more than two or at most three may be used of the same subject. Here too Demosthenes is our canon. The right occasions are when emotions come flooding in and bring the multiplication of metaphors with them as a necessary accompaniment. (2.) "Vile flatterers, mutilators of their countries, who have given away liberty as a drinking present, first to Philip and now to Alexander, measuring happiness by the belly and the basest impulses overthrowing liberty and freedom from despotism, which Greeks of old regarded as the canons and standards of the good."[85] In this passage the orator's anger against traitors obscures the multiplicity of his metaphors. (3.) This is why Aristotle and Theophrastus say that there are ways of softening bold metaphors —namely by saying "as if," "as it were," "if I may put it so," or "if we may venture on a bold expression." Apology, they say, is a remedy for audacity. (4.) I accept this doctrine, but I would add—and I said the same about figures—that strong and appropriate emotions and genuine sublimity are a specific palliative for multiplied or daring metaphors, because their nature is to sweep and drive all these other things along with the surging tide of their movement. Indeed it might be truer to say that they *demand* the hazardous. They never allow the hearer leisure to count the metaphors, because he too shares the speaker's enthusiasm.

(5.) At the same time, nothing gives distinction to commonplaces and descriptions so well as a continuous series of tropes. This is the medium in which the description of man's bodily tabernacle is worked out so elaborately in Xenophon and yet more superlatively by Plato.[86] Thus Plato calls the head the "citadel" of the body; the neck is an "isthmus" constructed between the head and the chest; the vertebrae, he says, are fixed underneath "like pivots." Pleasure is a "lure of evil" for mankind: the tongue is a "taste-meter." The heart is a "knot of veins" and "fountain of the blood that moves impetuously round," allocated to the "guard-room." The word he uses for the various passages of the canals is "alleys." "Against the throbbing of the heart," he continues, "in the expectation of danger and in the excitation of anger, when it gets hot, they contrived a means of succor, implanting in us the lungs, soft, bloodless and with cavities, a sort of cushion, so that when anger boils up in the heart, the latter's throbbing is against a yielding obstacle, so that it comes to no harm." Again: he calls the seat of the desires "the women's quarters," and the seat of anger "the men's quarters." The spleen is for him "a napkin for the inner parts, which therefore grows big and festering through being filled with secretions." "And thereafter," he says again, "they buried the whole under a canopy of flesh," putting the flesh on "as a protection against dangers from without, like felting." Blood he called "fodder of the flesh." For the purpose of nutrition, he says also, "they irrigated the body, cutting channels as in gardens, so that the streams of the veins might flow as it were from an incoming stream, making the body an aqueduct." Finally: when the end is at hand, the soul's "ship's cables" are "loosed," and she herself "set free." (6.) The passage contains countless similar examples; but these are enough to make my point, namely that tropes are naturally grand, that metaphors conduce to sublimity, and that passages involving emotion and description are the most suitable field for them. (7.) At the same time, it is plain without my saying it that the use of tropes, like all other good things in literature, always tempts one to go too far. This is what people ridicule most in Plato, who is often carried away by a sort of literary madness into crude, harsh metaphors or allegorical fustian. "It is not easy to understand that a city ought to be mixed like a bowl of wine, wherein the wine seethes with madness, but when chastened by another, sober god, and achieving a proper communion with him, produces a good and moderate drink."[87] To call water "a sober god," says the critic, and mixture "chastening," is the language of a poet who is far from sober himself.

DIGRESSION: GENIUS *VERSUS* MEDIOCRITY

(8.) Faults of this kind formed the subject of Caecilius' attack in his book on Lysias, in which he had the audacity to declare Lysias in all respects superior to Plato. He has in fact given way without discrimination to two emotions: loving Lysias more deeply than he loves himself, he yet hates Plato with an even greater intensity. His motive, however, is desire to score a point, and his assumptions are not, as he believed, generally accepted. In preferring Lysias to Plato he thinks he is preferring a faultless and pure writer to one who makes many mistakes. But the facts are far from supporting his view.

(XXIII.1.) Let us consider a really pure and correct writer. We have then to ask ourselves in general terms whether grandeur attended by some faults of execution is to be preferred, in prose or poetry, to a modest success of impeccable soundness. We must also ask whether the greater *number* of good qualities or the greater good qualities ought properly to win the literary prizes. These questions are relevant to a discussion of sublimity, and urgently require an answer. (2.) I am certain in the first place that great geniuses are least "pure." Exactness in every detail involves a risk of meanness; with grandeur, as with great wealth, there ought to be something overlooked. It may also be inevitable that low or mediocre abilities should maintain themselves generally at a correct and safe level, simply because they take no risks and do not aim at the heights, whereas greatness, just because it is greatness, incurs danger. (3.) I am aware also of a second point. All human affairs are, in the nature of things, better known on their worse side; the memory of mistakes is ineffaceable, that of goodness is soon gone. (4.) I have myself cited not a few mistakes in Homer and other great writers, not because I take pleasure in their slips, but because I consider them not so much voluntary mistakes as oversights let fall at random through inattention and with the negligence of genius. I do, however, think that the greater good qualities, even if not consistently maintained, are always more likely to win the prize—if for no other reason, because of the greatness of spirit they reveal. Apollonius makes no mistakes in the *Argonautica*; Theocritus is very felicitous in the *Pastorals,* apart from a few passages not connected with the theme; but would you rather be Homer or Apollonius? (5.) Is the Eratosthenes of that flawless little poem *Erigone* a greater poet than Archilochus, with his abundant, uncontrolled flood, that bursting forth of the divine spirit which is so hard to bring under the rule of law? Take lyric poetry: would you rather be Bacchylides or Pindar? Take tragedy: would you rather be Ion of Chios or Sophocles? Ion and Bacchylides are impeccable, uniformly beautiful writers in the polished manner; but it is Pindar and Sophocles who sometimes set the world on fire with their vehemence, for all that their flame often goes out without reason and they collapse dismally. Indeed, no one in his senses would reckon all Ion's works put together as the equivalent of the one play *Oedipus.*

(XXXIV.1.) If good points were totted up, not judged by their real value, Hyperides would in every way surpass Demosthenes. He is more versatile,[88] and has more good qualities. He is second-best at everything, like a pentathlon competitor; always beaten by the others for first place, he remains the best of the non-specialists. (2.) In fact, he reproduces all the good features of Demosthenes, except his word-arrangement, and also has for good measure the excellences and graces of Lysias. He knows how to talk simply where appropriate; he does not deliver himself of everything in the same tone, like Demosthenes. His expression of character has sweetness and delicacy. Urbanity, sophisticated sarcasm, good breeding, skill in handling irony, humor neither rude nor tasteless but flavored with true Attic salt, an ingenuity in attack with a strong comic element and a sharp sting to its apt fun—all this produces inimitable charm. He has moreover great talents for exciting pity, and a remarkable facility for narrating myths with copiousness and developing general topics with fluency. For example, while his account of Leto is in his more poetic manner, his Funeral Speech is an unrivalled example of the epideictic style.[89] (3.) Demosthenes, by contrast, has no sense of character. He lacks fluency, smoothness, and capacity for the epideictic manner; in fact he is practically without all the qualities I have been describing. When he forces himself to be funny or witty, he makes people laugh at him rather than with him. When he wants to come near to being charming, he is furthest removed from it. If he had tried to write the little speech on Phryne or that on Athenogenes,[90] he would have been an even better advertisement for Hyperides. (4.) Yet Hyperides' beauties, though numerous, are without grandeur: "inert in the heart of a sober man," they leave the hearer at peace. Nobody feels frightened reading Hyperides. But when Demosthenes begins to speak, he concentrates in himself excellences finished to the highest perfection of his sublime genius—the intensity of lofty speech, living emotions, abundance, acuteness, speed where speed is vital, all his unapproachable vehemence and power. He concentrates it all in himself—they are divine gifts, it is almost blasphemous to call them human—and so outpoints all his rivals, compensating with the beauties he has even for those which he lacks. The crash of his thunder, the brilliance of his lightning make all other orators, of all ages, insignificant. It would be easier to open your eyes to an approaching thunderbolt than to face up to his unremitting emotional blows.

(XXXV.1.) To return to Plato and Lysias, there is, as I said, a further difference between them. Lysias is much inferior not only in the importance of the good qualities concerned but in their number; and at the same time he exceeds Plato in the number of his failings even more than he falls short in his good qualities.

(2.) What then was the vision which inspired those divine writers who disdained exactness of detail and aimed at the greatest prizes in literature? They saw many things. One was the fact that nature made man to be no humble or lowly creature, but brought him into life and into the universe as into a great festival, to be both a spectator and an enthusiastic contestant in its competitions. She implanted in our minds from the start an irresistible desire for anything which is great and, in relation to ourselves, supernatural. (3.) The universe therefore is not wide enough for the range of human speculation and intellect. Our thoughts often travel beyond the boundaries of our surroundings. If anyone wants to know what we were born for, let him look round at life and contemplate the splendor, grandeur, and beauty in which it everywhere abounds. (4.) It is a natural inclination that leads us to admire not the little streams, however pellucid and however useful, but the Nile, the Danube, the Rhine, and above all the Ocean. Nor do we feel so much awe before the little flame we kindle, because it keeps its light clear and pure, as before the fires of heaven, though they are often obscured. We do not think our flame more worthy of admiration than the craters of Etna, whose eruptions bring up rocks and whole hills out of the depths, and sometimes pour forth rivers of the earth-born, spontaneous fire. (5.) A single comment fits all these examples: the useful and necessary are readily available to man, it is the unusual which always excites our wonder.

(XXXVI.1.) So when we come to great geniuses in literature—where, by contrast, grandeur is not divorced from service and utility—we have to conclude that such men, for all their faults, tower far above mortal stature. Other literary qualities prove their users to be human; sublimity raises us towards the spiritual greatness of god. Freedom from error does indeed save us from blame, but it is only greatness that wins admiration. (2.) Need I add that every one of those great men redeems all his mistakes many times over by a single sublime stroke? Finally, if you picked out all the mistakes in Homer, Demosthenes, Plato, and all the other really great men, and put them together, the total would be found to be a minute fraction of the successes which those heroic figures have to their credit. Posterity and human experience—judges whose sanity envy cannot question—place the crown of victory on their heads. They keep their prize irrevocably, and will do so, "So long as waters flow and tall trees flourish."[91]

(3.) It has been remarked that "the failed Colossus is no better than the

Doryphorus of Polyclitus."[92] There are many ways of answering this. We may say that accuracy is admired in art and grandeur in nature, and it is *by nature* that man is endowed with the power of speech; or again that statues are expected to represent the human form, whereas, as I said, something higher than human is sought in literature. (4.) At this point I have a suggestion to make which takes us back to the beginning of the book. Impeccability is generally a product of art; erratic excellence comes from natural greatness; therefore, art must always come to the aid of nature, and the combination of the two may well be perfection. It seemed necessary to settle this point for the sake of our inquiry; but everyone is at liberty to enjoy what he takes pleasure in.

SIMILES

(XXXVII.) We must now return to the main argument. Next to metaphors come comparisons and similes. The only difference is. . . . [Lacuna equivalent to about three pages]

HYPERBOLE

(XXXVIII.1.) . . . such expressions as: "Unless you've got your brains in your heels and are walking on them."[93] The important thing to know is how far to push a given hyperbole; it sometimes destroys it to go too far; too much tension results in relaxation, and may indeed end in the contrary of the intended effect. (2.) Thus Isocrates' zeal for amplifying everything made him do a childish thing. The argument of his *Panegyricus* is that Athens surpasses Sparta in services to the Greek race. Right at the beginning we find the following: "Secondly, the power of speech is such that it can make great things lowly, give grandeur to the trivial, say what is old in a new fashion, and lend an appearance of antiquity to recent events."[94] Is Isocrates then about to reverse the positions of Athens and Sparta? The encomium on the power of speech is equivalent to an introduction recommending the reader not to believe what he is told. (3.) I suspect that what we said of the best figures is true of the best hyperboles: they are those which avoid being seen for what they are. The desired effect is achieved when they are connected with some impressive circumstance and in moments of high emotion. Thucydides' account of those killed in Sicily is an example: "The Syracusans came down and massacred them, especially those in the river. The water was stained; but despite the blood and the dirt, men continued to drink it, and many still fought for it."[95] It is the intense emotion of the moment which makes it credible that dirt and blood should still be fought for as drink. (4.) Herodotus has something similar about Thermopylae: "Meanwhile though they defended themselves with swords (those who still had them), and with hands and mouths, the barbarians buried them with their missiles."[96] What is meant by fighting armed men with mouths or being buried with missiles? Still, it is credible; for we form the impression that the hyperbole is a reasonable product of the situation, not that the situation has been chosen for the sake of the hyperbole. (5.) As I keep saying, acts and emotions which approach ecstasy provide a justification for, and an antidote to, any linguistic audacity. This is why comic hyperboles, for all their incredibility, are convincing because we laugh at them so much: "He had a farm, but it didn't stretch as far as a Laconic letter." Laughter is emotion in pleasure. (6.) There are hyperboles which belittle as well those which exaggerate. Intensification is the factor common to the two species, vilification being in a sense an amplification of lowness.

WORD-ARRANGEMENT OR COMPOSITION

(XXXIX.1) There remains the fifth of the factors contributing to sublimity which we originally enumerated. This was a certain kind of composition or word-arrangement. Having set out my conclusions on this subject fully in two books, I shall here add only so much as is essential for our present subject.

EFFECT OF RHYTHM

Harmony is a natural instrument not only of conviction and pleasure in mankind, but also to a remarkable degree of grandeur and emotion. (2.) The flute fills the audience with certain emotions and makes them in a manner of speaking beside themselves and possessed. It sets a rhythm, it makes the hearer move to the rhythm and assimilate himself to the tune, "untouched by the Muses though he be."[97] The notes of the lyre, though they have no meaning, also, as you know, often cast a wonderful spell of harmony with their varied sounds and blended and mingled notes. (3.) Yet all these are but spurious images and imitations of persuasion, not the genuine activities proper to human nature of which I spoke.[98] Composition, on the other hand, is a harmony of words, man's natural instrument, penetrating not only the ears but the very soul. It arouses all kinds of conceptions of words and thoughts and objects, beauty and melody—all things native and natural to mankind. The combination and variety of its sounds convey the speaker's emotions to the minds of those around him and make the hearers share them. It fits his great thoughts into a coherent structure by the way in which it builds up patterns of words. Shall we not then believe that by all these methods it bewitches us and elevates to grandeur, dignity, and sublimity both every thought which comes within its compass and ourselves as well, holding as it does complete domination over our minds? It is absurd to question facts so generally agreed. Experience is proof enough.

(4.) The idea which Demosthenes uses in speaking of the decree[99] is reputed very sublime, and is indeed splendid. "This decree made the danger which then surrounded the city pass away like a cloud (*touto to psēphisma ton tote tē polei peristanta kindunon parelthein epoiēsen hōsper nephos*)." But the effect depends as much on the harmony as on the thought. The whole passage is based on dactylic rhythms, and these are very noble and grand. (This is why they form the heroic, the noblest meter we know.) . . . [A short phrase missing] . . . but make any change you like in the order: "*touto to psēphisma hōsper nephos epoiēse ton tote kindūnon parelthein,*" or cut off a syllable: "*epoiēse parelthein hōs nephos.*" You will immediately see how the harmony echoes the sublimity. The phrase *hōspēr nephos* rests on its long first unit (– –) which measures four shorts; the removal of a syllable (*hōs nephos*) at once curtails and mutilates the grand effect. Now lengthen the phrase: "*parelthein epoiēsen hōsperei nephos.*" It still means the same, but the effect is different, because the sheer sublimity is broken up and undone by the breaking up of the run of long syllables at the end.

EFFECT OF PERIOD STRUCTURE

(XL.1.) I come now to a principle of particular importance for lending grandeur to our words. The beauty of the body depends on the way in which the limbs are joined together, each one when severed from the others having nothing remarkable about it, but the whole together forming a perfect unity. Similarly great thoughts which lack connection are themselves wasted and waste the total sublime effect, whereas if they co-operate to form a unity and are linked by the bonds of harmony, they come to life and speak just by virtue of the periodic structure. It is indeed generally true that, in periods, grandeur results from the total contribution of many elements. (2.) I have shown elsewhere[100] that many poets and other writers who are not naturally sublime, and may indeed be quite unqualified for grandeur, and who use in general common and everyday words which carry with them no special effect, nevertheless acquire magnificence and splendor, and avoid being thought low or mean, solely by the way in which they arrange and fit together their words. Philistus, Aristophanes sometimes, Euripides generally, are among the many examples. (3.) Thus Heracles says after the killing of the children: "I'm full of troubles, there's no room for more."[101] This is a very ordinary remark, but it has become sublime, as the situation demands.[102] If you re-arrange it, it will become apparent that it is in the composition, not in the sense, that Euripides' greatness appears. (4.) Dirce is being pulled about by the bull: "And where it could, it writhed and twisted round, / Dragging at everything, rock, woman, oak, / Juggling with them all."[103] The conception is fine in itself, but it has been improved by the fact that the word-harmony is not hurried and does not run smoothly; the words are propped up by one another and rest on the intervals between them; set wide apart like that, they give the impression of solid strength.

FEATURES DESTRUCTIVE OF SUBLIMITY

(1) *Bad and Affected Rhythm*

(XLI.1.) Nothing is so damaging to a sublime effect as effeminate and agitated rhythm, pyrrhics (⏑⏑), trochees (–⏑ or ⏑⏑⏑) and dichorei (–⏑–⏑); they turn into a regular jig. All the rhythmical elements immediately appear artificial and cheap, being constantly repeated in a monotonous fashion without the slightest emotional effect. (2.) Worst of all, just as songs distract an audience from the action[104] and compel attention for themselves, so the rhythmical parts of speech produce on the hearer the effect not of speech but of rhythm, so that they foresee the coming endings and sometimes themselves beat time for the speaker and anticipate him in giving the step, just as in a dance.

(2) *The "Chopped Up" Style*

(3.) Phrases too closely knit[105] are also devoid of grandeur, as are those which are chopped up into short elements consisting of short syllables, bolted together, as it were, and rough at the joints.

(3) *Excessive Brevity*

(XLII.) Excessively cramped expression also does damage to sublimity. It cripples grandeur to compress it into too short a space. I do not mean proper compression, but cutting up into tiny pieces. Cramping mutilates sense; brevity gives directness. Conversely with fully extended expressions: anything developed at unseasonable length falls dead.[106]

(4) *Undignified Vocabulary*

(XLIII.1.) Lowness of diction also destroys grandeur.

The description of the storm in Herodotus is magnificent in conception, but includes expressions which are below the dignity of the subject.[107] "The sea seethed" is one instance: the cacophony does much to dissipate the sublime effect. "The wind slacked" is another example; yet another is the "unpleasant end" which awaited those who were thrown against the wreckage. "Slack" is an undignified, colloquial word; "unpleasant" is inappropriate to such an experience. (2.) Similarly, Theopompus first gives a magnificent setting to the descent of the Persian king on Egypt, and then ruins it all with a few words:

"What city or nation in Asia did not send its embassy to the King? What thing of beauty or value, product of the earth or work of art, was not brought him as a gift? There were many precious coverlets and cloaks, purple, embroidered, and white; there were many gold tents fitted out with all necessities; there were many robes and beds of great price. There were silver vessels and worked gold, drinking cups and bowls, some studded with jewels, some elaborately and preciously wrought. Countless myriads of arms were there, Greek and barbarian. There were multitudes of pack animals and victims fattened for slaughter, many bushels of condiments, many bags and sacks and pots of onions and every other necessity. There was so much salt meat of every kind that travellers approaching from a distance mistook the huge heaps for cliffs or hills thrusting up from the plain."

(3.) He passes from the sublime to the mean; the development of the scene should have been the other way round. By mixing up the bags and the condiments and the sacks in the splendid account of the whole expedition, he conjures up the vision of a kitchen. Suppose one actually had these beautiful objects before one's eyes, and then dumped some bags and sacks in the middle of the gold and jewelled bowls, the silver vessels, the gold tents, and the drinking-cups —the effect would be disgusting. It is the same with style: if you insert words like this when they are not wanted, they make a blot on the context. (4.) It was open to Theopompus to give a general description of the "hills" which he says were raised, and, having made this change,[108] to proceed to the rest of the preparations, mentioning camels and multitudes of beasts of burden carrying everything needed for luxury and pleasure of the table, or speaking of "heaps of all kinds of seeds and everything that makes for fine cuisine and dainty living." If he had wanted at all costs to make the king self-supporting, he could have talked of "all the refinements of maîtres-d'hôtel and chefs." (5.) It is wrong to descend, in a sublime passage, to the filthy and contemptible, unless we are absolutely compelled to do so. We ought to use words worthy of things. We ought to imitate nature, who, in creating man, did not set our private parts or the excretions of our body in the face, but concealed them as well as she could, and, as Xenophon says,[109] made the channels of these organs as remote as possible, so as not to spoil the beauty of the creature as a whole.

CONCLUSION OF CHAPS. 39–43

(6.) There is no urgent need to enumerate in detail features which produce a low effect. We have explained what makes style noble and sublime; the opposite qualities will obviously make it low and undignified.

APPENDIX: CAUSES OF THE DECLINE OF LITERATURE

(XLIV.1.) I shall not hesitate to add for your instruction, my dear Terentianus, one further topic, so as to clear up a question put to me the other day by one of the philosophers.

"I wonder," he said, "and so no doubt do many others, why it is that in our age there are minds which are strikingly persuasive and practical, shrewd, versatile, and well endowed with the ability to write agreeably, but no sublime or really great minds, except perhaps here and there. There is a universal dearth of literature." (2.) "Are we to believe," he went on, "the common explanation that democracy nurtures greatness, and great writers flourished with democracy and died with it? Freedom, the argument goes, nourishes and encourages the thoughts of the great, as well as exciting their enthusiasm for rivalry with one another and their ambition for the prize. (3.) In addition the availability of political reward sharpens and polishes up orators' talents by giving them exercise; they shine forth, free in a free world. We of the present day, on the other hand," he continued, "seem to have learned in infancy to live under justified slavery, swathed round from our first tender thoughts in the same habits and customs, never allowed to taste that fair and fecund spring of literature, freedom. We end up as flatterers in the grand manner." (4.) He went on to say how the same argument explained why, unlike other capacities, that of the orator could never belong to a slave. "The inability to speak freely and the consciousness of being a prisoner at once assert themselves, battered into him as they have been by the blows of habit. (5.) As Homer says,[110] 'The day of slavery takes half one's manhood away.' I don't know if it's true, but I understand that the cages in which dwarfs or Pygmies are kept not only prevent the growth of the prisoners but cripple them because of the fastening which constricts the body. One might describe all slavery, even the most justified,[111] as a cage for the soul, a universal prison."

(6.) "My good friend," I replied, "it is easy to find fault with the present situation; indeed it is a human characteristic to do so. But I wonder whether what destroys great minds is not the peace of the world, but the unlimited war which lays hold on our desires, and all the passions which beset and ravage our modern life. Avarice, the insatiable disease from which we all suffer, and love of pleasure are our two slavemasters; or perhaps one should say that they sink our ship of life with all hands. Avarice is a mean disease; love of pleasure is base through and through. (7.) I cannot see how we can honor, or rather deify, unlimited wealth as we do without admitting into our souls the evils which attach to it. When wealth is measureless and uncontrolled, extravagance comes with it, sticking close beside it, and, as they say, keeping step. The moment wealth opens the way into cities and houses, extravagance also enters and dwells therein. These evils then become chronic in people's lives, and, as the philosophers say, nest and breed. They are soon busy producing offspring: greed, pride, and luxury are their all too legitimate children. If these offspring of wealth are allowed to mature, they breed in turn those inexorable tyrants of the soul, insolence, lawlessness, and shamelessness. (8.) It is an inevitable process. Men will no longer open their eyes or give thought to their reputation with posterity. The ruin of their lives is gradually consummated in a cycle of such vices. Greatness of mind wanes, fades, and loses its attraction when men spend their admiration on their mortal parts and neglect to develop the immortal. (9.) One who has been bribed to give a judgment will no longer be a free and sound judge of rightness and nobility. The corrupt man inevitably thinks his own side's claim just and fair. Yet nowadays bribery is the arbiter of the life and fortunes of every one of us—not to mention chasing after other people's deaths and conspiring about wills. We are all so enslaved by avarice that we buy the power of making profit out of everything at the price of our souls. Amid such pestilential corruption of human life, how can we expect any free, uncorrupt judge of great things of permanent value to be left to us? How can we hope not to lose our case to the corrupt practices of the love of gain? (10.) Perhaps people like us are better as subjects than given our freedom. Greed would flood the world in woe, if it were really released and let out of the cage, to prey on its neighbors. (11.) "Idleness," I went on to say, "was the bane of present-day minds. We all live with it. Our whole régime of effort and relaxation[112] is devoted to praise and pleasure, not to the useful results that deserve emulation and honor. (12.) 'Best to let these things be,'[113] and proceed to our next subject. This was emotion, to which we promised to devote a separate treatise. It occupies as I said, a very important place among the constituents of literature in general, and sublimity in particular. . . ." [A few words missing at the end]

PLOTINUS

(205–269/270 A.D.)

INTRODUCTION

The principal source of biographical information about Plotinus is the Life of Plotinus written by his most eminent student, Porphyry. From this and other sources we learn that the eminent Neoplatonist philosopher was born in Egypt and lived the early part of his life there. He attended the lectures of various philosophers at Alexandria but without enthusiasm until he came under the influence of Ammonius Saccas, with whom he studied until 242 A.D. At that time he joined the Persian expedition of Emperor Gordian in the expectation of becoming more closely acquainted with Persian philosophy, but when Gordian died the expedition failed and Plotinus went to Rome where he founded his own school. He conceived of a plan to establish a city, Platonopolis, which was to be the realization of Plato's *Republic*; but, although his friend, Emperor Gallienus, showed interest in the project, the plan was never realized. With regard to Plotinus' personality we know that he had a great reputation for kindness and was named the guardian of the children of a number of his friends. He lived an intensely spiritual life and, according to Porphyry, he achieved ecstatic union with God four times in the six years during which Porphyry was his disciple. It was Porphyry who divided his writings into six books of nine chapters each and it is from the chapter divisions that the title *Enneads* (units of nine) was derived for the work as a whole.

As in the case of his predecessor, Plato, Plotinus' aesthetic theory is intimately connected with metaphysical considerations. Characteristically, Plotinus rejects the commonly held position (propounded by the Stoics) that beauty results from the existence of symmetry in all the parts of an object. He cites entities such as the virtues and the soul to which symmetry in the ordinary sense does not apply and yet which must be considered supremely beautiful. Plotinus solves this difficulty by adopting the Platonic position that beauty results from a communion of all things that are called beautiful and the always existing ideal form of beauty. The beautiful object achieves essential unity through its participation in the absolute principle of beauty. The task of judging beauty is attributed to a faculty of the soul which is capable of perceiving the presence of the ideal unifying principle of beauty in material things whether they be letters and words, colors and lines, or sounds and harmonies.

Plotinus' comments on art do not derive from an inquiry into "aesthetics"; instead, his position is essentially *theological,* proceeding directly from a concept of God. What Plato called "the One" is now emphasized as a totally active force, radiating outwards as the source and sustaining principle of all being. This premise allows for an elevation of the status of art. According to Plotinus, the artistic imitation is not merely a static copy of the objects it represents: it is also a manifestation of the *divine idea* which the object itself imitates. Plotinus supports this thesis by declaring that art can imitate objects which have never yet existed or which are incapable of sensuous apprehension; as an example he cites the representation of Zeus by Phidias, who had to envision the form that the great Olympian god might take if he were to manifest himself to our senses.

Plotinus is important, of course, for carrying Platonic themes into Hellenistic criticism. But his work also has great significance for the whole subsequent history of Western poetics: he is the first real "Neoplatonic" critic. Plotinus developed a strategy by means of which later critics, from Augustine to Shelley, could reconcile Platonic "imitation" with reverence for art. In short, the aesthetic experience could be interpreted as an encounter with a higher spiritual reality.

The translation of the selections used here is by Stephen MacKenna in Plotinus, *The Enneads,* 4th ed. rev. by B. S. Page (London: Faber and Faber; New York: Pantheon Books of Random House, 1969) and has been reprinted by permission of the publishers.

from THE ENNEADS

BEAUTY

(1.) Beauty addresses itself chiefly to sight; but there is a beauty for the hearing too, as in certain combinations of words and in all kinds of music, for melodies and cadences are beautiful; and minds that lift themselves above the realm of sense to a higher order are aware of beauty in the conduct of life, in actions, in character, in the pursuits of the intellect; and there is the beauty of the virtues. What loftier beauty there may be, yet, our argument will bring to light.

What, then, is it that gives comeliness to material forms and draws the ear to the sweetness perceived in sounds, and what is the secret of the beauty there is in all that derives from soul?

Is there some one principle from which all take their grace, or is there a beauty peculiar to the embodied and another for the bodiless? Finally, one or many, what would such a principle be?

Consider that some things, material shapes for instance, are gracious not by anything inherent but by something communicated, while others are lovely of themselves, as, for example, virtue.

The same bodies appear sometimes beautiful, sometimes not; so that there is a good deal between being body and being beautiful.

What, then, is this something that shows itself in certain material forms? This is the natural beginning of our inquiry.

What is it that attracts the eyes of those to whom a beautiful object is presented, and calls them, lures them, towards it, and fills them with joy at the sight? If we possess ourselves of this, we have at once a standpoint for the wider survey.

Almost everyone declares that the symmetry of parts towards each other and towards a whole, with, besides, a certain charm of color, constitutes the beauty recognized by the eye, that in visible things, as indeed in all else, universally, the beautiful thing is essentially symmetrical, patterned.

But think what this means.

Only a compound can be beautiful, never anything devoid of parts; and only a whole; the several parts will have beauty, not in themselves, but only as working together to give a comely total. Yet beauty in an aggregate demands beauty in details: it cannot be constructed out of ugliness; its law must run throughout.

All the loveliness of color and even the light of the sun, being devoid of parts and so not beautiful by symmetry, must be ruled out of the realm of beauty. And how comes gold to be a beautiful thing? And lightning by night, and the stars, why are these so fair?

In sounds also the simple must be proscribed, though often in a whole noble composition each several tone is delicious in itself.

Again since the one face, constant in symmetry, appears sometimes fair and sometimes not, can we doubt that beauty is something more than symmetry, that symmetry itself owes its beauty to a remoter principle?

Turn to what is attractive in methods of life or in the expression of thought; are we to call in symmetry here? What symmetry is to be found in noble conduct, or excellent laws, in any form of mental pursuit?

What symmetry can there be in points of abstract thought?

The symmetry of being accordant with each other? But there may be accordance or entire identity where there is nothing but ugliness: the proposition that honesty is merely a generous artlessness chimes in the most perfect harmony with the proposition that morality means weakness of will; the accordance is complete.

Then again, all the virtues are a beauty of the soul, a beauty authentic beyond any of these others; but how does symmetry enter here? The soul, it is true, is not a simple unity, but still its virtue cannot have the symmetry of size or of number: what standard of measurement could preside over the compromise or the coalescence of the soul's faculties or purposes?

Finally, how by this theory would there be beauty in the intellectual-principle, essentially the solitary?

(2.) Let us, then, go back to the source, and indicate at once the principle that bestows beauty on material things.

Undoubtedly this principle exists; it is something that is perceived at the first glance, something which the soul names as from an ancient knowledge and, recognizing, welcomes it, enters into unison with it.

But let the soul fall in with the ugly and at once it shrinks within itself, denies the thing, turns away from it, not accordant, resenting it.

Our interpretation is that the soul—by the very truth of its nature, by its affiliation to the noblest existents in the hierarchy of being—when it sees anything of that kin, or any trace of that kinship, thrills with an immediate delight, takes its own to itself, and thus stirs anew to the sense of its nature and of all its affinity.

But, is there any such likeness between the loveliness of this world and the splendors in the supreme? Such a likeness in the particulars would make the two orders alike: but what is there in common between beauty here and beauty there?

We hold that all the loveliness of this world comes by communion in ideal-form.

All shapelessness whose kind admits of pattern and form, as long as it remains outside of reason and idea, is ugly by that very isolation from the divine reason-principle. And this is the absolute ugly: an ugly thing is something that has not been entirely mastered by pattern, that is by reason, the matter not yielding at all points and in all respects to ideal-form.

But where the ideal-form has entered, it has grouped and coordinated what from a diversity of parts was to become a unity: it has rallied confusion into co-operation: it has made the sum one harmonious coherence: for the idea is a unity and what it molds must come to unity as far as multiplicity may.

And on what has thus been compacted to unity, beauty enthrones itself, giving itself to the parts as to the sum: when it lights on some natural unity, a thing of like parts, then it gives itself to that whole. Thus, for an illustration, there is the beauty, conferred by craftsmanship, of all a house with all its parts, and the beauty which some natural quality may give to a single stone.

This, then, is how the material thing becomes beautiful—by communicating in the reason-principle that flows from the divine.

(3.) And the soul includes a faculty peculiarly addressed to beauty—one incomparably sure in the appreciation of its own, when soul entire is enlisted to support its judgment.

Or perhaps the faculty acts immediately, affirming the beautiful where it finds something accordant with the ideal-form within itself, using this idea as a canon of accuracy in its decision.

But what accordance is there between the material and that which antedates all matter?

On what principle does the architect, when he finds the house standing before him correspondent with his inner ideal of a house, pronounce it beautiful? Is it not that the house before him, the stones apart, is the inner idea stamped upon the mass of exterior matter, the indivisible exhibited in diversity?

So with the perceptive faculty: discerning in certain objects the ideal-form which has bound and controlled shapeless matter, opposed in nature to idea, seeing further stamped upon the common shapes some shape excellent above the common, it gathers into unity what still remains fragmentary, catches it up and carries it within, no longer a thing of parts, and presents it to the inner ideal-principle as something concordant and congenial, a natural friend: the joy here is like that of a good man who discerns in a youth the early signs of a virtue consonant with the achieved perfection within his own soul.

The beauty of color is also the outcome of a unification: it derives from shape, from the conquest of the darkness inherent in matter by the pouring-in of light, the unembodied, which is a rational-principle and an ideal-form.

Hence it is that fire itself is splendid beyond all material bodies, holding the rank of ideal-principle to the other elements, making ever upwards, the subtlest and sprightliest of all bodies, as very near to the unembodied; itself alone admitting no other, all the others penetrated by it: for they take warmth but this is never cold; it has color primally; they receive the form of color from it: hence the splendor of its light, the splendor that belongs to the idea. And all that has resisted and is but uncertainly held by its light remains outside of beauty, as not having absorbed the plenitude of the form of color.

And harmonies unheard in sound create the harmonies we hear and wake the soul to the consciousness of beauty, showing it the one essence in another kind: for the measures of our sensible music are not arbitrary but are determined by the principle whose labor is to dominate matter and bring pattern into being.

Thus far of the beauties of the realm of sense, images and shadow-pictures, fugitives that have entered into matter—to adorn, and to ravish, where they are seen.

(4.) But there are earlier and loftier beauties than these. In the sense-bound life we are no longer granted to know them, but the soul, taking no help from the organs, sees and proclaims them. To the vision of these we must mount, leaving sense to its own low place.

As it is not for those to speak of the graceful forms of the material world who have never seen them or known their grace—men born blind, let us suppose—in the same way those must be silent upon the beauty of noble conduct and of learning and all that order who have never cared for such things, nor may those tell of the splendor of virtue who have never known the face of justice and of moral-wisdom beautiful beyond the beauty of evening and of dawn.

Such vision is for those only who see with the soul's sight—and at the vision, they will rejoice, and awe will fall upon them and a trouble deeper than all the rest could ever stir, for now they are moving in the realm of truth.

This is the spirit that beauty must ever induce, wonderment and a delicious trouble, longing and love and a trembling that is all delight. For the unseen all this may be felt as for the seen; and this the souls feel for it, every soul in some degree, but those the more deeply that are the more truly apt to this higher love—just as all take delight in the beauty of the body but all are not stung as sharply, and those only that feel the keener wound are known as lovers.

(5.) These lovers, then, lovers of the beauty outside of sense, must be made to declare themselves.

What do you feel in presence of the grace you discern in actions, in manners, in sound morality, in all the works and fruits of virtue, in the beauty of souls? When you see that you yourselves are beautiful within, what do you feel? What is this Dionysiac exultation that thrills through your being, this straining upwards of all your soul, this longing to break away from the body and live sunken within the veritable self?

These are no other than the emotions of souls under the spell of love.

ON THE INTELLECTUAL BEAUTY

(1.) It is a principle with us that one who has attained to the vision of the intellectual cosmos and grasped the beauty of the authentic intellect will be able also to come to understand the father and transcendent of that divine being. It concerns us, then, to try to see and say, for ourselves and as far as such matters may be told, how the beauty of the divine intellect and of the intellectual cosmos may be revealed to contemplation.

Let us go to the realm of magnitudes:—suppose two blocks of stone lying side by side: one is unpatterned, quite untouched by art; the other has been minutely wrought by the craftsman's hands into some statue of god or man, a Grace or a Muse, or if a human being, not a portrait but a creation in which the sculptor's art has concentrated all loveliness.

Now it must be seen that the stone thus brought under the artist's hand to the beauty of form is beautiful not as stone—for so the crude block would be as pleasant—but in virtue of the form or idea introduced by the art. This form is not in the material; it is in the designer before ever it enters the stone; and the artificer holds it not by his equipment of eyes and hands but by his participation in his art. The beauty, therefore, exists in a far higher state in the art; for it does not come over integrally into the work; that original beauty is not transferred; what comes over is a derivative and a minor: and even that shows itself upon the statue not integrally and with entire realization of intention but only in so far as it has subdued the resistance of the material.

Art, then, creating in the image of its own nature and content, and working by the idea or reason-principle of the beautiful object it is to produce, must itself be beautiful in a far higher and purer degree since it is the seat and source of that beauty, indwelling in the art, which must naturally be more complete than any comeliness of the external. In the degree in which the beauty is diffused by entering into matter, it is so much the weaker than that concentrated in unity; everything that reaches outwards is the less for it, strength less strong, heat less hot, every power less potent, and so beauty less beautiful.

Then again every prime cause must be, within itself, more powerful than its effect can be: the musical does not derive from an unmusical source but from music; and so the art exhibited in the material work derives from an art yet higher.

Still the arts are not to be slighted on the ground that they create by imitation of natural objects; for, to begin with, these natural objects are themselves imitations; then, we must recognize that they give no bare reproduction of the thing seen but go back to the reason-principles from which nature itself derives, and, furthermore, that much of their work is all their own; they are holders of beauty and add where nature is lacking. Thus Pheidias wrought the Zeus upon no model among things of sense but by apprehending what form Zeus must take if he chose to become manifest to sight.

(2.) But let us leave the arts and consider those works produced by nature and admitted to be naturally beautiful which the creations of art are charged with imitating, all reasoning life and unreasoning things alike, but especially the consummate among them, where the molder and maker has subdued the material and given the form he desired. Now what is the beauty here? It has nothing to do with the blood or the menstrual process: either there is also a color and form apart from all this or there is nothing unless sheer ugliness or (at best) a bare recipient as it were the mere matter of beauty.

Whence shone forth the beauty of Helen, battle-sought; or of all those women like in loveliness to Aphrodite; or of Aphrodite herself; or of any human being that has been perfect in beauty; or of any of these gods manifest to sight, or unseen but carrying what would be beauty if we saw?

In all these is it not the form-idea, something of that realm but communicated to the produced from within the producer, just as in works of art, we held, it is communicated from the arts to their creations? Now we can surely not believe that, while the made thing and the reason-principle thus impressed upon matter are beautiful, yet the principle not so alloyed but resting still with the creator—the idea primal and immaterial—is not beauty.

If material extension were in itself the ground of beauty, then the creating principle, being without extension, could not be beautiful: but beauty cannot be made to depend upon magnitude since, whether in a large object or a small, the one idea equally moves and forms the mind by its inherent power. A further indication is that as long as the object remains outside us we know nothing of it; it affects us by entry; but only as an ideal-form can it enter through the eyes which are not of scope to take an extended mass: we are, no doubt, simultaneouly possessed of the magnitude which, however, we take in not as mass but an elaboration upon the presented form.

Then again the principle producing the beauty must be, itself, ugly, neutral, or beautiful: ugly, it could not produce the opposite; neutral, why should its product be the one rather than the other? The nature, then, which creates things so lovely must be itself of a far earlier beauty; we, undisciplined in discernment of the inward, knowing nothing of it, run after the outer, never understanding that it is the inner which stirs us; we are in the case of one who sees his own reflection but not realizing whence it comes goes in pursuit of it.

NOTES

ARISTOPHANES: THE FROGS

1. Armor for the leg below the knee.
2. This seems to be a slip of memory on the part of Aristophanes. *The Persians* is reliably dated 472 B.C., *The Seven Against Thebes* 467 B.C.—R.L.
3. The heroine of a lost play named after her. Her story is similar to that of Phaidra, insofar as she made advances to Bellerophon, her husband's guest, was refused, and told her husband that Bellerophon had tried to seduce her.—R.L.
4. No one is willing to be *trierarch*. The *trierarchy,* a special duty or liturgy imposed on rich citizens, involved the outfitting and upkeep of a trireme (war galley), as well as the nominal command of the vessel on active service.—R.L.
5. *His nurses . . . life?* The nurse-procuress could be Phaidra's nurse in *Hippolytus*. In *Auge,* the heroine gave birth in the temple of Athene. In *Aeolus,* Makareus and Kanake, brother and sister, are involved in a love affair. For musings on life, see the fragment from Euripides' lost *Polyeidus*: "Who knows if life be not thought death, or death be life in the world below?" There is a similar thought in the lost *Phrixus.*—R.L.

PLATO: INTRODUCTION

1. See Richard P. McKeon, "The Concept of Imitation in Antiquity," in *Critics and Criticism: Ancient and Modern,* ed. by R. S. Crane (Chicago, Ill., 1952), pp. 147–75, and W. J. Verdenius, *Mimesis: Plato's Doctrine of Artistic Imitation and Its Meaning to Us* (Leyden, 1962).
2. Allen H. Gilbert, "Plato's *Ion,* Comic and Serious," in *Studies in Honor of De W. T. Starnes* (Austin, Texas, 1967), pp. 259–69.

PHAEDRUS

1. A sanctuary and oracular shrine of Zeus, located in the mountains of Epirus.

GORGIAS

1. Originally, choral hymns that were sung to Dionysus. Developed into a formal art form by Arion of Corinth (ca. 600 B.C.) and introduced into Athens by Lasus

of Hermione, dithyrambic poetry became one of the competitive subjects at the Greek festivals. In Plato's time it was the most important type of lyric poetry.

ION

1. Professional reciters of poetry.
2. Greek festival celebrated annually at Athens.
3. Or, "I think I have well deserved the golden crown given me by the Homeridae."—JOWETT'S EDITORS. The latter were reciters of Homer's poetry and claimed to be his descendants.
4. Mythical attendants of the nature goddess Cybele, who engaged in orgiastic ritual dances.
5. See Note 1 to *Phaedrus.*
6. Originally, a choral song in honor of Apollo or his sister Artemis.
7. *Iliad* XXIII.335.
8. *Iliad* XI.639–40.
9. *Iliad* XXIV.80
10. *Odyssey* XX.351.
11. *Iliad* XII.200.

THE REPUBLIC
Book III

1. Spoken by the ghost of Achilles, *Odyssey* XI.489.
2. *Iliad* XX.64.
3. Said by Achilles when he tries, in vain, to embrace the ghost of Patroclus, *Iliad* XXIII.103.
4. *Odyssey* X.495.
5. *Iliad* XVI.856.
6. *Iliad* XXIII.100.
7. *Odyssey* XXIV.6 (refers to the souls of the slain suitors of Penelope).
8. Appropriate.
9. Mourning his friend Patroclus, *Iliad* XXIV.10.
10. Perhaps in a metaphorical sense, "reeling." Plato has slightly altered the text of Homer.—JOWETT'S EDITORS.
11. *Iliad* XVIII.23.
12. When he saw Achilles mistreating the body of his son Hector, *Iliad* XXII.414.
13. The speaker is Thetis, the mother of Achilles, *Iliad* XVIII.54.
14. Zeus when he saw Hector pursued by Achilles, *Iliad* XXII.168.
15. *Iliad* XVI.433.
16. *Iliad* I.599.
17. *Odyssey* XVII.383ff.
18. Or, "if his words are accompanied by actions."—B.J.
19. *Iliad* IV.412.

20. *Iliad* III.3.
21. *Iliad* IV.431.
22. Spoken by Achilles to his king Agamemnon, *Iliad* I.225.
23. Odysseus is the speaker, *Odyssey* IX.8.
24. *Odyssey* XII.342.
25. *Iliad* XIV.294ff.
26. *Odyssey* VIII.266.
27. Odysseus is speaking, *Odyssey* XX.17.
28. Quoted by Suidas (a historical and literary encyclopedia compiled about 1,000 A.D.) as ascribed to Hesiod.
29. *Iliad* IX.515.
30. *Iliad* XXIV.175.
31. Cf. *Republic* X.595.
32. *Iliad* XXII.15ff.
33. *Iliad* XXI.130, 223ff.
34. *Iliad* XXIII.151.
35. *Iliad* XXII.395.
36. *Iliad* XXIII.175.
37. From the *Niobe* of Aeschylus.
38. Agamemnon and Menelaus, *Iliad* I.15.
39. A wreath or garland worn on the head.
40. Juror.
41. I.e. the four notes of the tetrachord.—B.J.
42. Socrates expresses himself carelessly in accordance with his assumed ignorance of the details of the subject. In the first part of the sentence he appears to be speaking of paeonic rhythms which are in the ratio of 3⁄2; in the second part, of dactylic and anapaestic rhythms, which are in the ratio of 1⁄1; in the last clause, of iambic and trochaic rhythms, which are in the ratio of 1⁄2 or 2⁄1.—B.J. In classical prosody, a long syllable is the equivalent of two short ones. The dactylic (—∪∪) and anapaestic (∪∪—) feet, each consisting of one long and two shorts, thus have a 1:1 ratio; the iambic (∪—) and trochaic (—∪) a 1:2 or 2:1 ratio; and the paean (first p., —∪∪∪; second p., ∪—∪∪; third ∪∪—∪; fourth, ∪∪∪—) a 3:2 ratio.

THE REPUBLIC
Book X

1. Stories taken from epic poetry often served as the plots of Greek tragedies. Thus Homer was considered the first tragic poet.
2. Or (probably better), "we have been accustomed to assume that there is one single idea corresponding to each group of particulars; and to these we give the same name (as we give the idea)."—JOWETT'S EDITORS, note abridged.
3. Or, "with his nouns and verbs."—B.J.
4. Dactylic hexameter.
5. Or, "law and the principle which the community in every case has pronounced to be the best."—JOWETT'S EDITORS.

6. Reading and sense uncertain. The origin of all these quotations is unknown.—JOWETT'S EDITORS.
7. I.e. imitative poetry. The word imitation, in the recent argument, had not the same sense as in Book III; but it has always been implied that there might be poetry which is not imitative.—JOWETT'S EDITORS.
8. Text doubtful. Perhaps "you demanded . . . this admission should be made."—JOWETT'S EDITORS.
9. *Odyssey* XI–XII.
10. I.e. those who were not incurable, but had further punishment to endure.—JOWETT'S EDITORS.
11. War galley; the earliest kind of a Greek warship.

LAWS

1. *Laws* V.741E.
2. *Laws* VI.764C.
3. *Laws* VI.765D.
4. Cf. *Republic* X.607A.
5. Or, . . . "even though the pleasure of music is not counted."—JOWETT'S EDITORS.
6. *Laws* I.644D.E.
7. *Laws* I.628.
8. *Odyssey* III.26ff.
9. The shortest metrical foot in classical verse, consisting of two short syllables (⏑⏑).
10. The solemn dance of the chorus in Greek tragedy.
11. Cf. *Republic* III.398A and X.607A.
12. Public square in which the popular political assembly met.

ARISTOTLE: INTRODUCTION

1. For a full discussion of this problem see O. B. Hardison's commentary in L. Golden and O. B. Hardison, Jr., *Aristotle's Poetics: A Translation and Commentary for Students of Literature* (Englewood Cliffs, N.J., 1968), pp. 230–37.
2. On the basis of the evidence from Book 10 of the *Republic,* the "copying" theory of imitation which is mentioned in the text has generally been attributed to Plato. Some scholars, however, having surveyed the entire corpus of Plato's work, have also attributed to him a more sophisticated view of imitation. See Richard McKeon, "Literary Criticism and the Concept of Imitation in Antiquity," in *Critics and Criticism: Ancient and Modern,* ed. R. S. Crane (Chicago, 1952), pp. 160–68; W. J. Verdenius, *Mimesis: Plato's Doctrine of Artistic Imitation and Its Meaning to Us* (Leyden, 1962); and L. Golden, "*Mimesis* and *Katharsis,*" *Classical Philology,* LXIV (1969), 143–53.
3. See, for example, Suzanne Langer, *Feeling and Form* (New York, 1953), p. 352: " 'Imitation' is used by Aristotle in much the same sense in which I use 'semblance' "; Roman Ingarden, "A Marginal Commentary on Aristotle's *Poetics* —Part II," tr. Helen Michejda, *Journal of Aesthetics and Art Criticism,* XX (1961–62), 282: "It

seems probable that Aristotle had in mind the same thing that in my book, *Das literarische Kunstwerk*, I called 'objective consistency' . . . within the framework of the world presented in the work"; and Northrop Frye, *Anatomy of Criticism* (Princeton, N.J., 1957), p. 113: the fictive imagination involves the "transmutation of experience into mimesis, of life into art, of routine into play."

4. *Aristotle's Theory of Poetry and Fine Art,* 4th ed. (New York, 1951), pp. 121–62.
5. "The Mimetic Principle" in *The World's Body,* 2nd ed. (Baton Rouge, La., 1968), pp. 196–97.
6. *Aristotle's Poetics* (Note 1), pp. 281–96.
7. An excellent warning against the confusion of the aesthetic principles of the *Poetics* with the non-aesthetic principles of the *Politics* has been given by Richard McKeon (Note 2), pp. 165–66.
8. For a discussion of Lessing's view see Ingram Bywater, ed., *Aristotle on the Art of Poetry* (London and New York, 1909), pp. 160–61.
9. Gerald F. Else, *Aristotle's Poetics: The Argument* (Cambridge, Mass., 1957), pp. 224–32, 423–47.
10. S. O. Haupt, *Wirkt die Tragödie auf das Gemüt oder den Verstand oder die Moralität der Zuschauer?* (Berlin, 1915) and *Die Lösung der Katharsis Theorie des Aristoteles* (Znaim, 1911).
11. Leon Golden, "Catharsis," *Transactions of the American Philological Association,* XCIII (1962), 51–60. See also his "*Mimesis* and *Katharsis,*" *Classical Philology,* LXIV (1969), 145–53.
12. H. D. F. Kitto, "Catharsis," in *The Classical Tradition: Literary and Historical Studies in Honor of Harry Caplan* (Ithaca, N.Y., 1966), pp. 133–47.
13. See J. M. Bremer, *Hamartia: Tragic Error in the Poetics of Aristotle and in Greek Tragedy* (Amsterdam, 1969); R. D. Dawe, "Some Reflections on *Ate* and *Hamartia,*" *Harvard Studies in Classical Philology,* LXXII (1968), 81–123; Martin Ostwald, "Aristotle on *Hamartia* and Sophocles' *Oedipus Tyrannos,*" in *Festschrift Ernst Kapp* (Hamburg, 1958), pp. 93–108.
14. "Tragedy and the Common Man," in Sylvan Barnet *et al,* eds., *Aspects of the Drama* (Boston, 1962), p. 64.

THE POETICS

1. See Plato, Note 1 to *Phaedrus.*
2. Dramatic representations of short scenes from daily life, involving dancing, music, and dialogue.
3. Poetry originally concerned with texts taken from the epic and presented with a flute or lyre accompaniment.
4. There is a lacuna in the text at this point where the name of another writer of nomic poetry was probably mentioned.
5. This poem is no longer attributed to Homer.
6. A form of drama in which the chorus was dressed as satyrs. In historical times a satyr play was presented as the fourth play in a tetralogy produced at Athenian dramatic festivals. The theme of the satyr play was mocking or "satirical" in tone,

contrasting with the seriousness of the other three dramas associated with it. Aristotle viewed the satyr play as a stage in the development of mature tragedy.

7. Athenian magistrates.
8. There is no word in the Greek text for "proper," but I have followed the practice of several other translators who add a modifier to the term "magnitude" where it is logically warranted. The term "representation" has also been added to the final clause of this sentence because of Aristotle's insistence that the pleasure of tragedy is achieved *through imitation* (Chapter XIV, lines 15–16).
9. Text is corrupt here.
10. A lost play by the 4th century tragic poet Theodectes.
11. Unknown. Possibly, a variant title for a tragedy by Sophocles.
12. The *Cresphontes* and the *Iphigenia,* the former no longer extant, are plays by Euripides. We have no further information concerning the *Helle.*
13. According to some scholars, a play by Euripides; others believe it to be a work of the dithyrambic poet Timotheus.
14. Euripides' play about the Amazon queen.
15. Medea escaped in a magic chariot in Euripides' tragedy.
16. A birthmark on the descendants of the armed men who, as legend has it, sprang up when Cadmus sowed the dragon's teeth at Thebes.
17. A lost drama by Sophocles.
18. Having had her tongue cut out by Tereus, Philomela disclosed the story of her rape through the web she wove.
19. The second play of the Aeschylean trilogy known as the *Oresteia.* The play describes Orestes' murder of his mother Clytemnestra, in vengeance for her killing of his father Agamemnon, and the subsequent madness visited upon him by the Erinyes in punishment for his crime.
20. Nothing more is known of these two plays, the *Tydeus* and the *Phinidae.*
21. Text is in dispute here.
22. The *Phthiotian Women* and *Peleus,* neither now extant, were probably written by Sophocles.
23. The *Daughters of Phorcis* and *Prometheus* are both by Aeschylus.
24. Opening line of the *Iliad.*
25. The passage that begins here is corrupt and difficult to interpret.
26. There is a lacuna in the text here. Massilia (Marseilles) was founded by Greeks from Phorcis.
27. "At her right breast" (*Iliad* V.393). Two words meaning "right" are quoted to illustrate Aristotle's point here.
28. This passage offers a number of difficulties in text and interpretation. The essential point is that the prose lines quoted can be technically turned into verse if enough licenses are allowed. The first phrase may be translated "I saw Epichares going to Marathon." The text of the second phrase is corrupt and does not have a clear meaning as it stands.
29. A lost play.
30. "Someone small, worthless, and unseemly" (*Odyssey* IX.515).
31. "Having set down [for him] an unseemly chair and a small table" (*Odyssey* XX.259).

32. "The shores cry out" (*Iliad* XVII.265).
33. One of the poems of the Trojan cycle once attributed to Homer. It described Paris' abduction of Helen and is no longer extant.
34. Part of the ancient epic cycle of poems composed after the Homeric epics by poets who are now unknown. The work has not survived.
35. The *Award of the Arms* may refer to the existing play *Ajax* of Sophocles or to a lost tragedy by Aeschylus. A play entitled *Neoptolemus* is attributed by Suidas (a literary and historical encyclopedia compiled around the year 1,000) to a tragic poet named Nicomachus. We have no further record of *Eurypylus,* the *Beggar,* and the *Return Voyage* as titles of tragedies.
36. Sophocles' *Laconian Woman* is lost. A play entitled the *Sack of Troy* is attributed to Iophon, who was the son of Sophocles and a tragic poet in his own right. Sophocles' *Sinon* has not survived. The *Women of Troy* is an extant play by Euripides.
37. Dactylic hexameter.
38. Musical competitions and athletic contests held, in honor of Apollo, every four years in Delphi.
39. Probably a lost play by Aeschylus.
40. There is a lacuna in the text here that I have filled by translating Bywater's suggested reading, *hēmarte de di'.*
41. "First of all, the mules" (*Iliad* I.50).
42. *Iliad* X.316.
43. *Iliad* IX.202.
44. *Iliad* XVIII.489.
45. The problem here is that words that are spelled the same way change their meaning when given different accents. In the first phrase quoted, *didomen* can be either a present indicative or an infinitive used as an imperative, depending on the way it is accented; in the second phrase, *ou* can be either a relative pronoun or a negative adverb, depending on the way it is accented.
46. The problem treated here is the effect that punctuation has on the meaning of a sentence. Thus, by means of different punctuations the word "before" in Empedocles' statement could be referred either to the phrase that precedes it, "things unmixed," or to the word that follows it, "mixed."
47. The word "more" has a form in Greek that can also be translated as "full."
48. In Homer, Icarius is Penelope's father.
49. Translating *kai ei adunaton,* suggested by Vahlen to fill a lacuna in the text at this point.

DEMETRIUS: ON STYLE

1. An apparent reference to *Rhetoric* III.viii.4–6, but Aristotle's discussion of rhythm does not deal with any theory of styles, nor does he use the adjective "impressive." —from G.M.A.G.
2. *History of the Peloponnesian War* II.48.
3. Here Demetrius makes an important advance when he speaks of the *general*

rhythmic character of a clause without trying to analyze it into exact feet. The sentence quoted is *tōn men peri ta mēdenos axia philosophountōn* ("they were philosophizing about matters of no importance," the rhythm of which is ——UUU—UU—UUUUU——). Thus it neither begins nor ends with a paeon; yet it is termed generally paeonic.—G.M.A.G.

4. Demetrius' example here is an unidentified clause: *hēkōn hēmōn eis tēn chōrān* in which all the syllables are long. The term "heroic meter" usually refers to the dactylic hexameter. His example has no dactyl and only four feet. Thus it can be said to be heroic only in the same general sense as the clause from Theophrastus was called paeonic.—G.M.A.G., note abridged.
5. The opening words of Thucydides' *History of the Peloponnesian War* and Herodotus' *Histories.*
6. *History of the Peloponnesian War* II.102.
7. *Aias d' ho megas aien ep' Hektori chalkokorustē* (*Iliad* XVI.358).
8. *History of the Peloponnesian War* II.49.
9. *Republic* III.411A–B.
10. *Odyssey* IX.190.
11. *Men* and *de* ["on the one hand" and "but on the other"] is the simplest way to express an antithesis in Greek. . . . We do not possess the context of the sentence here quoted: *hē men gar nēsos hēn echomen dēlē men kai porrōthen estin, hupsēlē kai tracheia, kai ta men chrēsima kai ergasima mikra autēs esti, ta de arga polla, smikras autēs ousēs.* (The island we occupy is visible from afar, high and rough, and the parts of it that are workable and cultivated are small, but the uncultivated parts are large, considering its size.) Actually, the *de* answers the last *men* only. *Men* was used alone when the second member of an antithesis remained unexpressed.—G.M.A.G.
12. *Iliad* II.497.
13. *Phaedrus* 246E.
14. *Iliad* XIV.433 or XXI.I.
15. *Odyssey* V. 203.
16. Demetrius quotes the first four words only of the Homeric line *kai nu k'oduromenoisin edu phaos ēelioio* (the light of the sun set upon their lamentations) from the scene of Patroclus' burial, *Iliad* XXIII.154.—G.M.A.G.
17. *Odyssey* XII.73. Substitution of the nominative for the genitive.
18. *Iliad* II.671. Epanaphora is the repetition of the same word at the beginning of succeeding clauses, here also succeeding lines. Dialysis (disconnection) is the name here given to lack of connectives, elsewhere also called asyndeton.—G.M.A.G.
19. The source of the quotation is unknown. The term synapheia is here used of the repetition of the *same* connective (*kai*). This figure is called *polysyndeton* by Quintilian (IX.iii.51).—G.M.A.G.
20. Demetrius expects his readers to remember Homer's description of the waves breaking on the shore in *Iliad* XIII.798–800: "Many a clashing wave of the loud-roaring sea, high-arched, white-crested; first one comes, then another. . . ."—G.M.A.G.
21. A brief and inexact quotation from *History of the Peloponnesian War* IV.12.—G.M.A.G., note abridged.
22. Anadiplōsis is the immediate repetition of a word. This sentence is not found in

Herodotus' description of the Caucasus, but a near-anadiplōsis does occur in his *Histories* I.203, where he says of the Caucasus: "Of mountains in number the greatest, and in greatness the highest."—G.M.A.G.

23. Isocrates was notorious for his avoidance of hiatus, that is, the clash of vowels which comes from a word that ends in a vowel being followed by one that begins with a vowel.—G.M.A.G.
24. All Demetrius' examples are proper names, except *chiōn.*—G.M.A.G.
25. The example (omitted in translation) of sounds that lose by being elided is an unidentified sentence: *panta ta nea kai kala estin* (all that is young is also beautiful) where the last two words would normally be elided into *kal' estin* or, and this is the form he gives, *kala 'stin* to avoid hiatus.—G.M.A.G.
26. The seven vowels in Greek are: a, e, ē, i, o, u, ō; ē and ō were always long; a, i, and u could be long or short.—G.M.A.G.
27. *Odyssey* XI.595–98. The Sisyphus passage was a favorite with critics. . . . Here, however, Demetrius quotes only three words and is concerned with the hiatus between the last two.—G.M.A.G.
28. *History of the Peloponnesian War* VI.1. Here again Demetrius quotes only three words with a hiatus between the first two.—G.M.A.G., note abridged.
29. *History of the Peloponnesian War* I.24. This example (omitted in translation) has many long syllables:

    tāūtēn kătŏkēsăn mēn Kērkȳrāīoī ōīkīstēs dĕ ĕgĕnĕtŏ
    (the Corcyraeans colonized it. The founder was),

    but our immediate concern is the hiatus in *oi* and *e* in the last four words.—G.M.A.G., note abridged.
30. This is a sound point that Aristotle does not make in his discussion of metaphors, and Demetrius may well be deliberately improving on him. The reference is to *Iliad* XX.218.—G.M.A.G.
31. *On the Crown* 136.
32. The reference is to *Rhetoric* III.xi.3–4, where Aristotle says that such metaphors put the action vividly before our eyes. He gives the same examples as Demetrius, namely, *Iliad* IV.126 and XIII.799.—G.M.A.G., note abridged.
33. *Iliad* XIII.339.
34. *Iliad* XXI.388.
35. *Anabasis* I.viii.18.
36. The quotation may be from the didactic poet, Theognis of Megara (6th century B.C.) or from the tragic poet of the last 5th century B.C.—G.M.A.G.
37. The "eyes of the vine" means the buds, and *ophthalmos* (eye) was used in many other common metaphors. A modern equivalent would be "the eye of a needle." —G.M.A.G.
38. The instances given in this section are *sphondulos* which means both vertebra and the whorl of a spindle; *kleis,* key and also collar-bone; and *ktenes,* ribs, incisor teeth, and also the comb of a loom.—G.M.A.G.
39. *Cyropaideia* I.iv.21. The distinction here is between the prose simile and the Homeric kind here called *parabolē poiētikē* (poetic comparison). It is a distinction that needed making and is not made by Aristotle.—G.M.A.G.
40. The Greek examples in the last sentence are *nomothetēs*, lawgiver, and *architektōn*,

but architect is not an English compound, nor is master-builder a single word.—G.M.A.G.

41. Demetrius' example, *sitopompia* for *hē pompē tou sitou* is not particularly impressive either in Greek or in English. Eyelid or flagstaff might be more impressive.—G.M.A.G., note abridged.
42. *Anabasis* I.v.2. The word translated "relays" is *diadechomenoi,* which is a compound word, so that this is not a digression.—G.M.A.G.
43. *Odyssey* IX.394. "Sizzled" is used of the Cyclops' eye when the burning stake is driven into it. "Lapping" is used of wolves and dogs in *Iliad* XVI.161.—G.M.A.G., note abridged.
44. *Historia Animalium* II.497 and 610.
45. *Allēgoria* seems to be used here in the general sense of meaning something else than one says rather than in our more restricted sense of allegory. The meaning of the example is that the whole city and country will be devastated.—G.M.A.G., note abridged.
46. The line (about the cupping-glass) is used by Aristotle both in *Rhetoric* III.ii.12 and *Poetics* 1458A.—G.M.A.G.
47. I.e., Dionysius was once a great ruler like you, but he is now living in Corinth as a private citizen.—from G.M.A.G.
48. The Greek for "to pass over in silence," that is, not to express what is implied, is *aposiōpēsis.* Repetition here is *dilogia,* that is, repeating words from one clause to another—G.M.A.G., note abridged.
49. *Anabasis* I.viii.20.
50. Ibid I.viii.10.
51. Demetrius here quotes only in part *Iliad* XVI.358, which he quoted in full, as an example of dysphony, in section 48 (see Note 7). Here our attention is drawn to the repetition of the long *a* and *ai* sounds in *Aias d'ho megas aien* . . . but we are meant to remember the line as a whole which contains both repetition of sound and lack of euphony.—G.M.A.G., note abridged.
52. *Odyssey* XIX.7–13.
53. Probably awnings or drapes.—from G.M.A.G.
54. *Iliad* XII.113.
55. *History of the Peloponnesian War* IV.64 and *Odyssey* XIX.172.
56. The lacuna indicated in the text must have contained not only some such expression as is added here, but also a reference to the fourth kind. It can be supplied from Aristotle's account in *Rhetoric* III.iii.1–4 which Demetrius is obviously following. —G.M.A.G.
57. Demetrius gives one example:

    hēḳōn hēmōn eis tēn chōrān, pāsēs hēmōn ōrthēs ōusēs,

    of which he gave the first five words as an example of "heroic" meter in section 42 (see Note 4). All the syllables are long.—G.M.A.G., note abridged.
58. Some name has obviously dropped out. It may have been any lowly or weak character. The suggestion of Thersites, the ugly and obstreperous rank-and-filer in *Iliad* II will do as well as any other.—G.M.A.G.
59. *Anabasis* IV.iv.3.

60. Source unknown.
61. Magistrate.
62. Hesiod, *Work and Days* 40.
63. The first two examples are used by Dolon of the horses of Rhesus: "they are whiter than snow, and run like the wind" in *Iliad* X.437. This certainly does not seem frigid. The third is from *Iliad* IV.443 and describes Eris or Strife. Here Demetrius' criticism is more justified.—G.M.A.G.
64. Demetrius is still dealing with the impressive style.—G.M.A.G.
65. Source of the quotations is unknown.—G.M.A.G.

HORACE: INTRODUCTION

1. See Richard McKeon's "Literary Criticism and the Concept of Imitation in Antiquity," in *Critics and Criticism: Ancient and Modern,* ed. R. S. Crane (Chicago, 1952), especially pp. 168–72.
2. *Works,* ed. Albert Feuillerat (Cambridge, Mass., 1922–23), III, 9.
3. See Marvin T. Herrick's *The Fusion of Horatian and Aristotelian Literary Criticism, 1550–1580* (University of Illinois Studies in Language and Literature, XXXII, no. 1; Urbana, Ill., 1946).

ARS POETICA

1. The *Ars Poetica* is a letter of advice addressed to a father and his two sons bearing the family name of Piso.
2. People saved from a shipwreck placed a picture on the scene as a votive offering in the temple.
3. Horace refers to the days of old when such men as M. Cornelius Cethegus wore a loincloth (*cinctus*) under the toga instead of the tunic of later times.
4. Perhaps a reference to the Portus Julius, an artificial harbor formed by constructing a channel to connect Lake Lucrinus with Lake Avernus.
5. Probably the draining of the Pontine Marshes.
6. Horace may be referring to the straightening of the course of the Tiber to prevent flooding of farm land.
7. Dactylic hexameter.
8. The elegiac couplet, consisting of a hexameter and a pentameter.
9. The iambic trimeter was the measure used in dialogue both in comedy and tragedy.
10. A lightweight shoe worn by ancient Greek and Roman comic actors.
11. The high, thick-soled shoe worn by ancient Greek and Roman tragic actors.
12. Chremes is a name used by the Roman poet Terence in his comedies. Peleus and Telephus are mythical figures (the father of Achilles and the son-in-law of Priam, respectively) and Euripidian characters.
13. Epic poets, probably later than Homer, whose subjects were the legends revolving around the Trojan and Theban wars.
14. A paraphrase of the opening lines of the *Odyssey*.

15. The mythical warrior Meleager, uncle of Diomedes, a hero in the Trojan war, dies before the latter is born.—The "twin eggs" refer to the birth of Helen of Troy. Zeus had visited her mother Leda in the form of a swan, and she produced two eggs. From one Helen emerged and from the other Castor and Pollux.
16. Campus Martius in Rome.
17. Tragedy or "goat song" was supposed to take its name from the prize in a competition: a he-goat. This derivation, however, is no longer accepted.
18. See Note 6 to Aristotle's *Poetics.*
19. Typical characters (slave, maid, old man) in the New Comedy.
20. Epithet given by the poet's admirers.
21. They produced hellbore, medicine made from a herb supposedly effective in the treatment of madness.
22. A female monster; a bugbear.
23. An ancient classification of Roman citizens into *seniores* and *iuniores.*
24. Booksellers in ancient Rome.
25. Region in ancient Macedonia. The Pierian Spring was sacred to the Muses, and its water was said to be a source of inspiration.
26. A festival at Delphi, including musical and athletic contests—next in importance to the Olympic games.

QUINTILIAN: INSTITUTIO ORATORIA

1. *Phaenomena* 1.
2. *Iliad* XXI.196.
3. Beginning; introduction.
4. Antilochus in the *Iliad* XVIII.18.
5. Phoenix, *Iliad* IX.529.
6. *Iliad* XXIV.486ff.
7. Refers to copying by dividing the surface of the picture to be copied, and of the material on which the copy is to be made, into a number of equal squares.—H.E.B.
8. The Annales Maximi kept by the Pontifex Maximus, containing the list of the consuls and giving a curt summary of the events of each consulate.—H.E.B.
9. Would seem to be.

"LONGINUS": INTRODUCTION

1. Roy Arthur Swanson, "'Longinus': Noesis and Pathos," *Classical Bulletin,* XLVI (November, 1969), 1–5.
2. See Samuel Holt Monk, *The Sublime: A Study of Critical Theories in Eighteenth-Century England* (New York, 1934).
3. See the "Introduction" to *"Longinus" on the Sublime,* ed. D. A. Russell (Oxford, 1964), pp. xlvii-xlviii.
4. "On the Relation of Analytical Psychology to Poetic Art," tr. H. G. and Cary F. Baynes, in *Modern Continental Literary Criticism,* ed. O. B. Hardison (New York, 1962), p. 286.

5. *Anatomy of Criticism* (Princeton, 1957), p. 65.
6. "Longinus and the 'New Criticism,'" in *Collected Essays* (Denver, 1959), p. 511.
7. See especially Elder Olson, "The Argument of Longinus' *On the Sublime*," in *Critics and Criticism: Ancient and Modern,* ed. R. S. Crane (Chicago, 1952); and Hoyt Trowbridge, "'Leda and the Swan': A Longinian Analysis," *Modern Philology,* LI (November, 1953).

ON SUBLIMITY

1. This is to translate *bathous.* The simple, 18th-century emendation *pathous* means "emotion." The English word "bathos" seems to have acquired its meaning from a misunderstanding of the passage.—D.A.R. See Pope's *Peri Bathous*; *or, Martinus Scriblerus, His Treatise of the Art of Sinking in Poetry* (1727/28).
2. *Orations* XXIII.113.
3. Aeschylus, fragment 281 in Nauck's *Tragicorum Graecorum Fragmenta* (ed. 2). But it is not certain that the passage is not rather by Sophocles. The speaker is Boreas, the North Wind, who is enraged with King Erechtheus of Athens because he will not give him his daughter Orithyia. As the passage is incomplete, the point of some of the critical comment is lost.—D.A.R.
4. Fragment 701, Nauck, op. cit.—D.A.R.
5. Presumably in the lost passage.—D.A.R.
6. In the 8th century B.C. According to other sources this war lasted 20 years.—D.A.R., note abridged.
7. Dionysius II, expelled in 356.—D.A.R.
8. The word *korē* means both "girl" and "pupil"; Xenophon replaces it by *parthenos,* which means unambiguously "maiden."—D.A.R.
9. *Iliad* I.225.
10. . . . The "unveiling ceremony" was normally held on the third day after the marriage.—D.A.R.
11. *Laws* 741C.
12. *Laws* 778D.
13. *Histories* V.18.
14. See chapters 23 and 38.—D.A.R.
15. Or "and coined words."—D.A.R.
16. *Sunthesis;* Latin "compositio," but narrower in sense than "composition" in non-technical English. See chaps. 39–42.—D.A.R.
17. *Odyssey* XI.315–17.
18. *Odyssey* XI.563. Note that this is not an example, but a simile illustrating the point that ideas in themselves can be grand.—D.A.R.
19. Parmenio said to Alexander that if he were Alexander he would be content, and would not go on fighting. "So would I, if I were Parmenio," replied Alexander.—D.A.R.
20. *Iliad* IV.440ff., where Strife is described as having her head in the sky and walking on the earth. "Longinus" means that Homer too is a colossus of cosmic dimensions. —D.A.R.
21. *Shield of Heracles* 267.

22. *Iliad* V.770–2.
23. See *Iliad* XXI.388 and XX.61ff.
24. See *Iliad* XIII.18ff. and XX.60.
25. Controversy about the genuineness of this reference to Genesis i has raged since the 18th century.—D.A.R., note abridged.
26. *Iliad* XVII.645ff.
27. *Iliad* XV.605ff.
28. Spoken by Nestor, *Odyssey* III.109ff.
29. For these various stories, see *Odyssey* X.17ff., X.237ff., XII.447ff., XXII.79ff.—D.A.R.
30. Sappho, fragment 31. See D. L. Page, *Sappho and Alcaeus,* chap. 2.—D.A.R., note abridged.
31. From a lost poem attributed to Aristeas of Proconnesus, a prophet of Apollo said to have travelled in Siberia in the 7th century B.C.—D.A.R., note abridged.
32. *Iliad* XV.624ff.
33. *Phaenomena* 299.
34. The example from Archilochus cannot be certainly identified. That from Demosthenes (*On the Crown* 169) describes the alarm at Athens when news arrived of Philip's occupation of Elatea (339 B.C.).—D.A.R., note abridged.
35. *Theaetetus* 144B.
36. *Republic* IX.586A (slightly abridged).
37. Text uncertain: perhaps "the reproduction of beauty of form. . . ."—D.A.R.
38. *Work and Days* 24: healthy rivalry contrasted with the strife that produces war. —D.A.R.
39. A Stoic definition.—D.A.R.
40. Euripides, *Orestes* 255–57. Orestes sees the Furies.—D.A.R.
41. Euripides, *Iphigenia in Tauris* 291. Again Orestes and the Furies.—D.A.R.
42. *Iliad* XX.170.
43. Fragment 779, Nauck op. cit. . . . The passages quoted [from Euripides' lost *Phaethon*] seem to be from a messenger's speech recounting Phaethon's fall.—D.A.R.
44. Fragment 935, Nauck op. cit. Perhaps from the *Alexandros.* As the context is lost, we do not know the point.—D.A.R., note abridged.
45. Aeschylus, fragment 58, Nauck, op. cit.; Euripides, *Bacchae* 726.—D.A.R., note abridged.
46. Final scene of *Oedipus Coloneus.*
47. Probably in the lost *Polyxena.*—D.A.R., note abridged.
48. Euripides, *Orestes* 264–65.
49. Demosthenes, *Oration,* XXIV.208.
50. I.e. after Philip's victory at Chaeronea (338 B.C.). The speech is not extant.—D.A.R.
51. *Oration* XVIII.208.
52. From the lost comedy *Demoi.* Eupolis parodies Euripides, *Medea* 395ff.—D.A.R.
53. See below, chap. 35.—D.A.R.
54. Note that these remarks are themselves cast as rhetorical questions.—D.A.R.
55. Demosthenes, *Orations* IV.10.
56. Ibid., 44.
57. *Hellenica* IV.iii.19.
58. *Odyssey* X.251–52.

59. Demosthenes, *Orations* XXI.72.
60. Probably a few words are missing here.—D.A.R.
61. *Histories* VI.11.
62. Polyptoton is the occurrence of the same word in various inflexions. It is not certain whether "Longinus" thinks of accumulation (*athroismos*), variation (*metabole*), and climax as species of it or as distinct.—D.A.R., note abridged.
63. *Oedipus Tyrannus* 1403ff.
64. A line of an unknown tragedy.—D.A.R.
65. *Menexenus* 245D. Not quoted in any other extant part of this book.—D.A.R.
66. Demosthenes, *Orations,* XVIII.18.
67. Herodotus, *Histories* VI.21.
68. Or, "it is a mark of emotion to pluralize them unexpectedly."—D.A.R.
69. *Cyropaedia* VII.i.37.
70. *Iliad* XV.697.
71. *Phaenomena* 287.
72. *Histories* II.29.
73. *Iliad* V.85.
74. *Iliad* XV.346.
75. Fragment 30, Jacoby.—D.A.R.
76. *Oration* XXV (a spurious speech). The passage is from §27.—D.A.R.
77. *Odyssey* IV.681ff.
78. *Menexenus* 236D.
79. *Cyropaedia* I.v.12.
80. *Histories* I.105.
81. 801B.
82. "Pathos" (emotion) characterizes truly "sublime" writing; "ēthos" (realistic depiction of manners or humors) belongs rather to lower, more human and even comic, genres; cf. the *Iliad-Odyssey* contrast, IX.13–15. "Hēdonē" (pleasure, charm) is the typical aim and effect of this second kind of literature.—D.A.R., note abridged.
83. Fragment 96, Bergk, *Poetae Lyrici Graeci.* "Filly" is a probable, but not certain, supplement. "Longinus'" text here is uncertain. Perhaps: ". . . But not Anacreon's I turn my mind. . . ' ."—D.A.R.
84. *Histories* VI.75, VII.181.
85. Demosthenes, *Orations* XVIII.296.
86. Xenophon, *Memorabilia* I.iv.5ff; Plato *Timaeus* 65C–85E ("Longinus" picks various details out of this long passage, and runs them together).—D.A.R., note abridged.
87. *Laws* VI.773C.
88. Or perhaps "fluent."—D.A.R.
89. The speech in which the myth of Leto was told is lost: the Funeral Speech is extant (*Oration* 2). "Epideictic": i.e. written as a demonstration of skill; the term applies to panegyrics, etc. Cf. chap. 8.—D.A.R.
90. The first is lost; the second is *Oration* 3 (5).—D.A.R.
91. "Epigram on the tomb of Midias," ascribed to Homer; see Plato *Phaedrus* 264D. —D.A.R.
92. It is not certain whether "Longinus" means the Colossus of Rhodes or some other large statue.—D.A.R., note abridged.
93. Demosthenes, *Orations* VII.45—a speech generally thought to be spurious.—D.A.R.

94. *Panegyricus* 8.
95. *History of the Peloponnesian War* VII.84.
96. *Histories* VII.225.
97. Euripides, fragment 663, Nauck, op. cit.—D.A.R.
98. Presumably in the work referred to in chap. 39.1.—D.A.R.
99. The decree making provision for war after Philip's occupation of Elatea.—D.A.R., note abridged.
100. Presumably in the two books on "composition."—D.A.R.
101. Euripides, *Hercules Furens* 1245.
102. Or, "in accordance with its structure."—D.A.R.
103. From Euripides' lost *Antiope* (fragment 221, Nauck, op. cit.). The Greek contains the words *perix helixas* and *petran drun,* and these are the effects to which "Longinus'" comment refers.—D.A.R.
104. Of a play, presumably.—D.A.R.
105. Obscure: is this the same as the "chopped up" manner or a separate fault?—D.A.R.
106. Again an obscure section; partly because "Longinus" seems to intend it as an example of "brevity."—D.A.R.
107. *Histories* VII.188, 191; VIII.13.
108. Translation doubtful. Perhaps "and then make a change of arrangement and proceed. . . ."—D.A.R.
109. *Memorabilia* I.iv.6.
110. *Odyssey* XVII.322–33.
111. Translate as though the adjective *dikaios* means the same as it does just above; but perhaps [it should read] "justly exercised," i.e., humane.—D.A.R.
112. Or, "all our effort and all that we undertake."—D.A.R.
113. Euripides, *Electra* 379.

BIBLIOGRAPHY

GENERAL INTRODUCTION

Atkins, J. W. H. *Literary Criticism in Antiquity*. 2 vols. See under Plato bibliography.

D'Alton, J. F. *Roman Literary Theory and Criticism: A Study in Tendencies*. London: Longmans, Green, 1931.

Else, Gerald F. "Classical Poetics." *Encyclopedia of Poetry and Poetics,* ed. by Alex Preminger, Frank J. Warnke and O. B. Hardison, Jr. Princeton: Princeton University Press, 1965.

Gomme, A. W. *The Greek Attitude to Poetry and History*. Berkeley: University of California Press, 1954. An important study by one of the foremost scholars of the 20th century who combines eminence as an historian with literary sensitivity.

Grube, G. M. A. *The Greek and Roman Critics*. See under Plato bibliography.

Harriott, Rosemary. *Poetry and Criticism before Plato*. London: Methuen, 1969. A useful survey of the early history of Greek literary criticism.

Jaeger, Werner. *Paideia,* tr. by Gilbert Highet. 3 vols. Oxford: Oxford University Press, 1939–44. A profound and influential work that treats with great perception the major themes of Greek culture.

Kitto, H. D. F. *Poiesis*. Berkeley and Los Angeles: University of California Press, 1966.

Lanata, Giuliana, ed. and tr. *Poetica pre-Platonica: testimonianze e frammenti*. Florence: "La Nuova Italia," 1963. A useful collection of passages concerned with the nature of poetry from the works of earlier Greek authors.

Parsons, Edward A. *The Alexandrian Library*. New York: Elsevier, 1952.

Pfeiffer, Rudolf. *History of Classical Scholarship, from the Beginnings to the End of the Hellenistic Age*. New York: Oxford University Press, 1968.

Saintsbury, George. *A History of Criticism and Literary Taste in Europe*. 3 vols. Edinburgh and London: Blackwood, 1900–04. This work has been highly influential for decades and, with its limitations, is still useful today.

Sikes, E. E. *The Greek View of Poetry*. London: Methuen, 1931.

Snell, Bruno. *Poetry and Society*. Bloomington: Indiana University Press, 1961. A volume containing many stimulating ideas about Greek poetry by one of the most influential scholars of the 20th century.

Webster, T. B. L. "Greek Theories of Art and Literature down to 400 B.C." *Classical Quarterly,* XXXIII (1939), 166–79.

Wimsatt, W. K. and Cleanth Brooks. *Literary Criticism: A Short History*. Part 1. New York: Knopf, 1967. An important, thought-provoking book.

ARISTOPHANES

Cornford, Francis M. *The Origin of Attic Comedy,* ed. by Theodore H. Gaster. Garden City, N. Y.: Anchor Books, 1961. A recent reprinting of an early important and controversial study of the genesis of comedy in the Greek world.

Dover, K. J. *Aristophanic Comedy.* Berkeley: University of California Press, 1972. Best treatment to date.

———, ed. Aristophanes: *Clouds.* Oxford: Oxford University Press, 1968. This edition with introduction and commentary is now the standard Greek text of this important play.

Ehrenberg, Victor. *The People of Aristophanes.* 3rd rev. ed. New York: Schocken Books, 1962. A major study using the plays of Aristophanes as a source of information about ancient Athenian society.

Gomme, A. W. *More Essays in Greek History and Literature.* Oxford: Blackwell, 1962. This volume contains an essay entitled "Aristophanes and Politics" which is representative of the author's sensitive appreciation of the inter-relationships which exist between art and society.

Grube, G. M. A. *The Greek and Roman Critics.* See under Plato bibliography.

Jaeger, Werner. *Paideia: The Ideals of Greek Culture,* tr. by Gilbert Highet. 3 vols. Oxford: Oxford University Press, 1939–44. One of the most important and perceptive studies of Greek culture that we possess, this work contains a valuable section on "The Comic Poetry of Aristophanes."

Lever, Katherine. *The Art of Greek Comedy.* London: Methuen, 1956. A comparatively recent standard survey of the subject.

Littlefield, David J., comp. *Twentieth Century Interpretations of The Frogs.* Englewood Cliffs, N.J.: Prentice-Hall, 1968. A useful collection of scholarly views concerning this play.

Murray, Gilbert. *Aristophanes: A Study.* New York: Oxford University Press, 1933. A standard work by one of the most influential classicists of this century.

Norwood, Gilbert. *Greek Comedy.* London: Methuen, 1931. A now somewhat outdated but still useful survey of the subject.

Pickard-Cambridge, A. W. *Dithyramb, Tragedy, and Comedy.* 2nd edition, revised by T. B. L. Webster. Oxford: Clarendon Press, 1962. A standard and extremely important reference work.

Stanford, W. B., ed. Aristophanes: *The Frogs.* 2nd ed. London: Macmillan, 1963. This edition with introduction and commentary is now the standard Greek text of this important play.

Strauss, Leo. *Socrates and Aristophanes.* New York: Basic Books, 1966. A recent study by an imaginative and stimulating political philosopher.

Whitman, Cedric H. *Aristophanes and the Comic Hero.* Cambridge, Mass.: Harvard University Press, 1964. A major study of Aristophanes by a scholar widely known for his work on Homer and Sophocles.

PLATO

Atkins, J. W. H. *Literary Criticism in Antiquity.* Cambridge: Cambridge University Press, 1934, vol. I, pp. 33–70. This standard history of classical literary criticism is still a useful and reliable guide although somewhat dated in its approach to the subject.

Brumbaugh, Robert S. "A New Interpretation of Plato's Republic." *Journal of Philosophy,* LXIV (1967), 661–70.

Carter, Robert E. "Plato and Inspiration," *Journal of the History of Philosophy,* V(1967), 111–21.

Cherniss, Harold. "Plato (1950–1957)." *Lustrum: Internationale Forschungsberichte aus dem Bereich des klassischen Altertums,* IV (1959), 5–316; V (1960), 321–648; see especially 520–54.

Crombie, Ian M. *An Examination of Plato's Doctrine.* 2 vols. London: Routledge and Kegan Paul, 1962.

Gallop, D. "Image and Reality in Plato's *Republic*," *Archiv für Geschichte der Philosophie,* XLVII (1965), 113–31.

Gilbert, Allen H. "Plato's *Ion,* Comic and Serious." *Studies in Honor of De W. T. Starnes.* Austin: University of Texas Press, 1967, pp. 259–84.

Gould, Thomas R. "Plato's Hostility to Art." *Arion,* III (1964), 70–91.

Greene, W. Chase. "Plato's View of Poetry." *Harvard Studies in Classical Philology,* XXIX (1918), 1–76.

Grube, G. M. A. *The Greek and Roman Critics.* Toronto: Toronto University Press, 1965, pp. 46–65. A scholarly history of classical literary criticism by one of the leading authorities in this field which usefully brings up to date our knowledge of the relevant scholarship.

Havelock, Eric A. *Preface to Plato.* Cambridge, Mass.: Harvard University Press, 1963.

Henning, Roslyn B. "A Performing Musician Looks at the *Ion.*" *Classical Journal,* LIX (1964), 241–47.

Levinson, Ronald B. "Plato's *Phaedrus* and the New Criticism," *Archiv für die Geschichte der Philosophie,* XLVI (1964), 293–309.

Lodge, Rupert C. *Plato's Theory of Art.* London: Routledge and Kegan Paul, 1953. A scholarly and thorough study of Plato's treatment of art throughout the dialogues.

McKeon, Richard. "Literary Criticism and the Concept of Imitation in Antiquity." *Critics and Criticism: Ancient and Modern,* ed. R. S. Crane. Chicago: University of Chicago Press, 1952, pp. 147–75.

Maguire, Joseph P. "Beauty and the Fine Arts in Plato: Some *Aporiai.*" *Harvard Studies in Classical Philology,* LXX (1965), 171–93.

———. "The Differentiation of Art in Plato's Aesthetics." *Harvard Studies in Classical Philology,* LXVIII (1964), 389–410.

Morrow, Gen R. *Plato's Cretan City: A Historical Interpretation of the Laws.* Princeton: Princeton University Press, 1960. This major scholarly work is the definitive study of Plato's *Laws.*

Murphy, Neville R. *The Interpretation of Plato's Republic.* Oxford: Oxford University Press, 1951. A standard, scholarly study of the *Republic.*

Philip, J. A. "*Mimesis* in the *Sophistes* of Plato," *Transactions of the American Philological Association,* XCII (1961), 453–68.

Ringbom, Sixten. "Plato on Images," *Theoria,* XXXI (1965), 86–109.

Steward, Douglas J. "Man and Myth in Plato's Universe." *Bucknell Review,* XIII, (1965), 72–90.

Tate, J. "'Imitation' in Plato's *Republic.*" *Classical Quarterly,* XXII (1928), 16–24.

———. "Plato and 'Imitation.'" *Classical Quarterly,* XXVI (1932), 161–69.

Verdenius, W. J. *Mimesis: Plato's Doctrine of Artistic Imitation and Its Meaning to Us.* Leiden: Brill, 1949. An important and perceptive study which emphasizes the positive values which Plato attributes to artistic *mimesis.*

Warren, John G. *Greek Aesthetic Theory: A Study of Callistic and Aesthetic Concepts in the Works of Plato and Aristotle.* New York: Barnes and Noble, 1962. This study of the important concepts of classical aesthetics is specifically directed at the student of modern literature.

ARISTOTLE

1. *Bibliographies of Studies on Aristotle's* Poetics.

Cooper, Lane, and Alfred Gudeman. *A Bibliography of the Poetics of Aristotle.* New Haven, Conn.: Yale University Press, 1928.

Else, Gerald F. "A Survey of Work on Aristotle's *Poetics,* 1940–1952." *Classical Weekly* (now *Classical World*), XLVIII (1955), 73–82.

Herrick, Marvin T. "A Supplement to Cooper and Gudeman's Bibliography of the *Poetics* of Aristotle." *American Journal of Philology,* LII (1931), 168–74.

2. *Texts, Translations, and Commentaries on the* Poetics.

Butcher, S. H. *Aristotle's Theory of Poetry and Fine Art.* New York: Dover Publications, 1951. Butcher offers a helpful translation and a fine series of essays on selected topics in the *Poetics* that manifest excellent literary judgment and perceptive insight into Aristotle's theory of literature. The Greek text which he prints is now out of date.

Bywater, Ingram. *Aristotle on the Art of Poetry.* London and New York: Oxford University Press, 1909. Bywater's Greek text remains authoritative for the study of the *Poetics* although it has recently been improved upon in some details. His commentary and translation, directed mainly at the illumination of philological rather than literary problems, are a model of their type and offer immense assistance to the student of this work.

Cooper, Lane. *Aristotle on the Art of Poetry.* Ithaca, N.Y.: Cornell University Press, 1947. Cooper extensively amplifies and therefore extensively interprets the actual text of the *Poetics* for his readers.

Else, Gerald F. Aristotle: *Poetics.* Ann Arbor: University of Michigan Press, 1967. A translation revised from the author's 1957 edition of the *Poetics* for greater fluency and easier use by those not in command of the Greek text. The translation still depends in various places on Else's own text and interpretation of the work.

———. *Aristotle's Poetics: The Argument.* Cambridge, Mass.: Harvard University Press, 1957. A stimulating and controversial edition which makes many new suggestions about the text and interpretation of the *Poetics.* Even where Else's suggestions are not accepted they offer an excellent point of departure for rethinking important concepts in the *Poetics.*

Fergusson, Francis, ed. *Aristotle's Poetics.* New York: Hill and Wang, 1961. The editor's introduction is perceptive and provides a number of references to classical and modern literature in illustration of Aristotle's meaning. Butcher's translation is presented in this text but without his commentaries.

Gilbert, Allan H., tr. Aristotle's *Poetics,* in *Literary Criticism: Plato to Dryden,* New York: American Book Co., 1940, pp. 63–124. A sound translation making use of a number of important 20th century editions of the *Poetics* and especially those of Gudeman and Rostagni.

Golden, Leon and Hardison, O. B. *Aristotle's Poetics: A Translation and Commentary for Students of Literature.* Englewood Cliffs, N.J.: Prentice-Hall, 1968. The translation aspires to be both literal and idiomatic and the commentary provides a chapter-by-chapter discussion of all of the major concepts in the *Poetics.* New interpretations of important ideas are presented together with a review of standard scholarly opinions.

Grube, G. M. A. *Aristotle on Poetry and Style.* New York: Library of Liberal Arts, 1958. A sound and literal translation together with a good general introduction to the *Poetics.* Relevant sections of Aristotle's *Rhetoric* are included in this edition.

Gudeman, Alfred. *Aristoteles' PERI POIETIKES.* Berlin and Leipzig, 1934. Greek text, notes and extensive commentary making significant use of the Arabic tradition of the *Poetics.*

Hardy, J. Aristote: *Poétique* (Collection des Universités de France publiée sous le patronage de l'Association Guillaume Budé). Paris, 1952. A scholarly Greek text and very useful French translation of facing pages. This edition with its perceptive notes is a major aid to the understanding and interpretation of the *Poetics.*

Kassel, Rudolf. *Aristotelis de Arte Poetica Liber* (Oxford Classical Texts). Oxford: Oxford University Press, 1965. This is an updating of Bywater's original Oxford text which takes into consideration all of the sources for Aristotle's original text. An informative preface describes the state of our knowledge of the text of the *Poetics* at the present time.

Lucas, D. W. Aristotle: *Poetics.* Oxford: Clarendon Press, 1968. Kassel's Oxford text is reproduced with valuable and extensive notes and appendices of varying quality on the major ideas presented in the *Poetics.*

Potts, L. J. *Aristotle on the Art of Fiction.* Cambridge: Cambridge University Press, 1959 (2nd print. rev.). A not always idiomatic translation that is challenging for some of the interpretations it puts upon the Greek. Brief but useful introduction and notes accompany the translation.

Rostagni, Augusto. *Aristotele Poetica.* Turin: Chiantore, 1945. One of the most distinguished of modern editions of the *Poetics.* An extensive and scholarly introduction and detailed commentary accompany the Greek text.

Telford, K. *Aristotle's Poetics: Translation and Analysis.* Chicago: Regnery, 1965. A literal translation together with a chapter-by-chapter commentary that sets the argument of the *Poetics* against the background of Aristotle's general philosophical mood.

Valgimigli, E., ed. Aristotle: *De Arte Poetica. Guillelmo de Moerbeke, Interprete.* Revised with prefaces and indices added by A. Franceschini and L. Minio-Paluello. Bruges: Brouwer, 1953. A major scholarly edition which presents the text of William of Moerbeke's important and extremely literal Latin translation of the *Poetics.*

3. *Interpretative Studies of Major Themes in the* Poetics.

Braam, P. van. "Aristotle's Use of *Hamartia.*" *Classical Quarterly,* VI (1912), 266–72.

Dale, A. M. "Ethos and Dianoia: Character and Thought in Aristotle's *Poetics.*" *AUMLA: Journal of the Australasian Universities Language and Literature Association,* XI (1959), 3–16.

Dawe, R. D. "Some Reflections on *Ate* and *Hamartia.*" *Harvard Studies in Classical Philology,* LXXII (1967), 89–123.

Else, Gerald F. " 'Imitation' in the Fifth Century." *Classical Philology,* LIII (1958), 73–90.

Golden, Leon. "Catharsis." *Transactions of the American Philological Association,* XCIII (1962), 51–60.

———. "Is Tragedy the 'Imitation of a Serious Action'?" *Greek, Roman and Byzantine Studies,* VI (1965), 283–89.

———. *"Mimesis* and *Katharsis."* *Classical Philology,* LXIV (1969), 145–53.

Goldstein, Harvey D. "Mimesis and Catharsis Reexamined." *Journal of Aesthetics and Art Criticism,* XXIV (1966), 567–77.

Gomperz, Theodor. *Zu Aristoteles' Poetik,* II, III. Vienna, 1896.

———. "Ein Beitrag zur Kritik und Erklärung der Kapitel 1–6." *Sitzungsberichte der Kaiserlichen Akademie der Wissenschaften in Wien.* Philosophisch-Historische Classe, I–VI (1888), 543–82.

Gresseth, Gerald K. "The System of Aristotle's *Poetics.*" *Transactions of the American Philological Association,* LXXXIX (1958), 312–35.

Harsh, Philip, W. "Hamartia Again." *Transactions of the American Philological Association,* LXXVI (1945), 47–58.

House, Humphry. *Aristotle's Poetics: A Course of Eight Lectures,* rev. by C. Hardie. London: R. Hart Davis, 1956.

Jones, John. *On Aristotle and Greek Tragedy.* London: Oxford University Press 1962.

Kerrane, Kevin. "Aristotle's *Poetics* in Modern Literary Criticism" (unpublished doctoral dissertation, University of North Carolina, 1968).

Lucas, D. W. "Pity, Terror, and *Peripeteia.*" *Classical Quarterly,* XII (1962), 52–60.

McKeon, Richard. "Literary Criticism and the Concept of Imitation in Antiquity." *Critics and Criticism: Ancient and Modern,* ed. R. S. Crane. Chicago: University of Chicago Press, 1952, pp. 147–75.

Montmollin, Daniel de. *La Poétique d' Aristote: Texte primitif et additions ultérieures.* Neuchâtel: Messeiller, 1951.

———. "Le Sens du terme *philanthropon* dans *La Poétique* d'Aristote." *Phoenix,* XIX (1965), 15–23.

Murray, Gilbert. "An Essay in the Theory of Poetry." *Yale Review,* X (1921), 482–99.

Olson, Elder, ed. *Aristotle's Poetics and English Literature: A Collection of Critical Essays.* Chicago: University of Chicago Press, 1965.

Ostwald, Martin. "Aristotle on *Hamartia* and Sophocles' *Oedipus Tyrannus.*" *Festschrift Ernst Kapp.* Hamburg, 1958, pp. 93–108.

Solmsen, Friedrich. "The Origins and Methods of Aristotle's *Poetics.*" *Classical Quarterly,* XXIX (1935), 192–201.

Stanford, W. B. "On a Recent Interpretation of the Tragic Catharsis." *Hermathena,* LXXXV (1955), 52–56.

Vahlen, Johannes. *Beiträge zu Aristoteles' Poetik.* Leipzig, Berlin, 1914.

DEMETRIUS

Atkins, J. W. H. *Literary Criticism in Antiquity,* vol. II, pp. 175–209. See under Plato bibliography.

Grube, G. M. A. *A Greek Critic: Demetrius on Style.* Toronto: University of Toronto Press, 1961. An important, recent edition of Demetrius which takes some controversial positions about this critic.

———. "The Date of Demetrius on Style." *Phoenix* (1964), 294–302.

———. *The Greek and Roman Critics,* pp. 110–21. See under Plato bibliography.

Roberts, W. Rhys, ed. *Demetrius on Style.* Cambridge: Cambridge University Press, 1902. A standard, authoritative edition of Demetrius.

Schenkeveld, Dirk M. *Studies in Demetrius On Style.* Amsterdam: Hakkert, 1964.

HORACE

Atkins, J. W. H. *Literary Criticism in Antiquity,* vol. II, pp. 47–103. See under Plato bibliography.

Brink, Charles O. *Horace on Poetry.* Cambridge: Cambridge University Press, 1963 (vol. I, Prolegomena, 1963; vol. II, Commentary, 1971.) A major work of scholarship on Horace's literary theories by one of the leading scholars in this field.

D'Alton, J. F. *Roman Literary Theory and Criticism: A Study in Tendencies.* London: Longmans, Green, 1931.

Dilke, O. A. W. "When Was the *Ars Poetica* Written?" *Bulletin of the Institute of Classical Studies,* University of London, V (1958), 49–57.

Duckworth, George. "Horace's Hexameters and the Date of the *Ars Poetica.*" *Transactions of the American Philological Association,* XCVI (1965), 73–95.

Elmore, Jefferson. "A New Dating of Horace's *De Arte Poetica.*" *Classical Philology,* XXX (1935), 1–9.

Fairclough, H. Rushton. "Horace's View of Relations Between Satire and Comedy." *American Journal of Philology,* XXXIV (1913), 183–93.

Fiske, George C. "Lucilius, the *Ars Poetica* of Horace, and Persius." *Harvard Studies in Classical Philology,* XXIV (1913), 1–36.

———. *Lucilius and Horace, a Study in the Classical Theory of Imitation.* (University of Wisconsin Studies in Language and Literature, VII. Madison, 1920.)

———. and Grant, Mary A. "Cicero's *Orator* and Horace's *Ars Poetica.*" *Harvard Studies in Classical Philology,* XXXV (1924), 1–74.

Fraenkel, Eduard. *Horace.* Oxford: Oxford University Press, 1957. A very important study of the poet's work by one of the most prominent and influential 20th-century scholars.

Frank, Tenney. "Horace on Contemporary Poetry." *Classical Journal,* XIII (1917–18), 550–64.

———. "Horace's Definition of Poetry." *Classical Journal,* XXXI (1935–36), 167–74.

Getty, Robert J. "Recent Work on Horace." *Classical World,* LII (1959), 167–88, 246–47.

Greenberg, Nathan A. "The Use of *Poiema* and *Poiesis.*" *Harvard Studies in Classical Philology,* LXV (1961), 263–89.

Grube, G. M. A. *The Greek and Roman Critics,* pp. 231–55. See under Plato bibliography.

Hack, Roy K. "The Doctrine of Literary Forms." *Harvard Studies in Classical Philology,* XXVII (1916), 1–65.

Haight, Elizabeth H. "Horace on Art: *ut pictura poiesis.*" *Classical Journal,* XLVII (1952), 157–62.

Hendrickson, George L. "Satura—the Genesis of a Literary Form." *Classical Philology,* VI (1911), 129–43.

Herrick, Marvin T. *The Fusion of Horatian and Aristotelian Literary Criticism, 1531–1555.* (University of Illinois Studies in Language and Literature, XXXII, no. 1. Urbana, 1946).

La Drière, Craig. "Horace and the Theory of Imitation." *American Journal of Philology* LX (1939), 288–300.

Rudd, Niall. "The Poet's Defense." *Classical Quarterly,* XLIX (1955), 142–56.

Smith, W. K. "The Date of the *Ars Poetica.*" *Classical Philology,* XXXI (1936), 163–66.

Solmsen, Friedrich. "Propertius and Horace." *Classical Philology,* XLIII (1948), 105–09.

DIONYSIUS OF HALICARNASSUS

Atkins, J. W. H. *Literary Criticism in Antiquity,* vol. II, pp. 104–36. See under Plato bibliography.

Bonner, S. F. *The Literary Treatises of Dionysius of Halicarnassus.* Cambridge: Cambridge University Press, 1939.

Grube, G. M. A. "Dionysius of Halicarnassus on Thucydides." *Phoenix,* IV (1950), 95–110.

———. *The Greek and Roman Critics,* pp. 207–30. See under Plato bibliography.

———. "Thrasymachus, Theophrastus and Dionysius of Halicarnassus." *American Journal of Philology,* LXXIII (1952), 251–67.

Roberts, W. Rhys, ed. Dionysius of Halicarnassus: *On Literary Composition.* London: Macmillan, 1910. This is the standard scholarly edition of Dionysius' work.

Wilkinson, L. P. *Golden Latin Artistry.* Cambridge: Cambridge University Press, 1962, *passim.*

QUINTILIAN

Atkins, J. W. H. *Literary Criticism in Antiquity,* vol. II, pp. 254–98. See under Plato bibliography.

Carver, P. L. "Quintilian's Approach to Literature." *University of Toronto Quarterly,* VII (1937), 77–94.

Clark, Donald L. *Rhetoric in Greco-Roman Education.* New York: Columbia University Press, 1957.

Cousin, Jean. *Etudes sur Quintilien.* 2 vols. Paris: Boivin, 1936 and "Quintilien 1935–1959." *Lustrum,* VII (1962), 289–331.

Grube, G. M. A. *The Greek and Roman Critics,* pp. 284–307. See under Plato bibliography.

Gwynn, Aubrey. *Roman Education from Cicero to Quintilian.* Oxford: Oxford University Press, 1926.

Kennedy, George A. "An Estimate of Quintilian." *American Journal of Philology,* LXXXIII (1962), 130–46, and *Quintilian.* New York: Twayne, 1969.

Laing, Gordon J. "Quintilian, the Schoolmaster." *Classical Journal* XV (1920), 513–34.

Leddy, J. F. "Tradition and Change in Quintilian." *Phoenix,* VII (1953), 47–56.

Marrou, H. I. *A History of Education in Antiquity,* tr. by George Lamb. New York: Sheed and Ward, 1956.

Odgers, Merle M. "Quintilian's Use of Earlier Literature." *Classical Philology,* XXVIII (1933), 182–88.

"LONGINUS"

Atkins, J. W. H. *Literary Criticism in Antiquity,* vol. II, pp. 210–53. See under Plato bibliography.

Boyd, M. J. "Longinus, the Philological Discourses and the Essay on the Sublime." *Classical Quarterly,* n.s. VII (1957), 39ff.

Brody, Jules. *Longinus and Boileau.* Geneva: Droz, 1958.

Grube, G. M. A. *The Greek and Roman Critics,* pp. 340–53. See under Plato bibliography.

———. "Notes on the *peri hypsous.*" *American Journal of Philology,* LXXIII (1952), 251–67.

Henn, T. R. *Longinus and English Criticism.* Cambridge: Cambridge University Press, 1934. A useful study of the influence of "Longinus" on English literary criticism which illustrates "Longinus'" major concepts with passages taken from English literature.

Monk, Samuel H. *The Sublime: A Study of Critical Theories in Eighteenth-Century England.* New York: Modern Language Association of America, 1935.

Olson, Elder. "The Argument of Longinus' *On the Sublime.*" *Critics and Criticism: Ancient and Modern,* ed. R. S. Crane. Chicago: University of Chicago Press, pp. 232–59.

Roberts, W. Rhys. "Longinus on the Sublime." *Philological Quarterly,* VII (1928), 209ff.

Russell, Donald A. *"Longinus" On the Sublime.* Oxford: Oxford University Press, 1964. A recent scholarly edition of the Greek text with useful introduction and notes.

Segal, Charles P. "*Hypsos* and the Problem of Cultural Decline in the *De sublimate.*" *Harvard Studies in Classical Philology,* LXIV (1959), 121ff.

Swanson, Roy Arthur. "'Longinus': Noesis and Pathos." *Classical Bulletin,* XLVI (1969), 1–5.

Tate, Allen. "Longinus and the 'New Criticism'." *Collected Essays.* Denver: Swallow Press, 1959.

Trowbridge, Hoyt. " 'Leda and the Swan': A Longinian Analysis." *Modern Philology,* LI (1953), 118–29; cf. rebuttal by Leo Spitzer in *Modern Philology,* LI (1953), 271–76.

PLOTINUS

Aubin, P. "L'Image dans l'oeuvre de Plotin." *Recherches de Science Religieuse,* XLI (1953), 348–79.

Bréhier, Emile. *The Philosophy of Plotinus,* tr. by Joseph Thomas. Chicago: University of Chicago Press, 1958. This authoritative study of the thought of Plotinus is a standard reference work on the subject.

Grube, G. M. A. *The Greek and Roman Critics,* pp. 354–55. See under Plato bibliography.

Inge, W. R. *The Philosophy of Plotinus.* 3rd ed. 2 vols. London and New York: Longmans, Green, 1929. This work, containing some controversial judgments, makes an important contribution to the interpretation of Plotinus.

Keyser, Eugénie de. *La Signification de l'art dans les Ennéades de Plotin.* Louvain: Bibliothèque de l'Université, 1955.

Merlan, Philip. *From Platonism to Neoplatonism,* 2nd ed. The Hague: Nijhoff, 1963.

Rich, A. N. M. "Plotinus and the Theory of Artistic Imitation." *Mnemosyne,* XIII (1960), 233–39.

Rist, John M. *Plotinus: The Road to Reality.* Cambridge: Cambridge University Press, 1967. An important study, on an advanced level, of specialized problems in the philosophy of Plotinus.

Trouillard, Jean. *La Purification plotinienne.* Paris: Universitaires de France, 1955.

Whittaker, Thomas. *The Neo-Platonists: A Study in the History of Hellenism.* 2nd ed. Cambridge: Cambridge University Press, 1918.

MEDIEVAL
LITERARY CRITICISM

O. B. Hardison, Jr.

GENERAL INTRODUCTION

There is at present no authoritative work on the history of medieval criticism. The explanation is first, doubtless, that scholars have not thought it worth the effort. Few people read medieval poetry and fewer still are interested in the critical theories that lie behind it. But there is another reason than lack of general interest. The subject is particularly difficult to define. Studies tend either to be too narrow and hence to distort by exclusiveness, or too inclusive and hence to lose focus. First and foremost, medieval literature is international, not national. Yet, outside of departments of comparative literature, the orientation of modern literary studies is strongly nationalistic. One of the standard treatments of medieval criticism in use today is J. W. H. Atkins' *English Literary Criticism: The Medieval Phase* (1952). Atkins' approach is not merely biased, it is fatal to the subject. The habit of dividing literary subjects along national lines leads Atkins to treat Bede and Alcuin in detail, while ignoring the late classical authors who were their primary sources; to treat John of Salisbury and John of Garland while ignoring Bernard Silvestris, Hugh of St. Victor, Conrad of Hirsau, and Gervase of Melcheley, among others.

Again, literary criticism is related to, but different from the history of aesthetics and the history of style. Medieval aesthetics has been treated by Edgar de Bruyne, while stylistics has been analyzed by Hans Glunz. Neither de Bruyne nor Glunz, however, had any intention of writing a history of criticism. De Bruyne is interested in the idea of beauty and its manifestation in medieval architecture, music, painting, and sculpture, as well as literature. Plotinus and St. Thomas are key figures in his study, although they are secondary in the history of medieval criticism. Again, Glunz's analysis of medieval stylistics takes him beyond the limits of treatises on literary theory and into analysis of the verbal texture of medieval poems.

Finally, it cannot be stressed too often that rhetoric and poetic are two different disciplines during the Middle Ages. C. S. Baldwin's *Medieval Rhetoric and Poetic* (1928), heavily indebted to Edmond Faral, is perhaps our closest approximation to a modern history of medieval criticism. Baldwin rightly points out that rhetorical doctrine was absorbed wholesale in many critical documents and had a pervasive influence on others. This leads him to the assumption that medieval poetic is merely a variant of medieval rhetoric, an assumption that is simply not valid. Baldwin's treatment of the *artes poeticae* of the twelfth and thirteenth centuries is a useful summary of their debt to rhetoric, particularly to the pseudo-Ciceronian *Rhetorica ad Herennium.* But it distorts the *artes* by ignoring the central fact that the rhetorical content has been adapted to artistic purposes. In other words, far from illustrating a confusion of rhetoric with poetic, the *artes* reveal a lively consciousness of the differences between them. The rhetorical approach also commits Baldwin to extended treatment of documents that are not primarily critical, like Alcuin's *Rhetoric,* while causing him to neglect such large and important segments of medieval criticism as allegory, the *accessus* (or list of authors), and scholastic treatises on poetry.

For present purposes, we will define literary criticism as a group of texts dealing with the history and theory of literature (in its narrower sense as against general discussions of art, the beautiful, and the like), literary creation, and the analysis of specific literary works. Biblical exegesis is an enormous subject in its own right. It will be mentioned from time to time simply because it is too large to be ignored. Certain challenges that it posed for criticism—for example, the assimilation of Hebrew literary forms into Graeco-Roman tradition and the extension of literary chronology to periods earlier than Homer—have a direct bearing on specific late classical developments. Others—whether a Christian should study pagan authors, the relation of biblical to secular allegory, and the concept of inspiration—provided standard critical topics throughout the whole period from Augustine to Boccaccio and gave rise to different responses at different times. But as a subject biblical exegesis is not literary criticism, and a history of medieval criticism must avoid the tendency to become excessively involved in the area covered so well by Henri de Lubac's *Exégèse médiévale.*

If we limit the topic successfully, we still have to come to terms with several problems. For example, what is the dividing line between "medieval" and "classical"? To select a historical date such as the conversion of Constantine is wholly unsatisfactory, for certain types of criticism that are generally considered typically medieval were commonplace before Plato. Allegorical criticism, for example, began with Theagenes of Rhegium in the sixth century B.C. and has a continuous history throughout the classical period. Alexandrian critical theory as exemplified in the works of Philo Judaeus, Clement of Alexandria, and Origen extends from the first century B.C. to the second century A.D., a period roughly coincident with the golden and silver ages of Roman literature. When we move to the Latin west, a still more curious situation presents itself. If Statius is "classical," is Tertullian "medieval"? If Augustine and Jerome are "medieval," are Servius, Donatus, and Macrobius "classical"? To ask questions like these is to call attention to the fact that the terms "classical" and "medieval" refer less to chronology than to cultural perspective.

Certain elements of the classical tradition were absorbed easily and naturally by medieval authors, while others—classical drama, for example—were intractable and were either neglected or had to be modified profoundly before being assimilated. Macrobius and Boethius are in the first category. They were read easily throughout the Middle Ages. At the same time, both were conscious of the whole body of classical tradition. They can be considered either "classical" or "medieval" with equal validity. On the other hand, Vergil and Ovid are unambiguously classical. They were read universally during the Middle Ages, but—as we know from Fulgentius, Bernard Silvestris, Bercorius and Boccaccio—their work was only admitted to the canon of medieval classics after it had been distorted almost beyond recognition. This process of assimilation by distortion was quite conscious.

In his *Clerical Institute* Rabanus Maurus advised, "If we wish to read the poems and books of the gentiles because of their flowers of eloquence, we must take as our type the captive woman in Deuteronomy . . . If an Israelite should want her as a wife, he should shave her head, cut off her nails, and pluck her eyebrows. When she has been made clean, he can then embrace her as a husband. By the same token, we customarily do this when a book of secular learning comes into our hands. If we find anything useful in it we absorb it into our teaching. If there is anything superfluous concerning idols, love, or purely secular affairs, we reject it. We shave the head of some books, we cut the nails of others with razor-sharp scissors." This expresses quite accurately the process whereby much pagan literature was assimilated by medieval culture. It could be called assimilation by selection and—in many cases—by distortion.

Second, there is the problem of systems of classification. The late classical period was fascinated to the point of obsession with terminology. Rhetoric was particularly fruitful of systems and terms. It bequeathed to the Middle Ages the system of the three (or four) styles, the division of figures into schemes and tropes, figures of amplification, figures of thought, and figures of words, the debate over the importance of talent in comparison to art, the doctrine of imitation in the sense of copying the masterpieces, the distinction between matter (*res*) and language (*verba*), the concept of decorum in terms of age, sex, and status, and the formulas for compositions such as encomium, epithalamium, and epicede, to name only a few of the more prominent topics. Poets assimilated most of these and added many schemata derived from poetics rather than rhetoric: the division of a critical essay into sections on *poesis* (general questions of poetry), *poema* (types of poetry), and *poeta* (the character and education of the poet), the system of genres, the conventions of classical prosody, the concept of imitation as "making," the question of whether poetry lies, the instruct and delight formula, and many others.

Allegory is a topic in itself. At least five distinct systems were commonplace by the fifth century: allegory as etymology, allegory as euhemerism (the theory that mythological figures are based on historical persons), allegory as doctrine related to science, ethics, or religion, and allegory as divinely inspired truth concealed under the veil of fiction either to protect it from the eyes of the unenlightened or because transcendent vision can only be expressed in symbols and metaphors. To these systems Christian writers beginning, apparently, with John Cassian (360–435), added a sixth, the idea that scripture (and eventually, secular poetry) has four levels of meaning: literal, allegorical, moral, and anagogical (spiritual).

The fact that during the Middle Ages certain terms and categories were isolated, analyzed, and defined through standardized formulas is demonstration of their central relevance to medieval critical theory. They run continuously through critical treatises from the fourth to the seventeenth century. They can be examined individually, and when approached in this way they emerge as critical themes which can be used as evidence of the continuity of medieval thought. Their deeper significance, however, is not their persistence as *topoi*, but their specific implications in different periods and different contexts, and it is this deeper significance which constitutes their chief interest here.

Christopher Caudwell once observed that the practice of criticism is something like carving a chicken. There are any number of ways in which the job can be done but there is only one right way and that is along the joints. In medieval criticism the joints are the classifications used at various times during the period for different kinds of knowledge. For most of the Middle Ages this means classifications based on the divisions in the trivium of grammar, rhetoric, and logic, and the quadrivium of arithmetic, geometry, music, and astronomy. If, for example, we take the trivium as our point of reference, we find that poetic can be considered a part of grammar or of rhetoric or of logic. Each placement results in distinctive forms of criticism related to the function which the placement implies. At the same time, subject matter frequently overlaps categories. To take the most obvious example, one finds the "colors of rhetoric"—that is, rhetorical imagery—included in both grammatical and rhetorical treatises of the late classical period. Their appearance in grammatical treatises doubtless reflects the exigencies of pedagogy: as the student was introduced to literary texts in the grammar curriculum it was only natural to begin teaching him the stylistic techniques that he would study, in more detail, as a part of rhetoric. The overlap is not the result of positive theory but of convenience. As the treatises collected by Heinrich Keil in his *Grammatici Latini* (1897–1923) and Carolus Halm in his *Rhetores Latini Minores* (1863) amply demonstrate, when late classical authors wrote as professional grammarians and rhetoricians they generally had a very clear sense of the difference between the two disciplines.

POETRY AND GRAMMAR

The most traditional and enduring "placement" of medieval poetic is in the grammar curriculum. Quintilian provided the basic formula relating poetic to grammar in his definition of grammar as "the science of correct speaking and the reading of the poets" (*Institutio Oratoria* I.iv.2). Book X of the *Institute* begins with an outline of the most elaborate formal literary curriculum that we possess from antiquity. It is a list of Greek and Roman authors to be studied for their eloquence and imitated in composition exercises involving translation and paraphrase as well as in original essays on set topics. The list in the *Institute* is the forerunner of the medieval *accessus* and a precedent for the emphasis on imitation and composition that formed a key element in the curriculum of the Cathedral schools of the twelfth century.

The association of grammar with "reading of the poets" can be traced through late classical treatises such as *De Arte Grammatica* of Victorinus, which follows Quintilian in defining grammar as "the science of interpreting the poets and historians and the method of correct speaking and writing," through discussions of the trivium by Cassiodorus and Rabanus Maurus. John of Salisbury sums up the matter for the twelfth century by observing that "poetry belongs to grammar, which is the mother and source of its study." It is no accident, then, that throughout the Middle Ages grammatical tradition preserves a strong attachment to pagan literature and a vivid memory of the commonplaces of classical criticism. This is to say that the grammar curriculum is the chief vehicle of medieval humanism. Although displaced in the thirteenth century in the wake of the so-called "battle of the liberal arts," grammar re-emerged in the fourteenth and fifteenth centuries in the treatises of humanist educators like Vittorino da Feltre, Guarino da Verona, and Erasmus, all of whom believed that the study of literature —and "reading the poets"—should be the center of the humanistic curriculum.

The association of poetry with grammar gave rise to three characteristic types of treatise. The first is the commentary or gloss. This sort of commentary is not an essay. Although a medieval gloss generally begins with a brief, generalized discussion of the life of the author whose works are being explained, followed by comments on the form and style of the works themselves—as exemplified by the commentaries of Donatus on Terence and Servius on Vergil—it consists chiefly of notes on individual words and lines of the text. These notes have a practical purpose. The poets were not read for aesthetic reasons but to develop eloquence, or, among Christian writers like Bede, Cassiodorus, and Rabanus Maurus, as preparation for interpreting scripture. Obviously, before the student can make use of the poets he must understand them. The grammatical commentary defines unfamiliar expressions, explains hard constructions, points out striking rhetorical figures, and may, on occasion, draw moral lessons or provide allegorical explanations of mythological allusions. The major extant commentaries date, with one exception, from the late classical period. They are the commentaries of Servius on Vergil, Aelius Donatus on Terence, and Arcon and Porphyrion on Horace. Typical of the numerous later commentaries in the same tradition are those by Remigius of Auxerre and Scotus Erigena on Martianus Capella, and the so-called *Scholia Recentiora,* dated after the eleventh century, on Terence. The exception to the rule that the major commentaries are pre-Carolingian is the twelfth century *Glossa Ordinaria* of Nicholas of Lyra, the standard high medieval commentary on the Bible.

A second specialized type of criticism created by the association of poetry with grammar is the *ars metrica.* Classical grammar involved the study of spelling, syllabification, and vowel quantities. Typically, a full-scale treatment of grammar required three books. In the third book, treatment of vowel quantities broadened out into a discussion of prosody. These discussions served a double purpose. They illustrated the quantities of various syllables together with such practices as elision and poetic license. And they prepared the student for "reading the poets" by introducing him to the standard poetic forms. The basic literary theory shared by the treatises on *ars metrica* is that poetry is not a matter of content or method but of versification. Poetry is to be distinguished not from history but from prose. In this system function follows form. That is, a work is "heroic" as much because it uses heroic meter (dactylic hexameter) as for its content. Beyond this, the typical *ars metrica* gives formulas for nine (or eight or ten) basic meters, usually beginning with dactylic and including anapest, troche, iamb, choriamb and the like. The meters are usually treated in detail; thirty-two "figures" are recognized as appropriate for heroic meter. Further instruction is given in such stanzaic forms as Sapphic, Alcaic, and Anacreontic.

The major late classical essays on the *ars metrica* are collected in Volume VI of Keil's *Grammatici Latini.* Bede's *De Arte Metrica,* which is in Keil's seventh volume, is of special interest on two counts. It consistently balances Christian, including biblical works, against their pagan counterparts. And it contains one of the earliest formal discussions of accentual prosody, which is "composition determined not by metrical practice, but by the number of syllables as determined by their sound [*iudicium aurium*] as in the songs of the popular poets."

Bede's treatise is the forerunner of a group of Latin treatises written between the eleventh and fourteenth centuries with the generic title *ars rhythmica,* as well as one of the true masterpieces of medieval criticism, Dante's *De Vulgari Eloquentia* (ca. 1304–07). The same tradition is evident in vernacular treatments of prosody, beginning with Eustace Deschamps' *L'art de dictier* (1392) and moving through the essays of the *seconde rhetorique* to Renaissance treatises on prosody including Trissino's *Poetica,* Du Bellay's *Deffence et illustration de la langue françoyse,* and George Gascoigne's *Certain Notes of Instruction.*

The list of curriculum authors in Book X of Quintilian's *Institute* establishes a precedent for medieval lists of *auctores* (standard authors). The critical interest of such lists comes from the fact that from the very beginning the tradition was comparative. Quintilian's list of Greek and Roman authors is, as has been noted, a precedent for the formal rhetorical comparison of a Roman work to the Greek work that is imitated. Plutarch compares Terence and Menander; Aulus Gellius, Vergil and Pindar; and Macrobius, whose *Saturnalia* provides the most elaborate examples of poetic (as against rhetorical) comparison, sets Vergil against Homer, Theocritus, and Hesiod among the Greeks, and Livius Andronicus and Ennius among the Romans. When the tradition was assimilated by the Christian authors, comparisons were drawn between Latin and Hebrew authors. Jerome was fond of such comparisons. "David" he remarked, "is our Simonides, our Pindar, our Horace," and it is to Jerome that Latin tradition owes its conception of Job as a tragedy, Pentateuch as heroic poem, and Ecclesiastes as an elegy. Bede, as we have seen, takes the same approach. Job to him is an heroic poem, while Deuteronomy and Psalms 118 and 119 are elegies. The Song of Songs is a biblical drama; Ecclesiastes is the biblical equivalent of the "narrative" form illustrated in antiquity by the *Georgics* and the *De Rerum Natura*; and Job is an example of the "mixed" form used by Homer in the *Iliad* and Vergil in the *Aeneid*.

Beginning in the early eleventh century, perhaps much earlier, the tradition of lists of authors was formalized in a group of treatises with the generic title *accessus ad auctores*. The earliest extant example of the type is an *accessus* by Bernard of Utrecht to the *Eclogue* of Theodulus, evidently the sole survivor of a large number of similar works. The formula for the *accessus* is given in the most complete example of the form that we possess, the *Dialogus Super Auctores, Sive Didascalon* of Conrad of Hirsau (ca. 1070–1150). Conrad explains: "You should not overlook that in explaining books, the ancients considered seven topics: author, title, type of poem, intention of the writer, order, number of books, and explanation [of the text]." The proximate source for this form of treatment—and presumably one of the "ancients" whom Conrad had in mind—is Servius; but behind Servius we can detect the influence of sophistic rhetoric.

What is important is that in order to provide the necessary information Conrad runs through a whole series of classical distinctions and definitions: the meaning of prose, rhythm, and meter; the definition of poet ("he is called a maker of fictions or a creator because he says false things instead of true or mixes the false with the true"); the difference between *poema, poesis,* and *poeta* (or "*poetria*"); the nature of bucolic, comic, tragic, and satiric poetry; the three styles; and so forth. This is followed by discussions of the *auctores* themselves, who are arranged from easy to difficult. The final subject is scripture—a reminder that according to Augustine, Cassiodorus, and Rabanus Maurus, the chief justification for the study of secular letters was as preparation for interpreting the Bible. The list is: Donatus (the *Ars Minor*), Cato (the *Distichs*), Aesop, Avianus, Sedulius, Juvencus, Prosper of Aquitaine, Theodulus, Arator, Prudentius, Cicero (*De Amicitia, De Senectute*), Sallust, Boethius, Lucan, Horace, Ovid, Vergil (incomplete), and scripture. While there is no attempt at pairing or contrasting Christian and pagan authors, the differences between Christian and pagan outlooks, and the dangers of paganism, are regularly stressed.

As Bruno Sandkühler has shown, the *accessus* tradition lies behind Dante's

Epistle to Can Grande della Scala. The *accessus* supplements the other two treatise types produced by the association of poetry with grammar—the commentary-gloss and the *ars metrica*—as a vehicle for medieval humanism. It is a precedent for, if not an influence on, the new "canon of the classics" developed for the Renaissance curriculum. A trace of the *accessus* tendency to include Christian along with pagan classics is found in John Colet's regulations for St. Paul's School, which stipulate that the schoolboys be introduced to classical eloquence not through Cicero but through Lactantius, a safe Christian author believed by early humanists like John Colet to have attained a near-Ciceronian eloquence.

RHETORIC AND POETIC

The typical forms of medieval grammatical criticism are clearly defined. The case is by no means so plain for medieval rhetorical criticism. In some ways, rhetoric and poetic are more closely interrelated during the classical period than during the Middle Ages. As the classical section of this volume shows, only one ancient document, Aristotle's *Poetics*, treats poetry without drawing heavily on rhetoric. Much of what passes for classical literary criticism—the work of Dionysius of Halicarnassus, Demetrius *On Style*, and Longinus *On the Sublime*, for example—is really oratorical criticism which is applicable to poetry. Horace's *Ars Poetica* draws in part on Alexandrian poetic theory (itself deeply influenced by rhetoric), but its debt to Roman rhetoric is pervasive. The topics of imitation, of the training of the poet, of talent (*physis*) versus experience (*episteme*) and learning (*melete*), of decorum of character, of the three styles and their correlative faults, and of the dual function of poetry to instruct and delight all have close parallels in Ciceronian rhetoric, from which they were probably taken. We know further that the Gorgian figures so important in sophistic rhetoric were thought in antiquity to have been derived from the poets and that this same sophistic tradition later produced formulas for epideictic orations like the encomium and epithalamium that were copied in occasional poetry. Classical rhetorical manuals regularly quote poetry to illustrate effective expression, while a major purpose of "reading the poets" in the grammar curriculum was to acquaint the student with the rhetorical figures that he would later use in prose orations.

This overlap is symptomatic of confusion only if we insist that poetic and rhetoric must be kept absolutely separate. The concept of an absolute separation of the two disciplines was not even generally available until the sixteenth century, when the *Poetics* again became current; but even if it had been, the practical and didactic temper of classical criticism would have insured its rejection. The same is true of late classical and early medieval criticism, with the ironic qualification that the closest approximation to a theory of art for art's sake during the period under consideration was the flowering of epideictic oratory and literary

Asianism during the late classical period. Both of these developments were stimulated by rhetorical rather than poetic theory.

Throughout the Middle Ages rhetorical theory impinges on critical thought. This is most obvious in the case of the rhetorical figures which were known through the *Ad Herennium*, the *De Inventione*, late classical essays on the rhetorical colors, and grammatical treatises like the *Ars Grammatica* of Donatus. We also hear frequent echoes in medieval criticism of some of the larger issues of rhetoric. The system of the three styles, for example, was adopted by Augustine in the *De Doctrina* and recurs in the *Scholia Vindobonensia* on Horace, Conrad of Hirsau's *Didascalon*, Geoffrey of Vinsauf's *Documentum de Arte Dictandi et Versificandi*, John of Garland's *Poetria*, John of Salisbury's *Metalogicon*, and elsewhere.

On the other hand, not all rhetorical treatises are directly relevant to medieval poetic theory. Works like Bede's *De Schematibus et Tropis*, Alcuin's *Rhetoric*, and Geoffrey of Vinsauf's *De Coloribus Rhetoricis* are purely rhetorical, referring to prose rather than poetic composition. This is true also of the *artes dictaminis* (treatises on letter-writing) and the *artes praedicandi* (arts of preaching) of the high Middle Ages. In the history of criticism such works are significant for the light they frequently throw on literary topics rather than as primary documents.

In terms of sources, the primary document for rhetorical criticism *qua* criticism throughout the Middle Ages was Horace's *Ars Poetica*. This work was evidently regarded by medieval scholars as part of grammar rather than rhetoric. Horace was one of the standard *auctores*, and the *Ars Poetica* was used in conjunction with "reading the poets." Thus, on the basis of classification we would have to regard treatises influenced by the *Ars Poetica* as part of the tradition of grammatical rather than rhetorical criticism, in spite of their heavy debt to formal rhetoric.

During the late classical period three documents illustrate formal and self-conscious rhetorical criticism. The first of these is the incomplete treatise *On the Sublime*, which is traditionally assigned to "Longinus." The essay is of great interest as an assertion of the claims of genius over training and skill, and of the primacy of imagery over arrangement. Each of these questions was debated in ancient rhetoric, and each is touched on in Horace's *Ars Poetica*. The position which "Longinus" takes on each of these topics is the opposite to that taken by Horace, and by and large the anti-Horatian stance would have been congenial to Latin authors after the Silver Age. However, *On the Sublime* had no discernible influence during the Middle Ages, and it was not translated into Latin until the 16th century. If it is a third-century document and its author was indeed, as tradition once had him, a pupil of Plotinus, it illustrates the late classical Neoplatonic aesthetic which also appears to have encouraged late classical Asianism. But until the matter of dating is settled this remains wholly conjectural.

The two late classical examples of rhetorical criticism which were unquestionably available, at least sporadically, to medieval readers are the *Interpretationes Vergilianae* of Tiberius Claudius Donatus and the lengthy discussion of Vergil in Books V and VI of Macrobius' *Saturnalia.* Both of these are fourth-century works. The *Interpretationes* begins with a prologue in the form of a letter from Donatus to his son. In it the father complains that the grammarians cannot appreciate Vergil. They are concerned with elementary matters fit only for school boys. Vergil was a master of all departments of rhetoric and therefore only an orator can appreciate his achievement. This prelude does not lead, as we might expect, to Vergil's use of schemes and tropes. Donatus was a good Ciceronian, and was able to consider the larger questions implicit in his approach. The resulting analysis is a wide-ranging, often philosophical treatise with something of the sophistication, if not the artistry, of Cicero's *De Oratore.* Vergil, we learn, had a dual purpose—to celebrate the early history of Rome and to praise the *Gens Julia* (the house to which Julius Caesar belonged). He was deeply learned, particularly in moral philosophy, and his work can be read as a guide to the conduct of life as well as a repository of much useful knowledge (*doctrina*). Donatus frequently notices Vergil's use of figurative language, and contends that he was a master in this department as well as in arrangement and invention, but the discussion never becomes a list of "colors." The result is not a grammatical commentary-gloss but a series of intelligent, informed essays covering all twelve books of the *Aeneid.* If the criticism is somewhat arid to modern tastes, this is because rhetoric itself is out of favor today and not because of the author's inadequacy.

The *Saturnalia* is quite different, in some ways more conventional. During the Silver Age, the question "Is Vergil an orator or a poet?" was sufficiently commonplace to become a standard topic for school exercises, called *controversiae.* The *Saturnalia* is an extended dialogue covering a large variety of subjects in the manner of Aulus Gellius' *Attic Nights.* In Book IV Symmachus, one of the speakers, discusses Vergil's use of the rules of rhetoric. His command of language is illustrated by citations of the numerous appeals to emotion and figures woven into the *Aeneid.* In Book V and Book VI the *controversia* topic is revived. Vergil's ability to use the four styles of oratory is demonstrated, with the conclusion that he combines the virtues of the ten Attic orators. The discussion then turns to Vergil as an imitator, in the rhetorical sense of one who follows great models. Homer, of course, comes first, but Roman authors are also cited—principally Ennius. Innumerable examples are given of passages in which Vergil parallels his sources closely. Although there are similar comparative treatments of poetry in "Longinus," Plutarch, and Aulus Gellius, no other classical or late classical work treats imitation so extensively.

As we move from the late classical to the Carolingian period and beyond, the tradition of purely rhetorical criticism disappears. In its place, we have grammatical treatises which draw most of their substance from rhetoric. The *artes poeticae* of the twelfth and thirteenth centuries rely heavily on the *Rhetorica ad Herennium* and variously contain brief sections on arrangement, memory, delivery, the three styles, imitation, art versus talent, and the like. They have been treated by Faral and Baldwin as prime examples of rhetorical criticism and as illustrations of the medieval confusion of rhetoric and poetic. On the other hand, there was a lively debate during the twelfth and thirteenth centuries concerning the relative importance of the disciplines of the trivium, and this debate reflects the very opposite of confusion. It shows that the authors involved had a very acute understanding of the subjects appropriate for the three departments of the trivium. They disagreed because of their recognition of the implications inherent in the available alternatives. The debate is summarized by John of Salisbury in the *Metalogicon.* It does not concern the relation of poetic to rhetoric but the claim that poetry is an art independent of both disciplines:

> Poetry stays so close to the things of nature that many have refused to include it in grammar, asserting that it is an art in its own right and is no more related to grammar than to rhetoric, though it is related to both and has precepts in common.

John of Salisbury emphatically believed that, in spite of its relation to rhetoric, poetry belongs with grammar, and it is most likely that the authors of the *artes poeticae* agreed with him. We know from the *Metalogicon* that the Cathedral schools required imitation as well as passive reading of the *auctores.* The *artes poeticae* were textbooks designed for this curriculum, and therefore—in spite of their rhetorical content—they must be considered part of grammar rather than rhetoric. True rhetorical criticism along the line of Donatus and Macrobius did not reappear in Europe until the educational reforms and the controversy over imitation in the fifteenth century.

LOGIC AND POETRY

When we move from rhetoric to logic, the third of the disciplines of the trivium, we enter a clearly defined area associated with a specific period of medieval history. The link between poetry and logic was made by late classical commentators on Aristotle, most notably Alexander of Aphrodisias. The option of associating poetry with logic had no attraction for the early Middle Ages. We have hints of it during the twelfth century in the explanations of Bernard of Utrecht and Conrad of Hirsau of the relation of the *accessus* formula to Aristotle's four causes, and in the thirteenth century in the preference of Gervase of Melcheley for a logical rather than a rhetorical system of classifying figures. Further indications of a new view of poetry are evident in the debate over the liberal arts, in which the Cathedral schools stood by grammar and the *auctores,* while the *avant garde* representing the newly-emergent universities insisted that logic should be the queen of the trivium. To quote *The Battle of the Seven Arts* of Henri d'Andeli (ca. 1250):

> Paris and Orleans are at odds.
> It is a great loss and a great sorrow,
> That they do not agree.
> Do you know the reason for this discord?
> It is because they differ about learning;
> For logic, who is always wrangling,
> Calls the *auctores* authorlings
> And the students of Orleans mere grammar-boys . . .
> However logic has the students
> Whereas grammar is reduced in numbers.

The main impulse for a revaluation of the placing of poetry in the curriculum came from Arabic Spain. The question of "the division of the sciences" had been treated by al-Farabi (d. 950) and Averroes (1126–98), who taught that Aristotle considered poetic a part of the *Organon.* The revival of Aristotelian philosophy which is intimately associated with scholasticism was made possible initially by wholesale translation into Latin of Arabic commentaries and translations, and the concept of poetic as a part of logic was one of the ideas that accompanied them. Since this placing was apparently an authoritative Aristotelian doctrine, it had considerable prestige. Its implications, however, were anti-humanistic. To make poetic a part of logic is to assert that it is an "instrument" or "faculty" without content—a technique for manipulating symbols like demonstrative logic, dialectic, and sophistic—rather than a "science" like politics or astronomy. The theory is developed in several scholastic treatises—in the Latin translation of al-Farabi's *Catalogue of the Sciences* by Gerard of Cremona, in the treatise *On the Division of the Sciences* by Dominicus Gundissalinus, and in the translation by Hermannus Alemannus of Averroes' *Commentary on the Poetics of Aristotle.*

The problem is that to define poetic as a "faculty" rather than a "science" is to deny its immemorial claim to providing instruction as well as delight. Throughout the Middle Ages one of the standard defenses of reading the *auctores* had been that they provided useful *doctrina* (general knowledge) and, above all, moral instruction through examples. This didactic bias is as common in the *accessus* tradition as it is to allegorical readings of Vergil and Ovid. The moral utility of Christian poetry, was, of course, obvious. That of the ethnic writers was considered "Egyptian gold," as Augustine put it, which Christians could use for their own profit, just as the Hebrews were allowed to take the gold of their heathen masters on their departure from Egypt. But to deny that poetry is a "science" is to deny that it has any ethical content. According to Gundissalinus, it is merely the technique of creating illusions. The implication is that poetry may well be a pleasant recreation, but it is essentially trivial. This is a challenge to the whole rationale of medieval humanism. In particular, it is a direct attack on the humanism of Chartres.

Echoes of the debate which the logical "placing" of poetry stimulated can be heard in St. Thomas and Roger Bacon, who are willing to concede that poetry has a dual place in the system of the sciences—as a technique it is part of logic; as an activity it is a kind of ethical teaching or a method of creating moral examples. More radical responses are evident in Dante, whose *Epistle to Can Grande della Scala* explicitly states that the *Divine Comedy* is a part of moral philosophy, and who interprets three of his *canzoni* in the *Convivio* as allegories of the ennobling effect of love, the value of philosophical studies, and the nature of true nobility, respectively. Mussato and Boccaccio agree with Dante that poetry teaches virtue. They add the considerably more audacious claim, based on Aristotle's *Metaphysics,* that poetry is allied to theology. That the controversy was a bitter one is evident from Petrarch's *Invective Against a Physician* and Boccaccio's defense of poetry in the *Genealogy of the Gentile Gods,* both of which record the bitter attacks of clerics against the new concepts. The revival of Platonism in the fifteenth century, it may be added, intensified the debate by providing fresh arguments in the running battle between humanists like Landino and Politian and Thomistic conservatives like Savonarola. It passed into the sixteenth century as a standard topic—the placement of poetry among the sciences—to be dealt with at the beginning of any full-scale critical essay.

POETRY AND THE QUADRIVIUM

Beyond grammar, rhetoric, and logic are the sciences of the quadrivium. There is no medieval treatise on poetry and arithmetic although we know that "numerical composition" was regarded as a legitimate device for imitating the divine numbers which are the basis of creation. St. Augustine's *De Musica* contains a lengthy analysis of the relation between musical rhythms and classical meters. Again, however, no medieval treatise exists which deals specifically with poetry and music, unless the theoretically rather barren treatises on the *ars rhythmica* are included in this category. The sense of the real and symbolic importance of harmony in poetry may be assumed from de Bruyne's treatment of twelfth-century aesthetics and is obviously relevant to such developments as the trope and the sequence. Dante treats the relation of music to the *canzone, ballata,* and other vernacular verse forms in Book II of the *De Vulgari Eloquentia,* but his treatment is technical, with nothing to offer concerning an underlying theory.

In fact, the first critical treatise to pay serious attention to the relation of poetry to music is Book I of Coluccio Salutati's *De Laboribus Herculis,* which belongs to the fifteenth century.

In medieval criticism the major "type" created by placement of poetry outside the trivium is the result of considering poetry a part of philosophy or theology. To do justice to this concept it would be necessary to refer to anthropology. We know that primitive poetry is often considered prophecy or revelation, and that, in fact, it embodies a world-view which is the primitive equivalent of formal philosophy. In this sense medieval critics who found inspired revelations in texts like the Bible, the *Hermetica,* Ovid's *Metamorphoses,* and Vergil's *Aeneid* may have been nearer the truth than nineteenth-century philologists.

The tradition of allegorical criticism is diffuse and was so even in antiquity. The practice of classifying the kinds of wisdom derived from the poets into scientific ("natural" or "physical"), ethical, and religious (or "rational") knowledge has been traced to Theagenes of Rhegium in the sixth century B.C. It was associated with Stoicism in antiquity and is evident, for example, in Cicero's *De Natura Deorum.* The standard Roman formulation is by Varro, and it is commonplace in late classical criticism. Macrobius writes at the conclusion of the commentary of the *Somnium Scipionis*:

> There are three branches of the whole field of philosophy—moral, physical, and rational. Moral philosophy is a guide to the highest perfection in moral conduct, physical philosophy is concerned with the physical part of the divine order, and rational philosophy discusses incorporealities, matter apprehended only by the mind . . .

As is clear from Macrobius, the allegorical approach is based on the assumption that poetry is not a part of grammar, rhetoric, or logic, but of philosophy proper. "I must declare," he writes in his commentary on the *Somnium Scipionis,* "that there is nothing more complete than this work which embraces the entire body of philosophy." Equally well developed in antiquity is the practice of using etymologies as a key to allegorical intentions. Plato's *Cratylus* and *Republic* furnish instances. The best ancient example of sustained allegorizing is the *Questiones Homericae* by Heraclitus, probably written in the first century A.D., which treats the *Iliad* and the *Odyssey* in detail, frequently using etymology and extracting all of the standard types of *doctrina* from the two works.

The techniques and commonplaces of Stoic criticism were absorbed by the late classical period, but the philosophical point of view to which they were subservient changed to Neoplatonic. This is reflected in emphasis on religious as against scientific and moral allegory, and in the strong insistence of critics on the importance of inspiration. For late classical and medieval critics allegory is not simply disguised textbook lore, but divinely revealed truth which is not available to discursive reason.

The extensive influence of Platonic thought on late classical authors and the persistence of a Platonic tradition throughout the Middle Ages has been documented, most notably by Raymond Klibansky in *The Continuity of the Platonic Tradition in the Middle Ages* (1939). This influence is based in part on the remarkable achievement of pagan Neoplatonists beginning with Plotinus (205–269/70), and in part on Alexandrian authors—Philo Judaeus, Clement of Alexandria, and Origen. A few Platonic texts, most notably Calcidius' translation of the *Timaeus,* were continually available in the West after the decline of Greek studies, but the major vehicles for Latin Neoplatonic tradition were Latin works which had themselves been influenced by Neoplatonism. Servius, Macrobius, and Boethius are especially important among the secular writers in this regard, while Augustine is the chief Latin patristic source for medieval Neoplatonism.

The assumptions on which Neoplatonic critical theory is based are spelled out by Proclus (ca. 410–85) in his discussion of the poetic questions in the *Republic.* As his citations of the *Phaedrus* and *Ion* show, the precedent for his theory is to be found in Plato himself. The theory begins, however, with an idea that Plato explicitly denies in the *Republic.* For Proclus, poetry is a higher version of truth than is available through contemplation of the visible world. This sort of poetry is not an imitation of nature, or, to use a common medieval analogy, a "mirror of custom." It is possible because the poet draws on a mental faculty that goes beyond reason. This faculty, the "intellect" or *mens,* is intuitive. It does not observe or reason things out but responds directly to inspiration. Consequently the deepest truths in poetry are transcendent, having the quality of revelation. Being transcendent they are necessarily obscure. To draw on a concept familiar in Alexandrian biblical criticism, they are "accommodated" to the limits of human understanding by being expressed as symbols and analogies. Because they are realities, they are supremely valuable. At the same time, precisely because they are a kind of revelation, they carry with them a radiance, a supernatural beauty, which is objectified through exquisite imagery and language. Of course, the fact that poetry can express these truths does not mean that they are the only truths with which it is concerned. In addition to divine wisdom, poets also present the truths of reason—of science, and ethics. This level of truth is important, and Proclus places special emphasis on the ethical lessons in poetry. Finally, there is an element in poetry that depends on appearance—the subrational faculties associated with sensation. This kind of poetry is the least valuable sort, but it has its uses. Since it directly reproduces sensory information, even when such information is faulty, it corresponds to the Socratic category of imitative poetry in the tenth Book of the *Republic.* The complex of ideas offered by Proclus, then, includes poetry as revelation, the poet as inspired seer, the poetic faculty as supra-rational, allegory as a veil or as an accommodation, with ornamentation and adornment correlative to the inner beauty of the work, and ethical teaching as an important but subsidiary poetic function.

Similar ideas can be found in varying combinations in the commentary of Philo Judaeus on Genesis, the commentary of Porphyry on the cave of the nymphs episode in Homer, the essay of Plutarch on the Isis and Osiris myth (*Moralia* V.1) and the commentary of Macrobius on the *Somnium Scipionis.* Related texts, which stress the ethical utility of poetry without going into its "mystical" aspects, are the two essays on Homer in Maximus Tyrius' *Dissertations* and Plutarch's "How a Young Man Should Study the Poets" (*Moralia* I.2).

The medieval continuation of this tradition involves the new question of whether pagans can ever have been inspired and what the source of inspiration really is. It was difficult throughout the whole history of allegorical criticism for Christians to answer these questions without appearing to undermine the unique authority of scripture. By and large, they accepted the idea that the Holy Spirit had, indeed, inspired the pagans; and by and large they incurred the hostility of more conservative clerics for this suspiciously deistic teaching. The doctrine is Alexandrian. It is most evident in the *Miscellanies* (*Stromata*) of Clement of Alexandria and various essays by Origen. The prime example and probably the most convincing proof of its validity—for Latin critics—was Vergil's sixth ("Messianic") eclogue, which was universally considered an inspired prophecy of the birth of Christ. That many other teachings of Vergil were considered anticipations of Christian truth is evident from the *De Continentia Vergiliana* of Fulgentius. Cassiodorus uses the metaphor of planting for this idea: "In the origin of spiritual wisdom, as it were, evidences of these matters were sown abroad in the manner of seeds, which instructors in secular letters later most usually transferred to their own rules." The corollary of this point of view is that pagan mythology can be a veil for higher truth. Fulgentius wrote a much-used compendium of allegories of the ancient pantheon, the *Mythologiarum Libri Tres.* The tradition reached its medieval culmination in the works *Epître d'Othéa* of Christine de Pisan, the *Ovidius Moralizatus* of Bercorius, and Boccaccio's *Genealogy of the Gentile Gods.*

Much medieval biblical criticism and much of the thought of high medieval mysticism echoes the same theory which justifies allegorical reading of pagan literature. For present purposes, the earliest critical document to have a more or less continuous influence on medieval criticism is the commentary on the *Somnium Scipionis* of Macrobius. Here the Platonic influence is everywhere apparent. The "dream" itself, which formed the concluding section of Cicero's *De Republica,* is an imitation of the "Vision of Er" episode that closes Plato's *Republic.* In it the elder Scipio appears to his son in a dream to disclose the secrets of the after-life. The text is thus a precedent for a favorite medieval genre, the dream allegory, as well as for the convention, used by Fulgentius, of presenting allegedly inspired truths through a superhuman agent. The commentary proper is an extended analysis of these truths. Although its debts are manifold, it relies especially heavily on a lost *Commentary on the Timaeus* by Porphyry.

In the second chapter of Book I, Macrobius defends the right of philosophy to use fictions. Here, and again in the conclusion of Book II, it is clear that he considers his text allegorized philosophy. Menander, Apuleius, and Petronius, he observes, used fables to delight, while Aesop used them to teach. Philosophers use them to present natural, physical, and rational (i.e., incorporeal) truths. They do this because Nature herself veils her secrets. In a particularly interesting passage, Macrobius offers what amounts to his own theory of accommodation. He observes that fables can be used in reference to the soul and divine matters, but that "similes and analogies are frequently used for the highest, most difficult truths such as the nature of the highest good and the divine intellect." The comment which follows deals with a miscellany of topics suggested by the text. There are chapters on numerology (I.6, II.2), prophecy (I.7), the cardinal virtues (I.8–9), the Zodiac (I.12), astronomy (I.15–22), the earth (II.5–9), and the soul (II.12–17). In short, all three kinds of philosophy are shown to be present in the text. Of particular interest, because it is recurrent in the allegorical tradition throughout its history, is the evident predilection for cosmological allegory. This is present in the *Timaeus* itself. It recurs in Philo Judaeus, who reads Genesis as a kind of Christian *Timaeus;* in Porphyry's essay *On the Cave of the Nymphs;* in Augustine's commentary on Genesis; and in such Renaissance works as Pico's *Heptaplus* and John Colet's *Letters to Radulphus on the Mosaic Account of Creation.*

The purely critical tradition next reappears after Macrobius in *The Exposition of the Content of Vergil According to Moral Philosophy* of Fulgentius, written in the late fifth or sixth century. This work has no obvious source. At times it seems to echo Heraclitus' discussion of the *Odyssey* in his *Questiones Homericae,* at times Servius, and, at least in its use of Vergil's ghost to expound his philosophy, the *Somnium Scipionis.* Any echoes, however, must be at two or three removes. A modest Platonic coloring is given by references to Plato, Porphyrius, and the late classical Latin poem *On the God of Socrates;* but the citations are all minor and appear to be from a handbook rather than the authors themselves.

As the title of the work announces, it treats poetry as philosophy with the emphasis on moral philosophy. We learn that Aeneas represents mankind. The *Aeneid* is an allegory of human life from birth to maturity. Each of its episodes is exemplary, and the characters typically represent virtues to be imitated or vices to be shunned. The Cyclops is vanity, Dido lust, Deiphobus cowardice,

Turnus rage, Anchises parental authority, the golden bough knowledge, Lavinia "the path of labor," and so on. When he has completed the *Aeneid,* the reader has a full knowledge of the virtuous life.

The strong moral bias of the *Exposition* resembles that found in ancient Stoic allegories, but, as we have seen from Proclus, it is perfectly compatible with the Platonic tradition as well. It is qualified in two important ways. First, Fulgentius makes it perfectly clear that Vergil "included the secrets of almost every art" in his works. Fulgentius states that he has avoided most of these secrets because they are "more dangerous than praiseworthy" for the age—that is, they are not suitable for Christians. We are reminded of the comparison of pagan literature to the gentile woman whose nails and hair must be trimmed before she can be married to an Israelite. It is evident from the list of secrets Fulgentius will not reveal that many of them are related to "rational" or "divine" philosophy. Second, Fulgentius often remarks that Vergil's teachings correspond to those revealed to Christians by the Holy Spirit. At one point he quotes the first Psalm, "Blessed is he who walks not in the counsel of the ungodly" to illustrate the parallel. Vergil replies, "I rejoice . . . at these sentiments. Athough I did not know the full truth concerning the nature of the righteous life, still, truth sprinkled its sparks in my darkened mind with a kind of blind favor." Thus, in addition to being a compendium of moral philosophy, the *Aeneid* contains adumbrations of Christian revelation. Its more abstruse doctrines remain mysterious, even dangerous, but they are there for the reader who is bold enough to lift the veil of Vergil's fiction.

The continuity of allegorical interpretation during the Carolingian period is obvious from biblical commentaries and allegorical interpretations of liturgy, especially the *Liber Officialis* of Amalarius of Metz. Theodolphus of Orleans touches on secular allegorizing in a reference to "books which I used to read and how the fables of the poets are mystically employed by philosophers." He mentions Vergil, Ovid, and Prudentius, adding "in their writings although there are many frivolities, a great many truths are hidden under the veil of falsehood. The pen of the poets gives us falsehood, of the Stoics, truth. But the poets often turn their falsehoods to truth. Thus Proteus symbolizes truth, Virgo justice, Hercules virtue, and Cacus crime." The next full-scale critical essay in the Fulgentian tradition, however, is the commentary on the first six books of the *Aeneid* by Bernard Silvestris, written in the twelfth century. Bernard's first sentence asserts, with a bow to Macrobius, that "Vergil was concerned with two kinds of doctrine in the *Aeneid*—. . . he both taught the truth of philosophy and did not neglect poetic fable." He continues with comment on the dual function of the poet to teach and instruct and with the observation that poems can follow a natural or artificial order. The latter point is important to Vergil because, "His procedure is this. Under the veil of fable he described what the human soul placed in a human body in the temporal world should do or endure. And in writing this he followed the natural order, and thus he used both kinds of narrative order—as a poet he used the artificial, and as a philosopher the natural."

All of this represents a considerable advance in sophistication beyond Fulgentius. The commentary proper, while far more copious, is in a less involuted style than Fulgentius. The first Book of the *Aeneid* is an allegory of infancy, the second of childhood, the third of adolescence, the fourth of youth, and the fifth of young manhood. The sixth occupies four-fifths of Bernard's commentary. It contains Vergil's most profound philosophic lore, and Bernard provides an almost word-for-word gloss, drawing heavily on Macrobius for its strategies and Boethius for many of its generalizations. The basic concept, however, remains Fulgentian. The episode in the underworld summarizes all human experience, and the descent of Aeneas, like that of Orpheus and Hercules, is an allegory of the wise man studying human experience, "so that recognizing its fragility and turning away from it, he may concern himself with higher things (*invisibilia*) and recognize the Creator more readily from knowledge of his creations."

Bernard's sources are Fulgentius and Macrobius, with supplementary debts to Boethius, Calcidius (commentary on the *Timaeus*), and a miscellany of less frequently cited writers—Horace, Ovid, Servius, and others. It seems unlikely, however, that Bernard would have made the effort if he had not been deeply involved in the Neoplatonic revival that followed in the wake of Scotus Erigena's translation of the works of Dionysius the pseudo-Areopagite at the end of the tenth century. We can follow the influence of this movement on secular poetry in Bernard's *Microcosmus* and *Megacosmus* and Alanus de Insulis' *De Planctu Naturae* and *Anticlaudianus*. If this is a valid suggestion, Bernard's interest in allegory is connected directly with Platonism through Dionysius, as well as indirectly through Macrobius, Calcidius, and Fulgentius.

During the fourteenth century the allegorical tradition continued to flourish. In France it is evident in the allegorical mythology of Christine de Pisan and Peter Bercorius. In Italy it appears in Dante's *Convivio,* which uses the tradition of biblical, rather than classical allegorizing to draw truths concerning the psychology of love, the importance of philosophy, and the nature of true nobility from three of Dante's *canzoni.* In general, the *Convivio* concentrates on truth available to reason, and Dante is careful to distinguish between "poet's allegory" and theological allegory of the sort elicited from scripture. The *Divine Comedy* is said in the *Epistle to Can Grande della Scala* to belong to the category of moral philosophy, and Dante's Fulgentian tour of the underworld consists largely in *exempla* of the vices. The *Paradiso,* however, begins with a retelling of the fable of Marsyas flayed after his singing contest with Apollo interpreted as an allegory of the departure of the soul from the body during flights of inspiration. It treats those highest mysteries that Macrobius said could only be presented through "similes and analogies." All human agencies—Beatrice and eventually even St. Bernard—finally leave Dante as he ascends the levels of a Dionysian heaven toward a final, transcendent vision which can only be expressed in terms of the imagery of light.

If Dante writes a poem justifying the claim of the poets to divine inspiration, Albertino Mussato and Boccaccio translate Dante's achievement into critical theory. In both of them the claim emerges in the form of an assertion: the poets are not only teachers of ethics, they are also—perhaps primarily—theologians. The only thing new about this claim, which goes back to Aristotle's *Metaphysics,* is the explicitness with which it is made. The critics are quite conscious of what they are doing. "Cavillers," as Boccaccio calls them, assert that poetry is a tissue of lies, that it is idolatrous, that it is morally depraved, and that it should be banished from a Christian society even as Plato banished it from his *Republic.* The mythological interpretations of the *Genealogy of the Gentile Gods* (Books I-XIII) answer the charge by showing that ancient myths are allegories of moral truth, and, on occasion, adumbrations of Christian revelation. Books XIV and IV defend Boccaccio's critical position. The early poets—the *prisci poetae*—were theologians writing directly from divine inspiration. Rightly understood, the fables of the poets are wholly edifying. Although sacred allegory is obviously distinct from secular allegory, at least one modern poet—Dante—has demonstrated that poetry can be a vehicle for the deepest of theological truths. Petrarch, Boccaccio's friend and mentor, has many of the same points to make about poetry in his letters and his *Invective Against a Physician,* on which Boccaccio leaned heavily in Book XIV of the *Genealogy.* However, in the context of Petrarch's work, the claims for supernatural vision and the importance of allegory are less pronounced than in Boccaccio. Petrarch admits the importance of both, but he seems more interested as a critic in eloquence, imitation, and moral instruction. His humanism tends to be conservative, classical, civic, while Boccaccio's is more radical and anticipates the work of the Florentine Neoplatonists of the fifteenth century—Ficino, Landino, Pico, and Politian.

To summarize, the four "placings" of poetry which are most important during the Middle Ages are as a part of grammar, of rhetoric, of logic, and of philosophy. The grammatical placement is the most persistent and is the vehicle of medieval humanism, if that term is understood as referring to the continuity of the classical tradition. Rhetorical placement seems to disappear after the late classical period, although, as we have seen, much rhetorical lore was absorbed by treatises on poetry and the *artes poeticae* were used in the grammar curriculum. Logical placement is associated specifically with scholasticism. Philosophical placement, like grammatical placement, is continuous from the late classical period through the Renaissance. It is associated with Platonism and its orthodoxy frequently tends to be suspect because it purports to find evidence of divine inspiration and adumbrations of Christian truth in secular works.

PERIODS OF MEDIEVAL CRITICISM

The placing of poetry among the disciplines of the trivium and quadrivium provides the threads that connect different periods of criticism from the fourth to the fourteenth century. Medieval criticism, however, is anything but continuous. At times a given tradition is dominant, at times it is muted, and at times it may simply disappear.

It is useful to think of medieval criticism as divided into five periods, the first and last of which are transitional. The periods are:

I. Late Classical (1st c. B.C. to 7th c. A.D.)
II. Carolingian (8th c. to 10th c.)
III. High Medieval (11th c. to 13th c.)
IV. Scholastic (13th c. to 14th c.)
V. Humanist (14th c. to 16th c.)

The last three of these periods overlap one another. During the twelfth century the Platonizing humanism of Chartres was already in conflict with the scholasticism of Paris. Later, in spite of the triumph of humanism, scholasticism continued to be important in criticism throughout the Renaissance, as numerous essays on the relation of poetry to logic testify. There is also a question of whether the humanism of Petrarch and Boccaccio is a new movement or merely a new phase of twelfth-century humanism. Burckhardt's emphasis on the novelty of the Renaissance is to be balanced against increasingly conspicuous evidence emphasized by Paul Kristeller and Eugenio Garin, among others, of its ties with the past. As Richard Schoeck recently observed of medieval rhetoric, "One may feel secure in holding the conclusion that from the late thirteenth century to the end of the fifteenth, for all of the changes and developments, there is an essential continuity."

LATE CLASSICAL PERIOD

The late classical period is the most various of those to be considered. This is not surprising. Pretty much the full range of the classical tradition was available in the Latin West through the end of the fourth century. The critical works of Heraclitus, Plotinus, Prophyry, and Proclus were not translated, but the ideas which they had to offer were assimilated by Latin writers. Philo Judaeus, Clement, and Origen were thoroughly digested by the Latin fathers, especially Ambrose and Augustine. The rhetorical treatises of Cicero and Quintilian were available both directly and in digest in the treatises reprinted in Halm's

Rhetores Latini Minores and in Christian adaptations, of which Augustine's *De Doctrina Christiana* is the most important. Horace was known and read continuously. In general, however, the late classical works most important for medieval criticism are the redactions, commentaries, and collections written between the fourth and seventh centuries.

If we look back on this body of material, we can perhaps gain a sense of why parts of it were valuable and parts simply ignored. To say that a new culture was emerging is not quite adequate. Early Christians were not drifting unwittingly in a new direction. They were fully aware of being the Chosen People, and to a large extent the new culture was conscious fabrication intended to fit the New Dispensation. It is hard to find a Christian work that deals with pagan thought between Tertullian and Cassiodorus that does not reveal a full awareness of this fact.

From the point of view of the New Dispensation the problem was one of assimilation. Pagan culture, said Augustine in the *De Doctrina,* is like the gold that the prudent Hebrews took with them on their flight to Egypt. It was too valuable to discard but, being pagan, it was suspect. This is particularly true of pagan poetry and its corollary, pagan mythology. Tertullian rejected ancient drama in the *De Spectaculis* as depraved and idolotrous. Jerome was taunted in a dream for being more of a Ciceronian than a Christian and once called secular poetry "the wine of demons." St. Augustine, former rhetor and author of a treatise *On the Apt and the Beautiful,* recalled in the *Confessions* how he used to weep over the death of Dido in the *Aeneid,* while Lactantius suggested that the classical gods are fallen angels in disguise.

Given many different shades of opinion, the first and most basic justification for literary study was practical. Poetry had been included in the classical grammar curriculum to teach eloquence, not for aesthetic reasons. It could be used to teach the same skill to Christians, who needed linguistic skill both to wage the wars of truth and to interpret scripture. St. Augustine's *De Doctrina Christiana* is a highly intelligent adaptation of Cicero and "the rules of Tychonius" to the teaching of scriptural exegesis and preaching. The *Institutes of Divine and Secular Letters* of Cassiodorus is more comprehensive than the *De Doctrina* but has the same object. Knowledge of the liberal arts "as it seemed to our Fathers, is useful . . . since one finds this knowledge diffused everywhere in sacred literature." The same argument was used by Gratian in *The Concord of Discordant Causes* to justify secular literature in the twelfth century:

> We read that Moses and Daniel were learned in *all* the wisdom of the Egyptians and Chaldeans. We read that our Lord ordered the children of Israel to spoil the Egyptians of their gold and silver: the moral interpretation of this teaches that should we find

in the poets either the gold of wisdom or the silver of eloquence, we should turn it to the profit of salutary learning. In Leviticus we also are ordered to offer up to the Lord the first fruits of honey, that is, the sweetness of human eloquence.

The dominant mode of early medieval criticism was therefore practical. The key pagan documents were those useful in the grammar curriculum—the commentaries of Servius on Vergil and Donatus on Terence, Horace's *Ars Poetica,* treatises on the *ars metrica,* and summaries of critical doctrine in grammar texts, such as Diomedes' *Ars Grammatica.* This material was easily assimilated by writers who were self-consciously Christian. Christian poets like Prudentius, Sedulius, and Juvencus used the forms and style of ancient poetry for scriptural and devotional subjects. Isidore of Seville derived a considerable miscellany of information about poetry from Diomedes, Evanthius, Donatus, and other sources, which he duly passed along to the later Middle Ages in his *Encyclopedia.* Bede restated the commonplaces on classical prosody in his *De Arte Metrica,* adding examples from Christian poetry and a chapter on the new rhythmic versification. His summary of the rhetorical figures in *De Schematibus et Tropis* is propadeutic to biblical studies and uses illustrations from scripture.

Medieval assimilation of pagan tradition created special problems in the area of literary history. The list of authors in Book X of Quintilian's *Institute* is limited to Greece and Rome, as are the comments on literary history in works like Horace's *Ars Poetica,* Evanthius' *De Fabula,* and Diomedes' *Ars Grammatica.* Christians, however, found themselves committed to a radical enlargement of the curriculum to include Old Testament authors on the one hand, and a rapidly growing body of Christian literature on the other. This had three results. First, the chronology of world literature was revised. With this revision the classical assumption that classical literature is self-contained and self-influenced was called into question. Being older than Greek literature, Hebrew literature may have influenced classical works. Second, the forms of Hebrew literature had to be described. The possibility of Hebrew influence on the classics encouraged speculation that much of the Old Testament is in forms analogous to those used by the Greeks and Romans. At the very least, however, the suggestion that the Song of Songs is a pastoral or an epithalamium and Job a tragedy implies a significant broadening of classical genre concepts. Third, a list of curriculum authors is also a canon of the classics. As Christian authors were added to the list and Greek authors disappeared, the concept of the classical tradition itself began to change. This change was accelerated by allegorical distortions of true classical authors like Vergil and Ovid, and by the ornate style of the literary parts of the Old Testament, which reinforced the widespread early medieval taste for Asiatic style.

It is impossible to do justice here to these developments. For chronology (and its corollary the indebtedness of Greek to Hebrew literature) the important precedents are the *History of the Jews* by Josephus, Philo's commentary on Genesis, the *Chronicle* of Eusebius, and the *Miscellanies* of Clement of Alexandria. Jerome's translation of Eusebius provided the Latin West with a system of dates beginning with the Creation which allowed Greek and Roman history to be plotted against Hebrew history. A looser system, used by Augustine in *The City of God,* divided history into six ages—from Creation to Noah, from Noah to Moses, from Moses to David, from David to the prophets, from the prophets to Christ, and from Christ to the Last Judgment. Greek civilization does not emerge in this system until the third age.

On the basis of the enlarged chronology, Jerome asserted that Hebrew literature influenced the classics and that the Old Testament anticipates classical forms. The Psalms are in iambics, Alcaics, and Sapphics, while Deuteronomy, Isaiah, and Job are in mixed pentameters and hexameters. Isidore wavers, but his *Encyclopedia* asserts that Moses used heroic verse in Deuteronomy long before Homer, and "it is apparent that the study of poetry was much older among the Hebrews than among the Gentiles." Bede's *De Arte Metrica* incorporates these ideas into formal criticism. In addition to repeating the commonplaces concerning the use of classical prosody in scripture, he notes that Hebrew poets anticipated the three classical manners of imitation. The pure mimetic, or dramatic, manner is used in the Song of Songs; the pure narrative in Ecclesiastes, and the "mixed"—the manner used by Homer and Vergil—in the Book of Job. The *De Arte Metrica* also illustrates the new canon of the classics by adding Prudentius, Arator, Sedulius, and Ambrose to the list of classical poets.

If grammar is the dominant mode of late classical criticism, Neoplatonism is its sub-dominant mode. The Greek background includes Philo Judaeus, Clement, and Origen in the Hebraeo-Christian tradition, and Plotinus, Iamblicus, Porphyry, and Proclus among the pagans. The basic Latin critical documents are Macrobius on the *Somnium Scipionis* and Fulgentius' *Exposition* of the *Aeneid.* These documents are supplemented by a general late classical interest in Neoplatonism evident in Augustine and Boethius, in Calcidius' commentary on the *Timaeus,* in the fashion of scriptural allegory, and in two much-admired allegorical poems, the *Psychomachia* of Prudentius and the *Marriage of Philology and Mercury* by Martianus Capella. The commentary of Servius on the *Aeneid* demonstrates that grammatical criticism could take on a Neoplatonic coloring. In general, however, grammatical criticism is conservative. It concentrates on practical matters which aid understanding and imitation, and secondarily on the moral values of literature. Neoplatonic criticism recognizes the moral utility of literature, but its interest is centered on the esoteric wisdom which poets conceal in their fables. If the grammatical and Neoplatonic traditions are not separate in the late classical period, they tend to diverge.

THE CAROLINGIAN PERIOD

The Carolingian period saw a flowering of poetry comparable to a "revival of classical antiquity" in little. Manitius records an impressive number of commentaries on classical, late classical, and Christian authors including works by Rabanus Maurus, Lupus of Ferrières, Remigius of Auxerre, and Scotus Erigena. In his commentary on Prician and in his *Clerical Institute* Rabanus repeats the grammatical commonplaces on poetry and offers a standard defense of reading pagan literature. We know from Theodolphus of Orleans that the pagan poets were read and regularly allegorized, and the *Liber Officialis* by Amalarius of Metz, an interpretation of Gregorian liturgy, illustrates how far the allegorical method could be taken. Rhetorical theory of the period is summarized in Alcuin's *Rhetoric.* This work is of particular interest in the history of medieval style. It is Ciceronian in scope and is evidently intended as a corrective to late classical emphasis on the oratory of display and the "rhetorical colors"—the lists of figures which were supposed to make the display impressive. De Bruyne therefore considers Alcuin a central figure in the history of the conflict between Attic and Asiatic ideals of style.

It is disappointing to find that in spite of all this literary activity there is only one purely critical document from the Carolingian period. This is the *Scholia Vindobonensia* on Horace's *Ars Poetica.* Although the work was attributed to Alcuin by Zechmeister, its nineteenth century editor, it is clearly much later.

In spite of its title the *Scholia* is more than a gloss on the model of Servius. It follows Horace line-by-line, but the result is more of a running discussion of critical theory—a kind of "close reading"—than a series of footnotes. It offers a considerable body of information concerning classical poetic theory along with a good deal of misinformation. In general, it is conservative, and we are probably not wrong in assuming that it was intended as an aid to the reading of Horace in the grammar curriculum. Its chief sources other than the *Ars Poetica* itself are the commentaries of Porphyrion and Arcon on Horace and of Servius on Vergil, the *Ad Herennium* and the rhetoric of Victorinus, Hyginus on mythology, the poetry of Ovid and Vergil, and (evidently) the *Rhetoric* and *Dialectic* of Alcuin.

At the beginning, poetic art is defined as "the art of making [*fingendi* —probably in the sense of 'making fictions'] and composing; Greek *poesis* means 'artifact' [*figmentum*] in Latin." The species of poetry are defined as "humble, middle, and serious" and are related to characteristic stylistic errors. The comment is based on the discussion of the three styles of oratory and their related vices in the *Ad Herennium* (IV. 8–12), which the scholiast attributes to Cicero. Line 45 of the *Ars Poetica* leads to a discussion of artificial and natural order. Later (l. 46), we learn that an author should strive for *facundia*—"beautiful and moderate expression" which is attained by restrained and careful use of language. This is supplemented by the observation (l. 87) that rhetorical "colors" distinguish and ornament the subject treated and make it "sweeter" (*dulcior,* l. 99). The comment obviously refers to the rhetorical figures (*colores rhetoricae*), but it is quite different in tone from the high medieval *artes poeticae,* in which the "colors" are of central importance. Character depends (l. 114 ff.) on nation, age, and status, a point illustrated by a list of types including the old man, the hero, the pious man, the matron, the prostitute, the merchant, and the farmer.

The discussion of drama (ll. 182 ff.) reveals the confusion that developed after the decline of the classical theatre. The scholiast correctly defines the varieties of classical drama, the *togata* (based on Roman life), *palliata* (Greek inspired), and *praetextata* (based on history), but he shows no understanding whatever of terms that relate to performance. The five act convention is explained as follows: "The first act is for the old men, the second for youths, the third for matrons, the fourth for the servant and maid, and the fifth is for the pimp and the prostitute." The chorus is not part of the action but a group of well-wishers who listen to the dramatic recitation (l. 195). A curious passage explaining the convention of action offstage (l. 182: *res aut agitur in scenis*) is interpreted by Zechmeister as a statement that biblical plays—specifically, a play about Herod's feast—were being performed at the time the commentary was written. Actually, it is at the most a reference to a literary recitation, which is evidently what the scholiast understood by drama. One point which the scholiast gets right is verisimilitude. Here and later (l. 340) he warns against impossible and unbelievable episodes. De Bruyne considers this a key feature of *Scholia* since it is an implicit criticism of the exotic style and subject matter of early medieval allegory.

Once past drama, the scholiast is back on reasonably firm ground. He sides with Horace in minimizing the value of genius. Poetry is nourished by grammar, rhetoric, and logic, and its content is ethics and the sciences of the quadrivium. Poems profit by offering moral instruction and arousing patriotism, and they delight through fables and comedies.

In sum, the *Scholia* gives us what we would expect from a scholar following the tradition of Alcuin. It intelligently supplements Horace by drawing on rhetoric, it subordinates genius to learning, and it recognizes both the moral and recreative aspects of poetry. Its key doctrines are stylistic restraint and verisimilitude. The misinformation is a by-product of the age rather than a failure on the part of the scholiast. In view of the poetic fashions of the late classical period its omissions are as significant as what it contains. There is no direct mention of allegory. There is no special pleading for classical poets and no statement that they anticipate Christian truths. Even Horace's assertion that it is pointless to try to save a man bent on suicide (1. 467) is allowed to pass without moralizing. Finally, the scholiast is as conservative as Alcuin himself on the subject of style. He points out that there are three styles but does not express preference for the grave (or elevated) variety. He does not list rhetorical figures or show marked enthusiasm for rhetorical ornament. If anything, his comments on *facundia* indicate a bias in favor of stylistic restraint. In all of these respects the *Scholia Vindobonensia* is a poetic cousin of Alcuin's *Rhetoric*. It is not "representative" of the Carolingian period since we know that other kinds of criticism continued to flourish, but it represents an important, perhaps temporarily dominant current of critical thought.

THE HIGH MIDDLE AGES

As we move toward the twelfth century, the critical texts become more numerous and the problem of understanding the factors that influenced them more complex. In one way or another the intellectual ferment caused by a reawakened interest in Neoplatonism underlies the most significant intellectual developments of the period. A major cause of this ferment was the translation by Scotus Erigena of the works of Dionysius the pseudo-Areopagite at the end of the tenth century. Dionysius offers a Christian theology completely dominated by the metaphysics of Plotinus. He had a special claim to authority during the Middle Ages since he was believed to be the Dionysius who conversed with St. Paul on the Areopagus. Supplemented by a miscellany of late classical works—especially the commentary of Calcidius on the *Timaeus,* Macrobius on the *Somnium Scipionis* and Boethius *On the Consolation of Philosophy*—Dionysius provided the basis for an articulated form of mysticism involving the concept of a "negative theology" and a distinct process (the *scala perfectionis*) whereby one moves from the material world to a vision of God. We see this mysticism in the works of Bernard of Clairvaux and St. Bonaventura. Its corollary is a renewed emphasis on the supra-rational, on inspiration, on the intellect (*mens*) as against the reason, and on visionary experiences which can only be communicated through symbols. The treatises of Dionysius *On the Heavenly Hierarchy* and *On the Ecclesiastical Hierarchy* provided a new geography of heaven and a new sense of the ways in which the visible world is a shadow of the invisible one. His symbolism pointed the way to a new interest in the transcendent and new ways of expressing transcendent experience. His God is an architect or a geometer making a world from numbers, or, alternately, a musician creating harmonies out of the discord of matter. As experienced by the Dionysian mystic, God is also light, an emanation from the source of light, and a radiance that shines in the beauty of the created world.

Dionysius is not the unique source of the various ramifications of high medieval Platonism, but many of them find precedent in his work, and the stimulus which it provided led to more energetic exploration of complementary works and more daring speculation by medieval authors themselves—a daring particularly evident in the *Megacosmus* and *Microcosmus* of Bernard Silvestris and in his *Commentary on the First Six Books of the Aeneid*. Its influence is also evident in the revival of grammatical humanism in the twelfth century as reflected in the series of *artes poeticae* that begins with Matthew of Vendôme's *Ars Versificatoria* composed at Orleans around 1175 and extends to Gervase of Melcheley's *Ars Poetica* of around 1215. There is evidence that Bernard Silvestris influenced the *ars poetica* tradition strongly. Matthew of Vendôme was his student at Orleans, and Gervase of Melcheley refers to a lost treatise on poetry by Bernard on which he drew for his own work. If such a treatise existed, it was in all probability the parent of the *ars poetica* tradition. In view of Bernard's keen interest in Platonic philosophy, which often gives his work a pagan or naturalistic tone, this text would undoubtedly be of great interest.

Indirect evidence of the Platonic influence on the *artes poeticae* is provided by Geoffrey of Vinsauf's *Poetria Nova*. Like all of the authors in the tradition, Geoffrey drew heavily on the figures in the *Rhetorica ad Herennium*. But he was not content simply to list figures. Throughout his treatise he emphasizes the inward, intellectual element in art. Geoffrey says nothing about imagination; the *Poetria* is a textbook and it naturally concentrates on what can be taught. While Geoffrey recognizes the importance of genius, he insists that experience and judgment are essential to the poet. In this he is closer to Cicero and Horace than to pagan Neoplatonists. In place of imagination, Geoffrey stresses the shaping power of the mind:

> If a man has a house to build, his impetuous hand does not rush into action. The measuring line of his mind first lays out the work, and he mentally outlines the successive steps in a definite order. The mind's hand shapes the entire house before the body's hand builds it. Its mode of being is archetypal before it is actual. Poetic art may see in this analogy the law to be given to poets . . . let the mind's interior compass first circle the whole extent of the material . . . When due order has arranged the material in the hidden chamber of the mind, let poetic art come forward to clothe the matter with words.

The images of the poet as architect, of planning a work by circling it with the compass of the mind, and of language as "clothing" for the poetic conception—all have their parallels in twelfth century poems, including Bernard Silvestris' *Megacosmus* and *Microcosmus,* which describe the creative activities of God. The theme of inwardness extends in the *Poetria* to language and imagery. The inner meaning of words is more important than their appearance—that is, in

Geoffrey's terms, their sound. By the same token, intention has precedence over ornament. Ornament is essential, and Geoffrey devotes over two-thirds of the *Poetria* to an extended treatment of figures, but ornament should always be appropriate. It is consistently described in terms of light imagery. The figures are "colors" or many-colored "flowers," and they are the outward expression of an inward "radiance."

The title *Poetria Nova* calls attention to the fact that the work differs from the *Ars Poetica. Poetria* was a common title for the *Ars Poetica* during the Middle Ages. Geoffrey's *Documentum de Mode et Arte Dictandi et Versificandi,* which is usually considered simply a prose version of the *Poetria Nova,* quotes the *Ars Poetica* extensively. The verse essay, however, contains no quotations from Horace, and does not even refer to him by name. The reason is plain. The *Poetria Nova* is a new poetic, not a redaction of Horace. Its novelty is its philosophy of art: the artist as creator, the superiority of mind to the materials of poetry, and ornament as the objectification of inner radiance.

If the philosophical background of the *artes poeticae* is Platonic, their immediate purpose was educational. John of Salisbury describes the teaching methods of the twelfth-century grammar curriculum in a famous tribute to Bernard of Chartres:

> Bernard of Chartres, the richest fountain of literary learning in modern times, taught the authors in this way: he pointed out what was simple and what conformed to rule; he called attention to grammatical figures, rhetorical colors, and sophistic fallacies; he showed where a given text was related to other disciplines . . . He expounded the poets and orators to those of his students who were assigned as preliminary exercises the imitation of works in prose or verse. Pointing out skillful connections between words and elegant closing rhythms, he would urge his students to follow in the steps of the authors . . . He bade them reproduce the very image of the author, and succeeded in making a student who imitated the great writers himself worthy of posterity's imitation. He also taught, among his first lessons, the merits of economy and the laudable adornment of thought and expression. (*Metalogicon* I.24)

The *artes poeticae* are manuals for the "preliminary exercises" involving "imitation of works in prose or verse." This explains their conservative tendencies—their heavy cargo of the figures which produce "laudable adornment," their careful illustration of each figure given, and their emphasis on the practical aspects of criticism rather than imagination, arcane philosophy and allegory.

The *accessus* tradition of the High Middle Ages is equally practical. Insofar as Platonism created a generally liberal intellectual climate and encouraged the emphasis of the Cathedral schools on the *auctores,* it encouraged the *accessus* tradition, but the works themselves are compendia and lack the larger philosophical interest which we find, for example, in the *Poetria Nova.*

A medieval *accessus* is a formal introduction to one or more of the curriculum authors. The earliest example of the form is the introduction by Bernard of Utrecht to the *Eclogue* of Theodulus, a much admired Christian imitation of Vergil composed in the tenth century. There is every reason to believe that the tradition was well established when Bernard began writing. Father Quain considers Servius an important precedent and traces the basic formula of the *accessus* to Hellenistic logic. According to this formula, a proper introduction to a work must include author, title, genre, intention, arrangement, number of books, and explanation. The best example of the type to survive is, as has been noted, the *Didascalon* of Conrad of Hirsau, written in the early twelfth century.

Conrad begins the *Didascalon* with a brief survey of standard poetic topics such as *poeta, poema, poesis,* the major genres, occasional forms like panegyric and epitaph, poetic arguments (which are explained in terms of Cicero's *Topics*), natural and artificial order, allegory, and the three styles as illustrated by Vergil's *Bucolics, Georgics,* and *Aeneid.* Much of Conrad's material is taken from Bernard of Utrecht. Directly or indirectly it goes back to late classical compendia like Diomedes' *Ars Grammatica* and Isidore's *Encyclopedia.*

This general survey is followed by introductions to the "authors" themselves. They are arranged from easy to difficult beginning with Donatus, whose *Ars Minor* provides a concise introduction to grammatical concepts and who is especially authoritative because he was a teacher of St. Jerome. The *Distichs* of Cato come next. They are filled with useful moral sentiments (*sententiae*) and are part of ethical as distinguished from natural philosophy. Two more pagans, Aesop and Avianus, are followed by Sedulius. Pagans, Conrad observes, sometimes experience bits of the truth, but Sedulius versified scripture and wrote expressly to lure readers away from seductive pagan poetry. Five more Christians are listed: Juvencus, Prosper of Aquitaine, Theodulus, Arator, and Prudentius. Conrad mentions the hymns of Prudentius but concentrates on the *Psychomachia* which shows how to avoid vice and is based on the technique of personification. We then return to the ancients and prose: Cicero, with emphasis on the *De Amicitia* and *De Senectute,* and Sallust's *Catiline's Conspiracy.* The *Consolation of Philosophy* teaches patience, and Boethius himself is a superb stylist as well as the best of all authorities on the seven liberal arts.

Lucan and Horace come next. The *Ars Poetica* is intended to correct bad poets and help those in need of advice. Curiously, Conrad believes its normal medieval title, *Poetria,* means "a woman studious of poetry" (*mulier carminis studens*). His explanation is that Horace began with the image of a woman beautiful above but a fish below, showing that he thought of poetry as feminine. Horace's odes are more suspect, and many of them are immoral (*viciosa*). This leads to comments on the dubious character of other pagan poets. Ovid is particularly dangerous. He teaches idolatry in the *Metamorphoses* and depicts the gods as animals. St. Paul has warned us about this sort of thing in his Epistle to the Romans (1:18–23). Terence, Juvenal, Statius, Persius, Homer, and Vergil are less dangerous. They are full of valid moral sentiments and have often been used by Christian authors. St. Paul quoted Menander and Augustine drew on Horace and Vergil.

The introductions to Juvenal, Homer, Persius, and Statius follow. They are incomplete. Vergil is given fuller treatment. The notion that in the *Bucolics* and *Georgics* "the poet included a full review of the liberal arts" is an echo of the Fulgentian tradition if not of the *Exposition* itself. Most of Conrad's discussion of the *Aeneid* has been lost. It is followed by comments on reading scripture. The disciplines of the trivium help us with the literal sense; those of the quadrivium are useful for its allegorical senses. Near the end, secular knowledge is defended in the venerable Augustinian way as Egyptian gold.

Conrad's list gives us an idea of the canon of the classics for the Cathedral schools. It includes Christian as well as pagan authors, and prose alternates with poetry. In general the selection is stylistically conservative—Martianus Capella is conspicuous by his absence. Interpretation is heavily and explicitly didactic. Equally important is the idea of imitation. Conrad asserts that all the great authors practiced imitation: Terence followed Menander; Horace, Lucinius (i.e., Lucilius); Sallust, Livy; Statius, Vergil; Boethius, Martianus Capella; and Theodulus, Vergil's *Bucolics*. Clearly the *accessus* is intended for the curriculum described by John of Salisbury. It provides historical and critical information which complements the practical instruction of the *artes poeticae*. The list of *auctores* is crowned by scripture. We are reminded that the basic justification for reading the poets was the preparation they provided for reading the Bible.

The twelfth-century Renaissance stimulated the writing of several general surveys of knowledge following the "Institute" tradition of Quintilian, Cassiodorus, and Rabanus Maurus. Hugh of St. Victor's *Didascalicon* has little to say about grammar and rhetoric and nothing about poetry. It concentrates almost entirely on biblical studies. Conversely, John of Salisbury's *Metalogicon* is extremely important for both its description of the grammar curriculum and its use of the *auctores,* and for the light it casts on the controversy between advocates of literary studies, generally associated with the Cathedral schools, and advocates of logic, generally associated with the University of Paris. John of Salisbury complains bitterly over the scornful attitude of the *avant garde* toward the older curriculum: "Poets who related history were considered reprobates, and if anyone applied himself to studying the ancients, he became a marked man and a laughing-stock to all."

The same controversy recurs in the literature of "the battle of the liberal arts," which raged during the thirteenth century and which derives its title from a poem on the subject by Henri d'Andeli, written around 1250. Paris, Henri d'Andeli tells us, stands for logic. The university men ridicule the study of the *auctores* and the emphasis on grammar of the Cathedral school of Orleans.

Evidently, humanists were fully conscious of themselves as a party united by a shared set of assumptions. Grammar and the *auctores* were the vehicles for the movement, and they were, as we have seen, intimately related. Consequently the controversy between the humanists and the scholastics tended to settle around two topics: the value of grammar in comparison to dialectic, and the value of reading the *auctores* in comparison with more technical studies. Although *Metalogicon* is primarily a work on dialectic, John of Salisbury insists that logic by itself is "bloodless and barren, nor does it quicken the soul to yield fruit of philosophy." Furthermore, poetry is essential to the grammar curriculum, and grammar is "the mother and nurse of its study."

Gervase of Melcheley's *Ars Poetica* (ca. 1215–16) may illustrate a compromise between the older and newer points of view. In content and presumably in its place in the curriculum it belongs with the *artes poeticae* of the Cathedral schools. In form, however, it is scholastic. It abandons the rhetorical division of the figures used by Matthew of Vendôme and Geoffrey of Vinsauf in favor of a logical division into figures of identity, similitude, and contrarity—i.e., figures in which the words are proper to their subject, figures which depend on resemblance, and figures, like allegory and irony, which depend on differences.

SCHOLASTIC PERIOD

With Gervase we have already entered the scholastic phase of medieval criticism. This phase is characterized by the application of logical theory to poetry. Its dominant mode is Aristotelian, with most of the Aristotle coming second-hand from translations of Arabic texts and commentaries.

When we see twelfth-century humanism from a scholastic point of view, we understand why it appeared superficial. It is not analytic. It looks backward rather than forward, and it wastes its energies on grammar when the intricacies of logic and (by the middle of the thirteenth century) the whole of Aristotle's *Organon* offer both a challenge to the mature man and an exciting new method for solving the major problems of the Christian faith. As for poetry, it is essentially a diversion. At its best it teaches moral lessons through *exampla,* but those who are seriously interested in morality will consult Aristotle's *Ethics* rather than the *Aeneid.*

This does not mean that the scholastics ignored poetry. Following al-Farabi, they dutifully included chapters on poetry in treatises explaining the system of the sciences. In such works, poetry is placed within logic as the last of the treatises of the *Organon.* This placement makes it a "faculty" rather than a "science"—that is, a technique for manipulating language rather than a subject with its own content like physics or ethics. As a "faculty" it has a distinctive function—illusion—as against rhetoric, for example, which seeks to persuade, or dialectic, which seeks "probable demonstration." Along with this function it had a distinctive instrument paralleling the enthymeme (a syllogism in which one premise is unexpressed) of rhetoric and the "probable syllogism" of dialectic. The strictest (and most opaque) definition of the poetic instrument is "imaginative syllogism," a phrase used by Dominicus Gundissalinus in his treatise *On the Division of the Sciences.* By and large, the later scholastics were inclined to be more generous. Roger Bacon and St. Thomas were willing to regard poetry as both a faculty and a branch of moral philosophy with a definite "content." For St. Thomas, the characteristic instrument of poetry is example, which is a logical form that can be used to teach lessons in ethics.

The most important theoretical statement of the scholastic period is the *Commentary of Averroes on the Poetics of Aristotle* translated into Latin in 1256 by Hermannus Alemannus. Medieval readers learned from this work that Aristotle considered poetry a branch of logic and that metaphor is its characteristic instrument. They could also learn, and in considerably more detail, that poetry concerns "matters of choice." In this sense, it is a kind of praise or blame. It uses praise to "heighten" the virtues of good men and thereby stimulates the reader to emulation. Through blame poetry exposes vice to ridicule and thus causes the reader to shun it. The praise and blame formula and the logical placement of poetry coexist in the treatise. If Averroes realized their incompatibility, he made no attempt to reconcile them. The Arab commentary thus nicely complements the scholastic conclusion that poetry has a dual allegiance to logic and ethics.

The best illustration of practical criticism along scholastic lines is Dante's *Epistle to Can Grande della Scala.* As Bruno Sandkühler has shown, the Epistle follows the *accessus* pattern. Its distinctive feature is not its content but its conscious emphasis on exact definitions and logical distinctions, an emphasis that is a by-product of the scholastic habit of mind. It is so stylized, in fact, that its authenticity has been questioned. No matter who wrote it, however, its relation to the *accessus* is established firmly by Dante's list of topics to be covered: "There are six things to be inquired about at the beginning of any work, to wit, the subject, the author, the form, the end, the title of the work, and the genus of its philosophy." A brief résumé follows of the four levels of theological allegory. Dante then moves to the *accessus* topics. The placement of the *Divine Comedy* in ethical philosophy is typically scholastic in its precision: "The genus of philosophy under which the work proceeds in its whole and in part is moral activity or ethics, for the whole and the part are devised not for the sake of speculation but of possible action. For if in any place or passage the method of discussion is that of speculative thought, it is not for the sake of speculative thought but for the sake of practical activity, since, as the Philosopher says in the second of the *Metaphysics,* 'practical men now and then speculate on something or other'."

HUMANISTIC PERIOD

The last period of medieval criticism is fourteenth century humanism. The documents begin with Dante's *De Vulgari Eloquentia,* the first self-conscious treatment of the vernacular as a medium for great poetry. Dante's immediate successors, Petrarch, Mussato, and Boccaccio, can be seen either as the end of the medieval tradition or the beginning of the Renaissance. Both points of view are valid, but in a survey of medieval criticism, their link to the past must receive major emphasis. This link is evident in their reliance on traditional medieval sources and in the fact that they frequently repeat, though with greater vehemence and broader knowledge of classical literature, the arguments for liberal studies that we encounter in the twelfth century. Finally, all three authors were driven to write defenses of poetry because of attacks against it. Their opponents were conservative. Just as the humanists of Orleans were eclipsed in the thirteenth century by the logicians of Paris, the logicians, in turn, were beginning to feel threatened by the humanists of Florence, and they reacted violently. Many of their arguments against poetry are based on scholastic theory, and these arguments largely determine the content of the defenses.

Contemporary with the revival of humanism in Italy a group of French works appear which are best understood as a continuation of twelfth-century humanism untouched by the "new learning." The tradition of the *artes poeticae* and *artes rhythmicae* emerges in the treatises of Deschamps and the authors of its *seconde rhétorique* on French vernacular poetry. Fulgentian allegorizing continues unabated in the *Ovidius Moralizatus* of Petrus Bercorius, the *Fulgentius Metaforalis* of John de Ridevall; and the *Epître d'Othéa* of Christine de Pisan. It is complemented by the vogue of allegorical poetry illustrated by the *Roman de la Rose,* Chaucer's *Book of the Duchess,* and Gower's *Confessio Amantis.* Such works are of great literary interest, but they are not central to the history of criticism. We can also pass over the tradition of the *ars dictaminis* and *ars praedicandi.* These traditions were continuous from the twelfth century through the Renaissance, but they properly belong to the history of rhetoric.

It is in Italy, then, that the important critical developments occur. The reason for their occurrence—if we rely on the documents themselves—is that the humanists had begun to make claims for poetry that conservatives found unacceptable. When they stated their objections, the battle was joined. Petrarch's major statement on poetry is his *Invective Against a Physician.* Other statements are scattered widely through his letters, often as replies to specific questions or criticisms. Mussato's critical theory was formulated as a reply to a specific adversary, Fra Giovannino of Mantua. Boccaccio's most important essay, Book XIV of the *Genealogy of the Gentile Gods,* is an answer to charges made by unnamed "cavillers" who were obviously conservative clerics.

If we draw back from the debate a little way, we can see that the major point at issue was the placement of poetry among the sciences. The idea that poetry is (or can be) a kind of theology is explicit in Mussato and Boccaccio. The corollary of this position is that poets, like religious prophets, are divinely inspired. If so, poetic fables can be regarded as veils covering esoteric truths or as symbolic statements necessitated by the impossibility of directly expressing transcendent experiences in language. Obscurity may be inevitable in great poetry as in scripture. Moreover, since the *prisci poetae* were inspired theologians, such pagan poetry, especially mythological poetry, may anticipate the truths of Christian revelation.

St. Thomas himself had been willing to consider poetry an instrument of moral instruction. However, in the heat of debate the opponents of poetry reverted to a more radical position: poetry is simply a "faculty." It has no content and the claim that it teaches morality is exaggerated if not a lie. Petrarch's response was to reassert the traditional didactic theory of poetry. He flirted with the idea of the divinity of poetry and the theory of allegory, but typically he considers poetry a means of instruction and a storehouse of examples of eloquence. To the traditional belief that poetry offers *doctrina* he adds the idea, anticipated by Cicero's *Pro Archia Poeta,* that poetry arouses patriotism. He thus anticipates the association between poetry and nationalism which is a typical feature of sixteenth-century criticism.

The belief that poetry is inspired and that poets express esoteric wisdom in their fables is associated during the Middle Ages with Platonism. That a Platonic critical frame could accept didacticism without strain we know from Plato himself and Proclus. During the high Middle Ages and the early humanistic period, Platonic theory blended easily with Ciceronian and Horatian criticism. Petrarch and Boccaccio argue at length that poetry is morally uplifting and in no sense a threat to Christian orthodoxy. They differ somewhat in emphasis. In the Genealogy, instruction is a secondary rather than a primary function of poetry. The major emphasis, which Boccaccio shares with Mussato, is on poetry as theology. In this Boccaccio both echoes the theories of Proclus and anticipates those of the Florentine Platonists of the fifteenth century. Petrarch, conversely, anticipates the more sober strain in Renaissance humanism which runs through the work of the educators, the rhetorical theorists, and the philologists; and which emerges finally in the seventeenth century as an important component of neoclassic criticism.

The selections below are intended to illustrate, as fully as possible within the limited space, the scope and historical development of medieval criticism as outlined above. Where possible, I have used standard translations, as noted at the end of the introduction to each selection. In three cases—the selections from Evanthius, Fulgentius, and Averroes—I have made my own translations.

The problem of providing bibliography for a body of material as broad and as varied as that represented by the following selections is formidable. In the end it seemed best to include all bibliographies in a single section categorized according to period and, to a certain extent, according to topic. The alternative—providing a general bibliography after the General Introduction, and more specialized bibliographies after each specific introduction—would have involved much repetition of entries for general works and would have required frequent cross-checking by the reader with the attendant possibility of overlooking important items. Footnotes have been avoided in the introductions. The studies and editions used may be readily ascertained, however, by reference to the bibliography. In general, the bibliography emphasizes works in English and translations where these are available. It is selective. For Dante in particular, the body of relevant material is so large that no attempt has been made to cover it, and the interested reader is referred to the standard editions and bibliographies.

EVANTHIUS AND DONATUS

(4th century A.D.)

INTRODUCTION

Classical stage drama disappeared completely during the Middle Ages. Knowledge of classical drama, however, persisted. It is clear from the plays of Hroswitha of Gandersheim that Terence was read, at least sporadically, in the schools. During most of the Middle Ages the major source of information concerning classical drama was the body of definitions and descriptions preserved in encyclopedias, floralegia, and the like, and transmitted lovingly from generation to generation. Isidore of Seville's *Encyclopedia* (seventh century) and Vincent of Beauvais' *Speculum Morale* (thirteenth century) are particularly important in this regard.

A. P. MacMahon has documented the continuity of definitions of comedy and tragedy from the late classical period to the early Renaissance. Beginning in the fourteenth century classical drama began to be read and imitated. Knowledge of its history developed rapidly, as did understanding of the ways it was produced, its typical forms, and the classical terminology associated with it. The new knowledge did not replace the old but supplemented it. Humanists did not so much reject Isidore of Seville and Vincent of Beauvais, for example, as go behind them to the documents that were the ultimate sources of their information.

The three most important late classical sources of information about classical drama are the essays *On Drama* (*De Fabula*) of Evanthius and *On Comedy* (*De Comedia*) of Aelius Donatus, and the section on drama in Diomedes' *Ars Grammatica.* These essays directly or indirectly provided most of the historical information and the definitions incorporated into medieval tradition. During the Renaissance the essays of Evanthius and Donatus were widely reprinted in editions of Terence. They continued to be used extensively in critical treatises, commentaries, prefaces, and the like, through the seventeenth century.

Of Evanthius we know only that he was a fourth century grammarian. Throughout the Middle Ages it was assumed that his essay was by Donatus. Donatus, on the other hand, was so widely known during the Middle Ages that the term "donet," meaning a Latin grammar, became a common noun in Middle English. The two grammars of Donatus, referred to as the *Ars Major* and the

Ars Minor, were used widely through the sixteenth century. They are reprinted in Heinrich Keil's *Grammatici Latini.* Donatus' commentary on Terence, which is a sixth-century redaction of the original text, was widely reprinted during the Renaissance and is available in the edition of the commentary of Donatus on Terence by Paul Wessner, together with an excellent introduction summarizing available information on Donatus and the history of the text. *On Drama* and *On Comedy* are evidently based on standard handbook information that was the stock-in-trade of the Roman grammar schools. No specific source has been discovered for either essay. The occasional citation of conflicting opinions in both essays suggests that they are compilations from several works. Ultimately, they go back through the Roman schools and Alexandrian criticism to Theophrastus and Aristotle, especially Aristotle's essay *On the Poets.* MacMahon summarizes the evidence that they contain echoes of the *Poetics,* but the echoes, if they are there at all, are very faint.

On Drama begins with a brief history of tragedy and comedy. The standard etymologies of both forms are given. It is of some interest that Evanthius traces both forms to religious ceremonies. Tragedy arose from Bacchic festivals and comedy from festivals to Apollo. Evanthius agrees with Aristotle that tragedy was the earlier form. His reasoning involves a bit of elementary *ex post facto* anthropology: tragedy deals with somber events. It is therefore associated with the early stages of civilization—with "barbarism and brutality"—while comedy, which is lighter in tone, is associated with the time when "towns were founded and life became more mild and easier." Thespis and Eupolis "along with Cratinus and Aristophanes" are cited as the founders of tragedy and comedy. We then turn to a more detailed history of comedy, which moves, following Horace in the *Ars Poetica,* from old comedy to satyr play (branching off into Lucilian satire) to new comedy, "especially Menander and Terence." The section ends with observations on the decline of the chorus, on differences between Greek and Roman drama, and on meter. Like Aristotle, Evanthius considers Homer a teacher of dramatic poets. He adds the point, made also, for example, by "Longinus," that the *Iliad* anticipates tragedy, the *Odyssey,* comedy.

The essay continues with a discussion of Roman comedy. Terence emerges as the foremost Latin comic poet. He is praised for his relaxed meter, which is close to prose, for his characterization, including his willingness to defy convention, for his observance of comic decorum, and for his double plots. In the conclusion Evanthius lists the standard types and parts of Roman drama.

Probably the most important part of this section is the contrast between tragedy and comedy:

> In comedy the fortunes of men are middle-class, the dangers are slight, and the ends of the action are happy; but in tragedy everything is the opposite—the characters are great men, the, fears are intense, and the ends disastrous. In comedy the beginning is

> troubled, the end tranquil; in tragedy events follow the reverse order. And in tragedy the kind of life is shown that is to be shunned; while in comedy the kind is shown that is to be sought after. Finally, in comedy the story is always fictitious; while tragedy is often based on historical truth.

This definition omits any reference to staging. It points the way toward the later medieval conception of tragedy and comedy as poems to be recited rather than plays to be acted. This conception is illustrated by the "tragedies" narrated by Chaucer's Monk and by Dante's defense of the "comic" nature of *The Divine Comedy* in the *Epistle to Can Grande della Scala.* The Evanthius definition is structural, and its differentiation between tragedy and comedy is entirely different from that found in the *Poetics.* Aristotle was willing to approve a tragedy like *Iphigenia in Tauris*, which ends happily, and he cited the *Antheus* of Agathon to show that an entirely fictitious plot can be as satisfactory as an historical one. By contrast, Evanthius insists that the end of tragedy must be sad, and that the tragic action must be based on history. Again, Aristotle is indifferent to moral lessons. By contrast, Evanthius asserts that tragedy shows what is "to be shunned" and comedy, what is "to be sought after." In sum, this passage contains the seeds of the most widespread clichés of medieval dramatic criticism and of Renaissance theory and practice.

On Comedy repeats much that is found in Evanthius. Cicero's definition of comedy as "an imitation of life, a mirror of character, and an image of truth" was quoted widely during the Renaissance. It comes from Donatus, since it is not found in any of Cicero's extant works. The quotation from Horace's *Ars Poetica* confirms the outlines of the history given by Evanthius and Donatus. The remainder of the essay consists of technical terms, most of them already introduced by Evanthius. The summary of the parts of a classical drama—prologue, protasis, epitasis, and catastrophe—is of interest because of the influence of these terms, demonstrated by T. W. Baldwin in *Shakespeare's Five-Act Structure*, on Renaissance dramatic practice.

The translation here used is my own. For bibliography, see especially pp. 481–84.

Evanthius: ON DRAMA

Tragedy and comedy began in religious ceremonies which the ancients held to give thanks for a good harvest.

The sort of song which the sacred chorus offered to Father Bacchus when the altars had been kindled and the sacrificial goat brought in was called tragedy.

This is from *apo tou tragou kai tes oides*—that is, from "goat," an enemy of vineyards, and from "song." There is a full reference to this in Vergil's *Georgics* [II.380 ff.], either because the poet of this sort of song was given a goat, or because a goatskin full of new wine was the usual reward to the singers; or else because the players used to smear their faces with wine-lees prior to the introduction of masks by Aeschylus. "Wine-lees" in Greek is *truges*. And the word "tragedy" was invented for these reasons.

But while the Athenians were not yet confined to the city and Apollo was called "Nomius" [shepherd] and "Aguieus" [guardian]—that is, guardian of shepherds and villages—they erected altars for divine worship around the hamlets, farms, villages, and crossroads of Attica and solemnly chanted a festival song to him. It was called comedy *apo ton komon kai tes oides*—the name composed, as I think, from "villages" [*komai*] and "song" [*oide*]. Or else it was composed *apo tou komazein kai aidein*—going to a revel singing. This is not unlikely since the comic chorus was drunk or engaged in love making on the sacred day.

And once the historical sequence has been established, it is clear that tragedy appeared first. For man moved little by little from barbarism and brutality to a civilized condition. Later towns were founded and life became more mild and easier. Thus the matter of tragedy was discovered long before the matter of comedy.

Thespis is thought to be the inventor of tragedy by those who study ancient history. And Eupolis, along with Cratinus and Aristophanes, is thought to be the father of old comedy. But Homer, who is, as it were, the copious fountainhead of all poetry, provided exemplars for these sorts of poetry and established almost a law for their composition. We know that he wrote the *Iliad* in the form of a tragedy and that the *Odyssey* has the form of a comedy. In the beginning such poems were crude and not all polished and graceful as they later became. And after Homer's excellent and copious work they were regularized in their structure and parts by clever imitators.

Now that we have discussed the early history of the two forms in order to determine their origin, let us proceed to necessary matters. But, keeping within the limits of the title of this work, we will defer those subjects that are proper to tragedy for a later time, and will talk of the sorts of drama that Terence imitated.

Old comedy, like tragedy, was once simply a song, as we previously observed. The chorus sang it to a flute accompaniment while grouped around the smoking altar. At times the chorus walked, at times stood still, and at times it danced in circles. Then one character was taken from the group who spoke to the group, each taking alternate turns—that is, . . . [lacuna; perhaps the Greek word *amoibaios,* "alternately"]—and with a different melody. Then there appeared a second and a third character; and at length, as the number of characters was increased by various authors, masks and *pallia* [robes] began to be used, and boots and the comic sock and the other adornments and costumes used by the actors. Eventually, each type of character came to have his own costume. Finally, as there were actors who played in the first part, the second, the third, the fourth, and the fifth, the whole drama was divided into five acts.

While comedy was still, as it were, in its cradle and had hardly begun, it was called *archaia komoidia* and *ep'onomatos,* because it was "old" [*archaia*] in comparison to what has been discovered more recently. And *ep'onomatos* [by name] because the fable has, as it were, the historical validity of a true story, and real citizens are named and freely described.

The early poets, unlike the moderns, did not write fictional plots but wrote openly about things which citizens had done, often using real names. This was very beneficial to the morals of the society since every citizen avoided immorality in order not to become a public spectacle and a disgrace to his family. But as the poets came to use their pens with greater license and began to pillory good men right and left just for the fun of it, they were silenced by a law forbidding anyone from writing a poem slandering another person.

From this situation a new type of drama, satyr play, originated. "Satyr play" derived its name from satyrs, who are, as we know, supernatural beings always involved in games and wanton sports, although some wrongly think the word has a different derivation. Satyr play took the form of a poem which, through the device of crude and, as it were, rustic jesting, attacked the vices of citizens without mentioning specific names. This species of comedy was damaging to many poets since they were suspected by powerful citizens of making their deeds worse than they really were, and of disgracing the upper class by their manner of writing. Lucilius began composing this kind of poem in a new way, and he wrote "poesy"—that is, a single poem in several books.

Forced by the abuses already mentioned to give up satyr play, poets invented another kind of poem—*nea komoidia*—that is, "new comedy." This kind of poem was concerned with more typical situations and in general terms with men who live a middle-class life. It gave the spectator less bitterness and more pleasure, being close-knit in plot, true to life in characterization, useful in its sentiments, delightful for its wit, and apt in its prosody. Just as those earlier works were celebrated for their authors, so new comedy is the work of many earlier and later writers, and especially Menander and Terence.

Although a great deal can be said about these matters, it will be enough to instruct the reader, to summarize what the writings of the ancients say about the comic art. Old comedy consisted in the beginning of the chorus. Little by little it expanded, by increasing the number of characters, into five acts. Eventually, as the chorus was reduced and thinned out, it came about that in new comedy the chorus is not only not brought onstage, but there is not even a place left for it. As times became more leisurely, the audience grew more sophisticated and as the play changed from the acted part to the singing the spectators began to grow restless and leave. The poets learned from this and reduced the choral part, leaving almost no place for it. Menander left out the chorus for this reason and not for another, as some other writers think. Eventually the poets did not leave any place at all for the chorus. The Latin comic poets wrote in this way, and this is why it is difficult to decide where the divisions of the five acts occur in their plays.

Moreover the Greeks do not have prologues, which we Latins customarily include. Like the Greeks, all the Latin writers but Terence have *theoi apo mechanes*—that is, "gods from a machine"—to narrate stories. Besides, the other comic writers do not readily admit *protatika prosopa*—that is, characters drawn from outside the plot—while Terence often uses them since the plot becomes clearer through introducing them.

The ancient poets were rather careless in meter, demanding only an iamb in the second and fourth place. But they are outdone by Terence, who, by relaxing the meter, reduced it as far as possible to the nature of prose.

As for the laws of characterization in respect to moral habits, age, station in life, and type roles, no one was more diligent than Terence. He alone dared—since verisimilitude is required in fiction—to defy the comic prescriptions, and at times to introduce prostitutes who were not evil. There is both a reason given for their goodness and the fact itself gives a certain pleasure.

Terence did these things most artistically, and it is especially admirable that he kept within the bounds of comedy and tempered the emotional element so that he did not slide over into tragedy. This effect, along with others, was seldom achieved, we observe, by Plautus and Afranius and Appius and the many other comic poets. Among the other virtues, it is also admirable that Terence's plays are so well controlled in style that they neither swell up to tragic elevation nor degenerate into the baseness of mime.

Add that Terence never brings in abstruse material or things that have to be glossed by antiquaries, as Plautus often does, and that Plautus is more obscure than Terence in many places. Add that Terence is careful about plot and style; that he always avoided or was very circumspect about topics that could give offense; and that he joined the beginning, middle, and end so carefully that nothing seems extraneous and everything appears to be composed from the same material and to have a single body.

It is also admirable that he never brings four characters together in such a way that their differences are unclear. And further, that he never has a character address the audience directly, as though outside the comedy, which is a frequent vice of Plautus. It also seems laudable, among other things, that he chose to make his story more full by means of double plots. Except for *Hecyra*, which deals with the love of Pamphilus alone, the other five comedies have two young couples.

It is clear that after new comedy the Latins developed many kinds of drama. For example, the *togata*, based on Roman events and stories; the *prae-*

textata, from the dignity of its noble characters taken from Roman history; the *Atellana*, from the town of Campania where this kind of drama was first acted; the *Rinthonica*, from the name of the author; the *tabernaria* from the lowness of the plot and style, and the *mime* from constant imitation of base subject matter and wanton characters.

Of the many differences between tragedy and comedy, the foremost are these: In comedy the fortunes of men are middle-class, the dangers are slight, and the ends of the actions are happy; but in tragedy everything is the opposite—the characters are great men, the fears are intense, and the ends disastrous. In comedy the beginning is troubled, the end tranquil; in tragedy events follow the reverse order. And in tragedy the kind of life is shown that is to be shunned; while in comedy the kind is shown that is to be sought after. Finally, in comedy the story is always fictitious; while tragedy often has a basis in historical truth.

Latin dramas were first written by Livius Andronicus. The form was so new that he was both the author of his dramas and acted in them.

Comedies are either "active" or "quiet" or "mixed." The "active" are more turbulent, the "quiet" are more tranquil, and the "mixed" have elements of both.

Comedy is divided into four parts: prologue, protasis, epitasis, and catastrophe. The prologue is a kind of preface to the drama. In this part and this part only it is permissible to say something extrinsic to the argument, addressed to the audience and for the benefit of the poet or the drama or an actor. The protasis is the first act and the beginning of the drama. The epitasis is the development and enlargement of the conflict and, as it were, the knot of all the error. The catastrophe is the resolution of the course of events so that there is a happy ending which is made evident to all by the recognition of past events.

Donatus: ON COMEDY

Comedy is a form of drama dealing with the various qualities and conditions of civil and private persons. Through it one learns what is useful in life and what, on the contrary, is to be avoided. The Greeks define it as follows: "Comedy deals with the acts of private persons in a story that lacks serious danger." Comedy, says Cicero, is "an imitation of life, a mirror of character, and an image of truth."

Comedy received its name from an ancient custom. In early times this kind of song was sung "in the villages" [*apo tes komes*]—as is the case with the "crossroads festivals" [*compitalia*] in Italy. A term was added for the spoken part with which the audience was entertained during the changing of the events. That is, they were held by the acting out of the lives of men who live "in the villages" because of the middle state of their fortunes, not in royal palaces like the characters of tragedy. And comedy, because it is written to imitate life and character with verisimilitude, employs gesture and speech.

No-one knows who invented comedy among the Greeks. The Roman inventor is known. Livius Andronicus was the first Roman to write comedy, tragedy, and *fabula togata.* He said comedy is "a mirror of daily life" and the observation is just. When we gaze into a mirror we readily see the features of truth by means of the reflection. Likewise, by reading comedy we readily discover the image of life and custom.

The original concept came in from foreign cities and with foreign customs. When the Athenians, the guardians of Attic propriety, wanted to rebuke anyone for an immoral life, they used to gather together from all sides, happily and eagerly, at the villages and crossroads. There they used to describe the vices of individuals publicly and with proper names. Comedy was named from this custom.

At first they sang their songs in grassy meadows. And there was no lack of prizes to incite the wits of the more learned to writing. And gifts were offered to the actors to encourage them freely to use pleasing modulations of voice to gain sweet commendation. A goat [*tragos*] was given to them as a reward, because the animal was considered an enemy of vineyards. From this custom the name "tragedy" arose. Many authorities, however, prefer the idea that "tragedy" was derived from *amurca*—that is, oil-lees—which has a watery quality, the word being suggested by "trygodia" [from Greek *truges*, "lees"].

Since these revels were performed at ceremonies in honor of Father Bacchus, the writers of tragedy and comedy began to worship and venerate the spirit of this god as though he were present. This is the probable explanation of the matter: these primitive songs were written for the purpose of setting forth and celebrating the fame and glorious deeds of Bacchus.

Little by little the reputation of this art form grew. Thespis first brought it to the attention of all. Aeschylus wrote next, following the example of his predecessor. On these matters, Horace writes in the *Ars Poetica*:

> Thespis is said to have invented tragedy, a type unknown previously, and to have carried his plays around in carts, to be performed by actors whose faces were smeared with wine-lees. After him came Aeschylus, who introduced the tragic mask and robe. He designed a stage built of small planks and taught the players to speak in a grand manner and wear the tragic buskin. Then came

old comedy, which won popular praise, but the freedom it employed degenerated into excess and violence that had to be restrained by law. Prevented from attacking people's characters, the chorus lapsed into shamed silence. The Latin poets have left no style untried. Nor do those poets deserve the least honor who dared to forsake the track laid out by the Greeks and celebrate the deeds of their own country, whether in the tragedy *praetexta* or the *togata* form of comedy. [*Ars Poetica,* 274–88]

Drama is a general term. Its two chief parts are tragedy and comedy. Tragedy, if it concerns Roman subjects, is called *praetexta.* Comedy has many species. It is *palliata* or *togata* or *tabernaria* or *Atellana* or *mime* or *Rinthonica* or *planipedia.*

Planipedia is named from the baseness of the subject matter and the lowness of the actors, who do not act on a stage or platform in the boot or sock, but act "in bare feet"—or else because the subject matter does not include things appropriate for people living in houses with towers and large halls, but only things appropriate for those in low and humble places.

They say that Cincius Faliscus was the first to use masks in comedy, and in tragedy, Minucius Prothymus.

The titles of all comedies are taken from four areas: name, place, deed, and result. Names as exemplified in the *Phormio*, *Hecyra*, *Cruculio*, and *Epidicus.* Places in the *Andria, Leucadia,* and *Brundisina.* Deeds in the *Eunuchus, Asinaria,* and *Captivi.* Result in the *Commorientes*, *Crimen*, and *Heautontimorumenos.*

There are three forms of comedy. *Palliata* uses Greek dress; *togata* exhibits the sort of people who wear a Roman toga—many people call this form *tabernaria*—; and the *Atellana* which is based on wit and jests that have no value except their antiquity.

Comedies are divided into four parts: prologue, protasis, epitasis, and catastrophe. Prologue is the first speech, so called from Greek *protos logos* ["first word" or "first speech"] preceding the complication of the plot proper [*ho pro tou dramatos logos*]. There are four types. There is the *sustatikos*—the "commendatory"—where the poet or the story is praised. Then the *epitimetikos*—the "relative" prologue—where the poet either curses some rival or praises the audience. Then the *dramatikos*—"relating to the story"—which explains the argument of the drama. And there is the *miktos*—"mixed"—which includes all these things.

There is this difference according to some between a *prologue* and a *prologium*: a *prologue* is where the poet is vindicated or the story praised. A *prologium*, however, says something about the story.

Protasis is the first action of the drama, where part of the story is explained, part held back to arouse suspense among the audience. *Epitasis* is the complication of the story, by excellence of which its elements are intertwined. *Catastrophe* is the unravelling of the story, through which the outcome is demonstrated.

In most dramas the title came before the name of the author; in several the authors were named before the dramas. In ancient times there was a diversity of practice. For when men first presented dramas to the public, the titles were announced before the poet to prevent his being discouraged because of hostility. But when the poets had gained reputations as a result of presenting many dramas, then their names came first so that the name might draw attention to the drama.

It is clear that plays were presented at various kinds of games. There are four kinds of games which the officials provide for the public: the Megalenses, dedicated to the major gods, whom the Greeks call *megaloi* ["great"]; the *Funebres*, devised to draw the attention of the people while funeral ceremonies in honor of some noble person were performed; the *Plebei*, held for the benefit of the people; and the *Apollinares*, in honor of Apollo.

Usually, two altars were placed on the stage. The right one was sacred to Bacchus. The left was sacred to the god whose games are being celebrated. Thus Terence says in the *Andria*: "Take some consecrated boughs from the altar" [IV.iii.724].

They always have Ulysses wear a *pilleus* [cap] either because he once feigned madness so that he would not be recognized and forced to go to war, or because of his singular wisdom which often made him a protection and aid to his companions. He had a special talent for deception. Many commentators note that the inhabitants of Ithaca wore the *pilleus*, as do the Locrians. The costumes of Achilles and Neoptolemus include diadems although neither hero ever possessed the royal sceptre. Proof of this is the fact that they never joined the other Greek youths in the sacred oath to wage war on the Trojans, nor were they ever under the command of Agamemnon.

Old men in comedy wear a white costume, because white is associated with old age. Youths wear a varicolored costume. Slaves in comedy are clothed in a short garment in token of their age-old poverty, or so that their actions will be unencumbered. Parasites come on with a *pallium* [cloak] wrapped around them. The successful man has a white garment; the unlucky man wears an old one; the rich man a purple one; the poor man a Phoenician [reddish-purple] robe. A soldier wears a short purple cloak. A girl wears a foreign costume. A pimp wears a cloak of various colors; a prostitute wears a yellow one symbolizing greed.

Syrmata [robes with a long train] are named from the fact that they are dragged along the ground—this garment was invented by the luxurious Ionians. When worn by characters in mourning they symbolize carelessness resulting from self-neglect. Embroidered *aulaea* [curtains] are also spread out in front of the stage. This ornate decoration was taken from Attalus' palace in Pergamum all the way to Rome. Later, a *siparium* [comic drop-curtain] was used instead of *aulaea.* There was also a mimer's curtain used to block off the audience's view while the scene was being changed.

The actors spoke their lines in iambic dialogue, but the songs had melodies invented not by the poet but by a skillful musician. And a single song did not have a single melody. Rather, the melodies were often varied, and this is indicated by three numbers used to mark the comedies. These different numbers indicate the varying melodies of the song. The name of the musician who composed the melodies was placed at the beginning of the drama following the names of the author and principal actor.

Songs of this kind were played on flutes. When they were heard many of the spectators could tell what drama the players were going to present, even before the title was announced. The songs were played by matched flutes for the right and left hand, and by unmatched flutes. The flutes for the right hand played grave music and foreshadowed the serious kind of comedy. Those for the left hand foreshadowed the sportive kind of comedy by their high pitch. And when the drama called for flute playing for both right and left hands, both seriousness and sport were foreshadowed.

PROCLUS

(ca. 410–485)

INTRODUCTION

In Book X of the *Republic* Plato develops his famous theory of imitation. There is the idea of a bed, says Socrates, which is the true bed, eternal and changeless. Then there is a primary imitation of the bed by a carpenter. The material bed is necessarily imperfect and mutable, but since it is made by a craftsman it is relatively close to the idea. Finally there is a picture of a bed. The artist who paints it knows nothing of the craft of bed-making and studies only appearances. His bed is farthest from the true bed. If man's highest good is to know truth, art leads us away from truth. At best it is trivial; at worst it is positively harmful, as when Homer depicts the gods not as they are but as the myths reveal them—erratic, often cruel, and subject to the lowest human passions.

Elsewhere, in Plato's *Ion* and *Phaedrus* especially, there are suggestions of a different approach. In the *Ion* Socrates flirts with the idea that poets are inspired—that they see more, rather than less, than the average mortal.

The history of Neoplatonism as it impinges on art is the history of the substitution and elaboration of ideas in the *Ion* at the expense of those in the *Republic*. In this process the most important figure is Plotinus (205–269/70). The foundation of Neoplatonic aesthetics is *Enneads* I.6, "On the Beautiful." There we learn that beauty is more than a matter of symmetry; it is a joy felt by the soul in the perception of that which is akin to the soul—a delight in higher spiritual experience rather than appearances. God, the first principle, is both the Good and the Beautiful. The perception of true beauty does not involve gazing at material things but closing the eyes of sense and seeking transcendent vision. In *Enneads* V.8, this line of thought is carried further. True beauty is intelligible beauty. It is found in the work of artists—Plotinus cites statuary rather than poetry or music—as the form, or spiritual element, conferred on the material. Art is thus a higher, almost visionary activity. It imitates nature only in the sense that it imitates the source from which nature derives. Phidias did not use a model for Zeus but made him as he might be if he should decide to manifest himself to human eyes. This sort of creation takes place in the soul. The artist, by implication, is a visionary using faculties that transcend reason. His work communicates this vision and leads others along the path taken by the artist himself.

As important as these ideas are, it remained for Proclus, a late disciple of Plotinus, to relate them directly to literature. Neoplatonic critics had previously dealt with literature. Maximus Tyrius had devoted several essays in his *Dissertations* to poetic questions, especially the probity of Homer. Philo Judaeus, Clement, and Origen had used Neoplatonic concepts in biblical exegesis, and Porphyry had discovered allegory, in a manner analogous to that of Macrobius in his commentary on *Scipio's Dream,* in the cave of the nymphs passage in Homer. But Maximus Tyrius is pedestrian and Philo, Origen, and Porphyry are tied to specific texts and an allegorical method that limits their discussion of general critical issues. It is Proclus who first applies Neoplatonic theory to the outstanding problems of literary criticism. Although it is impossible to trace the influence of the essay here reprinted, the ideas which the essay brings into remarkably sharp focus form a leitmotif in medieval and Renaissance critical thought. They are paralleled in the fourth-century cult of the poet-seer as reflected in Servius and Macrobius, they recur in conjunction with the rediscovery of Dionysius the pseudo-Areopagite following the translation of his work into Latin in the tenth century by Scotus Erigena, they are found in the Platonizing authors of the twelfth-century Renaissance, especially Bernard Silvestris, and they impinge deeply upon humanistic defenses of poetry from Boccaccio to Sir Philip Sidney. Their hallmark is the idea that poetry is a more profound philosophy, a form of theology, a kind of vision. Their corollaries include: (1) the idea that poetry is necessarily allegorical (its vision is untranslatable; or it begins with images but ascends to truth; or its profound revelations must be concealed by the veil of fable from the profane rabble); (2) the notion of the poet as seer; (3) the positing of a faculty (imagination) higher than reason; (4) the idea that this faculty seems irrational to the uninspired, so that poets often are compared by the uninitiated to madmen and drunkards; (5) rejection of the classical theory of imitation (that poetry is an image of nature, a mirror of life); (6) qualification of the nearly universal idea that the chief benefit of poetry is that it teaches good morals (that poets must profit as well as delight); and (7) the idea that the experience of art is not an entertaining diversion but something akin to religious experience. In sum, Neoplatonic theories of literature leavened the rather dry and matter-of-fact critical tradition transmitted to the Middle Ages by writers like Horace, Cicero, and Donatus. They implemented the strong mystical tendency inherent in biblical exegesis and are involved, if only at third or fourth hand, in the conception of art evident in Bernard Silvestris, Alanus de Insulis, and Dante. After Marsilio Ficino had resurrected Plato in a Neoplatonic guise in the late fifteenth century, they provided a vital stimulus to the critical theory and literary practice of humanists during the sixteenth and seventeenth centuries. It is significant that rationalists like Castelvetro and Bacon attacked poetry for precisely the qualities emphasized in Neoplatonism—its claim to higher vision, its allegory, and its resistance to logical paraphrase. And it is significant that one of the most common Neoplatonic terms for inspiration (*enthusiasm*) became a term of ridicule in the eighteenth century.

Proclus wrote extensively on poetic questions in his voluminous commentaries on Plato. The essay reprinted here has been chosen because it is self-contained and because its general observations on literature are supplemented by specific comments intended to answer the objections which led Socrates in *Republic* X to banish Homer from his ideal state.

Proclus begins with psychology. He observes that there are three faculties in the soul. The first, which would later be called the intuition, intellect, or *mens,* is allied to the divine. The second is allied to human life and the world revealed to the senses. It is the rational soul which makes "intellect and science . . . the principle of its energy." Reason is a discursive faculty. It abstracts general principles from what is known, according to the rules of logical inference. The third faculty does not abstract but is captive of images as they enter the mind (and are combined by chance associations) from the senses. This faculty is *phantasia* or fancy.

Corresponding to the three lives of the soul, there are three kinds of poetry. The first exhibits what may literally be called "a rage for beauty." It is produced by "divine inspiration" and is related to a madness (*mania*) that is better than the "temperance" advocated by reason. Being concerned with beauty, it is also concerned with "adornment"—which is objectified in poetry as "measures and rhythms." The impulse evident here emerges during the Renaissance (in Tasso, for example) as a striving toward poetic "magnificence"—toward maximum use of the imagery, word effects, stanza forms, sheer variety, and the like—which is the concomitant of truly inspired poetry.

The kind of poetry produced by the reason is essentially didactic. It presents the lore of science in attractive forms and teaches "prudence and every other virtue to those of a naturally good disposition." Interestingly, the lowest type of poetry—that of the fancy—is equated with imitation. The Platonic distaste for artistic imitation is retained here, but in a context which completely overturns Plato's low estimate of artists. Being limited to "the world as it seems to be," "phantastic poetry" depends on appearances. It is less artistic than the poetry of reason which abstracts impressions into general systems. In a single paragraph, Proclus has repudiated the hallowed classical tradition that imitation, in the sense of mirroring life and custom, is the highest function of art.

For support, Proclus brings in the *Phaedrus* and the *Ion.* His citations reveal the profound ambiguity in Plato's view of art. They are valid, but they ignore the *Republic,* and, like most Neoplatonists including Ficino, Proclus reads the *Ion* as an exposition of "*furor poeticus,*" ignoring the fact that Socrates may be (probably is) speaking ironically when he couples enthusiasm and divine inspiration with madness. When Plato's reservations in the *Republic* finally are introduced, Proclus stresses that the tales of the gods are "concealed in these symbols, as under veils." The passing remark in *Republic* III that certain fables have a higher allegorical sense is taken as a *carte blanche* for mythology considered as allegory, while the later very strong attack on poets for falsifying the true nature of divinity is ignored. Likewise, in the discussion of imitative poetry, subdivided into the assimilative and phantastic categories, Proclus implies that Plato's discussion in the *Republic* is consciously limited to a single category of art rather than to art as a whole. Again, the approach is—if not a conscious distortion—an egregious case of special pleading.

The essay ends with a eulogy of Homer. Homer is a master of all three kinds of poetry "but especially the enthusiastic, according to which, as we have said, he is principally characterized." Likewise, Homer represented a model for tragic poets, particularly as these, being committed to pleasing the masses, draw on the phantastic elements in his work.

The essay ends with a brief explanation of why Plato criticizes Homer so severely. Plato wrote at a time when philosophy was "despised" and the worst sort of poetry was admired. Plato did not condemn Homer because of deficiencies in his moral outlook, but because the poets of Plato's day appealed to the lowest common denominator in society. Instead of instructing the masses they devoted their energies to entertainment by means of the lowest (imitative) form of poetry, concentrating on the least edifying emotions. The tragedians, who most appeal to a popular audience, are the worst offenders in this respect. In spite of this abuse, however, Homer remains pre-eminent among poets: "so far as he is possessed of the Muses, he is divine; but as far as he is an imitator, he is the third from the truth."

Thomas Taylor's translation, which was published in the preface to his edition of Aristotle's *Poetics, Rhetoric, and Nicomachean Ethics* (London, 1818), has been revised for this volume by Kevin Kerrane. For bibliography, see especially pp. 482–84.

PROCLUS ON THE MORE DIFFICULT QUESTIONS IN THE *REPUBLIC*: THE NATURE OF POETIC ART

There are three lives in the soul. The best and most perfect is through the faculty which allies and conjoins it with the gods, so that the soul lives a life united to them through the highest similitude. The soul, no longer existing in itself, but deriving life from a divine source infusing the mind, is filled with ineffable impressions of the divine, and connects like with like—its own light with that of the gods, and that which is most uniform in its own essence and life with that which is above all essence and life. The second life of the soul is through a faculty of middle dignity and power: the soul, not divinely inspired, realizes its own individuality by ordaining intellect and science as the principle of its energy, evolving the multitude of its reasons. It surveys the various mutations of forms, unites through abstraction the intellect and its object, and expresses in images an intellectual and intelligible essence. The third life of the soul is that which accords with its inferior faculties: the soul, expressing itself through them, employs phantasies and irrational senses, and is filled entirely with things of a subordinate nature.

Just as there are these three forms of life in souls, so poetry, as it proceeds from the various faculties, is diversified into the first, middle, and last modes of being. The first kind of poetry has the highest existence: it is full of divine goods, and it establishes the soul in the causes themselves of things, according to a certain ineffable union, leading that which is filled into sameness with its replenishing source. The soul subjects itself to spiritual illumination, and the divine is impelled to a communication of light—thus, according to the Oracle, "perfecting works, by mingling the rivers of incorruptible fire." This kind of poetry produces one divine bond, a union of participation, in which that which is subordinate partakes of that which is more excellent, so that the divine energy infuses all. The inferior nature withdraws, and conceals itself in that which is superior. This, then, in short, is an apparent madness better than temperance, and is distinguished by a divine quality. And as every different kind of poetry subsists according to a different hyparxis, or summit of divine essence, so this first kind of poetry, proceeding from divine inspiration, fills the soul with symmetry, and hence adorns even its least energies with measures and rhythms. And just as we define prophetic fury as according with truth, and the amatory inclinations as according with beauty, so in like manner we define the poetic mania as according with divine symmetry.

The second kind of poetry, which is subordinate to this first and divinely inspired species, and which has a middle existence in the soul, derives its being from a scientific and intellectual faculty. Hence this kind of poetry embodies the essence of things, strives to contemplate beautiful works and reasonings, and leads everything toward a measured and rhythmical interpretation. For you will find many works of good poets to be of this kind, rivaling the wisdom of great men—full of admonitions, the best counsels, and intellectual harmony. This kind of poetry teaches prudence and every other virtue to those of a naturally good disposition, and it explores and reflects on the periods of the soul, its eternal reasons, and various powers.

The third species of poetry, subordinate to these, is mingled with opinions and phantasies. It is composed by means of imitation; it is said to be

—and is nothing other than—imitative poetry. Sometimes it uses likeness-making alone, and sometimes it relies on a likeness that is only apparent, not real. It strongly intensifies very moderate passions, astonishing the hearers; using appropriate names and words, mutations of harmonies and varieties of rhythms, it changes the dispositions of souls. It indicates the nature of things not as they are, but as they appear to the many, being a certain adumbration, and not an accurate knowledge of things. It also establishes as its goal the delight of the hearers, and looks particularly to the passive part of the soul, which is naturally adapted to rejoice or be afflicted. But of this species of poetry, as we have said elsewhere, one division is *assimilative,* in which the imitation is accurate, while the other is *phantastic,* affording only apparent imitation.

Such, then, in short are the species of poetry. It now remains to show that these are also mentioned by Plato, and to treat other matters compatible with his teachings about each. First we shall discuss those wonderful conceptions of divine poetry which may be collected by anyone who reads Plato attentively. And once these are clear, I think it will be easy to understand the other two species of poetry.

In the *Phaedrus* Plato calls divine poetry "a possession from the Muses, and a mania" [244–45], and says that it is imparted from above to a tender and solitary soul. Its employment excites and inspires with Bacchic fury, in odes and other poetic forms, and its purpose is to instruct posterity in celebrating the infinite deeds of the ancients.

From these words it is perfectly evident that Plato identifies the original and first-operating cause of poetry as the gift of the Muses. For just as the Muses fill with harmony and rhythmical motion all the other divine creations, both the apparent and the unapparent, so in like manner they produce a vestige of divinity in those souls they take possession of, and this illuminates inspired poetry. I think that Plato calls such an illumination a *possession* and a *mania* because the whole energy of the illuminating power is divine, and because that which is illuminated gives itself up to this energy and, abandoning its own habits, yields to the force of that which is divine and uniform. He calls it a possession because the whole illuminated soul surrenders itself to the present effect of the illuminating deity. Plato calls it a mania because such a soul abandons its own proper energies for those of the illuminating powers.

In the second place, Plato describes the characteristics of the soul possessed by the Muses, and says that it ought to be tender and solitary. A soul hard and resisting, and disobedient to divine illumination, would oppose the energy of divinely inspired possession, because it would exist in itself rather than through the illuminating power, and it would be incapable of appreciating the gifts of this power. And a soul given over to various opinions, and filled with thoughts alien to a divine nature, would obscure the process of inspiration by mingling itself and its energies with those derived from the Muses. The soul which is to be possessed by the Muses must therefore be tender and solitary—so that it may be properly receptive to divinity and harmonize with it, and it should be unreceptive to and unmingled with other things.

In the third place, Plato mentions the common occurrence of such an aptitude in combination with possession and mania from the Muses. For to excite and inspire with Bacchic fury is the province both of that which illuminates and that which is illuminated, and the two processes become one: the divine force moving from above, and the soul surrendering itself to this motion. Excitation is a purified energy of the soul, lifting it from the world of matter and time and into divinity. Bacchic fury is a divinely inspired motion and, as it were, an unwearied dance upward toward the divine, giving perfection to the possessed. But again, a correct disposition of the soul is as necessary as the divine power, so that the possessed will not incline to that which is worse, but will easily be moved to a more excellent nature.

In the fourth place, Plato adds that the purpose of this divine poetry is to instruct posterity in celebrating the infinite deeds of the ancients. This implies that human affairs become more perfect and splendid when they are presented by a divinely inspired poet, and that such poetry produces true learning in its hearers. It does not aim primarily at the training of the young, but is directed more toward those already schooled in civic virtue, who still need a greater spiritual understanding of divine matters. More than any other kind of poetry, this species instructs the hearers, once its divine nature becomes manifest to them. Hence Plato very properly prefers this poetry, which subsists from the Muses in tender and solitary souls, to every other human art: "For the poet who approaches the poetic gates without such a mania will be imperfect, and his poetry, so far as it is dictated by prudence, will vanish before that which is the outcome of fury" [*Phaedrus* 245]. Thus does Socrates in the *Phaedrus* instruct us in the peculiarities of divine poetry—which differs both from divine prophecy and from prudent, calculated art—and he attributes to the gods its first unfolding into light.

Socrates' comments in the *Ion,* when he is discoursing with the rhapsodist about this species of poetry, confirm these views. Here Socrates states clearly that the poetry of Homer is divine, and that it is a source of enthusiastic energy to those conversant with it. For when the rhapsodist says that he can speak copiously on the poems of Homer, but not at all on the writings of other poets, Socrates explains this by saying: "It is not from technical skill that you speak well concerning Homer, but because you are moved by a divine power" [533D]. And the truth of this is indeed perfectly evident. For those who do something by means of art are able to produce the same effect in all similar situations. But those who work by means of divine inspiration on something truly harmonious cannot regularly produce the same effect when working with other, similar things. The rhapsodist receives divine inspiration when reciting Homer, but not when reciting other poets. Socrates then instructs us by using the stone commonly called Herculean as a clear analogy to perfect possession by the Muses: "This stone, then, not only draws to itself iron rings, but imparts to them a power to attract similar things, so as to enable them to draw other rings, and form a chain of rings, or pieces of iron, each hanging from the other" [533D-E].

Let us now consider Socrates' continued remarks on divine poetry. "Thus then," he says, "the Muse makes men divine; and, from these men thus inspired, others catch the sacred power to form a chain of divine enthusiasts" [533E]. Here, in the first place, he speaks of the divine cause in the singular number, calling it the Muse and not, as in the *Phaedrus,* a possession from the Muses. Socrates refers to the divine cause as a single mania affecting a whole multitude, in order to attribute all enthusiastic power to one spiritual substance, the primary principle of poetry. For poetry subsists uniformly and mysteriously in the first mover, but secondarily and indirectly in poets moved by that spiritual power, and still more indirectly in the rhapsodists, who are led back to the first cause through the agency of the poets. By thus extending the principle of divine inspiration as far as the rhapsodists, Socrates celebrates the fecundity of the first moving power. At the same time he clearly states that poets themselves participate in inspiration: the poets' ability through their poems to excite others to a divinely inspired state indicates that a divine nature is conspicuously present in their souls. Consequently, Socrates adds this comment: "The best epic poets, and all who similarly excel in composing any kind of verse to be recited, do not frame their admirable poems from the rules of art; but, possessed by the Muse, they write from divine inspiration. Nor is it otherwise with the best lyric poets, and all other fine writers of verse to be sung"[533E]. And again, afterwards, he says: "For a poet is a thing light and volatile, and sacred, nor is he able to write poetry till he becomes divine, and has no longer the command of his intellect" [534B]. And lastly, Socrates adds: "Hence it is that the poets indeed say many fine things, whatever their subject, just as you do concerning Homer; but not doing it through any rules of art, each of them succeeds through a divine calling in that species of poetry to which he is uniquely impelled by the Muse" [534C].

In all these citations, it is evident that Plato traces divine poetry to a divine cause, which he calls a Muse. In this he emulates Homer, who at one time refers to a multitude of Muses and at another to the union of the Muses in a single principle—as when he says "O Muses, sing" and "Sing me the man, O Muse." Midway between this divine cause of enthusiasm and the last echoes of inspiration in the responses of the rhapsodists, Plato locates poetic mania. Moving and being moved, filled from on high and transferring to others the illumination thus derived, the poetic mania joins together even the last participants in a communion with the divine substance.

With these things we may also bring into accord what the Athenian Guest says about poetry in the third book of the *Laws,* and what Timaeus says about poets. The Athenian Guest says that "poetry is divinely inspired," and that "it composes sacred hymns, and, with certain Graces and Muses, relates many things that have been truly transacted" [682]. Timaeus exhorts us to follow poets inspired by Apollo, in that they are "the sons of gods, knowing their fathers' concerns, even though their assertions are not probable and are unaccompanied by demonstrations." From all this it is easy to understand what Plato thought about divine poetry, and how he characterized inspired poets as special messengers of divine powers, eminently acquainted with the affairs of their fathers. When, therefore, Plato takes notice of mythical fictions, and corrects the more serious part of the writings of the poets—such as those dealing with bonds, castrations, loves, sexual connections, tears, and laughter among the gods—we must say that he also especially testifies that these things are properly presented as allegorical, concealing the idea as under veils. For whoever thinks that poets are particularly worthy of belief in affairs respecting the gods, even though they speak through inspiration rather than logical demonstration, must certainly admire the divine fables through which they deliver the truth concerning the nature of the gods. Whoever calls poetry divine cannot also ascribe to it an impious and exaggerated treatment of the divine. And whoever shows that the assertions of poets are attended with certain Graces and Muses must certainly judge an inelegant, unharmonious, and ungraceful phantasy to be very remote from the theory of poetic inspiration. Thus, when Plato in his *Republic* establishes by law that poetry and allegorical fables are not adapted to the ears of the young, he is very far from despising poetry itself; he merely protects the juvenile mind, which is inexperienced in hearing such things, from fiction of this sort. For, as he says in the *Second Alcibiades,* "The whole of poetry is naturally enigmatical, and is not obvious to the understanding of everyone" [147]. And hence in the *Republic* he clearly says that "youth is not able to distinguish what is allegory and what is not" [II.377]. We must say, therefore, that Plato entirely approves of inspired poetry, which he calls divine, and thinks it proper that those who compose it should be venerated in silence. This concludes our examination of the first kind of poetry, which subsists, from a divine origin, in tender and solitary souls.

Now let us contemplate that species of poetry which has a scientific knowledge of things, and which proceeds according to intellect and prudence. It reveals to men many spiritual essences, and brings to light many probable tenets in practical philosophy. It investigates the most beautiful symmetry in human behavior, and examines the disposition to vice. And it adorns all of these things with proper measures and rhythms.

The Athenian Guest in the *Laws* says that the poetry of Theognis is of this kind, which he praises beyond that of Tyrtaeus, because Theognis is a teacher of the whole of virtue, including the whole of political life. Theognis teaches a fidelity which receives its completion from all the virtues, expelling from politics that most pernicious vice sedition, and changing the lives of those who are persuaded. On the other hand, Tyrtaeus merely praises the habit of fortitude by itself, preaching it to those who neglect other virtues. But it will be better to listen to Plato's own words: "We also have the poet Theognis as a witness in our favor, who was a citizen of Megara in Sicily. For he says, 'Who keeps his faith amid seditious cries/Is worth his weight in silver and in gold.' We say therefore that such a person will conduct himself better in the most difficult kind of war, much in the same degree as justice, temperance, and prudence, when united with fortitude, are better than fortitude alone. For no one can be both faithful and effective in civil strife without the whole of virtue" [*Laws* I.630]. Here, therefore, Plato recognizes Theognis as partaking of political science, and all the virtues.

In the *Second Alcibiades* Plato, defining the most right and healthy mode of prayer, attributes it to a certain wise poet: "To me, Alcibiades, it seems probable that some wise man or other, happening to be connected with certain persons void of understanding, and observing them to pursue and pray for things for which it were better for them to be without, but which appeared to them good, composed for their use a common prayer in words like these—'King Jupiter, grant us what is good, whether or not it is the subject of our prayers, and avert from us what is evil, even if we should pray for it' " [142–43]. For only the scientific man, in whom a divine nature is adapted to the middle faculties of man, knows how to distinguish between good and evil in daily life. And on this account Socrates calls the poet who composed the prayer a wise man: through science alone, rather than through divine inspiration or right opinion, the poet formed a judgment on the natures and habits of those who prayed, and he reserved to the gods that which falls under their beneficent power. For it was the work of wisdom and science, and not of anything casual, to have converted those people through prayer to the one kingly providence of Jupiter, to have attributed the existence of good to the power of divinity, to have prevented the generation of true evils by calling upon the benevolence of a more excellent nature, and in short to have asserted that these things were unknown to those who prayed and were instead within the province of the divinity. Very properly, therefore, we say that such poetry is wise and scientific. For the poetry which is able to adapt truths to the middle faculties of man must itself exist by means of perfect science.

In the third place, let us now speak about imitative poetry, which, as we have already said, sometimes makes accurate likenesses of things, and at other times expresses things according to mere appearance. In the *Laws* the Athenian Guest clearly explains to us the assimilative part of this poetry, but in the *Republic* Socrates describes its phantastic part. And in the *Sophist* the

Eleatean Guest apprises us of how the assimilative and phantastic species of imitation differ from each other:

> GUEST: For I seem to perceive two species of imitation—one being the art of making likenesses, which is executed when someone produces an imitation by copying an original model in all proportions (length, breadth, and depth) and colors.
>
> THEAETETUS: Do not all imitators try to do this?
>
> GUEST: Not those who perform or paint any great work. For if sculptors, for example, were to follow the exact proportions of their models, then the upper parts, which we see from farther off, would appear smaller than they should be, and the lower parts would seem too large.
>
> THEAETETUS: Entirely so. And thus artists forego accuracy in their imitations; they do not produce in images truly beautiful proportions, but only those which appear to be so. [235].

Very properly, I think, does the Eleatean Guest at the end of the dialogue, wishing to bind the sophist by the definitive method, distinguish between assimilative imitation (in which the image is a true likeness of the model) and phantastic imitation (in which the likeness is only apparent).

In the second book of the *Laws* the Athenian Guest speaks only of assimilative poetry, and he discusses music which, rather than making pleasure its end, aims at a true imitation of its model. On the other hand, Socrates in the *Republic* deals with phantastic poetry. And having shown that a poet of this kind is third from the truth and merely derivative, Socrates compares such poetry to a picture which represents not the works of nature but of artificers—and these not as they truly are, but only as they appear to be. Thus Socrates clearly shows that the phantastic species of poetry aims only at delighting the audience. Of the two kinds of imitative poetry, the phantastic is inferior to the assimilative for this very reason: whereas assimilative poetry is concerned with accuracy of imitation, phantastic poetry is concerned merely with how the power of the phantasy can produce pleasure in the audience.

Such, then, are the species of poetry which Plato thought worthwhile to distinguish—one as better than science, another as scientific, a third as conversant with, and a fourth as falling off from, right opinion.

Having clarified these matters, let us now return to the poetry of Homer and contemplate every poetic habit that shines in it, especially those concerned with truth and beauty. When Homer is filled with enthusiastic energy, is possessed by the Muses, and communicates mystical ideas about the gods themselves, then he operates according to the first and divinely inspired principle of poetry. When he speaks of the life of the soul, the diversities in its nature, and its relation to civic virtue, then he especially speaks scientifically. When he presents forms of imitation truly similar to specific things and persons, then he employs assimilative imitation. And, finally, when Homer directs his attention not to the truth of things, but only as they appear to the multitude, and thus seduces the souls of his hearers, then he produces phantastic poetry.

I wish now to illustrate these poetic habits in Homer, beginning with phantastic imitation. He sometimes describes the rising and setting of the sun, not by accurately recounting in his verses each of these as it actually happens, but merely as it appears to us from a distance. These and all similar examples may be called the phantastic part of his poetry. But when Homer imitates heroes as warring or consulting or speaking according to the forms of real life—some as prudent, others as brave, and others as ambitious—then I would call this assimilative poetry. The scientific habit of poetry is manifested, I believe, when Homer unfolds and teaches the workings of the soul, based on his knowledge of the various faculties within it or of the relation between an image and the soul's use of it, or when he deals with the order of the elements within the universe (earth, water, fire, air), or other similar matters. And I would say that Homer is filled with enthusiastic energy, and is possessed by the Muses, when he devises fables that teach us about such mysteries as the demiurge, the triadic emanation of the one, the bonds of Vulcan, or the relation between the paternal ideas of Jupiter and the fertile divinity of Juno.

In addition, Homer's portrayal of Demodocus the bard [*Odyssey,* Book VIII] attributes to him an energy originating from the gods. Ulysses says that Demodocus was impelled by a god when he began his song, that he was divinely inspired, that the Muse loved him, and that God is the leader of the Muses: "The Muse, Jove's daughter, or Apollo, taught/Thee aptly thus the fate of Greece to sing,/And all the Grecians, hardy deeds and toils" [488–90]. It is a standard interpretation that Homer intended to represent himself in the character of Demodocus, and their personal calamities are indeed similar. There seems to be a direct reference to the fabled blindness of Homer in the statement that the gods "With clouds of darkness quenched his visual ray,/But gave him power to raise the lofty lay" [62–64]. Homer thus clearly contends that Demodocus says what he says by means of divine inspiration.

It is well that we have mentioned Demodocus and his inspired song, for it seems to me that the musicians Homer thought worthy of mentioning illustrate the various poetic habits discussed above. Demodocus, as we have said, was inspired, both in narrating divine and human concerns, and is said to have received his songs from the gods. On the other hand, the Ithacan bard Phemius is characterized merely according to a scientific knowledge of divine and human affairs. In Book I of the *Odyssey* Penelope addresses him: "Alluring arts thou knowest, and what of old/Of gods and heroes sacred bards have told" [337–39]. A third bard is the lyrist of Clytemnestra, who seems to have been an imitative poet, employing right opinion. He performed melodies of temperance for

Clytemnestra's benefit, and as long as he remained with her she perpetrated no unholy deed: the disciplining effect of his song converted her irrational tendencies into temperate behavior. A fourth musician, Thamyris, may be taken to represent the phantastic species of poetry. It is said that his song made the Muses indignant, so that they caused it to cease, for he practiced a music much more diversified and sensuous, and calculated to please the vulgar. By preferring a more varied music than the simpler mode adapted to the Muses, Thamyris is said to have fallen into contention with them, and to have lost the benevolence of the goddesses. The anger of the Muses does not refer to any passion in them, but indicates that Thamyris was unsuited to participate with them: his kind of song is phantastic and most remote from truth, calling forth the passions of the soul, and possessing no value with respect to imitation, right opinion, or science.

We may therefore behold all the kinds of poetry in Homer, but particularly the enthusiastic which, as we have said, principally characterizes him. Nor are we alone in this opinion: as we observed earlier, Plato himself in many places calls Homer a divine poet, the most divine of poets, and a proper imitator in the best sense. But imitative and phantastic poetry has a very obscure place in Homer's work, since he uses it merely in order to gain the credibility of the vulgar multitude, and only when it is totally unavoidable. If a man entered a well regulated city and beheld intoxication employed there for a certain useful purpose, he might decide to imitate not the prudence or whole order in the city, but intoxication itself alone. In such a case the city is hardly to be blamed for his conduct, which is due rather to the peculiar imbecility of his judgment. And in like manner, I think, the tragic poets, who emulate the phantastic species of Homer's poetry, should refer the principle of their error not to Homer, but to their own weakness. Homer may therefore be called the leader of tragedy, insofar as tragic poets emulate him in other respects and distribute the different parts of his poetry—imitating phantastically what he asserts assimilatively, and adapting to the ears of the vulgar what he composes scientifically. But Homer is not only the teacher of tragedy (for he is this merely by means of the phantastic element of his poetry), but he is also the teacher of all that is imitative in Plato, and of the whole theory of that philosopher.

It seems to me that the reason Plato wrote so severely against Homer, and against the whole species of imitative poetry, was the corruption of the times in which he lived. Philosophy was then despised, some calling it useless and others condemning it entirely. By contrast, poetry was then held in immoderate admiration. Its imitative power was the subject of emulation, and it was considered as adequate by itself for purposes of discipline. And poets, because they imitated everything, persuaded themselves that they knew all things, as is evident from what Socrates says in the *Republic.* Hence Plato, indignant at the prevalence of such an opinion, shows that poetry and imitation wander far from the truth imparted by philosophy, the savior of souls. In the same benevolent spirit in which he criticizes the sophists and popular orators for their inability to contribute anything to virtue, Plato also criticizes the poets—particularly the composers of tragedy, and those imitators who devise works to charm the audience without promoting virtue, enchanting the multitude without instructing them. And Plato considers that Homer deserves a similar criticism, insofar as he is the leader of this species of poetry and the model for the tragedians' emulation. It was necessary for Plato to do this in order to recall the men of his age from their total admiration of poetry, because their immoderate attachment to it led to a neglect of true discipline. And so with a view to the instruction of the multitude, to correct an absurd phantasy, and to exhort men to a philosophic life, Plato reproves the tragedians (who were then thought of as public teachers) for directing their attention to nothing rational. At the same time, Plato gives up his reverence for Homer and, ranking him in the same class with tragic poets, blames him as an imitator.

It should not seem strange for Plato to call the same poet both divine and third from the truth. For insofar as Homer is possessed by the Muses, he is divine; but insofar as he is an imitator, he is third from the truth.

FABIUS PLANCIADES FULGENTIUS

(ca. 500–600)

INTRODUCTION

The *Exposition of Vergil* was written probably in the sixth century A.D. by Fabius Planciades Fulgentius. Next to nothing is known of its author. He was obviously a Christian, probably a cleric, and he was deeply interested in pagan literature, especially its esoteric meanings. This interest is illustrated by two other works, the *Three Books of Mythology,* containing allegorical interpretation of the most important pagan myths, and a brief allegorical exegesis of the *Thebiad* of Statius.

Today it is easy to regard the *Exposition* as an absurd jumble of ideas totally foreign to the *Aeneid* as we now read it. However, as Domenico Comparetti has shown in his *Vergil in the Middle Ages,* Fulgentius was an influence on the interpretation of Vergil throughout the Middle Ages and on into the Renaissance. Among the authors who drew on his work are Bernard Silvestris, Francis Petrarch, Giovanni Boccaccio, and Christoforo Landino. Fulgentian concepts of epic poetry—if not Fulgentius himself—are evident in Tasso's essay on the allegory of *Gerusalemme Liberata* and in both Spenser's *Letter to Raleigh* explaining *The Faerie Queene* and in the poem itself. In other words, the *Exposition* was a living document, influencing both the theory of epic poetry and the way epic poets went about their task from the sixth to the sixteenth century. George Saintsbury sums up the liabilities and assets of the work:

> If it were not written in a most detestable style, combining the presence of more than the affectation and barbarism of Martianus [Capella] with a complete absence of his quaintness and full-blooded charm, it would be rather agreeable to read. Even as it is, it is full of interest.

The *Exposition* comes last in the series of Vergil commentaries that includes the work of Servius, of Macrobius, and of Tiberius Claudius Donatus.

These late classical commentaries are by-products of the "reading of the poets" which formed a regular part of the ancient grammar curriculum. Like the grammatical commentaries of Aelius Donatus on Terence and of Arcon and Porphyrion on Horace, the commentary of Servius on Vergil is essentially a series of footnotes to the text. In a sample analysis of Servius on *Aeneid* II, Bolgar finds that about 60 percent of the notes are on points of language, especially the meanings of unfamiliar words. Of the remaining 40 percent, many are brief allegorical explanations of myths and mythological details. For example, the golden bough given to Aeneas is the Pythagorean "Y," symbol of virtuous choice; Tartarus is equated with "earth," the river Styx symbolizes the anger and lust suffusing the temporal world, and its nine circuits represent the nine spheres. Julian Ward Jones has found 183 instances of allegorical interpretation in Servius. This is a tiny percentage of the whole commentary, and the Servian allegories are unrelated to each other—they do not add up to an allegorical reading of Vergil. What they illustrate is that by the fourth century allegorical readings of Vergil were accepted by learned pagans. As allegory gained prestige, especially in Christian circles where allegorical reading of the Bible was the rule rather than the exception, more ambitious allegorical readings of the *Aeneid* became inevitable.

The Vergil commentary of Tiberius Claudius Donatus takes quite a different approach. In an introductory letter to his son, Donatus complains of the superficiality of the grammarians. He will approach the *Aeneid* as an orator rather than a writer of linguistic footnotes. In fact, his commentary is a continuous essay rather than a gloss. Like a good Ciceronian, Donatus emphasizes Vergil's wisdom. The *Aeneid* contains a pattern of human life as well as many useful and pithy maxims. It is also a masterful exercise in rhetoric. Rather surprisingly, Donatus avoids the jargon and the mindless listing associated with treatises on "figures of diction and of thought" and the *colores rhetoricae.* His emphasis is on larger, less technical points—the order of the narration, the use of digressions, *doctrina,* transitions, set speeches, and the like.

Donatus begins by "placing" the *Aeneid* in a specific department of rhetoric. Its form is *certe laudativum;* that is, it is a poem of praise following the formulas of demonstrative (or epideictic) rhetoric. Other materials are brought in, but "they are used to add to the praise of Aeneas." The result is a long essay—rather tedious to the modern reader, but generally informed and balanced—unified by the theme of praise.

If Donatus retains a balanced perspective, we begin to encounter in Macrobius' *Saturnalia* the kind of bardolatry to which Vergil was subjected in the later Middle Ages. The *Saturnalia* is a rambling dialogue treating the Roman calendar, history, mythology, philosophy, and various scientific and literary topics. Books III to VI treat Vergil. Vergil is praised for his deep knowledge of Roman religious rites, his mastery of every rhetorical device and emotion;

his imitation of the major Greek and Roman authors; and above all for his prowess as an orator. In fact, he is superior to Cicero, for Cicero excelled in only one style, while Vergil excels in all three. If Quintilian compared Homer to an ocean, Macrobius compares Vergil to Nature herself.

Between these commentaries and Fulgentius' *Exposition* there is a gap of about two hundred years. The *Exposition* employs a labored, involuted Latin which looks barbarous today but was probably the result of conscious effort to write according to the formulas of Asiatic (as against Attic) style. In terms of content, we can detect echoes of earlier traditions, but—rather surprisingly—no direct borrowings.

The full title of Fulgentius' essay is *The Exposition of the Content of Vergil According to Moral Philosophy*. This accurately defines its purpose. Fulgentius is not interested in footnotes or glossing hard lines, nor is he particularly concerned to demonstrate Vergil's rhetorical skill. His main objects are, first, to show that Vergil concealed a consistent system of ethics under the veil of fable; and second, to outline this system. The *Exposition* is thus different in fundamental conception from earlier Latin commentaries. Servius produced a treatise for the grammar curriculum, and Donatus and Macrobius wrote rhetorical criticism. The *Exposition*, on the other hand, turns from the trivium to a formal category of advanced learning, ethics. At the same time, Fulgentius has obviously learned at first or second hand from his predecessors. The fashion of allegory *via* etymology had already been applied to the *Aeneid* by Servius. More interesting, because more influential on the shape of the essay as a whole, Fulgentius agrees with Donatus that the *Aeneid* is a poem of praise following the prescriptions of demonstrative rhetoric. Commenting on the word order of *arma virumque cano* (and assuming that *arma* symbolizes valor), he remarks, "According to logic one should mention the person first and then the things relating to the person, so that substance precedes accidents—for example, 'man' would come first and then 'arms,' since the virtue is in the person. But I wrote according to the formulas of praise, and therefore I mentioned the merit of the man before the man himself." The plot of the *Aeneid* is also based on praise. An oration in praise of someone is an encomium, and the rhetorical prescriptions for the encomium are precise. An encomium should begin at or before birth and should summarize the life of the subject in a series of representative episodes. The rationale of the encomium is not flattery but teaching by example. The episodes should therefore be idealized in the interests of moral instruction. The standard virtues both in oratory and epic poetry are fortitude and wisdom, but temperance, magnanimity, justice, chastity, piety, and the like are also appropriate.

Clearly, if an encomium is written to embody a moral system, a critic can reduce it back to this system. This is the approach taken by Fulgentius. Having established that the *Aeneid* is written according to the formulas of praise, he attempts to penetrate the fable in order to abstract its basic content.

The extent to which Fulgentius is willing to go in this direction is evident in his treatment of the first episode in the *Aeneid,* the shipwreck of the Trojans on the shore of Carthage. Normally, this is considered a prime example of the epic convention of *in medias res* (in the midst of things). But Fulgentius is committed to the position that the *Aeneid* is an encomium, and an encomium should begin *ab ovo*—at the beginning. His solution is to assert that the shipwreck episode is an allegory of the birth of the soul into a tempestuous and painful life. Thus, what appears superficially to be *in medias res* is in reality the first episode in the life of the encomium hero.

As we move forward, Fulgentius remains relentlessly chronological and relentlessly exemplary. Aeneas becomes a kind of everyman engaged in the struggles and trials that beset us all at various stages in life. The tale of his wanderings is an allegory of childhood. His love for Dido symbolizes the awakening of passion in the adolescent, and Mercury, who commands him to leave Carthage, symbolizes the reason that must control passion. The death of Anchises represents the freeing of youth from parental authority. The descent into the underworld represents the formal study of philosophy. Finally, books VII–XII, which recount the wars of the Trojans in Italy, are an allegory of the active man following the path of labor (Lavinia) and resisting the temptations of drunkenness (Metiscus) and rage (Turnus). Throughout this extraordinary reading, Fulgentius emphasizes the virtues suggested by the opening words *arma* and *virum*—that is, valor and wisdom. The order in which the good life is attained is, first, natural talent, the inborn ability to learn the ways of virtue; second, education; and third, what Fulgentius calls adornment, which is the embodiment of virtue in action and the benefits that come from such action.

To describe the mechanism whereby Fulgentius extracts moral philosophy from the *Aeneid* is useful, for the *Exposition* is the first sustained allegorical reading of a Latin poetic classic that has survived. Equally, if not more, significant are several themes that run through the *Exposition*: poetry as esoteric wisdom, the poet as inspired prophet, and poetic truth as revelation.

The first of these themes is plain enough in the assumption that Vergil concealed his teaching under the veil of fable. The veil is so heavy, in fact, that in the essay Fulgentius has to summon the ghost of Vergil to lift it. Before Vergil appears, Fulgentius explains that the *Eclogues* and *Georgics* contain "the secrets of almost every art." He will not explain them, however, because they are very dangerous—evidently, they might corrupt Christian readers. The "secrets" which interest Fulgentius are ethical, for in ethics pagan wisdom based on natural law supplements (and at times anticipates) Christian revelation. The motif of hidden wisdom is further objectified in the imagery of darkness and light which runs through the *Exposition.* As Vergil is about to appear, Fulgentius exclaims, "Send me now the Mantuan Bard, so that I can lead his fugitive meanings into the light." Later Vergil remarks that although he did not know the truths of revelation, "still, truth sprinkled its sparks in my darkened mind." Discussing the burial of Anchises, Vergil states that he wants the meaning of the episode "to shine out with perfect clarity." The magical bough is "golden" says Vergil, "because I wanted to symbolize the splendor of eloquence." The scenes which Aeneas witnesses in Hades show that "unless learning has been mastered and darkness dispelled by profound knowledge, one sees the empty shapes of dreams."

The second motif, the notion of the inspired bard, is evident throughout the *Exposition.* Fulgentius is taking the same position adopted by Macrobius in the *Saturnalia*, but his viewpoint is more mystical, less rationalistic. Vergil is more than a genius. He emerges as a *vates*, a prophet, who sees to the heart of every mystery. His wisdom is so profound, in fact, that a mere mortal cannot hope to understand it. Supernatural assistance is required, and this is provided by none other than the ghost of Vergil himself. "Behold," says Fulgentius, "he comes toward me well-filled with a draught of the spring of Mount Helicon. He is a proper image of a Bard with his tablets raised in order to treat his topic, and with a fixed frown murmurs some mysterious truth that wells up within him." This is more than a clever invention. It parallels the appearance of the elder Africanus to expound the secrets of the afterlife in *The Dream of Scipio,* and it foreshadows the appearance of Vergil as a guide to the underworld in *The Divine Comedy.* It is another way of affirming what the concept of the poet as *vates* directly asserts—that certain works contain supra-rational truths; that they are texts having the authority of direct revelation.

The third theme, poetic truths as revelation, complements the second. Although Fulgentius emphasizes that he is interested only in ethical lore, he occasionally rises to more challenging topics. He cites Vergil's Messianic *Eclogue,* which was the standard example throughout the Middle Ages of Vergil's mysterious prophetic ability. In five instances, he remarks that Vergil's insights parallel those in Scripture. When Vergil states that the *Aeneid* begins by celebrating virtue and wisdom, Fulgentius exclaims, "If I understand you, most excellent Bard, Holy Writ sang Christ, the Redeemer of our world, as virtue and wisdom, because Divinity assumed the shape of a perfect Man." When Vergil comments on the symbolism of the first line of the *Iliad*, Fulgentius adds, "You did not speak poorly in this. Divine Wisdom, far surpassing your understanding, began in like manner, saying 'Blessed is the man who walks not in the counsel of the ungodly'." It is here that Vergil admits that "truth sprinkled its sparks in my darkened mind." Again, when Vergil comments on the excellence of contrition, Fulgentius adds, "I approve your sentiment. Our divine and lifegiving teaching tells us that God does not despise a humble and contrite heart."

In these and similar passages there is an echo, however dim, of the view of pagan literature taken by Philo Judaeus, Clement of Alexandria, and Origen. For these Alexandrians, the divine *logos* manifested itself in all cultures although it revealed itself most fully in Scripture. Consequently, one could expect to find anticipations of scriptural truths throughout pagan literature, although only those who have been properly prepared by study and meditation should be encouraged to undertake the search.

The translation here used is my own. For bibliography, see especially pp. 482–85.

THE EXPOSITION OF THE CONTENT OF VERGIL ACCORDING TO MORAL PHILOSOPHY

[TO CALCIDIUS THE GRAMMARIAN]

O most holy of Deacons, because of my age I thought complete silence proper. Not only did my mind cease to recall what it had learned, but it was becoming forgetful that it lived at all. But because I am subject to the New Law of charity, and the rule of love makes refusal impossible, I have touched on the hidden natural lore of Vergil, avoiding those things which are more dangerous than praiseworthy. Woe to me, I say, should I know and possess anything improper.

Therefore I have omitted the *Eclogues* and *Georgics* in which are interwoven concepts so profound that in those books Vergil has included the inner secrets of almost every art. In the first, second, and third eclogue he has given in philosophic terms the characteristics of the three kinds of life [contemplative, active, voluptuary]. In the fourth he treated the art of prophecy. In the fifth, priestly matters. In the sixth, with his exquisite meters, the art of music, and in part of this eclogue he explained physiology according to the Stoic view. In the seventh he touched on botany. In the eighth he described the art of music and also magic, and at the end, omens, which he continued to discuss in the ninth. In the eighth he says:

Lo, while I hesitate to carry it away,
The ash itself has spontaneously
Enveloped the altar with flickering flames,
May the omen be good!
Something has been determined; and the dog Hylax barks at the gate.
[II. 105–7]

In the ninth he says: "I remember this was forecast by the oaks struck by heaven" [not *Eclogue* IX but I.17]; and again, "Wolves beheld Moeris first" [1. 54].

The first *Georgic* is astrological throughout and toward the end deals with omens. The second deals with physiognomy and medicine. The third deals entirely with augury. And he also touches on this subject in the sixth book of the *Aeneid,* where he says: "Plucking the topmost hairs between the horns,/[The priestess] lays them on the fire as first offerings" [245–46]. The fourth is wholly concerned with music, and has interpretative comments on the art of music at the end.

I have, then, omitted teachings exceeding the limits of the times so that he who seeks reputation will not end by fracturing his skull. Be content, my Lord, with the modest posy that I have picked for you from the flowery gardens of the Hesperides. For, if you seek golden apples, you must play Eurystheus[1] to some other stronger man, who, like Hercules, is willing to risk his life. You will be able peacefully to take many ideas from this posy which will gratify your wishes. Now, laying aside the rancid bitterness of the Hellebore of Chrysippus, I will say something pleasing to the Muses:

O Maids of Helicon—and I do not call
On Calliope alone—assist me.
Give your blessing to my mind.
I undertake a more difficult task.
A single Muse will not suffice.
Run, Pierian Maidens, you are my greatest care.
Strike the Arcadian lyre with an ivory plectrum.

I think this little invocation will satisfy the Vergilian Muses.

Send me now the Mantuan Bard in person, so that I can lead his fugitive meanings into the light. And behold—he comes toward me well filled with a draught of the spring of Mt. Helicon. He is a proper image of a Bard with his tablets raised in order to treat his topic, and with a fixed frown murmurs some mysterious truth that wells up from within him.

I said: "If you please, put aside your frowning expressions, o most famous of Italian poets. Sweeten the bitter sauce of your difficult ideas with the condiment of sweet honey. For I do not search your words for what Pythagoras says about harmonic numbers, or Heraclitus fire, or Plato ideas, or Hermes the stars, or Chrysippus numbers,[2] or Aristotle entelechies.[3] Nor am I interested in what Dardanus says about powers, or Battiades about daemons, or Campester about spirits of the underworld and ghosts. I seek only the easy things taught by grammarians to their childish pupils for monthly fees."

Then, wrinkling his brow, Vergil said: "I thought, little man, that you were too foolish for me to load my heavier burdens on your heart. You are more dense than a dirt clod and will sleep through anything weighty."

I said: "Save that sort of knowledge, I pray, for your Romans for whom it is honorable and harmless. It will be enough for me to touch the lowest hem of your robe."

He said: "As far as your coarse intelligence and the timidity of your age permit you to learn, I will dip out just a few drops from the fountain of my swelling genius and explain these matters to you. This small measure will prevent you from becoming so drunk that you get sick. Now make the seats of your ears vacant so that my words can enter."

And then, settling into the posture of an orator, with two fingers erect in the form of an "I" and the third pressing the thumb, he began: "In all my works I treated subjects relating to natural philosophy. And in the twelve books of the *Aeneid* I revealed fully the condition of man's life. And I began the exordium with 'Arms and the man I sing'—referring to virtue[4] by 'arms' and wisdom by 'man.' For perfection consists of virtue of body and wisdom of mind."

I said: "If I am not mistaken about your meaning, most excellent bard, Holy Scripture sang Christ the Redeemer of our world as virtue and wisdom because God assumed the condition of a perfect man."[5]

"He said: "You know what true Majesty has taught you. Meanwhile, I can only relate what I think. Now it is proper according to logic to speak of the person first and then the things relating to the person so that substance comes first and then the accidents—as it were, to mention 'man' first and then 'arms,' since virtue is inherent in the man. But because I wrote according to the forms of praise,[6] I mentioned the merit of the man before the man himself. Thus we come to the person with his merit already recognized. This, in fact, is how things are commonly done in letter-writing, where we first write 'Most excellent' and then the name of the man addressed."

"But to understand more readily that I have written in the form of praise, notice the wording of the lines that follow. I say 'an outcast through fate' and 'by the power of the gods' to show that Fortune was to blame for the flight of Aeneas, not lack of virtue. He exposed himself to danger because of the gods, not through lack of wisdom. This accords with the ancient maxim of Plato, 'The spirit of man is his god.'[7] If it is worthy, God will be kindly. And Carneades in the *Telesias* says, 'All Fortune resides in the intelligence of the wise man.' "[8]

"Moreover, I wanted to mention 'virtue' first then 'wisdom' because, although wisdom rules virtue, wisdom flourishes in a virtuous soul. A lack of virtue is a weakness in wisdom because when wisdom intends to do something, if the virtue to accomplish it is inadequate, wisdom is cut off in its effects and languishes."

"Now about beginning with 'arms'—I knew that the word 'man,' if placed first, would indicate the sex of the individual, not his honor. There are many men, but not all of them are praiseworthy. Therefore, I placed first the word suggesting the 'virtue' for which the man is praiseworthy. In this I followed Homer, who says, 'The wrath, O goddess, sing of Achilles' [*Iliad* I.1]—mentioning the wrath of the man before the man himself. Moreover, Homer symbolizes virtue in the figure of Minerva, and he writes: 'She caught the hair of Achilles' [*Iliad* I.197]."

I said: "You did not speak badly in this. Divine Wisdom, far surpassing your understanding, began in like manner, saying, 'Blessed is the man who walks not in the counsel of the ungodly' [Psalms 1:1]. Note that the most perfect teacher of the righteous life, the Prophet David, placed the reward for virtuous living—'blessedness'—before the sweat of the struggle."

He said: "I rejoice, little fellow, at these added sentiments, because, although I did not know the full truth concerning the nature of the righteous life, still, truth sprinkled its sparks in my darkened mind with a kind of blind favor."

"Now, as I began to say, 'virtue' is related to substance, and 'wisdom' is what controls substance. As Sallust said, 'All our strength is in our soul and body' [*On Cataline's Conspiracy*, I.2]."

"To satisfy your mind more fully, there are three phases in human life: first possession, second control of what you possess, and third graceful adorning of what you control. Note that these three phases are included in my first line; that is, 'arms,' 'man,' and 'first.' 'Arms'—that is, virtue—refers to a natural characteristic. 'Man'—that is, wisdom—to a mental characteristic. And 'first'—that is, foremost—to judgment. Thus the order is: to possess, to control, and to adorn."

"Thus through an historical allegory I have shown the whole condition of human life, which involves first nature, second learning, and third success. Be careful to understand these phases. As I said before, first comes inner capacity which is a gift of nature and permits man to improve—for you cannot educate a creature that is not born with the ability to be educated. Second comes learning which enhances nature as it improves. This is like gold, for gold is malleable and beautiful by nature, but it is brought to perfection by the hammer of the workman. Like gold, the mind is born capable of expansion. It improves because it was born, and success comes along to adorn what improves."

"These phases of life should be followed by the young children to whom my poem is taught. Every worthy person is born capable of education. The person is educated so that his natural capacity will not be wasted. He is adorned with success so that the gift of learning will not be useless. Plato, explaining the triple order of human life, said: 'Each good is either inborn, or learned, or imposed.'[9] It is born through nature, learned through study, and imposed through experience."

"Now, having completed the preliminaries, I proceed to the beginning of the story. But to make sure that I am not explaining my story to untutored ears, tell me the content of the first book. Then, if all is well, I will explain the book to you."

I said: "If the memory of past studies does not fail me, first Juno asks Aeolus to cause shipwreck of the Trojans. Aeneas escapes with seven ships. He reaches the shore of Libya. He sees his mother but does not recognize her. He and Achates are enveloped in a cloud. Then his soul is stirred by pictures. After dinner he is soothed by the music of a lyre. You now have a brief summary of the contents of the first book. Now I wish to know what you meant by them."

He said: "The shipwreck symbolizes the perils of birth in which the mother suffers birth-pangs, and the infant endures the danger of being born. All human beings necessarily share in this. And to make this meaning very plain, the shipwreck is caused by Juno, the goddess of childbirth. And she sends Aeolus: Aeolus in Greek is *eonolus* [aion + oloos]—that is, 'the destructiveness of time.'[10] As Homer says, 'The destructive wrath that brought woes innumerable on the Achaeans' [*Iliad* I.2]. And note what is promised to Aeolus: Deiopea, Juno's nymph, as his bride. *Demos* in Greek means 'public'; *iopa* is 'eyes' or 'vision.' To those being born the temporal world is dangerous. But an unclouded vision of perfection is promised by the goddess of birth to Aeolus. Next Aeneas escapes with seven ships. This is symbolic, for seven is the harmonic number of birth. I will briefly explain the reason for this if you like."

I said: "I discuss this sufficiently in the book that I recently wrote about medicine. There I commented on the whole arithmetic significance of seven and nine, and I would be wordy if I put in one book what I included in another. Anyone who wants to learn about such matters can read my book on physiology. Now I await what remains."

He said: "As I began to say, as soon as Aeneas reaches land, he sees his mother Venus but does not recognize her. This symbolizes infancy because those recently born can see their mothers from the moment of birth but do not immediately recognize and respond to them. Next Aeneas is enveloped in a cloud and recognizes his companions but cannot speak to them. Note how plainly I have depicted the characteristics of the very young children. They have the ability to recognize people but not to speak. And I placed Achates with Aeneas at the beginning. Achates is his arms bearer after the shipwreck, and he is also enveloped in the cloud. Achates is Greek *aconetos* [achos + ethos]; that is, 'the habit of sorrow.' Humanity is doomed to hardship from infancy, as Euripides says in the tragedy of *Iphigenia*:

> Nothing can be described that is so terrible—
> Be it physical pain or heaven-sent affliction—
> That man's nature could not bear it.[11]

That is: there is nothing so terrible and no experience so dire that human nature has not endured it. There is no armor against sorrow except tears. Infants console and call attention to themselves by crying. Although we are scarcely able to laugh by the fifth month, tears flow freely on the very threshold of life."

"That Aeneas vainly feasts his soul on a picture clearly symbolizes childish thought. An infant can see but he cannot understand what he sees—just as pictures can be looked at but lack rational meaning."

"Then Aeneas is taken to dinner and soothed by the sound of the lyre. Little children characteristically seek nothing more than to be pleased by sweet music and filled with food. And note the name of the lyre-player. Iopas in Greek is *siopas* [siope]—that is, the silence of a child. Infants are always soothed by the sweet words and songs of nurses; and to symbolize this I described Iopas with long hair like that of a woman [cf. *Aeneid* I.740]. And also, Aeneas sees Cupid [I.715–17]. Youth is always wanting or desiring something. And therefore I wrote the verse that comes in the second book after the lyre playing is over: 'Who could refrain from tears' [II.8]."

In the second and third books Aeneas is diverted by tales of the sort that usually amuse talkative young children. At the end of the third book [613ff.] Aeneas sees the Cyclops after Achaemenides describes them. *Achos* [achos] means sorrow in Greek; *ciclos* [kuklos] means 'circle.' Also, *pes* [pais] means 'boy.' The sense is that the child, when released from fear of his guardians, does not yet have rational knowledge of grief and gives himself over to the wandering of wild youth. The Cyclops is described as having a single eye in his forehead because the wandering of wild youth is not directed by a full or a rational vision, and the whole of youth rests on Cyclopean vanity. The single eye in the head of the Cyclops symbolizes that he cannot see and understand anything but vanity. The wise Ulysses put out the eye: that is, vainglory is blinded by the flame of reason. And I called him Polyphemus—that is, *apolunta femen* [apoleipo + pheme], which means 'loss of reputation' in Latin. For a blind later life follows youth's pride and indifference to reputation."

"To make the sequence perfectly obvious, Aeneas next buries his father. As the child grows up he rejects the force of paternal authority. He buries his father at the port of Drepanum [III.707]. *Drepanos* is *drimpedos,* and *drimos* [drimos] means 'keen' and *pes* [pais] 'boy.' This symbolizes the fact that immaturity rejects parental discipline."

"And now that the soul of Aeneas is free of his father's authority, in the fourth book he goes hunting and is aroused by the fire of love. Driven on by a storm and mist—symbolizing a disturbed mind—he commits adultery. And when he has dallied for a long time, he gives up his immoral love at the urging of Mercury. Mercury is the god of reason. This symbolizes that at the prompting of reason the more mature person breaks the bonds of lust. And indeed, the object of passion [i.e. Dido] dies when it has been rejected. Totally consumed, it wastes away to ashes. When lust is expelled from the youthful heart by reason, it flickers out and is buried in the ashes of oblivion."

"In the fifth book Aeneas is aroused by the memory of his father and engages in the sports of young men. This symbolizes that when one reaches the age of prudence, he follows examples provided by his father's memory and exercises his body in manly activities."

"Note that they engage in boxing. That is, Entellus and Dares [V.362ff] practice a manly sport. *Entellin* [entello] in Greek means 'command' and *derin* [dero] 'cudgel'—which masters often do when teaching."

"Then the ships are burned [V.641]. They are the dangerous instruments that lure a youth onto the stormy seas of vanity where he is constantly buffeted by tempests, as it were, of dangerous impulses. By the excellent fire of reason all these are destroyed, and, as knowledge is added to intelligence, they all vanish like dreams in the ashes of oblivion. And Beroë—that is, 'the order of truth'—makes the fire."

"In the sixth book Aeneas comes to the temple of Apollo and descends into the underworld. Apollo is the god of learning and he is a friend of the Muses. Now the shipwreck and dangers of youth are over, and Palinurus has been lost. Palinurus is *planonorus* [plane + horao]—that is, 'wandering vision.' Therefore in Book IV [363] I wrote concerning amorous glances, 'her silent glances *wander* over the whole man'; and also in the *Eclogues,* 'the *wandering* footsteps of a bull' [VI.58]."

"Having put these things behind him, Aeneas now comes to the temple of Apollo—that is, learning from studies. And there he ponders the course of his future life and seeks out the path to the underworld. This symbolizes that whenever anyone considers the future he must penetrate the hidden and secret mysteries of knowledge. And Aeneas must bury Misenus first [VI.227]. *Misio* [misos] in Greek means 'spite' and *enos* [ainos] 'praise.' Unless you reject ostentatious and vain praise you will never reach the secrets of wisdom. The appetite for vain praise never seeks truth but thinks that false things flatteringly attributed to the self are truly possessed. Also there is the contest between Misenus and Triton with his horn and shell [VI.171–76]. Note how precise the symbolism. The bubble of vain praise is puffed up by a windy voice and Triton destroys it. Triton is *tetrimemenon* [?tetinmenos] in Greek, which we Latins call 'contrition.' Contrition always deflates vain praise. And for this reason Tritonia is called the goddess of wisdom: contrition always makes a man wise."

I said: "Having better knowledge on this subject, I approve your sentiment. Our divine and life-giving teaching tells us that God does not despise a humble and contrite heart [Psalms 50:19]. And this is true and manifest wisdom."

He said: "To make my story fully and explicitly clear, I wrote that

Carineus [Corynaeus; VI.227] cremated the body of Misenus in a fire. *Carin* [charis] in Greek means 'favor'; and we call *eon* [aion] 'time.' This symbolizes that through the favor of time the ashes of vainglory are inevitably buried."

"But no one learns about hidden knowledge until he has plucked the golden bough; that is, the study of philosophy and letters. I intended the golden bough to symbolize knowledge, recalling that my mother dreamed she gave birth to a branch,[12] and because Apollo is painted holding a branch. Moreover, the bough is said to be *'apo tes rapsodias,'* that is, 'from writings' by Dionysius [?Thrax] in his book on Greek expressions. And I called the bough 'golden' because I wanted to symbolize the splendor of eloquence, recalling the saying of Plato that when Diogenes the Cynic attempted to steal Plato's estate, he found nothing there except a golden tongue. Tiberianus recounts this in his book *On the God of Socrates.*[13]

"I referred to ten golden apples in the *Eclogues*: that is, the polished eloquence of the ten eclogues. Hercules took golden apples from the Hesperides. And the Hesperian maidens are said to be Aegle, Hespera, Medusa, and Arethusa, which in Latin are study, understanding, memory, and eloquence. First comes study, second understanding, third memorization of what you understand, and then adorning in eloquent language what you retain. In a similar way virtue seeks to grasp the golden prize of learning."

I said: "Most learned man, you are surely speaking the truth. Just now I recalled a passage in Scripture which speaks of a golden tongue and virtuous skills stolen from iniquity,[14] just as eloquence may be recovered from the gentiles. But pray go on to what remains."

He said: "As I previously remarked, having taken up the golden bough, that is, learning, Aeneas enters the lower regions and investigates the secrets of knowledge. In the outer chamber of Hades he sees sorrow, disease, wars, discord, old age, and poverty. This symbolizes that when all things in the mind and heart of man are considered, when learning has been mastered and the darkness dispelled by higher knowledge, one sees that old age and its cousin death are empty dreams, and war the child of greed, and disease the offspring of disorder and intemperance, and quarrels the consequence of drunkenness, and hunger the handmaid of laziness and sloth."

"So Aeneas descends into Hades and there he witnesses the punishments meted out to evil men and the rewards of good ones and sees the sad confusion of lovers."

"Charon the ferryman carries him and he crosses Acheron. This river symbolizes the boiling emotions of youthful activity. It is called 'muddy' because youths do not have mature and clear ideas. *Acheron* [akairos] is Greek for 'without time.' Charon is *ceron* [kairos] which means 'time.' Therefore he is said to be the son of Polidegmon. *Polidegmon* [polus + deigma] is Greek for 'much knowledge.' This symbolizes that when one has reached the age of much knowledge he moves past time—muddied waters and the dregs of his own bad habits."

"He drugs three-headed Cerberus with a morsel dipped in honey [VI.420]. I [that is, here, Fulgentius] have already explained in my *Mythologies* that the Tricerberus story is an allegory of quarreling and legal wrangles. Petronius says of Euscios, 'Cerberus was a trial lawyer.'[15] For men learn quarreling slander and use eloquence in other people's affairs simply for money, when true learning should be used for improvement—as is seen even today among lawyers. The bitterness of altercation, treated with the honey of wisdom, regains its sweet taste."

"Now that Aeneas has been admitted to the secrets of wisdom, he looks on the shades of heroic men. That is, he considers the achievements and monuments of virtue. And he sees the punishment of Deiphobus. Deiphobus is Greek for either *Dimofobus* [deima + phobos] or *demofobus* [demios + phobos]—that is 'fear of terror' or 'fear of the people.' Whatever kind of fear is intended, it is properly depicted with hands cut off and blinded and without ears [VI.495–97]. The reason is that fear never perceives what it sees or knows what it hears or, lacking hands to feel, recognizes what it does. And Deiphobus was killed by Menelaus when sleeping. Menelaus is *menelau* [mene + laos] that is 'valor of the people,' for this valor always overcomes slothful fear."

"Then Aeneas sees Dido, now an empty shadow of love and lust. But to the wise man the memory of lust, even though it has been deadened by indifference, brings penitent tears."

"We have now reached the place where I say:

> In front stands the huge gate and pillars
> Of solid adamant, so that no human power
> Not even the sons of heaven, can uproot them in war.
> There stands the iron tower soaring high.
> [VI.552–55]

Note how obvious I have made this image of pride and vanity. I put adamantine columns on the tower because this kind of rock is indestructible. The Greek [*adoneo*] means, in fact, 'untouched'—for neither fear of the gods nor human virtue nor fear of a bad reputation can control pride. 'An iron tower soaring high' signifies high and unbending arrogance. And who sustains this arrogance but Tisiphone, meaning 'raging voice' [?*tisis* + *phone*]. When I said 'The Hydra still more cruel with fifty black and gaping throats' [VI.576], I symbolized nothing less than that the swelling vanity in the heart of proud men is worse than the hot air of boasting coming from their mouths. When I said 'Tartarus itself yawns open twice as far' [VI.577–78], this symbolizes the final punishment of pride. The punishment for pride is to be thrown down. The more arrogant a proud man is, the more anguish he will endure when his arrogance collapses. Whoever is raised up by pride will therefore be doubly struck down. On this subject, recall the epigram of Porphyrius:

> Fortune aids you Quintus (by my soul)
> And takes your sneering face all over town.
> By heaven it's true: You are some stinking hole:
> The bigger you get, the more men stare you down.[16]

"Next Aeneas sees the giants [VI.580] and Ixion [VI.601] and Salmoneus [VI.585] all damned to punishment for pride, and Tantalus also [VI.602]. Tantalus is Greek *teantelon* [?te + anta + ethelo]; that is, 'greedy to see,' for avarice is reluctant to use a thing and is fed merely by looking at it."

"But here the judge Rhadamanthus of Cnossos appears [VI.566–77]. Rhadamanthus is Greek *tarematadamonta* [ta rema + ta damonta]—that is, 'ruling the word'—and *gnoso* [gnosis] means 'understand.' That is, he who knows how to control the force of words punishes and denounces pride. Next, Aeneas is frightened by loud noise. That is, the honest man flees the call of pride and fears the punishment meted out to evil men. Then, fixing the golden bough on the sacred doorposts, he enters Elysium. This symbolizes that when the labor of learning is over, one celebrates a perfected memory. Learning is fixed in the memory forever, like the golden bough on the sacred doorposts.

"Aeneas enters the Elysian Fields. *Elisis* [eleusis] is Greek for 'freeing'—that is, after the fear of teachers, life becomes like a holiday. And Proserpine is queen of the Underworld. That is, memory is the queen of knowledge. Extending [*proserpens*] itself, it reigns forever in the liberated mind. The golden bough of learning is dedicated to memory. Concerning memory, Cicero used to say that it was the store-house of knowledge [*de Oratore* I.v.18]."

"In the Elysian Fields Aeneas first sees Musaeus [VI.66]—as it were, 'the gift of the Muses'—exalted above all the rest. Musaeus introduces him to his father Anchises and shows him the river Lethe. He is shown his father to emphasize the need to retain a grave character. He is shown Lethe to bring out the need to forget the levity of youth. And note the name Anchises. Anchises is Greek *ano scenon*—that is, 'living in one's homeland.' There is one God, Father and King of all, dwelling alone on high, who is discovered whenever knowledge points the way. Note what Anchises teaches his son:

> In the beginning an indwelling spirit
> Infused the heavens and the earth
> And the watery plains and the shining orb
> Of the moon and the stars of Titan
> [VI.724–25]

You can see that the creator must be God and that Anchises teaches about the hidden mysteries of nature, and describes the souls returning again and again from life, and reveals the future."

I said: "O truest of Italian bards, how could you have obscured your brilliant genius in the darkness of such a stupid line of defense? When you were writing allegorically in the *Eclogues,* you once said: 'Now a virgin returns and the reign of Saturn returns. / Now a new race is promised by high heaven.' [IV.6] But here, snoring out some sort of Academic tripe while your wit is drowsing, you say: 'Heavenly souls go up to heaven / And then return again to sluggish bodies.' [VI.720] Why did you put blackberries among so many sweet apples and obscure the torch of your brilliant genius?"

Smiling he said: "If I had not mixed something Epicurean in with so many Stoic truths, I would not have been a pagan. No people except you Christians on whom the sun of truth has shone can know all of the truth. But I did not come here to explain your Scripture and argue about what I should have known, but to explain those things that I did know. Now listen to what remains."

"In the seventh book Caieta the nurse is buried [VII.2]—that is, the heavy burden of fear of one's teachers. Caieta means 'forcer of youth.' Among the ancients *caiatio* meant 'the yielding of children.' Thus Plautus in his comedy *Cistolaria* wrote, 'Are you afraid your doxy will not *yield* herself to your arms?' And I made it very plain that Caieta symbolizes discipline when I said, 'Dying you gave eternal fame, O Caieta' [VII.2]. Although the discipline of learning is eventually removed, it passes on the eternal seed of memory."

"Therefore, having buried school matters, Aeneas arrives at his much-desired Ausonia—that is, 'increase of good' toward which the desire of wise men eagerly hastens. *Ausonia* is from *apo tu ausenin* [apo toi auxanein]—that is, 'of increase.' Another explanation is that even at this age the body continues to grow."

"Next he seeks Lavinia as his wife—that is, 'the path of hard work.' About this time of life, everyone chooses labors which increase his worldly advantages. And Lavinia is called the daughter of Latinus, a descendent of Caunus [i.e., Faunus; VII.47]. *Latinus* is from *latitando* [lying in wait] because hard work lies in wait in many different places. *Latona* is from *luna* [moon] because at one time she conceals her upper parts, at another her lower parts and then, at another, is entirely concealed. *Caunus* is *camnonus* [kamno + nous]—that is, mental labor. And Caunus is married to the nymph Marica—that is, *merica* [merimna] or 'counsel.' As Homer says, 'His heart within his shaggy breast was divided in *counsel*' [*Iliad* I.189]."

"In Book VIII Aeneas seeks Evander as an ally. *Evandros* [eo + andros] in Greek is 'good man.' This symbolizes that the perfected individual seeks the companionship of good men. From Evander he hears of the excellence of goodness—that is, the glory of Hercules [VIII.193ff.] and how he slew Cacus, a name [i.e., *kakos*] that means 'evil' among the Latins. Then he puts on the armor of Vulcan [VIII.612ff.]; that is, the protection of the alert intelligence against all the temptations of evil. *Vulcan* is *bulencauton* [boule + kautes], or, as we say, 'ardent wisdom.' All the virtues of the Romans are displayed on this armor because all happiness is either provided by or foreseen through the careful protection of wisdom. To act well is the harbinger of future good, and he who acts well insures good for himself. Thus wisdom both produces good things and can look forward to them."

"In Book IX, assisted by the arms of Vulcan, Aeneas fights Turnus. *Turnus* is *turosnus* [thouros + nous] in Greek—that is, 'raging mind.' The arms of wisdom and intelligence always oppose rage. As Homer says, '[Athena] spoke and led the raging Ares from battle' [*Iliad* V.35]."

"Next Aeneas kills Mezentius, the belittler of the gods [X.907–8]. God ordains all things and commands them to be good. But when the spirit which inhabits the body despises the good it fails in its proper duty and neglects goodness to its own harm. The wise man sallies out to slay wrongdoers and slays Mezentius and his son Lausus [X.815–16]."

"This symbolizes the wise man's conquest of his own soul. And who is said to be the friend of Turnus? Messapus—that is, *misonepos* [misos + epos], which is 'threatening speech' in Latin. As Euripides says in his tragedy of *Iphigenia*, 'Nothing can be described that is so terrible . . .' [*Orestes* 1]."

"After overcoming Messapus, victorious Aeneas gravely balances out the armor of Messapus on the scales and displays his effigy."

"Then Juturna is forced to desist from war [XII.875]. She was driving the chariot of her brother. Juturna symbolizes calamity because calamity always [*diuturne*] threatens. Calamity is the sister of rage. And the chariot of Turnus which she uses to drive him away and save him from death is also calamity because it can cause rage to go on without end."

"First Turnus had Metiscus as his driver. *Metiscos* [methusko] is Greek for 'intoxicated.' Intoxication first produces rage. Then calamity arrives to prolong rage. But while Juturna is said to be eternal, Turnus is mortal. Rage can cease in a short time, but calamity continues forever. And Juturna drives the chariot everywhere—that is, she continues for a long time. The wheels symbolize time. Fortune is said to have a wheel, symbolizing the mutability of time."

The end.

Farewell, my Lord. Read cautiously these thorny outgrowths of my heart.

Here ends the exposition of the content of Vergil according to moral philosophy by the distinguished Fabius Planciadis Fulgentius.

AVERROES

(1126–1198)

INTRODUCTION

Aristotle's *Poetics* was written between 347 and 322 B.C. In view of the prestige which the treatise now enjoys, it often comes as a surprise to the contemporary student of criticism to learn that after Aristotle's death the *Poetics* disappeared almost without trace from the ancient literary scene. Obviously the text must have been copied during the classical and Byzantine periods; otherwise we would have no manuscripts at all. The influence on all later manuscripts of a single source, the eleventh-century manuscript designated Paris 1741, indicates, however, that the manuscript tradition of the Greek *Poetics* is relatively uncomplicated. Evidently there was little demand for the work in antiquity. Efforts to reconstruct the history of the text before the eleventh century have produced tenuous, often contradictory results. The same may be said for efforts to trace the influence of the *Poetics* on post-Aristotelian criticism, such as those made by McMahon, Rostagni, and (most recently) C. O. Brink. If Aristotle's *Poetics* had any influence, it was via two or three intermediaries, which, by warping its thought to fit the prevailing assumptions of rhetorical criticism, obliterated just those qualities that are today considered characteristically Aristotelian. The fragmentary essay *On the Poets* appears to have been far more widely known than the *Poetics,* and Theophrastus, Aristotle's pupil and popularizer, had far more influence on later critical thought than his master.

The version of the *Poetics* that influenced the Middle Ages was not Greek but Arabic. According to the best guesses of Margoliouth and Tkatsch, the source of the Arabic tradition is a Greek manuscript dating before the year 700 and independent of the archetype that is the source of Paris 1741 and its descendents. As translated into Arabic (through Syriac) in the tenth century, this version of the *Poetics* departed widely in vocabulary from the original, and thus initiated the process of assimilating Aristotle by misinterpretation that continued throughout the later Middle Ages.

The next phase in the history of the medieval *Poetics* is the result of the adoption by Arab philosophers of a scheme originally formulated by Alexander of Aphrodisias and other late Greek commentators on Aristotle. According to this scheme, Aristotle divided human knowledge (*scientia,* often translated as "science") into four main branches. First come the instrumental sciences of the *Organon.* These are sciences of technique or "faculties," and they have no "content" in the Aristotelian sense of that term. The other three branches, which *do* have content, are the theoretic (including metaphysics, mathematics, astronomy, and physics), the practical (including politics, economics, and ethics), and the productive (including most professions and crafts). It is the *Organon* that is important for present purposes. Today, scholars agree that the *Organon* is made up of six works; namely, *Categories, On Interpretation, Prior* and *Posterior Analytics, Topics,* and *Sophistic Refutations.* To these six books the late Greek commentators and their Arab disciples added the *Rhetoric* and the *Poetics.* The most influential Arab expression of this theory is the *Catalogue of the Sciences* written by al-Farabi in the tenth century. This work was twice translated into Latin during the twelfth century, first by Gerard of Cremona and second by John of Seville. The theory which it proposes may be called the "context theory" of the *Poetics,* since it arises from the context within which Aristotle was thought to have placed his treatise. To include the *Poetics* in the *Organon* is to assert that it is an essay on method, and that the method itself is a "faculty" without "content." Furthermore, since each of the logical faculties was supposed to be distinguished from the others by its use of a unique logical device, the inclusion of *Poetics* in the *Organon* shifted emphasis from "imitation," the key term in the Greek *Poetics,* to the "device" which differentiates poetry from its sister faculties.

This interpretation ignores imitation, plot, characterization, catharsis, and most of the other subjects stressed by Aristotle in favor of an element—the imaginative syllogism—for which the reader of the Greek text will search in vain. It also ignores the moral "purpose" usually attributed to poetry in the Middle Ages, because to bring in moral questions would be to assign a "content" to poetry—in Aristotelian terms, to treat it as a sub-division of "practical science" rather than of the *Organon.*

The most important Arab student of the *Poetics* was Averroes (Ibn Rushd). Averroes is considered the greatest of the Arab philosophers of the Middle Ages, and he is also the Arab philosopher who most deeply influenced the Latin West. During his long and active career he wrote commentaries on all of Aristotle's major works, and all but two of these were translated into Latin during the scholastic renaissance of the thirteenth century. Medieval interest in the *Poetics* must therefore be understood as a by-product of scholasticism, and in particular, that phase of scholasticism which was a self-conscious revolt against the earlier, Platonizing tradition of medieval thought.

Two key ideas, both of them foreign to Aristotle, run through Averroes' commentary. The first is the notion derived from al-Farabi and Avicenna that poetry is a branch of logic. The second also owes something to earlier Arab commentaries, but its basic source would seem to be the vocabulary of the Arab translation. This is the idea that poetry can be defined as the art of praise and blame. Praise and blame are rhetorical techniques, explained at length in Books I and III of Aristotle's *Rhetoric*. They are brought into the *Poetics* in Chapter 4, where Aristotle asserts the first two forms of poetry were "lampooning verses" and "praises of famous men." Averroes could understand this theory much better than the complex theory of imitation developed in the first three chapters of the *Poetics*. Better still, it seemed consistent with what he knew of the history of Arab poetry, whose early forms tend heavily to invective and encomiastic verse. From this apparent point of contact between the *Poetics* and Arab literary tradition, Averroes moved outward to the genres and function of poetry. Not only did poetry originate in praise and blame, its major forms fall into one or the other category. Epic and tragedy are poems of praise; comedy (by which Averroes means satire) is a form of blame; and ode is a mixed form that employs both techniques. Good poets praise good men in order to lead their readers to virtue, while base poets satirize and vituperate evil men and thus war against vice. This approach, it should be noted, assigns poetry an ethical function and is incompatible (or, at least, hard to reconcile) with the theory that poetry is a branch of logic. Averroes either failed to perceive the conflict or was indifferent to it, for the two theories exist side-by-side in his commentary, and no effort is made to harmonize them.

The Arabic *Poetics* was translated in 1256 by Hermannus Alemannus, a monk living in Toledo. Twenty-three manuscripts of the Hermannus translation survive, and it was printed in 1481, thus becoming the first version of Aristotle's literary theory published during the Renaissance. Its compatibility with medieval critical ideas is attested by the fact that in 1278 William of Moerbeke, Bishop of Corinth, made a remarkably accurate translation from the Greek, which was, however, ignored; William's translation exists in only two manuscripts, both dating from the thirteenth century, and it was not printed until 1953. The obvious moral of this tale is that the late Middle Ages was not prepared to assimilate the *Poetics*. On the other hand, Averroes' commentary was easy to assimilate. The distortions which disconcert the modern reader are the very features which made the work intelligible and attractive to the medieval audience. In effect, it enlisted Aristotle in support of the most characteristic (and most un-Aristotelian) features of medieval poetic theory.

In a preface referring to both the *Rhetoric* and the *Poetics*, Hermannus discusses the placing of these works in Aristotle's system of the sciences and quite explicitly locates the *Poetics* in the *Organon*. To avoid possible confusion, Hermannus cites the two common rival theories of poetry—first, the theory that considered rhetoric and poetry a part of "civil" philosophy, by which he means "practical" or "moral" philosophy; and second, the theory associating poetry with grammar. The first theory, attributed justifiably to Cicero, is the didactic theory, which considers poetry a device of ethical instruction. It is commonplace in medieval criticism, and both Averroes and Hermannus subscribed to it in practice. In his preface, however, Hermannus takes pains to call attention to the *difference* between it and the allegedly Aristotelian theory, which emphasizes technique rather content. The second theory, which Hermannus attributes to Horace, leads to emphasis on the prosodic element of poetry. Classical grammar included the study of syllables and quantity, and hence the study of the various poetic meters. According to the grammarians, the difference between poetry and nonpoetry is the use of meter; and the differences between the various poetic genres are the meters themselves. This inverts the normal relation between form and content. Poetry becomes "heroic," for example, by using dactylic hexameter, and only secondarily by narrating the deeds of noble heroes. In the same way, the essence of elegy is the elegaic distich, of satire and comedy, iambic meter, of the ode, lyric strophes, and so forth. Again, Hermannus explicitly rejects the *ars metrica* in favor of the logical theory attributed to Aristotle and justified by "al-Farabi, Avicenna, Averroes, and various others."

Hermannus' emphasis on the logical "placement" of poetry is apparent from the first section of the commentary where, with the help of hints taken from Chapter 20 of the *Poetics*, poetry is defined in terms of its use of the technical device of *comparison*. The Aristotelian concept of poetry as an imitation of action, human character, and/or nature is replaced by the concept of poetry as the skillful manipulation of similes, metaphors, and analogies.

The relation of poetry to logic continued to be debated until late in the sixteenth century. On the other hand, the theory destined to have the greatest influence on later critics is the one which is dominant in the Averroes commentary. This is the theory of praise and blame. Returning to Averroes' discussion of Chapter 1 of the *Poetics*, we find that the initial definition of poetry, offered as a quotation from Aristotle himself, is as follows: "Aristotle says: Every poem and all poetic speech are either blame or praise (*aut vituperatio aut laudatio*). And this is evident from examination of poems themselves, especially the poems which are concerned with matters of choice, either honest or base." The passage is, of course, not in the *Poetics.* Like the definition of imitation, it is an interpolation required to reconcile the text with the presuppositions of the commentator. Unlike that definition, however, it has some Aristotelian precedent. Averroes has transposed the notion that the original poetic forms were encomia and lampooning verses from Chapter 4 to Chapter 1 and converted it from an observation about primitive poems to a categorical assertion about poetry in general.

The praise-blame theory was attractive to Averroes for two reasons. First of all, it furnished a point of contact between Arab and Greek poetry. Second, it justified poetry by making it an instrument of moral instruction. These ideas are combined in a comment on Chapter 2 of the *Poetics*, where, after remarking that the Greeks had many excellent poems of praise, Averroes adds, "Children should be brought up to read those poems which incite and incline one to acts of fortitude and magnificence. In their poems the Arabs treat only these two virtues, although they do not incite to these virtues because they are good in themselves but because they are a means of attaining honor and glory." The didactic motive is also reflected in an interpretation of Aristotle's "objects of imitation" as virtue and vice.

The exotic combination of additions, transposed passages, and warped interpretations continues in the later sections of the commentary. According to Aristotle, the *Iliad* anticipates tragedy in its seriousness, its sustained plot, and its emphasis on dialogue, while the *Margites* antcipates comedy by dramatizing "the ludicrous" rather than continuing the earlier Greek tradition of personal satire. Because he knew neither Homer nor Greek drama, Averroes failed completely to understand these distinctions. (His problems are portrayed amusingly but sympathetically in Jorge Luis Borges' short story "Averroes' Search.") Homer, he says, "established the first principles of these arts, and there was no one before him whose achievement either in praise or blame had anything worth mentioning." Tragedy is defined simply as the "*ars laudandi*"—the art of praising, while comedy is "*ars vituperandi*"—the art of rebuking "not only everything that is bad, but what is despicable and almost beyond cure; that is, what is base and almost worthless." If this not only misses but inverts Aristotle's thoughts about the geniality that Homer introduced into comic tradition, it also wholly ignores the distinction between dramatic and narrative form. We are reminded here of the medieval habit, illustrated in the work of Dante, Lydgate, and Chaucer among others, of referring to narrative poems as "comedies" or "tragedies." Averroes' commentary did not create this misconception but may well have encouraged it. Benvenuto da Imola, for example, found that the Averroes commentary provided just the theory needed to explain the organization of Dante's *Comedy*.

Needless to say, the confusion of the commentary concerning poetic form produces a distorted interpretation of the six "parts" of tragedy listed by Aristotle in *Poetics* 6. Plot becomes *sermo fabularis;* character *consuetudines,* a category that includes both actions and morals; thought becomes *credulitas;* diction *metrum;* song *tonus;* and spectacle something called *consideratio,* by which Averroes seems to mean the gestures and facial expressions used by orators to emphasize their arguments. Equally characteristic, the concepts of probability and necessity are interpreted morally, with the surprising result that the poet is denied the right to create fictions: "And it is evident from what has been said about poetic speeches that representations that are based on lies are not proper to the poet's work." Again, reversal is treated not as a sudden change in the action of a work but as a shift in poetic technique from praise to blame or vice versa.

As a final example of Averroes' misinterpretation of Aristotle, we can turn to his comments on *Poetics* 12, which deals with the Greek terms used to designate the structure of tragedy—parode, episode, stasimon, and the like. Averroes solves the problem by substituting terms from rhetoric:

> [Aristotle] mentions in this discussion the parts that are proper to Greek poems. Of these, the parts that are found in Arab poems are three. First comes the part that resembles the exordium of rhetoric. It is the part where the Arabs speak of houses and noble buildings and of ruins and remains. . . . And the second is the praise proper; and the third is the part that is like the rhetorical conclusion. And this third part is usually either an invocation or petition to the man being praised, or a commendatory section praising the value of the poem itself.

This is an outline of the contents of the classic Arabic ode form, the *quasīda.* Its chief significance, however, is its suggestion that the formulas of rhetoric for organizing speeches are equally applicable to literature. This would doubtless have seemed a gratifying confirmation of what many Latin readers of the commentary already believed. The original passage in the *Poetics,* conversely, would have been as unintelligible to them as to Averroes.

References to the Averroes commentary begin almost immediately after its translation into Latin. Roger Bacon referred to the translation of "master Hermannus" with qualified approval, and a fourteenth-century manuscript of what appear to be lecture notes on the commentary has recently been discovered by Professor William Boggess of the University of Georgia. The first critic to make extensive use of the commentary may have been Benvenuto da Imola, one of the fourteenth-century commentators on Dante. Benvenuto knew the Hermannus translation well. Confidently claiming "Aristotle's authority" for his definition, he asserts that "it is manifest to whoever contemplates the forces of poetry . . . that all poetic discourse is either praise or blame." Later he cites Averroes rather than Aristotle to support the idea that poetry is morally edifying. Evidently, he considered both writers equally authoritative and did not differentiate between them.

Benvenuto's general acknowledgment is complemented by his analysis of the structure of the *Divine Comedy.* It is, he believes, a poem fully in accord with Aristotle's rules. The *Inferno* is a work based on "blame." It consists of a series of vignettes showing the ugliness of vice and its terrible consequences. It thus warns the reader to reform. After the *Inferno* comes the first of two "reversals" of the sort advocated by Averroes. The *Inferno* stresses unhappiness, the despair of the damned. In the *Purgatory* the tone abruptly changes to hope. The *Purgatory* contains some "blame"; but however wicked, the characters in this section have redeeming qualities which are "praised" by Dante. The second reversal comes at the beginning of the *Paradiso*. Here the tone changes from hope to joyful fulfillment, and the technique from a mixture of blame and praise to unqualified praise of men of preeminent virtue whom the reader is encouraged to emulate. As Benvenuto remarks, "no other poet ever knew how to praise or blame with more excellence. . . . [Dante] honored virtue with encomia and lacerated vice and vicious men."

Although Benvenuto's commentary was known in the sixteenth century, he remains primarily a medieval figure. It is significant that the next critic to be influenced by the Averroes commentary is Coluccio Salutati. Salutati is the most famous of Petrarch's disciples and was regarded during the sixteenth century as a full-fledged humanist. Among his many works, his allegorical interpretation of the life of Hercules, *De Laboribus Herculis*, is especially significant. It stands midway between Boccaccio's *Genealogy of the Gentile Gods* and the allegorized mythologies of such sixteenth-century writers as Comes (or Conti) and Cartari. The first book of the *De Laboribus* is a little "art of poetry," in which Salutati offers a theory that in parts may be accurately described as Averroes expanded and ornamented by examples from the Latin classics. In Chapter 2 Salutati attempts to differentiate between rhetoric and poetic. This is difficult because, following Averroes, he believes that the two disciplines share the same "matter"—that is, praise and blame. They are eventually distinguished by the assertion that poetry is (1) in meter (an echo of the *ars metrica*) and (2) employs "imaginative and figurative discourse," an idea derived from Averroes' definition of imitation. Later, the tired classical definition of the orator as *vir bonus dicendi peritus*—the good man skilled in speaking—is reworked to apply to the poet, who is called a *vir optimus laudandi vituperandique peritus*—a perfect man skilled in praise and blame. Even Horace is assimilated into the system. The "delight and instruct" formula from the *Ars Poetica* is explained in the following way: "The reprehension of vice may profit right away, but does not immediately please; praise pleases but does not immediately profit. Therefore blame is primarily for utility, praise for pleasure; although in a secondary way the former may please and the latter profit." As is appropriate for a forward-looking humanist, Salutati compliments modern poets on their ability to "celebrate virtue and criticize vice" in the way prescribed in "[Aristotle's] little book."

Averroistic ideas remained attractive during the sixteenth century, although they were occasionally attacked and more frequently disguised by an increasingly heavy overlay of erudition. Savonarola, Robortello, Segni, Maggi and Lombardi, and Mazzoni all debate the "placing" of poetry among the sciences and all decide that poetic is at least in part a branch of logic. Pietro Vettori was not only aware of Averroes, he edited the commentary for the Giunta "Aristotle" of 1552, eight years before composing his own analysis of the *Poetics*. Almost every one of these writers cites the Averroes commentary directly and with respect, often to buttress his own position. As late as 1575, in fact, Alessandro Piccolomini appealed to "the authority of Averroes which has always had great force with me" to refute Robortello's theory of the origin of poetry. Throughout the sixteenth century, it may be added, the didactic theory of poetry existed side-by-side in rather uncomfortable proximity with more precisely Aristotelian doctrines. The fact is that the *Poetics* was difficult to accommodate to the moralistic attitudes of the humanists, whereas Aristotle as interpreted by Averroes is not only moral but oppressively so. In the early part of the century, before the publication of the great commentaries on the *Poetics*, the problem was not fully understood. Aulo Parrasio, for example, was responsible for the first of many efforts to harmonize Horace with Aristotle. His "Commentary on the *Ars Poetica*" appeared posthumously in 1531. Although one reference in the commentary seems to be to the Greek *Poetics,* the remainder of his allegedly Aristotelian principles are evidently quotations or paraphrases from Hermannus Alemannus. Obviously, such an approach became increasingly difficult as time went by. The tension between didacticism and Aristotelian criticism finally became an open break in Lodovico Castelvetro's *Poetica d'Aristotele vulgarizzata et sposta*, published in 1570. Although Castelvetro himself radically distorted the *Poetics*, his interpretation is free of the influence of Averroes. For this reason, he was viewed with suspicion by his great humanistic contemporary Torquato Tasso. In the *Discorsi del poema eroico,* published in 1594, Tasso attacked Castelvertro's rather hardheaded view that praise is irrelevant to heroic poetry. "Without doubt," Tasso wrote, "Castelvetro erred when he said that praise is not appropriate to the heroic poem, because if the heroic poet were to celebrate virtue, he would have to exalt it clear up to the heavens with his praises. On the other side, St. Basil says that Homer's *Iliad* is nothing but a praise of virtue, and Averroes has the same opinion in his commentary on poetry, and Plutarch too. . . . Therefore, leaving aside the followers of Castelvetro in their ignorance, let us follow the opinions of . . . St. Basil, of Averroes, of Plutarch, and of Aristotle himself."

In the last decade of the sixteenth century, in other words, the most eloquent spokesman of Italian humanism found Averroes not only worthy of citing, but in some respects more truly Aristotelian than the most informed student of the *Poetics* that the age produced.

The translation which follows is my own. The Roman numerals inserted in the translation are my suggestion (sometimes my guess) as to what chapter in the *Poetics* Averroes may be referring. For bibliography, see especially pp. 488–89.

(It is worth noting that Averroes uses several terms which are roughly equivalent to Greek *mimesis* and English "imitation." Among these are *assimilatio, representatio,* and *imitatio.* Although these terms are frequently used in doublets and even triplets, they are presumably not exact synonyms. In general I have translated *imitatio* as "imitation," *representatio as* "representation," and *assimilatio* as "likening." In spite of obvious drawbacks, this strategy recognizes (a) the difference between *imitatio* and *assimilatio,* and (b) the tendency of Averroes to view poetic imitation as the making of poetic images, as well as the process of representing characters and actions in poetry.)

THE MIDDLE COMMENTARY OF AVERROES OF CORDOVA ON THE *POETICS* OF ARISTOTLE

Hermannus Alemannus says: After finishing my translation of the *Rhetoric* of Aristotle with no small labor, wishing to set my hand to his *Poetics,* I encountered such great diffculty because of the diversity of the system of writing poetry in Greek and Arabic and because of the difficulty of the vocabulary and for many other reasons that I did not trust myself to be able to make a full translation of this work for Latin-speaking readers. Therefore I chose the commentary of Averroes on this work by Aristotle. The commentary explains what Averroes could understand of the *Poetics.* And I translated the commentary as well as I could into Latin.

Considerable aid in understanding the *Poetics* is provided by the *Ars Poetica* of Horace, just as Cicero's writings on rhetoric aid in understanding Aristotle's theory of rhetoric. Let the studious receive this translation if they will and rejoice that in it they have the completion of Aristotle's thought about logic.

Here begins the commentary of Averroes on the *Poetics* of Aristotle.

Averroes says: My intention in this work is to determine what is contained in Aristotle's *Poetics* concerning the universal rules of poetry common to all nations or most. Much of what is said in this book either deals with rules proper to Greek poems and Greek conventions or is not found in Arabic or is found in different forms.

[Chapter I] Aristotle says: My purpose is to discuss the art of poetry and the kinds of poem. Properly, one who wishes the rules of this art to proceed in an orderly sequence, should discuss first what each kind of poetry does, and the elements from which poetic compositions are formed, and how many subjects poetry has. Aristotle rightly concentrates on this material in his treatise and begins with those first principles that are natural to us in this subject.

Aristotle says: Every poem and all poetry are either blame or praise. This is apparent from examination of poems and the subjects that are proper to them which deal with matters of choice, both good and bad. This holds true for the arts of representation that follow the lead of poetry, like lyre or harp music or flute or pipe music and dancing, for these arts are adapted by nature to these two subjects. Poetry is based on image-making. There are three kinds of image-making or "likening"—two simple and one composite. The first of the simple forms is "likening" of one thing to another and the comparison of the first to the second. This is done in all languages by words proper to them, like the Latin words *quasi* [like] and *sicut* [as] and similar expressions called "particles of comparison"—

or else through the use of the thing which is "like" together with the thing to which it has "likeness" or in place of it. And in the art of poetry this is called a trope. For example, a certain poet[1] wrote concerning a man who was extremely generous, *He is a sea everywhere flooding the emptiness of those who approach him, and filling it in a copious tide.*

You should know that this category includes forms which the moderns call analogy and metaphor. For example, *the meadow smiles* or *he plows the sand* [i.e. "he labors in vain"]; and, as a poet[2] writes, *There are mares that in their youth reject the saddle and bridle, and female camels that cannot bear saddle bags.* And metaphors can very properly be called tropes on attributes or characteristics of a thing.

An analogy is a trope based on proportion. For example, when *a* is related to *b* as *c* is to *d*, then the word for *c* can be used for *a* and vice versa. The varieties of these tropes have already been treated in the *Rhetoric.*

The second of the two simple types is when the "likening" is reversed, as when you say, *the sun is like a woman* or *the sun is a woman*—not *this woman is like the sun* or *this woman is the sun.* The third kind is a composite of these two simple types.

Aristotle says: Certain men naturally imagine humans and represent them in actions—for example some men make representations using colors and shapes and sounds, and this either through art or habit on the part of the imitators themselves or through long-established artistic conventions. By the same token, some men are naturally drawn to representation by speech.

Image-making and representation in poetry involves three elements: harmony and rhythm, and likening. Each of these elements is sometimes found by itself and without another—as sound in pipe or flute music, and rhythm in dance. And representation or imitation occurs in language alone—that is, in representational or imaginative speeches composed without meter or rhythm. And sometimes all three elements are combined.

This occurs among the Arabs in the so-called "song" [i.e. the Mozarabic folkforms, *muwashshahah* and *ghazal*] recently discovered or invented by the inhabitants of this region [Spain] in their own language, that is, Arabic. This form of poem developed naturally and uses two elements [words and music] together. Natural forms are only discovered by peoples living close to nature. Indeed, *symphonia*, or rhyme, used not to exist in Arab poems—only meter by itself or meter with representation.

And since this was the case, there were three imaginative arts which created the imaginative effect: the art of rhyme, the art of meter, and the art of making representational speeches. This is the part of the art of logic with which this book [the *Poetics*] deals.

Aristotle says: Often we find compositions which are called poetry but which have no poetic invention except meter, like the compositions of

Socrates and the works of Empedocles on natural philosophy, in contrast to what is contained in the poems of Homer. In Homer's poems one finds both elements [representation and meter] together.

Aristotle says: Therefore no work can be properly called a poem unless it contains these two elements. The others are better called "this or that composition" than poems. Likewise the author of metrical works on natural philosophy should be called a "discursive author" rather than a poet. Also, imaginative speeches which include mixed meters are not poems. Aristotle observes that poems are found among the Greeks using rhythm or mixed meters. This, however, is not found among the Arabs.

It is now clear from what has been said how many manners of representation there are and from what arts representational works in language are composed so that the effect is achieved.

[Ch. II] Aristotle says: Since imitators and makers of likenesses wished through their art to impel people toward certain choices and discourage them from others, they had to treat subjects that, being represented, would suggest either virtues or vices. All action and character are concerned with one of these two—that is, virtue or vice. It necessarily follows that good and virtuous men represented only virtues and virtuous men; while bad men represented evil and evil men. Since all "likening" and representation occurs through showing the proper or the improper or base, it is evident that representation aims at nothing but the encouragement of what is proper and the rejection of what is base. Necessarily, then, there are imitators of virtue—that is, men who naturally incline to representing the more virtuous and better sorts of men—and imitators of evil, who are less perfect and nearer to evil men. From these two kinds of men, praise and blame arose—that is, praise of good men and blame of bad ones.

And because of this certain poets are especially adept at praise but not at blame. And conversely certain poets are adept at blame but not at praise. Moreover these two different approaches—that is, commendation of good and criticism of what is base—run through all imitative poetry. But these two differences are only found in the arts of "likening" and representation that use language—not in representation using meter or rhyme alone. And there are three types of poetry of "likening." First, there is "likening" which compares one thing to another, which is comparable, without showing virtue or vice, and aiming only at accuracy. This kind of "likening" is capable, as it were, of being modified and varied toward either of the two extremes. That is, it is sometimes used to show goodness through strong emphasis in this direction, and sometimes modified to show badness by a similar use of emphasis.

Aristotle says: This was the practice of Homer, whose "accurate likening" is used to express goodness and badness. The excellence of certain writers consists in accuracy alone, and of others in showing goodness and badness, and of others in the combination of both, as is the case for Homer. Aristotle gives examples of each kind of poetry, citing poets who were famous or notable among the Greeks and are in their histories and used each of the three manners of "likening" [i.e., accuracy, emphasis on good, emphasis on evil.]

It will not be hard for you to find examples of these in Arab poems, although as al-Farabi says, most Arab poems are simply intended to give pleasure. The sort of poem they call "elegy" is nothing but an incitement to sexual intercourse, which they hide and disguise under the name of love. Therefore children should be kept from reading such poems and instructed and exercised in poems that incite and encourage acts of fortitude and generosity. Indeed, in their songs the Arabs incite readers to these two virtues alone out of all the virtues. They do not do this simply for the sake of virtue but because through fortitude and generosity one achieves supreme honor and glory.

The kind of poetry which seeks only accuracy is common in Arab songs. Often they describe the properties and characteristics of metals and other minerals and even of things that grow in the earth and of animals. The Greeks do not often include such things in their poems except insofar as they contribute to the object of teaching readers to seek virtues or avoid vices or of instructing them in various other kinds of good that can be done or known.

From this passage in the *Poetics* it is clear that there are three kinds of "likening" and three differences. It is also clear what the three differences and three kinds are. And when one considers various poems it seems clear that there is no fourth kind of "likening" and no fourth difference among the kind.

[Ch. IV] Aristotle says: There seem to be two causes in human nature for the origin of poetry. First, the tendency to liken one thing to another and to represent one thing by another exists naturally in man from birth. Indeed, this tendency to liken and represent is found even in infants. This tendency is proper to man in contrast to the other animals. And the reason is that only man, among all the other animals is delighted by "likening" things that he has perceived in his mind, and by their representation and imitation. A sign of this—that is, that man naturally enjoys and rejoices in "likening"—is that we are delighted and rejoice in representations of certain things that did not delight us when we perceived them directly. We are especially delighted when the representation very artfully expresses the thing represented, as happens with the images of many animals, represented by skilled sculptors and painters. This is why we use examples in teaching—so that what we say can be more easily understood through use of the power of images. For the mind will grasp a subject more perfectly when it experiences the delight arising from examples. And learning is not only for philosophers but is for all men, who share in this to some degree with philosophers.

Learning proceeds naturally from one man to another in the way that a teacher is related to a pupil. Since examples are nothing but likenesses of things which have already been perceived in the mind, it is clear that they are used simply to make understanding what is said more rapid and more easy. They make understanding more rapid because of the pleasure of the image of the thing that they represent. And this is the first cause for the origin of poetry.

The second is the pleasure that man naturally takes in meter and melody. Concerning melody, it appears to be adapted to the meter by those who have a natural talent for hearing and judging melody and meter. Thus the natural pleasure of the soul in representation and meter and melody was the cause of the invention of the art of poetry—and specifically, by men who had a special natural talent for it.

As soon as people began to gather together and formed a social group, the art of poetry began to develop among them. The development was gradual, however. At first they discovered a small part of it, and then another part, until at length the art attained perfection. Also the kinds of poetry reached perfection according to the capacity of various types of men for greater or lesser delight in this or that kind of poetic song.

In addition, virtuous and noble souls naturally first discovered the art of songs praising and reciting beautiful and excellent deeds. Less noble souls discovered songs blaming and denigrating base and immoral deeds. However, the poet who intends to denigrate evil men and deeds must approve and praise good men and good and virtuous deeds so that by this means evil and ignoble deeds can be more fully revealed—i.e., so that when the poet has narrated bad deeds he has placed the opposite sort next to them.

This, then, is what is contained in the chapter [*Poetics* IV] concerning things that are common to all nations or most. The rest of what Aristotle says in it is all or mostly about matters that are proper to the poems of the Greeks and their poetic conventions. He defines the kinds of poetry that were written by the Greeks, and what natural origin and beginning each one had, and which of the parts preceded the other in its appearance, and especially the art of praise and blame, which was very highly regarded among the Greeks. He also tells who first began each of the standard kinds of poetry and who added to them and who perfected them. And in this chapter he especially praises Homer, noting that he provided the first principles of these kinds and that there was no one before him who achieved anything worth mentioning in the art of praise or the art of blame or any of the other poetic kinds known to the Greeks.

Aristotle says: The more defective and briefer kinds of verse came first in time because in the beginning human nature understood them more easily. "Briefer" refers to the kind of verse that is made up of few syllables. And "defective" refers to poetry that has few melodies or sections.

Aristotle says: A sign that these kinds of verse came first and first revealed themselves to men's souls is that, in arguments, the speakers often use half a verse of a poem for the sake of rapidity and leave off the other half, wishing to make their arguments brief. In my opinion, he is referring to what lawyers frequently do when they argue, as when they say, "No, no, no," raising their voice during this. And when they say, "This is not so," also raising and increasing the volume of their voice. Negative responses of this sort are close to being half-verses having melody and meter. But fuller and more complete verses did not appear until later, as happens also in other arts.

[Ch. V] Aristotle says: The art of blame seeks to represent not all that is evil, but what is debased and almost diseased; that is, what is so abject that it is almost beyond cure.

Aristotle says: The sign that these three elements should be present in evil that is almost beyond cure or despicable is that in the face of the despicable man these three elements appear. That is, a wrinkled and ugly expression, a contemptible disposition, and a lack of desire to improve. And the same is true, given the different emotion, of the face of an angry man. That is, the expression is twisted, there is certain narrow-mindedness, and there is a vehemence like fire against the man who offered the provocation.

Aristotle says: Excellent poems of praise [i.e., the epic] use a lengthy, not a short meter. Therefore later writers rejected the brief meter used formerly in this art and in other kinds of poetry. The most proper kind of meter is uniform, not mixed. But it is most important that this not lead to tedious lengthiness. And the end in respect to content—that is, what makes the content of the art of praise meaningful—is that it should be the likeness and representation of a complete virtuous act of choice which has universal application to virtuous activities and not a particular application to an individual instance of virtue. I add, a representation which arouses in the soul certain passions which move it to pity or fear or to other like passions which the representation arouses and stimulates by what it makes virtuous men imagine about virtue and corruption. Representation does not deal with dispositions that follow virtue because of wise habits and the like [i.e., when will is not involved], for one cannot represent these things in images.

Representation in language is completed when melody and meter are joined to it. Reciters of songs have other abilities, in addition to those which are found in meter and language, which make the language more representational—that is, movements of the head and changes of expression, as has already been explained in the *Rhetoric*.

The first of the parts of the art of praise is to express [in words] noble concepts through which imaginative stimulation occurs. Then those concepts are enhanced by melody and meter appropriate to what is being expressed. The melody of the poem prepares the soul to receive images of the thing represented. The melody makes the soul receptive and thus sensitive to the likeness and representation of the thing whose likeness is intended. Indeed, the melody proper to each kind of poem shapes the soul in a way appropriate to each kind through its harmony and composition. Thus we find that a sharp or acute tone fits a kind of speech for which a "heavy" tone is inappropriate. This is the opinion we should have about harmony and meter and their composition.

The impressions created by those who recite and represent and enhance the imaginative content of the poetic speeches themselves (which contain three elements—that is, likeness and rhythm and melody) are two in number. The first is the impression of character and habit—as when one recites the speech of an intelligent man or the speech of a wrathful man. The second is the impression of human belief or opinion. For the impression made by a man who speaks from factual certainty is different from the impression made by a man who is uncertain when he speaks. The impression made in reciting and representing speech in tragedy should be the impression and image of one who is certain, not doubtful, and saying serious, not playful things. Such speech resembles the speech of men of the finest character, thought, and actions. It is the impression of the deeds and fortunes of men like this that those who give [tragic] recitations must create.

And fables which involve likening and representation or imitation are imitative works conveying the two impressions just mentioned. I refer to a fable composed of material whose representation is based on either what the material truly is in itself, or on the material as it is conventionally feigned in poetry, even though it is a fiction. This is why poetic speeches are called "fables."

Reciters and enunciators, to sum up the matter, are men who have the ability to represent human character and belief [i.e., thought].

[Ch. VI] Aristotle says: In tragedy, that is, the art of praise, there should be six parts. These are: representational speeches in the form of fables [i.e., plot]; character; meter or accent; belief [i.e., thought]; deliberation; and melody. A sign of this is that all poetic speech is divided into the "likening" and the means by which the "likening" is expressed. And there are three parts through which "likening" is expressed—representation, meter, and melody. And there are three parts which are "likened" in the poetry of praise, character, belief, and deliberation. Deliberation is proof of the truth of a belief.

Thus there are six parts of tragedy. The most important parts of this song of praise are character and belief. Tragedy is not an imitation of men in themselves as they are perceived individually, but is a representation of their honest characters and praiseworthy actions and praiseworthy beliefs. And character includes actions and moral attitudes. Therefore character is one of the six parts, and therefore action and morals are included in this part.

"Deliberation" is the demonstration of the rightness of the belief which makes a man praiseworthy. It is not found at all in the poems of the Arabs, but it is found in legal speeches. And three things—that is, character and belief and signification—are represented by the three means by which representation occurs—that is, imaginative speech and meter and melody.

Aristotle says: The parts of spoken fable [i.e., plot] which make it representational are two in number. All representation either defines itself through representation of its contrary and is then changed to its proper intention—this is the technique that the Greeks call "indirection" [i.e., reversal]—or else it presents the thing itself making no mention of its contrary—and they called this "signification" [i.e., discovery]. The part which is, as it were, the principal and fundamental one of the six is representational speech used in fable [i.e., plot]. The second part is character. In early times representation concentrated on character—that is, it concentrated on the thing represented. And representation or imitation is indeed the main prop and foundation in the art because there is no delight in mentioning a subject without representing it. But there is delight and stimulus when it has been represented. Therefore we are usually not delighted by seeing the form of something existing in nature, but we are delighted by its representation and image in drawings and colors. This is why men practice the arts of painting and description.

The third part of tragedy is belief. This is the power to represent a thing as it is or is not. This resembles what we seek in rhetoric when we assert that a thing exists or does not exist, except that rhetoric does this through persuasive speech and poetry through representational speech—and this sort of representation is also found in legal speeches.

Aristotle says: The makers of the laws of Sparta were content to strengthen belief in the minds of the citizens by poetic speech; while later men began to travel the road of rhetoric.

The difference between poetic speech which depicts and influences belief and poetic speech which depicts and influences character is that the speech that influences character impels us to perform and do something or to reject and withdraw from it. But speech which influences belief only influences us to believe that something exists or does not exist, not to seek it or reject it.

The fourth part is the meter or rhythm. The perfection of this part is to be appropriate to the purpose or intention. At times a certain rhythm is appropriate to one purpose and not to another. The fifth part, in order, is melody. It is the most important part for impressing and moving the soul.

The sixth part is deliberation—that is, argument or proof, not using persuasive speech, of the correctness of belief or action. Persuasive speech is not involved in the poetic art nor is it appropriate. The poetic art uses representational speech. Indeed, the poetic art—and especially tragedy—does not consist of logical arguments or philosophical speculation. Therefore the poem of praise does not use the techniques of gesture or of facial expression as they are employed in rhetoric.

Aristotle says: The philosophic art which shows or teaches from what and how poems are composed is more important and more perfect than the making of poems themselves. Every theoretical art which includes under itself the techniques for performing its tasks is more worthy than the techniques which are included in it.

[Ch. VII] Since we have said what tragedy is and from what it is composed and how many parts it has and what they are, let us now speak of the matters which lend excellence and goodness to those elements from which poetry arises. We must speak of these things in respect to tragedy and the other forms of poetry, for they are, as it were, the first causes and basis of existence of these forms.

The principles from which arts arise are of two kinds. Some are necessary and others provide completion or adornment.

We may say, then, that tragedy should achieve the end appropriate to its purpose—that is, it should attain through 'likening' and representation the end which its nature permits it to attain. Several factors make this happen. First, what is intended should have a certain definite magnitude so that it is whole and complete. Now that is whole and complete which has a beginning, middle, and end. The beginning precedes the main subject and must not be mixed with the things to which it is a beginning. The end follows those things to which it is an ending and must not precede them. The middle follows and precedes. The middle is better than the two extremes, since it occupies a position between what precedes and what follows. In war the bravest men occupy the same position—that is, the middle position between the cowards and bold and rash men. This is the middle place, and for this reason excellence in composition is in the middle and the middle is derived from the extremes and the extremes are not derived from it. Nor should the middle be merely the middle in respect to composition and location, but also in magnitude and excellence. When this happens the poetic subject will have a beginning, middle, and end, and each one of the parts will have an appropriate size. Likewise, the whole composed of these parts will have a definite size and will not be indeterminate.

Excellence in composition arises from two factors. One is arrangement and the other is magnitude—for we do not say, when discussing the general characteristics of things, that a very small animal is excellent or beautiful.

Arrangement in poetic speech is like arrangement in lecturing. That is, if the lecture is shorter than it should be, it hinders understanding; and if it is too long, it is difficult to retain and encourages the learner to be forgetful. In this respect arrangement is like one's stance when observing the appearance of something visible. The view is good when there is a proper distance between the observer and the object—neither too close nor too far.

What happens in teaching also happens in poetic speeches. That is, if the poem of praise is briefer and more compressed than the subject demands, it will not include all the praise that the subject warrants; and if it is too long, its parts will not be retained in the memory of the audience, and as they hear the last parts they will forget the first ones.

Rhetorical speeches used in controversy as confirmation or refutation do not have a size naturally determined. This is why men needed to measure the time of an argument between adversaries by water clocks, as was the custom among the Greeks, who chiefly used enthymemes; or by sundials as is our custom, since in our legal wrangles we employ much material extrinsic to the argument in order to bolster our credibility. If tragedy consisted of argumentative speech, men would need to measure the time of the dispute either by water clocks or some other device; but since this is not the case, the poetic art should have a natural limit as do the magnitudes of things existing in nature. All living things, if they are not impeded in their growth by some unfortunate accident, reach a magnitude defined by nature, and this should be true of poetic speeches and especially the two kinds of representation that employ either change from representing the contrary of a thing to the thing itself, or direct representation of the thing without reference to its contrary.

[Ch. VIII] Aristotle says: If the composition of a poem is to be excellent and attractive it should not be drawn out by mention of all the things that happened to the single subject that the poem depicts. Many things happened to a single subject, and likewise, many actions are found in the same subject.

Aristotle says: And it seems that not all poets concentrated on a single subject. Rather, they skipped from subject to subject and did not concentrate on the same material—all, that is, except Homer.

You find this frequently in the poems of the Arabs, both in the new or modern poems [*muwashshahah, ghazal*]; and especially in their songs of praise [*quasīda*], when they have any subject to praise, like an energetic horse or a precious sword, they digress from the subject at hand and waste much time in praising whatever subject presents itself.

And to sum things up, art in this should imitate nature; that is, whatever is done should be done according to a single subject and a single end. This being so, it follows that "likening" and representation should have unity; and the subject treated through them should be one; and the parts should have a definite magnitude. And there should be a beginning, middle, and end, and the middle should be best, since matters which depend on arrangement for their unity—and also the excellence derived from proper arrangement—will not achieve their potential effect if they are not properly organized.

[Ch. IX] Aristotle says: It is clear from what has been said about the object of poetic speeches that representations which are false and made up are not part of the poet's work. These compositions are called proverbial tales and exemplary tales, as, for example, the stories in Aesop's book and similar fabulous writings. It is the poet's task to speak only of things that exist or may exist. Such things are presented as desirable or to be avoided or as accurate likenesses, as was observed in the chapter on representation. The composition of proverbs and fables is not the work of poets, although men compose proverbial tales and fables and such things in meter. Although they use meter, the effect of both proverbial tales and fables is achieved through the stories themselves as they would be even if meter were not used. They convey a kind of instruction in prudence. The poet does not contribute to the achievement of this effect by stimulating the imagination, only by meter. The maker of made-up proverbial tales and fables invents or feigns individual things which obviously do not really exist and gives them names. But the poet only gives names to things that exist. And at times poets speak in universal terms. Therefore the art of poetry is closer to philosophy than is the art of making up proverbial tales. And this is what Aristotle says about Greek poetry that imitates nature and about the poetry of societies living close to nature.

Aristotle says: In the art of praise or tragedy one should be sure that most of the things on which the imitative representation is based are things that exist in nature, not things that are made up or imaginary, with made-up names. For the poems are intended to influence voluntary choices. When their actions are possible and like real actions, their persuasive power stimulates the soul more deeply—that is, it arouses the poetic belief that moves the soul to seek something or reject it. In tragedy names are never given or made up for things that do not exist in nature—or only rarely—as, for example, when poets treat generosity as though it were a person and then attribute to this person actions proper to a generous man and represent him and write poem after poem in his praise. And if this is at times effective and no small help because of the similarity of the actions and passions of such a made-up subject to things existing in nature, it is not therefore proper to rely on such devices in tragedy. For this kind of imaginative stimulation is not what appeals to most people. Rather, most people deride it and attack or revile it. And among the Arabs the poetic excellence discussed in this chapter can be seen in the lines of al-Asa, although they do not incite to virtue:

> Because of my life many eyes have gazed
> At the light of a fire
> Burning on the mountain-tops.
> So that two cold eyes passing the night in its brilliance
> Grew warm from its radiance.

Given these facts, it is clear that the poet is not a poet except through the making of fables [i.e., plots] and meters or rhythms with a magnitude sufficient to produce likenesses and imitative representations. And the poet only uses "likening" for matters relating to choice that exist in nature. And it is his task to imitate and represent not only what exists, but also what people think can possibly exist. He is a poet in this latter function no less than when he treats things that exist. Nothing prevents him from treating those things as he treats things that exist today. This sort of invented fable is not lacking in poetic stimulation of the imaginaton.

The skilled or perfect poet does not need to enhance his representation through extrinsic aids like dramatic gestures and facial expressions. Only those who parade as poets (although they are really not poets) use these devices. True poets only use such devices when they wish, through this, to show up the practice of false poets. They do not use these devices against skillful poets.

At times perfect poets are forced by place and time to aid themselves by using devices that are extrinsic or outside of the basic elements of poetry. This is because imitation is not always of complete things whose imitation can be definite and complete, but also of incomplete things whose imitation in language is difficult. Aid in imitating these subjects is therefore provided by extrinsic devices—especially when the imitation involves belief. It is difficult to make the reader imagine things that are neither actions nor substances.

Sometimes extrinsic devices are mixed with poetic images. If this happens by chance and without being planned it is a marvel, since that which occurs because of chance is marvelous by its very nature.

[Ch. X] Aristotle says: The excellence of many poetic speeches consists in simple imitation not having much variation. And there are many whose excellence consists in variation of the "likening" and imitation. The same thing holds true in other activities, for certain activities are performed in a simple, single action, and some require complex actions. This is true in imitation or representation. Simple imitation is a form that uses one of the two ways of presenting the material —that is, either the one called "indirection" [i.e., reversal] or the one called "directness" or "direct presentation" [i.e., discovery].

A mixed imitation is one that uses both kinds—that is, it can begin with "indirection" and proceeds to "directness" or it can begin with "directness" and proceed to "indirectness." The form to be used is the one beginning with "indirection" and proceeding to "direction." There is a great difference between beginning with "indirection" and moving to "direction," and beginning with "direction" and moving to "indirection."

Aristotle says: I mean by indirection imitation of the opposite of what is to be praised, so that the soul first rejects and despises the one, and then there is a change from the negative to the imitation proper of what is to be praised. For example, if one should want to imitate or represent success and things related to it, he would begin first by imitation of failure and things related to it and then change to imitation of success and things pertaining to it. And he will do this by presenting the opposite of what he used to represent failure.

Direct imitation treats the thing itself.

Aristotle says: Directness is more excellent when mixed with indirectness.

Aristotle says: At times directness and indirectness are used for animate and inanimate things not to move people to seek or reject them but merely to arouse the imagination. I call this "accurate imitation." The method of "directness"—really, "directness" and "indirectness"—is most often applied to inanimate things in Arab poems. For example, there is the passage of the poet al-Mutanabbi,[3] who writes:

As often as you visited hidden doorways—
Visits more sly than those made by the wolf when all are asleep—
So often did I visit them;
And the blackness of the night protected me.
And I returned and the white dawn met me.

The first part of this poem is "direct" and the second part "indirect." Since the two parts include the two methods of imitation, they are excellent or beautiful in effect.

Aristotle says: Among men, "directness" and "indirectness" are used for inquiry and rebuttal.

The method of "directness" and "indirectness" can move the soul at times to pity and at times to fear. This is what is needed in the art of praising laudable and moral human actions and in blaming base and immoral ones.

Aristotle says: These two parts which we have described are parts of tragedy. There is a third part—that is, a part that generates animal passions, like pity and fear and sorrow. He includes in this category all pitiable events like dangers experienced by friends and deaths of parents and other similar things that often happen to men. These, indeed, are what arouse pity and fear. And this element forms a large proportion of the parts of Greek poems that incite to praiseworthy actions which the poem is written to praise.

[Ch. XII] Aristotle says: The qualitative parts of tragedy have been described. Now we must speak of the quantitative parts. He mentions in this section parts which are proper to Greek poems. Three of these parts are found among the Arabs. First, there is the part that appears in poems in the manner of a rhetorical exordium. This is the part where the Arabs mention mansions or noble buildings and ruins and remains. After this, they include preludes and consolations in it. The second part is praise itself. The third part is what resembles a rhetorical conclusion. Most of this part among the Arabs is either an address or prayer to the man they have praised or a commendation of the value of the poem itself.

The first part is more noteworthy and better known than the last. Therefore they call the change from the first part to the second a "following." And at times they go directly to praise, leaving out the exordium, as in the passage by Abu Tammam: "Certainly, I should hesitate both to speak and act." And there is the passage by al-Mutanabbi: "One enjoys what he has been accustomed to all his life, and the lance of Saifu ad-Daulati has been accustomed to pierce his enemies."

[Ch. XIII] After Aristotle completes his list of the parts of Greek poems, he says: We have now listed the parts of tragedy according to quality and quantity. Let us next discuss the matters from which the effect of the art of praise, that is tragedy, is derived, adding this to what has preceded.

[Ch. XIV] Aristotle says: As has been said, the composition of songs of praise should not be by simple imitation but should mix elements of all three methods together—that is, the methods of "directness," of "indirectness," and of imitations arousing or inducing the passions of pity and fear and thus moving the soul. The ode, that is the poem of praise, which intends to impel the reader to virtue should be composed of representations of virtues and of matters inducing fear and pity, from which perturbation arises, like misfortunes happening to good men without cause. Indeed, this constitutes a powerful stimulation of the soul to receive virtue.

A change by the poet from representation of virtue to representation of vice or from representation of virtuous men to representation of vicious men accomplishes nothing toward impelling a man or forcing him, as though terrified, toward virtuous actions, if the change creates neither intense love nor fear. Both of these emotions should be found in songs of praise. This happens when the change is from representation of virtues to representation of misfortune and the evil accidents happening to good and worthy men; or when there is a change from this to representing those who are extremely virtuous. Truly, these representations arouse the soul and make it eager to receive virtue. And you will find many representations included in legal speeches which are like those that Aristotle discusses, since these are speeches of praise inciting to praiseworthy actions. For example there is the story of Joseph and his brothers and other similar stories from past history, which are called "hortatory examples."

Aristotle says: Pity and compassion are aroused when we tell of misery and misfortune befalling one who did not merit it, and without cause. Terror and fear arise from telling such things because of the thought of deserved harm that could befall those who are less worthy than the characters in the poem—that is, the audience, who know that they are less worthy than the characters. Sadness and pity arise from telling such things because they happened to a man who did not deserve it. When one simply mentions virtues by themselves, this does not involve fear of loss, nor pity, nor love. A poet who wishes to move to virtue must therefore devote part of his representation to things that arouse sadness and terror and pity.

Aristotle says: Songs of praise which are beautiful and excellent in terms of the art of poetry are poems based on this sort of composition—that is, narration of virtue, and of sad events, and of things that arouse fear and move to pity and compassion.

Aristotle says: Those men err who criticize a poet who devotes part of his poem to fictional or historical tales and includes indications of how these parts are useful to the praise. And in poems of praise dealing with war, things are added that arouse and signify wrath. Wrath is a kind of sorrow and perturbation accompanied by a powerful desire for revenge. This being the case, recalling the murder of parents and similar events that have befallen active and virtuous men, can move and arouse in the hearers a zealous love of virtue and a fear they may someday be deprived of the benefits of virtue.

Some poets include representation of vices or defects in songs of praise because they give rise to a certain measure of "indirection." But the reprehension and ridicule of defects is more proper to satire than to tragedy. Therefore their presence in tragedy should not be related to its principal intention and should only be included for the sake of "indirection." And when there is mention of defects in a poem of praise, then there is no excuse for not immediately mentioning enemies of the man praised and those who hate him.

A poem of praise is written only to recall the deeds of friends and loved ones. Enemies of enemies and friends of friends are not commemorated in praise or blame, since they are neither friends nor enemies of the man praised.

Aristotle says: Fictional invention should be so fearful and sorrowful that it occurs "before your eyes" and has almost the reality of something seen. For when a fictional story is ambiguous and is based on doubtful material, it does not produce the action that it seeks to produce. For what a person does not believe cannot move him either to fear or pity. What Aristotle says here explains why many people who do not believe the stories in the Bible are vile and depraved. Men are naturally moved by two kinds of speech—logical and non-logical. The kind of man just mentioned is prevented from being moved by either of these two types of speech that one finds in the Bible.

Aristotle says: Certain poets include in tragedy representation of things that arouse admiration alone without fear or sorrow. You find many passages of this kind in the Bible, though songs praising virtue are not found in Arab poetry and are not found in our own day except in the Bible.

Aristotle says: There is absolutely no efficacy in this form of tragedy [i.e., of admiration]. The art of poetry does not seek any sort of pleasure but seeks the level of pleasure which moves to virtue through imagination. This is the pleasure proper to tragedy.

Aristotle says: We know the things whose representation produces pleasure without suffering of fear. Things whose representation produces suffering and fear along with pleasure can be determined by asking what the difficult and harsh experiences are among those which tend to befall mankind, and what things are small and unimportant so that great sorrow and fear do not arise from them. The ideal kinds are things that happen intentionally between friends like the slaying of parents and dangers and misfortunes and other similar injuries, and not what happens between enemies. One is not saddened nor is he pained or terrified by an evil act performed by enemies in the same way that he is saddened and offended by an evil act caused by friends. And if a certain degree of suffering results from the first sort of deed, it is not comparable to the suffering that comes from an evil act performed by loved ones—like the slaying of a brother by a brother or a father by a son or a son by a father. The story of Abraham is a case in point. He was commanded to sacrifice his most beloved son. This is truly pitiable and produces an extreme impulse toward suffering and pity and fear.

Aristotle says: Praise should only be of excellent actions proceeding from free choice and knowledge. Some actions are based on free choice and knowledge. Some are based on neither choice or knowledge. Some are based on knowledge but not on choice, and some on choice but not on knowledge. Likewise some things are done by agents who are recognized, and some by agents who are not recognized. A deed that is done in ignorance and without free choice is not worthy to be called "praise." The same is true of a deed done by agents who are not recognized. This is far more appropriate to fabulous tales than poems. Therefore it should not be represented. Deeds which clearly proceed from free choice and knowledge and agents who are recognized are most worthy to be called "praise" and true commendation.

[Ch. XV] Aristotle says: We have now sufficiently discussed the proper treatment of the things from which poems are made and how they are to be composed. We will now discuss character—that is, what qualities are to be represented in praise.

We say, then, that there are four aspects of character or qualities worthy and excellent to represent in praise—that is, qualities that seem excellent to the audience.

Certain ones are characteristics which are good and virtuous qualities innate to the man who is praised. The soul is receptive to the representation of qualities truly existing in the man praised. And there is some good in any kind of man, although some things not good may be found in the man.

Second are attributes pertaining to the subject of praise and appropriate to it. Some attributes pertain and are convenient to a woman and do not pertain to a man and are not appropriate to a man.

Third are characteristics existing or invented in terms of the completion of the whole, when it is possible to discover characteristics that are verisimilar and appropriate.

Fourth are characteristics which are moderate and means between extremes.

And the case in respect to these matters is such that no-one is praised on account of bad and perverse customs and character. Likewise, no-one is praised for qualities that are not appropriate to him, even if they are good qualities. Likewise no-one is praised for appropriate qualities if they are not highly probable on the basis of verisimilitude and appropriateness, or are not adequate to the purpose.

Qualities which are good and express good and praiseworthy character are such according to truth or the opinion of many; or are similar to these. All of these are proper to praise—that is, qualities that are good according to truth or are similar to those which are truthful or thought by many to be true or are similar to these.

Aristotle says: The epilogues or conclusions of poems or metrical compositions should state in summary form the subject commemorated and the qualities of character which gave rise to the praise, just as happens in rhetorical conclusions. Also the poet should exclude from his poem representations extraneous to the speech except what those to whom the speech is directed can tolerate. Thus he will not be criticized for too much or too little or wandering from the path of poetry.

Aristotle says: Likeness and representation relate to praise of things which are at the summit of virtue and goodness. Just as the skilled artist depicts an object as it is in reality, so that he can represent anger and humor and sloth by his paintings—though the characteristics of these are primarily of the soul—in the same way in his representation the poet should depict and form the object as it is in itself and as he is able to do it, so that he imitates and expresses the character and habits of the soul. Here Aristotle mentions the poet Homer and his poem in which he depicted the character of a certain man [Achilles—*Poetics* XV.1454B]. Poetry of this type—I mean a poem that causes a quality of the soul to be imagined and represents it—is illustrated by the passage in al-Mutanabbi describing a certain messenger of the Romans coming to the presence of a certain Arab king named Saifu ad-Daulati and written with the intention of celebrating the king. He wrote:

When he came to you,
For fear, the head almost denied the neck on which it was placed.
All his joints almost dissolved for terror.
As though between battle lines drawn up on either side
He advanced toward you,
While he forced his trembling legs forward
Though his shaky will wanted to turn them back.

Aristotle says: In arousing the imagination and in imitative representation the poet should employ materials that are customary, and in making metaphors he should not stray from the paths of poetry.

[Ch. XVI] Aristotle says: The kinds of indicative signs which function in this way are many. One is that the representation of visible things be by means of sensible images which, by their nature, leave the spectator in doubt, making him believe the things themselves that are represented are present because of the ability of the images to communicate the forms of the things being represented. For example, they call certain constellations "crab" and "spear-bearer" because on hearing these terms, one can imagine from their shape and organization the things which they symbolize, as though the images were the things themselves. Much metaphoric resemblance among the Arabs is of this sort. They call words of comparison "doubtfuls," and the more apt the images—that is, the expressions arousing the imagination so that it "doubts" whether or not the thing represented is truly present—the more perfect and artful the metaphor using them. And the more distant, the more imperfect the excellence of the metaphor. Imperfect metaphors are representations far removed from what they represent, and they are to be shunned or rejected. For example, there is the saying of the poet Imru'u 'l-Qais about a lean and bony mare: "Your horse is like an old spear-handle." And his other saying: "When she comes call her 'She-bear of fields covered by waves'; when she comes say 'Seductress, there are no footprints in the water.' "[4] This saying is more apt than the first because there is a certain amount of contrast in it.

Certain images represent concepts by sensible things when these things have characteristics analogous to the concepts. Through these characteristics it is possible for the concepts to be understood. For example there is the saying about a favor: "It is a chain around your neck." And gifts: ""They are shackles to the recipient." And as the poet al-Mutanabbi says: "The man who finds gifts and favors finds shackles." A great many such metaphors are found among the Arabs. And we should reject those metaphors which are inept and disproportionate and lack likeness. But this often is found in modern poems, especially in the poetry of Abu Tammam, as in his saying, "Do not water me with the water of reproach." Really, there is no relation between water and reproach. And even less apt is his saying, "Death is curdled milk and milk freshly drawn."

Just as one should reject metaphors distant from the things to which they are likened, so one should avoid metaphors based on ignoble things and derive them from noble things. Sometimes, however, metaphors based on noble things are used for base things, as in the poem of Abu Najm: "Now the sun is setting and you have not yet finished; the sun half hidden on the horizon is like a squinting eye or the orb of a one-eyed man." And as another poet said in praise of king Saifu ad-Daulati:

Now the Romans knew—miserable and ill-starred as they were—
That you would confront them and their senate
And they were like mice hiding in the walls
And you were like a cat ready to pounce on them.

Aristotle says: There are other kinds of poetic expression which are more proper for persuasion or creating belief than for arousing the imagination or poetic representation, and they are closer to rhetorical example than metaphors and poetic representations. The kinds of poetic expression that Aristotle mentions here occur frequently in the songs of al-Mutanabbi; for example, his saying, "Blackening your eyes with antinomy dust is not the same as having black eyes." And again, his saying: "When the sun has risen for you, you can forget about Saturn." A charming example of this sort is the saying of the poet Abu Firas al-Hamdani: "We men are not content with the mean./Either we are at the heart of everything that goes on in the world,/Or we lie quiet in our graves./To obtain glory we value our lives little/As a man little values a rich dowry/When he is about to wed a lovely and honest woman."

Aristotle says: The third kind of representation is that which arouses memories of someone. This is when the poet includes something in his poem which makes someone recall someone else, so that when anyone reads what is written about the other person he both remembers him and suffers and mourns him if he is dead, or longs for him if he is alive. This is frequently found in Arab poetry—as in the saying of the poet Mutammim ben Nuwaira:

When someone objects: "Whatever the grave, you mourn,
Renewing your sorrow at the grave of your friend—
What end is there of the sorrow of graves?"
To this I reply, "Common misfortunes recall private ones,
Thus any grave recalls the grave of Malik
And calls forth my own tears."

Many similar examples of commemorative songs are found among the Arabs, when they want to arouse sad memories of the dead or express the misfortunes and sorrows of lovers. And among the Arabs this sort of poetry is most often used in elegies and laments.

Aristotle says: The fourth kind of representation or imitation—that is, metaphoric "likeness"—is that which recalls that one person is like another of the same sort. This sort of "likeness" is only used for deeds and character, as when one says: "Lo, the second Plato approaches"—meaning that a Socrates approaches, who is like Plato in character, in the opinion of the speaker. And this is the kind of image used in the saying of the poet Imru'u 'l-Qais when he remarks of a certain man: "You can recognize in him his father and his father's whole character."

A statement of similarity is different from "likeness" based on metaphor. Such "likeness" leaves a certain amount of doubt. But a statement or an open assertion of similarity between two persons (that is, when one says, "this man is like that one") is a true statement of the similarity between them and is like the object of "accurate likening" [see above p. 351].

Aristotle says: The fifth kind is the one used by sophisticated poets and is hyperbole or lying exaggeration. This is frequently found in Arab poems. For example the saying of the poet an-Nabiga ad-Dubyani:

He sent forth his ravening dog
Swifter than the wind,
And made a roaring fire
On the stones of the street.

And again, the saying of the poet al-Mutanabbi: "Your enemy is scorned by every tongue;/The sun and the moon would be scorned/If they were your enemies." And his saying in the same work: "If your soul scorned the turning of the firmament,/Doubtless its turning would be somewhat impeded." A great many such hyperbolic expressions are found in Arab poems, but in the noblest book, that is the Koran, nothing like logical or sophistic expression occurs when this type of writing—that is, poetic writing—is being employed. However, this type of expression sometimes is put to good use in the work of poets who are learned and write about natural subjects, as one finds in the saying of al-Mutanabbi: "In the water where he watered the horses/There was no shallow place free of blood." And again, in another work:

You do not cover yourselves in purples and silk
For the sake of beauty.
But to conceal your beauty within;
You do not bind your hair for adornment
But fearing the loss of the charms you have.

Aristotle says: The sixth kind is famous and widespread and the Arabs use it—that is, when the qualities of an animate thing are attributed to an inanimate one, like speech or reason. The Greeks call this figure *prosopopeia* [personification] that is, the invention of a new person, as when speech and the power to reply are ascribed to inanimate objects. For example, a certain poet,[5] mourning the inhabitants of a certain palace, says:

O noble house!
I am moved to tears, seeing your solitude.
And the palace trembled
Pitying me for my many tears.
I say to it: "Where, I beseech you, are those who once lived in you,
Leading a happy life, secure, and enjoying their time?"
And the building replies: "Those who live in time have passed away with time—
And they have left me and I will also pass away,
Some day, as time decides.
Nothing remains that flows with the current of time."

There are many examples of this figure used in various ways among the Arab poets. Aristotle also mentions this figure in the *Rhetoric* and says there that Homer himself often uses it.

Aristotle says: Direct representation of something being praised and "indirection" are only used for actions of the will. This technique is frequently found in the Koran—that is, praise of worthy actions of the will and blame of unworthy ones—but it is rarely found in Arab poetry. And the Koran prohibits reading of poetic fictions except some few songs that tend to satirize or rebuke vices, and tragic commendation of virtues and encouragement to practice them.

[Ch. XVII] Aristotle says: The excellence of poetic narration and what brings it to the fulfilling of its goal is when the poet in his stories and narratives writes so vividly that the audience considers what is narrated almost before its mind and eyes, so that it both understands what is narrated, and also does not fail simultaneously to understand things which are not narrated. This is frequently apparent in skilled and experienced poets. However, the techniques of making the thing vividly present to the imagination is not found in Arab poems except in elegaic songs which treat the actions or deeds of lovers, or when the poets wish only to achieve imaginative accuracy. For example, there is the song of the poet Imru'u l-Qais on the dialogue of two lovers:

I burned for a flowing stream
When I knew her husband was sleeping;
But she, murmuring denial, said:
"Do you wish to ruin me?"
Do you not know that there are still people awake?
I replied: "I am tormented by a fire
Which I wish to extinguish."

Another example which employs only accuracy in the imaginative representation is the saying of the poet Du'r-Rumma describing a fire being kindled by striking flints:

A glowing spark, glinting like an eye,
Leaps forth as the blow is struck.
I say: "Choose a nest for it to rest in.
Supply dry tinder
Summon the breath of the wind to rouse it.
Hold your hand around it lest it go out."

The Arabs also use this technique in their poems when they narrate various events, such as wars and the like, where their stories can be tested. Mutanabbi the poet was best in this kind of representation, as is clear from his poems. It is said of him that he did not want to describe any deeds of king Saifu ad-Daulati, his master, that occurred when he himself was not present. He understood things that he witnessed for himself better than the things told him by others. Indeed, everyone does best in reporting those things that he has understood for himself and almost seen first-hand with all their accidents and circumstances. Such a man can best represent and express poetic figures—that is, through imaginative imitation and meter and melody.

Aristotle says: To list the kinds or modes of direct representation would be too long and take too much time. He means by this that there is a great diversity of the kind of poetry among the various nations and a great deal of it.

[Ch. XVIII] Aristotle says: Certain parts of every song of praise constitute the tying together, and certain parts the resolution. The thing that is closest to the parts of the Greek poems which constitute the "tying together" is the part of the song that we call "following" [see p. 361]. This is the part in which the elegiac section leads into the tragic section [i.e., the song of praise]. And, as has been said several times, this introduction has the nature of a prólogue to the other material of the song of praise so that the praise will seem more beautiful.

The resolution is the separation of one part from another; that is, it permits them to stand separately. The "tying together" is very frequent in modern poems, as can be seen in Abu Tammam:

> I have passed my year with camels
> In the boiling heat and caves of the desert.
> I have made a feast-day for the birds of the air
> With songs for dead animals.
> Far from me were the gardens of solace.
> Now, therefore, I have finally found rest
> Thinking of songs of praise.

After this prologue he begins the principal subject, extolling the man he intended to praise. Many examples of this sort are found among the Arabs.

The resolution, however, sometimes comes in without any preamble in connection with the principal subject of praise. This technique is frequently found among the Arabs.

Aristotle says: There are four species of poems of praise. There are simple ones, and there are the ones already discussed. The first is "indirectness"; the second is "directness"; the third is "passion" as they write about men in Hades, for there one finds continual sadness and inconsolable sorrow. The fourth is composed of two or all three of these. You should know that we do not find examples of those four species of poems of praise relating to acts of the will among the Arab poets. But they are frequent in holy writ—that is the Koran.

Aristotle says: Some poets are good at writing in long meters and some at writing short or brief meters. These are the forms that we call "curtailed." The reason is that a good and skilled poet should describe and delineate things according to their proper qualities and their true natures. These are varied according to the quantity and scarcity of the accidents and proper qualities pertaining to the things being treated. When the poet does this, the representation is good and apt, and the imaginative stimulation is not in excess of the qualities of the things and their true natures. And certain men are skilled by custom or nature at causing things to be imagined that have few proper qualities. Such poets make "curtailed" poems—not extended or lengthy ones.

Other poets have the opposite inclination. That is, they are excellent in meters of long lines. They are skilled by custom or nature at delineating things that have many accidents and proper qualities. Or it happens that both aids—that is, custom and nature—are joined in these poets.

Aristotle says: Certain representations and imaginative works are appropriate and adapted to lengthy meters and rhythms, and certain to short meters. At times, the meter or rhythm is appropriate and adapted to the subject and not to the imagery of the poem, and at times the reverse is true, and at times the meter and rhythm are inappropriate to both. Examples of these kinds of verse are difficult to find in Arab poems or cannot be found at all since the Arabs have only a few kinds of meter.

Aristotle says: Among the devices which accompany or relate to the basic materials of poetry are extrinsic ones like appearance, vocal inflections, and the rest which have already been mentioned. For the most part, poets employ these devices in songs involving passion. These are lamentations and other forms like those about men in Hades and in other similar situations.

[Ch. XIX] We have now discussed the parts of poems that are intrinsic and based on truth, which are the parts from which poems are composed and created. Therefore let us now discuss those extrinsic devices which add to the excellence of poems. Speaking generally, we say that these are types of gesture that are called for by those compositions called "poems of passion." Therefore when these devices are used, they should be used with this type of poetry. These types of gesture manifest the passions which the speech indicates, as though they most certainly happened.

You already know, from the *Rhetoric,* about speeches of passion [i.e. *pathos*] and the kinds of passion which these speeches use [cf. *Rhetoric* II]. These gestures are really more proper to the *Rhetoric* than to the *Poetics.* The passions expressed by rhetorical or poetic speech are fear, anger, love, hate, joy, and sadness, and the rest of these motions of the soul which are listed in the *Rhetoric.* It is clear that just as these kinds of speech induce these passions, likewise, the appearance and gestures of the speaker indicate the presence of the things arousing these passions and thereby arouse the passions themselves. The viewer or listener is therefore moved and perturbed and suffers. But one must not use these forms and gestures in poetry except in poetry of passion, either to exaggerate or diminish something or for sorrow or arousing fear—since the poetry of praise based on passionate speech employs these devices, as has already been said. They are used especially in passionate speeches that are not true—that is, which do not create vivid images. Passionate speeches that are vivid and imaginative and appropriate to the object of the speech do not need to use, in addition to speech, those things that enhance the poem extrinsically. Rather, they debase such speeches since they are only used in speeches that are too imperfect to achieve their objective unless extrinsic devices are added. They are defective and bad in themselves and without that efficacy that marked the speech of a certain poet[6] who wanted to stir up wrath in the soul of King Kortubi against a certain steward of his household. Before a great multitude of his people, he said to the king: "He through whom you reign and are exalted is considered a liar by your steward." Because this speech was effective in itself in arousing the wrath of the king, it does not need acting or gesturing on the part of the speaker.

Aristotle says: And sometimes the poet may use the extrinsic forms and figures in any sort of speech when he has been forced to do so by those who know the art of facial expression [i.e., actors]. I understand by figures of language or speech, the figures of declaration and of question and of petition and refusal. The figure of a man declaring something is different from that of one asking, and of one petitioning from one refusing. By this criterion, Aristotle can reject the figures that are extrinsic, since these make poetic speeches base. Therefore they should not be considered part of the art of poetry, but of some other art.

[Ch. XX] Aristotle says: Poetic speech consists of seven elements: syllable, copula or conjunction, disjunction, noun, verb, case, speech. The elements of syllables are indivisible—that is, letters. Not, however, all letters, but only those by nature fitted to the composition of syllables. This is the simplest of those elements from which speech is composed. Indeed, the cries or sounds of beasts cannot be divided into letters, and therefore we say that their cries are not composed of letters, nor is any part of their cry a letter.

The parts of a sound which form a syllable are the vowel and the consonant. There are two kinds of consonant—that which is not extended when spoken—like T in "TA" and "TE," and that which is extended, like R in "RE" and SC in "SCIN" and others, which are called semivowels. Vowels are sounds created by vibrations of the lips or teeth or some part of the throat or mouth. There is a vowel that is composite but inseparable. I understand by this that it is impossible to separate or detach the vowel from a consonant. And, I think, those letters are called vowels that among the Arabs are called "motives" and "letters of extension or protraction" and "liquid" or "soft" letters.

A semivowel is a letter that has a certain extension like a vowel but does not have an audible sound by itself. A consonant is a letter that makes a sound combined with a vowel but does not have an audible sound by itself. I understand here that it has an audible sound when it is joined to another and sounds along with it. And consonants have no sound except when joined to letters that sound, like *el* and *eb.* These consonants are what the Arabs call "quiet" and "mute" letters. They are varied according to the various configurations of the mouth and other places where they are produced and from which they come and according to short and long and acute and heavy, and generally according to the extremes and the means between them that are found in sounds and in rhymes and meters and the various poetic forms.

A syllable is a non-significant sound composed of vowels and consonants. What Aristotle says of letters is true. It is impossible to produce the sound of *el* or *em* with a single letter. Likewise the marks called *fatha* [f] and *damma* [d]; and no sound can be made except by joining both kinds of letter. However the existence of the sound *fatha* or *damma* is primary, and the vowel sound is secondary. In general, you should know that a sound is made up of two elements, one of which is, as it were, the matter—that is, the consonant—and the other the form—that is, the vowel. And those who speak Arabic call vowels "motive," "extensive," and "soft."

Aristotle says: A conjunction is a composite sound that does not mean anything by itself, like *and, then,* and *also,* and in general words of like meaning that are like the cords tying the parts of the statement together or else come at the beginning of a statement like *that* and *indeed*; and conditional expressions which establish continuity, like *if, when,* and the like.

Aristotle says: A disjunction is a composite sound that does not mean anything by itself and either separates words from each other, like *either* and *or,* and similar words; or indicates an exception, like *except, except for,* and similar words; or indicates contrast, like *but, however, but indeed,* and similar words. And these come either at the beginning or end or in the middle of the statement. Here, in our language, we understand by "a sound not meaningful by itself" simple sounds which have meaning when they are joined to other sounds—like particles of conjunction—not simple sounds like letters. For sounds that have meaning by themselves and are composed of several sounds—three or four or more—according to the rules of language are nouns and verbs. A noun is a sound or word that has meaning by itself and signifies a definite thing without an associated time concept. And none of the parts of a noun mean any of the separate parts of the thing. This applies to both simple and compound nouns. Nouns which are compounds of two nouns are not used so that one of their parts refers to some part of the thing to which the noun compounded from the two simple nouns refers—for example *equiferus* [*equi* + *ferus* = wild horse].

A verb is a sound or word that means something and includes the concept of the time related to what is meant. And none of its parts signifies any part of the thing meant. The temporal element of a verb distinguishes it from a noun. *Man* and *white* have no time concept; but *runs* and *ran* indicate present and past time.

Aristotle says: Case or inflection pertains to noun and to statement and to verb. An inflected noun is related to another noun as *of Socrates* or *to Socrates.* An inflected statement is, for example, one in the imperative or interrogative. And an inflected verb is past or future. An "upright" verb is one in the present tense. This is mostly proper to the Greek language. A statement is a composite expression each part of which has meaning by itself. It is called a "statement" according to one of two criteria. Either because it refers to a single thing or idea —like "man is an animal"—or because there is one factor binding it together —as we say that a syllogism is one statement and a rhetorical oration is one, and a poetical composition is one.

[Ch. XXI] Aristotle says: There are two kinds of noun: the simple, which is not composed of meaningful parts; and the compound, which is composed of meaningful parts although by them is meant a single thing that the nouns of which the word is composed do not mean—like *famulus solis* ["planet"] or *armiger* [knight].

Aristotle says: Every noun is either native to its language, or borrowed from another, or used metaphorically, or coined, or shortened [i.e. compressed], or extended [i.e. elongated], or altered. A native noun is common to its nation. A borrowed noun is one taken by poets and interpolated into their language from another, as happens in languages that are contiguous and exchange words with one another. A noun used metaphorically is when, for example, the word for the species is used for the genus—as when "slaughter" is called "death,"— or the genus is used for the species—as when "change" is called "motion"; or the name of the species is used for another—as when "robbery" is called "theft"; or when, in an analogy, that which is related to the second term is used for the third, or that which is related to the third is used for the fourth. [i.e., when, in the analogy *a* is to *b* as *c* is to *d, a* is used for *c,* or *b* is used for *d.*] For example, the ancients used to call "age" the "evening of life" and "evening" the "old age of the day." Clearly, the relation of old age to life is like the relation of evening to day.

A coined or made-up noun is one invented by the poet having its own special meaning, and the poet is the first one to use it. Such nouns are not found in Arabic. But they are found often in arts newly invented. And at times modern poets use them, basing their derivation on metaphor—as al-Mutanabbi did when speaking of a man prompt to do what he intended: "As soon as you think of a word in the present, you try to make it pass into the past." And at times they use an unorthodox inflexion, as when the impersonal verb *oportet* ["it is proper that . . ."] is used with a personal ending—*oporteo* ["I should"] or *oportuisti* ["you should have"].

Elongated and compressed words are not found among the Arabs.

An ornamental word is one whose parts are adorned by a special accent.

It has already been observed that by an "elongated word" Aristotle meant a word altered by addition or subtraction of a syllable. And although we have not remarked on the fact, Aristotle is referring to nouns that are difficult to pronounce. But it is evident from what Aristotle says that such nouns are composed by the Greeks from definite syllables. And a "compressed noun," in my opinion, is the kind that he called "varied." Also it seems from his discussion that this type is altered by cutting off a syllable—what we call *syncope.* "Altered" nouns, however, are metaphors based on resemblance—for example, the Greeks call a certain star "the vulture"—or else based on contrast—as when they call the sun "the dark orb"—or else on consequence as when they call a garland [*sepum* = ?*sertum*] "softness" and rain, "crops."

[Ch. XXII] Aristotle says: The speech that is easiest to understand is speech that is familiar and customary, which is not obscure to anyone. This is achieved by nouns that are familiar and from standard usage. The nouns that he refers to in his treatise are called "truthful" and "designative" and "standard." This is what you find in this poet and that. . . . I.e., poets who were famous among the Greeks. The reader should here refer to Arab poets in whose poems this kind of diction is found.

Aristotle says: Orations of moderate praise are composed of standard nouns and others—that is, metaphors and altered nouns and enigmas; for when a poem is wholly deprived of proper and standard words it becomes a riddle and an enigma. Riddles and enigmas are composed of borrowed and obscure—that is, metaphorical—nouns, and metaphors, and slang and analogies. An enigma is a speech that includes meanings which are impossible or difficult to reduce to a single sense. This is frequently found among Arab poets, especially in the poems of Duromati.

Noble poetic speech which is moderate or restrained is composed of nouns that are especially excellent according to usage and from the other kinds. And when the poet wants to say anything plainly and clearly he should use nouns that have a special clarity. And when he wants to present something as delightful and admirable he should use nouns of the other type. For this reason, we ridicule anyone who wants plainness and clarity and uses obscure nouns or slang or borrowed or coined ones. Likewise we ridicule anyone who wants to make anything delightful or admirable and uses words or nouns that are commonplace or trite, though a poet should beware the excessive use of unusual nouns. For he needs to make moderate use of enigmatic speech to prevent his speech from becoming wholly enigmatic. Also he should beware the excessive use of trite speech in order to avoid straying from the path of poetry into commonplace speech.

Aristotle says: The resemblance of certain words to certain others in quantity [i.e. sound] and the similar meanings of certain words, and their stress should be common to and involve all of the words that are in the poetic speech. And we find that some poets use "exact" words in places where they are ridiculous, but their poems do not lack the other two elements—that is accent and rhyme and likeness in quantity. This is emphatically true in all kinds of poetry. But poems that use a variety of kinds of nouns do this most obviously.

The resemblance of words in quantity which he mentions is the similarity of certain words in number of letters, whether they agree in respect to the whole word or to a part. Poets of our time call this resemblance and kinship.

Resemblance, or rhyme, has many varieties. Either the resemblance is complete, as when a poet[7] says: "Don't you see *death*? / I know *death* spares no one." Or it is in a part of the word and a part of the meaning. Or it is in part of the word and in all of the meaning. Or it is in all of the word. Or it is in part of the word only. Or it is all of the meaning or it is part of the meaning only.

An example of resemblance in part of the word and part of the meaning is provided by different forms of the same stem, as in the poet al-Mutanabbi: "*Giving* GROWS to the GROWTH of the *giver;* and *givers* are multiplied by the GROWTH of *giving.*"

An example of resemblance in part of the word and in all of the meaning is the common expression, "*Strike,* and may the *striking* be hard." Analogous nouns are an example of resemblance in all the word and part of the meaning or significance. Poets often use these. And an example of resemblance in all the word only is when one says: "One dog with the troops *dines*; / Another in the stars *shines.*" [In Latin, *castris* and *astris*]. And an example of resemblance in part of the word only is the saying of Seneca: "What is born with me [*oritur*] dies with me [*moritur*]." And an example of resemblance in part of the meaning only is different words signifying the same thing according to different manners of speaking and different roots—like *homo* [màn] and *anthropos* [man]. The etymology of homo is "*factus ex homo*" [made from earth]; of *anthropos, arbor inversa* [inverted tree]. Yet they are names of the same thing.

Rhyme among the Arabs is resemblance in quantity and in part of the word. It occurs in a single letter, the last, or two letters—and the moderns call this "consequence."

"Doubling" occurs in a speech in four ways. The first gives the thing and something like it, such as "sun and moon" or "night and day." The second gives the thing and something associated with its use, like "bow and arrow" or "horse and bridle." The third operates by analogy, like "king and god"—and an analogy pertains among four things. The poet al-Kumait is to be criticized in this respect in the poem praising his mistress for the serenity or calm of her face and the sweetness of her kiss, saying: "Complete in her face is serenity [serenit*as*] / Her kiss salivates so sweetly [suavit*as*]." For there is no similarity between serenity of face and sweetness of saliva.

And certain lines of Imru'u 'l-Qais to someone who criticized him are of this sort:

As if a horse I had never ascended [*ascendissem*]
  For the sake of pleasure;
As if a girl I had never attended [*tenuissem*]
  Adorned with bracelets;
As if a barrel of strong wine
  I had never upended [*salutassem*];
As if a horse after many laps
  Back to the race I had not remanded [*incitassem*].

Truly, the connection of these lines seems awkward. It is clear that the poet ought to have written in the reverse order. That is, the first two lines should have been the beginning of the second quatrain, and the two lines that begin the second quatrain should have come first.

A poem of al-Mutanabbi praising his master for self-control is of the same sort:

You stayed, and your death was certain if you stayed
As if you were in the eye of sleeping danger.
Your brave soldiers passed by you, wounded and beaten;
Because of your calm expression, they were encouraged.

As before, there would be metrical proportion in this, I think, if the first line came third and the third line came first. And the same thing has been said of the poetry of Omir-'l-Kaisi.

Aristotle says: Speech is changed or varied from truthful or standard speech when nouns are put in it that have resemblance in respect to accent and quantity, and that are borrowed, and that use the other devices of variation. A sign that poetic speech should be varied is that when truthful or standard speech is "varied" it is called a poem or poetic speech and it is found to have the effect of poetry. For example, one might say: "After we finished what needed doing in that place and the surveyor had measured the angles, we began to discuss what had recently happened to us. And the mules were sweating from the hardness of the journey."[8] This speech can be converted into a poem by avoiding standard diction through changing some of the words, as if one said: "We were conferring and we were arriving, and our carriers were sweating with effort."

Many similar speeches are found among the Arab poets. When you have carefully considered moving poems, you will find that they have elements of these kinds of ornament—that is, words rhyming together and meanings that clash or vice versa; and the other kinds of alteration, already mentioned, and metaphors and other figurative expressions and enigmatic obscurities, and the like. Speech that lacks these has nothing of a poetic nature except meter.

Variation from proper and standard speech is achieved by accents and rhyme and fitting metaphor and through "likeness" and, in general, through any sort of departure in language from standard usage—like addition and deletion of syllables, and inversions of syntax, and change from affirmation to negation and the reverse, and in general from a form to its opposite, and through all the techniques that fall under the heading of poetic license.

Examples of all of these devices are obvious enough, nor are you ignorant of the more obvious and common species, both simple and composite, included in the general categories. It would be extremely difficult to list all the species. Therefore Aristotle was content with a general summary.

The best of all styles is the one which is the most easy and clear and convincing. It is found only in the work of elegant and learned poets. Indeed, a sign of their skill is that they can use the techniques of style in a way that is convincing and clear. Then the poems are more readily accepted by the audience and the objects of the poetic speeches are understood; and they lead the soul of the audience wherever they want.

When the variation is emphatic, it leads to excellence in imagery and at the same time, a more complete understanding of the thing represented. And even among sluggish and stolid men, well proportioned variation produces moderate comprehension. For example, there is the saying from the Koran: "Until you can tell the black thread from the white." Certain readers thought that a real thread was being referred to until it was revealed further on that the reference should be understood as to the thread of dawn separating day from night.

Aristotle says: Compound nouns are proper for the meter in which the praises of good men of the past are sung, when the praise is directed to a specific individual. Compound nouns are rarely produced in the Arab language—as if one noun said "Abochemyn," deriving the noun from "Abus + chemzin."

Borrowed words or idioms—that is, words taken from foreign languages—are proper for the meter in which the poet foretells the future, or describes the delights of good men or the terrible misfortunes of bad ones.

These are two manners of poem known to the Greeks.

Metaphors are words used in a new sense and are appropriate for poems in which proverbs and wise maxims and famous and familiar histories are told.

[Ch. XXIII] Aristotle says: We have now sufficiently discussed the art of praise and the things common to the manners of poetry based on "likeness" and others. The procedure or method for historical poems in reference to the beginning, middle, and end is the same as the method of the parts of the art of praise. The same is true except when the representation is not of deeds themselves but of the historical periods in which they were done. In these historical poems one represents with historical accuracy the characters and conditions of men who preceded the moderns and the change of authority and kings and conditions and times.

Representation of this sort is rare in Arab literature. However, it is extremely frequent in the lawbooks. Aristotle mentions poets who were good at this sort of poetry, and praises Homer highly for his skill in the genre. Among the Arab poems that are commendable for this kind of writing is the song of al-Aswad ben Ya'fur about times gone by and the vicissitudes of those who were once glorious.

What hope now that the family of Mauthairrikin
Has left its home?
Leaving the land of Egidin and Alkawarniky
And Scedicy and Baraky
And the fortress of Scendedin,
They descended to Enkyratin
Where the waters of the Euphrates
Coming from Etwetin
Descended over them.
The winds flooded their dwellings
Rushing over them as though from a sluice.
I see now how the sweetness of life
And all its joys
Will one day
Cease and perish.[9]

[Ch. XXIV] Aristotle says: The parts of this kind of poem are the parts of the art of moderate praise—"indirectness" and directness, and the composite form using both of them. And at times it uses passions, as happens in the art of moderate praise.

He mentions differences between the art of praise and other kinds of poetry among the Greeks and the special practices that the other kinds of poetry follow in respect to accents and parts and representation and length, and that certain poems have longer meters and greater capacity than others. And he says which poets are proficient in these matters and which not; and in all these matters he praises Homer. All these matters are proper to the Greeks and certain ones are not found among the Arabs, either because they are not common to all or most nations or because it happens that in these areas the Arabs are by nature untalented. This seems most likely. Indeed, Aristotle did not concentrate, in the *Poetics,* on what was peculiar to the Greeks, but on what was naturally common to all nations.

Aristotle says: That part of a poem which speaks for the poet should be like a short prologue and brief in comparison to the section of the poem in which the representation occurs—as Homer did. Homer delayed only a short time in giving his prologue, and afterwards spaciously and copiously treated the subject of the representation, although he did not include anything in this beyond what was usual. For extraordinary things are received badly.

He says this, I believe, because different nations have different customs in their "likenings" on account of subjects common to each and unknown to other nations, from which each draws metaphors. For example, there is the sandy desert called Zorabim where many snakes and lizards live. It seems to those who approach it from a distance to be a lake, and the snakes and lizards appear to be fish. Therefore the Arabs commonly say about someone deceived in a similar way, "You have seen the fish and water of Zorabim." The saying in the Koran is based on this: "Those who abandon a task they have undertaken are like viewers of Zorabim."

Aristotle says: When a speech is composed that has no variation or representation, then words of clear meaning should be used; that is, words that refer directly to the things themselves, not to the contraries of the things or to different things. Their composition or structure should have the familiar quality much admired among the Greeks and their pronunciation should be easy.

It seems that there are many poems of this type which have what we call "decorous style" in Arabic. The style is also decorous when the speech offers open truth and is clear. True speech which deserves critical favor uses little ornamentation and few poetic metaphors.

[Ch. XXV] Aristotle says: The poetic errors for which the poet must answer are six in number. The first is when his representation offers something that is not possible—or rather something that is impossible. There is an example of this in the work of Ibnu 'l-Hutazz describing a half moon and saying, "Look at her. She is like a little silver ship weighed down with a cargo of amber." This is indeed impossible. However, it is pleasing because of the strength of the simile, and because the poet does not intend it to impel the reader to do anything or to prevent him from doing something. Also, the representation should be through something that exists or people think exists—like the representation of bad men as demons—or through something where existence is possible, either for the greater part of the poem or on the average. The ways existence may be expressed are more proper to rhetoric than to poetics.

The second kind of poetic error is distorted representation, as happens when a painter adds a limb to the shape he is painting that does not fit it or puts it in an inappropriate place. For example, if anyone should paint the back legs of a quadruped on the front or the front on the back. Examples of this error in Arab poetry should be carefully examined. In my view, the diction of certain modern poets of Andalusia is close to this error, when they describe a wounded horse returning from battle with the line, "Over his ears was a third ear which the flashing sword had made."

The third error is to represent rational beings by irrational ones. This also can be answered. But, indeed, there is little truth in such representation and much falsehood unless the poet adds characteristics which rational beings have in common with irrational ones. And at times this is acceptable because of custom. As, for example, the Arab custom of comparing women to goats and wild cows and youths to young kids.

The fourth error is to compare a thing to its contrary or something resembling its contrary. For example the Arabs customarily say of women of modest demeanor that they have "sick eye-lids." They intend thereby to prove the beauty of the eyes and the modesty of the glance. Another example, close to this, is the Arab saying, "They stretched out in the evening like men sick from too much generosity."[10] And again, "His tunic was ragged and he entered the house like one sick from shame."[11] All these examples use words contrary to the fitting attributes, and yet they deserve favor because of customary forms of speech.

The fifth error is to use words having two different but equally common meanings—like *percussio* meaning both the act of striking a blow and the sensation of the man struck, and other similar cases which are frequent in various languages.

The sixth error is to abandon the poetic representation and employ rhetorical persuasion and speeches creating belief, and especially when the speech is of the humble style, for moderate persuasion. The poem of Imru'u 'l-Qais making excuses for his cowardice is of this sort, where he says, "My right-hand men did not flee because of fear, but because of longing for their home." At times this sort of writing is not improper when it has any degree of probability or truth. For example, there is the saying of another poet[12] making excuses for his flight from battle: "God knows that I did not leave the conflict until my horse was badly wounded by a poisoned arrow. I knew that by staying I would be destroyed and would die without hurting the enemy. / Thus I drew back from them hoping for a time of revenge on the day of their ruin." Here the expression is decorous, especially because of its direct truth, although there is a small amount of variation by metaphor in it. Because of such passages, there is that saying,

> O people and society of Arabs—
> You are wise in making any deed seem attractive.
> You even know how to make flight from battle seem attractive.

Aristotle says: There are thus six kinds of error and an equal number of answers opposed to them. Therefore there are twelve kinds and topics pertaining to and proper to the poet—that is, six errors and six answers.

Examples of answers are not found among the Arabs, since our poets did not distinguish—in fact did not even know—those kinds of poetry.

This is the sum of what I, Averroes, have been able to understand of the subjects that Aristotle discusses in his poetic speeches common to all manners or kinds of poetry and especially of the art of praise, or tragedy. The rest of what he discusses in his book concerning the differences among the other Greek kinds of poetry and their differences from tragedy is proper to the Greeks. Moreover, we find nothing of certain matters which he mentioned in this book, as it has reached us. This means that the book was not completely translated and that it lacks discussion of the differences among many kinds of poetry which the Greeks wrote. Aristotle promised to speak of all these in the prologue of the *Poetics.* What is missing from the common kinds of poetry is a discussion of the art of reprehension or blame. However, the relevant points seem sufficiently obvious from what was said about the art of praise, since things can be known from their opposites.

You will see as you consider what I have written here that what writers in Arabic said about the rules of poetry is trivial and slight in comparison to what is found in this book of Aristotle and in his *Rhetoric.* As al-Farabi says about this, "It should not escape you how those rules were applied to the poems of the Greeks; and you should not fail to observe where the Greeks were right and where they were wrong in formulating their rules."

Here we bring our present task to an end.

The End. Thanks be to God. The year of our Lord 1256, the 17th day of March, in the noble city of Toledo.

GEOFFREY OF VINSAUF

(fl. ca. 1200)

INTRODUCTION

The *Poetria Nova* was written between 1200 and 1216. Its author was an Englishman. He was also the author of three other works: the *Documentum de Modo et Arte Dictandi et Versificandi,* the *Summa de Coloribus Rhetoricis,* and a short poem, the *Causa Magistri Guafredi Vinesauf.* From these works we learn that he studied at Paris, taught at Hampton in England, and at one point in his career made a trip to Rome. The *Poetria* has two dedications. The first is to Pope Innocent III, whom Geoffrey had obviously never met. The second, which occurs at the end of the work, is to a certain William, identified in two early manuscripts as (1) William of Wrotham, administrator of the navy and the stannaries, or (2) William, Bishop of London. Since this second dedication is chiefly an appeal for patronage, it implies no more familiarity with its recipient than the dedication to Innocent III.

Some fifty manuscripts of the *Poetria Nova* exist, twenty of them English. Evidently it was a popular textbook. In a well known passage in the *Nun's Priest's Tale* Chaucer salutes its author and refers to one of its more lugubrious set pieces, the "Lament" on the death of King Richard I:

> O Gaufred, deere maister soverayn,
> That whan thy worthy kyng Richard was slayn
> With shot, compleynedest his deeth so soore,
> Why ne hadde I now thy sentence and thy loore
> The Friday for to chide, as diden ye? (11. 527–31)

Clearly, the reference is ironic. It suggests that the name of Geoffrey was familiar to Chaucer's readers. It also suggests that Geoffrey was regarded with amused contempt, perhaps as a kind of medieval Edgar Guest.

The *Poetria* is written in quantitative dactylic hexameter. The versification is hardly inspired, but it is sufficiently accurate for Geoffrey to make a little joke in his dedication about the impossibility of fitting the name of Innocent III (Īnnŏcēns) into the meter. Geoffrey's *Documentum* covers much the same ground as the *Poetria* but is in prose. One's first impression is that we have here yet another example of the medieval practice of making verse redactions of prose works. However, the case is not quite this simple even if we could strain our credulity to the point of believing that Geoffrey would have versified the *Documentum* simply as an exercise. The *Documentum* is more down-to-earth than the *Poetria.* It lacks the dedication, the section comparing literary creation to architecture, the section on memory, and the epilogue. Its style is rather dry in comparison to the florid, discursive style of the *Poetria,* which is evidently designed to illustrate Geoffrey's principles about "serious" and "weighty" style; and its illustrations are brief. For example, it has nothing comparable to the long poem on Richard I illustrating the figures of amplification and the still longer poem to the Pope illustrating the figures of thought. On the other hand, there is important material in the *Documentum* that is not in the *Poetria.* The *Documentum* has an extensive treatment of transition (*prosecutio*) from the beginning of a work to its main body, which is balanced later by a section on endings. It also has a section on rules common to both the easy and difficult styles and discussions of how to treat "familiar matter," of inventing words, and of "humorous matter." Finally, there is a section on the low, middle, and elevated styles. In addition to this material, the *Documentum* uses much more quotation and citation than the *Poetria.* Horace's *Ars Poetica* is quoted or cited 22 times, Ovid 9 times, and Vergil, Statius, Juvenal, Sidonius, and Boethius one or more times. There are also allusions to Seneca, Lucan, Claudian, and Vegetius Renatus, a fourth-century authority on warfare.

This list of differences suggests several points about the two works. First, it suggests that the *Documentum* preceded the *Poetria.* Not only is it stylistically less ambitious, it is also less complete. The standard departments of rhetoric are invention, disposition, elocution, delivery, and memory. Assuming that the section of the *Poetria* comparing the conception of a work to the plan of a building refers generally to invention, the *Poetria* deals with all five departments. The *Documentum* has nothing which could be interpreted as referring to invention and lacks a discussion of memory.

Second, the *Documentum* relies more heavily on authority than the *Poetria.* In the *Documentum* Geoffrey quotes Horace's *Ars Poetica* frequently. This sometimes gives the *Documentum* greater range than the *Poetria* simply because Horace knew more about poetry than Geoffrey. But this advantage was probably not apparent to Geoffrey himself. In the *Poetria* we can detect at most two echoes of Horace. Beyond these, the discussion and examples are almost entirely Geoffrey's own, although, of course, his list of figures and their definitions come chiefly from the *Ad Herennium*, as do the same materials in the *Documentum.* Evidently, there was substantial assimilation of the *Ars Poetica* between the *Documentum* and the *Poetria.*

Third, if we add up the differences, it seems most likely that the *Documentum* should be understood as a general treatise intended for exercises in essay-writing and poetry, while the *Poetria* is a treatise intended specifically for aspiring poets. This would explain the large amount of technical matter in the *Documentum* on transitions, on the three styles, and on treating "familiar matter," as well as the more theoretical tone and florid style of the *Poetria.*

Neither the *Documentum* or the *Poetria* includes specific internal evidence on its placement in the trivium. The heavy reliance of both works on the *Ad Herennium* for treatment of the figures would suggest an allegiance with rhetoric rather than grammar. Moreover, the title *Poetria Nova* associates that work with the *Ad Herennium,* which was known during the Middle Ages as the *Rhetorica Nova,* in contrast to the *De Inventione,* known as the *Rhetorica Vetus.*

On the other hand, Horace's *Ars Poetica* was known as the *Poetria* during the Middle Ages, and it was generally understood as a treatise on poetry as it pertains to grammar. The extensive quotation from Horace in the *Documentum* and the title *Poetria Nova* suggest that the works should be associated with Horace and grammar rather than the rhetorical tradition in spite of their extensive use of rhetorical lore. The *Poetria* thus is Geoffrey's "New Art of Poetry" and is related to "reading the poets" rather than to rhetoric. Finally, there is the fact that the "theory of determinations" and "theory of conversions" found in both the *Documentum* and the *Poetria* have no precedent in the *Ad Herennium* and are clearly derived from grammar. While none of this evidence is conclusive, it supports the idea that the *Poetria* was intended for the grammar curriculum as a supplement to the *accessus* literature and the *artes metricae.*

The *Poetria Nova* has the following outline:

I. Dedication to Innocent III (lines 1–42)
II. Idea vs. subject matter in poetry (43–86)
III. Arrangement (87–201)
IV. Amplification and abbreviation (202–736)
V. Ornaments of style: difficult ornaments (737–1093)
VI. Easy ornaments (1094–1587)
VII. Theory of conversions (1588–1761)
VIII. Theory of determinations (1762–1841)
IX. Miscellaneous prescriptions; decorum (1842–1968)
X. Memory (1969–2031)
XI. Delivery (2032–2066)
XII. Epilogue (2067–2117)

The prominence given to amplification and abbreviation relates the *Poetria* to classical epideictic (or demonstrative) rhetoric. This branch of rhetoric was set aside for "praise and blame" according to a formula that appears as early as Aristotle's *Rhetoric* (I.3), and the figures of amplification and abbreviation—that is, heightening and diminution, or, occasionally, expansiveness and brevity—were always deemed especially appropriate to it. As legal and political oratory lost ground in the late classical period, and as ornamentation for its own sake became fashionable, epideictic rhetoric gained in favor. Its standard forms, particularly the encomium, epithalamium, and epicede (funeral oration), were taken over bodily as forms for occasional poetry, and its florid style was imitated assiduously by the poets.

To some degree the *Poetria* is a distant echo of that late classical fashion. The poetic strategies that it teaches are primarily for display, and its extended examples are clearly epideictic in nature—for example, the eulogy of Pope Innocent III, the lament for Richard and, later, for the Fall of Man, the generalized description of a beautiful woman, and the like. The basic devices are amplification and abbreviation, and the difficult and easy figures are subordinate to them. They are "ornaments" and "adornments" of the basic theme which enhance it like "a precious garment" (line 756), "a luminous mist" (1050), "blooms in the field" (1225), and the "colors" of a painter (*passim*). Although Geoffrey is not writing a treatise on epideictic rhetoric but a textbook for the grammar curriculum, praise and blame are never far from his mind. His first example of amplification is an example of "rebuke" (277). The theme of rebuke is repeated in references to "assailing" an adversary (433) and "rebuking" error (456). Conversely, we learn after the description of a banquet, "in this way you may celebrate the feasts of kings" (667), and that hyperbole "diminishes or heightens eulogy to a remarkable degree' (1020). Converting adjectives to nouns "intensifies or diminishes eulogy to a marked degree. Denunciation and panegyric offer suitable occasions for this technique" (1660–64). It is clear, incidentally, from the preceding quotation that amplification and abbreviation are understood by Geoffrey in their classical sense of heightening or diminishing a subject, and the fact that they make a poem longer or shorter is a secondary consideration.

If we stand back from the details, it is clear that a thematic motif runs through the *Poetria.* It is the motif of the primacy of the intellectual conception of the work over its materials. Geoffrey's artist is no Longinian genius excited to ecstasy and moved to utterance by a supernatural enthusiasm. In the ancient debate between the claims of genius (or inspiration) and craftsmanship, Geoffrey stands with Cicero and Horace: "Three things perfect a work: artistic theory by whose law you may be guided; experience, which you may foster by practice; and superior writers whom you may imitate. Theory makes the craftsman sure; experience makes him ready; imitation makes him versatile; the three together produce the greatest craftsman" (1705–9). Talent is needed, but without proper training and experience it will be useless. Geoffrey's artist is an artisan—an architect, to use his initial metaphor—rather than a vehicle for transcendent revelation: "The mind's hand shapes the entire house before the body's hand builds it. Its mode of being is archetypal before it is actual. Poetic art may see in this analogy the law to be given to poets" (47ff.). The material is like wax made pliant by the heat of the creative process: "If intense concentration enkindle native ability, the material is soon made pliant by the mind's fire" (215ff.). Words have internal and external qualities—meaning and sound—and the internal quality must receive first consideration: "First examine the mind of a word, and only then its face" (740). This does not mean that the adornments of the rhetorical figures are without value. Rather, it sets up a concept of decorum according to which the outer garment must suit the inner nature of the words in the composition: "There are judges of the proposed expression: let the mind be the first judge, the ear the second, and usage the third and final one to conclude the whole" (1967ff.). Finally, in reference to delivery: "The outward emotion corresponds with the inward; outer and inner man are affected alike" (2046ff.).

How much emphasis should be placed on these remarks? Geoffrey does not strike one as a creative or even very analytic thinker. The importance of craftsmanship, the themes of art, exercise and imitation, the concept of ornamentation via the rhetorical figures—all these ideas can be traced to the *Ars Poetica* and the *Ad Herennium* and are commonplace themes in medieval criticism. On the other hand, the dichotomy of mind versus material and the corollary emphasis on inner versus outer significance are too consistent and too carefully worked out to be accidental.

We know that there were two related currents of thought during the twelfth-century Renaissance. The first gave rise to the humanism of Bernard of Chartres and John of Salisbury. It was grammatical with an overlay of rhetoric derived chiefly from the *Ad Herennium* and Cicero's *De Inventione,* and it involved reading and imitation of the *auctores.* The second was more directly influenced by medieval Platonism as reflected in such works as Calcidius' translation and commentary on the *Timaeus,* Macrobius' commentary on the *Somnium Scipionis,* and Boethius' *Consolation of Philosophy,* and as renewed in the works of Dionysius the pseudo-Areopagite. Among the representatives of this school were mystics like Bernard of Clairvaux and two highly significant literary figures, Bernard Silvestris and Alanus de Insulis. Bernard Silvestris was particularly interested in literary theory. He evidently composed a treatise on the art of poetry, perhaps the first in the series of twelfth- and thirteenth-century *artes* exemplified here by the *Poetria Nova;* and his commentary on the first six books of Vergil's *Aeneid* has survived. His *Megacosmus* and *Microcosmus* belong with Alanus' *De Planctu Naturae* and *Anticlaudianus* as the outstanding examples for the twelfth-century Renaissance of the strain of Platonizing poetry celebrating the harmony and beauty of the visible world. In this tradition, the theme of what Alanus calls "God the elegant architect and golden maker of a golden artifact" runs strong, as does the belief that Nature is the book of God embodying invisible concepts in visible substances. Although the evidence is indirect, it is most likely that Geoffrey of Vinsauf's poet—who plans his work like an architect and embodies the ideas in material substance which must, however, always be treated in such a way as to reflect its inner meaning—is in the same tradition. Geoffrey is no mystic; if anything he is pedestrian. But in the *Poetria* he does seem to be reaching for a new poetic theory which improves on Horace precisely in its effort to shape the commonplaces of grammatical and rhetorical criticism with concepts derived from high medieval Platonism. The difference between Geoffrey's modest use of this material in what is essentially a textbook and an extended and more radical use of it can be estimated by a comparison of the *Poetria Nova* with the selections (below) from Boccaccio's *Genealogy of the Gentile Gods*.

The translation used here (and the notes) are by Margaret F. Nims, *The Poetria Nova of Geoffrey of Vinsauf* (Toronto: Pontifical Institute of Medieval Studies, 1967), by permission of the translator and of the President of the Pontifical Institute. The numbers inserted in the translation give the approximate location of every tenth line in the Latin text. For bibliography, see especially pp. 486–88.

from POETRIA NOVA

I. GENERAL REMARKS ON POETRY
Divisions of the Present Treatise

If a man has a house to build, his impetuous hand does not rush into action. The measuring line of his mind first lays out the work, and he mentally outlines the successive steps in a definite order. The mind's hand[1] shapes the entire house before the body's hand builds it. Its mode of being is archetypal before it is actual. Poetic art may see in this analogy the law to be given to poets: let the poet's hand not be swift to take up the pen, nor his tongue be impatient to speak; (50) trust neither hand nor tongue to the guidance of fortune. To ensure greater success for the work, let the discriminating mind, as a prelude to action, defer the operation of hand and tongue, and ponder long on the subject matter. Let the mind's interior compass first circle the whole extent of the material. Let a definite order[2] chart in advance at what point the pen will take up its course, or where it will fix its Cadiz.[3] As a prudent workman, construct the whole fabric within the mind's citadel; let it exist in the mind before it is on the lips.

When due order has arranged the material in the hidden chamber of the mind, let poetic art come forward to clothe the matter with words. Since poetry comes to serve, however, let it make due preparation for attendance upon its mistress. Let it take heed lest a head with tousled locks, or a body in rumpled garments, or any final details[4] prove displeasing, and lest in adorning one part it should in some way disfigure another. If any part is ill-groomed, the work as a whole incurs censure from that one part. A touch of gall makes all the honey bitter; a single blemish disfigures the entire face. Give careful thought to the material, therefore, that there may be no possible grounds for reproach.

Let the poem's beginning, like a courteous attendant, introduce the subject with grace. Let the main section, like a diligent host, make provision for its worthy reception. Let the conclusion, like a herald when the race is over, dismiss it honorably. In all of its parts let the whole method of presentation bring credit upon the poem, lest it falter in any section, lest its brightness suffer eclipse.

In order that the pen may know what a skillful ordering of material requires, the treatise to follow begins its course with a discussion of order. Since the following treatise begins its course with a discussion of order, its first concern is the path[5] that the ordering of material should follow. Its second care: with what scales[6] to establish a delicate balance if meaning is to be given the weight appropriate to it. The third task is to see that the body of words is not boorishly crude but urbane. The final concern is to ensure that a well-modulated voice enters the ears and feeds the hearing, a voice seasoned with the two spices of facial expression and gesture.

II. ORDERING THE MATERIAL

The material's order may follow two possible courses: at one time it advances along the pathway of art, at another it travels the smooth road of nature. Nature's smooth road points the way when "things" and "words" follow the same sequence, and the order of discourse does not depart from the order of occurrence. The poem travels the pathway of art if a more effective order presents first what was later in time, and defers the appearance of what was actually earlier. Now, when the natural order is thus transposed, later events incur no censure by their early appearance, nor do early events by their late introduction. Without contention, indeed, they willingly assume each other's place, and gracefully yield to each other with ready consent. Deft artistry inverts things in such a way that it does not pervert them; in transposing, it disposes the material to better effect. The order of art is more elegant than natural order, and in excellence far ahead, even though it puts last things first.

The first branch of order has no offshoots; the second is prolific: from its marvelous stock, bough branches out into boughs, the single shoot into many, the one into eight. The air in this region of art may seem murky and the pathway rugged, the doors locked and the theory itself entangled with knots. Since that is so, the words that follow will serve as physicians for that disorder. Scan them well: here you will find a light to dispel the darkness, safe footing to traverse rugged ground, a key to unlock the doors, a finger to loose the knots. The way is thrown open; guide the reins of your mind as the nature of your course demands.

Let that part of the material which is first in the order of nature wait outside the gates of the work. Let the end, as a worthy precursor, be first to enter and take up its place in advance, as a guest of more honorable rank, or even as master. Nature has placed the end last in order, but art respectfully defers to it, leads it from its humble position and accords it the place of honor.

The place of honor at the beginning of a work does not reserve its luster for the end of the material only; rather, two parts share the glory: the end of the material and the middle. Art draws from either of these a graceful beginning. Art plays, as it were, the conjurer: causes the last to be first, the future to be present, the oblique to be straight, the remote to be near; what is rustic becomes urbane, what is old becomes new, public things are made private, black things white, and worthless things are made precious.

If a still more brilliant beginning is desired (while leaving the sequence of the material unchanged) make use of a proverb,[7] ensuring that it may not sink to a purely specific relevance, but raise its head high to some general truth. See that, while prizing the charm of the unusual, it may not concentrate its attention on the particular subject, but refuse, as if in disdain, to remain within its bosom. Let it take a stand above the given subject, but look with direct glance towards it. Let it say nothing directly about the subject, but derive its inspiration therefrom.

This kind of beginning is threefold, springing up from three shoots. The shoots are the first, the middle, and the last parts of the theme. From their stem a sprig, as it were, bursts forth, and is thus wont to be born, one might say, of three mothers. It remains in hiding, however, and when summoned it refuses to hear. It does not as a rule come forward when the mind bids it; it is of a somewhat haughty nature, and does not present itself readily nor to all. It is reluctant to appear, unless, indeed, it is compelled to do so.

Proverbs, in this way, add distinction to a poem. No less appropriately do exempla[8] occupy a position at the beginning of a work. The same quality, indeed, shines forth from exempla and proverbs, and the distinction conferred by the two is of equal value. In stylistic elegance, proverbs alone are on a par with exempla. Artistic theory has advanced other techniques [for the poem's beginning] but prefers these two; they have greater prestige. The others are of less worth and more recent appearance; the sanction of time favors the two forms mentioned. Thus the way that lies open is more restricted, its use more appropriate, its art superior, as we see both from artistic principle and from practice. . . . (150)

III. AMPLIFICATION AND ABBREVIATION

For the opening of the poem, the principles of art outlined above have offered a variety of paths. The poem's development now invites you onward. Keeping to our image, direct your steps further along the road's course.

The way continues along two routes: there will be either a wide path or a narrow, either a river or a brook. You may advance at a leisurely pace or leap swiftly ahead. You may report the matter with brevity or draw it out in a lengthy discourse. The footing on either path is not without effort; (210) if you wish to be wisely guided, entrust yourself to a reliable guide. Reflect upon the precepts below; they will guide your pen and teach the essentials for each path. The material to be molded, like the molding of wax, is at first hard to the touch. If intense concentration enkindle native ability, the material is soon made pliant by the mind's fire, and submits to the hand in whatever way it requires, malleable to any form. The hand of the mind controls it, either to amplify or curtail.

A. Amplification

Repetition (*interpretatio, expolitio*). If you choose an amplified form, proceed first of all by this step: (220) although the meaning is one, let it not come content with one set of apparel. Let it vary its robes and assume different raiment. Let it take up again in other words what has already been said; let it reiterate, in a number of clauses, a single thought. Let one and the same thing be concealed under multiple forms—be varied and yet the same.

Periphrasis (*circuitio, circumlocutio*). Since a word, a short sound, passes swiftly through the ears, a step onward is taken when an expression made up of a long and leisurely sequence of sounds is substituted for a word. In order to amplify the poem, avoid calling things by their names; use other designations for them. (230) Do not unveil the thing fully but suggest it by hints. Do not let your words move straight onward through the subject, but, circling it, take a long and winding path around what you were going to say briefly. Retard the tempo by thus increasing the number of words. This device lengthens brief forms of expression, since a short word abdicates in order that an extended sequence may be its heir. Since a concept is confined in one of three strongholds—in a noun, or a verb, or a combination of both—do not let the noun or verb or combination of both render the concept explicit, but let an amplified form stand in place of verb or noun or both.

COMPARISON (*collatio*). A third step is comparison, made in accord with one of two laws—either in a hidden or in an overt manner. Notice that some things are joined deftly enough, but certain signs reveal the point of juncture. A comparison which is made overtly presents a resemblance which signs explicitly point out. These signs are three: the words *more, less, equally.* A comparison that is made in a hidden way is introduced with no sign to point it out. It is introduced not under its own aspect but with dissembled mien, as if there were no comparison there at all, but the taking on, one might say, of a new form marvelously engrafted, where the new element fits as securely into the context as if it were born of the theme. The new term is, indeed, taken from elsewhere, but it seems to be taken from there; it is from outside and does not appear outside; it makes an appearance within and is not within; so it fluctuates inside and out, here and there, far and near; it stands apart, and yet is at hand. It is a kind of plant; if it is planted in the garden of the material the handling of the subject will be pleasanter. Here is the flowing water of a well-spring, where the source runs purer; here is the formula for a skillful juncture, where the elements joined flow together and touch each other as if they were not contiguous but continuous; as if the hand of nature had joined them rather than the hand of art. This type of comparison is more artistic; its use is much more distinguished.

APOSTROPHE (*apostrophatio, exclamatio*). In order that you may travel the more spacious route, let apostrophe be a fourth mode of delay. By it you may cause the subject to linger on its way, and in it you may stroll for an hour. Take delight in apostrophe; without it the feast would be ample enough, but with it the courses of an excellent cuisine are multiplied. The splendor of dishes arriving in rich profusion and the leisured delay at the table are festive signs. With a variety of courses we feed the ear for a longer time and more lavishly. Here is food indeed for the ear when it arrives delicious and fragrant and costly. Example may serve to complement theory: the eye is a surer arbiter than the ear. One example is not enough; there will be an ample number; from this ample evidence learn what occasion suitably introduces apostrophe, what object it addresses, and in what form.

Rise up, apostrophe, before the man whose mind soars too high in prosperity, and rebuke him thus:

Why does joy so intense excite your spirit? Curb jubilation with due restraint and extend not its limits beyond what is meet [appropriate]. O soul, heedless of misfortune to come, imitate Janus: look to past and to future; if your venture has prospered, regard not beginnings but issues. From the sun's setting appraise the day, not from its rising. To be fully secure, fear the future. When you think that you have done all, the serpent lurks in the grass. Keep in mind, as example, the sirens; learn from them in a happier time ever to beware an unhappy. There is nothing stable in things of this world: after honey comes poison; dark night brings the day to a close, and clouds end calm weather. Though happily all man's affairs are subject to change, misfortune is wont to return with greater alacrity. . . .

Digression. If it is desirable to amplify the treatise yet more fully, go outside the bounds of the subject and withdraw from it a little; let the pen digress, but not so widely that it will be difficult to find the way back. This technique demands a talent marked by restraint, lest the bypath be longer than decorum allows. A kind of digression is made when I turn aside from the material at hand, bringing in first what is actually remote and altering the natural order. For sometimes, as I advance along the way, I leave the middle of the road, and with a kind of leap I fly off to the side, as it were; then I return to the point whence I had digressed. Lest this matter of digression be veiled in obscurity, I offer the following example:

The bond of a single love bound together two hearts; a strange cause divided them one from the other. But before they were parted, lips pressed kisses on lips; a mutual embrace holds and enfolds them both. From the fount of their eyes, tears flow down their cheeks, and sobs alternate with farewells. Love is a spur to grief, and grief a witness to the strength of love. Winter yields to spring. The air unclasps its robe of cloud, and heaven caresses the earth. Moist and warm, air sports with earth, and the feminine earth feels the masculine power of the air.[9] A flower, earth's child, bursts forth into the breeze and smiles at its mother. Their first foliage adorns the tips of the trees; seeds that were dead spring up into life; the promise of harvest to come lives first in the tender blade. Now is the season in which birds delight. This hour of time found the lovers apart, who yet through their love were not parted.

Description, pregnant with words, follows as a seventh means of amplifying the work. But although the path of description is wide, let it also be wise, let it be both lengthy and lovely. See that the words with due ceremony are wedded to the subject. If description is to be the food and ample refreshment of the mind, avoid too curt a brevity as well as trite conventionality. Examples of description, accompanied by novel figures, will be varied, that eye and ear may roam amid a variety of subjects.

If you wish to describe, in amplified form, a woman's beauty:

Let the compass of Nature first fashion a sphere for her head; let the color of gold give a glow to her hair, and lilies bloom high on her brow. Let her eyebrows resemble in dark beauty the blackberry, and a lovely and milk-white path separate their twin arches. Let her nose be straight, of moderate length, not too long nor too short for perfection. Let her eyes, those watch-fires of her brow, be radiant with emerald light, or with the brightness of stars. Let her countenance emulate dawn: not red, nor yet white—but at once neither of those colors and both. Let her mouth be bright, small in shape—as it were, a half-circle. Let her lips be rounded and full, but moderately so; let them glow, aflame, but with gentle fire. Let her teeth be snowy, regular, all of one size, and her breath like the fragrance of incense. Smoother than polished marble let Nature fashion her chin—Nature, so potent a sculptor. Let her neck be a precious column of milk-white beauty, (580) holding high the perfection of her countenance. From her crystal throat let radiance gleam, to enchant the eye of the viewer and enslave his heart. Let her shoulders, conforming to beauty's law, not slope in unlovely descent, nor jut out with an awkward rise; rather, let them be gracefully straight. Let her arms be a joy to behold, charming in their grace and their length. Let soft and slim loveliness, a form shapely and white, a line long and straight, flow into her slender fingers. Let her beautiful hands take pride in those fingers. (590) Let her breast, the image of snow, show side by side its twin virginal gems. Let her waist be close girt, and so slim that a hand may encircle it. For the other parts I am silent—here the mind's speech is more apt than the tongue's. Let her leg be of graceful length and her wonderfully tiny foot dance with joy at its smallness.

So let the radiant description descend from the top of her head to her toe, and the whole be polished to perfection.

If you wish to add to the loveliness thus pictured an account of attire (600):

Let her hair, braided and bound at her back, bind in its gold; let a circlet of gold gleam on her ivory brow. Let her face be free of adornment, lovely in its natural hue. Have a starry chain encircle her milk-white neck. Let the border of her robe gleam with fine linen; with gold let her mantle blaze. Let a zone, richly set with bright gems, bind her waist, and bracelets enrich her arms. Have gold encircle her slender fingers, and a jewel more splendid than gold shed its brilliant rays. Let artistry vie with materials in her fair attire; (610) let no skill of hand or invention of mind be able to add aught to that apparel. But her beauty will be of more worth than richness of vesture. Who, in this torch, is unaware of the fires? Who does not find the flame? If Jupiter in those days of old had seen her, he would not, in Amphitryon's shape, have deluded Alcmena; nor assumed the face of Diana to defraud you, Callisto, of your flower; nor would he have betrayed Io in the form of a cloud, nor Antiope in the shape of a satyr, nor the daughter of Agenor as a bull, nor you, Mnemosyne, as a shepherd; nor the daughter of Asopo in the guise of fire; nor you, Deo's daughter, in the form of a serpent; nor Leda as a swan; nor Danae in a shower of gold. (620) This maiden alone would he cherish, and see all others in her. . . .

OPPOSITION (*oppositio, oppositum*). There remains yet another means of fostering the amplified style: any statement at all may assume two forms: one form makes a positive assertion, the other negates its opposite. (670) The two modes harmonize in a single meaning; and thus two streams of sound flow forth, each flowing along with the other. Words flow in abundance from the two streams. Consider this example: "*That young man is wise.*" Affirm the youthfulness of his countenance and deny its age: "*His is the appearance of youth and not of old age.*" Affirm the maturity of his mind and deny its youthfulness: "*His is the mind of mature age and not of youth.*" The account may perhaps continue along the same line: "*His is not the cheek of age but of youth;* (680) *his is not the mind of youth but of age.*" Or, choosing details closely related to the theme, you may travel a rather long path, thus:

His face is not wrinkled, nor is his skin dry; his heart is not stricken with age, nor is his breath labored; his loins are not stiff, nor is his back bowed; physically he is a young man, mentally he is in advanced maturity.

In this way, plentiful harvest springs from a little seed; great rivers draw their source from a tiny spring; from a slender twig a great tree rises and spreads.

B. Abbreviation

If you wish to be brief, (690) first prune away those devices mentioned above which contribute to an elaborate style; let the entire theme be confined within narrow limits. Compress it in accordance with the following formula. Let *emphasis* be spokesman, saying much in few words. Let *articulus*, with staccato speech, cut short a lengthy account. The *ablative*, when it appears alone without a pilot, effects a certain compression. Give no quarter to *repetition.* Let skillful *implication* convey the unsaid in the said. Introduce no *conjunction* as a link between clauses—let them proceed uncoupled (*asyndeton*). Let the craftsman's skill effect a *fusion of many concepts in one,* (700) so that many may be seen in a single glance of the mind. By such concision you may gird up a lengthy theme; in this bark you may cross a sea. This form of expression is preferable for a factual account, in order not to enshroud facts discreetly in mist, but rather to clear away mist and usher in sunlight. Combine these devices, therefore, when occasion warrants: emphasis, articulus, ablative absolute, deft implication of one thing in the rest, omission of conjunctions between clauses, fusion of many concepts in one, avoidance of repetition. (710) Draw on all of these, or at least on such as the subject allows. Here is a model of abbreviation; the whole technique is reflected in it:

Her husband abroad improving his fortunes, an adulterous wife bears a child. On his return after long delay, she pretends it begotten of snow.[10] Deceit is mutual. Slyly he waits. He whisks off, sells, and—reporting to the mother a like ridiculous tale—pretends the child melted by sun. . . .

IV. ORNAMENTS OF STYLE

Whether it be brief or long, a discourse should always have both internal and external adornment, but with a distinction of ornament reflecting the distinction between the two orders. First examine the mind of a word, and only then its face; do not trust the adornment of its face alone. If internal ornament is not in harmony with external, a sense of propriety is lacking. Adorning the face of a word is painting a worthless picture: it is a false thing, its beauty fictitious; the word is a whitewashed wall and a hypocrite, pretending to be something whereas it is nothing. Its fair form conceals its deformity; it makes a brave outward show, but has nothing within. It is a picture[11] that charms one who stands at a distance, but displeases the viewer who stands at close range. Take care, then, not to be hasty, but be Argus in relation to what you have said, and, Argus-eyed, examine the words in relation to the meaning proposed. If the meaning has dignity, let that dignity be preserved; see that no vulgar word may debase it. That all may be guided by precept: let rich meaning be honored by rich diction, lest a noble lady blush in pauper's rags.

In order that meaning may wear a precious garment, if a word is old, be its phsyician and give to the old a new vigor. Do not let the word invariably reside on its native soil[12]—such residence dishonors it. Let it avoid its natural location, travel about elsewhere, and take up a pleasant abode on the estate of another. There let it stay as a novel guest, and give pleasure by its very strangeness. If you provide this remedy, you will give to the word's face a new youth.

Difficult Ornament

METAPHOR (*translatio*). The method suggested above affords guidence in the artistic transposition of words. If an observation is to be made about man, I turn to an object which clearly resembles man [in the quality or state of being I wish to attribute to him]. When I see what that object's proper vesture is, in the aspect similar to man's, I borrow it, and fashion for myself a new garment in place of the old. For example, taking the words in their literal sense, gold is said to be yellow; milk, white; a rose, very red; honey, sweet-flowing; flames, glowing; snow, white. Say therefore: *snowy* teeth, *flaming* lips, *honied* taste, *rosy* countenance, *milky* brow, *golden* hair. These word-pairs are well suited to each other: teeth, snow; lips, flames; taste, honey; countenance, rose; brow, milk; hair, gold. And since here the linking of aspects that are similar sheds a pleasing light, if the subject of your discourse is not man, turn the reins of your mind to the human realm. With artistic tact, transpose a word which, in its literal sense, applies to man in an analogous situation. For example, if you should wish to say: "Springtime makes the earth beautiful; the first flowers grow up; the weather turns mild; storms cease; the sea is calm, its motion without violence; the vales are deep, the mountains lofty"; consider what words, in a literal sense, express the analogous situation in our human life. When you adorn something, you *paint*; when you enter on existence, you *are born;* affable in discourse, you *placate;* withdrawing from all activity, you *sleep;* motionless, you *stand on fixed foot;* sinking down, you *lie;* lifted into the air, you *rise.* The wording is a source of pleasure, then, if you say:

Springtime paints the earth with flowers: the first blossoms are born; the mild weather soothes; storms, dying down, slumber; the sea stands still, as if without movement; the valleys lie deep; the mountains rise aloft. . . .

Art has woven other garments of less price, yet they, too, have a dignified and appropriate use. There are in all ten[13] tropes, six in this group, four [in addition to metaphor, onomatopoeia, antonomasia, and allegory] mentioned above. This decade of figures adorns expression in a way we term *difficult* in that a word is taken only in its figurative and not in its literal sense. All the tropes are of one general class, distinguished by the figurative status of the words and the uncommon meaning assigned them. Lest understanding be uncertain and hesitant here, the following examples will ensure confidence.

METONYMY (*denominatio*). Consider a statement of this kind: *The sick man seeks a physician; the grieving man, solace; the poor man, aid.* Expression attains a fuller flowering in this trope: *Illness is in need of a physician; grief is in need of solace; poverty is in need of aid.* There is a natural charm in this use of the abstract for the concrete, and so in the change of *sick man* to *sickness, grieving man* to *grief, poor man* to *poverty.*

What does fear produce? Pallor. What does anger cause? A flush. Or what, the vice of pride? A swelling up. We refashion the statement thus: *Fear grows pale, anger flushes; pride swells.* There is greater pleasure and satisfaction for the ear when I attribute to the cause what the effect claims as its own.

Let the comb's action groom the hair after the head has been washed. Let scissors trim away from the hair whatever is excessive, and let a razor give freshness to the face. In this way, art teaches us to attribute to the instrument, by a happy turn of expression, what is proper to the one who uses it. So from the resources of art springs a means of avoiding worn-out paths and of travelling a more distinguished route.

Again, a statement expressed in the following way adds luster to style: *We have robbed their bodies of steel, their coffers of silver, their fingers of gold.* The point here is not that zeugma adorns the words with its own figure of speech, but that when I am about to mention something, I withhold its form completely and mention only the material. Whereas a less elegant style mentions both, art is silent about one, and conveys both by a single term. This device brings with it three advantages: it curtails the number of words required, it constitutes a poetic adornment, and it is helpful to the meter. It curtails the number of words in that a single term is more succinct than a word-group; it constitutes a poetic adornment in that an expression of this kind is artistically more skillful; and it is helpful to the meter if an oblique case, whose form the meter rejects, requires such help. This is clear from the following example: *The finger rejoices in gold. Gold* is a shorter sound, *a ring of gold* is longer; the latter form names the object itself, the former conveys it more artfully; in the former [*aurum*] the meter admits of oblique cases, in the latter [*annulus auri*] it rejects them. (1000)

Instead of the thing contained, name that which contains it, choosing the word judiciously whether it be noun or adjective. Introduce a noun in this way: *tippling England; weaving Flanders; bragging Normandy.* Try out an adjective thus: *clamorous market-places; silent cloisters; lamenting prison; jubilant house; quiet night; laborious day.* Seek turns of expression like the following: *In time of sickness Salerno, with its medical skill, cures those who are ill. In civil causes Bologna arms the defenceless with laws. Paris, in the arts, dispenses bread to feed the strong.* (1010) *Orleans, in its cradle, rears tender youth on the milk of the authors.*

HYPERBOLE (*superlatio*). Give hyperbole rein, but see that its discourse does not run ineptly hither and yon. Let reason keep it in check, and its moderate use be a source of pleasure, that neither mind nor ear may shrink from excess. For example, employing this trope: *A rain of darts lashes the foe like hail; the shattered array of spears resembles a forest; a tide of blood flows like a wave of the sea, and bodies clog the valleys.* This mode of expression diminishes or heightens eulogy to a remarkable degree; (1020) and exaggeration is a source of pleasure when both ear and good usage commend it.

SYNECDOCHE (*intellectio*). If you intend to say: *I studied for three years,* you may, with happier effect, adorn the statement. The wording above is inelegant and trite; you may refine the inelegant, your file may renew the trite in this way: *The third summer came upon me in study; the third autumn found me engaged; the third winter embroiled me in cares; in study I passed through three spring times.* I word the statement more skillfully when, suppressing the whole, I imply that whole from the parts, in the way just exemplified. Part of the year may be wet. *The year is wet;* (1030) part may be dry: *The year is dry;* part may be hot. *The year is hot;* part may be mild: *The year is mild.* I attribute to the whole what characterizes a part of it. By this same mode of reckoning, you, Gion, will be accounted turbid and clear, narrow and broad, brackish and sweet, because of some varied part of your course. Again, by the same figure, a day is to be accounted dry and yet rainy because of a part of it. Since both forms of this figure are pleasing, you may give pleasure by either form.

CATACHRESIS (*abusio*). There is likewise an urbane imprecision of diction when a word is chosen which is neither literal nor precise in its context, but which is related to the literal word. For example, if one proposes to say: (1040): *The strength of the Ithacan is slight, but yet he has a mind of great wisdom*, let catachresis alter the wording thus: *Strength in Ulysses is short, wisdom in his heart is long*, for there is a certain affinity between the words *long* and *great*, as between *short* and *slight.*

In the figures given above there is a common element of adornment and weightiness, arising from the fact that an object does not come before us with unveiled face, and accompanied by its natural voice; rather, an alien voice attends it, and so it shrouds itself in mist, as it were, but in a luminous mist. (1050)

HYPERBATON (*transgressio*). A certain weightiness of style results also from the order of words alone, when units grammatically related are separated by their position, so that an inversion of this sort occurs (anastrophe [*perversio*]) :*rege sub ipso; tempus ad illud; ea de causa; rebus in illis* [under the king himself; up to that time; for this reason; in those matters]; or a transposed order of this sort (transposition [*transjectio*]): *Dura creavit pestiferam fortuna famen* [harsh fortune produced a pestilent famine]; *Letalis egenam gente fames spoliavit humum* [deadly famine robbed the destitute soil of produce]. Here words related grammatically are separated by their position in the sentence. Juxtaposition of related words conveys the sense more readily, but their moderate separation sounds better to the ear and has greater elegance. . . . (1060)

Easy Ornament

If a mode of expression both easy and adorned is desired, set aside all the techniques of the dignified style and have recourse to means that are simple, but of a simplicity that does not shock the ear by its rudeness. . . .

Figures of thought. There are other figures [besides those of speech] to adorn the meaning of words. (1230) All of these I include in the following brief treatment: when meaning is adorned, this is the standard procedure. *Distributio* assigns specific roles to various things or among various persons. At times, *licentia,* fairly and lawfully, chides masters or friends, offending no one with its words. At times, *diminutio* implies more in the subject than is expressed in words, and makes its point by understatement, though with moderation. So, too, *descriptio* presents consequences, and the eventualities that can ensue from a given situation. It gives a full and lucid account with a certain dignity of presentation. (1240) Or again, *disjunctio* distinguishes alternatives, accompanying each with a reason, and bringing both to a conclusion. Or single details are brought together, and *frequentatio* gathers up points that had been scattered through the work. *Expolitio.* By turning a subject over repeatedly and varying the figure, I seem to be saying a number of things whereas I am actually dwelling on one thing, in order to give it a finer polish and impart a smooth finish by repeated applications of the file, one might say. This is done in two ways: either by saying the same thing with variations, or by elaborating upon the same thing. We may say the same thing with variations in three ways; we may elaborate upon the same thing with variations in seven ways. (1250) You may read about all of these at greater length in Cicero. [By *commoratio*] I go deeply into one point and linger on in the same place; or [by *contentio*] I institute a comparison in which the positions set forth are antithetical to each other. *Similitudo.* Often from an object basically dissimilar I draw forth a point of resemblance. Or I present as exemplum, with the name of a definite authority, some statement he has made or some deed he has performed. *Imago.* Or I pass over the figures just mentioned, and, as another figure comes to the fore, I introduce a comparison of one thing with a similar thing by means of an appropriate image. *Effictio.* Or there is a figure allied to this last one, (1260) whereby I depict or represent corporeal appearance, in so far as is requisite. *Notatio.* Again, I set down certain distinguishing marks—very definite signs, as it were—by which I describe clearly the character of a man; this is a better and more effective figure. *Sermocinatio.* There is another figure whereby a speech is adapted to the person speaking, and what is said gives the very tone and manner of the speaker. *Conformatio.* Again, adorning the subject with a different kind of freshness, at one time I fashion a new person by giving the power of speech where nature has denied it. *Significatio.* At another, I leave to suspicion more than I actually put into words. (1270) *Brevitas.* Again, I compress the entire subject into a few words—those which are essential to it and no others. *Demonstratio.* At another time the subject is revealed so vividly that it seems to be present to the eyes; this effect will be perfectly achieved by five means: if I show what precedes, what constitutes, and what follows the event itself, what circumstances attend it, and what consequences follow upon it. . . .

UNDERSTATEMENT. If this statement is proposed: *My power is not slight, my dignity not insignificant,* I am implying more than I say, and the actual situation is of greater consequence than the words indicate. If I happen to be speaking on behalf of my friends, or on my own behalf, this manner of speech is in good taste, and I show becoming modesty in employing such an expression. In this way, the meaning makes its appearance veiled; the true situation is not clearly apparent; there is more consequence in the actual fact than the expression of it indicates.

HYPERBOLE. *From the numerous and great resources left by his father, the squanderer of wealth has not enough to conceal his poverty with a covering, nor even an earthen jug in which to beg a fire.* (1540) Here I speak in excessive terms about a thing that is in itself excessive. I chide immoderately what is not moderate; there is moderation neither in the actual situation nor in my expression of it. If the situation is more moderate than my words, still the excessive language does suggest that there is less excess in the fact itself.

AMBIGUITY. *That peerless man:* the word means *most excellent;* but *most vicious* glances at us obliquely: this is its meaning. The word belies its appearance, or else our perception errs. In such ambiguities, the actual fact is veiled and the mockery is obvious.

CONSEQUENCE. *The boy's ruddy color fled his cheeks when he saw the rods, and his countenance was bloodless.* Such pallor indicates that he was afraid. *A blush had spread over the maiden's face;* her appearance indicates that she was ashamed. *The stroller went sauntering on with hair adorned;* the manner of expression suggests dissolute conduct. Note the signs that accompany a given circumstance. Present the facts, but do not present them as such; rather, reveal only signs of the facts: show fear by pallor, sensuality by adornment, and shame by a sudden blush; show the thing itself by its definite signs, what is prior by what is consequent upon it: this complexion, this sex, this age, that form.

APOSIOPESIS. *Recently in another's chamber . . . but I will not say it.* In this way I break off my words, and I do not say *that man,* but *a man of such-and-such an age,* or *of a certain appearance.*

ANALOGY. *You are great, and the world supplicates you on bent knee. Although you have power to vent your rage, do not do so; remember Nero.* After introducing an analogy in this way, I add nothing further. . . .

Various Prescriptions

If you heed the directives carefully and suit words to content, you will speak with precise appropriateness in this way. If mention has perhaps arisen of an object, sex, age, condition, event, place, or time, it is regard for its distinctive quality that the object, sex, age, condition, event, time, or place claims as its due. Felicity in this matter is an admirable thing, for when I make an apt use of qualifying words [*determino*] I give the whole theme a finished completeness [*termino*]. An object described [*condita*] in its entirety is a dish well-seasoned [*condīta*]. Note this prescription and heed its tenor; it is a prescription that is valid for prose as well as for verse. The same principle of art holds good for both, although in a different way.

Meter is straitened by laws, but prose roams along a freer way, for the public road of prose admits here and there wagons and carts, whereas the narrow path of a line of verse does not allow of things so inelegant. Verse wishes its very words to be graceful in appearance, lest the rustic form of a word embarrass by its ungainliness, and bring shame to the line. Meter desires to appear as a handmaid with hair adorned, with shining cheek, slim body, and peerless form. The charming gracefulness of verse cannot find a group of words of equal sweetness to the ear. A line of prose is a coarser thing; it favors all words, observing no distinction except in the case of those which it keeps for the end of periods: such words are those whose penultimate syllable carries the accent. It is not desirable that other words hold this final position. Aulus Gellius reaches the same conclusion and subjoins his reason: lest otherwise the number of syllables be weak and insufficient to bring the line to a close. If the last word of a period should be, as it frequently is, of a different cursus, nevertheless the one suggested above is preferable in as much as sounder opinion supports it —and my authority here is Aulus Gellius.[14] For the rest, the method of prose and verse does not differ; rather, the principles of art remain the same, whether in a composition bound by the laws of meter or in one independent of those laws, although what depends upon the principles of art is not always the same. In both prose and verse see that diction is controlled in such a way that words do not enter as dry things, but let their meaning confer a juicy savor upon them, and let them arrive succulent and rare. Let them say nothing in a childish way; see that they have dignity but not pomposity, lest what should be honorable becomes onerous. (1880) Do not let them enter with unsightly mien; rather, see that there is both internal and external adornment. Let the hand of artistic skill provide colors of both kinds. . . .

V. MEMORY

If you wish to remember all that reason invents, or order disposes, or adornment refines, (1970) keep in mind this counsel, valuable though brief: the little cell that remembers is a cell of delights, and it craves what is delightful, not what is boring. Do you wish to gratify it? Do not burden it. It desires to be treated kindly, not hard pressed. Because memory is a slippery thing, and is not capable of dealing with a throng of objects, feed it in the following way. When you appease hunger, do not be so sated with food that you can have nothing further set before you. Be more than half, but less than fully satisfied. Give to your stomach not as much as it can hold, but as much as is beneficial; (1980) nature is to be nourished, not overburdened. To remain between satiety and hunger is the wiser practice. So, too, in drinking, you moderate drink in accordance with reason. Sip, do not swill; let drink be taken in an honorable [*honori*], not an onerous [*oneri*] fashion. Drink as a temperate man, not a tippler. The abstemious man arraigns wine with better grace than the drunkard refutes him.[15] Knowledge, which is the food and drink of the mind, should be tasted in accordance with the same rule. Let it feed the mind in such a way that it is offered as a delight, not a burden to it. Suppose you are to learn this entire discourse: divide it into very small parts. (1990) Do not take several at once; rather, take one at a time, a very short section, much shorter than your shoulders are capable and desirous of bearing. In this way there will be pleasure, and nothing burdensome in the burden. Let practice come as companion; while the matter is fresh and new go over it frequently and repeat it; then stop, rest for a little while, take a breathing space. After a short delay has intervened, another piece may be summoned up; when it has been memorized in the same way, let practice join both parts together in the cell mentioned above, let it consolidate them and cement them together. (2000) Join a third part to these two with a similar bond, and a fourth part to the other three. But, in following through these steps, you make a mistake if you do not consistently proceed in such a way that you stop short of weariness. This advice holds good for all the faculties of sense; it sharpens those that are dull, makes pliable those that are rigid, and raises to greater heights of excellence those that are acute and flexible. Whatever attempts more than these precepts accomplishes less. Therefore let this sound principle adapt to each man the weight he can bear, and be the one model for all.

To these methods add others which I make use of—and which it is expedient to use. When I wish to recall things I have seen, or heard, or memorized before, or engaged in before, I ponder thus: I saw, I heard, I considered, I acted in such or such a way, either at that time or in that place: places, times, images, or other similar signposts are for me a sure path which leads me to the things themselves. Through these signs I arrive at active knowledge. Such and such a thing was so, and I picture to myself such and such a thing.

Cicero relies on unusual images as a technique for training the memory; but he is teaching himself; and let the subtle teacher, as it were in solitude, address his subtlety to himself alone. But my own subtlety may be pleasing to me and not to him. It is beneficial to one whom it suits, for enjoyment alone makes the power of memory strong. Therefore have no faith in these or in other signposts if they are difficult for you, or if they are unacceptable. But if you wish to proceed with greater security, fashion signs for yourself, whatever kind your own inclination suggests. As long as they give you pleasure, you may be taught through their means. There are some men who wish to know, but not to make an effort, nor to endure the concentration and pain of learning. That is the way of the cat; it wants the fish, but not the fishing. I am not addressing myself to such men, but to those who delight in knowing, and also in the effort of acquiring knowledge.

VI. DELIVERY

In reciting aloud, let three tongues speak: let the first be that of the mouth, the second that of the speaker's countenance, and the third that of gesture. The voice has its own laws, and you should observe them in this way: the period that is spoken should observe its natural pauses, and the word its accent. Separate those words which the sense separates, join those that sense joins. Modulate your voice in such a way that it is in harmony with the subject; and take care that voice does not advance along a path different from that which the subject follows. Let the two go together; let the voice be, as it were, a reflection of the subject. As the nature of your subject is, so let your voice be when you rehearse it: let us recognize them as one.

Anger, child of fire and mother of fury, springing up from the very bellows, poisons the heart and soul. It stings with its bellows, sears with its fire, convulses with its fury. Under its emotion, a caustic voice speaks; an inflamed countenance and turbulent gestures accompany it. The outward emotion corresponds with the inward; outer and inner man are affected alike. If you act the part of this man, what, as reciter, will you do? Imitate genuine fury, but do not be furious. Be affected in part as he is, but not deeply so. Let your manner be the same in every respect, but not so extreme; yet suggest, as is fitting, the emotion itself. You can represent the manner of a rustic and still be graceful: let your voice represent his voice; your facial expression, his own; and your gesture his gesture—by recognizable signs. This is a carefully tempered skill; this method is attractive in the tongue that recites, and this food is a delight to the ear. Therefore, let a voice controlled by good taste, seasoned with the two spices of facial expression and gesture, be borne to the ears to feed the hearing. Strength issues from the tongue, for death and life depend upon the powers of the tongue, if haply it is aided by the tempering principles of facial expression and gesture. So, then, let all be in harmony: suitable invention, flowing expression, polished development, firm retention in memory. If discourses are delivered ineptly, they are no more to be praised than is a recitation charmingly delivered but without the other requirements mentioned.

DANTE

(1265–1321)

INTRODUCTION

Dante's *Divine Comedy* is usually considered the culmination of medieval poetry. His critical works are in the same sense a culmination of medieval poetics. Unlike most medieval critical works, they are highly original. They show an awareness of tradition, particularly scholastic tradition, but Dante was not a compiler or redactor like Vincent of Beauvais or Geoffrey of Vinsauf. He depended on his own direct experience as a poet for much of his knowledge, supplementing this with deduction based on forms of scholastic logic. His three major treatises are the *De Vulgari Eloquentia,* the *Convivio,* and the thirteenth of his *Epistles,* which is an exposition of the *Divine Comedy.* The first two works are incomplete. They were probably begun in 1304–6, during Dante's residence in Bologna in the years following his exile from Florence (1301) after the triumph of the "Black" party led by Gabrielli da Gubbio. The *De Vulgari* was planned in four books but it breaks off in the middle of Chapter 14 of Book II. The *Convivio* was planned as an encyclopedic work of fifteen books. The materials were to evolve naturally in the course of a detailed commentary by Dante on fourteen of his own *canzoni.* Only four books were completed. *Epistle XIII* is addressed to Can Grande della Scala and dedicates the *Paradiso* to him. If it is genuine, internal evidence suggests a date of around 1316–19. However, its genuineness has long been doubted. It is first mentioned around 1390, long after Dante's death; and it is a tissue of critical formulas. If not genuine, it remains an important document for the light it casts on the *Comedy* and for the summation it provides of medieval thought on allegory, literary genres, the system of styles, and related objects.

The *Convivio* is the least easy of Dante's critical works to "place" in medieval tradition. The title *Convivio*—or "banquet"—relates it ultimately to Plato's *Symposium,* and more proximately to such informal miscellanies as the *Noctes Atticae* of Aulus Gellius and the *Saturnalia* of Macrobius; but it is more formal than either of these. It is not a dialogue but a group of formal essays divided into chapters. Its approach is philosophical rather than grammatical or rhetorical, and the philosophy is deduced by allegorical readings of the poems under consideration. In this respect, it is close to the *De Continentia* of Fulgentius and the Vergil commentary of Bernard Silvestris. The immediate source for the work, apart from Dante's wish to justify himself and express his thoughts about an ideal society, seems to have been Brunetto Latini's *Tesoretto.*

The most interesting sections of the *Convivio* are the first book, which contains a lengthy discussion of Dante's reasons for choosing the vernacular rather than Latin, and the first Chapter of Book II, which is a little essay on the various allegorical senses to be found in a literary work. The consideration of the vernacular overlaps the *De Vulgari* and need not be taken up here. The discussion of allegory is the most detailed treatment of the subject which we have from Dante. If the *Epistle to Can Grande* is spurious, the discussion in the *Convivio* is the only extended treatment. Dante begins by distinguishing the literal from the other senses. The first non-literal sense is called "allegorical" since it presents meanings "hidden under the veil of the fables, and it is a truth concealed in a beautiful lie." Ovid, for example, relates that Orpheus charmed wild animals and moved stones and trees with his music. This is an allegory of the fact that the wise man can charm the hearts of ignorant and unruly men. Dante adds, "Indeed, the theologians understand this [allegorical] sense differently from the poets; but because my intention is to follow the fashion of the poets here, I take the allegorical sense in the way that it is used by the poets." The distinction between poetic and theological allegory is important and has been discussed frequently. Dante probably made it to placate the conservative theologians of the day who mistrusted and attacked the divine pretentions of the humanistic poetics—the claim that poetry is divinely inspired, that the poet is a *vates*—a prophet, and that poetry is a kind of revelation.

In context, the distinction between theological and poetic allegory is related to Dante's use of the term *favola,* which, in the later Middle Ages, almost always meant a fictional (i.e., lying) story. If they write *favole,* poets are in some sense committed to falsehood rather than truth. As Conrad of Hirsau put it, a poet is "a maker or former, because he says false things rather than true ones or mixes truth from time to time with his falsehoods." But the *favola* is only the "literal" level of secular poetry. Its higher senses may be both true and morally edifying. This provides the basis for Dante's distinction between theology and poetry. Essentially, theology is true in all senses—literal as well as allegorical—whereas poetry is false in its literal sense and true only in its higher meanings: "The subject of sacred [theology] is divine virtue; the ancient poets treat the Gods of the Gentiles as men. Theology and poetry are contradictory insofar as theology brings forward from the beginning nothing unless it is true; poetry brings forward things as true that are wholly false."

The second non-literal sense is defined as moral. It teaches useful lessons. Scripture is especially rich in this kind of allegory. The third is anagogical or spiritual. When David, for example, speaks of the exodus of the Israelites from Egypt, he not only refers to an historical event but also, anagogically, to the freeing of the spirit from a state of sin. Dante stresses the fact that the literal sense is important; it is the "outside" and one cannot come to the "inside" of a thing without passing through its "outside." His point is significant. Most obviously, he is saying that one cannot proceed immediately in criticism to the inner or higher sense of a work ignoring its "outside." One must begin with what it is, its surface texture, its story and language. By implication, the passage is an assertion of the unity of any work of art. A poem cannot any more be separated into "meaning" and "content" than the "inside" of something can be separated from the "outside." After further argument along this line, Dante ends with a statement of the critical method to be used in analyzing the *canzoni* to be considered in the later books of the *Convivio*: "Therefore, for this reason, I will regularly analyze the literal sense of each *canzone* first, and after that I will analyze the allegory, that is, what is the hidden truth, and from time to time I will touch on the other senses in passing, as time and place permit."

II

The *Epistle to Can Grande della Scala* is in every way a more mechanical piece of work than the *Convivio.* It is heavily scholastic and heavily "Aristotelian" in the negative sense of being dominated by nice logical distinctions and formal definitions. Based on the *accessus* (list of authors) tradition, it tells us, essentially, that the *Divine Comedy* is an allegory having the four levels of biblical allegory. If the work is genuine, Dante has either forgotten the distinction in the *Convivio* between poetic and theological allegory, or he is making a bolder claim for the *Comedy* than he was willing to make for his *canzoni.* We learn further that the subject and form of the poem are both double. On the literal level the subject of the *Comedy* is the state of souls after death; allegorically, the consequences of virtuous and sinful choices. The definition of the form of the poem is particularly redolent of scholastic method: "The form or mode of treatment is poetic, fictitious, descriptive, digressive, transumptive [metaphorical], and, with all, definitive, divisive, probative, improbative, and exemplary."

The *accessus* formula calls for an explanation of the work's title. Dante explains the word *comedy* in a substantial passage based directly or indirectly on the treatises on tragedy and comedy ascribed to Donatus. He further points out that the department of philosophy to which the poem belongs is ethics—an echo of medieval didacticism, although less ambitious than Boccaccio's claim that Dante wrote as a theologian. All of this is most useful to reader of the *Divine*

Comedy, but it is so stylized as to be impersonal, and it contributes much less than the *Convivio* and the *De Vulgari* to our sense of Dante as a literary critic.

III

Written at approximately the same time as the *Convivio, De Vulgari Eloquentia* is both more traditional and more radical. Its subject matter relates it to the mass of grammatical literature dealing with the *ars metrica* collected in Volume VI of Keil's *Grammatici Latini* and—for the late Middle Ages—in Giovanni Mari's *I trattati medievali di ritmica latina* (Milan, 1899). Mari's *Trattati* deal with accentual Latin meters, and rhymes and stanza forms, and presumably reflect the tradition that led to manuals on vernacular poetry. They anticipate the chapters in Book II of the *De Vulgari* that give the rules for writing *canzoni.* But concern for prosody and rhyme are all they have in common with Dante. They are derivative for the most part and offer no precedent whatever for the wide-ranging philosophical analysis of language which occupies Book I and the earlier chapters of Book II.

Dante was conscious of the originality of his work. He begins with the statement that "we do not find that anyone before us has treated the science of vernacular language," and later he remarks (I.10), "our purpose is to investigate matters in which we are supported by the authority of none"—a remarkable statement for an age almost supinely dependent on authority.

Several general themes of great interest run through the work. Speech is considered an innate faculty correlative to man's status as a rational being, but, at the same time, a divine gift, "inspired by the vivifying power" (I.5). The purpose of speech is social, for rational beings must have a medium for the "intercommunication" of their thoughts (I.3). Dante now moves from hypothesis to the record of history as he understood it. During the first age, from Adam to Nimrod, there was only one language with a single form: "And I say 'a form,' both in respect of words and their construction and of the utterance of this construction; and this form every tongue of speaking men could use, if it had not been dissipated by the fault of man's presumption" (I.6). That there was originally only one language and that this was Hebrew follows both from the Bible and from the fact that God intended language for "intercommunication." The primitive unity of man was soon destroyed, however, by the vanity that created the Tower of Babel. Since then, the number of languages has multiplied. "Intercommunication" has given way to lack of communication. And the process is continuing. Dante points out that in Italy alone there are some fourteen dialects with innumerable local variations (I.10) and that changes are still going on: "since man is a most unstable and changeable animal, no human language can be lasting and continuous, but must needs vary like other properties of ours, as for instance our manners and our dress" (I.9). Dante revised and deepened his view of language in human affairs later in his life (see *Paradiso* XXVI). His later view suggests an attitude toward linguistic change that anticipates what is today called "historicism."

The image which Dante's history gives us is partly anthropological, partly psychological. Language is the vehicle of human society and man finds fulfillment in it. It is bestowed on men by a loving God, but man frustrates God's wishes—and his own needs as a spiritual being—by vanity. As languages multiply and become ever more distinct, men grow more and more isolated from one another.

There are two remedies for this. The first is grammar, which attempts to formulate universal principles of language: "Hence were set in motion the inventors of the art of grammar, which is nothing else but a kind of unchangeable identity of speech in different times and places. This, having been settled by the common consent of many peoples, seems exposed to the arbitrary will of none in particular, and consequently cannot be variable. They therefore invented grammar in order that we might not, on account of the variation of speech fluctuating at the will of individuals, either fail altogether in attaining, or at least attain but a partial knowledge of the opinions and exploits of the ancients, or of those whom difference of place causes to differ from us" (I.9).

Dante's emphasis on community, the original function of speech, is reasserted here in the opposition of "common consent" to "arbitrary will" and the "will of individuals." Grammar enables us to move, even though the movement may be slight, away from diversity and toward the unity that was our primitive birthright.

The second way is the way of the poet. It forms the burden of the remainder of Book I. As an Italian who had self-consciously chosen the path of vernacular rather than Latin poetry, Dante was primarily interested in his own language. His survey of Italian dialects (I.10) shows that he was thoroughly aware of how numerous and how diverse they were. On the one hand, this poses an aesthetic problem: "As the Italian vernacular has so very many discordant varieties, let us hunt after a more fitting and an illustrious Italian language" (I.11). On the other hand, and perhaps more deeply, we have seen that for Dante variation in language is a movement away from divinely ordained unity. The aesthetic problem cannot be separated from a social one. The Florentine exile and later, in the *De Monarchia,* the apostle of secular unity through world government, could hardly have been unaware of the practical and at the same time politically radical implications of calling for a single "fitting and illustrious Italian tongue" sanctioned by poets and used in the great affairs of state: "if we Italians had a court it would be spoken at court. For if a court is a common home of all the realm and an august ruler of all parts of the realm, it is fitting that whatever is of such a character as to be common to all [parts] without being peculiar to any, should frequent this court and dwell there . . . hence it is that those who frequent all royal palaces always speak the illustrious vernacular. Hence also it is that our illustrious language wanders about like a wayfarer, and is welcomed in humble shelters, seeing we have no court" (I.18).

The language that Dante seeks will be "illustrious, cardinal, courtly, and curial" (I.16). His method of deducing it constitutes the first empirical linguistic survey ever made of a modern European language and anticipates the efforts of the Accademia della Crusca and the Académie Française by almost three hundred years. Dante's metaphor for the project, which conveys some of its excitement, is that of the hunt (I.xi.16). In considering each dialect, Dante seeks elements common to all. In other words, he is seeking (in terms of the hunt metaphor, attempting to "track down") something like the underlying "form of speech" which was instilled by God in the first soul (I.6) and which is revealed in the analytic studies of the grammarians (I.9). Certain dialects have little to offer grammarians. This is proven by the fact that poets to whom these dialects were native abandoned them for a higher kind of speech in their poems. The point is charming and persuasive, and it has a serious meaning. The poet depicted in the *De Vulgari* is a man especially sensitive to language. Whether by instinct or design the great Italian poets of the past have pointed the way to the "illustrious vernacular"; and future poets will insure its greatness when it has been fully revealed. We are far, here, from the divinely inspired seer of Boccaccio, but nearer, perhaps, to an understanding of the poet's social role which a twentieth-century critic could accept.

Three dialects particularly interest Dante. Sicilian itself is defective, but the language of the poets of the court of Frederick and Manfred "differs in nothing from that language which is the most worthy of praise" (I.12). This association of the best language with a noble and gracious court is presented in an empirical observation in Chapter 12, but it reappears as an integral part of Dante's definition in the requirement that the best language be "illustrious" and "courtly" (I.16).

In Chapter 16 Dante announces that the hunt—i.e., the empirical survey—is over, and that the next step will be logical analysis. All members of the same genus may be compared because of certain common properties. It is these common properties that constitute the language "whose fragrance is in every town, but whose lair is in none." The analysis ends with the famous definition, which establishes the "form of speech" of the ideal vernacular:

> We declare the illustrious, cardinal, courtly and curial vernacular language in Italy to be that which belongs to all the towns in Italy but does not appear to belong to any one of them, and by which all the municipal dialects of the Italians are measured, weighed, and compared. (I.16)

In this definition "illustrious" refers to the fact that the language "shines forth" from the surrounding dross. This has been demonstrated in its use by the many poets, nurtured on different dialects, cited by Dante in the preceding chapters. It also "illuminates" those who use it, in the sense of exerting a noble and refining power. Again we are reminded of Dante's conception of language as a vehicle of culture. It not only permits communication. When properly constituted, it elevates and liberates those who use it. Poetry was a cause as well as a manifestation of the greatness of King Frederick's court. Social cannot be separated from aesthetic considerations.

The term "cardinal" (Lat. *cardo*-hinge) is a description of the centrality of the ideal language among the multitude of dialects. "Courtly" refers to its appropriateness to educated society with the hint, perhaps, that it may have a unifying effect on Italy similar to that of a royal court. "Curial" (Lat. *curia,* a court of justice) alludes to the fact that the illustrious language has been judged proper by the "gracious light of reason" (I.18) which is the Italian equivalent of the German imperial court.

Book II may be treated summarily. Dante continues the analytic method initiated in the closing chapters of Book I. He shows that the illustrious language is suited only to noble men and worthy objects. The worthiest objects (II.2) are arms, love, and virtue, the objectives respectively of the vegetable, animal, and rational souls. The worthiest form of poetry is the *canzone* which "embraces the art of poetry" much as the illustrious vernacular is common to all dialects. Among styles, the tragic is the most worthy (II.4), and among standard Italian lines, the eleven-syllable line is superior, although lines of three, five, and seven syllables may also be used (II.5). In vocabulary, words which are "combed out," "glossy," and "shaggy," and "rumpled" will be most appropriate (II.7). The discussion is of interest to the history of style since it echoes the ancient distinction between the three styles (*humilis, mediocris, nobilis*) and the tradition linking these styles to literary types (for Dante, elegy is humble, comedy, middle, and tragedy, elevated). Dante's selection of the hendeca syllabic is not only appropriate for Italian, but echoes for the vernacular the standard preference of the *artes metricae* for the dactylic hexameter, the longest of regular Latin quantitative lines. His stylistic terms are unique to the *De Vulgari,* but the fondness of late classical and medieval authors for adjectives suggesting different stylistic ideals has been amply documented by de Bruyne in his discussion of the Attic-Asiatic controversy between the fifth and the ninth centuries. The remainder of Book II is more technical. Although Dante continues to work deductively, his prescriptions are really a summary of the rules that he and his fellow poets regularly followed.

In spite of being unfinished, the *De Vulgari* is the only medieval critical essay that ranks with the great classical and modern critical essays. Its assumption of the fundamental unity of man, its view of language as both an innate faculty and a creator of culture, its vision of the poet as a supreme master of language who uses his genius and skill to further the ends of language, and its consistent linking of social and cultural matters are ideas which remain worthy of respect in the twentieth century. But the *De Vulgari* is more than an expression of critical ideals. It is also a brilliant essay in speculative anthropology, an informed survey of Italian dialects, and the only medieval treatise dealing with prosody that breaks away from the tired stereotypes of the *artes rithmicae* and the *artes poeticae.*

The translation, here slightly modernized, and the notes are from A. G. Ferrers Howell and Philip H. Wicksteed, *A Translation of the Latin Works of Dante Alighieri* (London: Dent, 1904). For bibliography, see especially pp. 489–90. For a recent discussion of Dante's authorship of the *Epistle to Can Grande della Scala,* see Allan H. Gilbert, "Did Dante Dedicate the *Paradiso* to Can Grande?" *Italica,* XLII (1966), 100–24.

DE VULGARI ELOQUENTIA

BOOK I

I

Since we do not find that any one before us has treated of the science of the vernacular language, while in fact we see that this language is highly necessary for all, inasmuch as not only men, but even women and children, strive, in so far as nature allows them, to acquire it; and since it is our wish to enlighten to some little extent the discernment of those who walk through the streets like blind men, generally fancying that those things which are [really] in front of them are behind them, we will endeavor, the Word aiding us from heaven, to be of service to the vernacular speech; not only drawing the water of our own wit for such a drink, but mixing with it the best of what we have taken or compiled from others, so that we may thence be able to give draughts of the sweetest hydromel.[1] But because the business of every science is not to prove but to explain its subject, in order that men may know what that is with which the science is concerned, we say (to come quickly to the point) that what we call the vernacular speech is that to which children are accustomed by those who are about them when they first begin to distinguish words; or to put it more shortly, we say that the vernacular speech is that which we acquire without any rule, by imitating our nurses. There further springs from this another secondary speech, which the Romans called grammar. And this secondary speech the Greeks also have, as well as others, but not all. Few, however, acquire the use of this speech, because we can only be guided and instructed in it by the expenditure of much time, and by assiduous study. Of these two kinds of speech also, the vernacular is the nobler, as well because it was the first employed by the human race, as because the whole world makes use of it, though it has been divided into forms differing in pronunciation and vocabulary. It is also the nobler as being natural to us, whereas the other is rather of an artificial kind; and it is of this our nobler speech that we intend to treat.

II

This [then] is our true first speech. I do not, however, say "our" as implying that any other kind of speech exists beside man's; for to man alone of all existing beings was speech given, because for him alone was it necessary. Speech was not necessary for the angels or for the lower animals, but would have been given to them in vain, which nature, as we know, shrinks from doing. For if we clearly consider what our intention is when we speak, we shall find that it is nothing else but to unfold to others the thoughts of our own mind. Since, then, the angels have, for the purpose of manifesting their glorious thoughts, a most ready and indeed ineffable sufficiency of intellect, by which one of them is known in all respects to another, either of himself, or at least by means of that most brilliant mirror in which all of them are represented in the fulness of their beauty, and into which they all most eagerly gaze, they do not seem to have required the outward indications of speech. And if an objection be raised concerning the spirits who fell, it may be answered in two ways. First we may say that inasmuch as we are treating of those things which are necessary for well-being, we ought to pass over the fallen angels, because they perversely refused to wait for the divine care.[2] Or secondly (and better), that the devils themselves only need, in order to disclose their perfidy to one another, to know, each of another, that he exists, and what is his power: which they certainly do know, for they had knowledge of one another before their fall.

The lower animals also, being guided by natural instinct alone, did not need to be provided with the power of speech, for all those of the same species have the same actions and passions; and so they are enabled by their own actions and passions to know those of others. But among those of different species not only was speech unnecessary, but it would have been altogether harmful, since there would have been no friendly intercourse between them.

And if it be objected concerning the serpent speaking to the first woman, or concerning Balaam's ass, that they spoke, we reply that the angel in the latter, and the devil in the former, wrought in such a manner that the animals themselves set their organs in motion in such wise that the voice thence sounded clear like genuine speech; not that the sound uttered was to the ass anything but braying, or to the serpent anything but hissing.

But if any one should argue in opposition, from what Ovid says in the fifth book of the *Metamorphoses*[3] about magpies speaking, we reply that he says this figuratively, meaning something else. And if any one should rejoin that even up to the present time magpies and other birds speak, we say that it is false, because such action is not speaking, but a kind of imitation of the sound of our voice, or in other words, we say that they try to imitate us in so far as we utter sounds, but not in so far as we speak. If accordingly any one were to say expressly "Pica" [magpie], and "Pica" were answered back, this would be but a copy or imitation of the sound made by him who had first said the word.

And so it is evident that speech has been given to man alone. But let us briefly endeavor to explain why this was necessary for him.

III

Since, then, man is not moved by natural instinct but by reason, and reason itself differs in individuals in respect of discernment, judgment, and choice, so that each one of us appears almost to rejoice in his own species, we are of opinion that no one has knowledge of another by means of his own actions or passions, as a brute beast; nor does it happen that one man can enter into another by spiritual insight, like an angel, since the human spirit is held back by the grossness and opacity of its mortal body. It was therefore necessary that the human race should have some sign, at once rational and sensible, for the intercommunication of its thoughts, because the sign, having to receive something from the reason of one and to convey it to the reason of another, had to be rational; and since nothing can be conveyed from one reason to another except through a medium of sense, it had to be sensible; for, were it only rational, it could not pass [from the reason of one to that of another]; and were it only sensible it would neither have been able to take from the reason of one nor to deposit in that of another.

Now this sign is that noble subject itself of which we are speaking; for in so far as it is sound, it is sensible, but in so far as it appears to carry some meaning according to the pleasure [of the speaker] it is rational.

IV

Speech was given to man alone, as is plain from what has been said above. And now I think we ought also to investigate to whom of mankind speech was first given, and what was the first thing he said, and to whom, where, and when he said it; and also in what language this first speech came forth. Now, according to what we read in the beginning of Genesis, where the most sacred Scripture is treating of the origin of the world, we find that a woman spoke before all others, I mean that most presumptuous Eve, when in answer to the inquiry of the devil she said, "We eat of the fruit of the trees which are in Paradise, but of the fruit of the tree which is in the midst of Paradise God has commanded us not to eat, nor to touch it, lest peradventure we die." But though we find it written that the woman spoke first, it is, however, reasonable for us to suppose that the man spoke first; and it is unseemly to think that so excellent an act of the human race proceeded even earlier from woman than from man. We therefore reasonably believe that speech was given to Adam first by him who had just formed him.

Now I have no doubt that it is obvious to a man of sound mind that the first thing the voice of the first speaker uttered was the equivalent of God, namely *El,* whether in the way of a question or in the way of an answer. It seems absurd and repugnant to reason that anything should have been named by man before God, since man had been made by him and for him. For as, since the transgression of the human race, every one begins his first attempt at speech with a cry of woe, it is reasonable that he who existed before that transgression should begin with joy; and since there is no joy without God, but all joy is in God, and God himself is wholly joy, it follows that the first speaker said first and before anything else "God." Here also this question arises from our saying above that man spoke first by way of answer: If an answer, was it addressed to God? For if so it would seem that God had already spoken, which appears to make against what has been said above. To which we reply that he might well have made answer when God questioned him; but it does not follow from this that God uttered what we call speech. For who doubts that whatsoever is can be bent according to the will of God? For by him all things were made, by him they are preserved, and by him also they are governed. Therefore since the air is made to undergo such great disturbances by the ordinance of that lower nature which is the minister and workmanship of God, that it causes the thunder to peal, the lightning to flash, the water to drop, and scatters the snow and hurls down the hail, shall it not be moved to utter certain words rendered distinct by him who has distinguished greater things? Why not? Wherefore we consider that these observations are a sufficient answer to this difficulty, and to some others.

V

Thinking then (not without reason drawn as well from the foregoing considerations as from those which follow) that the first man directed his speech first of all to the Lord himself, we may reasonably say that this first speaker at once, after having been inspired by the vivifying power, spoke without hesitation.

For in man we believe it to be more characteristic of humanity to be heard than to hear, provided he be heard and hear as a man. If, therefore, that workman and origin and lover of perfection by his breath made the first of us complete in all perfection, it appears to us reasonable that this most noble of animals did not begin to hear before he began to be heard. But if any one raises the objection that there was no need for him to speak, as he was, so far, the only human being, whilst God discerns all our secret thoughts without any words of ours, even before we do ourselves, we say with that reverence which we ought to use in judging anything respecting the eternal will, that though God knew, nay, even fore-knew (which is the same thing in respect of God) the thought of the first man who spoke, without any words being said, still he wished that the man should also speak, in order that, in the unfolding of so great a gift, he himself who had freely bestowed it might glory. And therefore it is to be believed that it is by God's appointment that we rejoice in the well-ordered play of our emotions.

Hence also we can fully determine the place where our first speech was uttered; for if man was inspired with life outside Paradise, he first spoke outside; but if within, we have proved that the place of his first speech was within.

VI

Since human affairs are carried on in very many different languages, so that many men are not understood by many with words any better than without words, it is appropriate for us to make investigation concerning that language which that man who had no mother, who was never suckled, who never saw either childhood or youth, is believed to have spoken. In this as in much else Pietramala is a most populous city, and the native place of the majority of the children of Adam. For whoever is so offensively unreasonable as to suppose that the place of his birth is the most delightful under the sun, also rates his own vernacular (that is, his mother-tongue) above all others, and consequently believes that it actually was that of Adam. But we, to whom the world is our native country, just as the sea is to the fish, though we drank of Arno before our teeth appeared, and though we love Florence so dearly that for the love we bore her we are wrongfully suffering exile—we rest the shoulders of our judgment on reason rather than on feeling. And although as regards our own pleasure or sensuous comfort there exists no more agreeable place in the world than Florence, still, when we turn over the volumes both of poets and other writers in which the world is generally and particularly described, and take account within ourselves of the various situations of the places of the world and their arrangement with respect to the two poles and to the equator, our deliberate and firm opinion is that there are many countries and cities both nobler and more delightful than Tuscany and Florence of which we are a native and a citizen, and also that a great many nations and races use a speech both more agreeable and more serviceable than the Italians do. Returning therefore to our subject, we say that a certain form of speech was created by God together with the first soul. And I say "a form," both in respect of words and sentences and of the utterance of sentences; and this form every tongue of speaking men would use, if it had not been dissipated by the fault of man's presumption, as shall be shown further on.

In this form of speech Adam spoke; in this form of speech all his descendants spoke until the building of the Tower of Babel, which is by interpretation the tower of confusion; and this form of speech was inherited by the sons of Heber, who after him were called Hebrews. With them alone did it remain after the confusion, in order that our Redeemer (who was, as to his humanity, to spring from them) might use, not the language of confusion, but of grace. Therefore Hebrew was the language which the lips of the first speaker formed.

VII

It is, alas! with feelings of shame that we now recall the ignominy of the human race. But since it is impossible for us to avoid passing through it, we will hasten through it, though the blush of shame rises to our cheeks and our mind recoils. O thou our human nature, ever prone to sin! O thou, full of iniquity from the first and ever afterwards without cessation! Did it suffice for thy correction that, deprived of light through thy first transgression, thou wast banished from thy delightful native land? Did it suffice, did it suffice that through the universal lust and cruelty of thy family, one house alone excepted, whatsoever was subject to thee had perished in the Flood, and that the animals of earth and air had already been punished for what thou hadst committed? Certainly this should have been enough! But as men are wont to say in the proverb, "Thou shalt not ride on horseback before the third time," thou, wretched one, didst choose rather to come to a wretched steed.

See, reader, how man, either forgetting or despising his former discipline, and turning aside his eyes from the marks of the stripes which had remained, for the third time provoked the lash by his stupid and presumptuous pride! For incorrigible man, persuaded by the giant, presumed in his heart to surpass by his own skill not only nature, but even the very power that works in nature, who is God; and he began to build a tower in Sennear, which was afterwards called Babel, that is, confusion, by which he hoped to ascend to heaven; purposing in his ignorance, not to equal, but to surpass his Maker. O boundless clemency of the heavenly power! Who among fathers would bear so many insults from a son? But he arose, and, with a scourge which was not hostile but paternal and had been wont at other times to smite, he chastised his rebellious son with correction at once merciful and memorable. For almost the whole human race had come together to the work of wickedness. Some were giving orders, some were acting as architects, some were building the walls, some were adjusting the masonry with rules, some were laying on the mortar with trowels, some were quarrying stone, some were engaged in bringing it by sea, some by land; and different companies were engaged in different other occupations, when they were struck by such confusion from heaven, that all those who were attending to the work, using one and the same language, left off the work on being estranged by many different languages and never again came together in the same intercourse. For the same language remained to those alone who were engaged together in the same kind of work; for instance, one language remained to all the architects, another to those rolling down blocks of stone, another to those preparing the stone; and so it happened to each group of workers. And the human race was accordingly then divided into as many different languages as there were different branches of the work; and the higher the branch of work the men were engaged in, the ruder and more barbarous was the language they afterwards spoke.

But those to whom the hallowed language remained were neither present, nor countenanced the work; but utterly hating it, they mocked the folly of those engaged in it. But these, a small minority, were of the seed of Shem (as I conjecture), who was the third son of Noah; and from them sprang the people of Israel, who made use of the most ancient language until their dispersion.

VIII

On account of the confusion of tongues related above we have no slight reason for thinking that men were at that time first scattered through all the climates of the world, and the habitable regions and corners of those climates. And as the original root of the human race was planted in the regions of the East, and our race also spread out from there on both sides by a manifold diffusion of shoots, and finally reached the boundaries of the West, it was then perhaps that rational throats first drank of the rivers of the whole of Europe, or at least of some of them. But whether these men then first arrived as strangers, or whether they came back to Europe as natives, they brought a threefold language with them, and of those who brought it some allotted to themselves the southern, others the northern part of Europe, while the third body, whom we now call Greeks, seized partly on Europe and partly on Asia.

Afterwards, from one and the same idiom received at the avenging confusion, various vernaculars drew their origin, as we shall show farther on. For one idiom alone prevailed in all the country which from the mouths of the Danube, or marshes of Mæotis to the western boundary of England, is bounded by the frontiers of Italy and France and by the ocean; though afterwards through the Slavs, Hungarians, Teutons, Saxons, English, and many other nations it was drawn off into various vernaculars, this alone remaining to almost all of them as a sign of their common origin, that nearly all the above-named answer in affirmation *ìo*.

Starting from this idiom, that is to say eastward from the Hungarian frontier, another language prevailed over all the territory in that direction comprised in Europe, and even extended beyond. But a third idiom prevailed in all that part of Europe which remains from the other two, though it now appears in a threefold form. For of those who speak it, some say in affirmation *oc*,[4] others *oïl*, and others *sì*, namely the Spaniards, the French, and the Italians. Now the proof that the vernaculars of these nations proceed from one and the same idiom is obvious, because we see that they call many things by the same names, as *Deum, celum, amorem, mare, terram, vivit, moritur, amat,* and almost all other things. Now those of them who say *oc* inhabit the western part of the South of Europe, beginning from the frontier of the Genoese; while those who say *sì* inhabit the country east of the said frontier, namely that which extends as far as that promontory of Italy where the Gulf of the Adriatic Sea begins, and Sicily. But those who say *oïl* lie in some sort to the north of these last; for they have the Germans on their east and north; on the west they are enclosed by the English sea, and bounded by the mountains of Aragon; they are also shut off on the south by the inhabitants of Provence, and the precipices of the Apennines.

IX

We must now put whatever reason we possess to the proof, since it is our purpose to investigate matters in which we are supported by the authority of none, namely, the change which has passed over a language which was originally of one and the same form. [And] because it is safer as well as quicker to travel by known paths, let us proceed with that language alone which belongs to us, neglecting the others. For that which we find in one appears by analogy to exist in the others also.

The language, then, which we are proceeding to treat of is threefold, as has been mentioned above; for some of those who speak it say *oc*, others *sì*, and others *oïl*. And that this language was uniform at the beginning of the confusion (which must first be proved) appears from the fact that we agree in many words, as eloquent writers show, which agreement is repugnant to that confusion which expiated the crime [committed] in the building of Babel.

The writers of all three forms of the language agree, then, in many words, especially in the word *Amor*. Giraut de Borneil says: *"Sim sentis fezelz amics / per ver encusera Amor."*[5] The King of Navarre: *"De fine amor si vient sen et bonté."*[6] Messer Guido Guinizelli: *"Nè fa amor prima che gentil core / nè gentil cor prima che amor natura."*[7] Let us now inquire why it is that this language has varied into three chief forms, and why each of these variations varies in itself; why, for instance, the speech of the right side of Italy varies from that of the left (for the Paduans speak in one way and the Pisans in another); and also why those who live nearer together still vary in their speech, as the Milanese and Veronese, the Romans and the Florentines, and even those who have the same national designation, as the Neapolitans and the people of Gaeta, those of Ravenna and those of Faenza, and what is stranger still, the inhabitants of the same city, like the Bolognese of the Borgo S. Felice and the Bolognese of the Strada Maggiore. One and the same reason will explain why all these differences and varieties of speech occur.

We say, therefore, that no effect as such goes beyond its cause, because nothing can bring about that which itself is not. Since therefore every language of ours, except that created by God with the first man, has been restored at our pleasure after the confusion, which was nothing else but forgetfulness of the former language, and since man is a most unstable and changeable animal, no human language can be lasting and continuous, but must needs vary like other properties of ours, as for instance our manners and our dress, according to distance of time and place. And so far am I from thinking that there is room for doubt as to the truth of our remark that speech varies "according to difference of time," that we are of opinion that this is rather to be held as certain. For, if we consider our other actions, we seem to differ much more from our fellow-countrymen in very distant times than from our contemporaries very remote in place. Wherefore we boldly affirm that if the ancient Pavians were to rise from the dead they would talk in a language varying or differing from that of the modern Pavians. Nor should what we are saying appear more wonderful than to observe that a young man is grown up whom we have not seen growing. For the motion of those things which move gradually is not considered by us at all; and the longer the time required for perceiving the variation of a thing, the more stable we suppose that thing to be. Let us not therefore be surprised if the opinions of men who are but little removed from the brutes suppose that the citizens of the same town have always carried on their intercourse with an unchangeable speech, because the change in the speech of the same town comes about gradually, not without a very long succession of time, whilst the life of man is in its nature extremely short.

If, therefore, the speech of the same people varies (as has been said) successively in course of time, and cannot in any wise stand still, the speech of people living apart and removed from one another must needs vary in different ways; just as manners and dress vary in different ways, since they are not rendered stable either by nature or by intercourse, but arise according to men's inclinations and local fitness. Hence were set in motion the inventors of the art of grammar, which is nothing else but a kind of unchangeable identity of speech in different times and places. This, having been settled by the common consent of many peoples, seems exposed to the arbitrary will of none in particular, and consequently cannot be variable. They therefore invented grammar in order that we might not, on account of the variation of speech fluctuating at the will of individuals, either fail altogether in attaining, or at least attain but a partial knowledge of the opinions and exploits of the ancients, or of those whom difference of place causes to differ from us.

X

Our language being now spoken under three forms (as has been said above), we feel, when comparing it with itself, according to the three forms that it has assumed, such great hesitation and timidity in placing [its different forms] in the balances, that we dare not, in our comparison, give the preference to any one of them, except in so far as we find that the founders of grammar have taken *sic* as the adverb of affirmation, which seems to confer a kind of precedence on the Italians, who say *sì*. For each of the three divisions [of our language] defends its pretensions by copious evidence. That of *oïl*, then, alleges on its behalf that because of its being an easier and pleasanter vernacular language, whatever has been translated into or composed in vernacular prose belongs to it, namely, the compilations of the exploits of the Trojans and Romans, the exquisite legends of King Arthur, and very many other works of history and learning. Another, namely that of *oc*, claims that eloquent speakers of the vernacular first employed it for poetry, as being a more finished and sweeter language, for instance Peter of Auvergne and other ancient writers. The third also, which is the language of the Italians, claims pre-eminence on the strength of two privileges: first, that the sweetest and most subtle poets who have written in the vernacular are its intimate friends and belong to its household, like Cino of Pistoia and his friend[8]; second, that it seems to lean more on grammar, which is common: and this appears a very weighty argument to those who examine the matter in a rational way.

We, however, decline to give judgment in this case, and confining our treatise to the vernacular Italian, let us endeavor to enumerate the variations it has received into itself, and also to compare these with one another. In the first place, then, we say that Italy has a twofold division into right and left. But, if any should ask what is the dividing line, we answer shortly that it is the ridge of the Apennines, which like the ridge of a tiled roof discharges its droppings in different directions on either side, and pours its waters down to either shore alternately through long gutter-tiles, as Lucan describes in his second book. Now the right side has the Tyrrhenian Sea as its basin, while the waters on the left fall into the Adriatic. The districts on the right are Apulia (but not the whole of it), the Duchy [of Spoleto], Tuscany, and the March of Genoa. Those on the left are part of Apulia, the March of Ancona, Romagna, Lombardy, and the March of Treviso with Venetia. Friuli and Istria cannot but belong to the left of Italy, and the islands of the Tyrrhenian Sea, namely Sicily and Sardinia, must belong to, or be associated with the right of Italy. Now in each of these two sides, and those districts which follow them, the languages of the inhabitants vary, as for instance the language of the Sicilians as compared with that of the Apulians, of the Apulians with that of the Romans, of the Romans with that of the Spoletans, of these with that of the Tuscans, of the Tuscans with that of the Genoese, of the Genoese with that of the Sardinians; also of the Calabrians with that of the people of Ancona, of these with that of the people of Romagna, of the people of Romagna with that of the Lombards, of the Lombards with that of the Trevisans and Venetians, and of these last with that of the Aquileians, and of them with that of the Istrians; and we do not think that any Italian will disagree with us in this statement. Whence it appears that Italy alone is diversified by fourteen dialects at least, all of which again vary in themselves: as for instance in Tuscany the Sienese differ in speech from the Aretines; in Lombardy the Ferrarese from the Placentines; in the same city also we observe some variation, as we remarked above in the last chapter. Wherefore if we would calculate the primary, secondary, and subordinate variations of the vulgar tongue of Italy, we should find that in this tiny corner of the world the varieties of speech not only come up to a thousand but even exceed that figure.

XI

As the Italian vernacular has so very many discordant varieties, let us hunt after a more fitting and an illustrious Italian language; and in order that we may be able to have a practicable path for our chase, let us first cast the tangled bushes and brambles out of the wood. Therefore, as the Romans think that they ought to have precedence over all the rest, let us in this process of uprooting or clearing away give them (not undeservedly) precedence, declaring that we will have nothing to do with them in any scheme of a vernacular language. We say, then, that the vulgar tongue of the Romans, or rather their hideous jargon, is the ugliest of all the Italian dialects; nor is this surprising, since in the depravity of their manners and customs also they appear to stink worse than all the rest. For they say "*Mezzure, quinto dici?*"[9] After them, let us get rid of the inhabitants of the March of Ancona, who say, "*Chignamente scate sciate?*"[10] with whom we reject the Spoletans also. Nor must we forget that a great many canzoni have been written in contempt of these three peoples, among which we have noticed one correctly and perfectly constructed, which a certain Florentine named Castra had composed. It began: "*Una fermana scopai da Casciòli / Cita cita sen gia'n grande aina.*"[11] And after these let us weed out the people of Milan and Bergamo with their neighbors, in reproach of whom we recollect that some one has sung: "*Enti l'ora del vesper, / Ciò fu del mes d' ochiover.*"[12] After them let us sift out the Aquileians and Istrians, who belch forth with cruelly harsh accents, "*Ces fastu?*"[13] And with these we cast out all the mountainous and rural dialects, as those of Casentino and Prato, which by the extravagance of their accent always seem discordant to the citizens dwelling in the midst of the towns. Let us also cast out the Sardinians, who are not Italians, but are, it seems, to be associated with them; since they alone seem to be without any vulgar tongue of their own, imitating Latin as apes do men: for they say, "*Domus nova*"[14] and "*dominus meus.*"[15]

XII

Having sifted, so to speak, the Italian vernaculars, let us, comparing together those left in our sieve, briefly choose out the one most honorable and conferring most honor. And first let us examine the genius of the Sicilian, for the Sicilian vernacular appears to arrogate to itself a greater renown than the others, both because whatever poetry the Italians write is called Sicilian, and because we find that very many natives of Sicily have written weighty poetry, as in the canzoni, "*Ancor che l'aigua per lo focho lassi,*"[16] and "*Amor che lungiamente m'ài menato.*"[17] But this fame of the land of Trinacria[18] appears, if we rightly examine the mark to which it tends, only to have survived by way of a reproach to the princes of Italy, who, not in a heroic but in a plebeian manner, follow pride. But those illustrious heroes Frederick Cæsar[19] and his happy-born son Manfred, displaying the nobility and righteousness of their character, as long as fortune remained favorable, followed what is human, disdaining what is bestial; wherefore those who were of noble heart and endowed with graces strove to attach themselves to the majesty of such great princes; so that in their time, whatever the best Italians attempted first appeared at the court of these mighty sovereigns. And from the fact that the royal throne was Sicily it came to pass that whatever our predecessors wrote in the vulgar tongue was called Sicilian; and this name we also retain, nor will our successors be able to change it. Racha, racha![20] what is the sound now uttered by the trumpet of the latest Frederick?[21] What is that uttered by the bell of Charles II.? What is that uttered by the horns of the powerful Marquises John and Azzo? What is that uttered by the flutes of the other magnates? What but "Come, ye murderers; come, ye traitors; come, ye followers of avarice."

But it is better to return to our subject than to speak in vain: and we declare that if we take the Sicilian dialect, that namely spoken by the common people, out of whose mouths it appears our judgment should be drawn, it is in nowise worthy of preference, because it is not uttered without drawling, as for instance here: "*Tragemi d'este focora, se t'este a boluntate.*"[22] If, however, we choose to take the language as it flows from the mouths of the highest Sicilians, as it may be examined in the canzoni quoted before, it differs in nothing from that language which is the most worthy of praise, as we show further on.

The Apulians also, because of their own harshness of speech, or else because of their nearness to their neighbors who are the Romans and the people of the March [of Ancona], make use of shameful barbarisms, for they say, "*Volzera che chiangesse lo quatraro.*"[23]

But though the natives of Apulia commonly speak in a hideous manner, some of them have been distinguished by their use of polished language, inserting more *curial* words into their canzoni, as clearly appears from an examination of their works, for instance, "*Madonna, dir vi voglio,*"[24] and "*Per fino amore vo sì letamente.*"[25]

Wherefore it should become clear to those who mark what has been said above, that neither the Sicilian nor the Apulian dialect is that vulgar tongue which is the most beautiful in Italy, for we have shown that eloquent natives of those parts have diverged from their own dialect.

XIII

Next let us come to the Tuscans, who, infatuated through their frenzy, seem to arrogate to themselves the title of the illustrious vernacular; and in this matter not only the minds of the common people are crazed, but we find that many distinguished men have embraced the delusion; for instance Guittone of Arezzo, who never aimed at the curial vernacular, Bonagiunta of Lucca, Gallo of Pisa, Mino Mocato of Siena, and Brunetto of Florence, whose works, if there be leisure to examine them, will be found to be not curial but merely municipal. And since the Tuscans exceed the rest in this frenzied intoxication, it seems right and profitable to deal with the dialects of the Tuscan towns one by one, and to take off somewhat of their vain glory. The Florentines open their mouths and say, "*Manichiamo introque—Noi non facciano atro*";[26] the Pisans, "*Bene andonno li fanti De Fiorensa per Pisa*";[27] the people of Lucca, "*Fo voto a Dio che in gassarra eie lo comuno de Lucca*";[28] the Sienese, "*Onche renegata avesse io Siena!*"[29] "*Ch'ee chesto?*"[30] the Aretines, "*Vo tu venire ovelle?*"[31] (We do not intend to deal with Perugia, Orvieto, and Città Castellana at all, because of their close connection with the Romans and Spoletans.) But obtuse as almost all the Tuscans are in their degraded dialect, we notice that some have recognized wherein the excellence of the vernacular consists, namely, Guido, Lapo, and another, all Florentines, and Cino of Pistoja, whom we now undeservedly put last, having been not undeservedly driven to do so. Therefore if we examine the Tuscan dialects, reflecting how the writers commended above have deviated from their own dialect, it does not remain doubtful that the vernacular we are in search of is different from that which the people of Tuscany attain to.

But if any one thinks that what we say of the Tuscans may not also be said of the Genoese, let him but bear this in mind, that if the Genoese were through forgetfulness to lose the letter *z,* they would have either to be dumb altogether, or to discover some new kind of speech, for *z* forms the greatest part of their dialect, and this letter is not uttered without great harshness.

XIV

Let us now cross the leaf-clad shoulders of the Apennines, and hunt inquiringly, as we are wont, over the left side of Italy, beginning from the east.

Entering Romagna, then, we remark that we have found in Italy two alternating types of dialect with certain opposite characteristics in which they respectively agree. One of these, on account of the softness of its words and pronunciation, seems so feminine that it causes a man, even when speaking like a man, to be believed to be a woman. This type of dialect prevails among all the people of Romagna, and especially those of Forli, whose city, though the newest, seems to be the centre of all the province. These people say *deuscì* in affirmation, and use *"Oclo meo"*[32] and *"Corada mea"*[33] as terms of endearment. We have heard that some of them have diverged in poetry from their own dialect, namely the Faentines Thomas and Ugolino Bucciola.

There is also, as we have said, another type of dialect, so bristling and shaggy in its words and accents that, owing to its rough harshness, it not only distorts a woman's speech, but makes one doubt whether she is not a man. This type of dialect prevails among all those who say *magara,*[34] namely the Brescians, Veronese, and Vicentines, as well as the Paduans, with their ugly syncopations of all the participles in *tus* and denominatives in *tas,* as *mercò* and *bontè.* With these we also class the Trevisans, who, like the Brescians and their neighbors, pronounce *f* for consonantal *u*, cutting off the final syllable of the word, as *nof* for *novem,*[35] *vif* for *vivo,* which we disapprove as a gross barbarism.

Nor do the Venetians also deem themselves worthy of possessing that vernacular language which we have been searching for; and if any of them, trusting in error, should cherish any delusion on this point, let him remember whether he has ever said *"Per le plage de Dio tu non veràs."*[36]

Among all these we have noticed one man striving to depart from his mother-tongue, and to apply himself to the *curial* vernacular language, namely Ildebrandino of Padua.

Wherefore, on all the dialects mentioned in the present chapter coming up for judgment, our decision is that neither that of Romagna nor its opposite (as we have mentioned), nor that of Venice is that illustrious vernacular which we are seeking.

XV

Let us now endeavor to clear the way by tracking out what remains of the Italian wood.

We say, then, that perhaps those are not far wrong who assert that the people of Bologna use a more beautiful speech [than the others], since they receive into their own dialect something borrowed from their neighbors of Imola, Ferrara, and Modena, just as we conjecture that all borrow from their neighbors, as Sordello showed with respect to his own Mantua, which is adjacent to Cremona, Brescia, and Verona; and he who was so distinguished by his eloquence, not only in poetry but in every other form of utterance forsook his native vulgar tongue. Accordingly the above-mentioned citizens [of Bologna] get from those of Imola their smoothness and softness [of speech], and from those of Ferrara and Modena a spice of sharpness characteristic of the Lombards. This we believe has remained with the natives of that district as a relic of the admixture of the immigrant Longobards with them: and this is the reason why we find that there has been no poet among the people of Ferrara, Modena, or Reggio; for from being accustomed to their own sharpness they cannot adopt the courtly vulgar tongue without a kind of roughness; and this we must consider to be much more the case with the people of Parma, who say *monto* instead of *multo.* If, therefore, the people of Bologna borrow from both these kinds of dialect, as has been said, it seems reasonable that their speech should by this mixture of opposites remain tempered to a praiseworthy sweetness; and this we without hesitation judge to be the case. Therefore if those who place the people of Bologna first in the matter of the vernacular merely have regard in their comparison to the municipal dialects of the Italians, we are disposed to agree with them; but if they consider that the dialect of Bologna is, taken absolutely, worthy of preference, we disagree with them altogether; for this dialect is not that language which we term courtly and illustrious, since if it had been so, the greatest Guido Guinizelli, Guido Ghisilieri, Fabruzzo, and Onesto, and other poets of Bologna would never have departed from their own dialect; and these were illustrious writers, competent judges of dialects. The greatest Guido, wrote: *"Madonna lo fermo core"*;[37] Fabruzzo, *"Lo meo lontano gire"*;[38] Onesto, *"Più non attendo il tuo secorso, Amore"*;[39] and these words are altogether different from the dialect of the citizens of Bologna.

And since we consider that no one feels any doubt as to the remaining towns at the extremities of Italy (and if any one does, we do not deem him worthy of any answer from us), little remains to be mentioned in our discussion. Wherefore being eager to put down our sieve so that we may quickly see what is left in it, we say that the towns of Trent and Turin, as well as Alessandria, are situated so near the frontiers of Italy that they cannot possess pure languages, so that even if their vernaculars were as lovely as they are hideous, we should still say that they were not truly Italian, because of their foreign ingredients. Wherefore if we are hunting for an illustrious Italian language, what we are hunting for cannot be found in them.

XVI

After having scoured the heights and pastures of Italy, without having found that panther which we are in pursuit of, in order that we may be able to find her, let us now track her out in a more rational manner, so that we may with skillful efforts completely enclose within our toils her who is fragrant everywhere but nowhere apparent.

Resuming, then, our hunting-spears, we say that in every kind of things there must be one thing by which all the things of that kind may be compared and weighed, and which we may take as the measure of all the others; just as in numbers all are measured by unity and are said to be more or fewer according as they are distant from or near to unity; so also in colors all are measured by white, for they are said to be more or less visible according as they approach or recede from it. And what we say of the predicaments which indicate quantity and quality, we think may also be said of any of the predicaments and even of substance; namely, that everything considered as belonging to a kind becomes measurable by that which is simplest in that kind. Wherefore in our actions, however many the species into which they are divided may be, we have to discover this standard by which they may be measured. Thus, in what concerns our actions as human beings simply, we have virtue, understanding it generally; for according to it we judge a man to be good or bad; in what concerns our actions as citizens, we have the law, according to which a citizen is said to be good or bad; in what concerns our actions as Italians, we have certain very simple standards of manners, customs, and language, by which our actions as Italians are weighed and measured. Now the supreme standards of those activities which are generically Italian are not peculiar to any one town in Italy, but are common to all; and among these can now be discerned that vernacular language which we were hunting for above, whose fragrance is in every town, but whose lair is in none. It may, however, be more perceptible in one than in another, just as the simplest of substances, which is God, is more perceptible in a man than in a brute, in an animal than in a plant, in a plant than in a mineral, in a mineral than in an element, in fire than in earth. And the simplest quantity, which is unity, is more perceptible in an odd than in an even number; and the simplest color, which is white, is more perceptible in orange than in green.

Having therefore found what we were searching for, we declare the illustrious, cardinal, courtly, and curial vernacular language in Italy to be that which belongs to all the towns in Italy but does not appear to belong to any one of them, and by which all the municipal dialects of the Italians are measured, weighed, and compared.

XVII

We must now set forth why it is that we call this language we have found by the epithets illustrious, cardinal, courtly, and curial; and by doing this we disclose the nature of the language itself more clearly. First, then, let us lay bare what we mean by the epithet illustrious, and why we call the language illustrious. Now we understand by this term "illustrious" something which shines forth illuminating and illuminated. And in this way we call men illustrious either because, being illuminated by power, they illuminate others by justice and charity; or else because, having been excellently trained, they in turn give excellent training, like Seneca and Numa Pompilius. And the vernacular of which we are speaking has both been exalted by training and power, and also exalts its followers by honor and glory.

Now it appears to have been exalted by training, inasmuch as from amid so many rude Italian words, involved constructions, faulty expressions, and rustic accents we see that it has been chosen out in such a degree of excellence, clearness, completeness, and polish as is displayed by Cino of Pistoja and his friend in their canzoni.

And that it has been exalted by power is plain; for what is of greater power than that which can sway the hearts of men, so as to make an unwilling man willing, and a willing man unwilling, just as this language has done and is doing?

Now that it exalts by honor is evident. Do not they of its household surpass in renown kings, marquises, counts, and all other magnates? This has no need at all of proof.

But how glorious it makes its familiar friends we ourselves know, who for the sweetness of this glory cast [even] our exile behind our back. Wherefore we ought deservedly to proclaim this language illustrious.

XVIII

Nor is it without reason that we adorn this illustrious vernacular language with a second epithet, that is, that we call it cardinal: for as the whole door follows its hinge, so that whither the hinge turns the door also may turn, whether it be moved inward or outward, in like manner also the whole herd of municipal dialects turns and returns, moves and pauses according as this illustrious language does, which really seems to be the father of the family. Does it not daily root out the thorny bushes from the Italian wood? Does it not daily insert grafts or plant young trees? What else have its foresters to do but to take away and bring in, as has been said? Wherefore it surely deserves to be adorned with so great a name as this.

Now the reason why we call it "courtly" is that if we Italians had a court it would be spoken at court. For if a court is a common home of all the realm and an august ruler of all parts of the realm, it is fitting that whatever is of such a character as to be common to all [parts] without being peculiar to any, should frequent this court and dwell there; nor is any other abode worthy of so great an inmate. Such in fact seems to be that vernacular language of which we are speaking; and hence it is that those who frequent all royal palaces always speak the illustrious vernacular. Hence also it is that our illustrious language wanders about like a wayfarer, and is welcomed in humble shelters, seeing we have no court.

This language is also deservedly to be styled "curial," because "curiality" is nothing else but the justly balanced rule of things which have to be done; and because the scales required for this kind of balancing are only wont to be found in the most excellent courts of justice, it follows that whatever in our actions has been well balanced is called curial. Wherefore since this illustrious language has been weighed in the balances of the most excellent court of justice of the Italians, it deserves to be called curial. But it seems mere trifling to say that it has been weighed in the balances of the most excellent court of justice of the Italians, because we have no [Imperial] court of justice. To this the answer is easy. For though there is no court of justice of Italy in the sense of a single [supreme] court, like the court of the king of Germany, still the members of such a court are not wanting. And just as the members of the German court are united under one prince, so the members of ours have been united by the gracious light of reason. Wherefore, though we have no prince, it would be false to assert that the Italians have no [such] court of justice, because we have a court, though in the body it is scattered.

XIX

Now we declare that this vernacular language, which we have shown to be illustrious, cardinal, courtly, and curial, is that which is called the Italian vernacular. For just as a vernacular can be found peculiar to Cremona, so can one be found peculiar to Lombardy; and just as one can be found peculiar to Lombardy, [so] can one be found peculiar to the whole of the left side of Italy. And just as all these can be found, so also can that which belongs to the whole of Italy. And just as the first is called Cremonese, the second Lombard, and the third Semi-Italian, so that which belongs to the whole of Italy is called the Italian vernacular language. For this has been used by the illustrious writers who have written poetry in the vernacular throughout Italy, as Sicilians, Apulians, Tuscans, natives of Romagna, and men of both the Marches. And because our intention is, as we promised in the beginning of this work, to give instruction concerning the vernacular speech, we will begin with this illustrious Italian as being the most excellent, and treat in the books immediately following of those whom we think worthy to use it; and for what, and how, and also where, when, and to whom, it ought to be used. And after making all this clear, we will make it our business to throw light on the lower vernaculars, gradually coming down to that which belongs to a single family.

BOOK II

I

Urging on once more the nimbleness of our wit, which is returning to the pen of useful work, we declare in the first place that the illustrious Italian vernacular is equally fit for use in prose and in verse. But because prose writers rather get this language from poets, and because poetry seems to remain a pattern to prose writers, and not the converse, which things appear to confer a certain supremacy, let us first disentangle this language as to its use in meter, treating of it in the order we set forth at the end of the first book.

Let us then first inquire whether all those who write verse in the vernacular should use this illustrious language; and so far as a superficial consideration of the matter goes, it would seem that they should, because every one who writes verse ought to adorn his verse as far as he is able. Wherefore, since nothing affords so great an adornment as the illustrious vernacular does, it would seem that every writer of verse ought to employ it. Besides, if that which is best in its kind be mixed with things inferior to itself, it not only appears not to detract anything from them but even to improve them. Wherefore if any writer of verse, even though his verse be rude in matter, mixes the illustrious vernacular with his rudeness of matter, he not only appears to do well, but to be actually obliged to take this course. Those who can do little need help much more than those who can do much, and thus it appears that all writers of verse are at liberty to use this illustrious language. But this is quite false, because not even poets of the highest order ought always to assume it, as will appear from a consideration of what is discussed farther on. This illustrious language, then, just like our behavior in other matters and our dress, demands men of like quality to its own; for munificence demands men of great resources, and the purple, men of noble character, and in the same way this illustrious language seeks for men who excel in genius and knowledge, and despises others, as will appear from what is said below. For everything which is suited to us is so either in respect of the genus, or of the species, or of the individual, as sensation, laughter, war; but this illustrious language is not suited to us in respect of our genus, for then it would also be suited to the brutes; nor in respect of our species, for then it would be suited to all men; and as to this there is no question; for no one will say that this language is suited to dwellers in the mountains dealing with rustic concerns: therefore it is suited in respect of the individual. But nothing is suited to an individual except on account of his particular worth, as for instance commerce, war, and government. Wherefore if things are suitable according to worth, that is the worthy (and some men may be worthy, others worthier and others worthiest), it is plain that good things will be suited to the worthy, better things to the worthier, and the best things to the worthiest. And since language is as necessary an instrument of our thought as a horse is of a knight, and since the best horses are suited to the best knights, as has been said, the best language will be suited to the best thoughts. But the best thoughts cannot exist except where knowledge and genius are found; therefore the best language is only suitable in those in whom knowledge and genius are found; and so the best language is not suited to all who write verse, since a great many write without knowledge and genius; and consequently neither is the best vernacular [suited to all who write verse]. Wherefore, if it is not suited to all, all ought not to use it, because no one ought to act in an unsuitable manner. And as to the statement that every one ought to adorn his verse as far as he can, we declare that it is true; but we should not describe an ox with trappings or a swine with a belt as adorned, nay rather we laugh at them as disfigured; for adornment is the addition of some suitable thing.

As to the statement that superior things mixed with inferior effect an improvement [in the latter], we say that it is true if the blending is complete, for instance when we mix gold and silver together; but if it is not, the inferior things appear worse, for instance when beautiful women are mixed with ugly ones. Wherefore, since the theme of those who write verse always persists as an ingredient distinct from the words, it will not, unless of the highest quality, appear better when associated with the best vernacular, but worse; like an ugly woman if dressed out in gold or silk.

II

After having proved that not all those who write verse, but only those of the highest excellence, ought to use the illustrious vernacular, we must in the next place establish whether every subject ought to be handled in it, or not; and if not, we must set out by themselves those subjects that are worthy of it. And in reference to this we must first find out what we understand by that which we call *worthy*. We say that a thing which has worthiness is worthy, just as we say that a thing which has nobility is noble; and if when that which confers the habit is known, that on which the habit is conferred is [also] known, as such, then if we know what worthiness is, we shall know also what *worthy* is. Now worthiness is an effect or end of deserts; so that when any one has deserved well we say that he has arrived at worthiness of good; but when he has deserved ill, at worthiness of evil. Thus we say that a soldier who has fought well has arrived at worthiness of victory; one who has ruled well, at worthiness of a kingdom; also that a liar has arrived at worthiness of shame, and a robber at worthiness of death.

But inasmuch as [further] comparisons are made among those who deserve well, and also among those who deserve ill, so that some deserve well, some better, and some best; some badly, some worse, and some worst; while such comparisons are only made with respect to the end of deserts, which (as has been mentioned before) we call *worthiness*, it is plain that worthinesses are compared together according as they are greater or less, so that some are great, some greater, and some greatest; and, consequently, it is obvious that one thing is worthy, another worthier, and another worthiest. And whereas there can be no such comparison of worthinesses with regard to the same object [of desert] but [only] with regard to different objects, so that we call *worthier* that which is worthy of greater objects, and *worthiest* that which is worthy of the greatest, because no thing can be more worthy [than another] in virtue of the same qualification, it is evident that the best things are worthy of the best [objects of desert], according to the requirement of the things. Whence it follows that, since the language we call illustrious is the best of all the other forms of the vernacular, the best subjects alone are worthy of being handled in it, and these we call the *worthiest* of those subjects which can be handled; and now let us hunt out what they are. And, in order to make this clear, it must be observed that, as man has been endowed with a threefold life, namely, vegetable, animal, and rational, he journeys along a threefold road; for in so far as he is vegetable he seeks for what is useful, wherein he is of like nature with plants; in so far as he is animal he seeks for that which is pleasurable, wherein he is of like nature with the brutes; in so far as he is rational he seeks for what is right—and in this he stands alone, or is a partaker of the nature of the angels. It is by these three kinds of life that we appear to carry out whatever we do; and because in each one of them some things are greater, some greatest, within the range of their kind, it follows that those which are greatest appear the ones which ought to be treated of supremely, and consequently, in the greatest vernacular.

But we must discuss what things are greatest; and first in respect of what is useful. Now in this matter, if we carefully consider the object of all those who are in search of what is useful, we shall find that it is nothing else but safety. Secondly, in respect of what is pleasurable; and here we say that that is most pleasurable which gives pleasure by the most exquisite object of appetite, and this is love. Thirdly, in respect of what is right; and here no one doubts that virtue has the first place. Wherefore these three things, namely, safety, love, and virtue, appear to be those capital matters which ought to be treated of supremely, I mean the things which are most important in respect of them, as prowess in arms, the fire of love, and the direction of the will. And if we duly consider, we shall find that the illustrious writers have written poetry in the vulgar tongue on these subjects exclusively; namely, Bertran de Born on Arms, Arnaut Daniel on Love, Giraut de Borneil on Righteousness, Cino of Pistoja on Love, his friend on Righteousness. For Bertan says: "*Non posc mudar c'un cantar non exparja.*"[40] Arnaut: "*L'aura amara fals bruols brancuz clairir.*"[41] Giraut: "*Per solaz reveillar / que s'es trop endormitz.*"[42] Cino: "*Digno sono eo de morte.*"[43] His friend: "*Doglia mi reca nello core ardire.*"[44] I do not find, however, that any Italian has as yet written poetry on the subject of Arms.

Having then arrived at this point, we know what are the proper subjects to be sung in the highest vernacular language.

III

But now let us endeavor carefully to examine how those matters which are worthy of so excellent a vernacular language are to be restricted. As we wish, then, to set forth the form by which these matters are worthy to be bound, we say that it must first be borne in mind that those who have written poetry in the vernacular have uttered their poems in many different forms, some in that of canzoni, some in that of ballate, some in that of sonnets, some in other illegitimate and irregular forms, as will be shown farther on. Now we consider that of these forms that of canzoni is the most excellent; and therefore, if the most excellent things are worthy of the most excellent, as has been proved above, those subjects which are worthy of the most excellent vernacular are worthy of the most excellent form, and consequently ought to be handled in canzoni. Now we may discover by several reasons that the form of canzoni is such as has been said. The first reason is that though whatever we write in verse is a canzone, the canzoni [technically so called] have alone acquired this name; and this has never happened apart from ancient provision.

Moreover, whatever produces by itself the effect for which it was made, appears nobler than that which requires external assistance. But canzoni produce by themselves the whole effect they ought to produce; which ballate do not, for they require the assistance of the performers for whom they are written; it therefore follows that canzoni are to be deemed nobler than ballate, and therefore that their form is the noblest of any, for no one doubts that ballate excel sonnets in nobility of form.

Besides, those things appear to be nobler which bring more honor to their author; but canzoni bring more [honor] to their authors than ballate; therefore they are nobler [than these], and consequently their form is the noblest of any.

Furthermore, the noblest things are the most fondly preserved; but among poems canzoni are the most fondly preserved, as is evident to those who look into books; therefore canzoni are the noblest [poems], and consequently their form is the noblest.

Also, in works of art, that is noblest which embraces the whole art. Since, therefore, poems are works of art, and the whole of the art is embraced in canzoni alone, canzoni are the noblest poems, and so their form is the noblest of any. Now, that the whole of the art of poetic song is embraced in canzoni is proved by the fact that whatever is found to belong to the art is found in them; but the converse is not true. But the proof of what we are saying is at once apparent; for all that has flowed from the tops of the heads of illustrious poets down to their lips is found in canzoni alone. Wherefore, in reference to the subject before us, it is clear that the matters which are worthy of the highest vulgar tongue ought to be handled in canzoni.

IV

Having then labored by a process of disentangling [to show] what persons and things are worthy of the courtly vernacular, as well as the form of verse which we deem worthy of such honor that it alone is fitted for the highest vernacular, before going off to other topics, let us explain the form of the canzone, which many appear to adopt rather at haphazard than with art; and let us unlock the workshop of the art of that form which has hitherto been adopted in a casual way, omitting the form of ballate and sonnets, because we intend to explain this in the fourth book of this work, when we shall treat of the middle vernacular language.

Reviewing, therefore, what has been said, we remember that we have frequently called those who write verse in the vernacular poets; and this we have doubtless ventured to say with good reason, because they are in fact poets, if we take a right view of poetry, which is nothing else but a rhetorical composition set to music. But these poets differ from the great poets, that is, the regular ones, for the language of the great poets was regulated by art, whereas these, as has been said, write at haphazard. It therefore happens that the more closely we copy the great poets, the more correct is the poetry we write; whence it behooves us, by devoting some trouble to the work of teaching, to emulate their poetic teaching.

Before all things therefore we say that each one ought to adjust the weight of the subject to his own shoulders, so that their strength may not be too heavily taxed, and he be forced to tumble into the mud. This is the advice our master Horace gives us when he says in the beginning of his "Art of Poetry" ["Ye who write] take up a subject [suited to your strength"].

Next we ought to possess a discernment as to those things which suggest themselves to us as fit to be uttered, so as to decide whether they ought to be sung in the way of tragedy, comedy, or elegy. By tragedy we bring in (*sic*) the higher style, by comedy the lower style, by elegy we understand the style of the wretched. If our subject appears fit to be sung in the tragic style, we must then assume the illustrious vernacular language, and consequently we must bind up a canzone. If, however, it appears fit to be sung in the comic style, sometimes the middle and sometimes the lowly vernacular should be used; and the discernment to be exercised in this case we reserve for treatment in the fourth book. But if our subject appears fit to be sung in the elegiac style, we must adopt the lowly vernacular alone.

But let us omit the other styles and now, as is fitting, let us treat of the tragic style. We appear then to make use of the tragic style when the stateliness of the lines as well as the loftiness of the construction and the excellence of the words agree with the weight of the subject. And because, if we remember rightly, it has already been proved that the highest things are worthy of the highest, and because the style which we call tragic appears to be the highest style, those things which we have distinguished as being worthy of the highest song are to be sung in that style alone, namely, Safety, Love, and Virtue, and those other things, our conceptions of which arise from these; provided that they be not degraded by any accident.

Let every one therefore beware and discern what we say; and when he purposes to sing of these three subjects simply, or of those things which directly and simply follow after them, let him first drink of Helicon, and then, after adjusting the strings, boldly take up his *plectrum*[45] and begin to ply it. But it is in the exercise of the needful caution and discernment that the real difficulty lies; for this can never be attained to without strenuous efforts of genius, constant practice in the art, and the habit of the sciences. And it is those [so equipped] whom the poet in the sixth book of the *Æneid* describes as beloved of God, raised by glowing virtue to the sky, and sons of the Gods, though he is speaking figuratively. And therefore let those who, innocent of art and science, and trusting to genius alone, rush forward to sing of the highest subjects in the highest style, confess their folly and cease from such presumption; and if in their natural sluggishness they are but geese, let them abstain from imitating the eagle soaring to the stars.

V

We seem to have said enough, or at least as much as our work requires, about the weight of the subjects. Wherefore let us hasten on to the stateliness of the lines, in respect of which it is to be observed that our predecessors made use of different lines in their canzoni, as the moderns also do; but we do not find that any one has hitherto used a line of more than eleven or less than three syllables. And though the Italian poets have used the lines of three and of eleven syllables and all the intermediate ones, those of five, seven, and eleven syllables are more frequently used [than the others], and next to them, that of three syllables in preference to the others. But of all these the line of eleven syllables seems the stateliest, as well by reason of the length of time it occupies as of its capacity in regard to subject, construction, and words: and the beauty of all these things is more multiplied in this line [than in the others], as is plainly apparent; for wherever things that weigh are multiplied so also is weight. And all the teachers seem to have given heed to this, beginning their illustrious canzoni with a line of eleven syllables, as Giraut de Borneil: "*Ara auzirez encabalitz cantars.*"[46]

And though this line appears to be of ten syllables, it is in reality of eleven, for the last two consonants do not belong to the preceding syllable. And though they have no vowel belonging to them, still they do not lose the force of a syllable; and the proof of this is that the rhyme is in this instance completed by one vowel, which could not be the case except by virtue of another understood there. The king of Navarre writes: "*De fine Amor si vient sen et bonté,*"[47] where, if the accent and its cause be considered the line will be found to have eleven syllables. Guido Guinizelli writes: "*Al cor gentil repara sempre Amore.*"[48] The Judge [Guido] delle Colonne of Messina: "*Amor che lungiamente m' ài menato.*"[49] Rinaldo d'Aquino: "*Per fino amore vo sì letamente.*"[50] Cino of Pistoja: "*Non spero che già mai per mia salute.*"[51] His friend: "*Amor che movi tua vertù da cielo.*"[52] And though this line which has been mentioned appears, as is worthy, the most celebrated of all, yet, if it be associated in some slight degree with the line of seven syllables (provided only it retain its supremacy), it seems to rise still more clearly and loftily in its stateliness. But this must be left for further explanation.

We say also that the line of seven syllables follows next after that which is greatest in celebrity. After this we place the line of five, and then that of three syllables. But the line of nine syllables, because it appeared to consist of the line of three taken three times, was either never held in honor or fell into disuse on account of its being disliked. As for the lines of an even number of syllables, we use them but rarely, because of their rudeness; for they retain the nature of their numbers, which are subject to the odd numbers as matter to form. And so, summing up what has been said, the line of eleven syllables appears to be the stateliest line, and this is what we were in search of. But now it remains for us to investigate concerning exalted constructions and pre-eminent words; and at length, after having got ready our sticks and ropes, we will teach how we ought to bind together the promised faggot, that is the canzone.

VI

Inasmuch as our intention has reference to the illustrious vernacular, which is the noblest of all, and we have distinguished the things which are worthy of being sung in it, which are the three noblest subjects, as has been established above, and have chosen the form of canzoni for them, as being the highest form of any, and have also (in order that we may be able more perfectly to give thorough instruction in this form) already settled certain points, namely the style and the line, let us now deal with the construction.

Now it must be observed that we call construction a regulated arrangement of words, as "Aristotle philosophised in Alexander's time," for here there are five words arranged by rule, and they form one construction. Now in reference to this we must first bear in mind that one construction is congruous, while another is incongruous; and inasmuch as, if we recollect the beginning of our distinction, we are only pursuing the highest things, the incongruous construction finds no place in our pursuit, because it has not even proved deserving of a lower degree of goodness. Let therefore illiterate persons be ashamed—I say, let them be ashamed of being henceforth so bold as to burst forth into canzoni, for we laugh at them as at a blind man making distinctions between colors.

It is, then, it seems, the congruous construction after which we are following. But here we come to a distinction of not less difficulty before we can reach that construction which we are in search of, the construction, I mean, which is most full of refinement. For there are a great many degrees of constructions; namely, [first] the insipid, which is that of uncultivated people; as, "Peter is very fond of Mistress Bertha." [Then] there is that which has flavor but nothing else, which belongs to rigid scholars or masters; as, "I, greater in pity than all, am sorry for all those who, languishing in exile, only revisit their native land in their dreams." There is also that which has flavor and grace, which belongs to some who have taken a shallow draught of rhetoric; as, "The praiseworthy discernment of the Marquis of Este and his munificence prepared for all makes him beloved." Then there is that which has flavor and grace and also elevation, which belongs to illustrious writers; as, "Having cast the greatest part of the flowers out of thy bosom, O Florence, the second Totila went fruitlessly to Trinacria." This degree of construction we call the most excellent, and this is the one we are seeking for, since, as has been said, we are in pursuit of the highest things. Of this alone are illustrious canzoni found to be made up as [that by] Giraut de Borneil,

Si per mon Sobre-totz no fos.[53]
[that by] Folquet of Marseilles,
Tan m' abellis l'amoros pensamens.[54]
[that by] Arnaut Daniel,
Sols sui qui sai lo sobraffan quem sortz.[55]
[that by] Aimeric de Belenoi,
Nuls hom non pot complir addreciamen.[56]
[that by] Aimeric de Pegulhan,
Si com l'arbres que per sobrecarcar.[57]
[that by] the King of Navarre,
Ire d'amor qui en mon cor repaire. [58]
[that by] Guido Guinizelli,
Tegno de folle 'mpresa a lo ver dire.[59]
[that by] Guido Cavalcanti,
Poi che di doglia cor conven ch'io porti.[60]
[that by] Cino of Pistoja,
Avegna che io aggia più per tempo.[61]
[that by] his friend,
Amor che nella mente mi ragiona.[62]

Nor, reader, must you be surprised at our calling to memory so many poets; for we cannot point out that construction which we call the highest except by examples of this kind. And it would possibly be very useful in order to the full acquirement of this construction if we had surveyed the regular poets, I mean Virgil, Ovid in his *Metamorphoses*, Statius, and Lucan, as well as other writers who have employed the most lofty prose, as Titus Livius, Pliny, Frontinus, Paulus Orosius, and many others whom friendly solitude invites us to consult. Let, then, those followers of ignorance hold their peace who praise up Guittone of Arezzo and some others who have never got out of the habit of being plebeian in words and in construction.

VII

The next division of our progress now demands that an explanation be given as to those words which are of such grandeur as to be worthy of being admitted into that style to which we have awarded the first place. We declare therefore to begin with that the exercise of discernment as to words involves by no means the smallest labor of our reason, since we see that a great many sorts of them can be found. For some words are *childish*, some *feminine*, and some *manly*; and of these last some are *sylvan*, others *urban*; and of those we call urban we feel that some are *combed-out* and *glossy*, some *shaggy* and *rumpled*. Now among these urban words the combed-out and the shaggy are those which we call *grand*; whilst we call the glossy and the rumpled those whose sound tends to superfluity, just as among great works some are works of magnanimity, others of smoke; and as to these last, although when superficially looked at there may be thought to be a kind of ascent, to sound reason no ascent, but rather a headlong fall down giddy precipices will be manifest, because the marked-out path of virtue is departed from. Therefore look carefully, Reader, consider how much it behooves thee to use the sieve in selecting noble words; for if thou hast regard to the illustrious vulgar tongue which (as has been said above) poets ought to use when writing in the tragic style in the vernacular (and these are the persons whom we intend to fashion), thou wilt take care that the noblest words alone are left in thy sieve. And among the number of these thou wilt not be able in any wise to place childish words, because of their simplicity, as *mamma* and *babbo, mate* and *pate*; nor feminine words, because of their softness, as *dolciada* and *placevole*; nor sylvan words, because of their roughness, as *greggia* and *cetra*; nor the glossy nor the rumpled urban words, as *femina* and *corpo*. Therefore thou wilt see that only the combed-out and the shaggy urban words will be left to thee, which are the noblest, and members of the illustrious vulgar tongue. Now we call those words *combed-out* which have three, or as nearly as possible three syllables; which are without aspirate, without acute or circumflex accent, without the double letters *z* or *x*, without double liquids, or a liquid placed immediately after a mute, and which, having been planed (so to say), leave the speaker with a certain sweetness, like *amore, donna, disio, vertute, donare, letitia, salute, securitate, defesa.*

We call *shaggy* all words besides these which appear either necessary or ornamental to the illustrious vulgar tongue. We call *necessary* those which we cannot avoid, as certain monosyllables like *sì, no, me, te, se, a, e, i, o, u,* the interjections, and many more. We describe as *ornamental* all polysyllables which when mixed with combed-out words produce a fair harmony of structure, though they may have the roughness of aspirate, accent, double letters, liquids, and length; as *terra, honore, speranza, gravitate, alleviato, impossibilità, impossibilitate, benaventuratissimo, inanimatissimamente, disaventuratissimamente, sovramagnificentissimamente,* which last has eleven syllables. A word might yet be found with more syllables still; but as it would exceed the capacity of all our lines it does not appear to fall into the present discussion; such is that word *honorificabilitudinitate,* which runs in the vernacular to twelve syllables, and in grammar to thirteen, in two oblique cases.

In what way shaggy words of this kind are to be harmonised in the lines with combed-out words, we leave to be taught farther on. And what has been said [here] on the pre-eminent nature of the words to be used may suffice for every one of inborn discernment.

VIII

Having prepared the sticks and cords for our faggot, the time is now come to bind it up. But inasmuch as knowledge of every work should precede performance, just as there must be a mark to aim at, before we let fly an arrow or javelin, let us first and principally see what that faggot is which we intend to bind up. That faggot, then (if we bear well in mind all that has been said before), is the canzone. Wherefore let us see what a canzone is, and what we mean when we speak of a canzone. Now canzone, according to the true meaning of the name, is the action or passion itself of singing, just as *lectio*[63] is the passion or action of reading. But let us examine what has been said, I mean whether a canzone is so called as being an action or as being a passion. In reference to this we must bear in mind that a canzone may be taken in two ways. In the first way, as its author's composition, and thus it is an action; and it is in this way that Virgil says in the first book of the *Æneid,* "I sing of arms and the man." In another way, when, after having been composed it is uttered either by the author or by some one else, whether with or without modulation of sound; and thus it is a passion. For in the first case it is acted, but in the second it appears to act on some one else; and so in the first case it appears to be the action of some one, and in the second it also appears to be the passion of some one. And because it is acted on before it acts, it appears rather, nay, altogether, to get its name from its being acted and being the act of some one than from its acting on others. Now the proof of this is, that we never say "This is Peter's canzone," meaning that he utters it, but meaning that he has composed it.

Moreover, we must discuss the question whether we call a canzone the composition of the words which are set to music, or the music itself; and, with regard to this, we say that no music [alone] is ever called a canzone, but a sound, or tone, or note, or melody. For no trumpeter, or organist, or lute-player calls his melody a canzone, except in so far as it has been wedded to some canzone; but those who write the words for music call their words canzoni. And such words, even when written down on paper without any one to utter them, we call canzoni; and therefore a canzone appears to be nothing else but the completed action of one writing words to be set to music. Wherefore we shall call canzoni not only the canzoni of which we are now treating, but also ballate and sonnets, and all words of whatever kind written for music, both in the vulgar tongue and in Latin. But, inasmuch as we are only discussing works in the vulgar tongue, setting aside those in Latin, we say that of poems in the vulgar tongue there is one supreme which we call canzone by super-excellence. Now the supremacy of the canzone has been proved in the third chapter of this book. And since the term which has been defined appears to be common to many things, let us take up again the common term which has been defined, and distinguish by means of certain differences that thing which alone we are in search of. We declare therefore that the canzone as so called by super-excellence which we are in search of is a joining together in the tragic style of equal stanzas without a *ripresa*,[64] referring to one subject, as we have shown in our composition "*Donne che avete intellecto d'amore.*"[65] Now the reason why we call it "a joining together in the tragic style" is because when such a composition is made in the comic style we call it diminutively *cantilena*, of which we intend to treat in the fourth book of this work. And thus it appears what a canzone is, both as it is taken generally, and as we call it in a super-excellent sense. It also appears sufficiently plain what we mean when we speak of a canzone, and consequently what that faggot is which we are endeavoring to bind up.

IX

Inasmuch as the canzone is a joining together of stanzas, as has been said, we must necessarily be ignorant of the canzone if we do not know what a stanza is, for knowledge of the thing defined results from knowledge of the things defining; and it therefore follows that we must treat of the stanza, in order, that is, that we may discover what it is, and what we mean to understand by it. And in reference to this matter we must observe that this word has been invented solely with respect to the art [of the canzone]; namely, in order that that in which the whole art of the canzone is contained should be called stanza, that is a *room* able to hold, or a receptacle for the whole art. For just as the canzone embosoms the whole theme, so the stanza embosoms the whole art; nor is it lawful for the subsequent stanzas to call in any additional scrap of the art, but only to clothe themselves with the art of the first stanza; from which it is plain that the stanza of which we are speaking will be the delimitation or putting together of all those things which the canzone takes from the art; and if we explain them, the description we are in search of will become clear. The whole art, therefore, of the canzone appears to depend on three things: first, on the division of the musical setting; second, on the arrangement of the parts; third, on the number of the lines and syllables. But we make no mention of rhyme, because it does not concern the peculiar art of the canzone, for it is allowable in any stanza to introduce new rhymes and to repeat the same at pleasure, but this would by no means be allowed if rhyme belonged to the peculiar art of the canzone, as has been said. Anything, however, relating to rhyme which the art, as such, is concerned to observe will be comprised under the heading "Arrangement of the Parts."

Wherefore we may thus collect the defining terms from what has been said, and declare that a stanza is a structure of lines and syllables limited by reference to a certain musical setting, and to the arrangement [of its parts].

X

If we know that man is a rational animal, and that an animal consists of a sensible soul and a body, but are ignorant concerning what this soul is or concerning the body itself, we cannot have a perfect knowledge of man, because the perfect knowledge of every single thing extends to its ultimate elements, as the master of the wise[66] testifies in the beginning of the *Physics*. Therefore in order to have that knowledge of the canzone which we are panting for, let us now compendiously examine the things which define its defining term[67]; and first let us inquire concerning the musical setting, next concerning the arrangement [of the parts], and afterwards concerning the lines and syllables.

We say, therefore, that every stanza is set for the reception of a certain ode; but they appear to differ in the modes [in which this is done]; for some proceed throughout to one continuous ode, that is, without the repetition of any musical phrase, and without any diesis: and we understand by diesis a transition from one ode to another. (This when speaking to the common people we call *volta*). And this kind of stanza was used by Arnaut Daniel in almost all his canzoni, and we have followed him in ours beginning, "*Al poco giorno e al gran cerchio d'ombra.*"[68]

But there are some stanzas, which admit of a diesis: and there can be no diesis in our sense of the word unless a repetition of one ode be made either before the diesis, or after, or both. If the repetition be made before [the diesis] we say that the stanza has feet; and it ought to have two, though sometimes there are three; very rarely, however. If the repetition be made after the diesis, then we say that the stanza has verses. If no repetition be made before [the diesis] we say that the stanza has a *Fronte*; if none be made after, we say that it has a *Sirma* or Coda. See, therefore, Reader, how much license has been given to poets who write canzoni, and consider on what account custom has claimed so wide a choice; and if reason shall have guided thee by a straight path, thou wilt see that this license of which we are speaking has been granted by worthiness of authority alone.

Hence it may become sufficiently plain how the art of the canzone depends on the division of the musical setting; and therefore let us go on to the arrangement [of the parts].

XI

It appears to us that what we call the arrangement [of the parts of the stanza] is the most important section of what belongs to the art [of the canzone], for this depends on the division of the musical setting, the putting together of the lines, and the relation of the rhymes; wherefore it seems to require to be most diligently treated of.

We therefore begin by saying that the *fronte* with the verses, and the feet with the coda or *sirma*, and also the feet with the verses, may be differently arranged in the stanza. For sometimes the *fronte* exceeds or may exceed the verses in syllables and in lines; and we say "may exceed" because we have never yet met with this arrangement. Sometimes [the *fronte*] may exceed [the verses] in lines, and be exceeded by them in syllables; as, if the *fronte* had five lines, and each verse had two lines, while the lines of the *fronte* were of seven syllables and those of the verses of eleven syllables. Sometimes the verses exceed the *fronte* in syllables and in lines, as in our canzone *"Traggemi de la mente Amor la stiva."*[69] Here the *fronte* was composed of four lines, three of eleven syllables and one of seven syllables; for it could not be divided into feet, since an equality of lines and syllables is required in the feet with respect to one another, and also in the verses with respect to one another. And what we say of the *fronte* we might also say of the verses; for the verses might exceed the *fronte* in lines and be exceeded by it in syllables; for instance, if each verse had three lines of seven syllables and the *fronte* were made up of five lines, two of eleven syllables and three of seven syllables.

And sometimes the feet exceed the coda in lines and syllables as in our canzone, *"Amore che movi tua vertù da cielo."*[70] Sometimes the feet are exceeded by the sirma both in lines and syllables, as in our canzone, *"Donna pietosa e di novella etate."*[71] And just as we have said that the *fronte*, [though] exceeded [by the verses] in syllables may exceed them in lines, and conversely, so we say of the *sirma* [in relation to the feet].

The feet likewise may exceed the verses in number, and be exceeded by them; for there may be in a stanza three feet and two verses, or three verses and two feet; nor are we limited by that number so as not to be able to combine more feet as well as verses in like manner.

And just as we have spoken of the victory of lines and syllables in comparing the other parts of the stanza together, we now also say the same as regards the feet and verses [compared together]: for these can be conquered and conquer in the same way.

Nor must we omit to mention that we take feet in a sense contrary to that of the regular poets, because they said that a line consisted of feet, but we say that a foot consists of lines, as appears plainly enough.

Nor must we also omit to state again that the feet necessarily receive from one another an equality of lines and syllables, and their arrangement, for otherwise the repetition of the melodic section could not take place. And we declare that the same rule is to be observed in the verses.

XII

There is also, as has been said above, a certain arrangement which we ought to consider in putting the lines together; and therefore let us deal with this, repeating what we have said above respecting the lines.

In our practice three lines especially appear to have the prerogative of frequent use, namely, the line of eleven syllables, that of seven syllables, and that of five syllables, and we have shown that the line of three syllables follows them, in preference to the others. Of these, when we are attempting poetry in the tragic style, the line of eleven syllables deserves, on account of a certain excellence, the privilege of predominance in the structure [of the stanza]. For there is a certain stanza which rejoices in being made up of lines of eleven syllables alone, as this one of Guido of Florence: "*Donna me prega, perch' io voglio dire.*"[72] And we also say: "*Donne ch' avete intellecto d'amore.*"[73] The Spaniards have also used this line, and I mean by Spaniards those who have written poetry in the vernacular of *oc.* Aimeric de Belenoi [has written] "*Nuls hom non pot complir adrechamen.*"[74]

There is a stanza where a single line of seven syllables is woven in, and this cannot be except where there is a *fronte* or a coda, since (as has been said) in the feet and verses an equality of lines and syllables is observed. Wherefore also neither can there be an odd number of lines where there is no *fronte* or no coda, but where these occur, or one of them alone, we may freely use an even or an odd number of lines. And just as there is a certain stanza formed containing a single line of seven syllables, so it appears that a stanza may be woven together with two, three, four, or five such lines, provided only that in the tragic style the lines of eleven syllables predominate in number, and one such line begin. We do indeed find that some writers have begun with a line of seven syllables in the tragic style, namely, Guido dei Ghisilieri and Fabruzzo, both of Bologna, as thus: "*Di fermo sofferire,*"[75] and, "*Donna, lo fermo core,*"[76] and, "*Lo meo lontano gire,*" and some others also. But if we go carefully into the sense of these writers, their tragedy will not appear to have proceeded without a certain faint shadow of elegy.

With regard to the line of five syllables also, we are not so liberal in our concessions; in a great poem it is sufficient for a single line of five syllables to be inserted in the whole stanza, or two at most in the feet: and I say "in the feet," because of the requirements of the musical setting in the feet and verses.

But it by no means appears that the line of three syllables existing on its own account should be adopted in the tragic style; and I say, "existing on its own account," because it often appears to have been adopted by way of a certain echoing of rhymes, as may be discovered in that canzone of Guido of Florence, "*Donna me prega*," and in the following of ours: "*Poscia ch' Amor del tutto m' ha lasciato*."[77] And there the line of three syllables does not appear at all on its own account, but only as a part of a line of eleven syllables, answering like an echo to the rhyme of the line before.

This further point also must be specially attended to with regard to the arrangement of the lines, [namely] that if a line of seven syllables be inserted in the first foot, it must take up the same position in the second that it receives in the first. For insance, if a foot of three lines has the first and last of eleven syllables, and the middle one—that is the second—of seven syllables, so the second foot must have the second line of seven syllables and the first and last of eleven syllables, otherwise the repetition of the melodic section, with reference to which the feet are constructed, as has been said, could not take place; and consequently there could be no feet.

And what we have said of the feet we say of the verses also; for we see that the feet and the verses differ in nothing but position, the former term being used before the diesis of the stanza, and the latter after it.

And we declare also that what has been said of the foot of three lines is to be observed in all other feet. And what we have said of one line of seven syllables we also say of more than one, and of the line of five syllables, and of every other line.

Hence, Reader, you are sufficiently able to choose how your stanza is to be arranged as regards the arrangement which it appears should be considered with reference to the lines.

XIII

Let us apply ourselves to the relation of the rhymes, not [however] in any way treating of rhyme in itself; for we put off the special treatment of them (*sic*) till afterwards, when we shall deal with poems in the middle vulgar tongue.

At the beginning of this chapter it seems advisable to exclude certain things: one is the unrhymed stanza, in which no attention is given to arrangement of rhymes; and Arnaut Daniel very often made use of this kind of stanza, as here: *"Sim fos Amors de joi donar"*;[78] and we say: *"Al poco giorno."* Another is the stanza all of whose lines give the same rhyme; and here it is plainly unnecessary to seek for any arrangement [of rhymes].

And so it remains for us only to dwell upon the mixed rhymes. And first it must be remarked that in this matter almost all writers take the fullest license; and this is what is chiefly relied on for the sweetness of the whole harmony. There are, then, some poets who sometimes do not make all the endings of the lines rhyme in the same stanza, but repeat the same endings, or make rhymes to them, in the other stanzas: as Gotto of Mantua, who recited to us many good canzoni of his own. He always wove into his stanza one line unaccompanied by a rhyme, which he called the key. And as one such line is allowable, so also are two and perhaps more.

There are also some other poets, and almost all the authors of canzoni, who never leave any line unaccompanied in the stanza without answering it by the consonance of one or more rhymes.

Some poets also make the rhymes of the lines following the diesis different from the rhymes of the lines preceding it; while some do not do this, but bring back the endings of the former [part of the] stanza, and weave them into the lines of the latter part. But this occurs oftenest in the ending of the first line of the latter part of the stanza, which very many poets make to rhyme with the ending of the last line of the former part; and this appears to be nothing else but a kind of beautiful linking together of the whole stanza.

Also with regard to the arrangement of the rhymes, according as they are in the *fronte* or coda, every wished-for license should, it seems be conceded; but still the endings of the last lines are most beautifully disposed if they fall with a rhyme into silence.

But in the feet we must be careful; and [here] we find that a particular arrangement has been observed; and, making a distinction, we say that a foot is completed with either an even or odd number of lines, and in both cases there may be rhymed and unrhymed endings. In [the foot of] an even number of lines, no one feels any doubt [as to this]; but in the other, if any one is doubtful let him remember what was said in the next preceding chapter about the line of three syllables, when, as forming part of a line of eleven syllables, it answers like an echo. And if there happens to be an unrhymed ending in one of the feet, it must by all means be answered by a rhyme in the other. But if all the endings in one of the feet are rhymed, it is allowable in the other either to repeat the endings, or to put new ones, either wholly, or in part, at pleasure, provided, however, that the order of the preceding endings be observed in its entirety; for instance, if in a first foot of three lines, the extreme endings, that is, the first and last, rhyme together, so the extreme endings of the second foot must rhyme together; and according as the middle line in the first foot sees itself accompanied or unaccompanied by a rhyme, so let it rise up again in the second; and the same rule is to be observed with regard to the other kinds of feet. In the verses also we almost always obey this law; and we say "almost," because on account of the above-mentioned linking together [of the two parts of the stanza], and combination of the final endings, it sometimes happens that the order now stated is upset.

Moreover, it seems suitable for us to add to this chapter what things are to be avoided with regard to the rhymes, because we do not intend to deal any further in this book with the learning relating to rhyme. There are, then, three things, which with regard to the placing of rhymes it is unbecoming for a courtly poet to use, namely, [first], excessive repetition of the same rhyme, unless perchance something new and before unattempted in the art claim this for itself; just like the day of incipient knighthood, which disdains to let the period of initiation pass without any special distinction. And this we have striven to accomplish in the canzone, "*Amor, tu vedi ben che questa donna.*"[79]

The second of the things to be avoided is that useless equivocation which always seems to detract somewhat from the theme; and the third is roughness of rhymes, unless it be mingled with smoothness; for from a mixture of smooth and rough rhymes the tragedy itself gains in brilliancy.

And let this suffice concerning the art [of the canzone] so far as it relates to the arrangement [of the parts of the stanza].

XIV

Having sufficiently treated of two things belonging to the art in the canzone, it now appears that we ought to treat of the third, namely, the number of the lines and syllables. And in the first place we must make some observations with regard to the stanza as a whole; then we will make some observations as to its parts.

It concerns us therefore first to make a distinction between those subjects which fall to be sung of, because some stanzas seem to desire prolixity, and others do not. For whereas we sing of all the subjects we are speaking of either with reference to something favorable or else to something unfavorable, so that it happens that we sing sometimes persuasively, sometimes dissuasively, sometimes in congratulation, sometimes in irony, sometimes in praise, sometimes in contempt, let those words whose tendency is unfavorable always hasten to the end, and the others gradually advance to the end with a becoming prolixity. . . .

GIOVANNI BOCCACCIO

(1313–1375)

INTRODUCTION

From the point of view of the history of criticism, Giovanni Boccaccio is the foremost spokesman of the humanism that appeared (or reappeared) in Italy in the fourteenth century. The *Genealogy of the Gentile Gods*, while indebted to Boccaccio's friend and mentor Francis Petrarch, is the fullest summary we have of the early phase of the humanistic defense of secular literature.

In his preface Boccaccio tells us that he was in some sense commissioned to write the *Genealogy* by Donino of Parma, acting on behalf of Hugo IV, King of Cyprus from 1324–58. The commission was given during the 1340's. In 1350 Boccaccio met Bechino Bellincioni. He tells us near the end of Book XV that Bellincioni "began with wonderfully urgent importunity to rouse my mind from the drowsiness into which it had fallen over the work; and this he said he did at [King Hugo's] command." The task, however, was immense. Although Boccaccio addresses King Hugo in his conclusion as though the King, who died in 1359, is alive, the *Genealogy* continued to evolve during the 1360's; and, in fact, when Boccaccio heard in 1371 that the manuscript had been copied, he protested on the grounds that it was still incomplete. Evidently, the *Genealogy* was a life work extending from around 1343 to after 1370.

Boccaccio explains the method of the book in his preface:

> Before each book I plan to set a tree; at the root sits the father of the line, and on the branches, in genealogical order, all his progeny, so that you may have an index of what you are looking for in the book that follows. These Books you will find divided into chapters with proper and fuller rubrics corresponding to the mere name which you have already noted on the tree.
>
> I shall conclude with two books, in the first of which I shall reply to certain objections that have been raised against poetry and poets. In the second—and last of all—I shall endeavor to remove such criticisms as may possibly be leveled at me.

The result of this plan is an enormous compendium of classical mythology, arranged in terms of a genealogical scheme, followed by a two-book defense of poetry. If the size and rather wooden organization are typically medieval, the purpose and the range of scholarship are new. The *Genealogy* is a textbook for humanist poets. As we know from Bercorius, Christine de Pisan, John de Ridevall and others, classical mythology fascinated secular writers during the later Middle Ages. Knowledge of the myths, however, was limited, being based chiefly on Ovid, Servius, Fulgentius, and a few other classical and late classical authorities. In addition, there was the question of whether the pagan myths were idolotrous or obscene or both. The task that Boccaccio set himself was twofold. First, he had to collect and rationalize the enormous body of material waiting to be drawn from classical sources unknown or neglected during the Middle Ages. This meant not only the considerable number of Latin writers directly available to Boccaccio, but also a sampling of Greek writers whose work Boccaccio could consult with the aid of his friend Leontius Pilatus, a pupil of the famous Barlaam of Calabria. Second, he had to show, both specifically and in terms of general theory, that reference to and use of this material is entirely fitting a Christian poet.

Like most of his predecessors in the defense of pagan mythology, Boccaccio regarded the ancient myths as storehouses of wisdom concealed under the veil of fable. We must know the inner meaning as well as the story if we are properly to appreciate the achievement of the ancients. This leads to allegorical interpretation. Boccaccio knew several methods of allegorical interpretation and used them all as they seemed appropriate. Euhemerism and etymological interpretation are common in the *Genealogy*. So, also, is the classification of myth in terms of natural, ethical, and theological allegory. And so is the interpretation of myth according to the literal, allegorical, tropological (moral), and anagogical (spiritual) "levels" of scriptural interpretation. Sometimes the methods are used separately, sometimes in combination. The reader who is not overly concerned with consistency can end the mythological section of the work (through Book XIII) comfortably reassured that pagan myths almost always contain natural and moral truths, and, on occasion, adumbrations of the truths of Christian revelation embodied in their definitive form in the Bible.

The defenses of poetry contained in Books XIV and XV of the *Genealogy* have no obvious medieval precedent. The twelfth-century Renaissance had produced apologies for the liberal arts by men like John of Salisbury and Richard of Bury but no full-scale defenses of poetry. Moreover, the humanists of the twelfth century were all but eclipsed for some two centuries by the scholastics of Paris. Although it is becoming increasingly clear that there is much greater continuity than we formerly recognized between the French humanism of the twelfth century and the Italian variety of the fourteenth, the most obvious and primary influences on Boccaccio are classical and contemporary. The idea of a formal defense of poetry may have come originally via Cicero's *Pro Archia Poeta*, a spirited oration defending a minor Roman poet, which Boccaccio quotes at the end of Book XIV as a last, crushing rejoinder to the "enemies of poetry."

Two more recent authorities undoubtedly supplemented whatever influence Cicero may have had. Albertino Mussato (1261–1329) had already become involved in a much-publicized dispute with the Dominican Giovannino of Padua over the value of reading the poets, and his arguments outline the main topics later covered by Boccaccio. Above all, Boccaccio writes under the shadow of his friend Francis Petrarch. Petrarch's ideas about poetry are scattered throughout his letters and prose works. The oration which he delivered when crowned laureate in Rome in 1341 summarizes several of them. His fullest statement of these ideas, however, is his *Invective Against a Physician.* This work is not a defense of poetry so much as a defense of humane learning, but particularly at the end of Book I and the beginning of Book III, Petrarch lists most of the objections to poetry cited by Boccaccio and offers refutations much like those in the *Genealogy.* The *Invective* is thus not the source for the idea of a formal defense of poetry but it is a store-house of arguments, topics, and citations of authority on which Boccaccio leaned heavily.

The argument of the *Genealogy* opens with an attack on poetry's enemies, the dilettantes, the materialistic lawyers, and "other cavillers" (XIV.5). The "other cavillers" are associated with "sacred studies" and "mask themselves with sanctity." They are fond of quoting the line from Psalm 69 "The zeal of God's house hath eaten me up." They pretend to great knowledge but are really ignorant. The portrait reminds one of Erasmus' *Praise of Folly.* Although the "cavillers" are not specifically identified, it is obvious that they are clerics and an open secret that they are Dominicans of the same ilk as Giovannino of Padua. Boccaccio lists their objections to poetry, and the list provides the topics for the remainder of Book XIV. It testifies to the hostility and suspicion with which the dominant party of scholasticism greeted a rising (or reviving) humanism. In one way or another the controversy can be traced throughout the fifteenth century, down to the open warfare between Savonarola and the Florentine humanists during the 1490's.

The main charges against poetry are (1) that it is trivial, (2) that poets lie, (3) that poems are "false, lewd, and obscure," (4) that they corrupt readers, (5) that poets ape philosophers, (6) that it is a sin to read them, and (7) that Plato and Boethius rejected poetry. Boccaccio answers each charge in one or more chapters. Most of the charges are as old as "the ancient quarrel between the philosophers and the poets" mentioned by Socrates at the end of Republic X, but they appear here in a specifically Christian and late medieval guise.

Chapter 6 asserts that poetry is a divine gift, cites the *poesis*, *poeta*, *poema* triad inherited with modifications from Alexandrian criticism, and defends the utility of poetry with the claim that it is a "science." As is clear from an earlier chapter (XIV.4) Boccaccio has in mind the distinction between a "faculty" having no content and a "science" which does have content. The analysis of poetry's place in the scheme of knowledge was a central feature of scholastic poetic theory, and the typical scholastic position was that it belongs with the instrumental disciplines of the *Organon*—i.e., it is a part of logic and a faculty to be used on any "content" rather than depending on a content. This justified rejection of the claims of the poets to teaching wisdom, goodness, and higher truth. By claiming that poetry is a science rather than a faculty, Boccaccio is inverting the argument. For him and for later humanists, poetry contains a whole range of truths, from the most arcane verities of revelation to the useful truths of ethics and political science. The fact that it teaches these truths delightfully, according to the Horatian formula, gives it unique social utility.

Chapter 7 is a tissue of humanistic commonplaces. Poetry came from the "bosom of God." It is a gift possessed by a few men and not a skill to be learned, although writing good poetry demands familiarity with the lore of grammar, rhetoric, and moral philosophy. It is the result of inspiration, bringing forth "strange and unheard-of creations of the mind," and it "veils truth in a fair and fitting garment of fiction." The tone is Platonic. We are closer here to Macrobius and Proclus than to Horace. The chapter illustrates the nexus in humanist theory between inspiration, fondness for the marvelous ("unheard-of creations") at the expense of verisimilitude, and allegory. Naturally, poetry that meets these criteria will be obscure, a point that Boccaccio repeats in Chapter 12.

In Chapter 8 Boccaccio adds that poets were the first theologians. His claim is supported by a much-quoted sentence in Aristotle's *Metaphysics* (1000a9) and by the fact that in the earlier books of the *Genealogy* Boccaccio has demonstrated that ancient myths are frequently adumbrations of Christian truths. In the *Life of Dante* Boccaccio argues that "theology and poetry are in agreement as to their form of working, but in subject . . . they are not merely wholly diverse, but in some parts contradictory." Theology treats divine virtue, poets, the pagan gods and mortal men; theology (that is, scripture) is true in all four of the standard senses, poetry is false on the literal level and even "against the Christian religion." Boccaccio adds that when critics "foolishly blame the poets for this they rashly stumble into blaming that Spirit that is none other than the way, the truth, and the life." The *Genealogy* is more circumspect in that it does not claim that the Holy Spirit directly inspires secular poetry, but it tends in the same direction: poetry originated in "the bosom of God," and Dante (XV.6) was "a sacred theologian rather than a mere mythographer."

Taken together, Boccaccio's arguments are a daring assertion of the value of secular poetry. If they are valid, poetry must in some sense be a form of revelation and thus complementary—if not an alternative—to scripture. Here we have the fundamental reason for the hostility of the scholastic tradition to poetry. From the scholastic point of view, the humanist position is nothing less than a challenge to the unique authority of scripture.

The following chapters of Book XIV elaborate arguments already presented. The difficulty of relating Hebrew to Greek chronology makes it difficult (XIV.8) to decide where poetry originated. Boccaccio favors the Greeks. If the Hebrews bear the palm, the first poet was Moses "who wrote the largest part of Pentateuch not in prose but in heroic verse." Moses may, in fact, be the same person as Musaeus! If the Greeks invented poetry, the first poets were Musaeus, Linus, and Orpheus, who "under the prompting stimulus of the divine mind, invented strange songs in regular times and measure, designed for the praise of God." Fables (XIV.9) are exemplary (Aesop), mixed, historical, and fictional. All kinds except the last are found in the Bible, and "the writings of the Old Testament and the writings of the poets seem as it were to keep in step with each other." To reject fables is to reject the Bible; to call them lies is "to call the Holy Spirit, or Christ, the very God, liars." Wherever they are found their power "pleases the unlearned by its exterior appearance, and exercises the minds of the learned with its hidden truth." The latter point is illustrated in Chapter 10 by Vergil, Dante, and Petrarch; i.e., by both the ancients and the moderns. As for the "cavillers," "When they have made themselves clean, let them purify the tales of others, mindful of Christ's commandment to the accusers of the woman taken in adultery, that he who was without sin should cast the first stone."

Chapter 12 is of interest because of its treatment of poetic obscurity. Obscurity is inevitable in poetry that bodies forth truths unavailable to the reason, and biblical obscurity had long been explained by various doctrines including the idea of accommodation, the theory of allegory, and the notion that the highest truths should be clothed in the most elaborate (hence the most involuted) images. As Boccaccio remarks, scripture proceeds from the Holy Spirit and is "full to overflowing with obscurities and ambiguities." The function of poets is to write, not to "rip up and lay bare the meaning which lies hidden in his inventions." In the *Life of Dante* Boccaccio remarked that "anything gained with fatigue seems sweeter than what is understood without effort. The plain truth, since it is understood easily, delights us and passes from the mind. But, in order that it may be more pleasing because acquired with labor, and therefore better valued, the poets hide the truth beneath things appearing quite contrary to it." Here, he is content to quote Petrarch's *Invectives*: "What we acquire with difficulty and keep with care is always the dearer to us."

What stands out here, as elsewhere in Boccaccio's defense of poetry, is the habit of comparing the inspiration of the Muses with the inspiration of the Holy Spirit, the insights of the poets to the wisdom of the theologians, the obscurity of poetic fables to the difficulty of scripture.

In what ways, we might ask, is Christian revelation unique? What is special about the Bible if pagan poetry contains the same levels of meaning, the same literary devices, and the same truths? Of course, Boccaccio's contemporaries did not ask this. Instead, the "cavillers" attacked the pretensions of the poets, and the vehemence of their onslaught is a measure of the threat they felt to their own concept of the Christian tradition. Boccaccio, on his side, did not feel that he was undermining or betraying Christian tradition any more than Petrarch or Ficino or Erasmus. Literature for him, as for later humanists, should supplement and broaden Christianity, not replace it. From this point of view the "cavillers" are not true Christians but bigots. It is they, not Boccaccio, who would be forced if consistent to call the Holy Spirit a liar for using fables in scripture.

This is most of the story but not all of it. If any one, says Boccaccio, should confuse the old poets with "sacred" [i.e. Christian] theologians, "the veriest fool would detect the falsehood." At the same time "the old theology can sometimes be employed in the sense of Catholic truth if the fashioner of the myth should choose." After all the explanations, there is an ambivalence in Boccaccio's defense that is not present—or at least not nearly so obvious—in Petrarch. It is the ambivalence of a Platonizing Christianity, whether in Alexandria, in twelfth-century France, or Ficino's fifteenth-century academy. If Boccaccio's defense of poetry looks back, in this respect to Bernard Silvestris, it looks forward to Ficino, Landino, and a host of later humanistic defenders of art and poetry.

The translation, here slightly modernized, and the notes have been taken from Charles G. Osgood, *Boccaccio on Poetry* (Princeton: Princeton University Press, 1930). For bibliography, see especially pp. 489–90.

GENEALOGY OF THE GENTILE GODS

from BOOK XIV

V. Other Cavillers at the Poets and Their Imputations

There is also, O most serene of rulers, as you know far better than I, a kind of house established in this world by God's gift, in the image of a celestial council, and devoted only to sacred studies. Within, on a lofty throne, sits philosophy, messenger from the very bosom of God, mistress of all knowledge. Noble is her mien and radiant with godlike splendor. There she sits arrayed in royal robes and adorned with a golden crown, like the empress of all the world. In her left hand she holds several books, with her right hand she wields a royal sceptre, and in clear and fluent discourse she shows forth to such as will listen the truly praiseworthy ideals of human character, the forces of our Mother Nature, the true good, and the secrets of heaven. If you enter you do not doubt that it is a sanctuary full worthy of all reverence; and if you look about, you will clearly see there every opportunity for the higher pursuits of the human mind, both speculation and knowledge, and will gaze with wonder till you regard it not merely as one all-inclusive household, but almost the very image of the divine mind. Among other objects of great veneration there, behind the mistress of the household, are certain men seated in high places, few in number, of gentle aspect and utterance, who are so distinguished by their seriousness, honesty, and true humility, that you take them for gods not mortals. These men abound in the faith and doctrine of their mistress, and give freely to others of the fullness of their knowledge.

But there is also another group—a noisy crowd—of all sorts and conditions. Some of these have resigned all pride, and live in watchful obedience to the injunctions of their superiors, in hopes that their obsequious zeal may gain them promotion. But others there are who grow so elated with what is virtually elementary knowledge, that they fall upon their great mistress' robes as it were with their talons, and in violent haste tear away a few shreds as samples; then don various titles which they often pick up for a price; and, as puffed up as if they knew the whole subject of divinity, they rush forth from the sacred house, setting such mischief afoot among ignorant people as only the wise can calculate. Yet these rascals are sworn conspirators against all high arts. First they try to counterfeit a good man; they exchange their natural expression for an anxious, careful one. They go about with downcast eye to appear inseparable from their thoughts. Their pace is slow to make the uneducated think that they stagger under an excessive weight of high speculation. They dress unpretentiously, not because they are really modest, but only to mask themselves with sanctity. Their talk is little and serious. If you ask them a question they heave a sigh, pause a moment, raise their eyes to heaven, and at length deign to answer. They hope the bystanders will infer from this that their words rise slowly to their lips, not from any lack of eloquence, but because they are fetched from the remote sanctuary of heavenly secrets. They profess piety, sanctity, and justice, and often utter the words of the prophet, "The zeal of God's house hath eaten me up."[1]

Then they proceed to display their wonderful knowledge, and whatever they don't know they damn—to good effect too. This they do to avoid inquiry about subjects of which they are ignorant, or else to affect scorn and indifference in such matters as cheap, trivial, and obvious, while they have devoted themselves to things of greater importance. When they have caught inexperienced minds in traps of this sort, they proceed boldly to range about town, dabble in business, give advice, arrange marriages, appear at big dinners, dictate wills, act as executors of estates, and otherwise display arrogance unbecoming to a philosopher. Thus they blow up a huge cloud of popular reputation, and thereby so strut with vanity that, when they walk abroad, they want to have everybody's finger pointing them out, to overhear people saying that they are great masters of their subjects, and see how the grand folk rise to meet them in the squares of the city and call them "Rabbi," speak to them, invite them, give place, and defer to them. Straightway they throw off all restraint and become bold enough for anything; they are not afraid to lay their own sickles to the harvest of another; and, while they are basely defiling other people's business, the talk may fall upon poetry and poets. At the sound of the word they blaze up in such a sudden fury that you would say their eyes were afire. They cannot stop; they go raging on by the very momentum of their wrath. Finally, like conspirators against a deadly enemy, in the schools, in public squares, in pulpits, with a lazy crowd, as a rule, for an audience, they break out into such mad denunciation of poets that the bystanders are afraid of the speakers themselves, let alone the harmless objects of attack.

They say poetry is absolutely of no account, and the making of poetry a useless and absurd craft; that poets are tale-mongers, or, in lower terms, liars; that they live in the country among the woods and mountains because they lack manners and polish. They say, besides, that their poems are false, obscure, lewd, and replete with absurd and silly tales of pagan gods, and that they make Jove, who was, in point of fact, an obscene and adulterous man, now the father of gods, now king of heaven, now fire, or air, or man, or bull, or eagle, or similar irrelevant things; in like manner poets exalt to fame Juno and infinite others under various names. Again and again they cry out that poets are seducers of the mind, prompters of crime, and, to make their foul charge fouler, if possible, they say they are philosophers' apes, that it is a heinous crime to read or possess the books of poets; and then, without making any distinction, they prop themselves up, as they say, with Plato's authority to the effect that poets ought to be turned out-of-doors—nay, out of town, and that the Muses, their mumming mistresses, as Boethius says, being sweet with deadly sweetness, are detestable, and should be driven out with them and utterly rejected. But it would take too long to cite everything that their irritable spite and deadly hatred prompt these madmen to say. It is also before judges like these—so eminent, indeed, so fair, so merciful, so well-inclined—that my work will appear, O glorious Prince; and I know full well they will gather about it like famished lions, to seek what they may devour. Since my book has entirely to do with poetic material, I cannot look for a milder sentence from them than in their rage they thunder down upon poets. I am well aware that I offer my breast to the same missiles that their hatred has already employed; but I shall endeavor to ward them off.

O merciful God, meet now this foolish and ill-considered clamor of mad men, and oppose their rage. And thou, O best of kings, as I advance upon their line, support me with the strength of thy noble soul, and help me in my fight for thee; for courage and a stout heart must now be mine. Sharp and poisonous are their weapons, but weak withal. Foolish judges though they be, they are strong in other ways, and I tremble with fear before them, unless God, who deserteth not them that trust in Him, and thou, also, favor me. Slender is my strength and my mind weak, but great is my expectation of help; borne up by such hope, I shall rush upon them with justice at my right hand.

VI. Poetry Is a Useful Art

I am about to enter the arena, a manikin against these giant hulks—who have armed themselves with authority to say that poetry is either no art at all or a useless one. In the circumstances, for me first to discuss the definition and function of poetry would be hunting a mare's nest. But since the fight must be fought I wish these past masters of all the arts would declare upon what particular point they desire the contest to bear. Yet I know full well that with a sneer and a brazen front they will unblushingly utter the same ineptitudes as before. Come, O merciful God, give ear to their foolish objections and guide their steps into a better way.

They say, then, in condemnation of poetry, that it is naught. If such is the case, I should like to know why, through generation after generation, so many great men have sought the name of poet. Whence come so many volumes of poems? If poetry is naught, whence came this word poetry? Whatever answer they make, they are going out of their way, I think, since they can give no rational answer that is not directly against their present vain contention. It is absolutely certain, as I shall show later,[2] that poetry, like other studies, is derived from God, Author of all wisdom; like the rest it got its name from its effect. From this name "poetry" at length comes the glorious name of "poet"; and from "poet," "poem." In that case poetry apparently is not wholly naught, as they said.

If then it prove a science, what more will those noisy sophists have to say? They will either retract a little, or rather, I think, flit lightly over the gap thus opening in their argument to the second point of their objection, and say that if poetry *is* a mere art, it is a useless one. How rank! How silly! Better to have kept quiet than hurl themselves with their frivolous words into deeper error. Why, do not the fools see that the very meaning of this word "art" or "faculty" always implies a certain plenitude? But of this elsewhere. Just now I wish that these accomplished gentlemen would show how poetry can reasonably be called futile when it has, by God's grace, given birth to so many famous books, so many memorable poems, clearly conceived, and dealing with strange marvels. They will keep quiet at this, I think, if their vain itch for display will let them.

Keep quiet, did I say? Why they would rather die than confess the truth in silence, not to say with the tip of their tongues. They will dart off on another tack, and by their own arbitrary interpretation, will say, with slight addition, that poetry must be regarded a futile and empty thing, nay, damnable, detestable, because the poems which come of it sing the adulteries of the gods they celebrate, and beguile the reader into unspeakable practices. Though this interpretation is easy to refute—since nothing can be empty that is filled with adulteries—in any case it may be borne with a calm mind; nay their contention based upon it may be granted in all reason, since I readily acknowledge that there are poems of the kind they describe, and if the bad kind were to corrupt the good, then the victory would be theirs. But, I protest; if Praxiteles or Phidias, both experts in their art, should choose for a statue the immodest subject of Priapus on his way to Iole[3] by night, instead of Diana glorified in her chastity; or if Apelles, or our own Giotto—whom Apelles in his time did not excel—should represent Venus in the embrace of Mars[4] instead of the enthroned Jove dispensing laws unto the gods, shall we therefore condemn these arts? Downright stupidity, I should call it!

The fault for such corruption lies in the licentious mind of the artist. Thus for a long time there have been "poets," if such deserve the name, who, either to get money or popularity, study contemporary fashions, pander to a licentious taste, and at the cost of all self-respect, the loss of all honor, abandon themselves to these literary fooleries. Their works certainly should be condemned, hated, and spurned, as I shall show later.[5] Yet if a few writers of fiction erred thus, poetry does not therefore deserve universal condemnation, since it offers us so many inducements to virtue, in the monitions and teaching of poets whose care it has been to set forth with lofty intelligence, and utmost candor, in exquisite style and diction, men's thoughts on things of heaven.

But enough! Not only is poetry more than naught, but it is a science worthy of veneration; and, as often appears in the foregoing as well as in succeeding pages, it is an art or skill, not empty, but full of the sap of natural vigor for those who would through fiction subdue the senses with the mind. So, not to be tedious, it would seem that at the first onset of this conflict, these leaders have turned tail, and, with slight effort on my part, have abandoned the arena. But it is my present duty to define Poetry, that they may see for themselves how stupid they are in their opinion that poetry is an empty art.

VII. The Definition of Poetry, Its Origin, and Function

This poetry, which ignorant triflers cast aside, is a sort of fervid and exquisite invention, with fervid expression, in speech or writing, of that which the mind has invented. It proceeds from the bosom of God, and few, I find, are the souls in whom this gift is born; indeed so wonderful a gift it is that true poets have always been the rarest of men. This fervor of poesy is sublime in its effects: it impels the soul to a longing for utterance; it brings forth strange and unheard-of creations of the mind; it arranges these meditations in a fixed order, adorns the whole composition with unusual interweaving of words and thoughts;

and thus it veils truth in a fair and fitting garment of fiction. Further, if in any case the invention so requires, it can arm kings, marshal them for war, launch whole fleets from their docks, nay, counterfeit sky, land, sea, adorn young maidens with flowery garlands, portray human character in its various phases, awake the idle, stimulate the dull, restrain the rash, subdue the criminal, and distinguish excellent men with their proper reward of praise: these, and many other such, are the effects of poetry. Yet if any man who has received the gift of poetic fervor shall imperfectly fulfill its function here described, he is not, in my opinion, a laudable poet. For, however deeply the poetic impulse stirs the mind to which it is granted, it very rarely accomplishes anything commendable if the instruments by which its concepts are to be wrought out are wanting—I mean, for example, the precepts of grammar and rhetoric, an abundant knowledge of which is opportune. I grant that many a man already writes his mother tongue admirably, and indeed has performed each of the various duties of poetry as such; yet over and above this, it is necessary to know at least the principles of the other liberal arts, both moral and natural, to possess a strong and abundant vocabulary, to behold the monuments and relics of the ancients, to have in one's memory the histories of the nations, and to be familiar with the geography of various lands, of seas, rivers, and mountains.

Furthermore, places of retirement, the lovely handiwork of nature herself, are favorable to poetry, as well as peace of mind and desire for worldly glory; the ardent period of life also has very often been of great advantage. If these conditions fail, the power of creative genius frequently grows dull and sluggish.

Now since nothing proceeds from this poetic fervor, which sharpens and illumines the powers of the mind, except what is wrought out by art, poetry is generally called an art. Indeed the word poetry has not the origin that many carelessly suppose, namely *poio, pois,* which is but Latin *fingo, fingis*; rather it is derived from a very ancient Greek word *poetes,* which means in Latin exquisite discourse (*exquisita locutio*). For the first men who, thus inspired, began to employ an exquisite style of speech, such, for example, as song in an age hitherto unpolished, to render this unheard-of discourse sonorous to their hearers, let it fall in measured periods; and lest by its brevity it fail to please, or, on the other hand, become prolix and tedious, they applied to it the standard of fixed rules, and restrained it within a definite number of feet and syllables. Now the product of this studied method of speech they no longer called by the more general term poesy, but poem. Thus as I said above, the name of the art, as well as its artificial product, is derived from its effect.

Now though I allege that this science of poetry has ever streamed forth from the bosom of God upon souls while even yet in their tenderest years, these enlightened cavillers will perhaps say that they cannot trust my words. To any fair-minded man the fact is valid enough from its constant recurrence. But for these dullards I must cite witnesses to it. If, then, they will read what Cicero, a philosopher rather than a poet, says in his oration delivered before the senate in behalf of Aulus Licinius Archias,[6] perhaps they will come more easily to believe me. He says: "And yet we have it on the highest and most learned authority, that while other arts are matters of science and formula and technique, poetry depends solely upon an inborn faculty, is evoked by a purely mental activity, and is infused with a strange divine inspiration."

But not to protract this argument, it is now sufficiently clear to reverent men, that poetry is a practical art, springing from God's bosom and deriving its name from its effect, and that it has to do with many high and noble matters that constantly occupy even those who deny its existence. If my opponents ask when and in what circumstances, the answer is plain: the poets would declare with their own lips under whose help and guidance they compose their inventions when, for example, they raise flights of symbolic steps to heaven, or make thick-branching trees spring aloft to the very stars, or go winding about mountains to their summits. Perhaps, to disparage this art of poetry now unrecognized by them, these men will say that it is rhetoric which the poets employ. Indeed, I will not deny it in part, for rhetoric has also its own inventions. Yet, in truth, among the disguises of fiction rhetoric has no part, for whatever is composed as under a veil, and thus exquisitely wrought, is poetry and poetry alone.

VIII. Where Poetry First Dawned Upon the World

If you inquire, O King, under what sky, in what period, and by whose agency poetry first came to light, I hardly trust my ability to answer. One group of writers thinks it arose with the holy rites of the ancients, that is, among the Hebrews, since Holy Writ records that they were the first to offer sacrifice to God; for we read that the brothers, Cain and Abel, the first men born on earth, sacrificed to God; so also did Noah when the flood subsided and he went forth from the ark; and so Abraham for victory over his foes, when he offered Melchisedek, the priest, wine and bread. But since these accounts do not yield altogether the desired answer, writers of this opinion—rather by divination than proof, it must be said—insist that these rites were accomplished with some sort of formal discourse. They add that Moses, when, with the people of Israel, he had passed the Red Sea dry-shod, performed a complete sacrifice, since we read that he established rites, priests, and a tabernacle like the temple that was to be, and appointed prayers to placate the Divine Will. So it seems that poetry had its origin among the Hebrews not earlier than Moses, leader of the Israelites; and he led the people forth and performed his rites about the time that King Marathius of the Sicyoni died, which was the three thousand, six hundred and eightieth year of the world.

A second group would give the Babylonians the glory of inventing poetry. Among these the Venetian,[7] bishop of Pozzuolo, a tremendous investigator, was wont to argue at length in bantering fashion, that poetry was far older than Moses, having had its origin about the time of Nembroth. Nimrod, he said, was the founder of idolatry, for when he saw that fire was useful to men, and that he could, to some extent, foretell the future from its various motions and sounds, he averred that it was a god; wherefore he not only worshipped it instead of God, and persuaded the Chaldeans to do likewise, but built temples to it, ordained priests, and even composed prayers. Now, according to the Venetian these prayers showed that he employed formal, polished discourse. Possibly; but the Venetian never clearly showed his authority for his statement. Yet I have read often enough that religious worship, the study of philosophy, and the glory of arms all had their origin among the Assyrians. But I cannot easily believe, without more trustworthy evidence, that an art so sublime as that of poetry arose first among peoples so barbarous and wild.

The Greeks also maintain that poetry originated with them, and Leontius supports this view with all his might. I am a little inclined his way, as I recollect hearing my famous teacher once say that among the primitive Greeks, poetry had some such origin as this: While they were still rude, some of them, above the rest in intellectual power, began to wonder at the works of their Mother Nature; and as they meditated they came gradually to believe in some one Being, by whose operation and command all visible things are governed and ordered. Him they named God. Then, thinking that He sometimes visited earth, and considering Him holy, they raised buildings for Him at enormous expense, that He might on His visits find abiding places consecrated to His name. These we now call temples. Then, to propitiate Him, they devised peculiar honors to be rendered Him at appointed seasons, and called them rites. Finally, in their belief that, as He excelled all others in divinity, so ought He in honor also, they had silver tables made for His rites, and fashioned of gold the drinking-cups, candelabra, and whatever other vessels they used; they also selected men from among the wisest and gentlest of the people, whom they afterwards called priests, and these they would have appear in no common garb at the celebration of rites, but made them resplendent in costly robes with tiaras and crosiers. Then, since it seemed absurd for the priests to perform rites to the Deity in utter silence, they had certain discourses composed to show forth the praise, and great works of the Deity himself, to express the petitions of the people, and offer him the prayers of men in their various needs. And since it would appear inappropriate to address the Deity as you would a farmhand, an underling, or a familiar friend, the wiser among them wanted a polished and artistic manner of speech devised, and they committed this task to the priests. Some of these, though few —and among them, it is thought, were Musaeus, Linus, and Orpheus—under the prompting stimulus of the Divine Mind, invented strange songs in regular time and measure, designed for the praise of God. To strengthen the authority of these songs, they enclosed the high mysteries of things divine in a covering of words, with the intention that the adorable majesty of such things should not become an object of too common knowledge, and thus fall into contempt. Now since the art thus discovered seemed wonderful and wholly new, they named it, as I have said, from its *effect,* and called it poetry or *poetes,* that is, in Latin *exquisita locutio*; and they who had composed the songs were named poets. And, as the name favors the effect, the belief is that both the musical accompaniment of poetry and all its other accoutrements arose among the Greeks.

But the date of its origin is very doubtful. Leontius, for one, used to say that he had heard his teacher, Barlaam of Calabria, and other learned authorities on the subject, more than once assign the date to the time of Phoroneus, King of Argos, who came to the throne in the three thousand, three hundred and eighty-fifth year of the world. They also said that Musaeus, whom I mentioned above as one of the inventors of poetry, was eminent among the Greeks, and that Linus flourished about the same time; their fame, which is still great, bears witness even in our day that they presided over the rites of the ancients. To these is added Orpheus of Thrace; they are therefore considered the earliest theologians.

But Paul of Perugia used to infer from the same ancient authorities, that poetry was much younger, and alleged that Orpheus, who is recorded as one of the earliest poets, flourished in the reign of Laomedon, King of Troy, when Eurystheus ruled Mycenae, about the three thousand, nine hundred and tenth year of the world, that he was the Orpheus of the Argonauts, and not only a successor of Musaeus, but the teacher of the same Musaeus, son of Eumolpus. Such, at least, is the testimony of Eusebius in his *Liber Temporum.* Whence Paul's statement, cited above, that poetry was more recent among the Greeks than his opponents held. Leontius, however, in reply maintained that learned Greeks thought there were several by the name of Orpheus and Musaeus, but that the ancient Orpheus was a Greek contemporary with the ancient Musaeus and Linus, whereas it is a younger one who is called the Thracian. Indeed, since this younger Orpheus invented the rites of Bacchus, and the nocturnal gatherings of the Maenads, and made many innovations in the liturgy of the ancients, and especially had great powers of eloquence—all of which won him high esteem in his generation—he was therefore regarded as the great Orpheus by posterity. Perhaps this is the right view especially since some of the ancients bear witness that there were poets before the birth of the Cretan Jove, and it is known from Eusebius that Orpheus the Thracian flourished after Jove's rape of Europa.

But with scholars thus at variance, and me unable to find reliable evidence in ancient authors to support their theories, I cannot tell which to follow. It is at least evident from all accounts that, if one is to follow Leontius, poetry originated with the Greeks before it did with the Hebrews; if the Venetian, then with the Chaldeans before it did among the Greeks; but if we prefer to believe Paul, it follows that Moses was a master of poetry before either Babylonians or

Greeks. Aristotle,[8] to be sure, perhaps for reasons just urged, asserts that the first poets were theologians, by that meaning Greeks; and herein he favors somewhat the opinion of Leontius. Nevertheless I cannot believe that the sublime effects of this great art were first bestowed upon Musaeus, or Linus, or Orpheus, however ancient, unless, as some say, Moses and Musaeus were one and the same. Of the beast Nimrod I take no account. Rather was it instilled into most sacred prophets, dedicated to God. For we read that Moses, impelled by what I take to be this poetic longing, at dictation of the Holy Ghost, wrote the largest part of the Pentateuch not in prose but in heroic verse. In like manner others have set forth the great works of God in the metrical garment of letters, which we call poetic. And I think the poets of the Gentiles in their poetry—not perhaps without understanding—followed in the steps of these prophets; but whereas the holy men were filled with the Holy Ghost, and wrote under His impulse, the others were prompted by mere energy of mind, whence such a one is called "seer." Under fervor of this impulse they composed their poems. But since I have nothing further to say on the origin of poetry, do thou, O glorious King, choose whichever opinion accords with thy serene judgment.

IX. It Is Rather Useful Than Damnable To Compose Stories

These fine cattle bellow still further to the effect that poets are talemongers, or, to use the lower and more hateful term which they sometimes employ in their resentment—liars. No doubt the ignorant will regard such an imputation as particularly objectionable. But I scorn it. The foul language of some men cannot infect the glorious name of the illustrious. Yet I grieve to see these revilers in a purple rage let themselves loose upon the innocent. If I conceded that poets deal in stories, in that they are composers of fiction, I think I hereby incur no further disgrace than a philosopher would in drawing up a syllogism. For if I show the nature of a fable or story, its various kinds, and which kinds these "liars" employ, I do not think the composers of fiction will appear guilty of so monstrous a crime as these gentlemen maintain. First of all, the word "fable" (*fabula*) has an honorable origin in the verb *for, faris,* hence "conversation" (*confabulatio*), which means only "talking together" (*collocutio*). This is clearly shown by Luke in his Gospel, where he is speaking of the two disciples who went to the village of Emmaus after the Passion. He says: "And they talked together of all these things which had happened. And it came to pass, that, while they communed together, and reasoned, Jesus himself drew near, and went with them."[9]

Hence, if it is a sin to compose stories, it is a sin to converse, which only the veriest fool would admit. For nature has not granted us the power of speech unless for purposes of conversation, and the exchange of ideas.

But, they may object, nature meant this gift for a useful purpose, not for idle nonsense; and fiction is just that—idle nonsense. True enough, if the poet had intended to compose a mere tale. But I have time and time again proved that the meaning of fiction is far from superficial. Wherefore, some writers have framed this definition of fiction (*fabula*): Fiction is a form of discourse, which, under guise of invention, illustrates or proves an idea; and, as its superficial aspect is removed, the meaning of the author is clear. If, then, sense is revealed from under the veil of fiction, the composition of fiction is not idle nonsense. Of fiction I distinguish four kinds:[10] The first superficially lacks all appearance of truth; for example, when brutes or inanimate things converse. Aesop, an ancient Greek, grave and venerable, was past master in this form; and though it is a common and popular form both in city and country, yet Aristotle,[11] chief of the Peripatetics, and a man of divine intellect, did not scorn to use it in his books. The second kind at times superficially mingles fiction with truth, as when we tell of the daughters of Minyas at their spinning, who, when they spurned the orgies of Bacchus, were turned to bats; or the mates of the sailor Acestes,[12] who for contriving the rape of the boy Bacchus, were turned to fish. This form has been employed from the beginning by the most ancient poets, whose object it has been to clothe in fiction divine and human matters alike; they who have followed the sublimer inventions of the poets have improved upon them; while some of the comic writers have perverted them, caring more for the approval of a licentious public than for honesty. The third kind is more like history than fiction, and famous poets have employed it in a variety of ways. For however much the heroic poets seem to be writing history—as Vergil in his description of Aeneas tossed by the storm, or Homer in his account of Ulysses bound to the mast to escape the lure of the Sirens' song—yet their hidden meaning is far other than appears on the surface. The better of the comic poets, Terence and Plautus, for example, have also employed this form, but they intend naught other than the literal meaning of their lines. Yet by their art they portray varieties of human nature and conversation, incidentally teaching the reader and putting him on his guard. If the events they describe have not actually taken place, yet since they are common, they could have occurred, or might at some time. My opponents need not be so squeamish—Christ, who is God, used this sort of fiction again and again in his parables!

The fourth kind contains no truth at all, either superficial or hidden, since it consists only of old wives' tales.

Now, if my eminent opponents condemn the first kind of fiction, then they must include the account in Holy Writ describing the conference of the trees[13] of the forest on choosing a king. If the second, then nearly the whole sacred body of the Old Testament will be rejected. God forbid, since the writings of the Old Testament and the writings of the poets seem as it were to keep step with each other, and that too in respect to the method of their composition. For where history is lacking, neither one concerns itself with the superficial possibility, but what the poet calls fable or fiction our theologians have named figure. The truth of this may be seen by fairer judges than my opponents, if they will but weigh in a true scale the outward literary semblance of the visions of Isaiah, Ezekiel, Daniel, and other sacred writers on the one hand, with the outward literary semblance of the fiction of poets on the other. If they find any real discrepancy in their methods, either of implication or exposition, I will accept their condemnation. If they condemn the third form of fiction, it is the same as condemning the form which our Savior Jesus Christ, the Son of God, often used when He was in the flesh, though Holy Writ does not call it "poetry," but "parable," some call it "exemplum," because it is used as such.

I count as naught their condemnation of the fourth form of fiction, since it proceeds from no consistent principle, nor is fortified by the reinforcement of any of the arts, nor carried logically to a conclusion. Fiction of this kind has nothing in common with the works of the poets, though I imagine these objectors think poetry differs from it in no respect.

I now ask whether they are going to call the Holy Spirit, or Christ, the very God, liars, who both in the same Godhead have uttered fictions. I hardly think so, if they are wise. I might show them, your Majesty, if there were time, that difference of names constitutes no objection where methods agree. But they may see for themselves. Fiction, which they scorn because of its mere name, has been the means, as we often read, of quelling minds aroused to a mad rage, and subduing them to their pristine gentleness. Thus, when the Roman plebs seceded from the senate, they were called back from the sacred mount to the city by Menenius Agrippa, a man of great influence, all by means of a story. By fiction, too, the strength and spirits of great men worn out in the strain of serious crises, have been restored. This appears, not by ancient instance alone, but constantly. One knows of princes who have been deeply engaged in important matters, but after the noble and happy disposal of their affairs of state, obey, as it were, the warning of nature, and revive their spent forces by calling about them such men as will renew their weary minds with diverting stories and conversation. Fiction has, in some cases, sufficed to lift the oppressive weight of adversity and furnish consolation, as appears in Lucius Apuleius; he tells how the highborn maiden Charis, while bewailing her unhappy condition as captive among thieves, was in some degree restored through hearing from an old woman the charming story of Psyche.[14] Through fiction, it is well known, the mind that is slipping into inactivity is recalled to a state of better and more vigorous fruition. Not to mention minor instances, such as my own, I once heard Giacopo Sanseverino, Count of Tricarico and Chiarmonti, say that he had heard his father tell of Robert, son of King Charles,[15]—himself in after time the famous King of Jerusalem and Sicily—how as a boy he was so dull that it took the utmost skill and patience of his master to teach him the mere elements of letters. When all his friends were nearly in despair of his doing anything, his master, by the most subtle skill, as were, lured his mind with the fables of Aesop into so grand a passion for study and knowledge, that in a brief time he not only learned the liberal arts familiar to Italy, but entered with wonderful keenness of mind into the very inner mysteries of sacred philosophy. In short, he made of himself a king whose superior in learning men have not seen since Solomon.

Such then is the power of fiction that it pleases the unlearned by its external appearance, and exercises the minds of the learned with its hidden truth; and thus both are edified and delighted[16] with one and the same perusal. Then let not these disparagers raise their heads to vent their spleen in scornful words, and spew their ignorance upon poets! If they have any sense at all, let them look to their own speciousness before they try to dim the splendor of others with the cloud of their maledictions. Let them see, I pray, how pernicious are their jeers, fit to rouse the laughter only of girls. When they have made themselves clean, let them purify the tales of others, mindful of Christ's commandment[17] to the accusers of the woman taken in adultery, that he who was without sin should cast the first stone.

X. *It Is a Fool's Notion That Poets Convey No Meaning Beneath the Surface of Their Fictions*

Some of the railers are bold enough to say, on their own authority, that only an utter fool would imagine the best poets to have hidden any meaning in their stories; rather, they have invented them just to display the great power of their eloquence, and show how easily such tales may bring the injudicious mind to take fiction for truth. O the injustice of men! O what absurd dunces! What clumsiness! While they are trying to put down others, they imagine in their ignorance that they are exalting themselves. Who but an ignoramus would dare to say that poets purposely make their inventions void and empty, trusting in the superficial appearance of their tales to show their eloquence? As who should say that truth and eloquence cannot go together. Surely they have missed Quintilian's saying; it was this great orator's opinion that real power of eloquence is inconsistent with falsehood. But this matter I will postpone that I may come to the immediate subject of this chapter. Let any man, then, read the line in Vergil's *Bucolics*: "He sung the secret seeds of Nature's frame,"[18] and what follows on the same matter: or in the *Georgics*: "That bees have portions of ethereal thought / Endued with particles of heavenly fires."[19] with the relevant lines; or in the *Aeneid*: "Know first that heaven and earth's compacted frame, / And flowing waters, and the starry frame, etc."[20]

This is poetry from which the sap of philosophy runs pure. Then is any reader so muddled as not to see clearly that Vergil was a philosopher; or mad enough to think that he, with all his deep learning, would, merely for the sake of displaying his eloquence—in which his powers were indeed extraordinary—have led the shepherd Aristeus into his mother Climene's presence in the depths of the earth, or brought Aeneas to see his father in Hades? Or can anyone believe he wrote such lines without some meaning or intention hidden beneath the superficial veil of myth? Again, let any man consider our own poet Dante as he often unties with amazingly skillful demonstration the hard knots of holy theology; will such a one be so insensible as not to perceive that Dante was a great theologian as well as philosopher? And, if this is clear, what intention does he seem to have had in presenting the picture of the griffon[21] with wings and legs, drawing the chariot on top of the austere mountain, together with the seven candlesticks, and the seven nymphs, and the rest of the triumphal procession? Was it merely to show his dexterity in composing metrical narrative? To mention another instance: that most distinguished Christian gentleman, Francis Petrarch, whose life and character we have, with our own eyes, beheld so laudable in all sanctity—and by God's grace shalll continue to behold for a long time; no one has saved and employed to better advantage—I will not say, his time, but every crumb of it, than he. Is there anyone sane enough to suppose that he devoted all those watches of the night, all those holy seasons of meditation, all those hours and days and years—which we have a right to assume that he did, considering the force and dignity of his bucolic verse, the exquisite beauty of his style and diction—I say, would he have taken such pains merely to represent Gallus begging Tyrrhenus[22] for his reeds, or Pamphilus and Mitio[23] in a squabble, or other like pastoral nonsense? No man in his right mind will agree that these were his final object; much less, if he considers his prose treatise on the solitary life, or the one which he calls *On the Remedies for all Fortunes,* not to mention many others. Herein all that is clear and holy in the bosom of moral philosophy is presented in so majestic a style, that nothing could be uttered for the instruction of mankind more replete, more beautified, more mature, nay, more holy. I would cite also my own eclogues, of whose meaning I am, of course, fully aware; but I have decided not to, partly because I am not great enough to be associated with the most distinguished men, and partly because the discussion of one's attainments had better be left to others.

Then let the babblers stop their nonsense, and silence their pride if they can; for one can never escape the conviction that great men, nursed with the milk of the Muses, brought up in the very home of philosophy, and disciplined in sacred studies, have laid away the very deepest meaning in their poems; and not only this, but there was never a grumbling old woman, sitting with others late of a winter's night at the home fireside, making up tales of Hell, the fates, ghosts, and the like—much of it pure invention—that she did not feel beneath the surface of her tale, as far as her limited mind allowed, at least some meaning—sometimes ridiculous no doubt—with which she tries to scare the little ones, or divert the young ladies, or amuse the old, or at least show the power of fortune.

XII. The Obscurity of Poetry Is Not Just Cause for Condemning It

These cavillers further object that poetry is often obscure, and that poets are to blame for it, since their end is to make an incomprehensible statement appear to be wrought with exquisite artistry; regardless of the old rule of the orators, that a speech must be simple and clear. Perverse notion! Who but a deceiver himself would have sunk low enough not merely to hate what he could not understand, but incriminate it, if he could? I admit that poets are at times obscure. At the same time will these accusers please answer me? Take those philosophers among whom they shamelessly intrude; do they always find their close reasoning as simple and clear as they say an oration should be? If they say yes, they lie; for the works of Plato and Aristotle, to go no further, abound in difficulties so tangled and involved that from their day to the present, though searched and pondered by many a man of keen insight, they have yielded no clear nor consistent meaning. But why do I talk of philosophers? There is the utterance of Holy Writ, of which they especially like to be thought expounders; though proceeding from the Holy Ghost, is it not full to overflowing with obscurities and ambiguities? It is indeed, and for all their denial, the truth will openly assert itself. Many are the witnesses, of whom let them be pleased to consult Augustine,[24] a man of great sanctity and learning, and of such intellectual power that, without a teacher, as he says himself, he learned many arts, besides all that the philosophers teach of the ten categories. Yet he did not blush to admit that he could not understand the beginning of Isaiah. It seems that obscurities are not confined to poetry. Why then do they not criticize philosophers as well as poets? Why do they not say that the Holy Spirit wove obscure sayings into his works, just to give them an appearance of clever artistry? As if He were not the sublime Artificer of the Universe![25] I have no doubt they are bold enough to say such things, if they were not aware that philosophers already had their defenders, and did not remember the punishment[26] prepared for them that blaspheme against the Holy Ghost. So they pounce upon the poets because they seem defenseless, with the added reason that, where no punishment is imminent, no guilt is involved. They should have realized that when things perfectly clear seem obscure, it is the beholder's fault. To a half-blind man, even when the sun is shining its brightest, the sky looks cloudy. Some things are naturally so profound that not without difficulty can the most exceptional keenness in intellect sound their depths; like the sun's globe, by which, before they can clearly discern it, strong eyes are sometimes repelled. On the other hand, some things, though naturally clear perhaps, are so veiled by the artist's skill that scarcely anyone could by mental effort derive sense from them; as the immense body of the sun when hidden in clouds cannot be exactly located by the eye of the most learned astronomer. That some of the prophetic poems are in this class, I do not deny.

Yet not by this token is it fair to condemn them; for surely it is not one of the poet's various functions to rip up and lay bare the meaning which lies hidden in his inventions. Rather where matters truly solemn and memorable are too much exposed, it is his office by every effort to protect as well as he can and remove them from the gaze of the irreverent, that they cheapen not by too common familiarity. So when he discharges this duty and does it ingeniously, the poet earns commendation, not anathema.

Wherefore I again grant that poets are at times obscure, but invariably explicable if approached by a sane mind; for these cavillers view them with owl eyes, not human. Surely no one can believe that poets invidiously veil the truth with fiction, either to deprive the reader of the hidden sense, or to appear the more clever; but rather to make truths which would otherwise cheapen by exposure the object of strong intellectual effort and various interpretation, that in ultimate discovery they shall be more precious. In a far higher degree is this the method of the Holy Spirit; nay, every right-minded man should be assured of it beyond any doubt. Besides it is established by Augustine in the *City of God,* Book Eleven,[27] when he says: "The obscurity of the divine word has certainly this advantage, that it causes many opinions about the truth to be started and discussed, each reader seeing some fresh meaning in it." Elsewhere he says of Psalm 126: "For perhaps the words are rather obscurely expressed for this reason, that they may call forth many understandings, and that men may go away the richer, because they have found that closed which might be opened in many ways, than if they could open and discover it by one interpretation."

To make further use of Augustine's testimony (which so far is adverse to these recalcitrants), to show them how I apply to the obscurities of poetry his advice on the right attitude toward the obscurities of Holy Writ, I will quote his comment on Psalm 146: "There is nothing in it contradictory: somewhat there is which is obscure, not in order that it may be denied thee, but that it may exercise him that shall afterward receive it," etc.

But enough of the testimony of holy men on this point, I will not bore my opponents by again urging them to regard the obscurities of poetry as Augustine regards the obscurities of Holy Writ. Rather I wish that they would wrinkle their brows a bit, and consider fairly and squarely, how, if this is true of sacred literature addressed to all nations, in far greater measure is it true of poetry, which is addressed to the few.

If by chance in condemning the difficulty of the text, they really mean its figures of diction and rhetorical imagery and the beauty which they fail to recognize in alien words, if on this account they pronounce poetry obscure—my only advice is for them to go back to the grammar schools, bow to the rod, study, and learn what license ancient authority granted the poets in such matters, and give particular attention to such alien terms as are permissible beyond common and homely use. But why dwell so long upon the subject? I could have urged them in a sentence to put off the old mind, and put on the new and noble; then will that which now seems to them obscure look familiar and open. Let them not trust to concealing their gross confusion of mind in the precepts of the old orators; for I am sure the poets were ever mindful of such. But let them observe that oratory is quite different, in arrangement of words, from fiction, and that fiction has been consigned to the discretion of the inventor as being the legitimate work of another art than oratory. "In poetic narrative above all, the poets maintain majesty of style and corresponding dignity." As saith Francis Petrarch in the Third Book of his *Invectives,* contrary to my opponents' supposition, "Such majesty and dignity are not intended to hinder those who wish to understand, but rather propose a delightful task, and are designed to enhance the reader's pleasure and support his memory." "What we acquire with difficulty and keep with care is always the dearer to us"; so continues Petrarch. In fine, if their minds are dull, let them not blame the poets but their own sloth. Let them not keep up a silly howl against those whose lives and actions contrast most favorably with their own. Nay, at the very outset they have taken fright at mere appearances, and bid fair to spend themselves for nothing. Then let them retire in good time, sooner than exhaust their torpid minds with the onset and suffer a violent repulse.

But I repeat my advice to those who would appreciate poetry, and unwind its difficult involutions. You must read, you must persevere, you must sit up nights, you must inquire, and exert the utmost power of your mind. If one way does not lead to the desired meaning, take another; if obstacles arise, then still another; until, if your strength holds out, you will find that clear which at first looked dark. For we are forbidden by divine command to give that which is holy to dogs, or to cast pearls before swine.

XXII. The Author Addresses the Enemies of Poetry in Hope of Their Reform

And now, O men of sense, ye will do wisely to calm your indignation and quiet your swollen hearts. Our contest has grown perhaps too bitter. You began by taking up the cudgel against an innocent class of men, with the intention of exterminating them. I came to their defense, and, with God's help and the merits of the case, did what I could to save deserving men from their deadly enemies. Yet, if the poets in person had fairly taken the field against you, you would see how far their powers surpass both yours and mine, and repent at the eleventh hour. But the fight is over; with some glory of war, and a good deal more sweat, we have reached the point where the lust for victory may be a bit qualified, and we may part company with a fair settlement. Come then, let us freely unite to rest from our labors, for the prizes of the contest have been awarded. You forfeit to me your theory, and I to you a bit of consolation; this leaves ample room for peace. I have no doubt you are willing, since you are sorry to have begun the contest, and by this arrangement we shall both enjoy its benefits. To prove my sincerity, I, who am the first to tire of it, will be the first to resume friendly relations; that you may do likewise, I beg of you to consider with fair and unruffled mind the few words which I, in all charity and friendship, am about to say to you.

You recall, gentlemen, that, as well as I could, I have shown you the nature of poetry, which you had counted as naught, who the poets are, their function, and their manner of life, whom you cried out upon as depraved liars, moral perverters, corrupt with a thousand evils. I have shown also the nature of the Muses, whom you had called whores and consigned to the houses of prostitution. Yet being actually so worthy of regard as I have shown, you should not only cease to condemn them, but should cherish, magnify, love them, and search their books to your improvement. And that old age may not prevent you, or the popularity of other arts, try your best to do what an aged prince was not ashamed to attempt; I refer to that shining example of all virtues, famous King Robert of Sicily and Jerusalem, who besides being king, was a distinguished philosopher, an eminent teacher of medicine, and an exceptional theologian in his day. Yet in his sixty-sixth[28] year he retained a contempt for Vergil, and, like you, called him and the rest mere story-tellers, and of no value at all apart from the ornament of his verse. But as soon as he heard Petrarch unfold the hidden meaning of his poetry, he was struck with amazement, and saw and rejected his own error; and I actually heard him say that he never had supposed such great and lofty meaning could lie hidden under so flimsy a cover of poetic fiction as he now saw revealed through the demonstration of this expert critic. With wonderfully keen regret he began upbraiding his own judgment and his misfortune in recognizing so late the true art of poetry. Neither fear of criticism, nor age, nor the sense of his fast expiring lease of life were enough to prevent him from abandoning his studies in the other great sciences and arts, and devoting himself to the mastery of Vergil's meaning. As it happened, an early end broke off his new pursuit, but if he might have continued in it, without doubt he would have won much glory for the poets, and no little advantage for the Italians engaged in such studies. Will you, then, hold that gift not worth the taking which was holy in the sight of this wise king? Impossible! You are not mere tigers or huge beasts, whose minds, like their ferocity, cannot be turned to better account.

But if my pious expectation is doomed to disappointment, and the heat of your hatred still burns against them who deserve it not, then whenever your tongues itch to be at it again, I beseech you, for the sake of your own decency, mind my words. I adjure you, by the sacred breast of philosophy, which in other days has nourished you, not to rush in headlong fury upon the whole company of poets. Rather, if you have sense enough, you must observe right and timely distinction among them—such distinction as only can bring harmony out of discord, dispel the clouds of ignorance, clear the understanding, and set the mind in the right way. This you must do if you would not confuse the poets we revere—many of them pagans, as I have shown—with the disreputable sort. Let the lewd comic writers feel the stream of your wrath, the fiery blast of your eloquence; but be content to leave the rest in peace. Spare also the Hebrew authors. Them you cannot rend without insulting God's majesty itself. I have already cited Jerome's statement that some of them uttered their prophetic song in poetic style as dictated by the Holy Ghost. By the same token must Christian writers escape injury; for many even of our own tongue have been poets—nay, still survive—who, under cover of their compositions, have expressed the deep and holy meaning of Christianity. One of many instances is our Dante. True, he wrote in his mother tongue, which he adapted to his artistic purpose; yet in the book which he called the *Commedia* he nobly described the threefold condition of departed souls consistently with the sacred teaching of theology. The famous modern poet Petrarch has, in his *Bucolics*,[29] employed the pastoral guise to show forth with marvellous effect both the praise and the blame visited by the true God and the glorious Trinity upon the idle ship of Peter. Many such volumes are there which yield their meaning to any zealous inquirer. Such are the poems of Prudentius, and Sedulius, which express sacred truth in disguise. Arator, who was not merely a Christian, but a priest and cardinal in the church of Rome, gave poetic form to the Acts of the Apostles by recounting them in heroics. Juvencus, the Spaniard, also a Christian, employed the symbolic device of the man, the ox, the lion, and the eagle, to describe all the acts of Christ our Redeemer, Son of the Living God. Without citing further examples, let me say that, if no consideration of gentleness can induce you to spare poets of our own nation, yet be not more severe than our mother the Church; for she, with laudable regard, does not scorn to favor many a writer; but especially hath she honored Origen. So great was his power in composition that his mind seemed inexhaustible and his hand tireless; so much so that the number of his treatises on various subjects is thought to have reached a thousand. But the Church is like the wise maiden who gathered flowers among thorns without tearing her fingers, simply by leaving the thorns untouched; so she has rejected the less trustworthy part of Origen, and retained the deserving part to be laid up among her treasures. Therefore distinguish with care, weigh the words of the poets in a true balance, and put away the unholy part. Neither condemn what is excellent, as if, by raising a sudden hue and cry against poets, you hoped to seem Augustines or Jeromes to an ignorant public. They were men whose wisdom equalled their righteousness; they directed their attack not against poetry, or the art of poetry, but against the pagan errors contained in the poet's works. At these they hurled fearless and outspoken condemnation because it was a time when Catholic truth was surrounded and beset with harassing enemies. At the same time they cherished them and ever recognized in these works so much art, and polish, such seasoning of wisdom and skillful application of ornament, that whoever would acquire any grace of Latin style apparently must derive it from them.

Finally in the words of Cicero pleading for Archias:[30] "These studies may engage the strength of our manhood and divert us in old age; they are the adornment of prosperity, the refuge and solace of adversity; delightful at home, convenient in all places; they are ever with us through the night season; in our travels; in our rural retreats. And if we may not pursue them ourselves nor enjoy them in person, yet should we admire them as seen in others," etc. Poetry, then, and poets too, should be cultivated, not spurned and rejected; and if you are wise enough to realize this there is nothing more to say. On the other hand, if you persevere in your obstinate madness, though I feel sorry for you, contemptible as you are, yet no writing in the world could help you.

from BOOK XV
Proem

I have now steadied and trimmed my little craft, O most clement King, by such means as I could, for fear she be driven ashore by the wash of a stormy sea or the counterforce of the wind, with joints sprung and timbers crushed. And I have spread above her such protection as seemed opportune against lowering clouds that dissolve in rain or deadly flashes of lightning, lest she be either swamped or burned. Finally I have made her fast to the rocks, with ropes and hawsers, that the ebb tide might not drag her into the depths. But mortal precaution avails naught against the wrath of God; and I have therefore resolved that the fate of my venture must be left in His hands without Whose favor naught shall endure. May He in His mercy keep her!

VIII. The Pagan Poets of Mythology Are Theologians

There are certain pietists who, in reading my words, will be moved by holy zeal to charge me with injury to the most sacrosanct Christian religion; for I allege that the pagan poets are theologians—a distinction which Christians grant only to those instructed in sacred literature. These critics I hold in high respect; and I thank them in anticipation for such criticism, for I feel that it implies their concern for my welfare. But the carelessness of their remarks shows clearly the narrow limitations of their reading. If they had read widely, they could not have overlooked that very well-known work on the *City of God*; they might have seen how, in the Sixth Book, Augustine cites the opinion of the learned Varro, who held that theology is threefold in its divisions—mythical, physical, and civil. It is called mythical, from the Greek *mythicon*, a myth, and in this kind, as I have already said, is adapted to the use of the comic stage. But this form of literature is reprobate among better poets on account of its obscenity. Physical theology is, as etymology shows, natural and moral, and being commonly thought a very useful thing, it enjoys much esteem. Civil or political theology, sometimes called the theology of state worship, relates to the commonwealth, but through the foul abominations of its ancient ritual, it was repudiated by them of the true faith and the right worship of God. Now of these three, physical theology is found in the great poets since they clothe many a physical and moral truth in their inventions, including within their scope not only the deeds of great men, but matters relating to their gods. And particularly, as they first composed hymns of praise to the gods, and, as I have said, in a poetic guise, presented their great powers and acts, they won the name of theologians even among the primitive pagans. Indeed Aristotle himself avers that they were the first to ponder theology; and though they got their name from no knowledge or lore of the true God, yet at the advent of true theologians they could not lose it, so great was the natural force of the word derived from the theory of any divinity whatsoever. Aware, I suppose, that the title "theologian" once fairly won, cannot be lost, the present-day theologians call themselves professors of sacred theology to distinguish themselves from theologians of mythological cast or any other. Such distinction admits no possible exception as implying an injury to the name of Christianity. Do we not speak of all mortals who have bodies and rational souls as men? Some may be Gentiles, some Israelites, some Agarenes, some Christians, and some so depraved as to deserve the name of gross beasts not men. Yet we do not wrong our Savior by calling them men, though with His Godhead He is known to have been literally human. No more is there any harm in speaking of the old poets as theologians. Of course, if any one were to call them sacred, the veriest fool would detect the falsehood.

On the other hand there are times, as in this book, when the theology of the ancients will be seen to exhibit what is right and honorable, though in most such cases it should be considered rather physiology or ethology than theology, according as the myths embody the truth concerning physical nature or human. But the old theology can sometimes be employed in the service of Catholic truth, if the fashioner of the myths should choose. I have observed this in the case of more than one orthodox poet in whose investiture of fiction the sacred teachings were clothed. Nor let my pious critics be offended to hear the poets sometimes called even sacred theologians. In like manner sacred theologians turn physical when occasion demands; if in no other way, at least they prove themselves physical theologians as well as sacred when they express truth by the fable of the trees choosing a king.

NOTES

FULGENTIUS: EXPOSITION OF THE CONTENT OF VERGIL

1. He imposed the twelve labors on Hercules.
2. A reference to the theory of the Greek Stoic philosophers about the number of human souls (which remains constant).
3. States of completion or perfection; actuality as contrasted with potentiality.
4. *Virtus.* Alternately, "courage." Here and below, the term "virtue" has been chosen because it fits best in later contexts. The formula anticipates the medieval prescription for the epic virtues of *fortitudo* and *sapientia* (fortitude and wisdom).
5. I Corinthians 7:24.
6. *Materiam laudis,* that is, the formulas of epideictic rhetoric, the rhetorical formulas of praise and blame.
7. Cf. *Corpus Hermeticorum,* ed. A. D. Nock (Paris, 1945), XII.1.
8. Work unknown.
9. Not by Plato. Helm cites Tertullian, *On Modesty* 1.
10. Here and below the Greek readings in brackets are conjecture. Fulgentius does not explain his often bizarre etymologies.
11. The quotation is from *Orestes* 1–3. The error in ascription probably derives from an anthology of quotations used by Fulgentius.
12. The story is told by Donatus in his *Life of Vergil.*
13. A book *On the God of Socrates* was written by Apuleius. The reference by Fulgentius is unclear.
14. Cf. Ezekiel 7:20.
15. Reference unclear.
16. *Epigrams,* ed. Kluge (Leipzig, 1926), p. 37.

AVERROES: THE MIDDLE COMMENTARY ON THE POETICS OF ARISTOTLE

1. Abu Tammam, a "modern." For these and later citations see: W. F. Boggess, "Hermannus Alemanus' Latin Anthology of Arabic Poetry," *Journal of the American Oriental Society* 88 (1968), 657–70.
2. Zuhair, Boggess, pp. 665–67.
3. Normally referred to by Hermannus as Abitaibl (Abi at-Tayyibi), cf. Boggess, p. 669.

4. Meaningless, cf. Boggess, p. 661 for the original and an Italian translation.
5. Quais al-Majnum ben 'Amir.
6. Unknown.
7. Abi ben Zaid.
8. Probably by Kutayyir 'Azza; cf. Boggess, p. 663.
9. For the proper Arabic place names, see Boggess, p. 664.
10. By Samardal ben Sarik; cf. Boggess, p. 664.
11. Laila al-Akyaliya.
12. Harit ben Hisam; Boggess, p. 664.

GEOFFREY OF VINSAUF: POETRIA NOVA

1. Geoffrey makes frequent use of corporal metaphors.
2. For metrical reasons, the author consistently uses the term *ordo* for the more technical term *dispositio*.
3. Limit. (To the Greeks and Romans, Cadiz, the ancient Gades, was long the westernmost point of the known world.)
4. Geoffrey refers, again in a corporal metaphor (head, body, final details) to the three parts of a composition: beginning, middle, end.
5. I.e., natural order or the order of art.
6. That is, amplified or abbreviated treatment, as the dignity of the subject demands.
7. The author understands by the term *proverbium* any general truth drawn from observation or experience.
8. The term *exemplaris imago* (illustrative image) renders more precise what Geoffrey understands by the term exemplum. All the exampla he offers as models in this treatise are exemplary images rather than stories.
9. The topos of *Mater Terra* (mother earth) and *Pater Aether* (father air) appears frequently in classical and medieval times.
10. The story of the snow child was a popular theme in the Middle Ages.
11. Horace, *Ars Poetica* 360ff.
12. The word's "native soil" (*proprium locum*) refers to its literal meaning rather than to its position in the sentence. To "take up an abode on the estate of another" is to assume metaphorical meaning.
13. In his discussion of the tropes, the author follows the treatment in *Ad Herennium* IV.xxxi.42–xxxiv.46. But Goeffrey lists only nine figures (anastrophe and transposition are included under hyperbaton), omitting the tenth, *circumitio* or periphrasis.
14. The reference is to Aulus Gellius' *Noctes Atticae* I.vii.20.
15. The source of this rather obscure line is Sidonius' *Epistles* I.ii.6: "There is more reason for the thirsty to criticize the infrequent filling of goblets than for the intoxicated to refrain from them."

DANTE: DE VULGARI ELOQUENTIA

1. A liquor consisting of honey diluted in water; when fermented, it becomes mead.
2. I.e., "They anticipated the divine solicitude for their well-being." The expression

"divine care" appears to be used as meaning "the time appointed by God's providence."

3. Lines 295–99.
4. *Oc*-Lat. *hoc* (this); *oïl* results from the combination of affirmative *hoc* with *ille* (he). The speakers of the language of *oc* are not inaptly called Spaniards, since a dialect of the language we now call Provençal prevailed over the whole of Aragon and Catalonia.
5. "If a faithful friend heard me, I would make accusation against love."
6. "From pure love proceeds wisdom and goodness."
7. "Before the gentle heart, in nature's scheme / Love was not, nor the gentle heart ere love." (Rossetti's tr.). These are the third and fourth lines of the first stanza of the canzone whose first line is quoted in Book II.v.
8. Dante.
9. "Sir, what are you saying?"
10. Meaning uncertain.
11. "I met a peasant girl (?) from Cascioli; she was slinking off in a great hurry."
12. "At the hour of evening, in the month of October."
13. "What are you doing?"
14. "New house."
15. "My lord."
16. "Even though through fire water forsakes [its great coldness]."
17. "O love, who long has led me." This line and the preceding one are the opening lines of two canzoni by Guido delle Colonne, a judge and notary of Messina (fl. 1257–88). "Weighty poetry" refers to the dignity of its subject matter.
18. Ancient name of Sicily.
19. Frederick II, crowned emperor in 1220.
20. An expression of contempt taken from Matthias 5:22.
21. I.e., Frederick II, king of Sicily from 1296–1337.
22. "Draw me from these fires, if it is thy will." The third line of a poem in the form of a dialogue between a lover and his mistress.
23. Meaning uncertain.
24. "Lady, I will tell you (how love has seized me)." The first line of a canzone by Jacopo da Lentino (fl. first half of 13th century).
25. "For pure love I go so joyfully." The first line of a canzone by Rinaldo d'Aquino, a contemporary of Jacopo.
26. "Let us eat meantime—we do nothing else."
27. "Truly the soldiers of Florence are going through Pisa."
28. "Thank God the commonwealth of Lucca is in a happy state" (?).
29. "Would that I had never forsworn Siena!"
30. "What is this?"
31. "Will you come somewhere?"
32. "My eye."
33. "My heart."
34. "Would it were so."
35. *Novem* is the Latin for "nine" (Ital. *nove*).
36. "By God's wounds thou shalt not come."
37. "Lady, the steadfast heart."

38. "My going afar."
39. "No more do I await thy succor, Love."
40. "I cannot choose but utter a song."
41. "The bitter blast strips bare the leafy woods."
42. "For the awakening of gallantry which is too fast asleep."
43. "Worthy am I of death."
44. "Grief furnishes my heart with daring."
45. A small stick or quill for striking the strings of the lyre.
46. "Now you shall hear perfect songs."
47. See Note 6.
48. "To the gentle heart love ever flies for shelter."
49. See Note 17.
50. See Note 25.
51. "I have no hope that ever for my well-being."
52. "Love who wieldest thy virtue from heaven" (Rossetti's tr.).
53. "Were it not for my all-excelling one."
54. "So pleasing is to me the amorous thought."
55. "I alone am he who knows the excessive grief which rises [in my heart]."
56. "No man can properly fulfill [what he has in his heart]."
57. "Even as the tree which through being overladen."
58. "Sorrow of love which in my heart abides."
59. "To say the truth, I hold his conduct foolish [who yields himself to one too powerful]."
60. "Since I must needs bear a heart of woe."
61. "Albeit my prayers have not so long delayed" (Rossetti's tr.)
62. "Love that discourses to me in my mind."
63. The Latin *lectio* is retained since there is no word in English which expresses at once the "action" and "passion" of reading.
64. The words "without *ripresa*" (*sine responsorio*) are added to distinguish the canzone from the ballata. The *ripresa* was the opening portion of the ballata, and was repeated at its close.
65. "Ladies that have understanding of love." This is the first line of the first canzone in Dante's *Vita Nuova.*
66. Aristotle.
67. The stanza.
68. "To the short day and the great sweep of shadow."
69. "Love drags the plough-pole of my mind."
70. See Note 52.
71. A very pitiful lady, very young" (Rossetti's tr.). The second canzone of the *Vita Nuova.*
72. "A lady prays me, therefore I will speak." The opening line of Guido Cavalcante's celebrated canzone on the nature of love.
73. See Note 65.
74. See Note 56.
75. "Of steadfast endurance."
76. See Notes 37 and 38.

77. "Now that love has entirely forsaken me."
78. "If love were as bountiful in bestowing joy upon me [as I am towards her in purity and sincerity of affection]."
79. "Love, you can well see that this woman."

BOCCACCIO: THE GENEALOGY OF THE GENTILE GODS

1. David, Psalm 69:9.
2. XIV.8.
3. There is no such story. Boccaccio probably means Ovid's obscene tale of Priapus and Lotis, *Fasti* I.415–40.
4. Cf. Homer, *Odyssey* VIII.266–366.
5. XIV.19.
6. *Pro Archias* 18.
7. Paolino, bishop of Pozzuoli, 1324–44.
8. *Metaphysics* II.iv.12. Aristotle, of course, means only authors of theogonies.
9. Luke 24:14–15.
10. Cf. Macrobius, *Somnium Scipionis* I.2., with some suggestion of Cicero's *De Inventione* I.27.
11. *Rhetoric* II.20.
12. Daughters of Minyas . . . Acestes. Ovid, *Metamorphoses* III.582–686; IV.31–415.
13. Judges 9:8–15.
14. *The Golden Ass* IV.21.
15. Charles II. of Anjou.
16. Horace, *Ars Poetica* 333.
17. John 8:7.
18. VI.49 (Dryden's tr., as are the two following quotations).
19. IV.322–23.
20. VI.980–81.
21. Dante, *Purgatory* XXIX.108ff.
22. Petrarch, *Eclogue* 4.
23. Characters in Petrarch's *Eclogue* 6.
24. *Confessions* IV.16.
25. Wisdom 7:21, 22.
26. Mark 3:29.
27. Chapter 19.
28. In fact, it was his sixty-fourth, as he was born in 1278.
29. *Eclogues* 6, 7.
30. *Pro Archia* 16, 17.

BIBLIOGRAPHY

Section I: General; II. Classical and late Classical Sources; III. Christian and Early Medieval; IV. Carolingian; V. The XII Century Renaissance; VI. Scholastic Poetics; VII. Late and Post-Medieval Texts of Importance.

I. GENERAL

Arbusov, Leonid. *Colores Retorici.* Göttingen: Vandenhoeck & Ruprecht, 1948.

Atkins, J. W. H. *English Literary Criticism: The Medieval Phase.* London: Methuen, 1952. Limited to English authors, this volume is rather one-sided in view of the European scope of medieval thought.

Baldwin, Charles S. *Medieval Rhetoric and Poetic.* New York: Macmillan, 1928. The best survey currently available in English, but weakened by its exclusion of non-rhetoric poetic theory and now dated.

Beardsley, Monroe C. *Aesthetics from Classical Greece to the Present.* New York: Macmillan, 1966.

Bolgar, Robert R. *The Classical Heritage and Its Beneficiaries.* London: Cambridge University Press, 1954. Primarily concerned with influences rather than critical theory.

Bruyne, Edgar de. *Etudes d'esthétique médiévale.* 3 vols. Brussels: De Tempel, 1946 and (a 1-volume abridgment) *The Esthetics of the Middle Ages,* tr. by Eileen B. Hennessey. New York: Ungar, 1969. To date the definitive study of medieval aesthetics.

Buck, August. *Italienische Dichtungslehren vom Mittelalter bis zum Ausgang der Renaissance.* Tübingen: Niemeyer, 1952.

Comparetti, Domenico. *Vergil in the Middle Ages,* tr. by E. F. M. Benske. New York: Stechert, 1929. A pioneering work; useful for discussion of Vergilian exegesis.

Curtius, Ernst Robert. *European Literature and the Latin Middle Ages,* tr. Willard Trask. New York: Pantheon, 1953. A brilliant study of poetic themes and *topoi.* Much incisive discussion of rhetorical and literary theory.

Daniélou, Jean. *From Shadows to Reality: Studies in the Biblical Typology of the Fathers,* tr. Dom W. Hibbard. Westminster, Md.: Newman Press, 1960.

Gilson, Etienne. *A History of Christian Philosophy in the Middle Ages.* New York: Random House, 1955.

Glunz, Hans. *Die Literärästhetik des europäischen Mittelalters.* 2nd ed. Frankfurt a. M.: Klostermann, 1963. Emphasis is on stylistics rather than critical theory *per se.*

Halm, Karl. *Rhetores Latini Minores.* Leipzig: Teubner, 1863. Reprinted Dubuque, Iowa: Brown, 1964. A basic collection.

Keil, Heinrich. *Grammatici Latini.* 7 vols. and suppl. Leipzig: Teubner, 1857–80. Definitive collection of texts.

Klibansky, Raymond. *The Continuity of the Platonic Tradition During the Middle Ages.* London: Warburg Institute, 1939. The basic study.

Lubac, Henri de. *Exégèse médiévale. . . .* 4 vols. Paris: Aubier, 1959–64. Standard.

Manitius, Max. *Geschichte der lateinischen Literatur des Mittelalters.* 3 vols. Munich: Beck, 1911–31. The foundation on which much medieval scholarship rests.

Migne, Jacques Paul. *Patrologiae Cursus Completus. Series Graeca.* 161 vols. in 166. Paris, 1857–80.

———. *Patrologiae Cursus Completus. Series Latina.* 221 vols. Paris: Garnier, 1844–64 (see also supplements and indexes). Basic although many texts are now available in superior modern editions.

Montano Rocco. *L'estetica nel pensiero cristiano.* Milan, 1955. A collection of excerpts, with discussion. Emphasizes Neo-platonic aesthetics, esp. those associated with Chartres and its influences.

Monumenta Germaniae Historica, ed. H. G. Pertz and others. Berlin, 1826– . See esp. *Auctores Antiquissimi* (15 vols.) and *Poetae Latini Medii Aevi* (5 vols.). Like Migne, a magisterial collection.

Norden, Eduard. *Die antike Kunstprosa.* 5th ed. 2 vols. Stuttgart: Teubner, 1958. A standard study, extended to the Renaissance, of "art prose" derived from the Asiatic tradition in rhetoric.

Paetow, Louis J. *The Arts Course at Medieval Universities with Special Reference to Grammar and Rhetoric.* Urbana: University of Illinois Press, 1910.

Raby, F. J. E. *A History of Christian Latin Poetry in the Middle Ages.* 2nd ed. Oxford: Clarendon Press, 1953.

———. *A History of Secular Latin Poetry in the Middle Ages.* 2nd ed. 2 vols. Oxford: Clarendon Press, 1957.

Robertson, D. W. *A Preface to Chaucer: Studies in Medieval Perspectives.* Princeton: Princeton University Press, 1962. Emphasis is on biblical exegesis and allegorical and symbolic interpretation as well as its relation to secular literature.

Robins, Robert H. *Ancient and Medieval Grammatical Theory in Europe. . . .* London: Bell, 1951.

Saintsbury, George. *A History of Criticism and Literary Taste in Europe.* 3 vols. Edinburgh and London: Blackwood, 1900–04. (Vol. I: Classical-Medieval). Dated but the medieval section remains useful. Should be checked regularly against more recent scholarship.

Sandkühler, Bruno. *Die frühen Dantekommentare und ihr Verhältnis zur mittelalterlichen Kommentartradition.* Munich: Hueber, 1967. Discusses the influence of the *accessus* tradition.

Sandys, John E. *A History of Classical Scholarship.* 3 vols. Cambridge: Cambridge University Press, 1920. (Vol. I: Classical-Medieval).

Schanz, Martin, *Geschichte der römischen Literatur.* Vol. I (to Justinian); vol. II (the 4th Century); vol. III (with Carl Hosius and Gustav Krüger: the 5th and 6th Centuries). Munich: Beck, 1904–13. Massive and (for the time of its publication) definitive.

Seznec, Jean. *The Survival of the Pagan Gods,* tr. B. F. Sessions. New York: Pantheon, 1953. Interpretation of classical myth in medieval art and literature.

Smalley, Beryl. *The Study of the Bible in the Middle Ages.* 2nd ed. Oxford: Blackwell, 1962.

Spengel, Leonhard von. *Rhetores Graeci.* 3 vols. Leipzig: Teubner, 1853–56. A collection of basic texts.

Wimsatt, William K. and Brooks, Cleanth. *Literary Criticism: A Short History*. New York: Knopf, 1957.

II. CLASSICAL AND LATE CLASSICAL SOURCES

Atkins, J. W. H. *Literary Criticism in Antiquity*. 2 vols. Cambridge: Cambridge University Press, 1934.

Auerbach, Erich. *Literary Language and Its Public in Late Latin Antiquity and the Middle Ages*, tr. Ralph Manheim. New York: Pantheon, 1965.

Baldwin, Charles C. *Ancient Rhetoric and Poetic*. New York: Macmillan, 1924.

Burgess, Theodore. *Epideictic Literature*. (University of Chicago Studies in Classical Philology, III. Chicago, 1902). Epideictic (or demonstrative) rhetoric was extremely popular in late antiquity and influenced medieval and Renaissance authors.

Clark, D. L. *Rhetoric in Graeco-Roman Education*. New York: Columbia University Press, 1957.

Clark, M. L. *Rhetoric at Rome* [through St. Augustine]. London: Cohen & West, 1953.

Ernesti, Johann Christian. *Lexicon Technologiae Graecorum Rhetoricae*. Leipzig, 1795. Reprinted Hildesheim: Olms, 1962.

———. *Lexicon Technologiae Latinorum Rhetoricae*. Leipzig: Fritsch, 1797.

Fisk, George. *Cicero's de Oratore and Horace's Ars Poetica*. (University of Wisconsin Studies in Language and Literature, XXVII. Madison, 1929).

Grube, G. M. A. *The Greek and Roman Critics*. Toronto: University of Toronto Press, 1965.

Henderson, Charles. "Lexicon of Stylistic Terms Used in Roman Literary Criticism." 3 vols. Unpubl. University of North Carolina dissertation, 1955.

Kennedy, George. *The Art of Persuasion in Greece*. Princeton: Princeton University Press, 1963.

McMahon, A. P. "Seven Questions on Aristotelian Definitions of Tragedy and Comedy." *Harvard Studies in Classical Philology*, XI (1929), 97–198. Shows the continuity of certain definitions throughout the Middle Ages and into the Renaissance.

Quadlbauer, Franz. *Die antike Theorie der Genera Dicendi im lateinischen Mittelalter*. (Sitzungsberichte der Österreichischen Akademie der Wissenschaften. Philosophisch-Historische Klasse, CCXLI.2. Vienna, 1962). The vicissitudes of ancient theory in the Middle Ages.

Survival of Classical Authors

Crossland, Jessie. "Lucan in the Middle Ages." *Modern Language Review*, XXV (1930), 32–51.

Landi, C. "Stazio nel medio evo." *Atti dell' Accademia Padovana*, XXXVII (1921), 201–32.

Manitius, Max. *Analekten zur Geschichte des Horaz im Mittelalter*. Göttingen, 1893.

———. "Beiträge zur Geschichte des Ovidius und anderer römischer Schriftsteller im Mittelalter." *Philologus*. Supplementband VII (1899), 723–68.

Munari, Franco. *Ovid im Mittelalter*. Zurich: Artemis, 1960.

For Vergil, see Comparetti, section I.

Allegory

See Lubac, Daniélou, section I.

Hanson, R. P. C. *Allegory and Event: A Study of the Sources and Significance of Origen's Interpretation of Scripture.* London: S. C. M. Press, 1959.

Heraclitus. *Allégories d'Homère,* ed. and tr. Félix Buffière. Paris, 1962. A little known but important classical interpretation of the *Iliad* and *Odyssey.*

Hersman, A. B. *Studies in Greek Allegorical Interpretation.* Chicago: Blue Sky Press, 1906.

Hollander, Robert. *Allegory in Dante's Commedia.* Princeton: Princeton University Press, 1969.

Pépin, Jean. *Mythe et allégorie.* Paris: Aubier, 1958.

Tate, J. "The Beginnings of Greek Allegory." *Classical Review,* XXXI (1927), 214–15.

———. "Plato and Allegorical Interpretation." *Classical Quarterly,* XXIII (1929), 142–54; XXIV (1930), 1–10.

———. "On the History of Allegorism." *Classical Quarterly,* XXVIII (1934), 105–14.

(For the later tradition of Byzantine allegorism, see Cornutus. *Theologiae Graecae Compendium,* ed. Karl Lang. Leipzig: Teubner, 1881; Psellus. *Allegoriae;* and Tzetzes, *Allegoriae Iliados,* both ed. P. Boissonade. Lyons, 1851).

Neoplatonism

Whittaker, Thomas. *The Neo-Platonists: A Study in the History of Hellenism.* 2nd ed. Cambridge: Cambridge University Press, 1918.

GREEK AUTHORS:

Maximus Tyrius. *Dissertations,* tr. Thomas Taylor. 2 vols. London: Whittingham, 1804.

Plotinus. *Opera,* ed. Paul Henry and Hans-Rudolf Schwyzer. Paris: Desclée de Brouwer, 1951– . This critical edition will be in 4 vols.

———. *Ennéades,* ed. and tr. Emile Bréhier. 6 vols. in 7. Paris: Société d'édition "Les belles lettres," 1924–38.

———. Enneads, tr. Stephen MacKenna. 4th ed., rev. B. S. Page. London: Faber and Faber, 1969.

Henry, Paul. *Plotin et l'occident: Firmicus Maternus, Marius Victorinus, St. Augustine, et Macrobe.* Dubuque, Iowa: Brown, 1965. (Repr. of Spicilegium Sacrum Lovaniense, études et documents, fasc. XV).

Keyser, Eugénie de. *La Signification de l'art dans les Ennéades de Plotin.* Louvain: Bibliothèque de l'Université, 1955.

Porphyry. *De Antro Nympharum.* In *Opuscula Selecta,* ed. August Nauck. Leipzig: Teubner, 1886. An example of Neoplatonic exegesis of the "cave of nymphs" episode in Homer.

Dörrie, Heinrich et al. *Porphyre: Huit exposés suivis de discussions.* Geneva: Foundation Hardt, 1965. (See esp. J. Pépin. "Porphyre exégète d'Homère").

Proclus. *Eis tes Politeias Platonos Hypomnema.* 2 vols. Leipzig: Teubner, 1899–1901.

———. "Proclus on the More Difficult Questions in the *Republic*: The Nature of Poetic Art," tr. Thomas Taylor. In "Preface" to *The Rhetoric, Poetics, and Nico-*

machean Ethics of Aristotle, ed. T. Taylor. 2 vols. London, 1818. Proclus provides the best exposition of Neoplatonic literary theory.

Friedel, A. J. *Die Homer-Interpretation des Proklos.* Würzburg, 1923.

Rosán, Laurence. *The Philosophy of Proclus: The Final Phase of Ancient Thought.* New York: Cosmos, 1949.

Late Latin Authors

Arcon. See Porphyrion.

Donatus, Aelius. *Commentum Terenti,* ed. Paul Wessner. 2 vols. Leipzig: Teubner, 1902–5.

———. *Ars Minor* and *Ars Maior* in Keil. *Grammatici Latini,* IV.

———. *The Ars Minor of Donatus,* tr. W. J. Chase. (University of Wisconsin Studies in the Social Sciences and History, XI. Madison, 1926).

The standard grammarian throughout the Middle Ages.

Donatus, Tiberius Claudius. *Interpretationes Vergilianae,* ed. Heinrich Georges. 2 vols. Leipzig, 1905–6. A rhetorical exegesis of Vergil.

Evanthius. *De Comoedia et Tragoedia.* In *Commentum Terenti,* ed. Paul Wessner, vol. I (repr. Teubner, 1969). Often attributed to Aelius Donatus in the Middle Ages. A basic statement about comedy and tragedy.

Macrobius. *Commentary on the Dream of Scipio,* tr. William H. Stahl. New York: Columbia University Press, 1952.

———. *The Saturnalia,* tr. Percival V. Davies. New York: Columbia University Press, 1969.

Whittaker, Thomas. *Macrobius, or Philosophy, Science, and Letters in the Year 400.* Cambridge: Cambridge University Press, 1923. Macrobius is a major source of medieval Neoplatonism, and his influence persists into the Renaissance.

Martianus Capella. *De Nuptiis Philologiae et Mercurii,* ed. Adolf Dick. Stuttgart: Teubner, 1969. Best edition to date; a new one by James Willis is in preparation. A favorite medieval allegory, containing much aesthetic and rhetorical lore in a flamboyant style.

Martianus Capella and the Seven Liberal Arts. Vol. I. The Quadrivium of Martianus Capella, Latin Traditions in the Mathematical Sciences 50 B.C.–A.D. 1250, by William H. Stahl. With a Study of the Allegory and the Verbal Disciplines by Richard Johnson with E. L. Burge. New York: Columbia University Press, 1971.

Plutarch. *Moralia,* ed. and tr. Frank C. Babbitt. 15 vols. London: Heinemann, 1927–31 (Loeb Classical Library). See esp. I.2 ("How a Young Man Should Read the Poets") and V.1 ("On Isis and Osiris").

———. "How a Young Man Should Study Poetry." In *Essays on the Study and Use of Poetry,* ed. and tr. with an introduction by Frederick M. Padelford. New York: Holt, 1902. (Yale Studies in English, XV). A treatise emphasizing the didactic function of literature.

Porphyrion. *Arconis et Porphyrionis Commentarii in Q. Horatium Flaccum,* ed. Ferdinand Hauthal. 2 vols. Berlin, 1864–66. Two late classical commentaries on Horace (useful for *Ars Poetica*).

Servius. *Servii Grammatici qui Feruntur in Vergilii Carmina Commentarii,* ed. Georg Thilo and Herman Hagen. 2 vols. Leipzig and Berlin: Teubner, 1923. Reprinted, 3 vols. Hildesheim: Olms, 1961. A new edition, *Servianorum in Vergilis Carmina Commentariorum Editionis Harvardianae Volumen,* ed. Edward K. Rand et al., has been in preparation since 1946 when vol. II (*Aeneid* I–II) appeared (Lancaster, Pa.: American Philological Association); vol. III (*Aeneid* III–IV) was published in 1965.

Jones, Julian Ward. "An Analysis of the Allegorical Interpretation in the Servian Commentary on the *Aeneid.*" Unpub. University of North Carolina dissertation, 1959.

Servius provided the standard commentary-gloss on Vergil from the 4th century through the Renaissance.

III. CHRISTIAN AND EARLY MEDIEVAL

Augustine. *Opera.* In Migne. *Patrologiae . . . Latina* XXXII–XLVII. A modern edition (Corpus Christianorum. Series Latina) has been in progress since 1954 (Turnhout: Brepols).

———. *On Christian Doctrine,* tr. D. W. Robertson, Jr. New York: Liberal Arts Press, 1958. Basic for its presentation of a "Christian rhetoric."

———. *On Music,* tr. R. C. Taliaferro. Annapolis, Md., 1939. Deals extensively with prosody.

Eskridge, Thomas B. *The Influence of Cicero upon Augustine in the Development of His Oratorical Theory.* Menasha, Wisc. 1912.

Knight, W. F. *St. Augustine's De Musica: A Synopsis.* London, 1949.

Basil the Great. "On the Right Use of Greek Poetry." In *Essays on the Study and Use of Poetry,* ed. and tr. by F. M. Padelford. New York: Holt, 1902. (Yale Studies in English, XV). Emphasis on the ethical benefits to be derived from a right use of pagan authors.

———. *Exegetic Homilies,* tr. Sister Agnes C. Way. Washington, D.C.: Catholic University of America Press, 1963. (The Fathers of the Church. A New Translation, vol. XXXXVI).

Bede. *De Arte Metrica* and *De Orthographia.* In Keil. *Grammatici Latini* VII.

———. *De Schematibus et Tropis.* In Halm. *Rhetores Latini Minores.* Tr. by G. H. Tanenhaus in *Quarterly Journal of Speech,* 48 (1962).

Cassiodorus. *Opera.* In Migne. *Patrologiae . . . Latina* LXIX–LXX. A modern edition (Corpus Christianorum. Series Latina) has been in progress since 1958 (Turnhout: Brepols).

———. *An Introduction to Divine and Human Readings,* tr. Leslie W. Jones. New York: Columbia University Press, 1946. An early attempt to formulate a Christian curriculum.

John Cassian. *Opera.* In Migne. *Patrologiae . . . Latina* XLIX–L.

Translations: In *Select Library of the Nicene and Post-Nicene Fathers of the Christian Church.* 2nd series, ed. Henry Wace and Philip Schaff. 14 vols. Oxford: Parker, 1891–1905, vol. XI. Cassian was important in the development of allegorical exegesis.

Clement of Alexandria. *Stromata.* in Migne. *Patrologiae . . . Graeca* VIII–IX. See esp. I.14, 21 (Greek debt to Hebrew) and VI. 15, 16 (Allegory).

Translations: In *The Ante-Nicene Christian Library,* ed. A. Roberts and J. Donaldson. London, 1867–72, vols. IV, XII.

Chadwick, Henry. *Early Christian Thought and the Classical Tradition: Studies in Justin, Clement, and Origen.* New York: Oxford University Press, 1966. Alexandrian and Christian Neoplatonism.

Fulgentius. *De Continentia Vergiliana.* In *Opera,* ed. Rudolf Helm, Leipzig, 1898. For the Middle Ages, the basic allegorical reading of Vergil.

———. *Fulgentius the Mythographer,* tr. Leslie Whitbread. Columbus: Ohio State University Press, 1972.

Liebeschütz, Hans. *Fulgentius Metaforalis: Ein Beitrag zur Geschichte der antiken Mythologie.* Berlin, 1926. (Studien der Bibliotek Warburg, IV).

Isidore of Seville. *Etymologiarum sive Originum Libri XX,* ed. W. M. Lindsay. 2 vols. Oxford: Clarendon Press, 1911. Contains much literary lore. The standard medieval encyclopedia before Vincent of Beauvais.

Jerome. *Opera.* In Migne. *Patrologiae . . . Latina* XXII–XXV. A modern edition by P. Lagarde et al. (Corpus Christianorum, Series Latina) has been in progress since 1958 (Turnhout: Brepols).

Translations: In *Select Library of the Nicene and Post-Nicene Fathers of the Christian Church.* 2nd series, vol. VI.

The Homilies of Saint Jerome, tr. by Sister Marie Liguori Ewald. Washington: Catholic University of America Press, 1964–66. (The Fathers of the Church. A New Translation, vols. XLVIII and LVII).

Selected Letters, tr. Paul Carroll. Chicago, 1958. Comments on the theory of translation, the relation of biblical to classical literature, literary style, the value of pagan authors, etc.

Lactantius. *Opera.* In Migne. *Patrologiae . . . Latina* VI–VII; also, ed. by Samuel Brandt and G. Laubmann. 3 vols. Leipzig: Freytag, 1890–97. (Corpus Scriptorum Ecclesiasticorum Latinorum, vols. XIX, XXVII.1, XXVII.2).

Translations: In *The Ante-Nicene Christian Library,* vols. XX–XXII.

The Divine Institutes, tr. by Sister Mary Francis McDonald. Washington: Catholic University of America Press, 1964. (The Fathers of the Church. A New Translation, vol. XLIX).

Lactantius assimilates much classical tradition to a Christian frame of reference.

Origen. *Opera.* In Migne. *Patrologiae . . . Graeca* XI–XVII.

Translations: In *The Ante-Nicene Christian Library,* vols. X, XXIII.

Tertullian. *Opera,* ed. E. Dekkers et al. 2 vols. Turnhout: Brepols, 1954 (Corpus Christianorum, Series Latina I–II).

———. *De Spectaculis.* In *Tertullian, Apology, De Spectaculis,* with an English translation, by T. R. Glover. London: Heineman, 1931. (Loeb Classical Library). Arguments against classical drama. Tertullian provides the forerunner of most later attacks on the theatre and related public spectacles.

IV. CAROLINGIAN

Alcuin. *Disputatio de Rhetorica.* In Halm. *Rhetores Latini Minores.*

———. *The Rhetoric of Alcuin and Charlemagne,* tr. W. S. Howell. Princeton: Princeton University Press, 1941.

A balanced rhetoric influenced by the Ciceronian tradition.

Amalarius of Metz. *Opera,* ed. J. M. Hanssens. 3 vols. Vatican City: Biblioteca Apostolica Vaticana, 1948–50. Allegorical interpretation of Christian liturgy.

Gariépy, Robert J. *Lupus of Ferrières and the Classics.* Darien, Conn., 1967. Continuity of classical literature.

Rabanus Maurus. *De Clericorum Institutione.* In Migne. *Patrologiae . . . Latina* CVII. In the tradition of Cassiodorus and Lactantius.

Remigius of Auxerre. *Opera.* In Migne. *Patrologiae . . . Latina* CXXXI.

———. *Commentum in Martianum Capellam,* ed. Cora E. Lutz. 2 vols. Leiden: Brill, 1962–65. Exegesis of *On the Marriage of Philology and Mercury.*

Scholia Vindobonensia ad Horatii Artem Poeticam, ed. Joseph Zechmeister, Vienna, 1877. Extremely important for Carolingian poetic theory. Actually, more of an extended essay on the *Ars Poetica* than a series of notes in the style of Servius.

V. THE XII CENTURY RENAISSANCE

General

Faral, Edmond, *Les Arts poétiques du XIIe et du XIIIe siècle.* Paris: Champion, 1924. Reprinted 1958.

Kelly, Douglas. "The Scope of the Treatment of Composition in the Twelfth- and Thirteenth-Century Arts of Poetry." *Speculum,* XLI (1966), 261–78.

Mari, Giovanni. *I trattati medievali di ritmica latina.* Milan: Hoepli, 1899. Medieval treatises on accentual prosody.

Murphy, James J., ed. *Three Medieval Rhetorical Arts.* Berkeley: University of California Press, 1971.

ARTES PRAEDICANDI (Arts of Preaching):

Charland, Th.-M. *Artes Praedicandi.* Paris: Vrim, 1936.

COMMENTARIES:

An Anonymous Medieval Commentary on Juvenal [XII–XIII Century], ed. Robert J. Barrett. Darien, Conn., 1967.

Representative examples of a very popular genre.

Commentarius Recentior. In *Scholia Terentiana,* ed. Friedrich Schlee. Leipzig: Teubner, 1893.

Commentum Bernardi Silvestris super Sex Libros Eneidos Vergilii, ed. Wm. Riedel. Greifswald, 1924.

Stock, Brian. *Myth and Science in the Twelfth Century: A Study of Bernard Silvester.* Princeton: Princeton University Press, 1972.

Wetherbee, Winthrop. *Platonism and Poetry in the Twelfth Century: The Literary Influence of the School of Chartres.* Princeton: Princeton University Press, 1972.

DICTAMINA (LETTER WRITING) AND OTHER FORMS

Breitow, A. *Die Entwicklung mittelalterlicher Briefsteller bis zur Mitte des 12. Jahrhunderts.* Greifswald, 1908.

Haskins, Charles H. "Italian Treatises." In *Mélanges H. Pirenne,* Brussels, 1926, pp. 101–10. Treatises on letter-writing; derived from rhetorical tradition.

———. *The Renaissance of the Twelfth Century.* Cambridge, Mass., 1927. Reprinted New York: Meridian, 1957. Still a basic survey.

Rockinger, Ludwig von. *Briefsteller und Formelbücher des elften bis vierzehnten Jahrhunderts.* Munich, 1863. Reprinted (2 vols.) New York: Franklin, 1961.

Hieronimus, J. P. and Cox, Josiah, eds. *Two Types of XIII Century Grammatical Poem.* Colorado Springs, 1929. (Incl. the paraphrase of the *Ars Minor* of Donatus by Henry of Avranches).

Huygens, R. B. C. *Accessus ad Auctores.* Brussels: Latomus, 1954. The "introduction to the classics" of the later Middle Ages.

Quain, E. A. "The Medieval Accessus ad Auctores." *Traditio,* III (1945), 215–64.

RHETORIC (TO XV CENTURY):

Allen, Judson B. *The Friar as Critic: Literary Attitudes in the later Middle Ages.* Nashville: Vanderbilt, 1971.

Baltzell, Jane. "Rhetorical Amplification and Abbreviation and the Structure of Medieval Narrative." *Pacific Coast Philology,* II (1966), 32–38.

Murphy, James J. "The Earliest Teaching of Rhetoric at Oxford." *Speech Monographs,* XXVII (1960), 345–47.

———. "The Arts of Discourse, 1050–1400." *Mediaeval Studies,* XXIII (1961), 194–205.

———. "The Medieval Arts of Discourse: An Introductory Bibliography." *Speech Monographs,* XXIX (1962), 71–78.

———. "A New Look at Chaucer and the Rhetoricians." *Review of English Studies,* n.s., XV (1964), 1–20.

———. "Rhetoric in Fourteenth-Century Oxford." *Medium Aevum,* XXXIV (1965), 1–20.

———. "A Fifteenth-Century Treatise on Prose Style." *Newberry Library Bulletin,* VI (1966), 205–10.

Authors

For John of Garland, Matthew of Vendôme, Geoffrey of Vinsauf, Everardus, see Faral, V. General.

For treatises on prosody, see Mari, V. General.

Conrad of Hirsau. *Dialogus super Auctores,* ed. R. B. C. Huygens. Brussels: Latomus, 1955. The fullest of the treatises in the *accessus* tradition.

Geoffrey of Vinsauf. *Poetria Nova,* tr. Margaret F. Nims, Toronto: Pontifical Institute of Medieval Studies, 1967.

Gervase of Melcheley. *Ars Poetica,* ed. Hans-Jürgen Gräbener. Münster: Aschendorff, 1965. (Forschungen der Romanischen Philologie, XVII). Interesting for the scholastic influence evident in its classification of figures.

Henri d'Andeli. *The Battle of the Seven Arts,* ed. and tr. L. J. Paetow. Berkeley: University of California Press, 1914. The debate between medieval humanism and the emergent scholasticism of the universities.

Hugh of St. Victor. *Didascalicon,* tr. Jerome Taylor. New York: Columbia University Press, 1961.

John of Salisbury. *Metalogicon* (1929) and *Policraticus* (2 vols., 1909), both ed. C. C. J. Webb. Oxford: Clarendon Press. Basic works of medieval humanism.

———. *Metalogicon,* tr. Daniel D. McGarry. Berkeley: University of California Press, 1955.

———. *Policraticus,* tr., in part, by John Dickinson in *The Stateman's Book of John of Salisbury.* New York: Knopf, 1927.

Liebeschütz, Hans. *Medieval Humanism in the Life and Writings of John of Salisbury.* London: Warburg Institute, 1950.

Ryan, Sister Mary Bride. *John of Salisbury on the Arts of Language in the Trivium.* Washington: Catholic University of America Press, 1958.

Richard of Bury, *Philobiblon,* ed. and tr. E. C. Thomas. Oxford: Blackwell, 1960.

VI. SCHOLASTIC POETICS

General

Mandonnet, Pierre. *Siger de Brabant et l'Averroïsme latin au XIIIe siècle.* 2nd ed. 2 pts. Louvain: Université de Louvain, 1908–11. The context for the translation and influence of Averroes' commentaries on Aristotle.

McKeon, Richard. "Rhetoric in the Middle Ages." *Critics and Criticism: Ancient and Modern,* ed. R. S. Crane. Chicago: Chicago University Press, 1952, pp. 260–96.

Renan, E. *Averroes et l'Averroïsme.* Paris: Calman Lévy, 1852. Dated and inaccurate, but some sections remain useful.

Authors

al-Farabi. *Catálogo de las ciencias,* ed. and tr. Angel González Palencia. 2nd ed. Madrid: Consejo Superior de Investigaciones Cientificas. . . , 1953. (Incl. tr. into Latin by Gerard of Cremona, ca. 1150). Discusses the placement of poetry among the sciences.

AVERROES-HERMANNUS ALEMANNUS AND THE POETICS:

"Averrois Cordubensis Commentarium Medium in Aristotelis Poetriam," ed. William F. Boggess. Unpubl. University of North Carolina dissertation, 1965. A Latin text based on the manuscripts. Does not use Arabic mss. extensively.

Lobel, E. "The Medieval Latin Poetics." *Proceedings of the British Academy,* XVII (1934), 309–34.

Luquet, G. H. "Hermann l'Allemand." *Revue de l'histoire des religions,* XLIV (1901), 407–22.

Margoliouth, David. *Analecta Orientalia ad Poeticam Aristotelis.* London, 1889. (Incl. fragmentary Latin version of Syriac tr. of the *Poetics,* ca. 900).

———. *The Poetics of Aristotle Translated from Greek into English and from Arabic into Latin.* London, 1911.

Franceschini, E. "La Poetica di Aristotele nel secolo XIII." *Atti del Real Instituto Veneto,* XCIV (1935), 523–48.

Marsa, E. "Ruggero Bacone e la Poetica di Aristotele." *Giornale critico della filosofia italiana,* XXXII (1953), 457–73.

Tkatsch, Jaroslav. *Die arabische Übersetzung der Poetik des Aristoteles.* 2 vols. Vienna and Leipzig, 1928–32. The standard treatment.

Dominicus Gundissalinus. *De Divisione Philosophiae,* ed. with introduction by Ludwig Baur. Münster: Aschendorff, 1903. (Beiträge zur Geschichte der Philosophie des Mittelalters. Texte und Untersuchungen, IV.3–4.). A Latin treatise with discussion of the "placing" of poetry. Arabic influences.

William of Moerbeke. *Aristotelis de Arte Poetica,* ed. E. Valgimigli. Paris, 1953. (Aristoteles Latinus, XXXIII). A translation directly from the Greek which, however, failed to achieve the popularity of the Averroes commentary.

VII. LATE AND POST-MEDIEVAL TEXTS OF IMPORTANCE

General

Trabalza, Ciro. *La critica letteraria del rinascimento.* Milan: Vallardi, 1915.

Vossler, Karl. *Poetische Theorien in der italienischen Frührenaissance.* Berlin: Felber, 1900.

Zabughin, Vladimiro. *Vergilio nel rinascimento italieno da Dante a Torquato Tasso.* 2 vols. Bologna: Zanichelli, 1921–23.

None of these works is as detailed or as comprehensive as the materials require. Zabughin is thorough but limited rather narrowly to Vergil and Italy.

Authors

BERSUIRE, PIERRE (PETER BERCORIUS) AND THE OVIDE MORALISE

Ovide Moralisé, ed. C. de Boer and J. van't Sant. *Verhandelingen der Koninklijke Akademie van Wetenschappen.* 5 vols. Amsterdam: Müller, 1915–38. Ovid with moral allegories. Immensely popular in the late Middle Ages.

Born, L. K. "Ovid and Allegory." *Speculum,* IX (1934), 362–79.

Ghisalberti, F. "L'Ovidius Moralizatus di Pierre Bersuire." *Studi romanzi,* XXII (1933), 5–136.

Tuve, Rosemond. *Allegorical Imagery.* Princeton: Princeton University Press, 1964.

Boccaccio, Giovanni. *Genealogia Deorum Gentilium,* ed. Vincenzo Romano. 2 vols. Bari: Laterza, 1951.

———. *Boccaccio on Poetry,* tr. Charles G. Osgood. Princeton: Princeton University Press, 1930. Books XIV and XV are the first full-scale "defense of poetry" of the Renaissance. Much influenced by Petrarch.

Dante. *De Vulgari Eloquentia,* ed. Aristide Marigo. Florence: Le Monnier, 1968. (English tr. in *A Translation of the Latin Works of Dante Alighieri,* by A. G. F. Howell and P. H. Wicksteed. London: Dent, 1904).

———. *Convivio,* ed. Maria Simonelli. Bologna, 1966. (English tr. by William W. Jackson. Oxford: Clarendon Press, 1909).

———. *La corrispondenza poetica di Dante Alighieri e Giovanni del Virgilio,* ed. E. Bolisani and M. Valgimigli. Florence: Olschki, 1963.

———. *Dante and Giovanni del Virgilio.* Comment and translations by Philip H. Wicksteed. Westminster, 1902.

———. *Epistle to Can Grande della Scala.* In *Opere,* Testo critico della Società dantesca italiana, ed. M. Barbi et al. Florence, 1921. (Epistola XIII). *Epistolae,* ed. and tr. Paget Toynbee. 2nd ed. Oxford: Clarendon Press, 1966.

Imola, Benvenuto de' Rambaldi da. *Commento latino sulla Divina commedia,* tr. (Italian) and ed. Giovanni Tamburini. 3 vols. Imola: Galeati, 1855–56. Influenced by Averroes' commentary on the *Poetics.*

Landino, Christoforo. *Disputationes Camaldulenses.* No modern ed. Allegorical interpretation of Vergil along the lines of Fulgentius.

Mussato, Albertino. See *Dante and Giovanni del Vırgilio* under Dante.

Dazzi, Manlio T. *Il Mussato preumanista (1261–1329): L'Ambiente e l'opera.* Venice: Neri Pozza, 1964. Early humanism.

Petrarch. *Opere.* Edizione nazionale. Florence, 1926–64. (Selected trs. in James H. Robinson and Henry W. Rolfe. *Petrarch: The First Modern Scholar and Man of Letters.* New York, 1898, reprinted Haskell House, 1970, and in Petrarch. *Letters,* sel. and tr. Morris Bishop. Bloomington and London: Indiana University Press, 1966.) Petrarch's critical theory is most evident in his "Invective Against a Physician" and his "Coronation Oration" delivered when he was awarded the laurel crown in 1341.

Bernardo, Aldo. "Petrarch and the Art of Literature." *Festschrift for Beatrice Corrigan.* Toronto: University of Toronto Press, 1972, pp. 19–43. The best overview of Petrarch's theory of literature.

Politian, Angelo. *Le Selve e la Strega,* ed. Isidoro del Lungo. Florence, 1925.

Pontanus, Iovianus. *I Dialoghi,* ed. Carmelo Previtera. Florence, 1943.

Salutati, Coluccio. *De Laboribus Herculis,* ed. B. L. Ullmann. 2 v. Zurich, 1951.

Savonarola, Girolamo. *De Divisione Scientiarum.* No modern ed. A restatement of the scholastic position concerning the placement of poetry among the sciences.

GLOSSARY AND INDEX OF PROPER NAMES

Abu Firas al-Hamdani (ca. 932–68, Arabic poet), 367

Abu Tammam Habib ibn Aws (ca. 805–ca. 845, Arabic poet and anthologist), quoted, 361, 366, 370

Accius, Lucius (170–ca. 90 B.C., Latin tragic poet; the last great dramatist of the Roman Republic), 164

Achaemenides (one of Odysseus' crewmen who is rescued from the Cyclops by the Trojans), 334

Achates (Aeneas' friend), 333

Acheron (in classical mythology, a river in Hades, q.v.), 336

Achilles (in Greek mythology, the son of Peleus and the goddess Thetis; the greatest Greek champion in the Trojan War and the hero of Homer's *Iliad*), 28, 42, 50, 53, 123, 134, 145, 156, 161, 179, 181, 195, 199, 205, 236 fn. 1, 3, 12–14, 237 fn. 22, 245 fn. 12, 308, 332, 365

Addison, Joseph (1672–1719, English essayist, poet, and statesman), 190, 191

Admetus (in Greek mythology, king of Pherae in Thessaly, who was told by Apollo that he must die unless someone was willing to die in his place; his wife Alcestis, q.v., was willing), 28

Adonis (in mythology, a beautiful youth loved by the goddess Aphrodite, q.v. Killed by a boar, he was permitted by Zeus to spend part of the year on earth with Aphrodite and part in the world below with Persephone, q.v. His death and rebirth symbolize the cycle of life), 33

Aegeus (legendary king of Athens; father of Agamemnon and Menelaus, qq.v. In Euripides' *Medea*, he meets Medea while he is searching for a cure for his childlessness and she is planning her vengeance on Jason. Aegeus promises her sanctuary after the deed, and she, in turn, promises him a magical cure), 137

Aegisthus (in Greek legend, the son of Thyestes and paramour of Clytemnestra, qq.v. The lovers murdered her husband Agamemnon. Avenging the death of his father, Orestes, q.v., killed them both), 121

Aeneas (son of Venus and Anchises, prince of Troy and reputed ancestor of the Romans), 325, 328, 331, 462, 465; as everyman, 279, 327; his story, according to Fulgentius, 333–40

Aeolus (in Greek mythology, god of the winds), 333

influential liturgical book of the early Middle Ages in the West), 280, 287

AMBROSE, SAINT (ca. 339–97, bishop of Milan, the first of the great Fathers of the Roman Catholic Church), 283, 286

AMMONIUS (2nd-century B.C. disciple of the scholar Aristarchus, q.v., whose work he continued in Alexandria), 203

AMMONIUS SACCAS (3rd-century Alexandrian philosopher, Neoplatonist, and teacher of Plotinus, q.v.), 226

AMPHIARUS (Amphiaraus, in classical mythology, husband of Eriphyle who forced him, against his will, to participate in the expedition of the Seven against Thebes. *See* Alcmaeon), 125

AMPHICRATES (fl. 90 B.C., Athenian orator and historian), 194, 195

AMPHION (legendary Greek musician who, by the power of his music, could move stones into place for building the walls of Thebes), 167

AMPHITRYON (in classical mythology, the husband of Alcmene, q.v. While he was away, Zeus assumed his shape and visited Alcmene. The latter bore him a child, Hercules, q.v., whom Amphitryon accepted as his son), 394

ANACHARSIS (6th-century Scythian prince and sage), 69

ANACREON (ca. 570–ca. 485 B.C., Greek lyric poet of remarkable imagination and wit), 214

ANCHISES (prince of Troy, father of Aeneas), 280, 327, 328, 338, 339

ANDROMACHE (in classical mythology, the wife of Hector, q.v.), 42

ANTILOCHUS (in Greek mythology, son of Nestor, described by Homer as a great warrior and fast runner), 44, 246 fn. 4

ANTIOPE (in classical mythology, the daughter of Nycteus, king of Boeotia. Visited by Zeus in the form of a satyr, she bore him two sons. She is the heroine of Euripides' tragedy *Antiope*), 394

ANTIPHATES (mythological king of the Laestrygonians, giants described in the *Odyssey*, X.100 ff.), 161

ANTIPHON (ca. 480–411 B.C., Athenian orator and teacher of rhetoric), 144, 172

APELLES (4th-century B.C. Greek painter), 456

APHRODITE (in Greek mythology, the goddess of sexual love, beauty, and fertility), 18, 53, 233

APOLLO (in Greek mythology, the god of the sun, prophecy, music and song; in art he is depicted as the ideal of manly beauty), 53, 56, 61, 167, 189, 241 fn. 38, 281, 300, 302, 308, 318, 321, 335, 336

APOLLONIUS RHODIUS (3rd-century B.C. Alexandrian poet and scholar), 190, 216, 217

ARATOR (a 6th-century Christian poet, born in Liguria, Italy), 269, 286, 292, 470

ARATUS (ca. 315–240/39 B.C., Greek poet and author of *Phaenomena*, a treatise in hexameters on the stars and weather), 180, 201, 211

ARCADIA (a mountainous region in the center of the Peloponnesus; its inhabitants were known for their contented pastoral way of life), 330

ARCHILOCHUS (Greek poet of the early 7th century; the reputed inventor of iambic poetry), 39, 40, 160, 201, 203, 217, 248 fn. 34

ARES (in Greek mythology, son of Zeus and Hera, and the god of war), 53, 130, 199, 205, 340

ARGONAUTS (the men who, about a generation before the Trojan war,

DEMETRIUS (the author of the treatise *On Style* who probably lived in the 1st century B.C. Nothing further is known about him), 140–41, 270; *On Style*, commentary, 140–41, 270

DEMETRIUS OF PHALERUM (b. ca. 350 B.C., Greek rhetorician, philosopher, and statesman), 140

DEMOCRITUS OF ABDERA (5th-century B.C. Greek philosopher), 165

DEMODOCUS (in Homer's *Odyssey*, the blind minstrel of King Alcinous, q.v. 321

DEMOSTHENES (384–322 B.C., the greatest of the Greek orators), 170, 176, 185, 206–207, 209, 210, 212, 214–15, 217–18, 221, 248 fn. 34; compared to Plato, 202–203; "Longinus" on, 189, 190, 193, 201

DESCHAMPS, EUSTACHE (1346?–1406?, French poet), 268, 296

DIANA (Roman goddess of the moon, the hunt, and fertility; in ancient times identified with the Greek goddess Artemis, q.v.), 158, 168, 394, 456

DICAEOGENES (tragic Greek poet of the second half of the 5th century B.C.), 124

DIDO (Queen of Carthage, who, in Vergil's epic, fell in love with Aeneas and killed herself when he left her), 279, 284, 327, 334, 337

DINARCHUS (ca. 360–ca. 290 B.C., Greek orator), 170

DIOMEDES (ancient king of Aetolia and one of the Greek heroes in the Trojan War), 52, 161

DIOMEDES (Latin grammarian of the late 4th century A.D.), 285, 292, 299

DIONYSIUS (Greek painter, mentioned by Aristotle in the *Poetics*; cannot be identified with certainty), 109

DIONYSIUS OF HALICARNASSUS (literary critic and historian of the 1st century B.C.), 170–71, 187, 270; *On Literary Composition*, commentary, 170–71

DIONYSIUS THE AREOPAGITE (according to tradition, a 1st-century Athenian converted to Christianity by St. Paul. The four Greek treatises erroneously attributed to him were, scholars agree, written much later, probably early in the 6th century), 289–90, 387

DIONYSIUS THE PSEUDO-AREOPAGITE. *See* Dionysius the Areopagite

DIONYSUS (in mythology, the god of vegetation, fertility, and wine. The cult of Dionysus spread from Thrace to Greece, where he was at times identified with Bacchus or Orpheus, qq.v. He was intimately associated with artistic creativity), 41, 130, 205, 231, 235 fn. 1

DOLON (Trojan spy in the *Iliad*), 136

DONATUS, AELIUS (influential 4th-century Latin grammarian and writer of commentaries), 264, 267, 285, 299–300, 311, 325, 407; *Ars Grammatica*, 271; *Ars Minor*, 269, 292, 300; *On Comedy* (*De Comedia*), 299, 301

DONATUS, TIBERIUS CLAUDIUS (late 4th-century writer of a commentary on Vergil's *Aeneid*), 272, 273, 324, 325, 326

DU BELLAY, JOACHIM (1552–60, French poet and critic), 268

ELECTRA (in mythology, daughter of Agamemnon and Clytemnestra and sister of Orestes, qq.v., whom she aided in avenging the death of their father), 174

ELIOT, T. S. (1888–1965, American poet, critic, and playwright), 158, 190

ELYSIUM (in Greek mythology, the region in the underworld reserved for the souls of the good and great. Also known as the Elysian Fields), 338

EMERSON, RALPH WALDO (1803–82, American poet, essayist, and philosopher), 24

FULGENTIUS, FABIUS PLANCIADES (ca. 500–600, mythographer and allegorical interpreter of Vergil), 265, 281, 286, 293, 296, 298, 324–29, 448; *De Continentia Vergiliana*, 278, 406; *The Exposition of the Content of Vergil* . . . , comments on, 279–80, 326–29; on Vergil, 278, 324–40; on Vergil's *Aeneid,* 324–28, 330–340; on Vergil's *Eclogues*, 327, 329–30, 335–36, 339; on Vergil's *Georgics*, 327, 329–30

FURIES (in classical mythology, goddesses whose function it was to punish crimes. They were known to the Greeks as the Erinyes, q.v., or—euphemistically—Eumenides and to the Romans as *Furiae* or *Dirae*), 248 fn. 40–41

GALLIENUS, PUBLIUS LICINIUS EGNATIUS (d. 268, Roman emperor), 226

GALLO OF PISA (ca. 1250–1300, Italian poet), 424

GALLUS, GAIUS CORNELIUS (ca. 69–26 B.C., Roman poet and politician; important for the development of the love elegy), 465

GANYMEDE (in Greek mythology, a handsome youth taken to Olympus by the gods to serve as their cup bearer), 137

GASCOIGNE, GEORGE (ca. 1530–77, English poet and playwright), 268

GELLIUS, AULUS (ca. 130–ca. 180, Latin writer, popular during the Middle Ages and the Renaissance), 268, 401–402; *Noctes Atticae* (*Attic Nights*), 272, 405, 474 fn. 14

GEOFFREY OF VINSAUF (fl. ca. 1200, English teacher of rhetoric), 271, 294, 383–88, 405; *Poetria Nova*, 290–92, 383–88 (commentary on); influences of Horace, 384–88

GERARD OF CREMONA (ca. 1114–87, Italian translator of numerous classical works from Arabic into Latin), 274, 342

GERVASE OF MELCHELEY (or Gervais of Melkeley, 13th-century English grammarian and poet), 263, 273–74, 290; *Ars Poetica*, 294

GHISILIERI, GUIDO (ca. 1244–ca. 1278, Italian poet), 426, 443–44

GIOTTO (ca. 1267–1337, Italian painter and sculptor), 456

GIRAUT DE BORNEIL. *See* Guiraut de Borneil

GLAUCUS (mythical figure who became immortal after eating a magic herb, leaped into the sea, and turned into a sea-god), 81

GORDIAN III (Roman Emperor, 238–44), 226

GORGIAS (ca. 483–376 B.C., leading Sophist and rhetorician of Leontini, Sicily), 176, 193

GOWER, JOHN (ca. 1330–1408, English poet and friend of Chaucer), 296

GREEKS, the origin of poetry, and, 451, 459–61

GUARINO DA VERONA (1374–1460, Italian classical scholar and teacher), 267

GUIDO GHISILIERI. *See* Ghisilieri, Guido

GUINIZELLI, GUIDO (ca. 1230–76, Italian poet), 419, 426, 436, 437

GUIRAUT DE BORNEIL (ca. 1165–1220, Provençal troubadour), 419, 432, 435

GUITTONE D'AREZZO (ca. 1225–ca. 1294, Italian poet), 424, 438

GYGES (king of Lydia, ca. 685–657 B.C.), According to Plato, Gyges, a shepherd of the king of Lydia, found a magic ring which made the wearer invisible. With the help of the ring, he eventually killed the king and took his place), 81

HADES (in classical mythology, the underworld inhabited by the souls of the dead; also the ruler of this lower world), 49, 65, 81, 126, 201, 328, 336, 370, 371, 465

HAEMON (in Greek legend, the son of Creon, king of Thebes. Haemon's

Homer (*cont'd*)
326; St. Basil on, 348; Vergil (Fulgentius) on, 332, 333, 339, 340

Horace (Quintus Horatius Flaccus, 65–8 B.C., Latin poet and critic), 106, 155–58, 178, 267, 269, 271, 281, 284, 290–91, 293, 297, 311, 325, 344, 450; *Ars Poetica*, 105, 107, 155–58, 190, 270, 285, 287–89, 292, 300–301, 306–307, 347–49, 434; influence on Geoffrey of Vinsauf, 384–88

Hroswitha of Gandersheim. *See* Roswitha of Gandersheim

Hugh of Saint-Victor (12th-century philosopher, theologian, and author of mystical works), 263, 293

Hydra (in Greek mythology, a water serpent with nine heads. If one was cut off, two new ones grew. Hercules, q.v., killed the monster by burning the necks as he cut off the heads), 337

Hyperides (389–332 B.C., Athenian orator with an occasional Demosthenes-like fervor), 205, 217

Iamblichus (ca. 250–ca. 325, Syrian Neoplatonist philosopher and student of Porphyry, q.v.), 286

Icarius (in Homer's *Odyssey*, the father of Penelope, the wife of Odysseus), 137, 241 fn. 48

Ida (mountain in Phrygia [central and northwestern Asia Minor], where, according to tradition, the shepherd Paris chose Aphrodite over the other two goddesses Hera and Athena—all of whom claimed the golden apple inscribed "to the Fairest"), 54, 148

Imru' al-Qays (6th-century Arab poet; probably the most famous poet of the pre-Islamic period), 366, 367, 369, 377, 381

Ino (in Greek mythology, a daughter of Cadmus, q.v., and Harmonia. When she took care of the infant Dionysus, q.v., the son of Zeus and Semele, Hera, Zeus' wife, afflicted her with madness), 161

Io (mythological priestess of Argos with whom Zeus fell in love. Afraid of being found out by his wife Hera, he changed Io into a heifer. Hera asked for the heifer and set the monster Argos to watch her. When Hermes, q.v., killed Argos, Hera tormented Io with a gadfly, which finally drove her to Egypt. There Zeus transformed her back into a woman), 161

Ion of Chios (about 490–before 421 B.C., Greek tragic, lyric, and elegiac poet), 24, 38–48, 217

Ionia (ancient Greek district on the western coast of Asia Minor), 210

Iopas (in Vergil's *Aeneid*, a bard at the court of Dido, q.v.), 334

Iphigenia (in classical mythology, Agamemnon's daughter who is sacrificed by her father for the benefit of the Greek army. Her story is treated by both Aeschylus and Euripides), 119, 124

Isidore of Seville, Saint (ca. 560–636, Spanish archbishop, theologian, historian, and encyclopedist), 285, 286, 292, 299

Isocrates (436–338 B.C., important Athenian orator and creator of a new prose style), 146, 194, 209, 219

Ixion (in classical mythology, king of the Lapiths, in Thessaly, who murdered one of his kin. Although purified by Zeus, he made plans to seduce Zeus' wife, Hera. Zeus punished him by fastening him for all eternity to a fiery wheel revolving in the depths of Tartarus, q.v.), 161, 338

Janus (ancient Roman god of beginnings and protector of gates. He is usually depicted as having two heads looking into opposite directions), 392

JEROME, EUSEBIUS HIERONYMUS, SAINT (ca. 348–ca. 420, Father of the Church and scholar who laid the foundations of medieval Bible interpretation), 264, 269, 284, 286, 292, 470

JOCASTA (mother and wife of Oedipus, q.v.), 211

JOHN CASSIAN (ca. 360–432/35, monk, theologian, and ascetical writer), 266

JOHN DE RIDEVALL (14th-century Franciscan writer of theological and philosophical works), 296, 448

JOHN OF GARLAND (ca. 1195–ca. 1272, English grammarian, poet, and humanist), 263, 271

JOHN OF SALISBURY (ca. 1115–80, English ecclesiastic scholar and classical writer), 263, 267, 271, 273, 291, 387; *Metalogicon*, 293, 294, 448

JOHN OF SEVILLE (12th-century writer and translator), 342

JOHN SCOTUS ERIGENA (ca. 810–ca. 877, Irish scholastic philosopher), 267, 281, 287, 289, 311

JOHNSON, SAMUEL (1709–84, English writer and critic), 107

JONSON, BEN (1572–1637, English poet, dramatist, and critic), 107, 157

JOVE. *See* Jupiter.

JUNG, CARL GUSTAV (1875–1961, Swiss psychiatrist), 191

JUNO (Roman goddess identified with Hera, q.v.), 321, 333, 454

JUPITER (the Roman king of the gods. *See* Zeus), 319, 321, 394, 454, 456, 460

JUTURNA (in classical mythology, a nymph beloved by Jupiter and immortalized by him as the goddess of lakes and streams; the sister of Turnus, q.v.), 340

JUVENAL (Decimus Iunius Iuvenalis, ca. 60–ca. 140, the greatest Roman satirist), 293, 384

JUVENCUS, GAIUS VETTIUS AQUILINUS (4th-century Spanish priest and the first Latin poet known to have treated a Christian subject with classical epic technique), 269, 285, 292, 470

KANT, IMMANUEL (1724–1804, German philosopher), 191

LACEDAEMON (Sparta, an ancient city in southern Greece), 29, 69

LACTANTIUS, LUCIUS CAELIUS FIRMIANUS (ca. 240–ca. 320, Christian apologist from North Africa. During the Renaissance he was referred to as the "Christian Cicero"), 270, 284

LAIUS (Oedipus' father who is unwittingly slain by his own son. His fate is described in Sophocles' *Oedipus Rex* and *Oedipus at Colonus*), 134

LANDINO, CRISTOFORO (1424–92, Italian humanist), 275, 282, 324, 452

LATINI, BRUNETTO (ca. 1220–ca. 1294, Italian politician, scholar, and encyclopedist; teacher of Dante), 406

LATINUS (according to Roman legend, the king of Latium and father of Lavinia), 339

LAVINIA (princess of Latium and the second wife of Aeneas), 280, 327, 339

LEDA (in classical mythology, daughter of Thestius, king of Aetolia. According to one legend, Zeus visited Leda in the form of a swan, and she bore two eggs. Helen, q.v., issued from one and Castor and Pollux from the other), 394

LESSING, GOTTHOLD EPHRAIM (1729–81, German dramatist and critic), 102

LETHE (in classical mythology, a river in Hades. Those who drank its water, forgot their past), 338

LETO (in Greek mythology, a Titaness, mother of Apollo and Artemis, qq.v.), 217

PATROCLUS (in Greek mythology, close friend of Achilles, q.v.), 28, 44, 51, 53, 181, 199, 236 fn. 3, 9

PAUSON (Greek painter, mentioned by Aristotle in the *Poetics*; cannot be identified with certainty), 109

PELEUS (mythological king of the Myrmidons; father of Achilles, q.v.), 53, 160, 245 fn. 12

PELION (mountain in East Thessaly, near the Aegean coast. *See also* Aloadae), 196

PELOPONNESUS (the large peninsula of south Greece that is connected with the mainland by the Isthmus of Corinth), 110, 211

PENELOPE (in Greek mythology, the daughter of Icarius and wife of Odysseus, qq.v.), 212–13, 236 fn. 7, 241 fn. 48, 321

PERSEPHONE (in Greek mythology, daughter of Zeus and Demeter, goddess of fertility; she was abducted by Pluto, the ruler of Hades, became his wife, but was allowed to return to earth for part of the year), 49

PERSIUS FLACCUS, AULUS (A.D. 34–62, Roman satirist), 293

PETER BERCORIUS. *See* Bersuire, Pierre

PETER OF AUVERGNE (fl. 1150–80, Provençal troubadour), 421

PETRARCH, FRANCIS (1304–74, Italian poet and humanist), 275; and Boccaccio compared, 282–83, 296, 297, 324, 347, 447, 451, 452, 465, 469; *Bucolics*, 470; influence on Boccaccio, 449, 465; *Invective Against a Physician*, 449, 451, 468; *On the Remedies for all Fortunes*, 465

PETRONIUS ARBITER (1st-century A.D. Roman writer), 279, 337

PHAETHON (in Greek mythology, the son of Helios, the sun-god), 204

PHIDIAS (ca. 490–ca. 430 B.C., Greek sculptor), 227, 232, 310, 456

PHILIP II (king of Macedon from 359–336 B.C., and father of Alexander the Great), 215

PHILISTUS (Sicilian historian of the late 5th century to mid-4th century B.C.), 221

PHILO JUDAEUS (ca. 20 B.C.–A.D. 50, Jewish philosopher), 264, 277, 279, 283, 286, 311, 328

PHILODEMUS (ca. 110–ca. 40/35 B.C., Greek philosopher, poet, and critic), 103, 155

PHILOXENUS (436/35–380/79 B.C., dithyrambic poet from Cythera), 109

PHOENIX (tutor of Achilles, q.v., and, in his old age, one of the ambassadors bringing Agamemnon's offer of reconciliation in the Trojan War), 53

PHORMIS (5th-century B.C. writer of Dorian comedy), 112

PHRYNICUS (Phrynichus, one of the earliest Athenian tragic poets who lived from the late 6th to mid-5th century B.C.), 211

PICO DELLA MIRANDOLA, GIOVANNI (1463–94, Italian philosopher and humanist), 279, 282

PINDAR (518–438 B.C., Greek lyric poet, capable of brilliant imagery), 217, 268, 269

PISONES (mentioned in Horace, *Ars Poetica;* possibly refers to Gn. Calpurnius Piso, consul in 23 B.C., and his two sons), 158, 159, 163, 245 fn. 1

PLATAEA (ancient city in south Boeotia, destroyed by Xerxes I of Persia in 480 B.C. because of the help rendered to Athens at the battle of Marathon; scene of Greek victory over the Persian general Mardonius in 479 B.C.), 206, 207

PLATO (ca. 429–347 B.C., Greek philosopher), 21–25, 264, 276, 279, 282, 297, 330, 367; and Aristotle compared, 21–22, 24, 25, 100, 103; Boccaccio, and, 449–50, 452, 454, 466; criticism of Homer, 322–23; Demetrius, and, 142, 144, 148;

Quintilian, Marcus Fabius (ca. 30/35–ca. 100, Roman rhetorician and literary critic), 178–80, 266–68, 283–84, 293, 326, 464; *Institutio Oratoria*, commentary on, 178–80, 266–68, 285

Rabanus Maurus (776?–856, archbishop of Mainz, Benedictine theologian, and prolific writer), 267, 296, 293; *Clerical Institute*, 265, 287

Ransom, John Crowe (1888– , American poet and critic), 100, 107

Remigius of Auxerre (ca. 841–908, Carolingian theologian, scholar, and humanist), 267, 287

Richard of Bury (1281–1345, English book collector and patron of learning), 448

Rinaldo d'Aquino (13th-century Italian poet), 436

Roswitha of Gandersheim (ca. 935–after 1000, German canoness and writer of Latin poems and plays), 299

Salamis (island off the southeastern coast of Greece, in the Gulf of Aegina, where in 480 B.C. the Greek fleet decisively defeated the Persian fleet), 132, 206–207

Sallust (Gaius Sallustius Crispus, ca. 86–ca. 35 B.C., Roman historian), 184, 269, 292–93; *On Catiline's Conspiracy*, 332

Salutati, Coluccio (1331–1406, Italian humanist and writer), 276, 347

Sappho (b. ca. 612 B.C., Greek poet unsurpassed in simple charm and emotional intensity), 151, 154, 189, 200

Sarpedon (leader of the Lycians [in SW Asia Minor], one of Priam's allies in the *Iliad*), 51, 211

Saturn (ancient Roman god of agriculture, later identified with the Greek god Kronos and thus considered the father of Jupiter, Juno, etc. He was thought to have been an early king of Rome, and his reign was referred to as the golden age), 339

Savonarola, Girolamo (1452–98, Italian religious reformer), 275, 347, 449

Scaliger, Julius Caesar (1484–1558, Italian scholar, critic, and physician), 107

Scotus Erigena. *See* John Scotus Erigena

Scylla (in Greek mythology, a sea nymph transformed into a monster living in a cave opposite the whirlpool Charybdis, q.v.), 161

Scythian (inhabitant of a region situated north and east of the Black and Caspian seas and known by the ancient name of Scythia. It is now part of the Soviet Union), 150, 213

Sedulius (5th-century Christian Latin poet), 269, 285, 286, 292, 470

Seneca, Lucius Annaeus (ca. 4 B.C.–65 A.D., Roman writer and philosopher), 376, 384, 428

Servius (4th-century Latin grammarian and writer of a commentary on Vergil), 264, 267, 269, 277, 279, 281, 285–87, 292, 311, 324, 448; on Vergil's *Aeneid*, 325–26

Shelley, Percy Bysshe (1792–1822, English poet), 24, 227

Sidney, Sir Philip (1554–86), English poet, critic, statesman, and soldier), 107, 157, 311

Silenus (in Greek mythology, a satyr and constant companion of Dionysus, q.v. In appearance—and sometimes in wisdom—he has been likened to Socrates), 94, 163

Simonides (ca. 556–468 B.C., Greek lyric and elegiac poet of Ceos; best known for his epitaph for the 300 fallen Spartans at Thermopylae), 205, 269

Sisyphus (in punishment for a life of deception and crime, he is depicted in

Ulysses (the Latin name for Odysseus, q.v.), 308, 321, 334, 398, 462

Venus (Italian goddess of love and beauty; identified, in classical Rome, with Aphrodite, q.v.), 333, 456

Vergil (Publius Vergilius Maro, 70–19 B.C., the greatest of the Latin poets), 159, 265, 267–69, 274, 276, 285–87, 292–93, 302, 451, 462, 469; *Aeneid*, 281, Bernard Silvestris on, 280–81, 387, 406, Boccaccio on, 464, Tiberius Claudius Donatus on, 325, Fulgentius on, 324–28, 330–40, Servius on, 325; Boccaccio on, 464–65; *Bucolics*, Boccaccio on, 464; Dante on, 435, 438–39; *Eclogues*, 327–30, 335–36, 339; Fulgentius on, 278–81, 324–40; Geoffrey of Vinsauf, and, 384; *Georgics*, Boccaccio on, 464, Fulgentius on, 327, 329–330; Macrobius on, 272, 325–26

Victorinus, Gaius Marius (4th-century Roman grammarian), 267, 287

Vincent of Beauvais (1190/1200-ca. 1264, French encyclopedist), 299, 405

Vittorino da Feltre (1378–1446, Italian scholar, educator, and humanist), 267

Vulcan (the Latin name for Hephaestus, q.v., god of fire and metalworking), 321, 340

Whitehead, Alfred North (1861–1947, English philosopher), 21

William of Moerbeke (ca. 1215–86, Belgian Dominican archbishop; prolific translator of Greek authors into Latin), 343

Xenarchus (late 5th-century writer of mimes), 108

Xenophanes (ca. 570–ca. 480 B.C., Greek philosopher who expressed skepticism of the anthropomorphic view of the gods and developed a monotheistic concept of deity), 136

Xenophon (ca. 428/27–ca. 354 B.C., important Greek historian and prolific writer), 142, 148–51, 153, 172, 194–96, 208, 211, 213, 215, 223

Zeus (in Greek mythology, the father of the Olympian gods; ruler of the heavens, god of the weather, protector of law and morals), 52–54, 77, 137, 144, 193–94, 199–200, 227, 232, 235 fn. 1, 236 fn. 14, 310

Zeuxis (Greek painter who lived in the late 5th and 4th centuries B.C.), 114, 137

Zoilus (4th-century B.C. Greek cynic philosopher, notorious for his carping criticism of Homer), 199

GENERAL INDEX

ABOUT THE EDITORS

ALEX PREMINGER is the editor of the *Princeton Encyclopedia of Poetry and Poetics* and other books; he is associate professor, Brooklyn College Library, the City University of New York. Senior editor of this project, he was also responsible for the concept and coordination of the book.

O. B. HARDISON, JR., has been Director of the Folger Shakespeare Library since 1969. Formerly professor of English and Comparative Literature at the University of North Carolina, he is the author, among other volumes, of *Christian Rite and Christian Drama in the Middle Ages.*

KEVIN KERRANE is co-editor of *The Art of Drama* and *The Art of Modern Drama* and associate professor of English at the University of Delaware.